THE INSTITUTIONAL INVESTOR SERIES IN FINANCE

GLOBAL FINANCIAL SERVICES

*Strategies for Building Competitive Strengths
in International Commercial
and Investment Banking*

Roy C. Smith
Ingo Walter

*Stern School of Business
New York University
and
INSEAD*

HARPER BUSINESS

A Division of Harper & Row Publishers, New York

*Grand Rapids, Philadelphia, St. Louis, San Francisco
London, Singapore, Sydney, Tokyo, Toronto*

To Marianne and Jutta

International Standard Book Number: 0-88730-335-8

Library of Congress Catalog Card Number: 90–32811

Printed in the United States of America

Library of Congress Cataloging–in–Publication Data

Smith, Roy C., 1938–
    Global financial services : strategies for building competitive
strengths in international commercial and investment banking / Roy
C. Smith and Ingo Walter.
      p. cm. — (The Institutional investor series in finance)
    Includes bibliographical references.
    ISBN 0-88730-335-8
    I. Walter, Ingo. II. Title. III. Series.
HG3881.S544 1990
332.1'5—dc20   90–32811
                                              CIP

90 91 92 93 HD 9 8 7 6 5 4 3 2 1

Contents

Preface

The purpose of this volume is to provide a comprehensive overview of the international banking and securities business—an industry that has become truly global in recent years and that is subject to continuing rapid evolution. The focus is on determinants of competitive performance in the international financial services industry, covering the entire range of commercial and investment banking activities carried out internationally.

The volume begins with brief discussions of the globalization process as its has occurred within both the commercial and investment banking segments in this industry—the importance of factors affecting international trade, monetary relations, corporate finance, and financial markets, and the pressures that have affected international markets for capital. The evolutionary developments in international finance are also described, including the divergences and convergences between the commercial banking and securities businesses.

There follows a discussion of the major segments of international commercial and investment banking services. Topics include criteria for selecting investment banking services; domestic and Eurobond new issues; competition in swaps and synthetics; international equity finance and direct investment; asset and liability management in the international context; trade financing; legal aspects of international lending; project financing; private banking; and investment management. Throughout, emphasis is placed on competitive performance of international commercial and investment banking activities. This includes origination, underwriting, and distribution of new international debt and equity issues; international mergers and acquisitions; and related topics. On the commercial banking side, we develop principles of international credit analysis and credit extension in the short and medium term; we discuss evaluation of foreign banks and establishment of cooperative arrangements, correspondent linkages, and joint ventures; and we analyze conditions that may affect international bank and nonbank relationships.

The next sections describe the structure of risk encountered in the international financial services industry. Included in these sections is an emphasis on country risk assessment and its relationship to the dynamics of competition in international financial services.

The theory of multinational corporations is applied to the financial services sector in an attempt to determine sources of competitive strength, market share, profitability, growth, and similar dimensions of performance by financial institutions in the global marketplace. Factors affecting top management decisions on whether and how to service international markets and on the implications for the structure of commercial banks and securities firms themselves, are examined. Likewise, we consider regulatory issues facing international commercial and investment banks; the volume closes with an assessment of public policy dimensions with respect to market access, efficiency, innovation, and financial stability.

We are indebted to an array of academics and bankers around the world, far too numerous to mention individually, with whom we have discussed these issues over the years, as well as to our MBA classes in international banking at New York University and INSEAD. Certainly not least, Dorothea Benson, Fergal Byrne, Amanda Lomas, Ann Rusolo, and Hugh Thomas contributed significantly to production of the manuscript for publication.

ROY C. SMITH
INGO WALTER
New York City
March 1990

Evolution of International Financial Services

1

The Continuous Restructuring of Global Financial Services

Financial people know in their bones that their profession goes back a long way. Its frequent association with "the oldest profession" may simply be because it is almost as old. After all, the technology of finance is very basic, requiring little more than simple arithmetic and minimal literacy, and the environment in which it applies is universal—that is, any situation that involves money, property, or credit, all of which have been in demand since man's earliest days.

These financial commodities have been put to use to facilitate trade, commerce, and business investment and to accommodate the accumulation, preservation, and distribution of wealth by states, corporations, and individuals. Financial transactions can occur in an almost infinite variety, yet they always require the services of banks, whether acting as principals or as agents, and markets in which to operate.

Banks, too, therefore have a long history: a history rich in product diversity, international scope, and, above all, continuous change and adaptation. Generally, the latter have been required to adjust to drastic changes in economic and regulatory conditions. During times of such changes, banks have collapsed, only to be replaced by others eager to try their hand in this traditionally dangerous but profitable business. New competitors have continually appeared on the scene, especially during periods of rapid economic growth, opportunity, and comparatively light governmental interference. Competitive changes have forced adaptations too, and in general they have improved the level and efficiency of services offered to clients, thereby increasing transactional volume. The one constant in the long history of banking is, perhaps, the sight of new stars rising and old ones setting. Some of the older ones have been able to transform themselves into players capable of competing with the newly powerful houses, but many have not. Thus, the banking industry has much natural familiarity with economic restructuring.

It is doubtful, however, that there has ever been a time in the long history of banking that the pace of restructuring has been greater than it is at present. Banking and securities markets during the 1980s in particular have been affected by a convergence of several exceptionally powerful forces—deregulation and reregulation, competition and disintermediation, and product innovation and technology—all of which have occurred in a spiraling expansion of demand for financial services across the globe. Bankers today live in interesting, yet exhausting and hazardous, times.

A brief examination of where we have come from should be useful in orienting ourselves to the present.

THE LEGACIES OF GLOBAL BANKING

History has revealed that both bankers and credit were plentiful and active in the ancient world. The recorded legal history of several great civilizations started with elaborate regulation of credit, such as the Code of Hammurabi, ca. 1800 B.C., where the famous Babylonian set forth, among other laws, the maximum rate of interest for loans of grain ($33\frac{1}{3}$ percent) and silver (20 percent).[1]

Maritime trade abounded in the Mediterranean and was already highly developed by the Greeks and the Phoenicians in 1000 B.C. Such trade involved long-distance shipment of commodities that were not locally available. Wherever such trade occurred there had to be a means of payment acceptable to both sides; often such payment could be obtained only through the good offices of a bank represented in both countries acting as a foreign exchange or bill broker.

Banks also helped the merchants, the shipowners, and, later, the public officials manage their money—sometimes by accepting it on deposit, and sometimes by investing it for them in precious metals, stones, or the financial assets of the day. One could make money on money long before Alexander the Great.

By the second century A.D., the Romans, then at their peak, had reorganized everything. Their power in the Mediterranean was absolute, peace reigned along its shores, piracy had been eliminated, trade flourished, and coinage was available throughout the empire. Bankers and financiers prospered. Will Durant described them as follows:

> One of the streets adjoining the forum became a banker's row, crowded with the shops of the moneylenders and money-changers. Money could be borrowed on land, crops, securities, or government contracts, and for

financing commercial enterprises or voyages. Cooperative lending took the place of [commercial] insurance; instead of one banker completely underwriting a venture, several joined in providing the funds. Joint-stock companies existed chiefly for the performance of government contracts . . . they raised their capital by selling their stocks or bonds to the public in the form of *partes* or *particulae*, i.e. "little parts," or "shares" [or "partnerships" or "participations"].[2]

Under other circumstances, this financial and commercial infrastructure might have grown to produce large international banking and trading companies similar to those that exist today. However, this didn't happen in the Roman period, largely because the state, focused as it was on conquest and strict control of its empire through efficient administration, reserved for itself the principal financial powers in the society. As the state was the principal holder of capital, it also became the principal dispenser of it, lending large sums to the public—a process that was no doubt accompanied by some degree of corruption. Perhaps to preserve this convenient arrangement, the Roman senate did not permit limited liability companies to be formed, thus keeping the private wealth of the empire where it could be best controlled— among individuals.

In any case, large banks and commercial houses never emerged in the Roman period, though banking transactions themselves were plentiful on a small scale. This may have proved to be a contributing cause in the decline of the empire, which suffered acute economic decay as well as political deterioration. In the third century, much economic difficulty was experienced, including the "great crash" of A.D. 259 (after the Emperor Valerian had been taken captive) when markets collapsed and there were runs on banks in various parts of the empire.[3]

During the following century, Roman economic decline was irreversible. Money and gold bullion were leaving the empire in a great payments drain (it ended up in the Near East and in India). The population was declining, and barbarians had to be brought in to replenish the dwindling supply of workers. Wealth had become highly concentrated at the top, and the *nouveau riche* had been suppressed. Society's savings were dissipated in consumption, and military conquests were no longer being undertaken to resupply the state with plunder and slaves. The empire itself was breaking into two parts, with most of the action taking place in the eastern capital, Constantinople. What was left of the "smart money" moved there.

The rest, sadly, we know, though one eminent historian of the period, Harold Mattingly, a distinguished Cambridge University scholar and expert on Roman finance, makes a curious observation:

> The possibilities at the disposal of an all-powerful state are enormous if it can [utilize] its resources in money, natural wealth and man-power. If the Roman State could have been administered by a syndicate of men of modern capacity in banking and industry, there might have been rationalization on a magnificent scale. The State might have been able to meet all demands upon it and still have left its subjects to enjoy a very fair measure of prosperity. If it failed to realize all these possibilities, that will have been due to lack of knowledge as well as lack of interest.[4]

The Roman Empire collapsed in the fifth century. It was succeeded by the Byzantine Empire, which ruled in the eastern Mediterranean until the Arab conquests of the seventh century. These conquests in turn diminished the scope and power of the Byzantine Empire.

In the western Mediterranean, trade between the great ports and up the rivers leading into them was sporadic (again interrupted by pirates) and almost totally lacking in finance. After the Arab conquests, Mediterranean trade flourished but European trade did not. For all practical purposes it was in limbo for several hundred years. From the viewpoint of European bankers and financiers, these truly were their "Dark Ages."

Where there was no trade, economic life fell back upon villages or counties. People consumed only what they grew, raised, or made themselves and no more. There were no surpluses beyond local needs, as there were no markets to send them to nor any way to send them. No trade, no money, no finance—there was nothing to do with money anyway. From this stagnant, landlocked condition, the feudal system emerged, digging its roots deeply into European life.

The Catholic Church, which was founded when the brutality of the all-conquering Romans was at its peak, emerged as a major social and economical force in Europe at this time. As an institution devoted to Christ's teaching of brotherly love and human equality before a single, caring and redemptive God, the Church had profound influence in establishing how people should live and treat each other. Naturally, people behaved much as before, but now they were told what was right and what was wrong according to a supreme being and what would happen to them if they offended God and were not subsequently forgiven.

Christ was not just a prophet, the Church declared, he was the son of God, and therefore an extremely authoritative source for these new teachings, which instructed mankind in God's will. According to the teachings, everyone was a sinner, but sinners could be forgiven. Men were supposed to treat their neighbors kindly; they were not to take advantage of them nor climb over them on their way up. These teachings, as further interpreted by holy men over the years, came to establish the standards of Christian morality, of good and evil, and of right and wrong in everyday life. How one had lived one's life would be judged at its end and rewarded either in heaven or in hell. It was a powerful notion because of the hope it contained, especially for a future life better than the miserable one that most people then lived, and it was a notion that spread throughout Europe.

The teachings of the medieval Church began with the idea that everyone should know his or her place and not unduly strive to improve it at the expense of others. Peasants should be happy enough as peasants. Upward mobility was not encouraged. One's future would be secure in the next life if one served God and trusted completely in Him. Kings, and their associated nobles, were those designated by God (through divine right) to rule. They should be obeyed and not interfered with (or revolted against).

Barbara Tuchman, in a fascinating report on the catastrophic four-teenth century—a century of great famine, the Black Death, and the Hundred Years War—notes that the Christian attitude toward commerce during the Middle Ages was "actively antagonistic":

> It held that money was evil, business was evil, that profit beyond a minimum necessary to keep the dealer alive was avarice (a sin), that to make money from the lending of money was usury (also a sin), and buying at wholesale and selling at retail was immoral and condemned by canon law. In short, as St. Jerome said: "A man who is a merchant can seldom, if ever, please God."[5]

By such a definition, businesspeople, merchants, and bankers were not only conceived in original sin, they lived in it daily, unless they were willing to give up their ambition. However, as Tuchman also points out: "As restraint of initiative, this was the direct opposite of capitalist enterprise. It was the denial of economic man, and consequently even more routinely violated than the denial of sensual man."[6]

The ways of man and those of heaven were in stark opposition to one another. When violations would occur, these sins would have to be atoned for—an atonement that resulted in an enormous accumulation of wealth and financial power in the Church itself.

This took some time to happen, however. While western Europe suffered dismally from A.D. 500 to A.D. 1000, the conflict was moot since there was very little commerce to tempt people into sin. However, the Vikings began voyages in the eighth century A.D., and for 200 or 300 years sailed and rowed their way up the rivers and into the lakes and seas of Europe, replanting the seeds of commerce and trade in their fearsome wake. After a while, it became easier and much more profitable for them to trade with their counterparts than to slaughter them, and economic life in northern and western Europe was reborn. At about the same time, Venice emerged as a principal entrepôt of trade and finance within southern Europe and between Europe and the Arab world.

With the rekindling of trade, of course, came opportunity for those seeking it—often, no doubt, those on the bottom rungs of society, as it was then inflexibly cast.

A French historian of the Middle Ages, Henri Pirenne, repeats the story of one St. Godric of Finchale as an example of the way the *nouveau riche* class was formed in the latter part of the eleventh century. Godric was born of poor peasant stock in Lincolnshire and forced, no doubt, to leave his parents' meager holdings to make his own way. He became a beachcomber, looking for wrecks, which were numerous at the time. Finding one, he put together a peddler's pack and set out on the road, where he fell in with a band of "merchants" (possibly bandits). In time he amassed enough money to form a partnership with others, owning a ship engaged in coastal trade, which subsequently branched out into long-distance trade, merchanting, and banking. He became very rich, subsequently made his peace with God, no doubt leaving much of his fortune to the Church, and later became a saint. Pirenne is emphatic that there were many Godrics operating at the time in Europe, though few among them were saints. They emerged as the bourgeoisie, and the commercial rebirth of Europe was soon an accomplished fact.

By the late twelfth century, business schools were in operation, and those seeking a career in commerce could learn basic reading, bookkeeping, and arithmetic. By the thirteenth century, banking and finance had become quite sophisticated. Great textile factories were established in Flanders, furnished with wool from Britain and flax from Egypt, and the cloth was sold all over Europe with financing provided by expatriate Italian bankers speaking French. By the four-teenth century, long-term credits were available from merchants seeking to place their excess cash and from bankers acting on their behalf.

Public authorities and noblemen were also borrowers. For example, when they needed to buy grain during a famine or outfit a regiment to be sent off to the Crusades, it was easier to borrow from moneylenders than to send one's plate to the local mint.

By the fifteenth century, the mighty house of Medici reigned supreme in Italy, with its various branches throughout Europe acting as merchants in wool and cloth, dealers in spices and silks, bankers, goldsmiths, shipowners, deposit takers, and foreign exchange brokers. The influence of the Medicis and other houses like them spread to the papacy and the Church and to princes and noble families all over the continent.

By this time the *modus operandi* of relations between merchants and the Church was reasonably well fixed, but it was complicated. To redeem his soul, the merchant would make contributions to the Church and its charitable works and alms-houses, perhaps leaving a substantial part of his fortune to the Church upon his death. He would also suffer, as an ordinary cost of doing business, numerous fines and other charges for violating commercial laws. He could purchase benefices or indulgences from the Church for hundreds of purposes. As a lowly member of the bourgeoisie, he also might be required to renounce high social position in his community, though it is unlikely that Lorenzo de' Medici ever did so.

On the other hand, having fulfilled these requirements, he would be left alone to grow as rich as he was able, to ascend in society, and to leave most of his fortune to his heirs. It was a delicate balance, but one that was efficient for both the Church and the emerging middle classes. Each became mutually supportive of the other, despite the unbridgeable chasm of their intellectual and spiritual positions, and each prospered.[7]

The more developed Italian banking became during the Renaissance, the more it was exposed to the great risks of the times—that is, the volatile shifts in political and religious power and influence. Even the Medicis could not endure the constant turmoil of the sixteenth century. They were succeeded in the world of merchants, after the Reformation, by German and Swiss protestant bankers, many of whom developed ties in Britain, Holland, and France. During the modern era, commercialism and finance were substantially freed of the stern admonitions of the church.

The Dutch moved especially quickly, having set up organized markets for trading in financial instruments by 1602. The Amsterdam

Stock Exchange followed in 1611, and trading and speculation in securities of all types developed rapidly. The tulip mania, in which the prices of bulbs temporarily reached extraordinary levels (one traded as high as £20,000), came in 1636. The Amsterdam market permitted various forms of short selling, puts and calls, and futures transactions in many different commodities (tulip bulbs being one) and securities, including shares of the dominant and prosperous Dutch East India Company. Insider trading was first made an illegal practice in Amsterdam in the seventeenth century. The shrewd and profit-minded Dutch traders knew that insider trading was not a victimless crime.[8]

By the beginning of the eighteenth century, trading in bills of exchange and other financial instruments (including shares of a limited number of corporations), took place daily in the city of London in an area called Exchange Alley. In 1720 this was the scene of the Great South Sea Bubble, in which thousands of British investors developed a mania for shares of a new company that would have monopoly rights to trade off the east coast of South America, the prospects for which were never much better than dim. Many people had bought their shares on margin, an early example of financial leverage at work. The bubble burst, of course.

In the late 1700s the American and the French revolutions changed forever the way ordinary people would think about their lives and how much they would come to value the freedom to take chances and venture their own capital for the chance at a better, more prosperous future. Also at this time Adam Smith's influential work, *The Wealth of Nations*, helped to ensure nearly 100 years of prosperous laissez-faire economic policy in Great Britain.

Britain's defeat of Napoleon at the battle of Waterloo in 1815 set the stage for nearly a century of economic dominance. It also was the occasion for the House of Rothschild to rise from obscurity to supreme prominence. The Rothschilds made a killing in the market by getting the jump on the outcome of the battle and the defeat of Napoleon and then misleading everybody else on the Exchange by first selling and then buying large amounts of British paper. The Rothschilds had earlier amassed a smaller fortune in buying and selling commercial bills from both sides all during the war. Their activities were neither illegal nor considered improper at the time, although they would be condemned today.

The great era of capitalism that followed the defeat of Napoleon was nourished by the Industrial Revolution and the ascendancy of "the people" in Europe and America. Since 1800 the general growth in people's economic well-being has been several times that which had been experienced over the preceding 4,000 years. In those areas of the world still ruled by conquerors or by religious groups, not much general improvement has been experienced. And in those areas where old regimes have been toppled by people's (i.e., communist) revolutions and capitalism has been stamped out, some, but far less, growth has occurred—a fact that has become painfully obvious in recent years. Indeed, the lack of adequate economic growth was a principal cause of the toppling of communist governments in Eastern Europe at the end of 1989.

THE ROOTS OF MODERN BANKING

Our modern economic and financial heritage begins with the advent of democratic capitalism, around the time of Adam Smith. Under this system the state does not prevent or discourage anyone who is willing to work hard enough, and who also has access to capital, from becoming a capitalist.

A hundred years after Adam Smith, England was at the peak of its power. Politically, it ruled 25 percent of the world's area and people. The British economy was by far the strongest and most developed in the world. Its competitors were still partly asleep. France was still reeling from a century of political chaos and a war with Prussia that had gone wrong. Germany was just starting to come together politically, but it still a had quite a way to go to catch up with the British in industrial terms. Although the rest of Europe did not pose a threat to British dominance, there was a potentially serious problem from reckless, often irresponsible competition from America, which fancied itself as a rising economic power. With this exception, the horizon was comparatively free of competitors. British industry and British finance were very secure in their respective positions of world leadership.

English financial markets had made it all possible according to Walter Bagehot, the editor of *The Economist* at the time, who published a small book in 1873 called *Lombard Street*, which described these markets and what made them tick. England's economic glory, he suggested, was based on the supply and accessibility of capital. After all, he pointed out, what would have been the good of inventing a railroad back in Elizabethan times if there was no way to raise the capital to build it? In poor countries there were no financial resources anyway, and in most European countries money stuck to the aristocrats and the landowners and was unavailable to the market. But in England, Bagehot boasted, there was a place in London called Lombard Street where "in all but the rarest of times, money can be always obtained upon good security, or upon decent prospects of probable gain." Such a market, Bagehot continues, is a "luxury which no country has ever enjoyed with even comparable equality before."

However, the real power in the market, he goes on to suggest, is its ability to offer the benefits of leverage to those working their way up in the system, whose goal it is to displace those people at the top. "In every district," Bagehot explains, "small traders have arisen who discount their bills extensively, and with the capital so borrowed, harass and press upon, if they do not eradicate, the old capitalist." The new trader has "obviously an immense advantage in the struggle of trade."

> If a merchant have £50,000 all his own, to gain 10 percent on it he must make £5,000 a year, and must charge for his goods accordingly; but if another has only £10,000 and borrows £40,000 by discounts (no extreme instance in our modern trade), he has the same capital of £50,000 to use, and can sell much cheaper. If the rate at which he borrows be 5 percent, he will have to pay £2,000 a year [in interest]; and if, like the old trader he makes £5,000 a year, he will still, after paying his interest, obtain £3,000 a year, or 30 percent on his own £10,000. As most merchants are content with much less than 30 percent, he will be able, if he wishes, to forego some of that profit, lower the price of the commodity, and drive the old-fashioned trader—the man who trades on his own capital—out of the market.

Thus, the ambitious "new man," with little to lose and access to credit through the market, can earn a greater return on his money than a risk-averse capitalist who borrows little or nothing. The higher return enables the new man to undercut the other man's prices and take business from him. True, the new man may lose on the venture and be taken out of the game, but there is always another new man on his way up who is eager to replace him. As the richer man has a lot to lose, he risks it less and thus is always in the game, continually defending himself against one newcomer or another until finally he packs it in, retires to the country, and invests in government securities instead.

"This increasingly democratic structure of English commerce," Bagehot continued, "is very unpopular in many quarters." On one hand, he says, "it prevents the long duration of great families of merchant princes . . . who are pushed out by the dirty crowd of little men."

On the other hand, these unattractive democratic defects are compensated for

> by one great excellence: no other country was ever so little "sleepy," no other was ever so prompt to seize new advantages. A country dependent mainly on great "merchant princes" will never be so prompt; there commerce perpetually slips more and more into a commerce of routine. A man of large wealth, however intelligent, always thinks, "I have a great income, and I want to keep it. If things go on as they are, I shall keep it, but if they change I *may* not keep it." Consequently he considers every change of circumstance a "bore," and thinks of such changes as little as he can. But a new man, who has his way to make in the world, knows that such changes are his opportunities; he is always on the lookout for them, and always heeds them when he finds them. The rough and vulgar structure of English commerce is the secret of its life.[9]

In 1902 a young American new man named Bernard Baruch took Bagehot's essay to heart and made himself the first of many millions in a Wall Street investment pool, buying control of a railroad on borrowed money.[10] The United States had come of age financially around the turn of the century, and Wall Street would soon displace Lombard Street as the world's center of finance.

Early in the century J. P. Morgan organized United States Steel Corporation, having acquired Carnegie Steel and other companies in a transaction valued at $1.5 billion, an amount worth perhaps $20 billion today. This was the largest financial deal ever made, until the RJR-Nabisco transaction in 1989, and it occurred in 1901 during the first of four merger booms to take place in the United States. Each of these booms was powered by different factors, but rising stock markets and easy access to credit were major contributors in each boom.

By the early 1900s New York was beginning to emerge as the world's leading financial center. While many American companies still raised capital by selling their securities to investors in Europe, they also sold them to American investors. These investors, looking for places to put their newly acquired wealth, also bought European securities, perhaps thinking they were safer and more reliable investments than those of American companies. By the early twentieth century, European issues in the New York market were commonplace. This activity proved especially beneficial during World War I, when both sides in the conflict sought funds from the United States although the allied powers raised by far the larger amounts.

After World War I, American prosperity continued while Europe's did not. Banks were busy raising money for corporations, foreign governments, and investment companies and were busy making large loans to investors buying securities. At this time banks were "universal"—that is, they were free to participate in commercial banking (lending) and investment banking, which meant the underwriting, distribution, and trading of securities in financial markets. Many of the larger banks were also involved in a substantial amount of international business. There was trade to finance all over the world, especially in such mineral-rich areas as Latin America and Australia. There were new securities issues (underwritings) to perform for foreign clients, which in the years before the 1929 crash accounted for approximately 25 percent of all securities business done. There were correspondent banking and custodial (safekeeping) relationships with overseas counterparts, and there was a variety of financial services to perform both for foreigners doing business in the United States and for Americans conducting business abroad.

The stock market crash in 1929 was a global event—markets crashed everywhere all at the same time, and the volume of foreign selling orders was high. The Great Depression followed, and the banks were blamed for it, although the evidence has never been strong to connect the speculative activities of the banks during the 1920s with either the crash or the subsequent depression of the 1930s. Nonetheless, the following three consequenes of these events greatly influenced American banking: (1) the passage of the Banking Act of 1933 which provided for the Federal Deposit Insurance system, and the Glass-Steagall provisions of the act, which completely separated commercial banking and securities activities; (2) the depression itself, which led in the end to World War II and a 30-year period of banking being confined to basic, slow-growing deposit taking and loan making within a limited local market only; and (3) the rising importance of the government in deciding financial matters, especially during the postwar recovery period. There was little for banks or securities firms to do until the late 1950s and early 1960s.

By then international business had resumed its rigorous expansion, and U.S. banks, following the lead of First National City Bank (now Citicorp), resumed their activities abroad. The successful recovery of the economies of Western Europe and Japan led to pressures on the fixed-rate foreign exchange system set up after the war. The

Eurodollar market followed, then the Eurobond market, and then the reattraction of banks and investment banks to international capital market transactions.

Next came the 1971 collapse of the fixed exchange rate system in which the dollar was tied to gold. Floating exchange rates set by the market replaced this system, obviating the need for government capital controls. In turn, this led to widespread removal of restrictions on capital flows between countries and to the beginnings of the global financial system that we have today.

This system, which is based on markets setting prices and determining the flow of capital around the world, has drawn in many new players—both users and providers of banking and capital market services. Competition among these players for funds, and the business of providing them, has greatly increased the stakes of individual institutions and indeed the risks of the banking and securities businesses.

The effects of competitive capitalism have been seen and appreciated during the past decade as they have not been since 1929. The 1980s witnessed further rounds of deregulation and privatization of government-owned enterprises, indicating that governments of the industrial countries around the world have found private sector solutions to problems of economic growth and development preferable to state-operated socialist programs. Thus there have been radical changes in Europe, where massive deregulation of financial markets in the United Kingdom and several other countries has occurred, and where the 1992 liberalization initiative promises similar effects on European business and finance. Deregulation in Japan has freed vast sums of capital for investment overseas and for the creation of active global securities markets in Tokyo.

Most businesses are now effectively global, especially financial businesses. Banking and capital market services have proliferated, and numerous new competitors have emerged on the scene—many of which are not banks at all. Indeed, some, like General Electric Capital Corporation, are customers of banks. New regulations are constantly being introduced, and old ones are being changed. Telecommunications provides an ease of access to information that separated banks from their clients, pushing much of today's business into trading markets in which advice and service are less valuable than the latest quotation posted by securities and foreign exchange traders. It is a time of great and widespread change, affecting everyone. It is a time of massive restructuring for all financial service firms.

This book attempts to wade into the chaos and confusion of today's global banking and capital market environment and highlight the central parts of it, so that each can be examined separately. The purpose is to gain a better understanding of the evolution of international banking and finance, the services represented in today's market, the competitive processes involved, and the impact these have on prominent public policy issues. By treating the services of commercial banks and investment banks separately, we are not acknowledging that these are or should be separated, we are simply using a traditional distinction for examining what these services are and how competition works in each.

Our main emphasis is on the issues of formulation, implementation, and evaluation of *competitive strategies* (i.e., strategies that succeed because they are ultimately shown to be competitive) for banks and capital market institutions. Each financial services business will have to reformulate its own global competitive strategy over the coming years. There is no single strategy that will work for all. Indeed, there are so many different types of firms, from different countries and possessing different strengths and weaknesses, that an enormous variety of different strategies is likely to result. Our effort in this book is to clarify the process of strategic determination in this period of enormous change, with its inescapable requirement for rethinking how individual businesses fit into the totality of global finance—rendering that process more understandable to students of the subject and to practitioners.

NOTES

1. Sidney Homer, *A History of Interest Rates*, 2nd ed. (New Brunswick, NJ: Rutgers University Press, 1963, 1977), p. 5.
2. Will Durant, *Caesar and Christ* (New York: Simon and Schuster, 1948), pp. 79–80.
3. Harold Mattingly, *Roman Imperial Civilization* (Garden City, NY: Doubleday Anchor Books, 1957), pp. 225–247.
4. Ibid., p. 241.
5. Barbara W. Tuchman, *A Distant Mirror* (New York: Alfred A. Knopf, 1978). p. 37.
6. Ibid., p. 38.
7. Henry Pirenne, *Economic and Social History of Medieval Europe* (London: Routledge & Kegan Paul Ltd., 1936), pp. 47–168.
8. Joseph de la Vega, *Confusions de Confusiones (1688)*, reprinted in *Publications Number 13*, (Cambridge, MA: Kress Library of Business

and Economics, Harvard Business School, 1957); from E. C. Bursk, et al. eds., *The World of Business*, 2 Vols. (New York: Simon & Schuster, 1962) 2: 794–97.

9. Walter Bagehot, *Lombard Street, A Description of the Money Market* (London: Henry S. King & Co., 1873), pp. 1–20.

10. Bernard M. Baruch, *Baruch: My Own Story* (New York: Henry Holt and Co., 1957), pp. 165–76.

2

International Commercial Banking

Involvement of commercial banks abroad can be traced to the ancient Egyptians and Sumerians, who used papyrus letters of credit and clay tablet "checks" to facilitate the flow of international trade. Bills of exchange made their appearance in Babylonia and Assyria as early as the twenty-first century B.C. The banking dynasties of the fifteenth and sixteenth centuries, dominated by the Medicis in Florence and the Fuggers in Frankfurt, often engaged in highly sophisticated cross-border operations, many of which were similar to some of today's basic commercial banking activities—lending to business, governments, and individuals; operating the payments function; providing an array of financial guarantees; providing foreign exchange services; and covering a broad range of information needs for clients. Similarly, the dominant British merchant banks were extremely active in the nineteenth century and made important contributions to the industrial development of the time.

Besides cross-border lending and investing, these forerunners of modern international banking maintained impressive direct links outside their home countries. The Medicis, for example, had numerous correspondent banking relationships throughout Europe, as well as branches in Rome, Venice, Milan, Paris, Avignon, Bruges, London, and Geneva. Each branch was capitalized separately, with majority ownership and control in the hands of the Medici family in Florence. Later, while Baring Brothers in London limited itself to strong correspondent banking links abroad and one representative office in the United States, other British merchant banks of the nineteenth century had impressive branch networks especially in Latin America and South Africa. In the 1860s, 5 British banks had operations in the state of California alone, while 22 operated in the Far East. The Rothschilds set up branches in Paris, London, Vienna, and Frankfurt, while Crédit Mobilier had banking affiliates in England, Spain, Germany, Italy, and the Netherlands.

Internationalization has taken on an entirely new meaning in the modern context, of course, and geographic interpenetration of financial institutions, with respect to various domestic and offshore markets, has become very significant indeed. Table 2–1 indicates the number of foreign banks that had a significant presence (branches or majority-owned affiliates) in the major industrial countries in 1970, 1980, and 1985, respectively. These data actually understate the degree of internationalization of banks, since forms of involvement other than branches or majority-owned subsidiaries are not captured in the statistics.

Foreign banks operating in the United States booked $411 billion in deposits (13 percent of the U.S. total) and $110 billion in business loans (22 percent of the total U.S. market and 50 percent of the New York City market) in 1986.[1] In dollar-denominated acceptance financing, they took 33 percent of the United States market. Japanese banks alone captured a 40 percent share of foreign bank assets in the United States and an 80 percent share of foreign banks' dollar-

Table 2–1. Foreign Banking Presence, by Host Country [a]

Country	1970	1980	1985
United States[b]	50	579	783
United Kingdom	95	214	336
Germany[b]	77	213	287
France[b]	58	122	147
Switzerland	97	99	119
Japan[b]	38	85	112
Luxembourg[b]	23	96	106
Belgium	26	51	58
Canada	0	0	58
Netherlands	23	39	44
Italy	4	26	40

a. The data are not fully comparable. Except for countries denoted (*b*), the totals include foreign banking institutions or families operating through branches of majority-owned subsidiaries (branches only for Italy.)

b. Totals include banking offices (branches only for Japan), so that foreign organizations represented by more than one entity are double-counted. At the end of June 1985, total represented foreign organizations numbered 350 in the United States, 95 in Germany, and 76 in Japan.

SOURCE: Bank for International Settlements, as reported in Morgan Guaranty Trust Company, *World Financial Markets*, Nov.–Dec. 1986.

Table 2–2. Total Assets ^a of the U.S. Offices of Foreign Banks, 1980–1986

Ten Largest Countries (1986)	1980	1981	1982	1983	1984	1985	1986
Canada	15,718,428	21,503,472	22,148,288	25,838,300	38,101,415	39,553,299	42,431,042
France	12,925,772	16,914,185	15,736,972	16,101,115	18,384,141	20,653,757	20,653,757
Germany, West (Fed. Rep.)	7,253,180	7,349,767	8,880,866	7,382,739	7,565,605	8,801,212	11,049,175
Hong Kong	11,920,682	12,983,516	16,707,658	19,705,400	17,288,573	23,376,817	24,920,412
Israel	4,097,400	4,239,426	6,084,051	7,096,780	7,863,308	7,812,780	8,074,245
Italy	9,216,825	10,891,512	14,718,455	17,523,890	23,931,971	29,090,071	36,445,780
Japan	72,484,137	88,646,854	113,005,182	125,982,961	151,259,221	178,761,678	245,571,205
Netherlands	3,668,150	4,813,409	5,284,834	4,894,644	5,335,755	7,134,185	8,539,678
Switzerland	11,312,568	11,225,989	12,929,098	13,215,445	15,280,357	18,338,243	24,518,535
United Kingdom	25,136,319	46,445,237	52,171,252	53,058,135	51,443,593	57,170,899	40,631,292
TOTALS:							
TEN COUNTRIES	173,733,461	225,043,367	267,666,656	290,799,409	336,453,939	390,692,941	462,835,121
ALL COUNTRIES	198,115,287	251,217,538	301,021,581	333,336,188	378,313,617	441,525,633	526,589,545

a. Assets in thousands of dollars.
SOURCE: Federal Reserve Board.

denominated acceptances. Meanwhile, the 30 Japanese banks in London held over 25 percent of all banking assets booked in the United Kingdom in 1986. Table 2–2 indicates the growth of foreign banks' assets in the United States in recent years, demonstrating once again the particular importance of Japanese institutions in this context. This is reinforced by Table 2–3, which shows U.S. foreign subsidiaries of Japanese banks.

Banking interpenetration has taken on other geographic patterns as well. Table 2–4 shows assets and market shares of banks from

Table 2–3. Subsidiaries of Japanese Banks in the United States

Subsidiary	Parent	State	Assets [a]
California First Bank	Bank of Tokyo, Ltd.	California	$5,699,514
Sanwa Bank California	Sanwa Bank, Ltd.	California	5,067,044
Bank of Tokyo Trust Co.	Bank of Tokyo, Ltd.	New York	4,559,058
Industrial Bank of Japan Trust Co.	Industrial Bank of Japan, Ltd.	New York	3,995,714
Fuji Bank & Trust Co.	Fuji Bank, Ltd.	New York	3,955,815
Bank of California	Mitsubishi Bank, Ltd.	California	3,760,907
Sumitomo Bank of California	Sumitomo Bank, Ltd.	California	2,665,621
IBJ Schroeder Bank & Trust Co.	Industrial Bank of Japan, Ltd.	New York	2,593,096
Mitsui Manufacturers Bank	Mitsui Bank, Ltd.	California	1,817,647
Mitsubishi Bank of California	Mitsubishi Bank, Ltd.	California	1,490,517
Tokai Bank of California	Tokai Bank, Ltd.	California	1,470,711
Daiwa Bank Trust Co.	Daiwa Bank, Ltd.	New York	1,242,555
LTCB Trust Co.	Long-Term Credit Bank of Japan, Ltd.	New York	459,573
Dai-Ichi Kangyo Bank of California	Dai-Ichi Kangyo Bank, Ltd.	California	229,638
Mitsubishi Trust & Banking Corp. (U.S.A.)	Mitsubishi Trust	New York	144,373
Kyowa Bank of California	Kyowa Bank, Ltd.	California	93,099
Dai-Ichi Kangyo Trust Co.	Dai-Ichi Kangyo Bank, Ltd.	New York	0
Mitsui Finance Trust Co.	Mitsui Bank, Ltd.	New York	0
Tokai Trust Co.	Tokai Bank, Ltd.	New York	0
Mitsubishi Bank Trust Co. of New York	Mitsubishi Bank, Ltd.	New York	n.a.
TOTAL			39,244,882

a. Assets in thousands of dollars as of June 30, 1987.

SOURCE: Bank of Japan.

Table 2–4. Cross-Penetration of Banking: The United States and the European Community

U.S. Banks in the European Community (end 1986)

Branches and subsidiaries of U.S. banks in	Total Assets [a]	Percentage of the local market
Belgium	11.7	5.8
France	13.4	2.2
Germany	19.0	1.4
Italy	8.2	1.7
Luxembourg	3.3	1.9
Netherlands	6.9	2.6
Spain	8.5	3.2
United Kingdom	129.3	12.4
TOTAL Eight European Community Countries	200.3	4.6

European Community Banks in the United States (end 1987)

U.S. branches and subsidiaries of banks from	Total assets [a]	Percentage of the U.S. market
Belgium	2.3	0.1
Denmark	1.7	0.1
France	25.0	1.0
Germany	13.5	0.6
Italy	41.0	1.7
Netherlands	8.7	0.4
Spain	5.6	0.2
United Kingdom	44.7	1.8
TOTAL Eight European Community Countries	142.5	5.9

a. Total assets in billions of dollars.

SOURCES: Federal Reserve, International Monetary Fund.

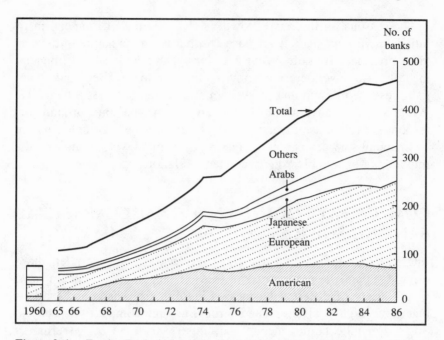

Figure 2–1. Foreign Banks in London. (*Source:* Noel Alexander Associates, March 1987; reprinted by permission)

selected European countries in the United States, and U.S. bank assets in these same countries, in the mid-1980s.

Major banking markets such as London and Zurich have likewise attracted significant numbers of foreign banks, as Figures 2–1 and 2–2 show. Both markets have a unique profile of attractions for foreign-based banking institutions and have developed in a unique way historically.

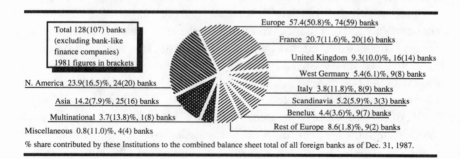

Figure 2–2. Foreign Banks' Presence in Switzerland. (*Source:* Association of Foreign Banks in Switzerland; reprinted by permission)

The reasons for the rapid growth in the activities of financial institutions in various markets are based primarily on the nature of the services provided. It is often (but not always) imperative for a financial institution to have a presence physically close to the client and an active presence in important markets in order to do business effectively. While a certain amount of business can certainly be done through correspondent relationships and travel, the increasingly complex nature of financial services and client needs has in many ways enhanced the importance of reliable "direct connect" relationships.

COMPOSITION OF INTERNATIONAL COMMERCIAL BANKING SERVICES

International commercial banking services closely parallel those offered in purely domestic markets (see Chapter 20). They encompass a great variety of different businesses involving products and markets that have highly differentiated structural and competitive profiles. Some are quite homogeneous and, unless distorted by government policies, have many of the attributes of efficient markets—intense competition, ease of entry and exit, low transaction and information costs, rapid adjustment to change, and very thin profit margins. Others involve substantial monopoly elements, with high degrees of product differentiation, natural barriers to entry, and substantial competitive power on the part of individual firms. There are at least six broad "product" categories.

First, there is *deposit taking* in onshore markets abroad and in offshore (Euro) markets, demand and time deposits of residents and nonresidents in foreign onshore accounts, and Eurodeposits in offshore accounts, which are deposits in foreign currencies not subject to full national regulating burdens. Deposits include those of individuals, corporations, governments, and other banks (redeposits). Competition for deposits is often intense, with funding costs dependent, in part, on the perceived safety and soundness of the institution, its sophistication, the efficiency of its retail deposit-gathering capabilities, and the range of customer services offered.

Second, and closely related, there are *international trading and dealing activities*—in foreign currencies, deposits, forward exchange contracts, financial futures and options, and gold and perhaps other commodities—all functionally linked to position the institution to profit from shifts in markets within acceptable limits of exposure to risk. A major determinant of profitability is the management of sources and uses of funds—mismatching the maturity structure of a part of the institution's assets and liabilities in the light of the shape of the yield curve, expectations about future interest rate movements, and anticipated liquidity needs. The financial institution must anticipate market developments more correctly and consistently than the competition, and it must move faster if it is to earn more than a normal return on its capital. The counterparties that it trades with in money and foreign exchange dealing, for example, must have different interest rate and exchange rate expectations or be slower and less sophisticated (and the institution itself has to be correct more of the time) if it is to excel in this activity. All of this must be accomplished in an environment in which each important player has simultaneous access to the same information. It is a fiercely competitive business.

Third, a traditional international financial product line encompasses *international trade and cash management services*. These involve international documentary collections, letters of credit, and acceptance financing. International trade services (ITS) have always been a mainstay of banks involved in global business. In banking they have been considered somewhat routine in nature, with relatively little scope for product differentiation and incremental returns. In recent years, however, there have been a number of innovations, particularly in the areas of process technology, systems, and data transmission, so that international trade services (particularly proprietary international cash management services supplied to multinational corporate clients and automated trade financing) have become much more attractive for banks.

In addition, standby letters of credit covering the issuance of debt by private firms and public-sector entities, as well as construction and related projects, have become an insurance-related and fee-earning activity that is not based on enlarging the balance sheet and, hence, can be attractive to banks. As a result of renewed interest in international trade and cash management services, competition between banks in this area has once again become heated. In part, this is due to some major institutions that have a strong interest in making up for lost ground in areas that they have long neglected in favor of more lucrative business opportunities.

Fourth, *international lending* remains a mainstay of the banking industry. This lending includes secured and unsecured loans to local corporations, banks, governments, multinational enterprises, and individuals domiciled outside the bank's home country, either in local or foreign currencies. Competition in this area varies from exceedingly intense in the Euromarkets to essentially monopolistic in some of the more protected onshore markets. Returns tend to vary with the degree of competition prevailing in the local environment, the complexity and riskiness of the deal, and the creditworthiness of the borrower. Specific dimensions of competitiveness in this area include the initiation and maintenance of contact with borrowers or other customers, the quality of credit evaluation, and questions of country risk. Specialized forms of international lending include syndicated loans and the financing of projects. In loan syndications the economic rents (i.e., compensation) are to a significant degree associated with lead management roles—namely, a bank's ability to obtain syndication mandates, to handle legal and information tasks as well as agency functions, and to develop networks of bank contacts and knowledge about their portfolios so that other participants can be brought into a transaction. Not every institution can cope successfully with all of these functions or can carry the often substantial underwriting risks involved, so that the fee-based returns from loan syndication activities can be substantial.

This is even more true of the financing of projects generally associated with energy or infrastructure development activities that are at least partly without recourse to the project's sponsors—e.g., energy or mining companies. It requires highly technical scientific and engineering capabilities within the bank and the ability to work with technical consultants. It also requires the capacity to assess a broad range of risks that run the gamut from project completion (delays, cost overruns) and *force majeure* to market prospects in natural resources or energy, and political change. Here, barriers to entry are quite high, and the structure of the market for lead positions in this business can perhaps be described as oligopolistic. International lease financing and ship and aircraft financing are other forms of specialized (asset-based) lending that require particular types of financial expertise and can generate substantial returns.

Fifth, besides trade-related and lending-related activities, there is also a range of services involving *underwriting and trading/dealing in domestic and international securities* issues (both foreign bonds and Eurobonds and notes) of various maturities, as well as futures, options, and (increasingly) equity shares. The origination, underwriting, and distribution of new securities in the international marketplace can be highly profitable, but, like syndicated lending, such activities require a high degree of distribution or placing power, extensive issuer contact, and the ability and willingness to take substantial underwriting risks. These activities also require a well-developed trading capability in secondary markets, since trading is a global, 24-hour business in many instruments and demands a strong presence in each time zone. This is the core business of investment banks in the United States and Japan, but in many other countries commercial banking and investment banking activities are combined in "universal" banking institutions.

Finally, there are *international personal banking and investment services*, fiduciary trust and investment activities for institutional clients, and retail banking abroad. These services include the issue of travelers' checks and travel-related services, stockbrokerage, securities custody and clearing, mutual funds, and meeting the financial needs of the wealthy. Such businesses involve specialized financial services and unique forms of competition and institutional cooperation. A significant worldwide market position is quite difficult to achieve, and yet it is often indispensable in offering a viable product (as is the case with travelers' checks). Retail banking in national financial markets abroad is not easy to penetrate, but product differentiation and infusion of new banking technologies can produce substantial returns to successful competitors who are able to gain access to local markets abroad.

If the variety and complexity of the kinds of international financial services are impressive, so too are the types of institutions that provide them. They range from enormous private and government-owned financial supermarkets, selling almost the entire range of products on a broad scale, to small specialist houses or boutiques that have carved out a position in international markets for a limited range of services. They also include predominantly domestic institutions that nevertheless have a substantial and often quite profitable international business (often conducted through correspondent relationships with foreign institutions). Across this product range, competition is frequently fierce. Yet, perhaps more than in some other industries, there is a substantial amount of cooperation as well, particularly in large or complex transactions.

PATTERNS OF INTERNATIONAL MARKET PENETRATION

Why do firms providing financial services, in particular commercial and universal banks, go international? Separate from the competitive distortions imposed by governments, there are a number of common sense explanations that often dictate the kinds of foreign affiliates established abroad by financial institutions.[2]

Customer Following

The number and complexity of international financial products just identified have increasingly called into question the feasibility of traditional correspondent banking relationships—largely associated with syndicated lending, trade-related financing, and foreign-exchange business—to service customer needs adequately. The addition of long-term financing, financing of projects, financial advisory services, and the like has often made it necessary to be physically close to the corporate customer in order to meet that customer's financial needs. When American-based multinational enterprises emerged as a major global economic force in the 1960s and early 1970s, it was only natural that U.S. commercial and investment banks would seek to follow their expansion into Canada, Latin America, and Western Europe. Having a presence in a country that is host to an affiliate of a multinational enterprise can cement a relationship that already exists at home. Decisions can be made more efficiently than through correspondent banking links. Higher priority is assigned to the client's needs.

Many American banks thus evolved into a "customer following" pattern that built on domestic client relationships by supplying financial services to affiliates of multinational enterprises in countries that received the bulk of foreign direct investment by American firms. In the 1970s and 1980s, when European, Canadian, and later Japanese investment in the United States took over as some of the most rapidly growing aspects of multinational corporate operations, foreign banks in turn followed their respective companies into the American market.[3] In essence, customer-following strategies derived from their close financial and institutional links to the major trading houses or manufacturing enterprises.

Customer-following behavior does not go unchallenged. Besides possible host government restrictions on the activities of foreign financial firms, indigenous banks also see local multinational affiliates as a fertile area for business development and often rise to the challenge.[4] Conversely, foreign-based financial institutions have attempted to use their natural multinational customer base to get a foothold in servicing the indigenous corporate community in host countries and possibly local retail customers as well.

Customer-following behavior has occasionally led to managerial tensions within multinational financial institutions. Multinational affiliates are often among the most creditworthy corporate customers in host country financial markets and, therefore, can command comparatively fine lending terms. Indigenous companies often have to pay higher rates on loans and, within accepted parameters of risk, may present more attractive financing prospects to foreign banks. Moreover, the companies present a potential opportunity, as they may subsequently move into foreign business environments where the bank is already present. Yet, neglect of multinational affiliates in local markets can strain bank relations with the parent corporation at home. It has always been difficult to weigh the profitability of the total relationship between banks and multinational enterprises against the alternatives that present themselves in various onshore banking environments abroad. Similar conflicts emerge in nonbank financial service firms but perhaps on a somewhat smaller scale.

Customer Leading

Apart from following their multinational customers into foreign markets, international banks sometimes lead them. They may be well established in a national business environment abroad and can provide useful information, contacts, advice, and financial services to foreign firms considering market entry. They can help lead the client into the foreign market, whether through *de novo* investments or acquisitions, and this can pay off in terms of new financing opportunities, fee-based service income, and future business with the multinational enterprises worldwide.

Again, foreign banks must compete with indigenous institutions for customer-leading activities. However, the foreign banks frequently seem to have an inside track because of existing banking and advisory relationships with the customer back home or possibly in third countries. Once a financial institution has learned how to engage in customer-leading activities, which often have many of the characteristics of investment banking, it can use its global presence to good advantage in obtaining maximum leverage. Customer-leading patterns have also emerged in the case of nonbank international investment houses, particularly among U.S. and Japanese securities firms.

Serving Local Markets

Besides exploiting the synergy that exists between multinational enterprises and financial institutions through customer-following and customer-leading behavior, there is a third option: seeking direct access to wholesale and retail customers in local markets. Astute research can reveal the essential competitive structure of national financial markets. Local banks may do a particularly poor job of deposit gathering or money dealing in the domestic financial market, or they may not be fully competitive on the lending side (e.g., in transaction efficiency, operations, and systems) or in providing ancillary services (e.g., financial advice). Such conditions translate either into high levels of profitability for local institutions, low levels of productivity, or both. They indicate a potentially strong opportunity for foreign-based competitors to penetrate the local market and provide better and less costly services to indigenous customers. If the foreigners can transfer product or process technologies, seeking local markets can be highly rewarding.

Such activity is not likely to go unnoticed by indigenous competitors. As long as foreign penetration of their traditional markets is small and not considered a material threat, little may happen. But once a particular threshold is reached, intense competition can break out, with local institutions adopting many of the financial innovations, business strategies, and managerial tactics of their foreign rivals. Clearly, banking customers will be the principal beneficiaries of the heightened efficiency and creativity that accompanies the higher level of competition. Alternatively, the local institutions may seek government protection to exclude or limit the foreign institutions. Or they may try to use their superior power in the marketplace to constrain foreign encroachment on the lending side or foreign access to funding sources in the local currency. Both kinds of responses will help to preserve financial inefficiency and banking profits in the local environment.

Local market-seeking activities of foreign banks or other firms providing financial services may be aimed at a number of different groups of customers: corporate, banking, government, and retail. The government market is probably the easiest to penetrate, in terms of foreign currency lending, followed by the indigenous banking sector. The number of local corporations that may be attractive to foreign banks is often extremely limited. Once a bank begins to seek clients beyond a small cadre of prime names that are the targets of virtually every other institution in the market, the list of potential customers— subject to substantial difficulties in evaluating credit risks in the local environment—may become rather short. In the investment business, exchange controls restricting residents from placing funds abroad often severely limit the value of foreign firms' financial services in the local market.

An interesting case of foreign market penetration by U.S. institutions in recent years has involved credit cards in Western Europe and Japan. With the domestic market virtually saturated and European and Japanese retail customers only beginning to accept credit cards as a means of payment in the 1980s, the prospects for transferring the necessary product and marketing know-how, as well as processing technologies, seemed very promising indeed.

In Europe, travel and entertainment cards such as American Express and Diners Club have been marketed to up-scale clients for a long time, but these cards did not make significant inroads until recently. They faced resistance from local banks, especially in Germany, where institutions placed a premium on cross-selling a variety of products to their customers. That this fear was not unfounded was underscored by American Express's purchase of a Frankfurt bank, as well as by the sale of insurance and other financial services through credit cards. Moreover, German retail bank marketing is heavily based on the client's physical presence inside the banking office, which widespread use of credit cards would obviously make far less necessary.

Following several attempts to impede entry by regulatory means and collaboration among banks in refusing credit card participation, the German banks launched their own "Eurocard" as a means of curbing the foreign incursions. The inroads continued, however, and in 1987 the German retailers announced a plan to issue charge cards themselves, to the great consternation of the banks. Given the pressures from competitors, bank resistance to charge cards was viewed as a lost cause, with the response focused on creation of a charge card for all of Europe complete with a common clearing and processing system—even as the U.S.-based charge card systems redouble their efforts to sign up increasing numbers of European bank issuers.

Japan eased limits on foreign bank card operations in the late 1970s, and both Visa International and MasterCard International began to compete with the local JCB card operations. The number of cards outstanding increased from 23.6 million in 1979 to 85 million in 1985. Each firm approached the market in a different way, with MasterCard franchisees issuing cards under their own names and Visa franchising though a 22-bank consortium called Visa Japan, Inc. Visa International also reached a marketing arrangement with the Japanese postal service's savings system, which accounts for roughly one-third of personal savings, a move that strained relations with the Visa Japan franchisees, which compete directly for savings with the post office.

American Express and Diners Club, meantime, dominated the upper end of the market, each with about 450,000 cards outstanding, and in 1987 Citibank launched a gold card as part of an effort to increase its small foothold in the Japanese retail market.

Japanese cardholders are not permitted to access a revolving line of credit through their cards. Rather, they must pay all balances in full at the end of each billing period. This regulation is a result of persistent lobbying on the part of local consumer finance companies, which see a distinct threat to their customer base.

Forms of Involvement

How foreign-based financial institutions choose to serve national markets depends on the specific types of services to be provided, the degree of control management wants to exercise, and the local restrictions. These forms of involvement include representative offices, consortium banks, minority participations, joint ventures, wholly owned subsidiaries, agencies, and full branches. Table 2–5 lists the various strengths and weaknesses associated with different forms of involvement.

INTERNATIONAL BANKING CENTERS

Beginning in the 1960s a good deal of international commercial banking expansion occurred in the Eurocurrency markets. These markets permit banks to take offshore deposits from, and make offshore loans to, nonresidents free from significant regulatory constraints imposed on banks in national or "onshore" markets. They also permit banks to accept deposits and make loans in various currencies on a separate set of books entirely divorced from similar activities within the domestic monetary system. For banks there are no reserve requirements, asset ratios, or other restrictions that form the basis of safety and soundness in domestic banking systems. Supervision of offshore branches is supposed to be exercised by the bank's home authorities, while other forms of offshore banking (e.g., subsidiaries and consortiums) are under the jurisdiction of the country in which the banking center is located. In principle, no offshore banking center is supposed to be able to escape prudential safety and soundness constraints (see Chapter 25), although there have been some instances of regulatory slippage fostered in part by regulatory competition among the offshore banking centers themselves.

Table 2–5. Relative Advantages of Alternative Forms of Organization

	Representative Office	"Shell" Branch	Affiliate	Subsidiary	Branch	Consortium and Joint Venture
Amount of investment required	Modest	Minor/modest	Moderate	Moderate/substantial	Moderate substantial	Moderate
Control over operation	Direct	Direct	Minor	Substantial/direct	Direct	Minor/moderate
Referral business	Favorable	None	Minor	Favorable [a]	Favorable	Minor/moderate
New business	Favorable	None	Limited potential	Favorable [a]	Favorable	Minor/moderate
Flexibility of operation	Relatively inflexible	None	Inflexible	Flexible [b]	Flexible [b]	Some flexibility
Manpower	Some manpower [d]	Minor	Minor	[c]	[c]	Modest

a. A subsidiary is likely to refer business to its own parent and is virtually capable as a branch of introducing new business to the group.

b. Under certain circumstances, subsidiaries can undertake business which cannot be undertaken by a branch. In addition, subsidiaries have "independent" management decision-making power which may give more flexibility than is enjoyed by a branch.

c. Difficult to categorize, since it depends on specific circumstances, the type of subsidiary of branch and the characteristics of the business to be undertaken (for example, retail or wholesale business).

d. In some instances, however, the scale of business carried out by a representative office is such as to require a substantial amount of manpower.

SOURCE: R. M. Pecchioli, *The Internationalization of Banking* (Paris: OECD Secretariat, 1983), p. 19.

While offshore banking is conducted in many countries around the world, the major centers are the Bahamas, Bahrain, the Cayman Islands, Hong Kong, London, Luxembourg, New York, Panama, Singapore, and (most recently) Tokyo. There are several factors that make a given locale attractive as an offshore banking center. The most important are permissive local regulation of administrative operations, foreign borrowing and lending, foreign exchange operations, and favorable tax treatment. Many centers permit business that is booked in their jurisdictions to be administered in another country, which allows substantial economies in staffing and other expenses. Additional factors important to the development of a center are the receptiveness and stability of the host government, time zone positioning, and, in the case of functional centers, the local supply of skilled labor and the sophistication of the local transport and telecommunications network.

Transactions and earnings in offshore banking centers are largely free of tax; even minimal levels of taxation can quickly price a center out of the market. Eurodeposits and redeposits within and among these centers serve to fund loans in various maturities, including major syndicated credits often involving dozens of banks (see Chapter 5). Sharing the long end of the market in several centers are Eurobonds, which are debt instruments of private and public issuers sold to non-residents in bearer form and, hence, generally free of tax and free from the kinds of tight regulatory and disclosure requirements usually found in domestic bond markets (see Chapter 14). Euroloans and Eurobonds have been joined by short-term Euronotes, which may be underwritten and distributed in the offshore markets and supported by note issuance facilities (NIFs), revolving underwriting facilities (RUFs), or other variants on these backstops provided by financial institutions (see Chapter 9).

The major areas of offshore activities for banking centers are: the funding, syndication, booking, and administration of loans; the underwriting, dealing in, and clearing of securities; and the management of tax-sheltered investments for nonresidents. The importance of these centers stems from the number of commercial banks, affiliates of these banks, and investment banks that operate in them, the volume of transactions they handle, and the significant earnings derived from them. Artificial barriers to entry and exit are minimal, competition is intense, and limited regulatory controls mean that spreads between deposit and lending rates are thinner than in most onshore financial markets.

Table 2–6 indicates the relative sizes of offshore markets in various financial centers. In New York, Tokyo, and Singapore they involve

Table 2-6. Characteristics of Selected Offshore Markets

	New York IBF Type [a]			London Type [b]		Tax Haven Type
	Tokyo	New York	Singapore	London	Hong Kong	Bahamas
Established	Dec. 1986 [d]	Dec. 1981	Nov. 1968	End 1950s	1957–1958	Late 1960s
Assets ($ billions) [c]	97 [d]	261	155	751	143	126 [e]
Taxation						
Corporate	48.3%	Max. 46%	40% + 10% of overseas profits	40%	18.5%	No
Other	Local (12.3%) and stamp duty	—	—	—	—	Registration and licensing fees
Securities business allowed?	No	No	Yes	Yes	Yes	No

a. Domestic and foreign transactions separated.

b. Domestic and foreign transactions integrated.

c. December 1985.

d. December 1986.

e. December 1984.

SOURCE: Bank of Tokyo, as reported in *The Economist*, February 21, 1987, p. 83. ©1987 The Economist Newspaper Ltd. All rights reserved.

accounts of nonresidents that are separate from domestic accounts and that benefit from reduced regulatory constraints. In London and Hong Kong regulatory constraints are minimal, so that transactions of residents and nonresidents need not be separated and "offshore" transactions really represent onshore transactions between nonresidents of the United Kingdom and Hong Kong. To this are added tax-haven incentives for nonresidents in countries like the Bahamas and the Cayman Islands, which represent "booking" rather than "functional" centers (the actual transactions are handled elsewhere).

SUMMARY

In this chapter we have introduced the internationalization and globalization of the commercial banking industry in a historical and behavioral context. We have also outlined the industry in terms of commercial banking services, or "products," that it supplies to wholesale and retail clients around the world. Some of these are highly localized or tailored to the idiosyncratic needs of a particular client or situation. Others are broad based and generic and are capable of being spread across wide markets.

It is important to remember the extreme complexity of the financial services industry today. It is not just one industry, but perhaps 20 or 30, each one driven by distinctive competitive criteria and having its own competitive dynamics in terms of its international evolution. This will become clear in later chapters, which examine the individual activity segments of the industry (see Part II, "Commercial Banking Services") and provide a coherent market model (see Chapter 20).

NOTES

1. Morgan Guaranty Trust Company, "America's Banking Market Goes International," *Morgan Economic Quarterly*, June 1986, pp. 1–6.
2. Ingo Walter, *Global Competition in Financial Services* (New York: Ballinger - Harper & Row, 1988), pp. 34–36.
3. R. M. Pecchioli, *Internationalization of Banking* (Paris: OECD Secretariat, 1983), p. 12.
4. Olivier Pastré, *Multinationals: Banking and Firm Relationships* (Greenwich, CT: JAI Press, 1981, pp. 147–48.

SELECTED REFERENCES

Aliber, Robert Z. "International Banking: A Survey." *Journal of Money, Credit and Banking*, November 1984.

American Bankers Association, *The Future Development of U.S. Banking Organizations Abroad*. Washington, D.C.: American Bankers Association, 1981.

Boston Consulting Group. *The Future of Wholesale Banking*. Rolling Meadows, IL: Bank Administration Institute, 1986.

Crane, Dwight B., and Hayes, Samuel L. III. "The New Competition in World Banking." *Harvard Business Review*, July–August 1982.

Davis, Steven I. *The Euro-bank*, 2nd ed. London: Macmillan, 1979.

Davis, Stephen I. *Excellence in Banking*. London: Macmillan, 1985.

Fieleke, Norman S. "The Growth of U.S. Banking Abroad: An Analytical Survey." In *Key Issues in International Banking*. Boston: Federal Reserve Bank of Boston, 1977.

Hogan, Warren E., and Pierce, Ivor F. *The Incredible Eurodollar*. London: Allen & Unwin, 1982.

Mathis, John F., ed. *Offshore Lending by U.S. Commercial Banks*, 2nd ed. Philadelphia: Bankers' Association for Foreign Trade and Robert Morris Associates, 1982.

McKenzie, George W. *Economics of the Eurodollar Market*. London: Macmillan, 1976.

Morgan Guaranty Trust Company, "America's Banking Market Goes International." *Morgan Economic Quarterly*, June 1986.

Office of Technology Assessment, U.S. Congress. *International Competition in Banking and Financial Services*. Washington, D.C.: OTA, July 1986. Mimeographed.

Organization for Economic Cooperation and Development. *Trade in Services in Banking*. Paris: OECD Secretariat, 1983.

Page, Diane and Soss, Neil M. "Some Evidence on Transnational Banking Structure." In *Foreign Acquisitions of U.S. Banks*. Washington: U.S. Government Printing Office, for the Office of the Comptroller of the Currency, 1982.

Pastré, Olivier. *Multinationals: Banking and Firm Relationships*. Greenwich, CT: JAI Press, 1981.

Pastré, Olivier. "International Bank-Industry Relations: An Empirical Assessment." *Journal of Banking and Finance*, March 1981.

Pecchioli, R. M. *Internationalization of Banking*. Paris: OECD Secretariat, 1983.

Sagari, Sylvia B. *The Financial Services Industry: An International Perspective*. Ph.D. dissertation, Graduate School of Business Administration, New York University, 1986.

Saunders, Anthony, and Walter, Ingo. "International Trade in Financial Services: Are Bank Services Special?" Paper presented at the *Symposium on New Institutional Arrangements for the World Economy*, 1987, University of Konstanz. Mimeographed.

Tschoegl, Adrian E. "Foreign Bank Entry into Japan and California." In *New Theories of the Multinational Enterprise*, edited by Allen M. Rugman. London: Croom Helm, 1982.

Tschoegl, Adrian E. "Size, Growth and Transnationality Among the World's Largest Banks." *Journal of Business*, 56 (1983).

U.S. Comptroller of the Currency. *Foreign Acquisition of U.S. Banks: Motives and Tactical Consideration*. Washington, D.C.: U.S. Government Printing Office, for the Office of the Comptroller of the Currency, 1982.

U.S. Comptroller of the Currency. *U.S. Banks' Loss of Global Standing*. Washington, D.C.: U.S. Government Printing Office, for the Office of the Comptroller of the Currency, 1984.

Walter, Ingo. *Barriers to Trade in Banking and Financial Services*. London: Trade Policy Research Centre, 1985.

Walter, Ingo. *Global Competition in Financial Services*. New York: Ballinger–Harper & Row, 1988.

3

Investment and Merchant Banking

International transactions involving loans and securities have occurred more or less continuously since the fifteenth century, when both commerce and conflict between the city-states of Europe had to be financed by means other than taxes. Those who provided the financing, like the Medicis of medieval Florence, had to be well connected with decision makers, had to maintain a wide network of sources of information and influence, and had to possess an exquisite sense of timing. They had to be clever, they had to be able to react quickly, and they had to be—or at least appear to be—unquestionably sound themselves. Though the business was imperiled by the intrigues of others as well as the risk of the market, the rewards could be very great for those who could compete in it successfully. Banker-adventurers have been closely involved with, or at least not far behind, most of the great events of modern European history, especially its colonial period. Financial skills have always been in demand, and many of the functions performed today are not very different from those carried out 500 years ago.

However, the scale and the volume of transactions, the speed at which they are conducted, and the vast array of products now available are far beyond anything our financial forefathers could have imagined, as is the extent to which the international component of finance has grown and become institutionalized.

The great players are no longer small private banking houses but substantial financial institutions whose activities span the globe. They come from America as commercial and investment banks; from Europe as merchant banks, banques d'affaires, and universal banks; and from Japan as long-term credit banks, city banks, trust banks, and securities firms. Though in some countries there are regulations that require separation between deposit taking and loan making on one hand, and securities underwriting and trading on the other, such regulations do not apply beyond the borders of the countries involved. The world beyond one's own borders is often referred to in financial parlance as "offshore," where home country regulations do not apply. For regulatory purposes, it is a virtually stateless world. There the various types of banks compete in Eurobond and equity securities and international investments of all types.

In recent years the volume of offshore bond and equity financing involving transactions between national markets has grown very rapidly. Linkages between these markets have increased to an extent that conditions in one market affect those in others, leading us to conceive of world financial markets as having become "globalized." In the case of major industrialized countries, barriers to cross-border financial transactions have declined to almost nothing. Deregulation of the financial services sector in many countries has led to increased competition and exposure to international markets. Prodigious improvements in telecommunications have made it possible for markets to become integrated. These developments have greatly expanded the range of alternatives available to those from all over the industrialized world who seek to raise money or invest it.

Major markets for securities, foreign exchange, and commodities are centered in New York, London, and Tokyo, and trading between these markets in almost all instruments goes on around the clock. The international securities business has become large, complex, diverse, highly competitive, and risky. In order to survive, today's players must continue to adapt to changes in the marketplace, particularly the international market in which traditional regulatory orderliness does not apply. The 1980s were and the 1990s will continue to be times of great competitive and strategic repositioning by the world's major financial institutions and providers of financial services of all types.

EUROPEAN ORIGINS

Banking in Europe has an extremely long, rich, and varied history. From widely different origins, banks of many types have evolved through time into what are thought of today as investment and merchant banks. In medieval Italy various northern cities developed deposit banking from pawnbroking and money changing. These banks became skilled in transferring money required for trade between Tuscany and other parts of Europe. They established branches or agencies in France, Spain, Belgium, Holland, Germany, and Britain. To secure advantages in these foreign arenas, including profitable export concessions and currency exchange, the Italians were persuaded to advance funds to English and other monarchs. Occasionally, a ruler defaulted, often bringing down whoever was then holding his paper. As the Italians faded, merchants from the south of Germany took their place in the sixteenth century. The famous Fuggers of Augsburg were merchants who traded all over Europe through "factories"— branches containing both a warehouse and a counting house in various countries.

The Fuggers are credited with developing the system of financial intermediation in which they would borrow from wealthy depositors to lend to others. Other merchants, such as the Rothschilds of Frankfurt, as well as goldsmiths and public notaries became increasingly active as financial intermediaries through the eighteenth and nineteenth centuries and came to be called *merchant bankers*. Often the transactions financed by the banks were international and involved trade with colonial areas, which frequently were short of credit.

By the nineteenth century, most such houses had left the commercial aspects of their business behind to specialize in the seemingly more profitable and less risky business of lending, usually against good collateral, to support trade between other parties. Often clients would ask their merchant bankers to "accept," or guarantee, receivables due from customers of the client—or the client's own obligations—to make payment for goods or services so that these notes could be discounted for cash at banks. In the United Kingdom, virtually all of today's merchant banks are designated accepting houses authorized to do business with the Bank of England. Many great names of finance, such as Rothschild, Baring, Morgan, and Lehman, began as merchants who later became bankers.[1]

Raising Funds and Managing Money

In addition to financing trade and commerce, merchant bankers often performed additional services for their clients. For those needing money for capital investments, they arranged loans in the form of secured or promissory notes. They sold these notes to investors, many of whom were purchasers of the trade paper that was also sold by the bank. For those with large fortunes seeking good-quality investments, merchant bankers offered advice and found opportunities. Some German bankers, many of whom were descendants of Jewish merchants and goldsmiths from Berlin, Hamburg, Frankfurt, and the Rhineland, evolved as *private bankers* to monarchs, governments, and large corporations, which were constantly seeking funds, and to wealthy families whose money required skillful management. Warburg, Bleichroder, and Rothschild are among the prominent European private bankers who have survived to the present. Other European banks, especially the Swiss, specialized in money management of funds left in the bank's custody by wealthy families and individuals. Political disruption, wars, and economic restrictions resulted in large amounts of private wealth flowing into Switzerland during the twentieth century. Here it could be left with the large banks in Zurich or Basel or with the smaller, more specialized and intimate private banks (e.g., Pictet, Hentsch, and Lombard Odier), which today are located mainly in Geneva.

In the latter part of the nineteenth century, a type of bank specializing in investments in industry, *banques d'affaires*, developed in France and Belgium. Banks such as the Banque de Paris et de Pays-Bas (Paribas) made loans and invested their own funds and clients' funds in securities, including common stock, in many companies included on long lists of industrial clients. Because of the substantial amount of capital required for these investments, only the larger banks developed industrial portfolios to any significant degree. Elsewhere in Europe, the larger German, Swiss, and other continental banks that engaged in all aspects of banking, from deposit taking to investment management, came to be called *universal banks*. These, especially the German universal banks, made substantial equity investments in their industrial clients, especially during the periods after the two world wars, and gained significant degrees of control over the German industrial structure.

INVESTMENT BANKING IN THE UNITED STATES

There were two main tasks to be accomplished by investment bankers in the United States during the nineteenth century: (1) the establishment of networks and connections through which European capital could be channeled into the United States, and (2) the organization of an internal American securities distribution system.

Several prominent London banks such as Baring Brothers and Rothschilds were represented in the United States by the 1840s—in the Rothschild's case by the wealthy, socially prominent, and powerful figure of August Belmont. London connections were vital to any ambitious American financial house, and several of these located representatives in England to look after their business there and to widen their circle of acquaintances. In the early 1800s Alexander Brown of Baltimore organized the London firm of Brown Shipley, headed by one of his sons, with branches in New York and Philadelphia headed by other sons. The New York branch ultimately became Brown Brothers Harriman & Co.

Another American, George Peabody of Boston, founded his own firm in London after representing others there for many years. In 1854 he accepted Junius S. Morgan, a dry goods merchant from Boston, as a partner. On Peabody's retirement to pursue a second career as a philanthropist, for which he was offered (but declined) a knighthood by Queen Victoria, the firm's name was changed to J. S. Morgan & Co. Later known as Morgan, Grenfell & Co., the firm was represented in New York and Philadelphia by Junius's son, J. Pierpont Morgan, who had set up his own firm in 1860. The younger Morgan went on to become the most important and celebrated investment banker in U.S. history.

Morgan's firm distributed stocks and bonds of U.S. corporations in Europe and later distributed stocks and bonds of European governments and corporations in the United States. It also organized some of the largest corporations in America, such as U.S. Steel in 1901, by merging several independent producers into a new giant, by capitalizing the new company with both debt and equity, and by underwriting the sale of these securities for distribution to investors through syndication operations in the United States and Europe. Much of what investment bankers in the United States do today, including mergers, acquisitions, the distribution of various kinds of securities, and the restructuring and recapitalizing of underperforming companies, was introduced well before World War I.

J. P. Morgan and his associates operated in a totally unregulated, unprotected environment that created many opportunities as well as many hazards for bankers. The relationships between banker and client were extremely close, with bankers and their partners occupying several seats on the boards of directors of client companies and participating actively in important management decisions. Rapidly growing, capital-intensive businesses benefited from these relationships because, through the sponsorship of well-known financiers, they could have access to the markets for working capital and investment funds.[2]

In the 1860s a number of Jewish banking firms with German origins, some of which had prospered during the American Civil War by selling U.S. government securities to investors in Germany, began to rise in prominence. Among these were J. & W. Seligman, Kuhn

Loeb, Lehman Brothers, and Goldman Sachs. All of these firms had strong European connections, which they were able to employ successfully in distributing U.S. securities. The Jewish firms were especially active around the turn of the century in selling securities of retailing and light manufacturing companies. Goldman Sachs and Lehman Brothers are credited with devising the first initial public offerings of common stock in the United States, with issues by General Cigar Manufacturing Co. and Sears Roebuck in 1906.[3]

The general distribution of securities in the United States developed slowly. The main activity of the domestic brokerage business was the sale of U.S. government securities, particularly those issued to finance various wars. The U.S. Treasury floated a $16 million war bond in 1813 to help finance the War of 1812, most of which could not be sold to the general public and had to be purchased by three wealthy New Yorkers. The Civil War produced somewhat better results. The first national brokerage effort was undertaken by J. Cooke, who sold large quantities of U.S. Civil War bonds through a national sales organization. Subsequently, Cooke applied his organization to the sale of municipal and some corporate (mainly railroad) securities. The Cooke firm failed in 1873 in one of the periodic panics that characterized nineteenth-century American finance. Other firms, of course, subsequently rose in its place. The First National Bank of New York, later called Citibank, which was founded in 1863, was active in investment banking and securities distribution until 1933.

After 1900 there was sufficient investment capital available in the United States for large issues to be completely taken up by U.S. investors. Indeed, in the period between the world wars, the U.S. market absorbed substantial issues of foreign securities, many of which were issued by Latin American governments that ultimately defaulted. To manage such large issues of securities, the "underwriting syndicate" was devised. Such syndicates were formed by grouping 100 or so securities firms into tiers, according to the financial capacity and prestige of individual firms. As a group these firms would purchase an entire issue of securities for resale over a period time, and in an orderly manner, to institutional, individual, and overseas investors.[4]

The 1920s were boom years, especially for the issuance of new corporate and investment company securities. Private banks, such as J. P. Morgan and Kuhn Loeb, dominated the new issues business, but well-capitalized securities affiliates of the major commercial banks, such as First National Corporation and Chase Securities Corp., were also active in bringing new issues to the market and in secondary market trading. During the feverish period of the late 1920's, many excesses occurred. Ultimately, the stock market crash of October 29, 1929 triggered the collapse of financial markets in other countries, and a combination of nonresponsive monetary policies and restrictive trade legislation helped to bring on the Great Depression of the 1930s. Banks were blamed for causing the crash and the subsequent hard times. Concerned by the collapse of banks around the country and inspired by the activist administration of a newly elected president, Franklin Roosevelt, the Congress passed legislation that had singular effects on the banking and securities businesses in the United States.

The trauma of the Great Depression, with its contraction of world trade and numerous sovereign debt defaults, caused a 30-year hiatus in international banking. The international environment of the 1930s and 1940s, characterized by waves of nationalism, socialism, and militarism was far less conducive to international finance than the previous 100 years of the Pax Britannica had been. Free market mechanisms were perceived to have failed, and governments assumed an unprecedented role in regulating economies. Bankers, wounded by failures and loan defaults and now subject to extensive government regulation, largely accepted their new role as managers of financial "public utilities," providing liquidity and financial services under careful supervision of regulators.

When the United States emerged from isolationism to support and fund the allied war effort and subsequently to help reconstruct an economically devastated Europe through the Marshall Plan, the government, not the banks, emerged as the provider of the necessary financial resources. Governments, in cooperation with one another, created the World Bank and the International Monetary Fund (IMF) at the Bretton Woods Conference in 1944, and these new institutions were designated to have the principal role in lending to poorer countries and to maintain a regime of stable currencies.

In the 1950s and early 1960s U.S. capital was exported abroad through direct foreign investment of U.S. multinational corporations, which attracted the banks again to the foreign environment. This environment expanded dramatically during the 1960s and 1970s.

The Glass-Steagall provisions of the Banking Act of 1933 required all banking institutions to discontinue participation in the corporate securities business. This resulted in the formation of two separate and distinct banking sectors in the United States: (1) *commercial banks* and (2) *investment banks*. The commercial banks were allowed to accept deposits (which were entitled to U.S. government insurance up to a stipulated maximum amount through the Federal Deposit Insurance Corporation, also created in 1933, and were entitled to borrow from the Federal Reserve, which would act as a lender of last resort. Investment banks, so named because they dealt in investment securities, were not banks at all; they were underwriters, brokers, and dealers in negotiable securities. With the exception of U.S. government securities and certain municipal securities, commercial banks were not permitted to participate in these businesses. Investment banks and other securities firms were made subject to regulation by the Securities and Exchange Commission, as provided for in the landmark Securities Acts of 1933 and 1934, which were enacted after the stock market crash of 1929.

Although denied access to the banking business, securities firms were allowed to finance customer purchases of securities under margin rules promulgated by the Federal Reserve and to underwrite issues of commercial paper, or short-term promissory notes, sold by top-rated corporations to raise working capital. Initially, commercial banks were not eligible to participate in the commercial paper business, which became exclusive to investment banks and those corporations large enough to issue their own paper directly. The Glass-Steagall provisions, however, did not apply outside of the United States, where vigorous competition between U.S. commercial banks and investment banks in both the banking and the securities businesses developed and has continued.

Many changes have occurred in recent years that have affected the division of labor between commercial banks, and the various investment and merchant banking organizations around the world. In the United States the securities business has grown much more rapidly since 1975 than the banking business, and many commercial banks, seeking to enter this promising field, have endeavored to secure changes and liberalizations to the Glass-Steagall legislation enacted over half a century earlier. As of the end of 1989, banks had succeeded in forcing the erosion of Glass-Steagall in many significant areas (including the ability to enter the commercial paper business), but the main prohibitions against underwriting corporate equity securities and engaging in the brokerage business remain in force. Major banks strongly oppose these restrictions and have engaged in vigorous efforts to promote a major legislative change to the Glass-Steagall legislation. Such efforts have had the support of the Treasury Department and more recently the Federal Reserve Board, though Congress remained substantially divided on the issue.

BANKING DIVISIONS IN JAPAN

During the American occupation of Japan following World War II, the occupation authorities under General Douglas MacArthur effected a number of major reforms to the structure of Japanese industry. The large industrial and financial holding companies called *zaibatsu* were broken up in the interest of restricting anticompetitive and politically powerful monopolies. At the same time, the equivalent of the U.S. Glass-Steagall legislation was inserted into the Japanese Securities and Exchange Act of 1948 as Article 65. Accordingly, Japanese commercial banking has since been separate from investment banking, which is conducted exclusively by securities firms. These are dominated in Japan by four large retail brokerage houses, Nomura, Daiwa, Nikko, and Yamaichi. The firms had been associated with *zaibatsu* before the war but were later restructured as independent companies. Each has about 100 branch offices throughout Japan that handle securities transactions for individuals, institutions, and corporations. Between them, the "big four," as they are known, account for approximately 40 percent of commissions earned and an even higher percentage of underwriting managerships. Article 65, like the U.S. Glass-Steagall provisions, does not apply outside Japan; however, the administrative jurisdiction of the Ministry of Finance does apply, and the activities of banks and securities firms, though liberalized greatly, are still subject to strict regulation.

It is generally assumed that the amendment or abolition of the Glass-Steagall Act will result in a similar change in Japan's Article 65, which has also been subject to controversy and challenge. Many foreign banks have already been able to bypass restrictions preventing them from participating in the securities business in Japan, and this has put further pressure on the Japanese government to provide similar advantages for their own banks by amending Article 65. Many new financial services have been introduced in Japan over the past few years, and the banks and securities firms have fought over who should have rights to which businesses. Because of the booming stock market, fixed commission structure, and the enormously increased importance of Japan as a financial center, the securities firms have grown more rapidly than banks. Today, the principal firms are not only equivalent in size to the formerly all-powerful banks, they are also much larger than any investment or merchant bank elsewhere in the world (see Table 3–1). Together with the commercial banks, they account for about 90 percent of the market value of equity of the top 50 investment and commercial banks in the world.

Table 3–1. Financial Data for the World's Leading Banks and Securities Firms

1988 World Ranking by Market Capitalization	Name of Institution	Market Value[a]	Total Assets[a]	Book Value[a]	Ratio of Market to Book Value	Ratio of Assets to Book Value
1	Industrial Bank of Japan	86.0	249.6	6.2	13.9	40.3
2	Sumitomo Bank	80.0	334.8	8.7	9.2	38.5
3	Fuji Bank	75.2	327.8	9.3	8.1	35.2
4	Mitsubishi Bank	71.3	317.9	8.2	8.7	38.8
5	Dai Ichi Kangyo Bank	70.9	352.6	8.5	8.3	41.5
6	Sanwa Bank	60.2	307.6	7.9	7.6	38.9
7	Nomura Securities	57.1	29.2	9.1	6.3	3.2
8	Long Term Credit Bank	36.9	168.9	4.1	9.0	41.2
9	Mitsui Bank[b]	33.9	188.2	4.8	7.1	39.2
10	Tokai Bank	33.7	213.6	5.4	6.2	39.6
11	Mitsubishi Trust & Banking	33.5	198.3	5.0	6.7	39.7
12	Sumitomo Trust & Banking	28.2	189.7	3.5	8.1	54.2
13	Bank of Tokyo	26.0	162.6	3.9	6.7	41.7
14	Daiwa Securities	24.7	35.8	5.6	4.4	6.4
15	Nikko Securities	21.3	20.3	4.1	5.2	5.0
16	Mitsui Trust & Banking	20.0	173.2	4.1	4.9	42.2
17	Taiyo Kobe Bank[b]	18.1	166.7	3.2	5.7	52.1
18	Nippon Credit Bank	17.6	110.0	2.4	7.3	45.8
19	Yamaichi Securities	17.3	22.9	4.0	4.3	5.7
20	Daiwa Bank	16.4	144.5	2.8	5.9	51.6
21	Yasuda Trust & Banking	15.7	147.2	3.3	4.8	44.6
22	Toyo Trust & Banking	12.9	119.7	2.7	4.8	44.3
23	Kyowa Bank	12.4	103.2	2.5	5.0	41.3
24	Bank of Yokohama	11.5	76.4	2.1	5.5	36.4
25	Saitama Bank	11.3	86.4	2.1	5.4	41.1

48

26	Deutsche Bank	11.3	171.5	6.5	1.7	26.4
27	American Express Corp.	11.1	117.0	4.8	2.3	24.4
28	Union Bank of Switzerland	9.5	110.9	6.7	1.4	16.6
29	Citicorp	8.2	203.4	9.9	0.8	20.5
30	Barclays Bank	8.1	189.3	14.9	0.5	12.7
31	Banco Bilbao-Vizcaya	8.0	62.4	4.1	2.0	15.2
32	Swiss Bank Corporation	7.5	102.6	6.1	1.2	16.8
33	Shizuoka Bank	7.4	41.6	1.7	4.4	24.5
34	National Westminister bank	7.0	176.5	10.7	0.7	16.5
35	Hokkaido Takushoku Bank	7.0	71.3	1.5	4.7	47.5
36	Credit Suisse	6.6	75.4	4.8	1.4	15.7
37	Chiba Bank	6.6	49.9	1.6	4.1	31.2
38	Banco Santander	6.4	29.3	2.0	3.2	14.7
39	J. P. Morgan	6.3	82.6	5.8	1.1	14.2
40	Hokuriku Bank	5.8	46.3	1.3	4.5	35.6
41	Joyo Bank	5.5	44.3	1.4	3.9	31.6
42	Nippon Kangyo Kakumaru	5.3	6.0	1.4	3.8	4.3
43	Dresdner Bank	5.6	129.5	4.3	1.3	30.1
44	New Japan Securities	5.0	8.2	1.0	5.0	8.2
45	Hachijuni Bank	5.1	31.7	1.0	5.1	31.7
46	Societe Generale	5.0	145.7	4.1	1.2	35.5
47	Ashikaga Bank	4.9	38.8	1.3	3.8	29.8
48	Bank of Fukuoka	4.8	35.2	1.2	4.0	29.3
49	Lloyds Bank	4.7	93.8	5.2	0.9	18.0
50	Toronto-Dominion Bank	4.7	43.2	3.1	1.5	13.9

a. In billions of dollars as of December 31, 1988

b. These banks announced a merger on August 29, 1989

SOURCES: *Euromoney*, March 1989 and June 1989; *Moody's International Manual*, 1989.

CHANGES IN BRITAIN—THE BIG BANG

From the early nineteenth century to the beginning of World War I, the United Kingdom was the dominant financial power in the world. However, it emerged a weakened victor from two world wars, and the loss of its colonial empire hastened Britain's decline relative to the rising powers of America, Japan, and continental Europe.

From the end of World War II through 1979, the United Kingdom labored under exchange controls designed to defend an overvalued pound. But even as the British economy diminished in world stature and sterling declined in international importance relative to the dollar as a reserve currency, London—because of its accumulation of know-how and its hands-off attitude regarding the regulation of offshore financial transactions—emerged as the world capital of the Euromarkets.

The election of Margaret Thatcher as prime minister in 1979 and the abolishing of exchange controls in that year, marked the beginning of a vigorous decade in the British economy, and ushered in a period when the cloistered domestic capital markets were opened to the rigors of international competition. As a result of an antitrust action filed against the London Stock Exchange by the previous Labour government, the Conservative government negotiated a settlement where by the Stock Exchange would cease its monopolistic practices. The changes that ensued came to be known as the "Big Bang."

Previous Stock Exchange rules had permitted the exchange to consider itself a closed shop. As in the case of "Mayday" in the United States, when negotiated brokerage commissions (as opposed to fixed-rate brokerage commissions) were introduced on the New York Stock Exchange on May 1, 1975, the rule change was forced by a threat of an antitrust action against the stock exchange by the government. Unlike Mayday, however, the Big Bang required that the entire London Stock Exchange system of dealing in debt and equity securities be scrapped and rebuilt.

First, negotiated commission rates were to be required. Second, brokers and jobbers, or market-makers (roughly equivalent to specialists on the New York Stock Exchange), would no longer be restricted to performing only their respective functions—that is, acting in a "single capacity." Members could now act in a "dual capacity," if they wished, as both brokers and jobbers (or as broker/dealers in American terms). Third, foreign and other nonmember securities firms could join the exchange and compete for business against the British firms.

Big Bang would also cause the market for government bonds (called *gilt-edged* securities or *gilts*) to be totally recast to resemble the U.S. system of having numerous authorized primary market dealers trading directly with the central bank. In addition, the stock market was to be rebuilt along the lines of the U.S. National Securities Dealer Quotation (NASDQ) system for electronic over-the-counter trading. Within a year following the rule changes, the trading volume on the London Stock Exchange had more than tripled, customers admitted receiving better and more advanced services, and the floor of the exchange itself was virtually deserted as trading became almost totally electronic. The pressure on profits for the many firms competing for business in the London market has been extreme, however, particularly in the slack period following the stock market crash of October 19, 1987.

Although the commercial banking and securities functions are separately regulated in Britain, there are now no prohibitions against banks engaging in underwriting, brokerage, and trading of securities, and most have gone into these businesses through subsidiaries.

Explosions similar to Big Bang have been heard around the world as financial markets were deregulated in the middle 1980s in Canada, Australia, France, and to some degree in Germany and Switzerland.

FREER ACCESS TO MARKETS BY FOREIGNERS

Prior to 1970, foreign firms were restricted from participating in indigenous securities markets just about everywhere. After Mayday in 1975, the New York Stock Exchange permitted foreign firms to become members, and a few (mainly Japanese) did so. With negotiated commission rates, however, most non-U.S. securities firms had only a limited incentive to join. They could save the expense of a large operation in New York and still get very competitive executions of orders for their customers by shopping among increasingly competitive, service-oriented U.S. brokers. Very few firms actually expected to challenge the U.S. investment bankers on their home ground, so they really did not need to be NYSE members.

Some Swiss, German, French, and British banks (and other European banks through minority interests) had owned securities affiliates in the United States before the passage of the International Banking Act of 1978. Consequently, they were grandfathered to conduct both banking and securities businesses in the United States. However, most foreign banks large enough to be able to finance major operations in the United States were, like their U.S. counterparts, prevented

from participating in the securities business. A few firms, such as
Paribas (one of the grandfathered banks) and S. G. Warburg (a British
merchant bank) who jointly purchased a majority interest in A. G.
Becker in 1976, attempted to compete in the U.S. domestic investment
banking business. The Paribas-Warburg venture was not successful,
however, as the Becker firm (then called Warburg-Paribas-Becker)
failed and was ultimately liquidated into Merrill Lynch in 1983.

In Europe the Big Bang was seen both as a success (from the
standpoint of users of capital market services) and as a wave of the
future. In its wake, liberalizations permitting foreign participation in national markets occurred in Germany and France. In Switzerland local
underwriting practices were relaxed sufficiently to allow foreign
firms to have a bigger share of participations in Swiss Franc–denominated issues led by the big three Swiss banks.

In Japan the opening of the Japanese capital markets to foreign issuers
and securities firms had been progressing gradually since the mid-
1970s. Foreign investment banks were permitted to open branches that
were licensed to engage in certain aspects of the securities business in
Japan in the early 1980s. As the Japanese became large-scale exporters
of capital, international securities firms rushed to open branches in
Tokyo, and pressure was applied to open the Tokyo Stock Exchange to
foreign membership. This was granted in 1986, when six non-Japanese
firms were allowed to join—three American investment banks (Merrill
Lynch, Goldman Sachs, and Morgan Stanley), two British merchant
banks (S. G. Warburg and an affiliate of Robert Fleming), and a British-
based stock brokerage owned by Citicorp (Vickers da Costa). Following
the initial opening of the exchange to foreign membership, several
additional securities licenses were granted to foreign firms, including
some controlled by non-Japanese commercial (or universal) banks.

Although it appears that the Japanese authorities did not wish to grant
highly controversial concessions to foreign banks that they could not
offer to their own banks, banking authorities in many countries threatened to rescind licenses granted to Japanese banks in their countries
unless reciprocal privileges were extended to their own banks in Japan.

FOREIGN OWNERSHIP OF FIRMS

The rapid growth of the securities business during the 1970s and
1980s placed increased importance on the ability of investment banks
to raise capital. In the United States there had been earlier invest-

ments in the capital stock of securities by foreign companies. Credit Suisse, one of the big three Swiss banks, had invested (through its 60 percent subsidiary, Credit Suisse First Boston) in a 39 percent interest in First Boston Corporation in 1978. Subsequently, in 1988 Credit Suisse First Boston and First Boston were merged into a new holding company, 44.5 percent of which was owned by Credit Suisse.

Lehman Brothers had sold a minority interest to Banca Commerciale Italiana in the early 1970s, an interest that remained until the acquisition of Lehman by Shearson American Express in 1984. Both of these investments were made at times when the American firms were suffering earnings and capital problems. A minority interest in Dillon Read was held by a Swedish group until the firm was sold to the Travelers Insurance Group in 1983. After Salomon Brothers's acquisition by Phibro in 1981, substantial minority interest in the firm was held for several years by Minorco, a major South African–controlled corporation.

By the mid 1980s other U.S. firms were raising capital by selling interests to foreign institutions. The Industrial Bank of Japan acquired a government bond dealer, Aubrey G. Lanston in 1986. Goldman Sachs sold a 12.5 percent nonvoting limited partnership interest to Sumitomo Bank; Shearson Lehman Hutton sold a 13 percent interest to Nippon Life; Paine Webber sold an 18 percent share to Yasuda Life; and Nomura Securities bought a 20 percent interest in Wasserstein, Perella & Co.

In Britain the build up to Big Bang saw 19 of the 20 largest brokerage firms sell out entirely to buyers from the United States, Germany, and Switzerland as well as to British institutions. Among these were the acquisition of Phillips & Drew by the Union Bank of Switzerland, which also was reported to have agreed to purchase the merchant bank, Hill Samuel, although the transaction was subsequently aborted. Security Pacific Bank of the United States acquired a controlling interest in Hoare Govett. Swiss Bank Corporation acquired Savory Milln, and Deutsche Bank secured a 5 percent interest in Morgan Grenfell & Co. In 1989 Deutsche Bank acquired 100 percent of Morgan Grenfell. All of the top London jobbers were also sold. Other merchant banks have also found themselves the target of open market purchases by unwanted parties.

Table 3–2 illustrates the international holdings of major competitors in the global securities business as of the end of 1989.

Table 3–2. International Holdings of Certain Investment and Merchant Banks (as of end-1989)

U.S. Investment Bank	%	Owned by
Shearson Lehman Hutton	13.0	Nippon Life Insurance
Goldman Sachs & Co.	12.5	Sumitomo Bank
Paine Webber	18.0	Yasuda Life Insurance
Drexel Burnham	35.0	Banque Lambert Group
First Boston	100.0	C. S. First Boston (44.5% owned by Credit Suisse)
Werrteim & Co.	50.0	J.H. Schroder
Aubrey G. Lanston	100.0	Industrial Bank of Japan
C. J. Lawrence	100.0	Morgan Grenfell
Kleinwort Benson Government Securities, Inc.	24.9	Fuji Bank
Wasserstein Pefella	20.0	Nomura Securities

Merchant Banks & U.K. Brokers	%	Owned by
Credit Suisse First Boston	100.0	C. S. First Boston (44.5% owned by Credit Suisse)
Morgan Grenfell & Co.	100.0	Deutsche Bank
Hoare Govett	100.0	Security Pacific
Vickers da Costa	100.0	Citicorp
Scrimgeour Kemp-Gee	100.0	Citicorp
L. Messel	100.0	Shearson Lehman Hutton
Laurie & Milbank	100.0	Chase Manhattan
Simon & Coates	100.0	Chase Manhattan
Phillips & Drew	100.0	Union Bank of Switzerland
James Capel	100.0	Hong Kong Shanghai
Savory Milln	100.0	Swiss Bank Corporation

SOURCE: *The Economist, Financial Times,* and various issues of Annual Reports

BUILD-UP OF OVERSEAS OPERATIONS

In the early 1980s international securities transactions expanded very rapidly indeed. The Eurobond market, inspired by a strong dollar and falling interest rates, became extremely active in both the issuance of new securities and in secondary market trading. Several very large issues were launched, including a $1 billion issue of convertible debentures for Texaco in 1984, the largest such issue ever undertaken. New types of securities proliferated, many linked to interest rate or currency swaps. Transactions in nondollar securities also expanded, especially after the dollar began to decline against major currencies in 1985. International issues of equity securities became very common and were in great demand. Firms also foresaw a substantial increase in the volume of business in the United Kingdom bond and equity markets following Big Bang.

For those firms seeking to carve out a secure position in the various European markets, a vast expansion of personnel, facilities, and commensurate overhead was required. Many U.S. firms saw the expansion of the Euromarkets and the unique opportunities associated with Big Bang to be very attractive and moved accordingly. Some U.S. firms had already become active in U.K. corporate finance— including mergers and acquisitions, equity, and real estate financings —and expected to increase their participation in these profitable areas over the ensuing years. For several U.S. houses, a tripling or quadrupling in the size of their London operations over a two- to three-year period would be necessary. Many of these firms were at the same time expanding rapidly in Tokyo, where trading with large financial institutions became a major business opportunity, and they were also evaluating new opportunities to set up or expand in Frankfurt, Zurich, Toronto, Paris, and Sydney. German, Swiss, and French banks expanded their London operations during this period, but not to the same extent as the U.S. firms. Japanese securities firms were mainly concentrating their efforts in London on handling the considerable volume of business brought to them by their Japanese clients, both corporate issuers and institutional investors; however, they also had their eyes on banking operations in London, for which all four of the major firms had received licenses by the end of 1987.

Some build-up in the United States by European and Japanese houses also took place during this period. British merchant banks added to their U.S. staffs, and some, like Kleinwort Benson, acquired modest-sized government bond dealers and swaps specialists. Five major European banks that were grandfathered to conduct investment banking operations in the United States (Deutsche Bank, Dresdner Bank, Paribas, Union Bank of Switzerland, and Swiss Bank Corporation) stepped up their activities through subsidiaries, but none have yet become a major factor in the securities business in New York. Japanese firms, while concentrating on Japanese business in the United States, were making some progress with American clients. A few new issues of U.S. corporate bonds were led by Japanese houses, and all of the "big four" had become primary government bond dealers by the end of 1987.

During the 1980s non-U.S. firms were not nearly as visible in the more lucrative areas of American investment banking, such as managing issues of common and preferred stock and arranging mergers and acquisitions, leveraged buyouts, junk bonds, or real estate financing. Even when the clients were non-U.S. corporations, the investment bankers handling these transactions were almost always U.S. firms. These highly specialized transactions were dominated by the top five to ten U.S. firms, which had the capital, the infrastructure, the contacts, and the know-how to remain on the leading edge of rapidly changing, complex, high value-added, and, accordingly, very profitable activities.

In Japan we have noted that the attraction of a dynamic local market and a huge flow of investment capital overseas drew many securities firms from Europe and the United States to expand their operations considerably. Under the best of circumstances, recruitment to expand a foreign firm's staff in Tokyo is difficult. It was especially difficult when it had to be done very quickly and at a time when the competition was also expanding in Japan. Nevertheless, most firms managed to do it, though perhaps not with maximum efficiency.

Following the acceptance of the original firms into membership in the Tokyo Stock Exchange, the participation of foreign firms in under-writings and government bond auctions was increased. At the same time, however, the Japanese authorities instituted a reduction of stock exchange commissions for those generating large volumes, which disproportionately reduced the revenues of the foreign firms whose business in Japanese securities was almost entirely institutional. Mean-while, the yen-dollar exchange rate was rising rapidly as were real estate costs and all other expenses of foreign firms in Tokyo. After the first few year's experience, most would agree that the Tokyo mar-ket had become too expensive and too competitive for all but the major international firms; however, the major firms had begun to earn substantial profits from securities activities in Japan.

INTERNATIONAL INVESTMENT BANKING SERVICES

There are now a broad range of international investment banking prod-ucts and services. Most of these are well integrated with their domestic market equivalents. Indeed, the words "domestic" and "international" are fading from use for certain types of services, such as the issuing of long-term debt or structuring portfolios for institutional investors. However, it is helpful in keeping track of the great variety of services now offered by the various firms from around the world to make two distinctions: (1) the division between home country clients and foreign clients and (2) the traditional division between services to those requir-ing access to capital and those requiring investments for capital.

Home country clients, from the United States, Europe, and Japan, have all seen a great proliferation of financial services, which has considerably widened the range of alternatives available to them. For example, when planning a debt financing, the choice is no longer between the bond market and a bank loan; it is between several capital market alternatives in the home market and several additional alternatives from the international and foreign markets. These latter alternatives include straight debt financing in one's own currency, financing in another currency swapped into the home country currency, or floating-rate financing converted into fixed-rate financing by means of an interest rate swap. Bond issues can be sold with detachable warrants that provide for the purchase by the holder of other securities of the issuer, either additional debt securities or equity securities, at a fixed price. There often can be as many as a dozen viable, price-competitive financing alternatives that an issuer must consider in making a selection.

The range of issuers whose securities are acceptable to the international markets has also expanded greatly since 1980. No longer must an issuer be a large, well-known corporation to be able to launch a Eurobond offering. In fact, many alternatives and ideas are provided to all sorts of potential issuers by aggressive, opportunistic bankers. So many alternatives backed by so much competitive energy has resulted in a great deal of international financing being completed in recent years, particularly in the Eurosecurities markets (see Figures 3–1 and 3–2).

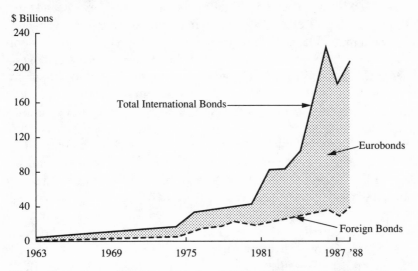

Figure 3–1. International Bond Markets 1963 to 1987. (*Source:* Morgan Guaranty Trust.)

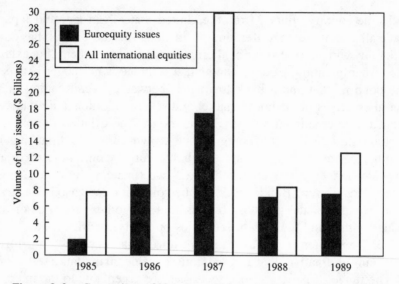

Figure 3–2. Comparison of New Issue Volume in Corporate Equity Securities, by Markets. (*Sources:* Goldman, Sachs & Co., *Investment Dealers Digest*, and *International Financial Review*.)

Many investment bankers believe they must maintain a first-rate capital markets team capable of offering a fully internationalized array of financing alternatives to avoid losing their traditional home country clients. Others, with fewer traditional clients, see opportunities for themselves in the situation. In any case, as clients have been drawn to the tempting offerings of a globalized marketplace, those bankers who have missed leading them there have been forced to follow along.

The same has been true of investor clients who, having discovered international portfolio diversification, require the same type of support services that they do when investing domestically. Investment research and a willingness to make secondary markets in issues are the most important of these. If U.S. brokers are not going to provide these services at a quality level at least as good as their foreign competitors, their share of the home country institution's commission volume will decline as business is directed to foreign firms. Institutional investors, particularly private pension funds, have expanded their international investments enormously in recent years (see Table 3–3), therefore it has become equally important, for both defensive and opportunistic reasons, for firms that offer services to investors to internationalize their businesses as well.

As bankers regard nondomestic country clients, they think in terms of three types of services: (1) executing transactions in the bank's

Table 3–3. Pension Assets of Major Countries (Total Size vs. Overseas Investments)

	Size of Pension Assets [a] (end 1989 US\$ bn)	Growth Rate 1989–94	Growth rate of Nondomestic Investment 1989–94	Size of Nondomestic Investment (1994 US\$ bn)
United States	\$ 2,425	7%	15%	\$ 180
Japan	513	13%	24%	125
United Kingdom	453	7%	9%	157
Netherlands	204	7%	16%	48
Canada	181	7%	28%	38
Switzerland	132	10%	17%	13
Germany	80	7%	9%	6
Sweden	60	8%	N.M.	4
Australia	42	16%	25%	21
Denmark	31	8%	—	—
France	19	8%	15%	1
Norway	11	9%	—	—
Ireland	9	9%	20%	5
Hong Kong	8	26%	26%	16
Belgium	6	15%	15%	4
Rest of the world	159	15%	18%	9
	\$ 4,333	8%	16%	\$ 617

a. Pension assets include both private sector and public sector pension funds.

SOURCE: InterSec Research Corp., March 1990

home country for the foreign-based clients, (2) executing transactions in third countries for them, and (3) executing transactions in the foreign client's own national market.

When a U.S. firm issues bonds in the United States for the Kingdom of Norway (called *Yankee bonds*) or assists a Swiss client in selling shares of IBM, then the firm is performing the first type of this service. Home country international services are the easiest to provide and probably the most profitable for investment banks. The competitive field is smaller, and the firm's domestic reputation is perhaps the most important factor in the awarding of the business to the banker. These services have been performed in one form or another for many years, particularly in the United States. British merchant banks have also provided foreign clients with British banking, corporate finance, money management, and underwriting services for many years, although the demand for *Bulldog bonds* and other strictly

British services has been modest. The Japanese securities firms owe their great international development of the 1980s to the provision of services linking the Japanese market with markets in Europe and the United States. Brokerage services in Japanese shares have been by far the most important of these, but the issuance of yen-denominated bonds in the Tokyo market (*Samurai bonds*) and the listing of shares on the Tokyo Stock Exchange have also been active businesses.

The execution of services in third countries, particularly the Euro-markets, is an important part of the international business of all invest-ment bankers. Originally, there was a significant competitive advan-tage associated with the arrangement of issues denominated in the bankers' own home currency. Eurodollar issues became associated with U.S. firms, Euro–Canadian dollar issues with Canadian firms, Euroyen with the Japanese, and so forth. Though this remains true on the whole, these divisions are much less adhered to today. The mar-kets have become exceedingly competitive, and participants now quote actively in all major currencies. Also, the arrangement of Eurotransac-tions for foreign clients has become quite common. It is not unusual for a Japanese firm to win a dollar mandate from a Swedish issuer, nor for a Euro-yen issue for a French company to be brought by a British firm. In the level playing field of the Euromarket, anything goes.

With so many participants, however, and so much emphasis on transactional relationships, price competition can be severe. The advantage goes to those competitors who have very close relationships with issuers (e.g., the relationships the Japanese securities firms have with their Japanese clients) or those who are capable of placing large amounts of bonds, usually with home country or otherwise captive investors. The Swiss banks manage very large sums of money for investment clients who are traditional buyers of Eurobonds, especially Eurodollar issues. When the dollar is attractive to these investors, they are very active buyers of Eurodollar bond issues brought by Ameri-can corporations. During such times, U.S. and Swiss firms will rank high in the Eurobond league tables. On occasions, such as between 1986 and 1989, when Japanese corporations were eager to escape restrictive new issue practices in their home market by issuing secu-rities in the Euromarkets, and/or when Japanese investors are eager to buy Eurosecurities of Japanese and other companies, the Japanese securities firms inevitably rank high in the underwriting league tables.

In addition to Eurobonds, banks today offer international equity underwritings. These can be arranged through the traditional Eurobond syndication method (discussed in Chapter 14) or they can involve home country issues with international tranches. If Nestle wants to sell shares outside of Switzerland, it can have its banker organize a distribution by inviting a group of international underwriters to purchase the shares just as if they were Eurobonds. If Sears Roebuck wants to sell a new issue of common stock, its U.S. investment banker may suggest that it provide for a portion of the issue, perhaps 15 percent, to be sold to overseas underwriters through a separate but simultaneous offering. This would broaden the company's base of international shareholders and attract worldwide demand for the issue as opposed to just U.S. demand. When the British government disposed of some of its industrial holdings in conjunction with its policy of privatization, foreign equity tranches were provided in the United States, Canada, Japan, and continental Europe for some of the larger issues such as British Gas and British Airways. In such cases it was necessary to integrate the underwriting systems in different countries to make the transaction work. In the case of the $12 billion issue of British Petroleum shares that was caught up in the stock market crash of October 1987, the U.S. and U.K. underwriting systems were integrated in such a way that the foreign underwriters, who participated in the two-week underwriting of the issue, were required to suffer losses estimated at an aggregate of more than $200 million on the transaction. Similar foreign tranches, not always involving similarly linked underwriting risks, have been arranged for privatization offerings in France, Germany, and Singapore.

The most difficult international securities services for a firm to offer successfully are those to be executed in national markets of foreign countries. Well-entrenched, effective national competition is difficult to dislodge. As noted earlier, the European banks permitted to perform investment banking services in the United States have not achieved a significant market share, although they have been competing in the American market for many years. In Japan, Germany, France, and Switzerland, foreign competitors have faced much the same story. In Britain, however, where Big Bang weakened the hold of British firms on their historical businesses and allowed foreign firms a much greater opportunity to offer new and competitive products and services to clients in the United Kingdom, freer and more intense competition has resulted. Foreign firms can perhaps hope to secure over time a prominent share of the market for securities services in the United Kingdom. Recent deregulation of securities markets in Canada and Australia may have a similar effect on foreign competition in those markets in the future, as may the broader European Community (EC) market after the 1992 liberalization initiative.

COMPETITIVE STRATEGIES OF MAJOR FIRMS

The securities business has experienced many changes in the past decade. Markets have become globalized creating a much broader range of financial alternatives for users of services. To be an effective competitor today, a firm must be able to provide a full range of expensive international capabilities. Competition in some sectors of the market, such as Eurobonds, has been intensified by the substantial increase in the number of participants. Increasingly, firms must use their own capital to take positions in tightly priced issues. On the other hand, the demand for capital market services as a whole has grown far more rapidly than has the demand for banking services in general during the past several years. More and more transactions, once considered the natural business of commercial banks, are migrating to capital markets in securitized form, where more competitive pricing can be obtained. Financing for working capital needs, more risky credit, and collateralized transactions can now be more cheaply obtained in the capital markets. Increasingly, investment bankers are being attracted to transactions in which they invest their own capital in bridge loans that will ultimately be repaid from a sale of securities. Commercial banks, on the other hand, have made substantial investments to increase their capital market capabilities.

In some countries there is also an increasing erosion of barriers requiring the separation of banking from securities businesses. Further deregulation in these areas is expected in the United States and in Japan. Home country competition will increase for those firms that have had the benefits of membership in small oligopolies that dominated the securities business in their country. Competition will come from other ambitious securities firms seeking to improve their share of the market in an environment in which it is much easier to do business with the traditional clients of other firms. It will come also from other suppliers of financial services, such as commercial banks in the United States, which previously have been excluded from dealing in securities by regulation, and from a variety of foreign securities firms and universal banks that will continue to expand in the home markets of others or acquire positions in firms that are already well established.

Investment banks and merchant banks, for the most part, have always taken pride in their ability to "live by their wits." Many have survived for 100 years or more in a risky and unpredictable business because they have done just that. The premium has been greater on the professional talent and flexibility of the firm than on the availability of capital. These conditions will no doubt continue into the future, but the globalization of markets, the corresponding internationalization of securities firms, the changes in the competitive climate, and the need to be active and competent in a large number of fields and geographic regions will certainly increase the importance of capital and managerial abilities of major firms in the future. Equally, major firms will have to refine their competitive strategies to make the most of their strengths and remedy their weaknesses. Each firm will find itself sufficiently different from others to justify a custom-made strategy. There will be room, in this context, for a great deal of variety among the players each of whom, however, will do well to heed the words of Casey Stengel, the celebrated American baseball manager who advised, "If you don't know where you're going, you might end up someplace else."

Many investment banks, merchant banks, and others aspire by the year 2000 to end up as one in a small and powerful elite world of financial players. To do so, their competitive strategies today must reflect that ambition. Not all will achieve the goal.

SUMMARY

The rapid rise in international investment banking activities represents a resumption of developments that began in the early nineteenth century and continued uninterrupted until the eve of the Great Depression. In the 1980s, half a century later, these developments are driven with unprecedented force by deregulation, competition, and telecommunications innovations. The separation of investment from commercial banking, built during the 1930s in the United States and during the 1940's in Japan, is now being dismantled while rapid innovation in financial instruments increases the scope of investment banking services.

Significant deregulation in the 1970's and 1980's has allowed foreign competitors freer access to domestic securities markets. This has complemented the simultaneous rise of the Euromarkets in globalizing securities markets. At the same time, investors have acquired an appetite for internationally diversified portfolios. Through foreign acquisitions, and expansion of overseas operations, and by crossing the dividing line between investment and commercial banking, about 50 banking houses throughout the world have emerged as serious competitors for providing the full range of international investment banking services. These houses are striving to become among the truly global investment powerhouses by the year 2000.

NOTES

1. Charles P. Kindleberger, *A Financial History of Western Europe* (Winchester, MA: Allen and Unwin, 1985), pp. 42–46.
2. Vincent P. Carosso, *Investment Banking in America* (Cambridge, MA: Harvard University Press, 1970) pp. 29–75.
3. *Ibid*, pp. 1–28.
4. Orlin Grabbe, *International Financial Markets* (New York: Elsevier, 1986).

4

The Globalization of Capital Markets [1]

During periods of great change, growth, or turmoil it seems to be common for single words or phrases to emerge as symbolic representations of the times. For example, there have been many "revolutions"—the industrial revolution, the cultural revolution, the green revolution, the environmental revolution, and so on. Likewise, there have been many "gaps" "crises," "booms," "bubbles," and "panics." All of which provide colorful imagery.

The phrasemakers of international finance appear to be limited to four- and five-syllable mouthfuls ending in "tion," but they certainly are not idle. In recent years we have been showered with new representational word-images that have become stand-ins in conversation for complex developments that are still evolving. We think we know what words such as institutionalization, deregulation, securitization, disintermediation, innovation, capitalization, and internationalization mean, but there is no standard of exactness. If we are off a bit, it usually does not matter very much. We may be more comfortable with the simpler "tion" words, like transaction, communication, and position, but these words too have taken on new meanings in the modern financial environment.

In this chapter we will consider the meaning of "globalization," a word in almost constant use in the context of capital markets. Clearly, what is intended to be represented in the term is the involvement of capital markets in different parts of the world with each other. By itself, such a concept is unphraseworthy simply because it is not at all new. Both those with money and those requiring money have crossed borders in search of each other for centuries without having been "globalized." However, the addition of two modern ingredients gives "globalization" its meaning.

First, the border crossings must not be opportunistic, smash-and-grab operations, they must involve a permanent, institutionalized structure that is based on linkages between markets. Second, the linkages result in a significant increase in the number and volume of transactions between markets, so that they begin to have some influence on the rate-setting mechanisms. As the process occurs, markets linked in this way become integrated, initially to a limited extent but more so as transactions volume increases.

If the only place where such integration existed was between the United States and, say, Canada, then the whole subject might be represented by the single phrase "North Americanization" of capital markets. But it is not. Financial integration is now in evidence between the capital markets of most of the principal industrialized nations. So we refer to the "globalization" of capital markets, a term that has become an accepted financial buzzword. It was preferred over "worldwidization" or even "internationalization," which after all has 8 syllables and 20 letters and in any case means something else (internationalization will be discussed later in this chapter).

In 1986 the Bank for International Settlements (BIS) published a volume entitled *Recent Innovations in International Banking*, which had been prepared by a study group of representatives from the central banks of each of its 10 member countries. The group's comments about global integration of financial markets go a long way to define what we *do* mean by "globalization":

> The roots of the present trend towards a global integration of financial markets go back to the 1960s when the development of the Euro-currency and Eurobond markets heralded the advent of truly international financial markets. However, owing to various regulations and exchange controls, the links between these international markets and the individual domestic markets remained in most cases rather loose or partial. It was only in the course of the 1970s, and particularly during the past five years, that international and domestic markets have become increasingly integrated. This has occurred as a result of macro-economic developments, deregulatory measures, technological changes and financial innovations. Since these changes have been neither smooth nor uniform, the outlines of what could be called truly global financial markets often appear as a patchwork of individually integrated financial instruments and channels of intermediation.[2]

Globalization clearly is what has been happening to international financial markets. Foreign exchange and commodities markets have been efficiently integrated for a long time. Markets for short-term credit have been integrated to a large extent through the banking system, and bond markets have become much more integrated since the removal of hindrances to cross-border capital flows. The spread between interest rates in the London interbank market and the U.S. market for certificates of deposits or between the new issue yields of Eurodollar and U.S. domestic bonds has narrowed as never before. The process is working between financial instruments denominated in other currencies too, although perhaps less completely. Equity markets lag behind the integration process, but even in this area of individualistic securities there is rapidly growing traffic in border-crossing transactions.

CAUSES OF GLOBALIZATION

During most of world's financial history, exchange rates were fixed against some standard. Currencies under pressure were defended in various ways, the most popular of which frequently involved controls on the import and export of foreign currency. These took various forms, from the prohibition of certain transactions to complex regulations designed to restrain but not totally prevent capital flows. However, with the collapse of the Bretton Woods agreement during 1971 to 1973 and the adoption of floating exchange rates thereafter, exchange controls were no longer necessary for the large industrial countries. The market would reprice currencies every day, which in turn set in motion the forces of supply and demand that would automatically eliminate balance of payments imbalances (but not imbalances in trade and capital flows). The causes and consequences of globalization are summarized in Table 4–1 and will be detailed in the following sections.

Deregulation

Deregulation of exchange controls began in 1974 when the United States withdrew its interest equalization tax and Office of Foreign Direct Investment (OFDI) controls. In 1973, the first oil price explosion occurred, requiring a further easing in the international transferability of capital. Still later, the scrapping of foreign exchange controls by the British and Japanese authorities, which was emulated by a number of other countries, left the principal industrial nations with virtually no regulatory barriers affecting capital flows between them. The result was that large sums began to move into various foreign investments. British

---

Table 4–1.   The Causes and Consequences of Globalization

Globalization Is Caused by:

- Deregulation Abroad
- Greater Institutionalization Abroad
- Success of Euromarkets
- Integration of Markets
- Technology and Know-How

Globalization Has Led to:

- Increased Cross-Border Investment
- Wider Range of Alternatives for Clients
- Three-Market Capability
- Management Complexities
- Need for Larger Firms
- Greater Commitment of Overseas Capital
- Greater Risk Exposure

---

pension funds could be freely invested in assets outside the United Kingdom. Japanese insurance funds could be invested in higher-yielding securities outside Japan, perhaps in the United States, Germany, or Hong Kong. Though conservatively managed institutions partake of new opportunities cautiously, as indeed those newly eligible did as well, between them they represented hundreds of billions of dollars of potential investment, even a small percentage of which would make a great difference to the international financial markets. The flowing of funds from domestic investments into international ones accelerated as more managers became familiar and confident in their abilities to competently manage funds in the new environment. As their commitments increased, so did liquidity and other kinetic qualities of the markets affected.

Deregulation, however, did not stop with foreign exchange controls and cross-border withholding taxes. It went further. A new spirit of free-market efficiency was in the air; it was fostered by President Reagan and Prime Minister Thatcher and later was promoted by many other countries. Internal financial markets were made freer and eventually became deregulated. This process began in the United States in 1975 with the Mayday reforms of the New York Stock Exchange, reforms of laws governing pension funds, easing of antitrust restrictions on mergers and acquisitions, and on the competitive activities of banks. The Big Bang—which totally reformed the British bond and equities markets—occurred in 1986, setting off a chain of other bangs around the world. Enhanced competition leading to enhanced performance in financial markets became the accepted standard in Australia, Canada, France, and, to a lesser extent, in the other European community (EC) countries and in Switzerland. As markets became more performance oriented, turnover and innovation increased. Funds that previously had been invested domestically were migrating to the unknown world of international finance, where excitement in the form of both exceptional rewards and exceptional risks was to be expected.

A further aspect of deregulation was the slow dismantling of restrictions on the participation in domestic securities markets by foreign financial firms. Banks had enjoyed comparatively liberal reciprocal branching privileges within the industrial countries for many years. By the end of the 1970s, the New York Stock Exchange had permitted foreigners to join, London had become the home of the Eurobond market and the principal location of U.S. securities brokers in Europe, and Tokyo had allowed foreign branches of securities firms to be opened. After Big Bang, the U.K. markets were completely opened to foreign competition, even at the cost of seeing British firms lose market share or go out of business. The Tokyo Stock Exchange allowed foreign members to join in 1986. Foreigners suddenly developed real competitive status in Toronto, Sydney, Frankfurt and Zurich. Although international financial houses had been active in these locations for some time, they were now allowed to conduct business locally as well. This resulted in an increase in the presence of the firms abroad and, of course, in the amount of international transactions that they could precipitate.

The march of deregulation has created two additional effects. First, it has developed a momentum of its own that appears to be accepted by the member countries of the EC as they approach the 1992 target deadline for complete harmonization of financial regulation. If this occurs, the restrictions on financial transactions between members may actually be less than those between various U.S. states—an event with great significance to the future financial and capital market activity level within Europe.

The second effect is the increasing requirement for various forms of re-regulation of previously deregulated areas to provide common standards by which participants can play. This rather complex subject is discussed more fully in Chapter 22.

Institutionalization

Prior to 1980 the most active international investors were the Swiss, British, and Dutch managers of funds owned by individuals or internationally active institutions, such as pension funds. The fund managers had developed their skills as a result of being required to find suitable investments for their clients outside of these countries, because domestic investment opportunities there were limited. They became particularly skilled at investing in the United States and in Japan and at managing the foreign exchange risks accompanying such transactions.

After 1980, however, as a result of the deregulatory actions described, large financial institutions were free to invest abroad, and they did so. At the same time, these institutions were growing at rates in excess of their underlying economies. Financial assets under management soared as a result of the inflation of the 1970s, the extraordinary growth of pension funds in Europe, Japan, and the United States, and the increases in the market value of funds under management.

These funds were managed by professional institutional money managers who had to look for outlets for large amounts of money that would require liquidity, trading support, and research assistance. Many of these money managers believed that they could not achieve the best return for their clients by keeping all of their investments in one country or in one type of instrument—they had to diversify. Bond investors began to look abroad for higher yields commensurate with acceptable levels of risk. Equity portfolio managers looking to invest in the chemical or automotive industries, learned that they should look at leading companies in these industries from around the world, and select a portfolio accordingly. Other managers saw more opportunities for speculation in various foreign countries (e.g., moving into the Spanish market ahead of the crowd, taking their profit, and moving on to another market, such as Norway).

Institutions making the conversion to international investing included many from Europe, the United States, and Japan, which by the mid-1980s was bursting with excess savings and huge trade surpluses. The investment of even a small percentage of the total funds under the control of these giant financial institutions around the world would represent a very large increase in the total cross-border investment pool. Institutional commitment to international markets is bound to be a continuously growing and powerful influence on global capital markets for many years to come.

Success of the Euromarkets

In the early 1960s an excess accumulation of dollars in the hands of Europeans resulted in the creation of the *Eurodollar*, the name given to dollar deposits in European banks, including the European branches of U.S. banks. These deposits were transferable, and a market for them developed. Eurodollars proliferated, especially after the closing of the U.S. gold window in 1971, which meant that the only recourse available to those outside the United States who were holding unwanted U.S. dollars was to sell them in the market to someone who did. In many countries dollars had to be turned in to the central bank for local currency. As central banks accumulated dollars, they were able to exchange them with the U.S. Federal Reserve for gold at a fixed price of $34 per ounce. After 1971 surplus dollars could only be sold in the market or invested in dollar securities.

Not long after Eurodollars were created, the Eurobond followed. The market for Eurobonds was novel for several reasons. It was completely outside of the regulatory reach of national governments, so that it became a laboratory in which free financial market behavior could be observed for the first time. What accepted practices it did possess were the result of benign but effective self-regulation. It became a market that linked very different issuers and investors from all over the world, and it became a hothouse for market innovation. As a result of these special features, and fueled by a large build-up of dollar holdings abroad, the Eurobond market has grown rapidly and is now recognized as one of the world's premier financial markets (see Table 4–2).

In the early years Eurobonds were mainly denominated in dollars. Since investors were almost always from countries other than the United States, the foreign exchange component of their incentive to invest differentiated the Eurobond market from the domestic bond market in the United States. During the period when the dollar was strong—or perhaps more accurately, when it was not weakening— the investors preferred dollars over other currencies and would take a somewhat lower return than U.S. investors might in order to own a dollar-denominated bond. But the investor did not want to buy the bond in the United States, where it would be subject to a withholding tax on interest payments and would be registered in the name of the owner for tax collectors all over the world to see. Eurobonds, on the other hand, would provide the same quality investment but would be

Table 4–2. Volume of New Issues of International Bonds and Domestic Bonds [a]

	1983	1984	1985	1986	1987	Compound Growth Rate (5 Years)
Eurobond Market						
U.S. dollars	38,428	63,593	97,782	119,096	56,727	10.23%
Deutsche marks	3,817	4,604	9,491	17,127	15,518	42.00%
Other European	2,986	7,017	15,881	27,223	37,696	88.50%
Canadian dollars	1,039					
Composite & dual	2,019	3,032	7,038	7,057	7,423	38.47%
Far East currencies	212	1,212	6,539	18,673	23,116	223.14%
Total Eurobonds	48,501	79,458	136,731	189,176	140,480	30.46%
Foreign Bond Market						
Yankee bonds	4,545	5,487	4,655	6,064	5,911	6.79%
Swiss francs	14,299	12,626	14,954	23,401	23,976	13.79%
Deutsche marks	2,671	2,243	1,741			
Yen	3,772	4,628	6,379	4,756	3,068	−5.03%
Others	2,541	2,969	3,297	4,240	3,856	10.99%
Total foreign bonds	27,828	27,953	31,026	28,461	26,811	7.24%
TOTAL INTERNATIONAL BONDS	76,329	107,411	167,757	227,637	177,291	23.45%
U.S. Bond Market						
U.S. Corporate and foreign bonds	68,370	109,903	119,559	231,936	208,670	32.17%
State & local obligations	53,700	50,400	136,400	30,800	31,300	−12.62%
U.S. government securities	254,400	273,800	324,200	393,500	311,500	5.19%
Total U.S. bonds	376,470	434,103	580,159	656,236	551,470	10.01%

a. In millions of dollars.

SOURCE: Morgan Guaranty Trust and the *Federal Reserve Bulletin*

exempt from withholding taxes and would be in bearer form, assuring anonymity.

Eurobond investors are a diverse group whose appetites can change quickly because of shifts in foreign exchange rates or changes in the political or regulatory climate of their countries. The Eurobond market, accordingly, is more volatile than its U.S. counterpart, and as a result a number of innovative features have been devised to either reduce or enhance volatility in order to sharpen investor interest. These innovations, which include the "bought deal," the zero coupon bond, the floating-rate note, and the currency swap, have helped advance integration between the Eurobond market and the domestic markets in other countries.

The growth in the Eurobond sector, in new issues, and in secondary market trading has fathered similar developments in money market instruments such as Eurocommercial paper (ECP), Note Issuance Facilities (NIFs), and Floating-Rate Notes (FRNs). It has also stimulated growth in the Euroequities markets, which include transactions involving common stock, convertible debentures, and debt with warrants attached to purchase shares of stock in the issuer. Most recently, the growth of the Eurobond market has fostered a major increase in "synthetic securities," which involve Eurobonds combined with interest rate or currency swaps. These developments are discussed in detail in Chapters 9, 12, 13, and 15.

Integration of Markets

The growth of activity in the Euromarkets has enhanced substantial integration between markets. With increased liquidity and turnover, especially among institutional investors, the Euromarket has become large and diverse enough to be able to attract significant daily activity from investors and issuers, particularly in the United States and in Japan. Thus, the prices for certain instruments popular among the three markets have become substantially the same. A 10-year U.S. Treasury security will trade at approximately the same price in London or Tokyo as it does in New York. Similarly, a 7-year Eurobond issued by General Motors could be expected to trade within 10 basis points (.10 percent) or so in each of the three cities. The Euromarket, however, does not perform equally well across the board. There is virtually no market in Europe for maturities beyond 15 years and often not for those beyond a 10-year maturity. Similarly there is no market for junk bonds, even for those rated at the Euromarket level.

Mortgage-backed and other asset-backed securities have been floated in the Euromarket, but only intermittently. Conversely, there is virtually no market in the United States for floating-rate notes or note issuance facilities.

Market integration across currencies has been occurring since Eurobond issuers have been able to float a new securities issue in currency other than U.S. dollars—that is, the Australian dollar, which is "converted" into U.S. dollars by means of a long-term Australian dollar–U.S. dollar currency swap. Similarly, issuers can link short-term and long-term markets in a single currency by means of interest rate swaps. When the market is in equilibrium, there will be no incentive to raise funds in this manner; however, when it is out of equilibrium, transactions will occur until market equilibrium is restored. In recent years roughly 40 to 50 percent of all Eurobonds have been "swap driven," or linked to swaps (see Chapter 15 and Table 15–1).

There are also linkages between debt and equity markets through Euromarket issues of convertible debentures and debt with equity purchase warrants. And there are linkages between cash and forward markets through the actions of hedgers, dealers, and the secondary trading operations of the financial futures exchanges in London, Tokyo, and Singapore (among others) with those in the United States.

Technology and Know-How

Without the silicon chip, world financial markets would not be nearly as active as they are today and concepts such as globalization and market integration would still be awaiting the invention of the bond math calculator.

Technology has given the international financial markets the ability to settle and deliver large numbers of transactions involving different locations, to keep track of more numerous and complex positions, to hedge positions with financial futures and options, to maintain a portfolio of swap transactions, and to transmit data internationally in large volume at comparatively low cost.

It also has made it possible to produce superior analytical work at a much faster pace, which has encouraged market operators all around the world to develop new financial products and ideas—hence the emphasis on innovation, innovation, and still more innovation. The newest products are the most profitable, but no product remains uncopied for more than 48 hours after being announced. New products solve old problems, or present new opportunities to their intended users, and they permit more transactions.

The system of applying computer, communications, and financial technology to create, execute, and settle transactions is highly effective. As transactions increase, so does market liquidity; as liquidity increases, volatility is reduced, at least from levels that it might otherwise reach. Thus, more transactions are attracted to the markets.

The technology component of market globalization is not without its problems, however. It is extremely expensive, it is difficult to work with for all but specially trained people, and it imposes unwanted dependencies and bottlenecks on all but the most technically competent firms. It also exposes firms to a variety of computer risks—risks that are perhaps greater in their international context than in the home market. Large computer installations must be maintained in London, Tokyo, and other locations. These are extremely difficult to administer by a firm's highly trained facilities experts, who are often far away. The international data they must handle is often exotic in comparison to domestic counterparts; the controls on the computer installations abroad and the access to communications and data processing systems may be less secure. The difficulty in replacing components in the event of a fire or other large-scale damage is considerable. The list of problems goes on—a list that must be solved by those determined to secure a prominent place in the globalized securities markets of the future.

CONSEQUENCES OF GLOBALIZATION

Cross-Border Investments

The principal consequence of globalization is the pooling of market capacity around the world to provide a larger common financial marketplace for all. This has enabled activity in financial commodities as well as singular financial instruments to grow rapidly. Globalization has provided investors around the world with a dynamic, cost-effective environment for making selections among financial alternatives.

Wider Range of Alternatives for Clients

In 1987, institutional bond investors in the United States were offered opportunities to purchase German government bonds *(Bundesanleihen, or "Bunds")* together with a currency swap or forward foreign exchange contract (a "covered" position) in order to improve U.S. dollar portfolio yields. "If the investor thinks German bonds will perform as well as (or better than) U.S. bonds over the coming month, you can pick up about 165 basis points by substituting a covered Bund for a Treasury currently in your portfolio, or by shorting a Treasury against a covered Bund position—without significant exchange rate risk."[3] Japanese investors have been provided with similar advice on how to manage their U.S. Treasury portfolios, which have been exposed to considerable foreign exchange risk.

Equity investors have also been looking at international opportunities very closely in recent years. Investors in the United States and Europe have admired how the Tokyo stock market bounced back after the stock market crashed in October 1987. By the end of 1987 it had almost returned to the peak price level existing before the crash, and it has reached new heights since that time. Foreign investors, though often puzzled by the Japanese market, have nonetheless cautiously returned to it.

Europeans and Japanese investors have reappeared in the New York markets, as have major corporations from those areas active in the acquisition of U.S. corporations. Cross-border equity investments were slowed by the market crash, but only briefly.

The opportunities for corporations seeking finance have also greatly expanded with globalization. There are many possibilities for companies that can finance in their home markets, or in international public or private markets, using their own currency or another that can be swapped or left alone to balance an existing foreign exchange position. Companies can also find expanded markets for their equity securities in a wider global marketplace. On the whole, they have a far greater range of alternatives than ever before (see Figure 4–1).

Three-Market Capability

London, Tokyo, and New York are the three principal centers of the globalized market described here. Transactions between them are continuous and take place in all types of debt, equity, and foreign exchange–linked securities. Market makers usually function as transactors within the domestic markets of their respective regions, as well as between markets. When traders in London come to work in the morning, they look forward to having orders to execute at the opening that came in during the night from colleagues in Tokyo. Before retiring for the night, many New York traders discuss their positions

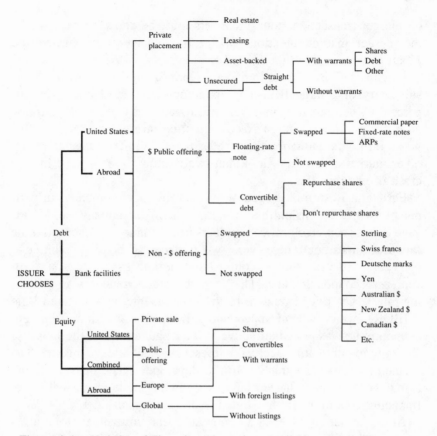

Figure 4–1. Varieties of Financing Alternatives Available to Major Corporations.

with their counterparts in Tokyo. Day and night, traffic is heading in both directions on each of the three great financial roadways that connect the financial capitals of Asia, America, and Europe.

The three markets are linked across the board—in debt securities, foreign exchange, commodities, equities, mergers, and real estate. They are linked by the transactions that are completed and by many that are not completed but that were considered as the principal alternative to another transaction that was completed.

For example, early in 1988, when Hoffmann La Roche tried to acquire Sterling Drug Co., the action brought in Eastman Kodak at a higher price. The Hoffmann La Roche deal was not completed, but its contribution was vital to the Kodak deal that was. When Pirelli, together with Michelin, tried to take over Firestone, Bridgestone of Japan came forward with a far higher bid. To advise large companies on merger transactions today, bankers must be knowledgeable about the merger market intentions of specific players from Europe and Japan as well as from the United States.

Late in 1987 Baskin-Robbins Ice Cream Co., a wholly owned U.S. subsidiary of a large British foods company, sold shares in its 50-percent-owned Japanese joint venture, B-R 31 Ice Cream Co., through an initial public offering in Tokyo at a price/earnings ratio of 38. This was a far higher valuation than the shares would have received in any other market at the time, less than two months following the market crash of October 1987.

Earlier, a Boston-based real estate development company, in partnership with the pension fund of a major British company, sold mortgage bonds secured by office buildings in Boston to a syndicate of nine Japanese investors. There were two tranches of bonds purchased— one was a 10-year current coupon tranche and the other was a 10-year zero coupon tranche. The current coupon tranche was a floating-rate issue, priced relative to the London Interbank Offered Rate (LIBOR), which was swapped into a fixed-rate obligation; the zero coupon issue was priced attractively to take advantage of the Japanese ability to avoid treating accrued interest as annual taxable income. The financing was very attractive to the developers. The banker putting it together obviously had to be very knowledgeable about real estate financing conditions in the United States and Japan.

At the beginning of 1988 a major European government took a 10-year yen loan from a large Japanese insurance company. The loan was priced very favorably and was callable at par after three years. The American firm that arranged the transaction recognized that at the time Japanese life insurers were prepared to provide extremely flexible and inexpensive call options for long-dated financings. Knowing that this particular sovereign borrower valued call flexibility highly, a transaction was quickly arranged.

At about the same time, an aggressive portfolio manager for one of New York's celebrated money management firms received a proposal from one of its brokers, based upon research done by the firm's financial strategies group, to take a position anticipating a move in the yen/Swiss franc cross-rate. The yen was still strengthening, relative to the dollar, but the Swiss franc was expected to lag. The position could be taken by buying a call option on yen struck at the current spot price and financing the purchase by selling a call on the Swiss franc, also struck at the spot exchange rate. The transaction would be self-financing and involve comparatively little downside risk relative to the dollar, the broker suggested. The portfolio manager took the recommended position.

These transactions are examples of global market transactions of various types. All of them occurred after the October 1987 stock market collapse. They continue to be created where the opportunities exist; only the takers need to be found.

Management Complexities

Senior managers of large investment banking institutions expecting to play a major role in globalized markets of the future must feel a little like the ambitious captain of an inland waterways vessel starting out on his first transatlantic voyage. "There's a lot of opportunity out there," he said, "but a helluva lot of ocean too." There is a lot of opportunity for securities firms that can structure themselves to be effective competitors in the global markets, but the cost and complexity of setting up multiple product lines in Tokyo, London, New York, and other promising places (e.g., Zurich, Toronto, Sydney, Hong Kong, Paris, and Frankfurt) is mind-boggling. Clearly, very few banks can do everything at once. For the rest, all of these possibilities are distracting temptations. (Further discussion of the issues related to the formulation of competitive strategy for the global market is continued in Chapter 20.)

Among the difficult management complexities that follow an effort to participate in globalized markets is the need to "internationalize" the firm. Apart from strategic and attitudinal considerations, this means recognizing the need for the firm to become much larger in size, to commit a large percentage of its capital overseas, and to greatly increase its risk exposure.

Need for Larger Firms

Between 1984 and 1987 many investment banking offices in London quadrupled in size. Such expansion was thought necessary in order for the firms to gear up to compete in the post–Big Bang environment in London, in which foreign firms would have access to all British markets for financial services. Those U.S. firms participating in the U.K. market would have to learn to be dealers and to be able to distribute British government securities (called "gilts"). They would have to be able to make markets and provide brokerage and block trading services in British stocks. They would have to increase their calling activities on British companies, including smaller ones that had not been covered before. They would have to be able to offer U.K. merger and corporate financing advice, real estate services, and pension fund assistance. All of this had to be done in competition with not only their American investment banking rivals, but their European, Japanese, and U.S. commercial banking competitors as well. Euromarket activities were expanding too, and they had to be provided for. Euroequities needed to be emphasized—more specialization in that area was required, and new opportunities to trade in Deutsche mark, Swiss franc, and French franc securities were developing quickly. All this expansion meant that more infrastructure would have to be provided. There was a need for more space, more computer and back office capacity, and more auditors, controllers, tax people, and other support staff. Previously, the foreign office had been run as a semiautonomous outpost of New York; now it would become a clone, but a clone that was doubling in size every year.

Tokyo was going through the same thing, at only a slightly slower pace. Memberships on the Tokyo Stock Exchange had been granted to foreign firms that frantically had to put together a staff that could function in the all-Japanese environment of the exchange. At the same time, the Japanese investors were consuming prodigious amounts of U.S. securities and Eurosecurities; trading, sales, and corporate finance people had to get on the job quickly, before the competition did.

Under the circumstances, it was no more possible to effect an orderly or cost-effective expansion in those cities at the time than it was to make an orderly and cost-effective invasion of Normandy in 1944—and then at least there was time for advance planning. It was no surprise when the firms discovered that they had overdone it. The sagging of the Eurobond market in the mid-1980s, the market crash in October 1987, the failure of the British Petroleum stock offering and other adventures of that year cooled the expansionary fever among international banks. Layoffs and "pruning" followed. Fears of difficult times ahead caused banks of all types to tighten their belts. But by the end of 1988 some additions to staff had resumed.

Today, many U.S. investment banks have 15 to 20 percent of their total staff located abroad; this percentage may increase somewhat as staffing requirements are filled out in Tokyo, Frankfurt, Zurich, Toronto and other locations. Manning overseas positions with U.S. expatriates is extremely expensive and requires cost-of-living and foreign exchange protection as well as tax equalization (among other benefits), and indeed can slow the necessary process of cultural assimilation. To be effective in Britain, a firm must rely on well-trained and fully competent British nationals to fill senior positions. However, it takes time to prepare nationals for senior positions and for them to be fully accepted by the head office.

Greater Commitment of Overseas Capital

Investment banks will also discover that foreign regulatory requirements for capital are considerable, and there is the possibility that these may increase. Previously, the Eurobond market never required any significant regulatory capital. Now it does. Subsequent to Big Bang and a reshaping of securities regulations in the United Kingdom, the London Stock Exchange absorbed the Eurobond Primary Market Dealers Association to preserve the self-regulatory status of Eurobond dealers. This resulted in the renaming of the Stock Exchange to the "International Stock Exchange" (ISE), and it made the principal Eurobond dealers subject to providing regulatory capital to support their Eurobond positions. Big Bang required further commitments of regulatory capital by those wishing to become primary market dealers in U.K. gilts and a further commitment for those becoming market makers in U.K. stocks. Tokyo, too, has developed strict regulations regarding regulatory capital and the cost of acquiring memberships on the exchange. Major firms have recently experienced a large increase in overseas regulatory capital requirements because of these changes.

Regulatory capital, of course, is effectively blocked capital. It cannot be used anywhere other than where it is supposed to be—that is, to support the safety and stability of the securities firms. For all practical purposes, this capital cannot be transferred or remitted to the parent unless the firm is in serious trouble or in liquidation. Once the firm commits its capital for regulatory purposes abroad, it is unlikely that it will ever have the use of that capital again in domestic operations unless it decides to eliminate or shrink its foreign operation.

Capital requirements in excess of regulatory capital are more flexible but still may be substantial. In the late 1980s many U.S. investment banks had between 20 to 25 percent of their total capital tied up outside of the United States. Ten years earlier this was less than 5 percent. The investment banking business is widely recognized as having become very capital intensive. Much of this is because of the greatly increased positions that the firms carry and the increasing involvement with various types of "merchant banking," activities in which the firms invest their own funds in equity or short-term loan positions in the deals they arrange. It should be clear, however, that a very large, unobserved component of the future capital intensity of the business will be in supporting the firms' individual commitments to the globalization of the financial marketplace.

Greater Risk Exposure

Much of this capital is needed to provide capacity for the firms to take risks. The risks are unavoidable if the firm wants to become a major global player, so they are not unexpected. The risks come in several forms—position risks, credit risks, systems risks, and management risks, which would include the risk of fraud or other forms of misbehavior while conducting business. All of these risks are harder to manage because they involve several additional international factors that do not exist at home and for which the staffs of most organizations are not yet properly trained.

The number of trading books that the average firm now maintains in foreign offices has increased severalfold over those of the early 1980s. Firms still trade in all sorts of U.S. and dollar-denominated securities, but now they also trade in various nondollar securities, swaps, foreign exchange, metals, oil, and futures and options involving most of these. More on-scene supervisors and controls are necessary to manage these risks, and they too are expensive.

Credit risks now involve exposures from all over the world and include many complex transactions with complicating time zone risks as well. For example, after the October 1987 stock market crash, several firms discovered that they were unable to collect on margin calls involving Hong Kong investors in options. The options had not been properly collateralized. Investment banks now must devote substantial attention and expense to building international credit analysis capability, much of which will have to be located abroad.

Systems and management risks are essentially the same as those experienced at home, but with rapid international expansion there is much more room for error. Away from the head office, close inspection of systems and facilities and supervision of large numbers of newly hired employees are much more difficult.

The costs and risks of internationalizing investment banking firms so that they can embark on the high seas of globalized capital markets are considerable. Until the incremental volume of transactions resulting from globalization is apparent, the costs will not be fully recouped. They should be capitalized and considered as a long-term investment by investment banking participants, undertaken for profit, opportunity, and the need to protect the client franchise at home. But the costs need not get out of control. Some temptations must be resisted until a later day; others simply must be refused. Expansion into dangerous areas of business should not be permitted until the necessary control systems and supervisors are in place. Everything does not have to be done at once; priorities must be set and insisted upon. Effecting the internationalization of a firm in these market circumstances is an extremely difficult task that requires substantial attention and resolute decision making on the part of the firm's most senior management. Those firms that master the management side of globalization (discussed in greater detail in Chapter 21) will have an enormous, and perhaps decisive, competitive advantage over those that do not.

SUMMARY

Global integration of financial markets is being driven by the worldwide search on the part of investors and issuers for more favorable returns and lower costs of funds, respectively, in securities packaged to meet their specific and varied needs. Meeting these objectives has been facilitated by improved communications, the erosion of barriers to capital flows, the modernization of key national financial systems, and the gradual liberalization of international trade in services. The cutting edge of globalization has been the Euromarkets—those loosely organized, virtually unregulated, over-the-counter global markets encompassing debt in a broad range of maturities and types of securities. The effect of globalization is to give participants in financial markets a wide range of viable alternatives. Centered in London, Tokyo, and New York, action in the global market is continuous. Its increased competition increases the pressure for and rate of financial innovation. The market places strict demands on participating financial houses—staffing, facilities, market intelligence and research, and changing regulatory requirements all involve significant costs. But those bearing the costs do so for the very considerable potential rewards that come from providing financial services to the leading issuers of securities and their investors throughout the world.

NOTES

1. This chapter originally appeared in Ron C. Smith, *The Global Bankers*, New York, E. P. Dalton, 1989.
2. Bank for International Settlements, *Recent Innovations in International Banking*, Basel, Switzerland: BIS 1986, p. 149.
3. Goldman, Sachs & Co., "Fixed Income Research", May 1987.

SELECTED REFERENCES

Aliber, Robert Z., *The Handbook of International Financial Management*. New York: Dow Jones-Irwin, 1989.

"A Survey of Wall Street." *The Economist*, July 11, 1987.

Bank for International Settlements. *Annual Report for 1987*. Basel, Switzerland: BIS, 1987.

Bank for International Settlements, Recent Innovations in International Banking (Basel, Switzerland: BIS, 1986).

Bank of England, "Developments in International Banking and Capital Markets." *Quarterly Bulletin*, March 1986.

"Euromarkets—Now for the Lean Years," *The Economist,* 1987.

Fisher, Frederick G. "Global Market Integration—An International Perspective." in *Investment Banking Handbook*, edited by J. Peter Williamson. New York: John Wiley & Sons, 1988.

Hormats, Robert D., *Reforming the International Monetary System*. New York: Foreign Policy Association, 1987.

Mayer, Martin. *The Money Bazaars*. New York; E. P. Dutton, 1988.

Morgan Guaranty Trust Co. "Global Financial Change." *World Financial Markets*, December 1986.

Morgan Guaranty Trust Co., "Global Growth and Adjustment at Risk." *World Financial Markets*, September–October. 1987.

Sampson, Anthony. *The Money Lenders*. London: Coronet, 1982.

"The World is their Oyster—A Survey of International Investment Banking," *The Economist* March 16, 1985.

Walter, Ingo. *Global Competition in Financial Services*. New York: Ballinger—Harper & Row, 1988.

Walter, Ingo, and Smith, Roy C. *Investment Banking in Europe—Restructuring in the 1990s*. Oxford: Basil Blackwell, 1990.

II

Commercial Banking Services

5

International Lending and Loan Syndication

International lending has changed dramatically in recent years. Highly rated corporations, public sector enterprises, and governments have largely migrated to the capital markets, where their own securities command terms that are competitive (and sometimes superior) to those of banks. The international financial disintermediation that has resulted has made straight bank-to-client lending to such borrowers largely obsolete. Even smaller and less highly rated borrowers have found it possible to tap the capital markets using various kinds of credit and liquidity backstops (see Chapter 6) issued by banks and other financial institutions. And due to the debt crisis of the 1980s confronting the developing countries, a major class of sovereign borrower for whom the capital markets have traditionally been closed has been out of the market—except for forced rescheduling and new-money packages undertaken as the debt crisis has worn on.

Nevertheless, international bank lending continues as an important component of the activities of global financial institutions. In times of financial instability, the capital markets tend to shrink and in some cases even disappear as viable sources of finance; this instability also causes borrowers to flock back to the banks. Banks could find themselves in the unenviable position of providing various kinds of backstop products for capital market issues at bargain-basement prices in good times and lending large amounts in times of trouble. For this reason, many creditworthy borrowers maintain bank lines even in the best of times, partly to make sure the banks are there when and if they are needed.

Furthermore, there are certain kinds of financing (e.g., short-term lending to finance merger, acquisition, leveraged buyout transactions, and longer-term lending on project financings) for which traditional bank loans are the best choice. This may be because the borrower cannot be sure precisely when the funds will be required or when they can be repaid out of the proceeds of stock or bond issues or asset sales, or it may be because the transaction is likely to encounter significant and unanticipated developments over its life that require a form of financing where the added flexibility is worth more than the added cost. Bank lending provides one of the few alternatives for close borrower-lender contact; therefore, it maintains significant advantages in contracting and information costs.

BANK LENDING FACILITIES

There are several ways to classify international bank lending. A bank may, for example, *lend to various types of clients out of branches or affiliates* in the countries in which it operates, funded by local currency deposits or local money market borrowings. This is purely local business, competing with local banks; for foreign-based banks to effectively go after this business, they must compete purely on price or they must develop some sort of market niche—special industry expertise, for example, or expertise in specific kinds of lending, such as asset-based financing (see Chapter 7). Foreign banks lending in local markets may also focus on affiliates of multinational companies based in their own home countries and on financing international trade transactions (see Chapter 8). Still, it remains essentially domestic lending, and the only thing international about it is the transfer of product or credit know-how, or client relationships, from the parent organization or from affiliates in third countries.

A second category is *direct cross-border lending by a bank or its branch or affiliate located in one country to clients located in another*. Such loans appear to be relatively minor in importance and to focus on special kinds of transactions as part of close relationships to particular clients, including foreign affiliates of multinationals, as part of workouts of earlier troubled loans, or in international private banking relationships (see Chapter 12). In many cases such loans take the form of Eurocurrency facilities funded out of the bank's Eurobook. The dominant form of international bank lending has been the *syndicated* loan, discussed in detail later in this chapter.

Lending facilities, whether direct or syndicated, can take a number of forms. The most important is revolving credit agreements (called "revolvers"), which permit clients to borrow, on demand, up to a certain maximum amount over an agreed period of time under an agreed interest formula. In return, the bank earns a commitment fee for standing ready to lend, whether or not such lending actually occurs. These are generally called "committed facilities," and the commitment is legally enforceable and covered by appropriate legal documentation. Committed facilities require the same kind of careful credit analysis as actual loans especially since, for some clients, committed facilities will be utilized only when capital market financing is restricted or too expensive. Such facilities often take the form of "backstop lines," which rating agencies like Moody's and Standard & Poor's require issuers of commercial paper to have in place in order to assure investors in such paper that the liquidity will be there when the paper matures.

Borrowers may also have in place "uncommitted facilities," which are not legally enforceable and hence involve lower fees to the borrower. Clients may find these attractive because of the lower cost and the small likelihood of difficulty in accessing financial markets in the foreseeable future. In the course of ordinary relationships with clients, banks will naturally have in place limits on the amount of lending exposure they are willing to incur, sometimes called "undisclosed, unadvised guidance lines," which may be increased or decreased at the bank's own discretion based on changing circumstances.

Whether committed or uncommitted, international bank lending facilities may be associated with various other banking products, especially those involving interest rate or exchange rate protection. Examples include: forward-rate agreements, which permit a client to lock in an interest rate today for a loan to be taken at some future date, interest rate "caps" or "collars," and "currency swaps," as discussed in Chapter 15. The bank, in turn, will hedge these transactions in the market and keep whatever spread it is able to earn in addition to the fee for the added value concerned.

BANK FINANCING OF FOREIGN GOVERNMENT ENTITIES

Lending to units of foreign governments took on major importance in the 1970s. The reasons include: (1) the rapid growth of balance-of-payments financing needs on the part of national governments, particularly after 1973; (2) the use of government agencies as intermediaries to secure external financing for a wide variety of ultimate borrowers domestically; (3) major borrowing needs on the part of governmental and quasi-governmental entities (e.g., power authorities, sewage systems, trading companies, airlines, shipping companies, etc.) both at the national and state or local levels; (4) active participation of governments as owners of manufacturing and trading companies, as well as financial houses and banks; and (5) the growing use of government guarantees to facilitate foreign borrowing on behalf of private ventures. In view of this, it is important to understand how lending to government entities differs from lending to private ones and what special kinds of factors determine international banking competitiveness, profitability, and risk in this aspect of the business.

The Nature of Foreign Government Borrowing

Government borrowing abroad may be undertaken by a national entity charged with managing the country's external finance, such as its central bank, monetary authority, ministry of finance, or a similar institution. It may also be undertaken by other government-owned authorities or corporations, often called "parastatals." In the latter case, the external borrowing generally must have the approval of a central coordinating agency such as the central bank, which is also often true of private borrowing abroad whether or not the country maintains a system of exchange controls.

Balance-of-payments borrowing is undertaken by countries with current account payments deficits that are not offset by private capital inflows, resulting in a balance-of-payments deficit at the existing exchange rate. The proceeds of external borrowing by the country's monetary agency are used to plug this gap under existing regimes exchange control regimes or to intervene in foreign exchange markets to support the external value of the national currency. Balance-of-payments borrowing may be *seasonal* or *cyclical*, in response to periodic underlying variations in export receipts and import disbursements or capital flows, or they may be *structural* due to an essentially permanent shock (e.g., an increase in oil import prices) that will take time for an economy to adjust to. They may also be *chronic* as a result of a more or less permanent excess of domestic absorption over production, capital flight due to lack of confidence in the country's future, and similar factors, whereby external borrowing helps to maintain domestic levels of living above those justified by the country's own means.

Seasonal and cyclical borrowing is essentially self-correcting and finds its everyday parallels in corporate working capital borrowing and personal finance. To the extent that such needs cannot be handled from a country's own reserves, short-term borrowings under bank credit lines, reviewed periodically, may be the way they are handled.

Structural borrowing is designed to ease the pain of adjustment to new economic realities and can also be fully justified provided the necessary adjustment actually does come about within an acceptable time frame. This is not the case for a country essentially living beyond its means and engaging in chronic external borrowing, its government unable or unwilling to take the steps needed to restore balance, which ultimately means a rough landing for debtors and creditors alike. Structural and chronic borrowing is generally (but not always) done on a medium-term basis, usually via loan syndications.

Fiscal borrowing concerns financing to cover a budgetary deficit; it is normally done internally with domestic financial institutions but often is forced to rely on foreign banks. Deficit financing domestically may be more inflationary than external borrowing (which makes more real goods and services available), and thus may be preferred where there is a choice. It is linked directly to the balance of payments and its financing, discussed above, and a chronic government deficit financed externally will have similar consequences. But in most cases, fiscal borrowing involves short-term loans made in anticipation of government receipts and, therefore, the loans are self-liquidating. The fact remains, however, that fiscal borrowing externally is not the same thing as fiscal borrowing internally.

Development borrowing involves the financing of intrastructure projects—schools, hospitals, roads, railways, airports, port facilities, communication networks, power grids, sewer systems, public housing, and a variety of other laudable purposes. Some of these projects are direct producers of foreign exchange (generating exports or saving on imports), while others are not. As distinct from development *project* lending, *program* lending may involve literacy training, vocational education, and so forth, with potentially far-reaching domestic and international consequences that are usually extremely difficult to forecast (see Chapter 7).

Syndication

Most major international lending facilities are syndicated. In simple form, a syndicated loan or credit facility involves the combined activities of a number of banks in the assembly of a relatively large medium-term credit to a single borrower, with one or several banks serving as lead managers.

The borrower has the advantage, under such arrangements, of being able to raise a larger sum than any single bank would be willing to lend, and to do so more efficiently and at a substantially lower cost than would be possible if borrowing from multiple sources on one's own. Moreover, the borrower enters the market fewer times, and thus may place future access to financing in less jeopardy. Borrower "visibility" is enhanced by major syndications involving a large group of banks, possibly making future financings considerably easier as well.

The lenders have the following advantages: (1) better diversification of their asset portfolios, (2) participation in lending they might not otherwise have access to, (3) cooperation with multiple banks (often home based in a number of different countries) having greater collective expertise and information than any single bank, (4) possibly reduced risk of borrower default against a syndicate of banks as compared with any single bank due to the enhanced penalties of such action for the borrower in terms of reduced future access to financial markets, and (5) certain legal protections inherent in syndicated loan agreements (see Chapter 10). Banks also find participation in a variety of syndicated loans to be an efficient way to obtain the necessary expertise, market exposure, and visibility without incurring unacceptable financial risks.

Despite these advantages, syndication has several drawbacks for borrowers, lenders, or both: (1) it tends to sharpen price competition; (2) it may reduce bank loyalty on the part of the client and cut or even substantially eliminate direct contact between the borrower and many of his creditors; (3) by promoting impersonal dealings, it may undermine the trust relationship that traditionally is at the heart of classic banking; and (4) it may reduce or distort the flow of information needed to make sound lending decisions.

Essentially, international syndicated loan facilities represent a cross between underwriting activities in investment banking and traditional commercial bank lending. They extend the scope of international banking activities beyond the limits often imposed by law at the national level in countries such as the United States, and they open medium-term financing opportunities to many borrowers who would not otherwise be able to obtain credit on comparable terms through the international or domestic securities markets, private placements, and other vehicles.

Historically, international syndications of medium-term credit facilities began in the late 1960s, when changes in interest rate levels and volatility increased the attractiveness of major financings on floating-rate terms, as opposed to fixed-rate bond issues, and when borrower needs outstripped the lending capabilities of individual banks. Its antecedents include the long-standing practice of multibank term lending to corporate customers in the United States, priced at or above the bank-administered domestic prime lending rate.

During the 1970s and 1980s, syndicated lending accounted for over half of all medium- and long-term borrowings in international capital markets, well over 80 percent of such borrowings by developing countries, and almost all such borrowings by communist countries. In terms of international bank lending in all maturities, including short-term credits, syndicated loans now comprise roughly half of the total.

A significant part of the enormous growth of syndicated lending during the 1970s can be traced to the balance-of-payments financing needs of non-oil-producing countries. The remarkably efficient performance of the Euromarkets in recycling the net investible surpluses of the OPEC countries to meet these needs was greatly assisted by syndication as an international lending technique. Chronic import requirements of the technologically and agriculturally backward communist countries generated further demand for medium-term syndicated credits. Large-scale lending for project financings (see Chapter 9) as well as the financing of mergers and acquisitions (M&A) and the financing of leveraged buyouts (LBO) are also done on a syndicated basis. Thus, while lending to developing countries and project financings took up the bulk of syndications in the 1970s, M&A and LBO syndications took their place in the latter part of the 1980s.

The geographic center for syndicated lending has always been London, with several hundred banks that are active in syndications physically represented there. London also has excellent transportation and communications facilities, and can provide the necessary human resources and technology. Dealings here are standardized in a single language. A second, much smaller, center in Hong Kong was developed to service the Asian markets. New York has played a relatively minor role, although bolstered somewhat by the creation of international banking facilities in 1981. In addition to these three cities, the actual booking of syndicated loan participations is done largely in the various offshore banking centers (e.g., Nassau, Luxembourg, and Bahrain); loan signings may occur in still different locations, depending on borrower and bank preference.

The Syndication Process

Borrower contact is maintained routinely by lending officers of major international banks. The better the "relationship" between a bank and the potential borrower, the better its information about evolving financing needs and the greater its chances of playing a significant role in meeting those needs.

In seeking syndication business, banks rely on (1) their own branches, representative offices, or other affiliates maintaining contact with the prospective borrower, (2) referrals from other units of the bank, (3) referrals through established corporate and other client relationships, (4) referrals from other banks anxious to render a service to their own clients, yet not in a position to take the leadership role themselves, and with whom good relations have been maintained, and (5) direct solicitations from potential borrowers or, in the event of joint lead-managed syndications, other banks.

Consortium banks were formed during the 1960s and 1970s in London and elsewhere to focus the syndication capabilities of multiple banks to provide the benefit of referrals from their shareholder banks. However, most consortium banks fell by the wayside in the 1980s. Along the same lines, less formal arrangements have been made (particularly among European banks) to jointly arrange syndications as an ongoing working relationship, drawing on the borrower contacts of the various participants. Finally, among the staffs of investment banks and other institutions, there are capable advisors to borrowers. One of the principal functions of these advisors is to facilitate capital-market access through introductions to competent banks active in the syndication of lending facilities.

At some point the potential client may make known an intention to borrow a specific sum (or general borrowing requirements over the next year or so) and may either explicitly or implicitly request proposals for structuring and pricing the necessary borrowing(s). Here the banks that are close to the borrower may have the inside track to win the business, although the borrower may also call for proposals through telexed solicitations or competitive bidding.

Knowing the borrower and conditions in international financial markets, a prospective *lead bank* will carefully draw up a proposal to arrange the facility, thereby seeking a *syndication mandate*. The proposal will specify pricing, terms, fees, and related pertinent aspects of the facility and will indicate whether the syndication will be *fully committed*, *partially committed*, or *best efforts* in nature. If it is fully committed, the proposing bank will undertake to provide the full amount of the loan to the borrower according to the terms of the mandate, whether or not it is successful in its efforts to interest other banks in participating in the deal. If it is partially committed, the bank will guarantee to deliver part of the facility, with the remainder contingent on market reaction to the loan. In a best efforts syndication, on the other hand, the borrower will only obtain the funds needed if sufficient interest and participation can be generated among potential participating lenders by the good faith efforts of the bank seeking the mandate.

By this time, or shortly thereafter, the bank may have brought in one or more co–lead managers to help with the syndication and share in the underwriting commitment, especially if the amount to be raised is very large or the deal is rather complex. Generally, the larger the facility, the larger the management group involved tends to be. It may include several *lead managers*, *managers*, and *comanagers*, with each group accepting a different share of the underwriting responsibility, and including several "brackets" of *participants*, whose role is confined to supplying funds.

The terms of the formal letter seeking the mandate will follow extensive discussions with the borrower and will be carefully tailored to its needs as well as market conditions. It will have to be fully competitive with other banks going after the same mandate—mandate-seeking generally requires leading off with the best possible offer—otherwise, further discussion will focus on competitors. The mandate letter will also specify exclusivity of the mandate and will repeatedly note the leading roles the bank is to perform in the syndication.

There are a variety of negotiable tradeoffs as between the term and size of the loan, drawdown schedule, grace period, amortization schedule, spread, fees, tax issues, borrower information, and legal covenants. In seeking a mandate, the prospective lead bank must strike a balance between what the borrower wants and what the market can live with—always keeping a watchful eye on what competitors may propose. Sophisticated borrowers will often accept "second best" proposals from highly responsible and prestigious lead banks over more "imaginative" or lower-cost bids from aggressive competitors if they feel that this will better serve their long-term standing in the market. Still, the tolerance for less than fully competitive bids is generally very low.

If the borrower decides to go ahead with the syndication, the mandate will be awarded to one of the competing banks or joint bidders who then becomes lead manager(s) of the syndicate. Suppose a single bank has won a mandate on a $100 million fully committed syndication and that the lead bank wishes to keep $15 million of this in its own portfolio—its *target take*. It will have to find a way to *sell down* the remaining $85 million to other banks and, to do so, will have to develop a *syndication strategy* that will successfully raise the required sum yet necessitate minimum sharing of the management fee that will be paid or the visibility it attracts for putting the deal together. Several other banks may have to be asked to jointly manage or comanage the facility, however, and will be allocated a portion of the total funds to be raised—part of which they will take into their own portfolios and the rest they in turn will sell down to other syndicate participants—in return for a proportionate share of the management fee.

The lead bank is generally expected to take a share in the facility that is at least as large as that of any other lender. The management group (lead manager(s), managers, and comanagers) may retain as much as 50 to 70 percent of the total deal for their own portfolios.

The syndicate will be put together by the lead manager and the management group on the basis of offering telexes or faxes to banks around the world, usually through their offices in such syndication centers as London and Hong Kong, on the basis of the agreed terms (a sample offering telex is shown in Figure 5–1). Especially in the syndication centers this may be followed up quickly with proposed documentation and personal discussions.

Deciding which banks to invite into the syndicate is a major part of a lead bank's task and will help determine its strategy. It must be able to judge the invitees' country and industry exposures, past client relationships, degree of sophistication in syndicated lending (especially in complex deals), its own relationships with invitees, and similar factors that will determine an individual bank's receptivity to the deal. In some cases, the borrower will also express a preference as to which banks should (and should not) be invited to participate. Contacting 200 or 300 banks to obtain 20 or 30 ultimate participants is not unusual. Banks invited to participate will usually decline, accept, or request further information on the basis of the offering telex, and their responses will be careful recorded by the lead manager or management group.

If there are several lead managers, one of them is assigned to keep track of responses from each of the banks that have been approached for various levels of participation and underwriting responsibility within the overall context of the syndication strategy. This can be rather complex when dozens of banks in a variety of countries are involved, with responsibility for contacting them divided among members of the management team.

Meanwhile, the lead manager will work on preparation of an *information memorandum*, in which the borrower will disclose financial and economic, and sometimes historical and political, facts pertinent to current and projected creditworthiness. This, together with a *term sheet* restating the terms of the loan, will be sent to interested banks and carefully prefaced by an emphatic disclaimer of all responsibility for its content on the part of the lead manager—a disclaimer is necessary to avoid possible legal liability to the participants in case of default or other problems with the facility that may arise later.

The information memorandum, although prepared by the borrower, will be carefully checked for accuracy and completeness by the lead bank. And since preparing a new information memorandum is time-consuming and costly—especially for borrowers thinly staffed for such work—this aspect sometimes becomes a bone of contention between the borrower and syndicate leadership. Yet it is critical in providing at least *pro forma* information to prospective lenders.

If things go well, the loan will be fully subscribed. If it is over-subscribed, participations will either be *prorated* among the interested banks or occasionally the total amount of the facility will be raised at the option of the borrower. In the latter case, however, prospective syndicate members may wish to reconsider their participation if they are less comfortable with a larger loan to the borrower in question. An oversubscribed syndication may well result in an unhappy borrower (who thinks the price is too high) or unhappy banks (who are unable to get as much of the loan as they were offered), and the competence of the lead manager will be called into question by both sides.

If insufficient funds are raised, then the borrower will have to make do with less (if the syndication is on a best efforts basis) or the banks in the management group will have to book the balance themselves and thereby exceed the target take if the syndication is fully committed. In such a case, the syndication is considered "unsuccessful," with potentially serious adverse consequences for the future prospects of the borrower as well as the lead manager(s) in the market. Again, the competence of the lead manager will be called into question.

Both undersubscribed and oversubscribed deals need to be avoided as much as possible. This is why tailoring the terms of the facility to perceived market receptivity—accuracy in pricing—is such an important determinant of competence in syndication leadership. Particularly desirable participations are those that present a favorable risk/return profile, both in comparison with other loans available in the market and with those offered in the months immediately ahead. Lead banks

Figure 5–1. Sample Offering Information

RE: **REPUBLIC OF RIVANA U.S.$100,000,000 EURODOLLAR LOAN**

THE UNDERSIGNED LEAD MANAGERS HAVE BEEN AWARDED A MANDATE TO ARRANGE A $100,000,000 LOAN FOR THE REPUBLIC OF RIVANA, WHICH HAS BEEN FULLY COMMITTED. AT THE SPECIFIC REQUEST OF THE REPUBLIC, WE ARE PLEASED TO INVITE YOUR INSTITUTION TO JOIN US AS A MANAGER ON A TAKE-AND-HOLD BASIS WITH A COMMITMENT OF U.S.$100,000,000.

THE PRINCIPAL TERMS OF THE FINANCING ARE AS FOLLOWS:

BORROWER:	THE REPUBLIC OF RIVANA.
AMOUNT:	U.S. DOLLARS 100,000,000.
PURPOSE:	THE PROCEEDS OF THE LOAN WILL BE USED TO PROVIDE GENERAL-PURPOSE FUNDS FOR THE REPUBLIC OF RIVANA.
INTEREST RATE:	3/4% P.A. OVER THE 3- OR 6-MONTH LONDON INTER-BANK OFFERED RATE FOR U.S. DOLLAR DEPOSITS FOR THE TERM OF THE LOAN.
FINAL MATURITY:	8 YEARS FROM THE DATE OF SIGNING THE LOAN AGREEMENT.
AVAILABILITY:	12 MONTHS FROM THE DATE OF SIGNING THE LOAN AGREEMENT.
GRACE PERIOD:	4 YEARS FROM THE DATE OF SIGNING THE LOAN AGREEMENT.
REPAYMENT:	9 SUBSTANTIALLY EQUAL SEMIANNUAL INSTALLMENTS COMMENCING 48 MONTHS FROM THE DATE OF SIGNING THE LOAN AGREEMENT.
PREPAYMENT:	PERMITTED WITHOUT PENALTY OF ANY INTEREST PAYMENT DATE GIVEN 30 DAYS ADVANCED NOTICE.
COMMITMENT FEE:	1/2% P.A. ON THE UNDRAWN PORTION OF THE LOAN COMMENCING UPON THE SIGNING OF THE LOAN AGREEMENT AND PAYABLE SEMI-ANNUALLY IN ARREARS.
MANAGEMENT FEE:	3/8% FLAT ON U.S.$10 MILLION TAKE AND HOLD. ANY ALLOCATION WILL BE MADE AT THE SOLE DISCRETION OF THE LEAD MANAGERS. BANKS WILL BE PAID 3/8% ON ANY FINAL ALLOCATED AMOUNT AND WILL RECEIVE MANAGER STATUS.

Figure 5–1.   (cont.)

AGENT:	SCHUBERT NATIONAL BANK OF NEW YORK.
GOVERNING LAW AND JURISDICTION:	THE LAW OF ENGLAND AND THE NONEXCLUSIVE JURISDICTION OF THE STATE AND FEDERAL COURTS IN THE STATE OF NEW YORK AND THE COURTS OF ENGLAND.
DOCUMENTATION:	THE CONCLUSION OF THIS TRANSACTION IS SUBJECT TO THE SIGNING OF A MUTUALLY SATISFACTORY LOAN AGREEMENT, WHICH WILL INCLUDE BUT NOT BE LIMITED TO USUAL EURODOLLAR CLAUSES SUCH AS INCREASED COST, RESERVE REQUIREMENTS, NEGATIVE PLEDGE, CROSS-DEFAULT, AND PARI PASSU PROVISIONS.
COUNSEL TO THE: LENDERS	SLAUGHTER AND MAY, ENGLISH LAW. MOSELEY, ARAFIN AND LEE, REPUBLIC OF RIVANA LAW.
INFORMATION MEMO-RANDUM:	ALL INFORMATION MEMORANDA REGARDING THE REPUBLIC WILL BE AVAILABLE UPON REQUEST.
TAXES AND WITH-HOLDINGS:	ALL PAYMENTS WILL BE MADE FREE AND CLEAR OF, AND WITHOUT DEDUCTION FOR, ALL PRESENT AND FUTURE TAXES, DUTIES, LEVIES, OR WITHHOLDINGS OF WHATEVER NATURE.

SIGNING OF THIS LOAN WILL BE IN HONG KONG IN MID-JANUARY 19XX.

IF YOU HAVE ANY QUESTIONS ON THE ABOVE TRANSACTION, PLEASE DO NOT HESITATE TO CONTACT ROBERT G. HAWKINS OR MARION EPPS, SCHUBERT NATIONAL BANK OF NEW YORK, HONG KONG (TEL: 00−0000) OR ROBERT F. WELLONS, SCHUBERT NATIONAL BANK OF NEW YORK, SINGAPORE (TEL: 000−000).

WE WOULD APPRECIATE RECEIVING YOUR RESPONSE BY TELEX TO ROBERT G. HAWKINS, SCHUBERT NATIONAL BANK OF NEW YORK, HONG KONG OFFICE, TELEX NO. SCBK 00−000 FAX NO. 00−000 BY CLOSE OF BUSINESS TUESDAY DECEMBER 16, 19XX.

REGARDS,
SCHUBERT NATIONAL BANK OF NEW YORK
(OTHER LEAD MANAGERS)

with a track record of spotting such deals are rewarded by further leadership roles and, obviously, by adding attractive paper to their own portfolios.

Along the way, a *loan agreement* will be drawn up (see Chapter 10), which spells out the rights and obligations of all parties to the deal, the governing law, and related matters. Drafting of the loan agreement, especially in complex deals, will be initiated during the syndication process, and various possible points of contention should be discussed with the borrower. Even after the successful completion of syndication, work on the loan agreement may well continue until all points are agreeable to both sides. No bank is finally committed in a syndication until it has agreed to the terms of the loan agreement, and, if no consensus can be reached on a point it has identified as vital, it can gracefully withdraw from the syndicate. However, most of the time the loan documentation seems to be sufficiently standard so that preparation time and acceptability questions are relatively minor problems.

Selection of competent legal counsel in syndicated loans is of utmost importance. Definition of the purpose of a loan in the loan agreement may or may not be helpful. On the one hand, it is the creditworthiness of the borrower that matters, not what the borrower intends to do with a specific block of funding. Excessive specificity in a loan agreement may unintentionally throw the loan into default, to the chagrin of borrower and lender alike. On the other hand, the purpose of a loan may be a good indicator of how the borrower is likely to conduct financial affairs in the years ahead or of the borrower's current financial condition; therefore, it could figure prominently in an overall assessment of the borrower's creditworthiness.

Publicity will eventually have to be arranged, a signing ceremony held, and arrangements made for signing of the loan agreement for those banks not present at the ceremony. The latter is often appropriately lavish, with formal lunches and dinners, complete with speeches, toasts, and mementos. Finally, an *agent* bank will be appointed early in the game. The job of the agent bank will be to run the books on the loan—a critical and influential role that the lead manager will usually want to keep for itself.

When multiple banks form the lead management group, they will split the main jobs between them. These jobs include: (1) preparing and distributing the information memorandum, (2) keeping track of syndication responses from potential participants, (3) negotiating the loan agreement, (4) arranging the signing, (5) handling publicity, and

(6) taking on the agency function. Those jobs providing the closest contact with the borrower or the greatest visibility in the market are the most sought after and will generally go to the dominant members of the group. But even the tasks of selecting menus and mementos, arranging seating charts, and protocol are better than nothing.

Figure 5–2 depicts a *tombstone*, an announcement of a typical full syndication that is a standard aspect of publicity on a deal. Note the prominence of the lead manager and the balance of the management group at the top, the agent bank (usually the lead manager that put the deal together) at the bottom, and the several brackets of participants in between the upper-bracket banks, which committed more funds and hence play a more important role in the deal than the lower-bracket ones.

There are a number of variants that deviate from this general *full syndication* pattern. If market conditions are not receptive to a full syndication, or if a borrower is regularly in the market for funds, a *club loan* may be arranged, wherein a separate information memorandum is not necessary and the lead bank together with the rest of the management group provide the entire amount of the loan themselves. In a *semisyndication*, an unusually large share of the funds is provided by the managers themselves; the balance is provided by a relatively small number of participants who generally know the borrower well and hence get involved on a more exclusive basis. Figures 5–3 and 5–4 give examples of club loans and semisyndications, respectively.

In *participation loans*, one or more banks will underwrite the entire financing and execute the loan agreement, later individually selling down participations to a small number of other banks without the formal structure of a full syndication. Also called a *preadvanced syndicate*, the borrower actually gets the money from the lead bank(s) before part of the loan is sold down on the basis of a participation certificate only and no borrower contact whatsoever. The same is true of *loan notes*, which are sold freely among any banks interested in booking participations in a particular transaction employing a loan note structure, sometimes on a competitive bidding basis.

The entire syndication process normally takes anywhere from two weeks to three months, depending on the borrower, the complexity of the deal, market conditions, competence of the managers, size of the loan, and similar factors. All out-of-pocket costs involved in the syndication—including legal fees, advertising, travel, and communications charges—are for the account of the borrower.

MANUFACTURERS HANOVER

This advertisement appears as a matter of record only

İKTİSAT BANKASİ T.A.Ş.

Iktisat Bankasi Turk A.S.

U.S. $30,000,000
Syndicated Loan

Arranger
Manufacturers Hanover Limited

Lead Managers
Banque Internationale à Luxembourg   Lloyds Bank Plc
London Branch

Managers
Manufacturers Hanover Trust Company New York   Atlantic Bank of New York

Berliner Bank Aktiengesellschaft Berlin   Société Nationale de Crédit à l'Industrie
Nationale Maatschappij Voor Krediet aan de Nijverheid

Participants
BfG: Bank (Schweiz) AG INGEBA   BANCA CRT– Cassa di Risparmio di Torino
New York Branch

Banca Popolare di Milano New York Branch   Banco de Fomento Nacional Brussels Branch

Bank for Foreign Economic Affairs of the USSR Zurich Branch Banque Internationale de Commerce

Banque Vernes et Commerciale de Paris   Bayerische Vereinsbank Aktiengesellschaft
(Groupe San Paolo)

Central-European International Bank Ltd. Budapest   Crédit Commercial de France

Itab Bank Limited   National Bank of Sharjah

National Westminster Bank Group   NMB Bank (France)

A/S Nordlandsbanken   Société Générale Paris

Agent Bank
Manufacturers Hanover Limited

December, 1988   *The Investment Banking Group*

Figure 5–2. Sample Tombstone Announcement. (*Source:* Adapted from Manufacturers Hanover Limited.)

102

Management Buy-Out
of

for
£55,200,000

SYNDICATED DEBT FINANCING

Arranged and underwritten by

Standard Chartered Bank

Participants

Bank of Scotland
Banque Française du Commerce Extérieur (London Branch)
Barclays Bank PLC
Canadian Imperial Bank of Commerce
The Industrial Bank of Japan, Limited
National Westminster Bank PLC
Société Générale

Standard ⚡ Chartered

July 1988

Figure 5–3. Sample Club Loan Offering. (*Source:* Adapted from Standard Chartered Bank.)

Vnesheconombank
Bank for Foreign Economic Affairs of the USSR

USD 150,000,000
Multi-Currency Syndicated Loan Facility

Lead-Managed by
Crédit Lyonnais
Compagnie Luxembourgeoise de la Dresdner Bank AG
— Dresdner Bank International —
Deutsche Bank Luxembourg S.A.
Westpac Banking Corporation

Managed by
Arab Banking Corporation (ABC)
Banque Nationale de Paris (Luxembourg) S.A.

Co-Managed by
Istituto Bancario San Paolo di Torino, Paris Branch
Österreichische Volksbanken-Aktiengesellschaft

Participants
Den Danske Bank
Melita Bank International Ltd.
Banco de Vizcaya, Paris Branch
Banque Hervet
Banque Vernes et Commerciale de Paris

Arranged By
Crédit Lyonnais

May 3, 1988

Figure 5–4. Sample Semisyndication Offering (*Source:* Adapted from Crédit Lyonnais.)

Maturities and Structure

Syndicated lending generally is medium term in nature, sometimes extending to 8 or 10 years. The banks involved thus frequently must take a relatively long view of the borrower's ability and willingness to service the loan, and this is one reason for the importance of government and government-guaranteed borrowing in this market. Countries are likely to be around for such periods, but the status of individual companies is less certain. Many private sector syndications are much shorter in maturity and are designed to be taken out by bond or stock issues or the proceeds of asset sales later.

Given borrower needs, maturities tend to follow market conditions and borrower creditworthiness. If financial markets are tight or have recently experienced a shock (e.g., debt-servicing difficulties by major borrowers, a significant bank failure, or imposition of government restrictions), maturities tend to get shorter. Obviously, the more creditworthy a given borrower is perceived to be, the longer banks are willing to go.

Syndicated loans usually involve a *drawdown schedule*, according to which the borrower will actually acquire the principal, generally related to the date on which the loan is signed. No interest is due on the undrawn amount, but the borrower usually pays a *commitment fee* to the banks for standing by to lend. Once the loan is drawn down, interest is payable, perhaps semiannually in arrears (e.g., at the end of the half-year period), and there may be a grace period of as much as four or five years during which no repayment of principal is due. Principal repayment may be made in a number of ways: (1) on a gradual amortization basis over the rest of the life of the loan, (2) all at once at the end (called a *bullet repayment*), or (3) on some other mutually agreed schedule. A borrower can generally repay the principal at any time without penalty, provided the borrower complies with provisions of prior notification (often 30 days prior to the next interest rate fixing), or a specified prepayment fee may be part of the loan agreement (see Figure 5–1).

Clearly, maturity and loan structure considerations must meet both borrower and market requirements. In devising an appropriate structure, the lead bank must use its expertise, market positioning, influence with the borrower, and creativity to bring the two sides together satisfactorily.

Unlike ordinary loans between a borrower and a lender, the terms of syndicated loans generally become publicly known. It is difficult to keep pricing, fees, maturity information, legal covenants, and borrower information confidential if it has to be fully disseminated among 20 or 50 or more banks in a major syndicated loan.

Borrowers and lenders constantly compare terms of syndications, both over time for individual borrowers and among borrowers, and precedent plays an important role in the market. A borrower will compare the terms he is offered with those he faced the last time he entered the market and those apparently being offered to others. If he shows up too frequently, if his creditworthiness is perceived to have deteriorated, if the purpose of the loan is questioned either in its own right or as an indication of his overall competence, or if others enter the market who are deemed to have better standing, he may have to live with higher costs, shorter maturities, or both. And what happens now will help set the stage for his next foray into the market.

Pricing

Syndicated loans in international banking are generally priced on an agreed-upon *floating base* rate of interest, in most cases the London Interbank Offered Rate (LIBOR), as a proxy for the banks' own cost of funds. To this floating base is added a *contractual spread*, which may be fixed for the entire life of the loan or may be *split*—that is, fixed at one spread for the first several years and another spread for part or all of the remainder. For example, the rate on a typical eight-year syndicated credit to a major borrower may be set at LIBOR $+ \frac{3}{4}$ percent for the first five years and LIBOR $+ \frac{7}{8}$ percent for the rest of the period.

Interest payable by the borrower is adjusted on a *rollover date* every three or six months, at the borrower's option, with the new period's base rate being specified in the typical loan agreement as the average LIBOR quoted two days earlier by selected *reference banks* that are members of the syndicate. The strongest of these banks can often attract three- or six-month deposits at a cost below LIBOR, or they may fund the loan in other maturities—depending on relative interest rates—in order to secure funding profits in addition to the contractual spread (see Chapter 13).

Most of the funds for syndicated lending in international banking are supplied by the Euromarkets and the major national money markets. In order to secure access to funds provided by smaller and regional banks, which may not have competitive access to funding in either of these markets, syndicated loans may also be priced at a contractual spread over U.S. prime or some other rate, with the base adjusted daily or weekly. This may be combined with a cap, floor, or collar defining maximum allowable deviations from, say, the 90-day certificate of deposit (CD) rate (adjusted for reserve requirements), in order to protect borrowers and lenders from significant movements in the base away from current money market rates. Prime-based pricing usually involves smaller spreads than LIBOR-based pricing, because reserve requirements on U.S. deposits keep the prime itself above LIBOR and some banks can fund themselves at significantly lower cost in the Euromarket. It coincides well with conventional pricing practices of the U.S. regional banks and permits borrowers access to these banks that might not otherwise be possible.

Note that whether LIBOR-based or prime-based pricing is used, floating-rate pricing in syndications places the basic interest rate risk (except that between rollover dates) on the borrower. Nevertheless, banks retain credit risk and country risk, as well as currency risk and funding risk—that is, the risk that funds in the needed currency may not be available when present funding has to be rolled over. Currency risk in U.S. dollar loans, for example, may be a concern for non-U.S. banks funding such loans in the Euromarket. The possibility that changing regulations may raise the cost of funding is a risk that the borrower must also bear, however, and thus is generally specified in loan agreements (*material adverse change*).

Special risks in syndicated loan pricing confront both borrowers and lenders as a result of possible shifts in the relationship between LIBOR and U.S. prime or similar base rates in other national financial markets. For example, a bank that funds a prime-based loan in the Euromarket at lower cost will gain or lose if the gap between the prime and LIBOR widens or narrows (e.g., as a result of changes in U.S. bank reserve requirements). Similarly, a borrower with a prime-based loan may lose if the gap widens or gain if it narrows. Caps or floors linked to U.S. CD rates, however, will substantially limit this risk for both sides—as does the prepayment option.

Spreads above the agreed floating-rate base naturally depend upon the assessed creditworthiness of the borrower in the view of the market from which the syndicate participants are drawn. Excessively fine spreads for a particular borrower will make for an unsuccessful syndication; overly wide spreads will unnecessarily inflate the borrower's cost of funds. Figure 5–5 shows how maturities and spreads have differed among syndicated loans to various country groups, reflecting assessments of relative creditworthiness, and how spreads have varied over time with changing Euromarket conditions. Note

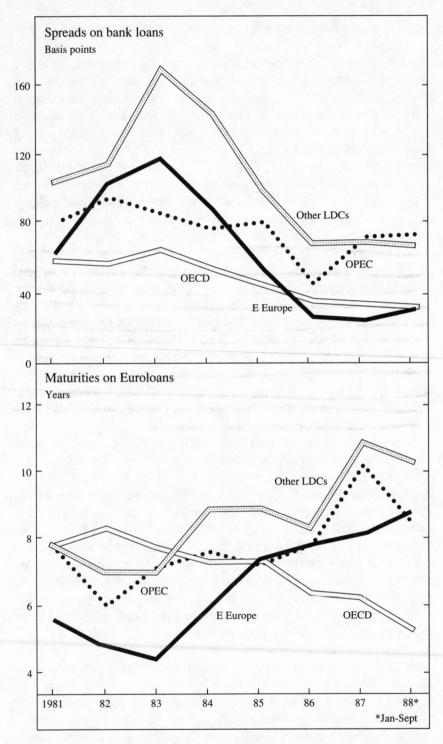

Figure 5–5. Maturities and Spreads among Syndicated Loans Made to Various Countries. (*Source:* OECD; reprinted by permission)

the above-average spreads traditionally paid by developing countries, their decline in the forced rollovers and new-money packages of the 1980s, and the commensurate (involuntary) increases in maturities during this period.

The possibility of widening or narrowing future spreads does leave banks with some residual interest rate risk. For example, a bank may participate in a very finely priced syndication now, but market conditions may dictate substantially fatter spreads for the same borrower a year or two later. This may be handled through *floating spreads*, a relatively unusual technique in which the spread is fixed for an initial period and then is reset annually based on the weighted average of syndicate members' quotes of what their spreads for that borrower would be under prevailing market conditions—limited by maximum and minimum allowable spreads and permitting the borrower to repay the loan without penalty if he objects to the revisions. While limited in use, this technique can protect both borrower and lender against major swings in Euromarket conditions, and it allows the lenders to adjust spreads periodically to reflect changes in borrower creditworthiness. Its practical usefulness in significant volume, however, can be called into question.

All payments of principal and interest in syndicated loans are specified *net to the lender*—that is, free and clear of all taxes levied by the borrower's country or fully creditable against the taxes levied in the bank's home country. Liability for taxes levied where the loan is booked is often negotiable.

Participants in syndicated loans tend to be comparatively steely-eyed in evaluating loan pricing since they, unlike the banks in the management group, have little or nothing to gain in terms of a relationship with the borrower. What's good for the lead managers is not necessarily good for the participants. Occasionally, however, banks will actively participate in syndications on the thinnest of spreads in order to contract volume business, compensate for slack loan demand elsewhere, secure entry into the market, or generate opportunities for funding profit. Participants that are led astray by sloppy risk assessment or portfolio management and become known in the trade as "stuffees"—much to the (usually temporary) delight of the lead managers.

In general, when interest rates are high, "effective" spreads (nominal spreads plus the interest equivalent of fees) on syndicated Eurocurrency credits tend to be narrow. This is because high interest rates raise the opportunity costs to banks of reserve requirements imposed at the national level, thereby driving funds into the Euromarkets where reserve requirements do not exist and thus easing the relative credit conditions under which syndications are carried out. Moreover, a higher LIBOR will tend to raise the return on bank capital relative to its cost of capital (assuming a given capital structure), and hence a particular target return on capital will permit lower effective spreads. Such conditions naturally attract more competitors to the market, and this ensures that narrower effective spreads actually come about.

A relatively low degree of interest rate volatility and the absence of market "shocks" such as bank failures and threats of regulatory controls will tend to reduce banks' funding risks and likewise encourage compressed effective spreads. The absence of borrower problems such as defaults or reschedulings will have a similar effect.

Naturally, lower nominal interest rates and increased perceived funding and lending risk tends to widen effective spreads. Factors that move effective spreads in one direction will move average maturities in the other direction because of the basic tradeoffs linking the two. The tighter credit conditions also tend to widen the degree of differentiation in loan terms between more and less creditworthy borrowers.

Fees

Of particular interest in evaluating the returns to banks from syndication activities are the fees paid by the borrower to the participants. These take several forms and may be present to varying degrees depending on the structure of a particular syndication.

First, the management groups in a particular syndication will have to be compensated for arranging and underwriting the loan, including assumption of the risks involved. This usually takes the form of a front-end *management fee*, which is usually a flat percentage of the total loan (e.g., 1%) payable at or shortly after the signing. The size and complexity of the loan, the nature of the borrower, competition among banks for the borrower's business, and similar factors figure into the negotiated size of the front-end fee.

A portion of the management fee may have to be shared by the syndicate manager(s) with other participants in order to successfully sell down a loan, especially a very large one. This *participation fee* takes the form of a flat percentage of each bank's final amount lent. It is often divided into size categories based on the level of participation by groups of banks.

Second, since a particular loan may not be drawn down immediately, but must be made available to the borrower over time as specified in the loan agreement, a separate *commitment fee* is often provided, generally a flat percentage (e.g., $\frac{1}{2}$%) on the undrawn portion of the loan, starting on the day of the signing and prorated among the participating banks.

Finally, the bank acting as agent in a syndication will normally negotiate an *agent's fee*, usually a fixed sum (e.g., $30,000 per year for the life of the loan) payable by the borrower up front or annually in recognition of that bank's responsibilities for running the books on the loan.

While the agent's fee and the commitment fee are clearly specified, the division of the management fee among syndicate participants is negotiable and may be quite complex. On a $100 million fully committed loan lead managed by a single bank that has negotiated a 1 percent management fee, or $1 million, the lead bank may decide it must distribute $750,000 among all banks in the "co–lead bank" category to ensure a successful syndication. The lead bank may also decide to withhold $\frac{1}{4}$% ($250,000) for itself as compensation for serving as "manager of the managers." This $\frac{1}{4}$ percent portion is called a *praecipium* and represents the unique return to lead manager(s) for arranging the deal.

It may now decide to offer a participation fee of $\frac{3}{4}$% of final participation to banks (including itself) that lend at least $10 million each (as they become co–lead managers), $\frac{1}{2}$% to banks participating at a level of $5 million or more, and $\frac{1}{4}$% to banks that take under $5 million. Suppose, of the $100 million total loan, the lead manager takes $15 million into its own portfolio, 4 co–lead managers are in at $10 million, 6 banks take $5 million, and 15 banks take $1 million. Of the available $750,000 in participation fees, the lead manager gets $112,500 ($\frac{3}{4}$% on its $15 million participation, or *final take*), co-managers get $300,000 ($\frac{3}{4}$% on $10 million x 4 banks), first-level participants get $150,000 ($\frac{1}{2}$% on $5 million x 6 banks), and second-level participants get $37,500 ($\frac{1}{4}$% on $1 million x 15 banks).

Under these conditions, a total of $600,000 in participation fees have been allocated, leaving $150,000 unallocated. This unallocated amount is called the *pool*, and it is normally distributed to the management group in proportion to their individual underwriting commitments. If these proportions are the same as the final take, the lead manager gets 15/55 × $150,000 = $40,909 and the co–managers get 10/55 × $150,000 × 4 banks = $109,091.

In this example, the returns to the lead manager out of the $1 million management fee are:

Praecipium	$250,000	
Participation	112,500	
Pool share	40,909	
	$403,409	(1 bank)

Each of the co-managers get:

Participation	$ 75,000	
Pool share	$ 27,273	
Total	$102,273	(4 banks)

Each of the first-level participants get:

Participation	$25,000	(6 banks)

Each of the second-level participants get:

Participation	$25,000	(15 banks)

All of this adds to $1 million: $403,409 + $102,273 × 4 + $25,000 × 6 + $2,500 × 15 = $1 million rounded off.

For the lead manager this means an immediate return of 2.69% of the final take ($15 million); for comanagers 1.02%; for first-level participants 0.5 percent; and for second-level participants 0.25%. But because these fees are *immediate*, the interest-equivalents based on the average life of the loan are proportionately higher in comparison to the contractual spread. Front-end fees, when calculated on an interest-equivalent basis over the average life of the loan, obviously raise the cost to the borrower and the returns to the lender and are thus fully comparable with fixed or split contractual spreads.

This illustrates the importance that fees can assume in evaluating a bank's overall return on syndication activity. The point for lead banks is to maximize fee income per dollar actually lent, and this obviously means being in a position to command the upper tiers of syndications where the bulk of the fee income (and the risks and required skills) are lodged. It also means, for the lead managers, strict confidentiality about the overall size of the fee and sharing that fee only to the extent necessary to ensure a successful syndication.

As components of returns to the participating banks (and costs to the borrower), spreads and fees are obviously related. Because higher contractual spreads may carry negative connotations about the borrower's creditworthiness, he may agree to fatter fees to compensate the lenders for fine spreads in order to improve his market positioning in future borrowings. Similarly, borrowers will sometimes undertake *benchmark financings*, borrowing via syndicated loans with extremely fine pricing when the borrower has no real need for funds (and is thus viewed by the market as particularly creditworthy) just to "show the flag" and try to improve future borrowing conditions. A borrower's "name" in the market evolves over a period of time, as does a bank's competitive positioning, and both have a great deal to do with the structure of pricing and fees.

The Agency Function

The task of servicing a syndicated loan falls upon the agent bank, usually the lead bank or one of the lead managers assigned the job. One view holds that the agency function is purely a clerical role with few substantive obligations to borrower and lender and little independent power of decision. An opposing view is that the agent represents a critical link among all parties over the life of a loan, with major responsibilities to all concerned—indeed that a syndicated loan cannot really be considered a "success" or "failure" until it has ultimately matured and that the agent plays a critical role in this determination.

The mechanical aspects of the agent's job involve running the books on the loan. This requires the following seven functions: (1) seeing that the terms of the loan agreement are complied with regarding drawdown, rollover, interest payments, grace period, and repayment of principal; (2) collecting of funds from participants as per the drawdown provisions and payment to the borrower; (3) periodic fixing of the interest rate on the floating base as per the contractual spread; (4) computing interest and principal due, collection from the borrower, and distribution to the lenders (not such a simple task when funds are due in one place and time and payable in another); (5) monitoring loan supports, such as collateral valuation, guarantees, and insurance; (6) evaluating and ensuring compliance with covenants in the loan agreement and informing participants, as necessary; and

(7) collecting periodic reports from the borrower, independent auditors, or other specified sources and distributing them to participants. Such tasks must be done reliably, efficiently, and promptly, yet they are little more than clerical in nature.

It is when trouble brews that the agency function may take on a more substantive meaning. The loan documentation will obviously specify under what conditions there is an event of default, but this may involve zero, partial, or full agent discretion. A capable agent bank that has attained this role by virtue of a superior track record in this function, participation in syndicate leadership, and a sizeable loan commitment for its own book is likely to have sufficient familiarity with the borrower and large enough stakes in the outcome to be trusted with some measure of discretion in problem situations, unless such decisions can only be made by a stipulated voting procedure among syndicate participants.

If a borrower does encounter difficulties, the syndicate leadership and/or the agent bank performs a critical role in explaining the problem to participants and creating a climate within which a workout can be accomplished—obviously in the fundamental interest of both sides. The role of agent took on enormous importance during the sovereign debt renegotiations throughout the 1980s.

Nevertheless, defining the agent's proper role is not an easy task. If the agent bank is also the lead manager and has long-standing ties to the borrower, there is potential for divided loyalties and conflicts of interest (e.g., what information obtained by the agent about the borrower's financial condition should be kept in confidence, and what should be passed on to participants?). Discretion also carries with it potential liability, which an agent bank may wish to avoid—laws differ, and are often rather fuzzy, about the division of an agent's responsibility to the borrower and the lender. And there is always the possibility, indeed the likelihood, that information distributed to syndicate members may reach the press and worsen the borrower's troubles.

Yet a continuing and digestible flow of information to syndicate participants may help to smooth problem situations before they become crises, provide sound advice to the borrower, and prepare the way for possible infusions of additional funds by syndicate members where workout situations are encountered.

It is in such cases that day-to-day borrower contact is especially critical, and this cannot possibly be provided by the whole syndicate. Here a certain degree of agent discretion, perhaps backed by a small committee representing syndicate members, and flexible interpretation of the terms of the legal documentation may lead to a better outcome than applying no flexibility at all. There must be mutual trust and commonality of interest, coupled with an adequate flow of information, for which no amount of legal language can effectively substitute.

The agency function is enhanced by the fact that borrower evaluation still tends to be inadequate in the case of many syndicate participants. They may be too small and have inadequate staff capabilities. The cost may be excessive. The time available before a decision has to be made may be too short. Yet the lead banks' own assessments cannot be made available because of the implied liability involved. Apart from the lead banks' efforts to ensure an accurate and complete information memorandum (almost always woefully deficient in defensible economic forecasts and invariably void of political risk assessment), there has been no good solution to this problem.

As one observer notes:

> Managers trust that participants will not vindictively pursue them for acting responsibly and in good faith, and participants must trust in the manager's integrity or ability, or decline the loan. . . . Banking skills include judging when incomplete information is sufficient for a sensible decision. . . . Most responsible managers try to exclude unsuitable participants from loans of unusual complexity or risk.[1]

Competitive Performance

Relatively few banks dominate international loan syndication activities. Table 5–1 gives the rankings for 1988 for lead banks on publicized Eurosyndications. The name of the game is obviously syndicate leadership, and in a market where news travels fast and rumors are rampant, a strong position is exceedingly difficult to attain and to hold.

Careful examination of tombstones over a period of time can yield valuable information about who is in the market, which banks are successfully competing for leadership roles, what kind of reception individual borrowers are getting, who is giving them financial advice, which banks are taking what kinds of loans into their portfolios, who is working with whom, and so on. Combined with gossip and regular leaks on pricing, fees, maturities, and related matters, this can give participants in daily contact with the market an excellent feel for what is going on.

Table 5–1. Top 50 Arrangers of Syndicated Loans in 1988 for Signed Facilities Only

Rank	Manager	$ million	Number
1	Citicorp	47,424.40	143
2	J. P. Morgan	43,655.90	108
3	Bankers Trust Company	28,819.10	115
4	Manufacturers Hanover	26,379.10	119
5	Chase Investment Bank	25,679.20	162
6	Chemical Bank	17,842.10	52
7	Barclays de Zoete Wedd	15,460.00	75
8	Midland Montagu	15,413.10	68
9	National Westminster Bank	13,241.00	70
10	CSFB	11,648.90	51
11	Bank of America International	11,156.60	66
12	Swiss Bank Corp.	10,298.80	33
13	Sumitomo Bank	6,974.48	40
14	SG Warburg	6,368.60	48
15	Grand Metropolitan Finance	6,000.00	1
16	Crédit Lyonnais	5,779.33	49
17	First National Bank of Chicago	5,525.26	24
18	Bank of Nova Scotia	4,771.67	18
19	Security Pacific Bank	4,642.72	34
20	HongkongBank Group	4,189.79	42
21	Westpac Banking	3,933.60	40
22	Union Bank of Switzerland	3,709.78	8
23	Industrial Bank of Japan	3,465.58	39
24	Toronto-Dominion Bank	3,372.65	16
25	Lloyds Merchant Bank	3,320.17	25
26	Bank of Tokyo	3,165.13	29
27	NM Rothschild & Sons	3,081.39	17
28	CIBC	3,065.85	14
29	Bank of Montreal	3,058.97	13
30	Baring Brothers	2,931.73	9
31	LTCB	2,744.34	15
32	ANZ-Grindlays Banking Group	2,694.14	18
33	Kleinwort Benson	2,676.54	10
34	Banque Indosuez	2,608.70	22
35	Minorco	2,389.08	1
36	Banque Nationale de Paris	2,328.05	31
37	Deutsche Bank	2,230.95	10
38	Société Générale	2,176.23	32
39	Standard Chartered Bank	2,123.29	29
40	Dai-Ichi Kangyo Bank	2,033.49	33
41	Morgan Grenfell	1,963.13	24

Table 5–1. (cont.)

Rank	Manager	$ million	Number
42	Banque Paribas	1,858.44	17
43	Merrill Lynch International Bank	1,847.48	19
44	Continental Illinois	1,706.71	21
45	Mitsubishi Trust & Banking Corp.	1,691.80	12
46	Commonwealth Bank of Australia	1,515.90	7
47	J. Henry Schroder Wagg	1,471.65	10
48	Mitsubishi Bank	1,305.74	31
49	Royal Bank of Canada	1,212.52	8
50	Tokai Bank	1,175.00	8

SOURCE: Euromoney Loanware.

The main ingredient of success in syndication leadership is the "name" of the bank and the reputation it has developed over the years in the market. A lead manager on a syndication carries heavy responsibilities to both borrowers and lenders. It must be absolutely forthright and reliable in dealings with participants. The lead bank must stay away from substandard deals and develop a pattern of offering participations that have attractive risk/return profiles. It must avoid the "hard sell," a difficult thing to do when things are not going well, and retain participant respect even in the heat of the syndication process. It must be thoroughly familiar with market conditions and individual banks' attitudes toward particular borrowers, and it must have developed a good overall working relationship with a broad array of banks—including participations and possible management roles in syndications led by others. The lead bank also must have a major presence in syndication centers, particularly London and Hong Kong, staffed by specialized support groups who can effectively bank up the lending officers at the customer end to win the mandate and at the same time are capable of structuring a syndicate and successfully getting the deal. Such individuals are generally bright, tactful, resourceful, and extremely tough bargainers.

At the other end of the deal, the successful lead bank must have established a sound working relationship with (and reputation among) potential borrowers, often covering the gamut of banking services, possibly a local presence, and a track record that evidences the bank's commitment in good times and bad. The bank must be a steady source of sound advice, even if this runs counter to current desires of the borrower. It must be able to convince the borrower of its strong position in the market and its ability to bring off a syndication on the most competitive terms possible. Its image of competence must be unquestioned and must be seen as an important factor in the market. Its bid for a mandate must naturally be highly competitive, whereby the borrower will weigh the bid against the service he expects to receive. Occasionally, borrowers will play rough, such as blackballing certain banks from participation, using a bank's local presence as leverage to secure improved terms, changing terms in the middle of a syndication, refusing to produce a new information memorandum, refusing certain loan agreement provisions, and the like. These too must be managed tactfully and firmly.

The need to get "close to" borrowers can be readily observed in syndications as banks scramble for the most visible positions and ones that will ensure borrower contact. It is also evident in the willingness of banks that lose a mandate to nevertheless participate in syndicate management under leadership of the winner.

Above all, banks must avoid errors. Misestimating market conditions or borrower acceptability may produce a "failed" syndication or an embarrassing return to the borrower for sweeter terms. Best efforts syndications can obviously fail outright, leading to red faces all around, a loss of fees, or a humiliating return to the market with sweetened terms. Renegotiated fully committed syndications have similar consequences. Both can strain relationships between syndicate leadership, the borrower, and participating banks and, if repeated too often, can severely erode the ability of those responsible to compete for syndications in the future.

Mishandling the job of agent, which is always possible in problem situations, can cause serious difficulties to borrower and syndicate participants alike. Even errors of judgment in arranging publicity, signings, and similar administrative details can have adverse consequences. When amplified by market gossip, these "black marks" can seriously erode a bank's competitive position for the most lucrative aspects of the business.

Since loan syndication is rather similar to the underwriting function for bonds and stocks in investment banking (discussed in Chapters 14 to 16), one might expect investment banks to play a much stronger competitive role in loan syndication than they apparently have. However, borrowers like to see those to whom they award syndication mandates take a substantial interest in the loan themselves, and in a fully committed deal they *must* be in a position to do so if necessary. Investment banks are generally unable or unwilling to do so. Similarly, syndicate participants like to see lead managers and agents with sizeable stakes in the game, whereas investment banks may be viewed as working primarily for the borrower's interests.

In the early days of international loan syndication, the status of the lead bank played a dominant role in determining the success of the deal. The lead bank was presumed to be intimately familiar with the borrower and, in being willing to provide the largest share of the funds and take on the underwriting commitment, must hold the borrower in high regard. Why should the Last National Bank of Omaha question its judgment and think twice about participating?

Some of this is still true—especially with respect to the demonstrated competence of the agent bank—but the Euromarket shocks of the 1970s, the LDC debt crisis of the 1980s, and pressure by bank regulators have tilted the balance toward a much more careful and detailed examination of the borrower by participating banks. Moreover, lead banks and their legal advisors have become almost paranoid about shedding all responsibility, moral or otherwise, for the ultimate outcome of a syndicated loan as far as the participating banks are concerned. Loan agreements generally require that participants have indeed made independent assessments of the borrower on the basis of adequate information. As noted, given the distribution of fees, the value of relationship, and similar considerations, the risk-return calculus of lead banks tends to be fundamentally different from that of the lower-bracket participants.

SUMMARY

Syndications have become an important component of international lending. Few banks that purport to provide a full range of services to their global client base are not actively involved in syndicated lending. We have seen that it has advantages for borrowers and lenders alike that clearly outweigh the disadvantages of complexity, impersonality, and lack of confidentiality. For large bank facilities in particular, there simply is no alternative to syndicated loans under present or prospective future market conditions.

This chapter spelled out the characteristics of success in syndicate leadership, which is where the real competitive game is played and where the real profits are lodged. Since the non–interest income involved is based on activities that are off the balance sheet of the bank, they tend to have a disproportionate influence on the value of the bank to its shareholders.

NOTE

1. T. H. Donaldson, *Lending in International Commercial Banking* (London: Macmillan, 1979), p. 72.

SELECTED REFERENCES

Bee, Robert N.   "Syndication." In *Offshore Lending by U.S. Commercial Banks*, edited by F. John Mathis. Washington, D.C.: Bankers' Association for Foreign Trade, 1975.

Donaldson, T. H.   *Lending in International Commercial Banking*. London: Macmillan, 1979, chapter 5.

Goodman, Laurie S.   "The Pricing of Syndicated Eurocurrency Credits." *Federal Reserve Bank of New York Quarterly Review*, Summer 1980.

Terrell, Henry, and Martinson, Michael G.   "Market Practices in Syndicated Bank Eurocurrency Lending." *Bankers Magazine*, November 1978.

6

Euronote Programs and Commercial Paper Issues

One of the most dramatic changes in recent years in the international capital markets has been the development of Euronote. Originally used as a cheap substitute for medium-term syndicated loans, Euronote programs sprouted a range of offshoots designed to provide top-quality corporate and sovereign borrowers with a flexible, cost-effective, short-term source of finance as well as a highly efficient means of securing medium-term floating-rate money. In general terms, a Euronote facility is a syndicated, underwritten, medium-term arrangement that enables borrowers to issue a stream of short-term promissory bearer notes on an assured rollover basis usually for maturities of one, three, or six months. The most significant further development of this general technique has been Eurocommercial paper (ECP). ECP programs again involve the issuance of short-term promissory bearer notes, but differ from the conventional Euronote in that they are nonunderwritten and have fixed maturities ranging from 7 to 365 days, thus offering both reduced costs and increased flexibility.

This chapter discusses the workings of Euronote and ECP programs and considers their growth and development against the financial background of the 1980s. It examines the major players in the market and the attractions it holds for them, followed by a discussion of pricing, terms, and distribution. The chapter concludes with a comparison of the U.S. domestic and ECP markets, and a summary of the current conditions and possible future developments.

Commercial paper has existed for more than 100 years in the United States (USCP). It is, like its European equivalent, a short-term promissory note sold without documentation by high-grade issuers to sophisticated investors (e.g., corporations, banks, and investment companies) who use the market to invest surplus cash at rates that exceed those available from the treasury bill market. Most paper is issued in maturities of 30 days or less and is rolled over at maturity. USCP is rated by rating agencies in the United States, as many investors are restricted from purchasing unrated paper. Issuers of paper must also provide committed bank loan backup facilities to assure the ability of cash to redeem maturing paper in the event of a market disturbance that might restrict rollovers. In order to meet the quality standards of the market, many issuers sell paper accompanied by a letter of credit from a major bank. Many international corporations and governments or agencies issue USCP; virtually all of this paper is placed with U.S. investors and not with investors outside the United States.

During the past several years, the USCP market has attracted most of the country's largest corporate borrowers, which are able to issue paper at borrowing rates substantially below banks' prime lending rates. Generally, the issuing rates available to international corporations in the U.S. market are lower than those available in the ECP market, so major U.S. market issuers generally do not issue ECP except when interested in developing new sources of finance. Though some USCP investors purchase ECP to obtain higher rates than are available in the U.S. commercial paper market, many are unfamiliar with the issuers and the arrangements for payment and delivery of paper (which are substantially different from those used in the U.S. market) and therefore do not invest. Moreover, the supply of available paper in the United States vastly exceeds that so far available in ECP, so that most investors are required to do their shopping in New York.

Non-U.S. issuers (especially large government issuers), however, frequently pay a slightly higher rate in the U.S. market where they may be less well known than a counterpart American issuer. Accordingly, for these issuers ECP rates may be more attractive and the market more convenient. As the ECP market has developed in size and liquidity, more first-rate issuers and investors have been attracted to it.

The ECP market has not generally required ratings from rating agencies, though the agencies are increasingly making these available, and not all programs require backup lines of credit. Most ECP programs, however, are created as a part of a Euro "Note Issuance Facility" (NIF), which provides a borrower with an assurance of a medium-term financing facility (provided by a syndicate of banks).

This facility allows the borrower to sell notes (i.e., ECP) to the market at a money market rate set by auction at the time of sale or to sell them at a rate reflecting an agreed maximum spread over a base rate, either LIBOR or the "bid" side of the London Interbank market rate for deposits (the LIBID).

The NIF can provide for a structure that permits auctioning off the notes at the time of their sale through a *tender panel*, that is, a designated group of banks (including some other than the NIF banks) and dealers who agree to tender, or bid, for notes when they are offered. The tender panel members may bid any rate they choose, so that their participation is in effect on a best-efforts basis. If the bids are not competitive with the maximum rates, none are accepted and the notes are instead purchased by the NIF banks. In the case of the Revolving Underwriting Facility (RUF), the designated sole placing agent (often not an underwriting bank), uses its best efforts to place the notes at rates below the maximum rate. If it is not successful, the underwriting banks either purchase the notes or offer a loan at the agreed maximum spread instead. The issuer pays arrangement and underwriting fees for a NIF and a RUF; the banks are not paid fees for their role on the tender panel—their compensation must come from the spread they would earn by reselling notes to the market at a slightly higher price than they paid for them. The structure is designed to give the borrower the best of both worlds—guaranteed rollover at an agreed spread for several years and the opportunity to sell paper at lower rates than the agreed rates when the conditions permit. The borrower may also sell notes either to a dealer or directly to the market itself on a nonunderwritten basis if preferred.

The borrower may also add a provision to the NIF or RUF agreement to permit the use of the facility for backstopping the issuance of USCP. In such cases, an undrawn portion of the facility is set aside for this purpose. The USCP will be sold and rolled over by a dealer in the United States, but only a portion of the facility will actually have to be made available in New York (in overnight funds)—an amount adequate to cover single-day rollovers. This portion of the facility is called a "swingline." The Euronote and ECP issuing process is illustrated in Figure 6–1.

Figures 6–2 and 6–3 present tombstones on typical NIF and RUF structures, respectively. The roles of arranger, underwriter, tender panel, and sole placing agent are clearly identifiable in these examples.

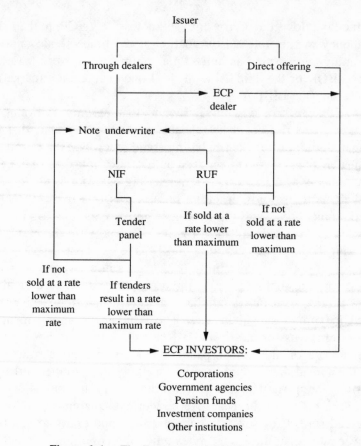

Figure 6–1. The Euronote and ECP Issuing Process.

Figures 6–4 and 6–5 present tombstones for U.S. domestic and ECP programs, respectively, and can be compared with the Euronote tombstones in the previous two figures.

The Euronote market has produced a bewildering number of variations on this basic theme, variations in which structuring and pricing are extremely flexible and can be closely matched to the borrower's requirements.

A popular variation is a NIF or RUF with a built-in provision for a letter of credit from a bank (usually with the lead bank in the facility) under which the notes (or USCP) are issued. This arrangement enables issuers of lesser credit standing to use the ECP or the U.S. commercial paper market or to borrow directly from the banks, whichever is cheaper. The "prime issuance facility" is similar to the NIF except that the maximum interest spread is expressed in terms of the U.S.

This announcement appears as a matter of record only — April 1988

AGL

THE AUSTRALIAN GAS LIGHT COMPANY

US$150,000,000
Note Issuance Facility

Arranged by

COUNTY NATWEST

Underwriting Banks

National Westminster Bank Group

Australian and New Zealand Banking Group Ltd. — **Bank of Montreal Asia Limited**

Banque Nationale de Paris — **CIBC Asia Limited**

Commonwealth Bank of Australia — **Die Erste österreichische Spar-Casse—Bank**
First Austrian Bank

Kyowa Finance (Hong Kong) Limited — **Mitsui Trust Bank (Europe) S.A.**

Union Bank of Switzerland
London Branch
— **Chase Manhattan Asia Limited**

Additional Tender Panel Members

Bankers Trust International Limited — **Commerzbank (South East Asia) Ltd.**

First Chicago Limited — **S.G. Warburg & Co. Ltd.**

Facility Agent

Nat West Investment Bank Limited

The Nat West Investment Bank Group

Figure 6–2. Sample Tombstone for a Typical NIF Structure. (*Source:* Adapted from NatWest Investment Bank Group, 1988)

Victorian Public Authorities Finance Agency
U.S. $100,000,000

Revolving Underwriting Facility

Guaranteed by

The Government of Victoria

Arranged by

Citicorp Investment Bank Limited

Underwriters

Algemene Bank Nerderland N.V. ● BankAmerica Capital Markets

Bank of Montreal Asia Limited ● The Bank of Tokyo (Holland) N.V. ● Banque Nationale de Paris

Barclays Bank PLC ● CIBC Capital Markets ● Citibank (Channel Islands) Limited

Commonwealth Bank of Australia ● Crédit Lyonnais, Singapore Branch ● Crédit Suisse

Duetsche Bank Luxembourg S.A. ● DKB International Limited

Fuji International Finance Limited ● The Industrial Bank of Japan (Luxembourg) S.A.

International Westminster Bank PLC ● Mitsui Finance Asia Limited

Nomura Europe N.V. ● Sanwa International Finance Limited

Security Pacific Hoare Govett Asia Limited ● Société Générale ● State Bank Victoria

Sumitomo Finance (Asia) Limited ● Swiss Bank Corporation ● Westpac Banking Corporation

Facility Agent

Citicorp Investment Bank Limited

Issuing and Paying Agent

Westpac Banking Corporation

December 21, 1987

CITICORP◆INVESTMENT BANK

Figure 6–3. Sample Tombstone for a Typical RUF Structure. (*Source:* Adapted from Citicorp Investment Bank, 1987)

This announcement appears as a matter of record only

Commercial Paper Program

established for

SSANGYONG (U.S.A.), INC.

a wholly owned subsidiary of

SSANGYONG CORPORATION

Seoul, Korea

Irrevocable Letter of Credit in support of
commercial paper issuance provided by

Bankers Trust Company

*The undersigned acted as advisor on the above
financing and will act as commercial paper dealer.*

 Merrill Lynch Money Markets Inc.
Merrill Lynch White Weld Capital Markets Group

Figure 6–4. Sample Tombstone for a U.S. Domestic Paper Program. (*Source:* Adapted from Merrill Lynch Money Markets, Inc. 1986)

127

PUBLIC LIMITED COMPANY

U.S.$250,000,000

Euro-Commercial Paper Programme

Dealers

Chase Investment Bank
Citicorp Investment Bank Limited
Credit Suisse First Boston Limited

Issuing & Paying Agent

The First National Bank of Chicago

Figure 6–5. Sample Tombstone for an ECP Program. (*Source:* Adapted from The First National Bank of Chicago, 1988)

prime instead of LIBOR or LIBID. In the "Transferable Revolving Underwriting Facility" (TRUF), the underwriting bank's contingent liability to purchase notes in the event of nonplacement is totally transferable (i.e., sellable) to other banks. Also making its appearance has been the "Borrowers' Option for Notes and Underwritten Stand-by" (BONUS), a Bank of America acronym for a facility allowing the borrower to tap both the USCP and ECP markets simultaneously. Then there is the "Grantor Underwritten Note" (GUN), a floating-note facility akin to a Euronote program whereby a group of banks (grantors) commit to purchase any notes "put" back to them by investors on any interest-fixing date on a medium-term floating-rate Euronote. Such "put" notes are then auctioned out to the market between the grantors.

Additional derivatives include the "Issuer Set Margin" (ISM), a method of pricing and distribution introduced by Merrill Lynch whereby the issuer, in consultation with the arranger, sets a price at the beginning of each tranche. Underwriters may then take up paper at this price up to the level of their underwriting commitment and place it themselves. Any unplaced paper becomes the arranger's responsibility. Finally, there is the "Multi-Option Financing Facility" (MOFF), introduced by J. P. Morgan in 1984. Under this method, the bank's medium-term commitment consists not only of Euronotes but extends to a wider range of instruments such as bankers' acceptances and short-term advances, possibly in a number of different currencies. Figure 6–6 presents a typical MOFF tombstone with the respective roles of the various participants clearly identified.

Banks find that these facilities meet several of their objectives. They are able to earn fees from arranging and participating in the facilities, which are expected to be undrawn for the most part, thus saving room on their balance sheets and increasing their overall return on assets. Banks also find that such facilities increase the bank's experience with pricing and distributing money market products and enable the banks to retain a meaningful role in business areas that have become subject to securitization. The facilities also offer a wide opportunity to demonstrate creativity and adaptability to client requirements.

HISTORICAL DEVELOPMENT

Although there had been attempts in the early 1970s to establish an international market for short-term corporate bearer notes, the first Euronote issue to attract serious attention was not undertaken until

USINOR SACILOR

FRF 1,350,000,000
Multi-Option Financing Facility
Incorporating a Letter of Credit Facility for the Issuance of U.S. Commercial Paper

Arranged by
BNP Capital Markets Limited   Crédit Lyonnais

Co-Arranged by
Banque Paribas

Lead Managed by

Banque Nationale de Paris	Crédit Lyonnais
Banque Paribas	Banco Central S.A. Succursala de Paris
Banque de l'Union Européenne	Caisse Centrale des Banques Populaires
Deutsche Bank AG Succursala de Paris	The Mitzui Bank, Ltd. Paris Branch

Managed by

Crédit Commercial de France	Crédit Suisse
The Fuji Bank, Limited Paris Branch	Groupe CIC (CIC Paris - BSD - CIAL - SNVS)
Lloyds Bank (France) Limited	The National Bank of Kuwait (France) S.A.
National Westminster Bank s.a.	The Sumitomo Bank, Ltd

Co-Managed by

Banco Bilbao Vizcaya S.A.	Banco di Roma (France) S.A.
Banco di Sicilia International S.A. Luxembourg	Banque de Neuflize, Schlemberger, Mallet
Banque Française du Commerce Extérieur	Bayerische Vereinsbank S.A. (SV France)
Crédit du Nord	NMB Bank (France)
Union de Crédit pour le Développement Régional - Unicrédit	Via Banque

Additional Tender Panel Members
Kleinwort Benson Limited   Westpac Banking Corporation

Facility Agent
Crédit Lyonnais

Tender Panel Agents

Domestic French Francs	Domestic Duetsche Marks	Eurocurrencies
Banque Paribas	Duetsche Bank AG	Crédit Lyonnais

Issuer of Letters of Credit
Banque Nationale de Paris

Figure 6–6. Sample Tombstone for a Typical MOFF Structure. (*Source:* Adapted from Crédit Lyonnais, 1989)

December 1978, when a program for the New Zealand Shipping Corporation was arranged. Real growth in the market was not seen until 1984. Between 1979 and 1983 there were just 86 Euronote facilities, with only $9 billion arranged.

Until this time, however, a large portion of arranged facilities were not used. The borrowers used the facilities when they needed standby credit capacity or when their efforts to sell ECP were unavailing. The principal investors in the market at the time were banks themselves— other banks looking for liquid assets that could be traded and the facilities-granting banks that would purchase the notes (being unable to sell them at lower rates) and use them as a substitute for loans. There were several hundred banks operating in Europe at the time, and enough became interested to provide a modest trading market in ECP. To expand further, the market needed more nonbank investors, which for the most part were not interested in purchasing additional bank paper or notes issued by other than the top-tier borrowers. In 1984 some $15 billion of Euronotes facilities came to the market.

In late 1984 and early 1985 Sweden held three Euronote auctions totaling $700 million as part of a $4 billion MOFF arranged by J. P. Morgan. Each of these was five times oversubscribed, with an average cost of LIBID minus 10 basis points, setting a new benchmark for borrowers and lenders alike for pricing and bidding in the market. These issues drew in many nonbank investors and moved the market ahead considerably.

The ECP market was pioneered by the Export Development Corporation of Canada (EDC), a Canadian government corporation. When EDC first came to market in 1983, it achieved rates 60 to 70 points below LIBID, beating rates at which it could be issued in the USCP market. European investors were extremely eager to purchase U.S. dollar paper at the time, when interest rates were falling and the dollar was rising against virtually all currencies. Canadian government paper was highly valued in Europe, more so perhaps at the time than in the United States. The paper was available on a bearer basis, making it attractive to tax-avoiding investors whose investments were handled by banks in Switzerland and other continental countries.

While only three facilities totaling $286 million were arranged in 1984, between January and November of 1985, 28 facilities for new issuers were arranged, for an aggregate of $6.1 billion. Figure 6–7 depicts the volume of Euronotes and ECP outstanding. New issues under active ECP programs rose from $4.5 billion early in 1986 to over $60 billion in mid-1988, with some 700 issuers involved.

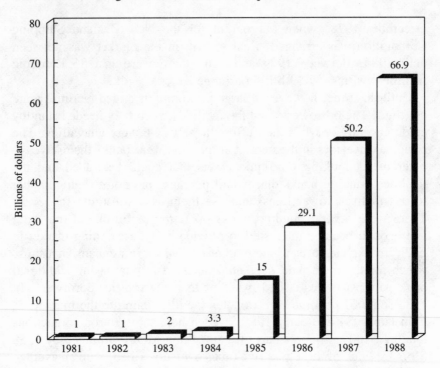

Figure 6–7. Growth in Amount of ECP and Euronotes Outstanding (in Billions of Dollars).

The growth and development of the Euronote market may be seen as intimately linked to the changes occurring throughout the world's capital markets in the 1980s. Prior to 1980 the predominant short-term Euro money market instruments were bank related—Eurodollar CDs, bankers' acceptances, and bank deposits. Even with the advent of the Euronote, nonbank investors tended at first to stay with these instruments, leaving Euronote investment to banks participating in the syndicated loan market. However, by mid-1982 fears over the extent of bank LDC exposures were precipitating a diversification of funds away from banks, and money market investors began to seek other vehicles for investment. Euronotes provided an ideal alternative.

Institutional investors, multinational corporations, and central banks entered the market. They were attracted not only by the opportunities for short-term asset diversification, but also by the greater liquidity and higher yields that were available. These nonbank investors were not "yield maximizers." They preferred a quality name at a modest rate to a "risky" name at a high rate, and they were prepared to pay for quality (in lower rates on the notes). Their opportunity cost was the bid rate on Eurocurrency bank deposits. The composition of the Euronote investor base thus changed significantly, and with it loan and Euronote spreads fell commensurately as LIBID became established as the market's reference point.

At the same time, the perspective was changing from the borrower's point of view as well. Disintermediation and securitization increased as quality borrowers realized that in many cases they could achieve financing more cheaply by going directly to the market rather than obtaining financing via the banks. Increasing globalization encouraged issuers to look beyond their own boundaries for sources of funds, and legal and fiscal restrictions on the issuance of short-term notes in a number of national money markets rendered supranational programs highly attractive.

There had long been a serious absence of investor alternatives at the short end of the market. Euronotes and subsequently ECP filled this gap, offering a flexible, liquid, high-yield instrument that increased options for investors and borrowers alike. For the investor, these alternatives provide another channel for short-term investment as well as a cash flow tool for the corporate treasurers. For the borrower, they provide a flexible debt management instrument as well as an effective means of liability management. Companies are as likely to use Euronotes or ECP to fund seasonal shortfalls in working capital as to reshape the maturity structure of assets and liabilities on their balance sheets.

THE PRINCIPAL PLAYERS

Investors in the Euronote/ECP market may be broken down into two broad segments with widely differing needs: (1) banks and other financial institutions looking for spreads linked to LIBOR or their own cost of funds (unattractive spreads will only be appropriate if the asset offers an attractive mismatch opportunity) and (2) nonbank investors, who have tended to become more sophisticated over time. The second group includes investors with natural short-term funds who originally were seeking security and aiming to keep risk to a minimum. Their investment opportunities consisted primarily of bank deposits, CDs, local government securities, and, occasionally, U.S. treasuries and USCP. Choices among these were affected by liquidity and yield requirements as well as by considerations of quality of risk and diversification. Over time, however, an increasing number of corporate treasurers became aware of the attractions and possibilities of Euronotes and ECP as sophisticated cash management tools. These investors eventually became the most important element of investor interest.

The emphasis between these two groups has shifted. It is estimated that even as late as 1985, 80 percent of Euronote investors were still banks, a figure that had fallen to 50 percent by 1988, with corporate and short-term fund managers accounting for the remainder.

As with investors, borrowers in the Euronote and ECP markets may be divided into two broad categories. The first group includes sovereign issuers, who were quick to see the opportunity to reduce the cost of medium-term borrowing. They welcomed the chance for a funding source beyond traditional syndicated bank loans and the opening of a new area of interest in sovereign debt at the short end of the market. The second category of borrowers includes corporate issuers, a group that itself may be subdivided between those companies viewed as high-quality credits and those of lesser credit standing. The former increasingly use uncommitted ECP programs, confident that the market has matured and deepened enough for such additional support to be superfluous. The latter still tend toward committed underwritten Euronote facilities in order to refinance existing bank lines yet generally achieve lower funding costs. As with investors, the relative weighting of borrowers in the market has shifted. Between 1978 and 1985 sovereign issuers accounted for 53 percent of new issue volume. This has gradually declined as corporate activity in the market has risen.

COST AND FLEXIBILITY

From the borrower's point of view, the advantage of Euronote financing over more traditional means such as floating-rate Eurobonds and syndicated loans is essentially twofold—it is cheaper and it is more flexible.

Periodic estimates suggest that the highest-rated issuers (mainly sovereign states and quasi-government bodies) can borrow in the short-term capital market at a rate of up to 15 basis points below LIBID. The highest-rated commercial companies and banks can borrow at a rate between 3 and 10 basis points below LIBID. Other issues must settle for a rate around 5 and 10 points above LIBOR, which is nevertheless cheaper than direct bank financing.

The savings come in several forms. First, Euronote programs separate the medium-term risk takers (the underwriters who back the

(the medium-term facility) and the short term providers of funds in-vestors who take up notes at each rollover point). This results in significant cost reductions against other medium-term debt as investors are content with a return commensurate with a short-term fixed-rate investment.

Second, a broad spectrum of buyers beyond the banking community is introduced to the issuer, which tends to produce lower cost funding. In addition, as name familiarity provides a powerful advantage, the very existence of one issue can lead to a circle of increased investor awareness and, consequently, improved funding.

Third, underwriting fees are relatively lower on Euronotes than on other instruments. With ECP there are no underwriting fees at all. Paperwork is kept to a minimum, with new issues normally arranged by telephone and documentation reduced to the note itself.

Flexibility comes in several forms. As Euronote programs are not locked into any one interest-fixing date, as are syndicated Euroloans or floating-rate notes in the Eurobond market (see Chapter 14), bor-rowers have more chances to take advantage of interest rate windows as they occur—clearly of great value in volatile market conditions. This speed of response is especially valuable in multioption facilities, which allow the borrower access to a range of currencies and credit forms so that issuers can react to arbitrage opportunities in virtually any currency base. They can play the yield curve and respond to par-ticular openings of investor interest. One large facility can serve to retire outstanding, more expensive credit and to rationalize debt man-agement requirements. For a competitive commitment fee, the bor-rower using Euronotes can access cheap funds as and when needed, expanding or contracting the level of debt at will, safe in the knowl-edge that if market conditions are not conducive to the notes' trading, funds are nevertheless assured. The broken or odd-dated maturities, which are a common feature of many ECP programs, also provide a great deal of flexibility, allowing issuers to tailor the period of their financings precisely to their specific funding requirements.

UNDERWRITERS AND ARRANGERS

As the debt crisis of the early 1980s contributed to the diversification of short-term investor interest away from the banks, so it also served to speed the pace of disintermediation in the world's capital markets. Debt securitization took much of their most profitable business away from the commercial banks, compressing spreads and forcing them into higher-risk lending, reducing the growth of term loan assets overall, and increasing the focus on contingent facilities and short-term lending. As part of this trend, banks became increasingly willing to underwrite Euronote facilities. These have a number of attractions for underwriters.

First, Euronote facilities tend to provide greater flexibility than other medium-term instruments. Although the underwriter is committed over the medium term, the nature of the commitment is intermittent, occurring at short-term intervals rather than continuously. The underwriter thus has a number of opportunities during the life of the arrangement to withdraw the commitment if any one of the conditions precedent to issuance (e.g., the creditworthiness of the issuer) is broken. Moreover, once the Euronote is issued, the underwriter no longer has the exposure on the books and can commit to other short-term assets until the maturity of the note. This makes possible a higher return on assets, since the same funds are effectively available to earn twice over. In addition, the underwriting fee on Euronotes is assured irrespective of the actual allocation of the notes.

Second, underwriters run lower risks with Euronotes than with other forms of underwriting in two respects. An underwriter is less likely to have to fund a Euronote than any other form of revolving credit. While the latter can be made operational simply on demand, Euronote funding depends upon the borrower's decision to issue and the borrower's inability to place the paper. The underwriter is thus two steps removed from the credit risk. In addition, Euronote programs can be designed to incorporate significant disincentives to discourage the issuer from drawing on the facility. And as long as the paper is held by third-party investors, the underwriters do not bear the risk of nonpayment or repayment of principal.

As would be expected, in keeping with financial risk/reward trade-offs, this combination of lower risk means that underwriters are willing to accept a lower underwriting fee on Euronotes than on a straight-forward credit facility, which is a clear attraction of the system to borrowers. With the growth of direct and dealer-placed ECP, banks naturally lose out on income from underwriting.

PRICING

As noted, Sweden's Euronote program in 1984–85 set a benchmark in the market for pricing. The coupon Euronotes carried in the early period was generally set in relation to LIBID, and subsequently it was set in relation to LIBOR. However, pressure grew, particularly in the ECP market, for a move away from using interbank rates as a reference point. It was argued that this was holding prices artificially high and that absolute pricing (as in paper sold purely at a discount) would be far preferable since it would allow easier comparison with USCP, for which such pricing is the norm.

Investors tend to prefer to purchase securities at or below rather than above par. Therefore, notes are typically issued with a low nominal interest rate but at a discount to their face value, thereby yielding a margin over their stated coupon. Indeed, most new ECP offerings (like USCP) carry a zero coupon and pay no interest at all, with the total return to the investor being the difference between the discounted cost at issue and the full repayment at par if held to maturity. For purely discounted paper, the normal calculation is

$$\text{Settlement proceeds} = \frac{\text{Face amount}}{1 + (Y \times N/360 \times 100)}$$

where Y = yield and N = days for settlement to maturity.

Clearly, the pricing of an ECP issue or Euronote program is critical and challenging, particularly in the absence of ratings. The lead manager needs to build a picture of the issuer in terms of creditworthiness and market perception. This involves the assessment of data specific to the company, including its current financial position and projections, its previous financing arrangements, and its credit rating, if any. Comparisons must also be made between the terms of floating-rate financing of similar companies and banks. Account must be taken of the existing state of the market and of any factors likely to affect it, such as prevailing central bank policies.

At the outset of the Euronote market, accurate pricing proved extremely difficult and there was little consistency in the prices achieved. This enabled lesser quality corporate names to acquire far cheaper financing than would otherwise have been possible, issuing Euronotes on occasions at premiums a mere 10 basis points over top-rated corporate names. This yield disparity reflected poorly developed trading activity rather than lack of investor interest in aggressively priced top-quality paper. The market also contributed to lower prices, generally due to the intense level of competition for mandates, as banks trying to gain market share proved willing to absorb many of the issuers' costs. The old days, when banks could rely on relationships to provide a steady source of business, were long gone. The reaction of many was to loss-lead on the products that were subject to the most intense competition in the hope of gaining other more lucrative business. As time passed, banks realized that they would have to compete effectively on each product separately, and the process of cross-subsidization declined.

In addition, the development of the ECP market led many bankers to raise fee levels on underwritten commitments, although this demand for extra compensation was to some extent offset by the need to remain competitive at very fine pricing, particularly for lesser-quality borrowers.

The threat of central bank regulation in the form of stricter capital requirements also increased upward pressure on prices. The rapid growth and evolution of the new financial instruments and the high level of competition in the market drew the attention of regulators to the mushrooming in bank off–balance sheet commitments (see Chapter 24), causing concerns about bank capital adequacy. The threat of regulation presented a serious impediment for the underwritten Euronote programs. It put pressure on banks to allocate commitments in a more discriminating way and to price them accordingly; this led the banks to increase their fees on those underwriting commitments they did make to compensate for the added capital allocation and reduced volume. Once again, better credits were encouraged to avoid using banks and to look to nonunderwritten facilities. Signs of these developments came as early as 1986, when the Bank of England assigned a risk ratio of 0.5 to Euronote underwriting commitments of banks under its supervision. The capital weighting in May 1988 by bank regulators under the auspices of the Bank for International Settlements confirmed this, reducing once again the attractions to bank arrangers of committed Euronote facilities and encouraging nonunderwritten forms of issuance.

Similarly, in the early stages of ECP, borrowers were able to command very competitive rates. Issuers could shop around for the finest terms as scores of institutions battled for market share. Increasingly, consolidation has occurred here as well, and by mid-1988 most observers agreed that agencies were concentrated in just four banks—Citicorp, Shearson Lehman Hutton, Swiss Bank Corporation Investment Banking, and Merrill Lynch. This concentration tended to shift the advantage from the issuers back to the placing houses.

RATINGS

The question of pricing disparities in the Euronote market was originally exacerbated by the absence of credit ratings for issuers. This resulted in a lack of any clear structure for the assessment of price/risk relationships. Ratings from one of the major agencies are increasingly common with ECP programs, as they have long been a feature of the USCP market—where lack of a rating is normally interpreted as inability to obtain a satisfactory one.

The two most important rating agencies in the United States are Moody's Investor Service, Inc. and Standard & Poor's Corporation. Moody's ratings of A1+, A1, A2, and A3 and Standard & Poor's ratings of P1, P2, and P3 represent the levels of investment grade paper in descending order. A rating is ordinarily sought from both agencies. There are two types of ratings: public and private. The public rating is used with public issues and cited in marketing releases and financial press, while the private rating tends to relate more to private placements and is more confidential in nature.

It is generally felt that the use of ratings adds order and structure to the market, assuring quality issuers of representative prices. It frees investors from detailed credit analysis, enabling them to make quick decisions, a particularly important factor in the short-term market. This in turn reduces the importance of an issuer's name being known to the investing public. The primacy of the "familiar name" syndrome declines and is replaced by more rigorous and standardized criteria.

Nevertheless, familiarity can be an advantage. In the ECP market, an unrated household name like Nestlé may still borrow at finer rates than a top-rated unknown borrower like Southern California Edison. And ratings can be a mixed blessing for some—while an A1/P1 rating can lead to significant cost savings, a nonprime rating can be worse than none at all. Another drawback is the length of the rating procedure, which can take up to 10 weeks. Nor is it inexpensive. Moody's has a charge of 0.02 percent of principal for a non-U.S. based borrower, subject to a range of $6,000 to $35,000 (reduced to $15,000 for pure Euro-issues). S&P's fees are between $15,000 and $30,000. There is evidence, however, that top-rated borrowers have subsequently realized interest savings on later Euro-issues that have more than made up for the cost of their original rating. The indications from the widening spreads between rated and unrated paper are that ratings are likely to play a greater role in ECP programs.

TERMS

The maturity of the "pure" Euronote tends to be of one, three, or six months, while ECP maturities are more varied, ranging from 2 to 365 days. Their average maturity tends to be longer than U.S. commercial paper—around 30 to 90 days as opposed to 22 to 30 days.

A major traditional drawback, as far as the development of the ECP market was concerned, was the limitation in choice of currencies available to the potential investor. This was at first restricted to the U.S. dollar and the European Currency Unit (ECU). Yet corporate treasurers often had funds only in Deutsche mark, for example, or in Swiss francs. Following authorization by a number of national authorities, ECP programs in a variety of currencies have been undertaken in recent years, including several with multicurrency options. For example, in 1986 the Bank of England permitted the issuing of sterling ECP. While nine-tenths of all paper issued is still denominated in U.S. dollars, there now is a range of currencies available to ECP borrowers, including the Dutch guilder, the Japanese yen, the Canadian dollar, and the Australian dollar.

Euronote program costs may be broken down into three main areas. The first cost is the periodic underwriting or facility fee, which is usually payable to the underwriting banks on the full, uncanceled nominal amount of the facility, whether it is used or not. The size of the underwriting fee varies according to the borrower and the structure of the deal. The second cost is the management fee, which is expressed as a percentage of the total nominal facility amount and is normally paid to the arranger on signing. It provides front-end compensation for structuring the deal. The third cost area includes the spread and the maximum interest yield, which are typically issued at a discount and therefore produce a margin over their nominal interest spread. The placing agents or tender panel members retain a proportion of this margin as compensation for the paper they distribute. If the paper is not placed and must be allocated to the underwriters, they receive the full margin. In some cases, underwriters have the option to make unsecured advances to the issuer at higher spreads if the market response is particularly poor and a significant amount of paper has been allocated to them. Thus they are partially protected against earning an insufficient return in the case of an adverse change in market conditions or a deterioration in the credit condition of the borrower during the life of the facility. Still, the maximum cost to the issuer is the contracted spread over the interest rate.

DISTRIBUTION

Due to the increasingly restrictive views of national regulatory authorities around the world, there has been a general tendency to separate the placement of Euronotes from the underlying backup or standby facility. The early development of the Euronote market as an underwritten market therefore obscured the role of placement. As the volume of business escalated, however, the importance of effective distribution became clearer. Institutions began to focus more attention on developing specific sales teams to cultivate investor interest and enhance placing power. As the issuer in the Euronote market is choosing the houses as tender panel members or sole placing agents that will best perform in the distribution of its paper on a renewed basis over a period of some 5 to 10 years, a primary consideration must be accountability and bank loyalty.

The principal aim of both issuers and underwriters is broad distribution of paper to genuine "end-user" investors. If low costs for issuers and reduced credit risks/increased returns for underwriters are to be achieved, substantial investor demand must be created so that at any rollover date demand will meet the supply of the issuer's paper. The distinction soon became apparent between those houses that could place short-term securities with genuine end-user investors and those that merely relied on passing unplaced paper on to the secondary market. Indeed, before long the former had squeezed the others from the market.

Leading banks in this market have proven themselves to be very innovative in the field of distribution and to be highly responsive to issuers' needs. A range of distribution methods has emerged, changing in popularity and appropriateness over time and circumstance.

The Sole Placing Agent

As discussed at the beginning of this chapter, under a RUF structure a single bank places the paper at a set price. This method, commonly used in the USCP market, was introduced to the Euronote market by Merrill Lynch in 1981. It provides a quick and clean method for the controlled and consistent placing of paper at consistent yields. Issuers can assign responsibility should the issue go badly. Distributors are assured of paper to place, and thus they can develop a diverse transactions base and a wide range of credits, maturities, and yields. The sole placing agent benefits from economies of scale, having a wide range of notes from different borrowers. However, the absence of competition in the placing process can lead to the economic benefits being retained by the agent rather than those benefits being passed on to the borrower. In addition, there was some early reaction from the commercial banks who resented being called in to underwrite when they had no share in the placement activity.

The Standard Tender Panel

The NIF structure was introduced in 1983, partly as a response to difficulties with the sole placing agent RUF structure. It took the form of an auction whereby members bid for each tranche of notes via telex. Notes are allocated to those offering the best prices. Underwriting banks are thus able to bid for paper at the time of issuance rather than merely collecting whatever cannot be sold at the agreed price. The system theoretically ensured wide distribution of paper, with the competitive element meaning that only the highest bids received allocation of paper. Issuers shared the advantage of the low yield and could expect the use of standby prices to be minimized as the underwriters themselves had the opportunity to place the paper.

In practice, however, the system had serious weaknesses. Bidding often bore no relation to the requirements of ultimate investors. Paper was loaded onto the market on a particular day at preset prices and maturities, irrespective of investor demand and market conditions. Inexperienced underwriters often bid too low and ended up dumping notes on the market. It was almost impossible for a tender panel member to develop a steady investor base for the paper of a given issuer, since he could never be sure of receiving an allocation and therefore always ran the risk of disappointing the very pool of investors he was trying to satisfy and enhance. The system was also unwieldy, often with between 30 to 60 tender panel members and with borrowers having to wait up to seven days for funds.

The Continuous Tender Panel

A development of the standard tender panel was introduced in 1984. One manager, similar in role to the bookrunner in traditional Eurobond issues (see Chapter 14), is responsible for the successful distribution of notes. Throughout the offering period, the manager quotes a "strike offering yield" (the yield offered to his own clients) and satisfies offers from panel members at or below that yield. This provides a realistic basis for tenders and a means of orderly and controlled distribution. Nevertheless, it is a cumbersome and relatively inflexible method in what has become an ever more freewheeling market. Tender panels have increasingly been viewed as suboptimal; although still in use, they are primarily for lesser credits—with sole placing agents viewed as the generally simpler and quicker approach, where possible.

Dual Placing Agents

This is a "competitive" form of the sole placing agent. Two dealers compete to place notes on a best efforts basis, which tends to lead to wider distribution and better prices.

Multiple Placing Agents

Under this structure, designated placing agents are given allocations of notes for resale to third parties or retention in their own accounts. As underwriters are certain of their allotment, they can make firm offers to investors. However, there is little incentive to establish a broad and genuine investor base, beyond the more obvious regulars, with the result that underwriters often end up competing with one another. This tends to drive up the yield level of offerings, which could adversely affect the costs of the borrower's subsequent issues.

The Tap Issue

This structure allows the borrower to release small amounts of notes onto the market in response to dealer demand. It does not need to be underwritten and consequently is usually associated with ECP. It is only appropriate for those borrowers without a pressing need for funds, but it can provide great flexibility in terms of odd issues and odd amounts of paper.

THE SECONDARY MARKET

While only a moderate secondary market exists in the U.S. commercial paper market, there was serious debate at the outset of ECP over the viability of a secondary market for Euronotes. Some believed that trading could be profitable if it developed in sufficient volume, with liquidity being the key to investor interest. It was suggested that in a sufficiently liquid market Euroinvestors would tend to ride the yield curve. For example, they could buy six-month paper and sell it after three months for a few points profit.

This view has been discredited, and the trading versus placement argument has been decisively resolved in favor of those houses that can place paper effectively with final investors. There is nevertheless a limited secondary market centered in New York and London, with the big banks communicating by telephone and acting as intermediaries between buyers and sellers. Mismatches between issuers and investors—in terms of timing, maturity, and yield—still require banks to carry some inventory. But a really active secondary market does not seem to add much value in this case.

ECP AND USCP

Although the ECP market still has nowhere near the depth of its U.S. counterpart, it has certain distinct advantages that have contributed to its rapid growth.

It offers longer maturities at competitive rates and covering a broader range. ECP caters to a global investor base, whereas demand in the U.S. market is still almost wholly domestic. Corporate treasurers, central and commercial banks and institutions, and investors from Australia, continental Europe, the Far East, the Middle East, and even the Eastern bloc are increasingly looking to the Euromarket to invest their surplus liquidity. This diverse investor base is allowing for the development of a far wider spread of maturities than in the U.S. domestic market.

Another key advantage is the speed at which the leading ECP houses are able to arrange and distribute deals. This is greatly helped by limited regulation. It is far easier for U.S. corporations with outstanding paper to issue in Europe than the reverse. It has also been suggested that a difference in the credit risk attached to issuers by investors in the two markets has been an instrumental factor. Whereas USCP investors have generally required a premium over domestic issues from foreign borrowers, no such systematic distinction regarding a borrower's nationality has been made in the ECP market.

There has been much discussion about the convergence of the USCP market and the ECP market. But there are obstacles. Quite apart from the relatively small size (see Figure 6–8) and average maturity, there are technical differences. Settlement in the United States, for example, can be done in the same day. It takes two days in the ECP market. In the United States most programs are backed by firm standby credit lines: this is not the case with ECP issues. While the yield differential has narrowed, there are still arbitrage possibilities, and it would seem that the goal of a future global commercial paper market—with large corporate names exchanging liquidity between

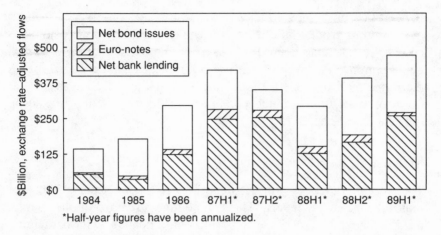

Figure 6–8. Funds Raised on International Markets. (*Source*: Bank for International Settlements)

themselves and banks acting in an intermediary role—is probably still some time away. Nevertheless, corporations are becoming ever more aware of the value of linkages between commercial paper markets. With a presence in both, borrowers can react instantaneously to windows in either. For example, using ECP as a backstop for USCP makes it possible to tap whichever source provides the cheapest funds on the day; this increased flexibility naturally results in reduced costs.

Euro Medium-Term Notes

By 1989 the Euro medium-term note (Euro MTN), initiated in 1986, had rapidly grown into an $8 billion market. This new market is modeled on the $90 billion medium-term note market in the United States, which was pioneered by General Motors Acceptance Corporation in 1972 to give it a flexible financing vehicle like USCP but with maturities of several years to match GMAC's auto financing needs. Filling the maturity gap between ECP and Eurobonds (see Chapter 14), Euro MTNs are seen by some as having the potential to displace the latter.

Typically, distribution of the notes is in the hands of four or five dealers who are not the underwriters of the issue and who more committed to maintaining a market in the notes that are the underwriters in the often illiquid Eurobond markets. The top dealers, Merrill Lynch (which leads the U.S. MTN market) and CSFB (which leads the Eurobond market), dominate through their ability to place the paper.

Euro MTNs have shown themselves to be highly flexible with maturities running from one to ten years, yields realized through floating-rate, fixed-rate, and deep discount zero coupon issues and multicurrency options. The rapidity with which tranches can be issued makes the Euro MTN a good funding vehicle for taking advantages of windows of opportunity in the changing yield curve and in the swap markets (see Chapter 15).

SUMMARY

The story of Euronote programs and Eurocommercial paper is one of rapid change at all levels. The competitive structure of the market has itself already undergone substantial modification, with bargaining power tending to shift away from borrowers. In the early days, top and lesser-quality names alike benefited from the intense competition among banks, which resulted from deregulation and disintermediation. They profited as well from a lack of investor sophistication. Today, an increasing number of corporate treasurers have a full understanding of the workings of the market and what is available to them. Distributive power has been concentrated in the hands of a few houses (see Table 6-2) that are more interested in volume and profitability than the number of dealerships they hold. Gone are the days of loss-leading for a place in the market. Attention is focused on courting the investor base in search of ever greater diversification of funding.

Other changes have occurred as well. Distribution methods have been modified to suit new conditions and demands. The use of ratings has increased with the need for investors to react quickly in fast-moving markets. The very nature of the instrument has evolved, with the nonunderwritten ECP now predominating over Euronote programs. These changes will continue. Given the pace of innovation, it is difficult to make firm predictions. New economic conditions will give rise to new requirements and new responses. The Euronote grew as a substitute for syndicated loans, floating-rate notes in the Eurobond market, and Eurocertificates of deposit issued by banks. Its success came in part from the events shaping the financial world at the time. As increasing globalization brought increasing competition, so the pace of product innovation quickened.

In its turn, ECP took the stage. As the Euronote market deepened, it became obvious that prime borrowers could dispense with underwrit-

Table 6–2. Top 30 Dealers in ECP, by Nominal Amount and Number of Deals

Rank	Bank	Amount [a]	1988 No. of deals	Share %
1	Citicorp Investment Bank	69,396.34	218	26.08
2	Swiss Bank Corporation	57,948.12	198	23.68
3	J. P. Morgan Securities	41,530.73	168	20.10
4	Merrill Lynch Capital Markets	58,104.69	160	19.14
5	Credit Suisse First Boston	41,302.29	144	17.22
6	Shearson Lehman Brothers International	55,862.74	133	15.91
7	S.G. Warburg	32,649.61	123	14.71
8	Chase Investment Bank	23,823.21	105	12.56
9 =	Morgan Stanley International	30,723.56	81	9.69
9 =	National Westminster Bank Group	19,023.57	81	9.69
11	Barclays Bank Group	18,007.99	80	9.57
12	Bankers Trust International	19,968.87	72	8.61
13	First Chicago	13,944.39	65	7.78
14	Union Bank of Switzerland	13,730.27	60	7.18
15	Bank of America International	11,685.89	55	6.58
16	Midland Montagu	11,339.39	50	5.98
17	Morgan Grenfell	8,352.17	41	4.90
18	SEB/Enskilda Securities	5,055.00	38	4.55
19 =	Manufacturers Hanover	5,860.00	37	4.43
19 =	Westpac Banking Corp.	5,743.99	37	4.43
21	Daiwa Securities	15,834.33	34	4.07
22	Goldman Sachs	13,069.60	32	3.83
23	Nomura Securities Co	6,105.32	31	3.71
24	Australia & New Zealand Banking Group	4,216.59	30	3.59
25	First Interstate Bank Group	6,225.00	29	3.47
26	Kleinwort Benson	4,596.17	26	3.11
27	Chemical Bank International Group	4,290.59	23	2.75
28	Lloyds Merchant Bank	5,874.63	22	2.63
29	Canadian Imperial Bank Group	5,786.50	21	2.51
30	Kansallis Banking Group	2,900.00	20	2.39

a. In millions of dollars.

SOURCE: "Annual Financing Report," *Euromoney*, March 1989, p. 30; reprinted by permission.

ten facilities altogether, thus reducing costs. ECP provided greater flexibility for borrowers and investors alike. It offered a faster and more efficient method of placement. These advantages led to a widening of the investor base and consequently further reduced costs and increased flexibility.

Euronote programs and subsequently ECP have had enormous success. They are perhaps best viewed as a complement to rather than a replacement for more traditional forms of bank finance, an additional financial string to the borrower's bow, offered as part of an increasingly efficient international money market.

SELECTED REFERENCES

Crabbe, Matthew, Grant, Charles, and French, Martin.   "The Euronote Explosion." *Euromoney*, November 1985.

"Eurocommercial Paper." *Bank of England Quarterly Bulletin*, May 1988.

Fingleton, Eammonn.   "Why Capital Ratios Are a Cause for Concern." *Euromoney*, June 1985.

Fisher, F. G.   *Eurobonds*. London: Euromoney Publications Plc, 1988.

Hobson, Dominic.   "Eurocommercial Paper—Four Banks Dominate the Market." *Financial Times*, May 25, 1988.

Pavey, Nigel.   "The Latest Twist to Note Facilities." *Euromoney*, April 1985.

Shireff, Davis.   "The Euronote Explosion." *Euromoney*, December 1985.

Wilson, Neil.   "Product for all Players?" *The Banker*, September 1989.

7

Asset-Backed Financing and Loan Securitization

The previous two chapters have discussed international commercial lending activities in terms of general obligations of borrowers, with full recourse to their balance sheets. There are, in addition, several specialized forms of lending that have limited recourse, or none at all. These can provide attractive lending opportunities but can expose banks to significant risks as well. Some such transactions, in which the asset is a major basis for the financing, also lend themselves to securitization and repackaging.

This chapter will discuss ship financing, commodities financing, and international leasing, as well as the securitization of mortgage and consumer lending. Trade financing is discussed in Chapter 8, and project financing is detailed in Chapter 9.

SHIP FINANCING

One of the most risky dimensions of international lending involves ship financing. This is because the economics of the financing leave little room for error. Shipping is a cyclical business. Shipowners often put up very little equity, and the value of used ships attached in cases of default may be little more than scrap value.

Ships are generally financed with a first mortgage, covering perhaps 70 or 80 percent of the cost. The remainder may be financed by the shipyard or the export finance agency of the exporting country, with the shipowner putting up a trivial amount of equity. Since the secondary ship market is so uncertain and becomes critical at precisely the time when conditions in the industry are likely to be at their worst, other sources of comfort must be sought. Shipowners usually "charter," or lease, the ships they own to operating companies (e.g., major oil companies, grain transporters, container lines, cruise lines, or small freight carriers) under one of two basic types of charters. The first of these is a "bare boat charter" in which the operator is responsible for all operating charges and risks of the vessel, including its being unable to sail on schedule because of mechanical problems. The operator bears all of the costs of labor, fuel, insurance, maintenance, and repairs. The other type of charter is a "time charter" in which the operator rents the ship from the owner for a specified time, but the owner bears the aforementioned costs and risks. Charters may range from a comparatively short-term leasing arrangement to one of 10 years or more. If a vessel is to be operated under a succession of short-term charters but seeks longer-term financing, then the banks carry the risk that successive "charter hire payments" will be sufficient to cover the required amounts of debt service on their loans. In such cases, the credit standing of the shipowner is of paramount importance. On the other hand, when a shipowner has arranged an adequate long-term bare boat charter with a major oil company, the shipowner's own creditworthiness is of lesser importance.

Ship financing can be a risky business, and history is littered with cases of bank-owned ships sold at great losses or scrapped. To be in this business, a bank must develop not only a firm understanding of the shipping business and the reputation of shipowners (and their ability to comply with the terms of charters as well as their ability to operate ships profitably), but a "sixth sense" as well.

To the extent that financial projections are reliable, they will cover the operator's cash flows, cost structures, competition, demand conditions, and related variables. Banks must be familiar with admiralty law and the laws of Panama, Greece, and Liberia, which are the countries of registry for much of the world's tonnage. In case of difficulties leading to a ship having to be "arrested," or seized by its creditors, the bank must be fast on its feet in order to prevent the values underlying its claim from slipping away.

With the high risks can come high returns, and the spreads on shipping loans are commensurately high. This has from time to time attracted inexperienced banks into shipping loans, often to their great distress. The risks also prevent shipping loans from being easily syndicated, sold, or participated out. Also, ships do not lend themselves to financing via securities issues because of risk-related issues and the need for flexibility in the case of restructuring.

COMMODITIES FINANCING

Another aspect of international asset-based financing involves commodities—grains, timber, oil, pulp, natural fibers, etc.—traders of which are heavily financed with short-term bank debt. The traders' profit margins are small, and turnover is rapid, with the liquidation of assets expected to provide fully for debt service. There is generally little sense in looking to the commodity trading company for recourse because companies that deal in commodities frequently take speculative positions that could wipe them out, so financing must be structured fully along asset-based lines. Commodity traders—as opposed to dealers—generally match buy and sell orders. The commodities are presold; therefore, the final customer's ability to pay becomes determining. Commodities companies may specialize in one commodity, or they may cover a variety in a highly specialized business.

Banks in the business of financing commodities must assure themselves of the credit quality of the ultimate buyers, the diversification of the commodity firm's exposure to buyers, and the volume of business. Critical are the firm's own financial controls, its own credit standing, and its ability to hedge its exposure. Financing is often in the form of letters of credit (see Chapter 8) including back-to-back letters of credit and transferable letters of credit that are the ultimate responsibility of the borrower. Nevertheless, the commodities themselves are the underlying security, so that evidence of quantity, quality and ownership (e.g., warehouse receipts, bills of lading, etc.) are critical for banks engaged in this business.

Like much of asset-based financing, this is a specialized activity that requires banks to have equally specialized knowledge. It can be quite lucrative, especially when the bank gets paid handsome spreads for effectively taking risks associated with top-quality customers such as the multinational oil or grain companies.

The commodity expertise acquired by banks in asset-based commodity financing is increasingly being applied by certain banks to a profitable new risk-sharing instrument—the commodity swap. As the name implies, commodity swaps are based on interest rate and currency swaps discussed in Chapter 15. A *commodity swap* is an agreement to exchange at a specific date (or dates) in the future an amount of a specific commodity for a cash payment. The payment between swap counterparties is on a net cash basis, using the market price of the commodity prevailing at the future date in place of physical commodity delivery. The commodity swap performs some of the hedging functions of the futures market, but it is more flexible.

A future market transaction takes place on an organized exchange that only trades in specific commodities with maturity of the contracts at specific dates (usually no more than a year in the future with contracts at three-month intervals). Contracting parties in futures place offsetting bets with the exchange standing between, effectively guaranteeing that the betters will abide by their contracts. Since the value of the contract bet is marked to zero each day (using the contract prices of new betters), contract parties receive or must pay the daily change in the value of the futures price.

In contrast, commodity swaps can be tailor-made for long-dated and odd-dated maturities. Moreover, they can be written for any good, rather than just for the limited set of commodities and maturities traded on fixed commodity exchanges. For example, a small travel tour operator may wish to offset the risk of airline fares increasing—an event occasioned by the rise in airline fuel costs. But there are no futures markets in airline fuel. A large bank that can manage its portfolio to reduce different risks is a good candidate for providing service of assuming commodity price risk. If that bank has obtained the requisite commodity expertise through asset lending and financial engineering skills acquired by participation in the swaps market, it requires few additional skills to set up commodity swaps. Moreover, the credit risk associated with contracting with the small tour operator can be assumed as part of normal corporate lending.

INTERNATIONAL LEASE FINANCING

Another important form of asset-based financing involves leasing of mobile capital goods. These can include aircraft, barges, containers, drilling rigs, power generation equipment, computers, production machinery, medical equipment, materials-handling equipment, and the like. Banks in the United States are restricted in their lease-financing activities to those in which leasing is the "functional equivalent of the extension of credit" (Federal Reserve Regulation Y), although this restriction does not hold in most of the rest of the world.

In leasing, the lessor owns the equipment and leases it to an operator, recovering the lease payments and the residual value, which cover the acquisition cost plus profit. Lessors may or may not have the option to acquire the equipment during or at the end of its useful life. Such "financial leasing" is distinguished from "operating leasing," where the lessor is responsible for maintaining and insuring the equipment and covering any applicable taxes. Financial leases cannot be canceled, whereas operating leases are used by customers to cover their short-term equipment needs and can be canceled at any time.

American banks are specifically forbidden to engage in speculative operating leasing in anticipation of customer needs, which means that operating leases are generally relegated to specialized leasing firms that finance themselves with bank loans and in the capital markets, with full recourse to the lessor on the basis of credit standing.

There are two types of financial leases. Straight leasing involves 100 percent bank financing on equipment procured according to the customer's specifications, with the asset acquired by the bank and delivered to the customer against assignment of the leasing documentation. Lessor and lessee may get together on the basis of a long-standing banking relationship, or they may be brought together by a broker. Alternatively, the lease may be structured through a leasing company, which pledges the equipment as well as lease revenues, with full recourse.

Leveraged leasing is generally done through a separate leasing affiliate of a bank holding company and an ownership trust, which owns the equipment. The bank contributes a small part of the required funds in the form of equity (generally at least 20 percent), and the leasing affiliate borrows the remainder on a long-term basis from banks or institutional lenders such as insurance companies. The institutional lenders have recourse to the equipment and to hike lease payments only; they do not have recourse to the leasing affiliate of the bank.

Leasing tends to be heavily tax-driven. Lessees are able to deduct lease payments as part of the cost of doing business, while the lessor deducts both interest costs and depreciation on the asset. Internationally, "double dip" tax-driven leases may be possible if interest and depreciation expenses can be deducted in both of two tax jurisdictions because of the structure of the lessor arrangements for the lease. For example, lessors organized in the United Kingdom have been able to set up tax-paying branches in the United States that have been able to deduct against U.S. taxes; at the same time similar deductions have been allowed against the branch's parent company back home.

International leasing is a specialized business and is the domain of a number of important nonbank players. These include the major aircraft leasing firms, such as Guinness Peat Aviation (GPA) of Ireland and International Lease Finance Company (ILFC) of the United States, which provide operating and financial leases to airlines that cannot afford to purchase their aircraft outright or that have temporary capacity needs or special tax considerations. By careful diversification across customers, these lessors attempt to limit their exposure to risk. However, they are still heavily exposed to the risk embedded in the industry of the lessees (e.g., airlines), and the opportunities for hedging their assets or equipment orders are relatively narrow.

The international boom in the aircraft industry in the mid-to-late 1980s provided an ideal environment for the expansion in aircraft financing. With Boeing, the world's leading manufacturer of aircraft, estimating that the world market for new commercial aircraft over the 1990s will be 8,000 planes valued at over $500 billion, the boom is likely to continue. Increasingly, leasing has displaced straight bank lending and export credit financing (see Chapter 8) of aircraft purchases. A lease (which effectively uses the aircraft asset as security) can have maturities of 20 to 30 years, matching the aircraft's expected life span and far exceeding the usual tenor of a sovereign guaranteed export credit. The asset may be of greater security value than the credit of the purchasing country. In recent years, aircraft financing for the flag carriers of Zambia, Ethiopia, Poland, Brazil, and other third-world countries have been arranged despite the impaired status of their sovereign bank loans. Moreover, the tax advantages of leasing can lower the all-in cost of financing to amounts competetive with those of export credit loans at concessionary rates of interest. At present, Japanese banks account for about half of the worldwide aircraft lease financing (75 percent excluding the United States), taking advantage of tax advantages of Japanese-based leases estimated to equal up to 17 percent of the purchase price. In other industries nonfinancial companies, such as General Electric Capital and General Motors Acceptance Corporation (GMAC), engage in a broader array of leasing activities. In turn, they finance themselves (against their own creditworthiness) with bank debt, commercial paper, medium-term notes and an array of other types of debt.

LOAN SECURITIZATION

"Securitization" is a term frequently used to describe a major change that has taken place in the international banking and capital markets. Strictly speaking, the term refers to the process of packaging illiquid financial assets held on the books of banks, savings and loan associations, mortgage lenders, insurance companies, and other financial institutions in such a way as to be able to sell participations in the package to capital market investors. A number of residential mortgages, for example, can be sold to a single-purpose trust, with the trust paying for these mortgages out of the proceeds from the sale of trust certificates representing proportionate ownership of the trust assets.

In a broader context, however, securitization has come to represent a general trend of movement of nonmarketable assets off of the balance sheets of financial institutions into the vast pool of marketable assets in the securities market. The new securities sold by one group of investors, however, are bought by other institutions where they are held as marketable instruments available for trading at any time.

Securitization occurs when an asset holder finds it desirable to liquidate or restructure an investment portfolio. This may be for reasons of profitability, because of mismatches between assets and the funding for them, or because of the need to adjust the overall size and capacity of the asset holder's balance sheet. Securitization also occurs when the traditional customers of these institutions discover alternate ways to finance at lower costs from other sources. When this happens, the flow of business into the traditional institutions is reduced.

The process of securitization of loans has been greatly accelerated by the considerable structural changes that have occurred in the international capital markets over the past two decades.

An early example of securitization was the growth in outstanding issues of commercial paper in the United States in the late 1960s. During this period, banking regulations limited the interest rates that banks could pay on deposits. The effect was to drive large corporate depositors to the commercial paper market where "market" rates could be obtained. These regulations and other tight-money policies at the time reduced the growth rate of bank loans, thus driving those companies needing working capital financing into the commercial paper market. Short-term loans, then, were flowing from the banks into the market where they were financed by nonbank sources, namely other financial institutions and corporations.

Figure 7–1 illustrates the shift of traditional bank-financing business from banks' balance sheets to the securities market during the 1980s — hence the sharp decline in the banks' share of all net new corporate borrowing since 1979.

The decline in the share of new credit financing passing through banks has been particularly dramatic. Various reasons have been put forward for this shift.

First, a general decline in long-term interest rates after 1981 (from the high rates that had been pervasive in the late 1970s) and a restoration of a positively sloped yield curve increased the attractiveness of fixed-rate financial instruments.

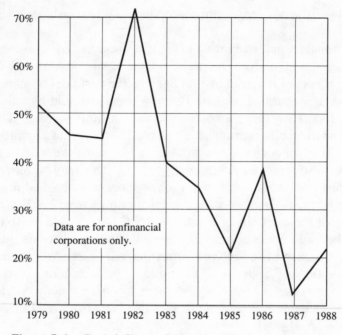

Figure 7–1. Banks' Share of Net New Corporate Borrowing.
(*Data*: Federal Reserve Board)

Second, U.S. banks had overextended themselves on developing country loans, leaving the banks with poor quality balance sheets. This eroded the credit standing of bank certificates of deposit and raised their funding costs as investors began looking for alternatives—in short, it meant that many high-grade companies could sell their own securities at rates lower than the rates at which banks could raise funds, thus making bank financing a high-cost source of funds.

Third, the growing LDC debt burden forced many banks to restrict growth in assets (in order to protect their deteriorating capital ratios) and to take more seriously the issue of liquidity. On the asset side, this meant selling off loans already on their books; on the liability side, it meant funding themselves in nontraditional ways with term debt. Thus, banks themselves became important borrowers in international capital markets, motivated by a need to issue new capital to strengthen their capital bases, to achieve better matches between asset and liability maturities, and to take advantage of capital market conditions to lower their overall cost of funds.

Fourth, constraints on the banks led to a very large increase in "off-balance sheet" activity, or contingent liabilities to offer financing in the future under specified circumstances, which for regulatory and accounting purposes were not recorded on the face of banks' balance sheets. The range of this type of business, which generated fees without using up balance sheet capacity, was only limited by the imaginations of the banks. They included guarantees, letters of credit, activities as lessors, participations in interest rate and currency swap transactions, and various forms of standby and backup note issuance facilities. These activities permitted the banks to recapture some of the business lost to securitization, to increase their returns on assets, and to improve capital ratios. At the same time, off-balance sheet activity and securitization increases the difficulty of determining a banker's aggregate risk exposure, a matter that has led to new rules for preserving bank capital adequacy (see Chapter 26).

Fifth, the growth in the volume, depth, and turnover of capital markets—caused by the increased globalization, deregulation, and institutionalization discussed in other chapters—created an enormous pool of financial assets seeking investment opportunities. These were found in Eurocommercial paper, mortgaged-backed securities, "junk bonds" (loans to lower-grade credits had previously been the preserve of banks), and more recently in bonds backed by a wide variety of different types of assets. The appeal of lower rates, more suitable maturity structures, and other special features available in the capital market drew even more business away from traditional lenders in a classic example of disintermediation.

As a growing share of credit flows outside traditional banking channels and through the capital markets, there are significant "adverse selection" problems. If higher-quality corporations are the predominant borrowers leaving the banking system for access directly to financial markets, one would expect that the overall level of risk associated with remaining bank assets will increase. This is not a problem if the banks are able to factor the higher risk into interest charges, but it does become a problem if this process is impeded by competition.

On the other hand, the capital markets have less information on which to base ongoing credit decisions and much less access to supervision. Thus, the relationship between ultimate borrowers and lenders is more distant, which may have implications for market access as well as possible future financial restructurings. Equally, there are questions about the presumption that securitized assets are more liquid than conventional bank loans. If a large number of creditors of a single borrower wish to liquidate their holdings simultaneously, liquidity may disappear; the risk is that liquidity will disappear just when it is most important.

Loan Securitization in the Mortgage Market

Several forms of securitization represent relatively recent innovations in asset transformation. One of the most dramatic examples of recent securitization activity began in the mortgage market. Its subsequent success prompted many firms to apply the same procedure to other types of loans and receivables. It is in essence a form of trust financing that turns illiquid mortgage assets or secured loans into tradeable financial instruments backed by the security that supported the original loans. Thus far, residential and commercial mortgage loans, automobile loans, credit card receivables, loans to finance recreational vehicles and boats, computer and manufacturing leases, and financial receivables have all served as collateral to back new securities issues.

There have been three basic types of loan-backed securities, all of which developed from the secondary mortgage market, pass-throughs, mortgage-backed bonds, and pay-throughs.

Pass-throughs

In a pass-through, a portfolio of mortgages that have similar maturity, interest rate, and credit quality are placed in trust and investors purchase certificates of ownership in the trust. The mortgages associated with the portfolio are assigned by the loan originator to the trust. The trust collects interest and principal and passes it on to investors. For these services, the originator extracts a servicing fee. This function may be passed on to another servicing institution.

Pass-throughs are owned by the final investor and, since they are not debt obligations of the originator, they do not appear on the originating bank's balance sheet. The best-known pass-throughs are backed by the Government National Mortgage Association (GNMA), or Ginnie Mae, and are collateralized by mortgages guaranteed by the Federal Housing Administration (FHA) or the Veterans Administration (VA). GNMA guarantees the payment of both interest and principal. Since Ginnie Maes are backed by government-guaranteed mortgages and also have the counterguarantee of a federal agency there is little or no default risk associated with these securities. For this reason, there is an active and well-developed domestic and international secondary market that assures liquidity.

Pass-throughs are more significant in the government-backed sector than in the purely private sector. Since BankAmerica's first private sector pass-through in 1977, the market for such securities has grown substantially; however, it still remains relatively small. Non-guaranteed private sector pass-throughs are backed by conventional mortgages, and the pool of mortgages is then usually insured privately before being securitized. Mortgage pass-throughs have been most popular with savings and loan associations. At the end of 1988, pass-throughs accounted for about 15% of the savings institutions' assets, 8% of insurance company assets, 7% of commercial bank assets, and 5% of pension fund assets.

Mortgage-backed Bonds

Mortgage-backed bonds (MBBs) are securities collateralized by a port-folio of mortgages that is a debt obligation of the issuer. Therefore, MBBs are reported as liabilities on the issuer's balance sheet, while the mortgages themselves act as collateralization and represent the issuer's assets. MBBs generally have a maturity of between 5 to 12 years, with interest paid semiannually. Unlike pass-throughs, the cash flows associated with the mortgage do not go directly to the investors, and the credit risk of the mortgages remains with the financial institution concerned.

Mortgage-backed bonds are typically overcollateralized, and if the collateral cover falls below a certain level stated in the bond indentures, the collateral must be topped up by the issuer. Overcollateralization allows the investor additional protection against default on individual mortgages in the portfolio, and it provides protection to bondholders from a fall in the market value of the collateral between valuation dates (usually every quarter). While bondholders could alternatively be covered for the risk of collateral erosion and default risk by extra yield, issuers tend to prefer overcollateralization, since they regularly receive principal and interest flows that can then be reinvested.

Unlike pass-throughs, MBBs are common in both the private and the government-backed sector in the United States. They are issued by savings and loan institutions, and by mutual savings banks. MBBs are less attractive than pass-throughs because they remain on a financial institution's books and thus do not avoid all the intermediation costs, including capital requirements, reserve requirements, and insurance charges.

Pay-throughs

The pay-through mortgage-backed security can be viewed as a hybrid of the pass-through and the MBB. The securities are collateralized by mortgage loans and remain on the originator's balance sheet as debt.

The principal and interest payments from the mortgages are in turn dedicated to the servicing of the bonds.

The most common pay-through is the collateralized mortgage obligation (CMO). The first CMO was issued by the Federal Home Loan Mortgage Corporation ("Freddie Mac") in 1983, and there have been a large number of variations since. In the initial Freddie Mac CMO, there were three maturity classes. Class 1 bondholders received that first installment of principal payments and any prepayments until Class 1 bonds were paid off. Class 2 and Class 3 bonds were handled similarly. Class 1 bonds were repaid within 5 years, Class 2 within 12 years, and Class 3 within 20 years.

This particular structure gives bondholders protection against being called by the issuer. Because of this cover as well as the range of maturities available, pay-throughs have attracted a segment of the investor base that was otherwise uninterested in mortgage-backed securities.

Although more common than MBBs, pay-throughs are still insubstantial when compared with pass-throughs. Between 1983 and 1988, pass-throughs guaranteed by a federal agency served as collateral for 45% of mortgage-backed issues, conventional mortgages accounted for 28%, and the rest were collateralized by a mixture of the two.

As Figure 7–2 shows, mortgage-backed securities originating in the United States can be packaged with a currency swap (see Chapter 15) and ultimately sold to Swiss-based investors.

Other Forms of Loan Securitization

Automobile installment loan-backed securities have also grown dramatically. The risk on car loan portfolios is considered to be quite tolerable. The possibility of reutilization of automobile loan receivables dramatically increases the flexibility that banks can have over their balance sheet assets. They can decide to keep the loan or pass it through, depending upon economic expectations and the state of their balance sheets in general. For automobile lenders, securitization gives them another degree of strategic freedom in managing their assets. Still, securitized automobile receivables are more attractive for some companies than others. For a company like GMAC, that has a very strong credit rating, the rate savings available to them from securitization are nominal.

In the United States there has also been the development of a secondary market in bank loans guaranteed by the Small Business Admin-

New Issue

August 1985

GLENDALE FEDERAL
SAVINGS AND LOAN ASSOCIATION

(Organized under the laws of the United States)

Swiss Francs 100 000 000

Mortgage collateralized 5½% Bonds 1985-1995

SODITIC S.A.

GOLDMAN SACHS FINANZ AG

MANUFACTURERS HANOVER (SUISSE) S.A.

BANK HEUSSER & CIE AG

CITICORP BANK (SWITZERLAND)

First Chicago S.A.

Nordfinanz-Bank Zürich

The Royal Bank of Canada (Suisse)

Amro Bank und Finanz	**Bank In Langnau**
Banque Bruxelles Lambert (Suisse) S.A.	**Banque de Dépôts et de Gestion**
Banque de Participations et de Placements S.A.	**Banque Pasche S.A.**
Banque Scandinave en Suisse	**Barclays Bank (Suisse) S.A.**
Chemical Bank (Suisse)	**Compagnie de Banque et d'Investissements, CBI**
Great Pacific Capital S.A.	**Kredletbank (Suisse) S.A.**
J.Henry Schroder Bank AG	**Société Générale Alsacienne de Banque**
	—Groupe Société Générale—

Figure 7–2. Sample Tombstone for a Mortgage-backed Securities Offering.

161

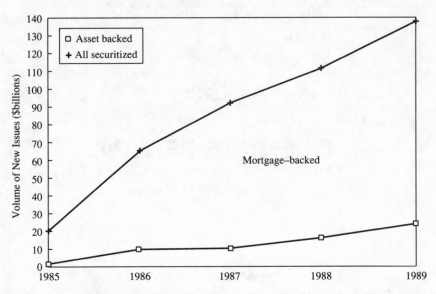

Figure 7–3.   Growth of Securitized Bank Loans (Securitized issues include real estate mortgage-backed securities and all other asset-backed securities, in billions of dollars of new issues.) (*Source*: Goldman, Sachs & Co., Investment Dealers Digest data bank.)

istration (SBA). Congress passed legislation that permitted trading in such loans in 1984.

The list of other assets that can be securitized is impressive. In March 1985, for example, Sperry Corporation (now Unisys) issued bonds backed by receivables in the form of computer leases.

There are problems associated with securitization of many receivables; however, most of them are technical in nature and can be overcome if the benefits outweigh the costs by a sufficient margin. Figure 7–3 indicates the growth of securitized bank loans in recent years.

Advantages to Issuers

Entities that have engaged in securitization can be broken into two distinct categories—nonfinancial institutions and financial institutions.

Nonfinancial Institutions

There are three generic benefits for corporations that engage in asset securitization. The first is liquidity, which is an important characteristic of marketable financial assets particularly in times of uncertainty. Financial assets that are illiquid have limited attractiveness and must be compensated for with a commensurately increased yield. Securitization allows investors to turn future uncertain payment streams instantaneously into cash. In general, the higher the degree of interest rate volatility of these assets, the more attracted they are to engaging in the securitization process.

Second, securitization also allows corporations and other issuers to access various new segments of the securities markets that can be more efficient in terms of transactions costs. Securities markets tend to be cheaper for issuers than direct loans, particularly when there is a wide spread between the credit ratings of a company and that of its clients. Due to investor preference for securities during the 1980s, issuers have been able to substantially reduce their cost of financing.

Third, securitization of a company's receivables allows it to diversify its investor base and to exploit new sources of capital, while leaving older sources unimpaired. Securitization is also attractive because the servicing of the obligation can continue without the client ever knowing that the debt has been sold. Securitization shrinks balance sheets and allows better use of capital.

The securitization process has significant effects on corporations. High technology and smaller companies can use their relationships with customers to raise capital at competitive rates. A firm's ability to sell receivables will have implications for how the company sells to clients and for the overall terms of credit it is able to extend to customers. The corporation can lengthen the terms for the clients, safe in the knowledge that it will be able to sell the receivables at a later stage and remove them from its balance sheet at short notice. This may give such firms advantages against their competitors. It has allowed small, independent companies with creditworthy customers the opportunity to access customer financing independent of its own balance sheet.

Securitization is most attractive for corporations with sizeable differentials between their own credit standing and that of their clients. The larger the differentials, the larger the scope for a reduction in the cost of financing. In the case of automobile companies, their balance sheets are reduced, and they can achieve a substantial increase in return on assets because servicing fees are still coming in.

Financial Institutions

Securitization is also attractive to financial institutions due to the possibility of avoiding intermediation taxes. The term "intermediation tax" is used to describe reserve and capital requirements as well as deposit insurance commissions.

Intermediation taxes have a primary function to limit the risk in the financial system. However, the structure of these taxes also tends to drive bank activities off the balance sheet. It also causes regulatory problems, reduces transparency, and potentially increases the risks within the financial system.

If a financial institution can sell a mortgage pass-through, it eliminates the underlying mortgage from its balance sheet and will no longer have to hold capital against that asset, thus freeing it up for other uses. Similarly, as the proceeds from the sale are not deposits, the issuer will not have to hold reserves or pay for deposit insurance against the proceeds.

The nature of intermediation taxes has an influence on the incidence of securitization. Since these taxes do not differentiate between low- and high-risk assets, the cost of funding low-risk loans (considering the intermediation taxes) may be significantly higher than costs faced by nonregulated competitors or by the borrowers themselves. This imperfection may drive financial institutions to substitute high-risk for low-risk assets. It has been suggested that securitization may no longer continue at its recent pace if these intermediation taxes are allocated more equitably over different classes of risk assets (see Chapter 26). The advantages to banks from securitization are greater as intermediation taxes increase.

Risk and Return Considerations

The return on an asset-backed security obviously depends upon its price and its coupon, both of which are related to the risk of the underlying assets. If a security's yield is greater than that of the underlying loan, there are no benefits from securitization. Several options are available to change the risk/return relationship associated with securitized assets. In the case of loan-backed bonds, for example, overcollateralization will reduce risk as well as return. There is also the possibility of insuring the securities themselves, in which case it is the insurer who bears the default risk—the insurer will have to evaluate the portfolio and will charge a premium commensurate with the underlying risk.

This indicates the importance of the ability to evaluate the pool of loans that underlies asset-backed securities. The securitization process is clearly dependent upon rating agencies' and investors' abilities to understand the loans. Highly complex loan portfolios or loans that have complex credit characteristics are unlikely to be well-suited to securitization. The success of securitization will also depend on the payment patterns and maturities. Loans with poorly defined payment patterns and with maturities of less than two years are unlikely to be candidates for securitization. In the latter case, the costs of securitization would not be recouped over such a short time period, and investors would not be as attracted by such short maturities.

The costs of securitization consist of administrative costs— primarily investment banking fees—as well as the costs associated with providing information to investors and rating agencies. The benefits from securitization include protection from interest rate risk, increased liquidity for original lenders and for investors, a more efficient transfer of resources from surplus to deficit financial sectors, and new and less expansive sources of capital for the original lenders.

It also serves to liquefy a bank's balance sheet and provide additional funding sources. Securitization is particularly common in the case of smaller loans, which would be difficult to sell individually. With the same nominal exposure, a bank in fact takes the credit risk of a large number of different borrowers, thus achieving greater diversification.

As the players become more experienced in the securitization process, the costs of securitizing tend to fall significantly. It is likely that the process will spread to other loan portfolios with the required securitization characteristics. If the process continues, and loans other than mortgages are securitized, the financial services industry will become increasingly fragmented. Banks will increasingly become loan brokers, warehousing loans before sale to final investors.

There are also significant implications for the competitive roles of banks vis-à-vis clients who finance their own customers' purchases. Competition that banks face for commercial and consumer loans include the captive finance affiliates of the large retail and manufacturing companies. These institutions will be in a better position to get consumers to finance their purchases directly through the retailer rather than through bank loans. If banks are unable to securitize commercial and industrial loans, they will effectively be tied into illiquid high-risk assets. Much depends on banks succeeding in securitizing their assets. If successful, the financial services industry is likely to become still more specialized and fragmented.

Ratings

One of the driving forces behind the growth in securitization has been the rating agencies. They have developed the capability to assess the risk inherent in these structures. Their analysis is conducted on two fronts—legal and credit. On the legal front, it is critical that the issuer of the securities, which is generally a shell company, be independent of the fate of the owners of the original securities. On the credit front, the major concern is the quality of the assets pledged, rather than the creditworthiness of the original owner of the receivables.

Future Course of Securitization

Some bankers see the securitization process spreading to assets that do not have predictable cash flows or that have cash flows that will only occur when the security is sold. Commodity-backed deals tied to the futures markets are one example.

The role of unsecured loans is a more complex issue. Although loan sales among banks have existed for years, in most cases control over loan pricing has been given to borrowers—which raises legal issues that make them exceedingly difficult to securitize. The quality of many banks' balance sheets means that buyers will not be willing to take part in a random, unsecured portfolio. The other alternative is to sell the best loans, which would compromise the overall asset quality and the banks' responsibility to their shareholders.

In a period of interest and exchange rate volatility, financial obligations can be attractive and will be turned into cash as soon as possible. The driving force is liquidity. Present criteria for securitization focus on assets with predictable payment streams—a payment history that can be tracked over a long enough period of time to satisfy investors and rating agencies.

It is argued by its strongest proponents that the market for further securitization is there, pending further regulatory changes. The demand for securitization on the part of banks and other originating institutions is indeed large, based on the outstanding volume of conventional loans.

SUMMARY

Asset-backed financing has seen a great deal of innovation and has taken on significant international dimensions. Some aspects, such as shipping and commodities financing, represent classic international banking products—albeit high-risk and specialized ones. Others, such as securitized mortgage loans, are relatively new and have grown rapidly, especially in the United States. They make possible the opening up of new sources of financing for borrowers and make liquid those financial assets that are themselves naturally illiquid. They add value both to issuers and investors—the essence of financial innovation. And they concentrate commercial banking and investment banking functions on highly specific financial needs.

SELECTED REFERENCES

Donaldson, T. H. *Lending in International Commercial Banking.* London: Macmillan, 1979.

Hempel, George H., Coleman, Alan B., and Simonson, Donald G. *Bank Management,* 2nd ed. New York: John Wiley & Sons, 1986.

Kochan, Nick. "Aircraft Finance Flying Higher." *Euromoney,* June 1989.

Marton, Andrew. "Mortgage Mania Circles the World." *Institutional Investor,* May 1985.

Roussakis, Emmanuel. *International Banking.* New York: Praeger, 1983.

Shapiro, Harvey D. "The Securitization of Practically Everything." *Institutional Investor,* May 1985.

8

Correspondent Banking
and Trade Financing

The dramatic changes that have taken place in the commercial banking environment have had far-reaching effects in all arenas of banking activity, including correspondent banking, which for a long time was treated as a relatively unimportant form of ancillary service offered by banks and given scant attention by senior management. With the restructuring taking place throughout the financial services industry, competitive pressures have forced commercial bankers to reassess their correspondent banking relationships. Correspondent banking around the world now faces its own distinct strategic challenges.

CORRESPONDENT BANKING SERVICES

Correspondent banking consists of banking services that are provided by banks to other banks. Typically, the banks buying and selling correspondent services are located in another city, state, or country. Correspondent banking services can be of a credit or noncredit nature, either domestic or international, with each market having very different characteristics. Due to logistical difficulties, a given bank can only have a limited number of correspondent relationships at a time. When a direct depository relationship does not exist, a third bank—the so-called reimbursement bank—is chosen to settle transactions.

For most banks, correspondent banking has been primarily an international rather than a national business. Domestic correspondent banking in most of the developed world has been limited to the payments function—the heart of any banking system—and interbank lending. This is not true of the United States, however, which has had a thriving domestic correspondent banking business due to the fragmented nature of the U.S. banking system and its traditional geographic limitations on banking activities.

The growth of international correspondent banking is closely linked to the growth in international trade. As the level of trade has grown, banks have increasingly had to service the needs of their clients in new international markets or lose business. As the U.S. dollar is the principal transactions currency, a large proportion of world trade is denominated in dollars, and banks throughout the world have had to access the U.S. payments system. American banks have been able to earn significant income providing U.S. dollar transactions and lines of credit to their foreign correspondents.

In recent years there has been a dramatic change in the distribution of earnings from correspondent banking activities. Until the 1980s the major banks' main earnings in this area came from the current balances ("nostro accounts") of their correspondents. With the rise in interest rates in the late 1970s and early 1980s, many minor banks started to economize on their holdings of nonearning assets, resulting in a consequent decline in the level of nostro balances held. Correspondent banking increasingly came to depend on other financial services as a source of income, and many major banks began to offer a wide range of new credit and consulting services to their correspondents. Consequently, there has been a shift from balance income to fee income.

Credit Services: Interbank Lending

A large amount of the international lending activities of commercial banks is comprised of bank-to-bank lending, and a significant portion of the international assets of a typical bank is comprised of interbank credits in one form or another. The major categories are the following: (1) lines of credit to permit financing of trade transactions; (2) clean loans or advances to finance specific imports or exports; (3) open facilities to borrow for general purposes; (4) medium-term loans or guarantees to finance imports; (5) interbank placement of funds for periods of up to one year; and (6) facilitating capital market access for correspondent banks.

As with other forms of corporate lending, the critical skill in correspondent banking is credit evaluation, which is a more complex task in an international context than in domestic lending. In the case of international lending, the banking system of the correspondent's home country must be examined, and the credit status of the bank itself must be evaluated. A thorough analysis of the macroeconomic condition of that country will also be necessary using standard country risk criteria (see Chapter 19).

Letters of Credit

The letter-of-credit business is an important part of both international trade financing and the correspondent banking business. A *letter of credit* is a written obligation by a bank for its client to honor an exporter's draft or any other demand for payment if and when the conditions specified on the letter of credit are satisfied. Letters of credit are one of the basic building blocks of international trade and are thus an important source of liquidity in the international economy. They facilitate international trade by removing any credit risk that might exist within the transaction. They also cover issuance of commercial paper and project financings (see Chapters 6 and 9). The basic function the bank provides is one of bearing the risk until the transaction is completed.

Bankers' Acceptances

Another area of trade financing that provides attractive business for the correspondent banks involves *bankers' acceptances*. When a bank "accepts" or pays against a draft on another bank in favor of a third party for payment in a certain period of time, a bankers' acceptance has been created. The old-style bankers' acceptance is becoming less predominant as wholesale interbank trade financing with bankers' acceptances becomes more common. This service enhances international liquidity, and the bank is rewarded for bearing risk.

The purchase and sale of bankers' acceptances is an important source of liquidity in many national markets due to the absence of suitable short-term assets. The growth of other markets for short-term assets and a loosening of monetary authorities' control of the money supply tend to reduce the attractiveness of bankers' acceptances as a money market instrument (as was the case with the rise of the commercial paper market in the United Kingdom). The bankers' acceptance market is very active in many countries providing substantial liquidity for those agents engaged in international trade.

Clearing House Functions

Correspondent banks typically handle the transactional requirements for other banks. These functions are normally paid for by fees, balances, or a combination of both. Due to the dollar's importance as an international unit of exchange worldwide, it was necessary to develop a settlement system to deal with payments processing and clearing. This task has been primarily undertaken by the large New York banks, and it represents their main correspondent banking role.

This function involves arranging details of transaction execution including debits and credits, advices, and account statements. The clearing function also involves the correspondent banks in bearing intraday risk. As payments are made in anticipation of later cover, these payments are often at risk for long periods of the day. Thus, the New York money center banks play a role different from that of a traditional correspondent bank supporting a nonbank client relationship. This sector of correspondent banking is truly interbank banking.

There are two main categories of risk that are borne by banks that perform the clearing house functions: (1) credit risk in making payments before the funds have been covered and (2) system risk due to the possibility of technical or operational failure in the system, in which case the banks could face significant interest costs.

In the international arena, local banks provide local check-clearing facilities as well as clearing facilities for foreign exchange contracts denominated in the local currency or in Eurocurrencies.

Payments and Collections

At the heart of any financial service is a payment. Most payments are accomplished through interbank account debiting and crediting. In recent years electronic instructions have replaced telexed instructions as the means of effecting transfer. Two networks, collectively owned by the banks that use them, dominate international payments. The Society for Worldwide International Funds Transfer (SWIFT) provides the international lines used for such interbank advice, while the Clearing House Interbank Payments System (CHIPS) is the system in operation in New York. They are connected by a system called "Gateway."

SWIFT carried up to 1.2 million messages per day in 1989, while CHIPS carried an average of 600,000 messages, daily transferring $700 billion. The rapidly increasing flow of payments—facilitated by automation—has caused banks to increase dramatically their intraday correspondent banking exposure as well as technological exposure to the systems that support them. The size of these exposures became painfully obvious to the Bank of New York on November 21, 1985 when, due to an in-house bank software failure, payment for a stream of securities purchased by Bank of New York could not be received.

By close of business, the Federal Bank of New York had extended a $23.6 billion overdraft to cover Bank of New York's shortfall. The problem, resolved by payment of the overnight interest charges of several million dollars from Bank of New York to the Federal Reserve, highlights the radically changed nature of payments exposures in particular and correspondent banking in general.

Correspondent banks can, through the agency function, act on behalf of clients to prepare and present negotiable instruments. Collections of this nature cover: (1) the settlement of terms of contracts; (2) sales and purchases of merchandise or securities; (3) security receipt and delivery services; (4) dividend receipts and coupon collections; and (5) provision of safekeeping services for assorted assets. At the international level, organizations such as Euroclear (Brussels) and Cedel (Luxembourg) provide many of these services, including securities lending and credit advances to participating forms in the Eurobond market. A network of custody banks in each case permits a wide range of transactions without bonds physically leaving the custody banks.

Foreign Exchange Services

Foreign exchange services have traditionally been an important component of correspondent banking services. With the increases in trade and international expansion of corporations, the demand for foreign exchange dealing has increased rapidly. This topic is examined in detail in Chapter 13.

Trade Development and Referrals

Correspondent banking relationships can provide an attractive means to serve clients, with prospects for development of collateral business. As foreign investment levels increase, business referrals and introductions become increasingly valuable. Introductions by correspondent banks can lead to new accounts in the local market and can generate the potential for international remittances and related fee-generating business. U.S. banks tend to have a preference for banks with large international correspondent networks due to the potential for overseas contact.

In addition, correspondents can serve as an information source for local bank clients. As correspondent banking relationships are often the first step in establishing a presence in a foreign market, a correspondent relationship provides vital information for banks considering a more sophisticated operation in the future. Banks can access their correspondents to provide local credit information, information on the regulatory environment, data on local economic and political conditions, and the like.

Other Services

Correspondent banks increasingly offer a range of additional services to their clients to increase their fee income. The key to success in this arena is to identify needs of correspondent banks. The range of services being offered is limited only by the needs of correspondent clients. Examples include First Tennessee Bank of Memphis, which has offered correspondents advice and help in establishing bank branches, and Wachovia First National Bank of Atlanta, which has offered seminars on bank management topics to its correspondents.

The change in the nature of the services offered has influenced the distribution of profits from different correspondent banking activities within the banks themselves. Bankers Trust, for example, has had a larger share of income from corporate finance and money market activities with correspondents than from correspondent balance earnings, with a significant part of its merger and acquisition activity coming from correspondent banks.

FINANCING INTERNATIONAL TRADE

Banks have been involved in the financing of international trade and effecting payments for international trade transactions since at least medieval times. The basic *transactions* services involve circumventing information and transactions costs for importers and exporters, making payment for international transactions as expeditiously and cheaply as possible, and providing associated foreign exchange and risk-shifting services. The basic *credit* services involve the direct extension of credit from the time merchandise leaves the factory door (and sometimes before that) to the time the buyer completes payment or, alternatively, making possible credit extension for this purpose by the financial market by providing backstops for the risk involved—all of this again in the most cost-effective available form. Variants of the basic trade finance transactions include forfaiting, international leasing, countertrade, and the use of electronic banking techniques.

Forms of International Payment

Probably the easiest and cheapest forms of payment for international trade transactions are made on an open-account or consignment basis, or against payment in advance. Both are possible only if the two parties know each other well and trust each other.

If a transaction is done on a consignment basis, the exporter ships the merchandise and sends the shipping documents to the importer, who is then able to claim the goods when they arrive. When the importer sells the merchandise, the proceeds minus the markup are sent to the exporter. The same thing happens when the transaction is done on an open-account basis, except that the importer remits payment to the exporter on arrival of the goods or within an agreed period of time thereafter. Selling on consignment loads the entire risk (that the merchandise will actually be sold and that the importer will actually pay), as well as the financing of the goods while in shipment and in the importer's inventory, on the exporter. Selling on open account also loads the credit risk, as well as part or all of the financing risk, on the exporter. Nevertheless, exporters may be willing to accept the risks involved in selling on consignment to better their competitive positions. Selling on open account is normally done when there is a tight connection between importer and exporter, as when the importer is an affiliate of the exporting company. Both forms of payment raise serious collection problems in the event of default, and all claims must be filed under the laws of the importer's country.

Payment in advance may be specified in cases in which the exporter is able to load onto the importer all of the risk (the risk that the goods will actually be shipped and will arrive as specified) and all the credit costs (the cost of credit during the time the goods are in transit and sometimes even as the goods go through the production process). This form of payment may be specified for certain types of custom-made products that cannot be sold to anyone else or in those cases in which the exporter has very substantial leverage.

In all three cases (payment in advance, consignment, and open account), banks get involved only in the payment function itself and will receive customary fees for this service as well as for the spot or forward exchange transactions involved (or possible trading gains in foreign exchange futures or options).

International Collections

Perhaps the most straightforward and substantive involvement of banks in international trade is collection of amounts due on arm's-length transactions between importers and exporters. Suppose the importer and exporter do not know each other well enough to create sufficient trust between them. The exporter would not want to ship merchandise on a straightforward basis, because he could not be sure that the importer would pay him. The importer could take care of this problem by simply paying in advance, but then he could not be sure that the merchandise was actually shipped by the exporter. This calls for an intermediary who takes care of the risk exposure on both sides.

The exporter prepares a "trade bill," or draft, that the importer is supposed to pay either when he takes possession of the merchandise ("documents against payment," or D/P draft) or when he accepts the draft (D/A draft) for payment at some specified future date, such as 30 or 90 days down the road. The exporter prepares the merchandise for shipment and obtains a "bill of lading" (B/L) from a common carrier (e.g., an airline or shipping company) attesting to the fact that the goods are as specified and that they were shipped on a specified date and along a specified route. The B/L and the D/P or D/A draft are sent to the exporter's bank, which in turn sends the draft and documents to its correspondent bank in the importer's country with instructions to hand over the documents (permitting the importer to claim the merchandise) against payment or against acceptance of the draft, as the case may be.

If it is a D/P draft, sometimes called a "sight draft," the payment is collected by the bank in the importer's country, transferred to the bank in the exporter's country, and credited to the exporter's account. No credit is extended, and the collection process is compensated by fees—plus a spread and fees on a foreign exchange transaction in the middle. The same thing happens if it is a D/A draft, now called a "time draft," except that the payment is collected for the account of the exporter on the specified date 30, 60, or more days in the future, after it has been accepted by the importer. The time draft may be held to maturity by the exporter, or it may be accepted by the importer's bank and either held to maturity by that bank or sold in the local bankers' acceptance market, with the discounted proceeds collected for the exporter immediately. In this case, credit is extended by the holder of the time draft, who collects the interest represented by the discount.

Figure 8–1 depicts the workings payment on a consignment and open-account basis, payment in advance, and international collections against sight and time drafts.

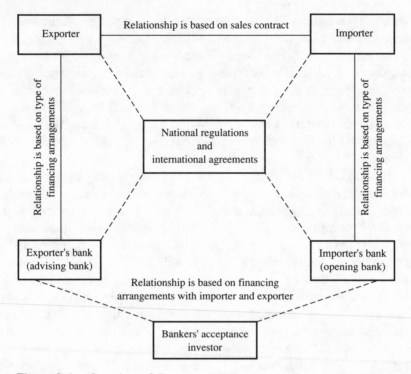

Figure 8–1. Overview of Payments Relationships. (*Source*: Ingo Walter (ed). *Handbook of International Business* (New York: Wiley, 1988) p. 1610; reprinted by permission.)

Letters of Credit

Documentary time drafts for collection provide one vehicle for financing international trade transactions, other than straightforward bank loans to the exporter or the importer. A time-honored alternative is the letter of credit (L/C) described earlier in this chapter. It efficiently and properly allocates the credit risks to those best able to carry them and at the same time greatly facilitates access to financing at the best available terms.

Assume the exporter and importer do not wish to extend credit to each other or to take payment risk. The exporter asks the importer to request his bank (the "opening bank") to issue an irrevocable L/C for the transaction amount in the exporter's favor. By doing so, the bank commits itself to paying the specified amount if the importer is unwilling or unable to pay—assuming the merchandise has been shipped precisely as specified in the terms of the L/C. The opening bank will then send the L/C to its correspondent bank in the exporter's country (the "advising bank"), which will forward it to the exporter. The transaction will then take place using a sight or time draft, as discussed earlier, with the credit risk covered by the opening bank. An L/C of this time will cover only a single transaction, with tight specification of what will be shipped and how it will be shipped.

If the exporter is unfamiliar or uncomfortable with the importer's bank, he may request that the opening bank's L/C be confirmed by the advising bank in his own country—a confirmed, irrevocable L/C. Should the importer default, the importer's bank will pay. Should both be unwilling or unable to pay, the advising bank will pay. Of course, the advising bank must be comfortable with the credit standing of the opening bank and with the country risk involved (e.g., the risk that exchange controls may be imposed that prevent the necessary currency from being made available to the importer or his bank). Again, the transaction will take place as specified earlier; in the case of a time draft, the acceptance can take place in the exporter's country and can be discounted in the local bankers' acceptance market at money market rates. Figure 8–2 shows how the process works.

In addition to unconfirmed and confirmed irrevocable letters of credit, there are other variants as well. *A revocable L/C* may be amended or canceled by the opening bank at any point; therefore it offers the exporter less protection and a lower price. *A revolving L/C* will cover multiple or continuous shipments of merchandise. If a revolving L/C is cumulative, any amounts used become reavailable once the transaction has been consummated, which is not the case in a noncumulative revolving L/C unless specifically amended. A *transferable L/C* permits the exporter to assign the proceeds to one or more secondary beneficiaries (e.g., subcontractors), while in a *back-to-back L/C* the exporter uses the first L/C (opened by the importer in his favor) as the basis for requesting his bank to open a second L/C in favor of his own supplier(s). The latter would tend to be used by exporters who are middlemen between domestic manufacturers and foreign buyers and who do not have sufficient credit standing of their own.

Banks have a number of opportunities to earn fee and interest income from international trade transactions covered by letters of credit. Fees go to banks for issuing and confirming the L/C, for collections, for foreign exchange transactions, for accepting time drafts, and (when the draft is held on the bank's own books) for extending credit—with the rate of interest reflected in the associated discount. Obviously, this is a highly competitive, transactions-

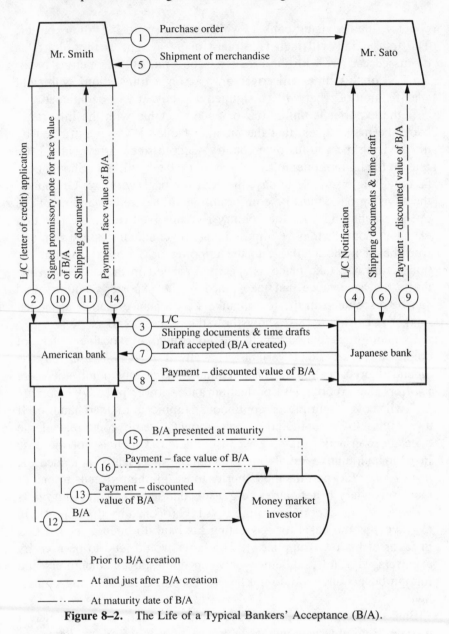

Figure 8–2. The Life of a Typical Bankers' Acceptance (B/A).

intensive business. Banks that are best at it have wide-ranging client bases involved in international trade and have designed procedures that are convenient to use, highly efficient, and error-free; they also have substantial networks of correspondent banks. Clients, for their part, understand that these services cost money and always have the opportunity to "unbundle," or separate the various components.

Forfaiting and International Factoring

Still another form of international trade financing, particularly common in Europe, is called "forfait" financing. Under this structure of medium-term export finance, a bank (forfaiting house) will buy from the exporter the obligations due him from importers in various countries without recourse to the exporter himself. The exporter will receive the discounted proceeds immediately—against evidence covering the quality, quantity, and shipment of the merchandise—with the discount reflecting both the interest charge and the credit risk (commercial as well as country) the forfaiter is assuming. The promissory notes involved are usually endorsed by the importer's bank. The notes, now endorsed by both the importer's bank and by the forfaiter, can then be held to maturity or resold in the market.

To some extent, a forfait transaction is similar to factoring, which is familiar in the United States and certain other domestic markets. *Factoring* is a process whereby a bank that believes it is wholly familiar with the customers of a particular client buys the client's accounts receivable on a nonrecourse basis at a discount. The goods have already been shipped and the bills sent out, and it is up to the bank to collect. Factoring is common in the garment industry. It is a specialized business in which risk must be carefully managed through intimate knowledge of the industry and the creditworthiness of customers and through diversification. It can be highly profitable for banks that know how to manage the risks involved. Internationally, factoring is more difficult because risk management is problematic—a domestic bank having the basis to understand the risks associated with a client's foreign customers and achieving appropriate diversification is difficult to imagine. One exception is two or more banks working together, swapping factored receivables involving customers in each bank's home country.

Government Export Financing, Backstops, and Countertrade

Governments in most industrial and many developing countries provide export assistance of various kinds in order to stimulate foreign sales of domestic companies. These involve guarantees covering commercial, political, and economic risks associated with the importing country, as well as concessionary financing of various types. In the United States, the Export-Import Bank (Eximbank) provides direct loans to exporters and importers, export credit insurance and guarantees, and backstops for banks involved in international trade financing. Medium-term support is discussed in Chapter 9. Short-term support, up to 180 days, is handled by the Foreign Credit Insurance Association (FCIA), which is run by Eximbank and private insurance companies. Export financing of commodity transactions is handled by the Commodity Credit Corporation (CCC). There are similar agencies in most other countries, such as Hermes in Germany and COFACE in France. All agencies permit lodging certain risks with the government at concessionary prices, thereby taking them out of the commercial market. Often these can result in very attractive profits for the banks involved, in the light of the limited risks they assume.

Banks in certain countries, such as Austria and Belgium, have become very active in arranging and facilitating "countertrade," "barter," "buybacks," "switchtrade," "offset," and other transactions with countries experiencing severe foreign exchange scarcity. For example, a company may ship a piece of capital equipment to a particular eastern European country; in return, it is obligated to take or buy for cash other specified commodities or arrange their sale to third parties. Or it may build a plant on a turnkey basis, for which it gets paid in a stream of production from that plant. The variants are numerous, and the business is highly specialized and risky. Normally the companies involved are in the best position to price countertrade services and to manage the risks. But even then there is no guarantee of enduring success, as companies like General Electric and Sears Roebuck have discovered. Banks in many countries get involved in facilitating such transactions, and some take on the role of principal as well. Enabling legislation permitting U.S. banks to engage in that activity exists, but success has been elusive.

CORRESPONDENT BANKING CUSTOMERS

There are three main categories of correspondent banking clients. The first category of clients consists of banks subcontracting back-office activities to larger banks. Over time, the incidence of smaller banks subcontracting operation functions to larger banks has grown. This demand for correspondent banking should be examined as part of a broader trend taking place throughout the banking industry with respect to banks' activities. In the past, many banks acted simultaneously as producer, wholesaler, and retailer of banking services. This is often no longer the case, with subcontracting activity occurring primarily in functions that are susceptible to economies of scale. There has been a considerable amount of debate as to the extent to which economies of scale are present in banking activities. There seems to be a consensus that technology-intensive banking activities offer the most potential for volume-related savings. The larger banks that have developed superior processing and transactions abilities have done so primarily due to investment in technology. They specialize in scale-intensive activities, with the correspondent banks acting in many ways as sales outlets.

The second category includes banks that face some sort of regulatory barriers with respect to the markets they can service. In the United States, this applies particularly to banks that have been limited from crossing state lines and thus have had to buy correspondent services from local banks in order to service their clients' needs. This function has typically been an important component of correspondent relationships. However, the increasing pace of deregulation with the onset of interstate banking has decreased this client motivation, and is less likely to be a driving force in the future. In the international market, the same driving force is present when national authorities discriminate in a more or less explicit fashion against foreign financial institutions entering or attempting to enter the local business market (see Chapter 26). In this case the bank will use a correspondent relationship to service its clients needs. Increasingly, foreign banks are succeeding in penetrating domestic markets themselves, as deregulation and competitive forces open domestic markets to international competition.

The third category of clients are banks that are involved in the interbank market—those buying funds to supplement their deposit bases. Over the years, banks have become more aware of the opportunity cost of funds and have reduced their level of nonearning assets to a minimum. Similarly, depositors have become more sensitive to interest rates. Banks are consequently having to rely on the interbank market to supplement loanable funds. The interbank market is a far less stable source of funds than deposits; this increases the level of risk for banks in the interbank market (see Chapter 13). As noted, the level of interbank lending has increased substantially over the last few years.

In the international correspondent banking market, the main motivation is twofold: (1) to satisfy customers' international needs and (2) to access new customers. Of all the vehicles available to a bank in penetrating the foreign market, a correspondent banking relationship can be particularly attractive. The final choice of such a vehicle will obviously depend on multiple factors. Banks will choose different vehicles according to their overall financial resources, their volume of international business, the overall strategy of the bank, and the structure and regulation of the banking industry in the country in question. The major determining factor, however, is usually the expected future volume of international business.

As discussed in Chapter 2, vehicles available for the transaction of international business include correspondent relationships, agencies, branches, consortium banks, local bank acquisitions, joint ventures, and merchant banks. Typically, correspondent banking is the most appropriate vehicle in the low-volume early stage of business. The decision to use a correspondent relationship is influenced also by the high costs associated with operating global branch systems. With access to national branch banking in foreign countries through correspondent relationships, a bank can easily obtain national access for certain services.

A particular attraction of an international correspondent relationship is that it allows the bank to take advantage of the business opportunities abroad while minimizing its operating costs. Another attraction is that local bankers are less threatened by correspondent relationships than by other forms of market penetration (e.g., branches). In fact, local banks tend to welcome correspondent relationships and generally will work to develop them. Overall, many banks have found that the expansion of correspondent networks can develop a greater customer base that can simultaneously be used as a basis for strategic marketing decisions. Offsetting these influences is the increasing complexity of financial services, which makes correspondent relationships a less-efficient means of servicing a client's international needs.

SUPPLIERS OF CORRESPONDENT BANKING SERVICES

In the domestic market, sales of correspondent services have been predominately money center, clearing, and universal banks in their respective countries, as well as some of the larger regional banks. In many countries, cooperative banks of various kinds have central organizations that provide many of these services within the structure of their own organizations (e.g., the Deutsche Genossenschaftsbank in Germany and Credit Agricole in France). In effect, banks that are active in correspondent banking services have developed the technological capability to undertake a significant part of other banks' payments and transactions needs by taking advantage of the possibility of achieving significant economies of scale through large volumes. Other regional and middle-sized banks have attempted to develop specialized services for other banks.

In the international arena, sellers of correspondent services have tended to be the banks with the larger branch networks. Due to foreign bank penetration in many national markets, local banks have increasingly tended to access correspondent networks directly rather than go through larger local banks with large foreign correspondent networks of their own. While it is rare to find a bank specializing totally in the provision of services for financial institutions, many banks are attracted to the business due to the possibilities to earn (partially soft) fee income.

Due to the highly regulated and protected environment in which financial services firms developed in many national markets, smaller banks and indeed a surprising number of larger banks remained rather unsophisticated with respect to management techniques and state-of-the-art financing techniques. As they faced an increasingly competitive environment, a growing market emerged for those banks with the requisite skills in-house to educate their smaller correspondents.

There also has been a need for banks to access foreign markets in order to provide a full service for their clients. In the nineteenth century the primary needs of traders were foreign currency and bills of exchange. As the businesses started to actually move in to the international markets themselves, their needs changed considerably. The globalization of international transactions has enabled many banks to expand their international activities.

In the U.S. domestic market prior to 1960, the main driving force in the development of correspondent banking was geography. Correspondent banking relationships enabled a bank to extend to its customers payment services outside the bank's own home market. Many correspondent banks built an international branch network in order to provide international payment services to domestic banks. During the 1960s and 1970s the emphasis in correspondent banking moved more toward providing a wider range of system-intensive processing services. Many of the smaller banks were no longer able to produce certain products in-house because they had insufficient volume to cover the development or purchase of the necessary software and hardware. Correspondent banks started offering back-office services such as check and credit card processing to smaller banks. This can be seen as part of an unbundling process whereby banks no longer engage in the production, wholesaling, and retailing of their products but have begun to specialize by function. During this period the correspondent banking business was driven by the need to maximize volumes in order to take advantage of the economies of scale available as a result of large fixed investments in systems and operations.

The development of the international money markets has changed correspondent banking ties considerably. Banks started to turn to international dealing, for the first time seeking large volumes of interbank funding that previously would not have been granted until an interbank relationship was significantly more developed. This increased the level of risk attached to interbank lending. The growth of the wholesale money markets has also changed the dynamics of banks' liability management activities. With the removal of regulations on deposit interest, banks had to pay more for funds, which decreased the attractiveness of retail deposits as compared with interbank lending. Many banks reassessed the viability of their retail branch networks, particularly as interest spreads declined to levels that threatened the economics of many retail networks. Retail funds nevertheless remained attractive primarily for their stability.

Developments in the market eroded the correspondent banks' hold on the payments business. The creation of Edge Act corporations by regional and established foreign banks in the United States, as well as the domestic penetration of new foreign banks, dramatically increased the level of competition in the international correspondent banking arena. Technological developments, often related to the payments process, reduced the demand for traditional correspondent services. Thus, the correspondent banking industry was beset by falling margins and at the same time encountered a decline in demand for their services.

The 1980s saw the continuation of many of these trends, with the deregulation of banking making itself felt. The main results were product proliferation and a more market-oriented awareness of the economics of the business. As expenditures on systems and operations capabilities have increased rapidly, so have expenditures on marketing.

The late 1980s brought the most revolutionary changes. Many banks starting to deal with correspondent banking in a strategic fashion for the first time. With high interest rates, banks began to face a higher opportunity cost of funds, and many correspondent banks became more aware of the levels of nostro balances that they had outstanding. This resulted in a dramatic drop in the level of compensating balances banks were willing to hold. Since the profitability of correspondent banking was very much dependent on these balances, many banks were forced to reassess their correspondent banking activities. Those banks that decided to stay in the business moved more toward fee-earning activities. As always, the onset of significant change created opportunities for some banks and difficulties for many others.

THE REGULATORY ENVIRONMENT

The regulatory setting facing correspondent banks has changed considerably since the Federal Reserve announced in May 1985 that new regulations would become effective in March 1986. These regulations were aimed at reducing banks' exposure to interbank money transfer networks. Banks must now obey self-imposed debit limits when they commit funds to any of the three transfer networks—CHIPS, CHESS, or Fedwire. The voluntary limits will be closely linked to bank capital ratios. Although the guidelines are voluntary, it is widely believed that if the limits are not followed they will become mandatory. The limits will affect three different transactions—bilateral limits between banks, debit limits on any one payments system, and debit limits to all payment systems combined.

The Federal Reserve's actions were a result of fears about the level of funds committed to the clearing systems. On CHIPS alone, the daily volume surpassed $200 billion in 1985, and the Federal Reserve estimated that the daily overdraft volume on all the networks combined was $100 billion daily. This overdraft is not explicitly covered by banks' capital bases and thus is a significant source of potential risk. The most worrisome feature is that many of the participating banks had no idea of their exposure to the system and indeed to other banks.

The Federal Reserve's announcement in May 1985 came after the banks themselves had become aware of the problem and had set about establishing bilateral limits of their own accord. Prior to the Federal Reserve's intervention, the regulation was governed by Rule 13 of the constitution of the New York Clearing House, which treated any payment that a defaulting bank sent as being null and void. However, the dramatic increases in dollar volume due to increases in the use of financial futures and foreign currency markets made it clear that Rule 13 could not be made to work.

Although the bureaucratic implications of the limits are potentially adverse, the majority of the U.S. banks support them. There are, however, several problems with the limits. First, with relatively static bank capital levels and increasing network volumes over time, the limits will effectively become tighter. Thus, a bank's capital may not be the best benchmark for setting limits. Second, for some of the smaller banks, the problem of measuring exposures on a moment-to-moment basis will create severe problems for information systems. Some of the banks have not had fast enough reporting systems to generate the necessary information. This problem has been intensified by the technological changes that have increased the speed of the payments system. Third, the limits may interfere with the banks' daily business, with some transactions having to wait overnight because the bank has already reached its exposure limit. This particular situation is complicated by the fact that daylight overdrafts are free while overnight overdrafts are not. Fourth, some bankers fear that the limits would benefit the banks with large limits and favor deposit-rich banks with large branch networks at the expense of other banks, such as relatively branchless wholesale institutions.

There is also an asymmetry between free daylight overdrafts and charges imposed for overnight overdrafts. Since it has now become possible to estimate a bank's exact daylight overdraft position, it is only a question of time before charges will be instituted.

The regulation that has taken place in the United States seems unnecessary in the United Kingdom. In the case of London's automated transfer system—CHAPS—clearing banks have always been required to guarantee every payment they received, which had the effect of building limits into the system from the outset. CHAPS, however, has had problems of its own, most notably the lack of a common interface to the system. CHAPS is normally approached through the clearing banks, each of which has its own distinct access system. Further problems are caused by the fact that the system closes just as the New York banks are opening. The various problems associated with the system have resulted in some banks boycotting the system.

AUTOMATION

High-technology systems have the potential to improve both the quality and the delivery of correspondent banking services by simplifying and reducing the costs of processing. In order to fully avail themselves of the technological possibilities, however, large up-front investments are necessary. This effectively prevents many of the smaller banks from getting involved.

There have been various pressures acting to increase the importance of the cash management function provided by correspondent banks. These include: (1) high real rates of interest, (2) the drop in interest in Eurocurrency loan participations, due in part to the LDC debt crisis; and (3) the large investments that banks have undertaken to build technologically sophisticated electronic systems that will improve money and other financial instrument transmission. As a result of these pressures, banks needed to maximize volume; therefore, they set about marketing very aggressively. Consequently, banks have been forced to reconsider their correspondent relationships. A good example is the SWIFT system, which obliges banks accessing the system to review their correspondent relationships and to direct business to other SWIFT members.

One of the greatest challenges facing banks wishing to offer correspondent services concerns the question of tracking the costs associated with correspondent banking in order to price activities accurately. However, the problem is not limited to tracking costs, which are only part of the pricing equation. Some bankers, for example, argue that cost-driven pricing overlooks the real value received by the buyers of correspondent banking services. With the general movement in banking from relationship-based to transaction-based activities, there is increasing pressure on banks to price their activities tactically rather than strategically. The old idea that 20 percent of a bank's clients provide 80 percent of their profits is no longer tenable in the current competitive environment, and the drive seems to be for each product to cover its own costs.

Strategic pricing is appropriate when the objective is to maintain a relationship. However, banks have to identify explicitly the benefits they expect to flow from the relationship. In the case of strategic pricing, banks examine the overall benefits of the relationship and are willing to accept losses on some products in the interest of maintaining an important relationship.

COMPETITIVE DYNAMICS

The competitive environment for correspondent banking has tradition-ally been very stable. Correspondent banking depended very much on the idea of reciprocity, and most of the players were relatively price inelastic. Correspondent banking was heavily dependent upon the quality of the personal relationships and banks tended to collab-orate, using one another's services and sharing business risks and information. Due to the changes in the competitive environment fac-ing all commercial banks, many have taken a cold, hard look at the profitability of their correspondent relationships. For those banks that are continuing, correspondent banking is typically treated as a profit center. But many banks selling correspondent banking services do not have the ability to assess the profitability very well—in particular to evaluate the costs associated with providing correspondent services—a serious shortcoming indeed. The U.S. market for correspondent banking has changed dramatically, mainly due to competition and Federal Reserve actions. There has been considerable consolidation in the market, with many of the marginal sellers of correspondent banking services dropping out and the larger banks increasing their market shares. Among these are Citibank, Chase Manhattan, Manu-facturers Hanover, and Chemical Bank. The mean number of banks served by correspondent sellers dropped from 82 in 1982 to 68 in 1985. Correspondent banks are also switching their relationships more often, which is generally felt to be a reflection of an increase in com-petitive pressures.

Buyers of correspondent banking services in both the domestic and international markets have become increasingly price sensitive. Traditionally, like many other areas in banking, correspondent bank-ing was more a question of diplomacy than it was a business. With banks buying correspondent services more tactically than strategical-ly, with the increase in transactions banking pervasive throughout the banking environment, and with the increasing tendency to price each product on a stand-alone basis, sellers of correspondent services have lost bargaining power.

In the international market, local banks increasingly have cor-respondent relationships with foreign banks in the local market rather than the larger local banks having international correspondent relationships. The existence of Edge Act corporations also increases the level of competition dramatically. Technological developments have also weakened the bargaining power of sellers in the domestic market considerably. Thus, while many of the smaller banks relied in the past on their correspondent banks to provide them with data processing activities, they now have the technology to do it themselves.

Correspondent banking is primarily a buyer's market. It has characteristics that are highly attractive to sellers—principally access to correspondent balances and further opportunities to earn "soft" fee income. Correspondent balances allow the banks to expand their deposit base, and the fees earned from correspondent services augment their income. The LDC debt crisis and capital adequacy problems have also influenced the correspondent banking business, increasing the conservative behavior of many of the players. The "flight to quality" witnessed after the 1983 debt crisis has had similar effects on the banks' relationships with each other. Banks have become much more aware of credit risk, especially in light of the Continental Illinois collapse, so that the bargaining power of buyers of correspondent banking services has increased significantly as increasing numbers of banks reassess the attractions of the services involved.

Moreover, traditional correspondent banking services are now being offered by nonbank financial services firms, and this has added a new dimension to the competitive environment. In particular, the rise of "bankers' banks" has caused problems for the traditional sellers of correspondent banking services. Bankers' banks have been established by groups of independent bankers on a cooperative basis to serve as an alternative to the orthodox correspondent banking services. They primarily help small banks to share loans; they provide a wide range of services as well, including data processing, profit analysis, and advertising services. This provision of services by bankers' banks has become significant because the Federal Reserve is charging for its payment services and has become a de facto competitor to many correspondent banks.

As in many other segments of the banking arena, the barriers to entry into correspondent banking have decreased considerably. This has been particularly troublesome in the case of some of the services traditionally offered by banks. Just as there has been fragmentation throughout the banking industry and just as corporations have found substitutions for banking services, the same is true of the banks themselves.

It is clear that each bank focusing on different segments of the market will adopt different strategies in order to fully serve their desired customer base. Banks that have chosen to act as clearing houses must provide personalized attention and transactions services but also require a large capital base and sophisticated risk management systems that control and sustain the exposure that significant clearing activity entails.

SUMMARY

The dramatic changes that commercial banks are facing in the competitive environment are reflected in correspondent banking. Deregulation is allowing nonbank institutions to compete for correspondent banking services. Increasing customer sophistication is forcing correspondents to minimize their holdings of nonearning assets. Deterioration in banks' balance sheets is forcing correspondents to instigate tighter credit assessments in their dealings with other banks. Technological innovation is changing the economics of correspondent banking and changing the ways banks do business. The development of transactions-oriented banking is forcing correspondents to reassess reciprocal relationships in terms of tighter cost-benefit analysis.

SELECTED REFERENCES

Anderson, Lynn. "Rational Pricing In An Irrational Environment." *The Banker,* February 1983.

Brittain, Ben. "Correspondent Bankers Close Ranks." *The Banker,* February 1983.

Eng, Maximo. "Financing International Trade." In *Handbook of International Business* edited by Ingo Walter. New York: John Wiley & Sons, 1988.

Evanoff, Douglas. "Priced Services: The Fed's Impact on Correspondent Banking." Federal Reserve Bank of Chicago, 1986. Mimeographed.

Keslar, Linda. "The Big Boys Muscle In." *Euromoney,* November 1985.

McDougall, Rosamund. "Exposure Explosure." *The Banker*, July 1989.

Rudy, John. "Correspondent Banking Comes Into Its Own." *The Banker,* February 1982.

Taplin, Peter. "Correspondent Banking: A U.K. Perspective." *The Banker,* February 1983.

Winder, Robert. "Raising The Price of CHIPS." *Euromoney,* November 1985.

9

Project Financing

The financing of large-scale projects such as pipelines, oil and gas production, tunnels and bridges, energy plants, major office buildings and similar long-gestation, highly capital-intensive ventures has evolved into a major competitive testing ground for international financial services firms. The sheer size of the financing needs that are frequently encountered, the high risks, the complex financial structuring, and the specialized risk-evaluation requirements have concentrated leadership in this business on the relatively few financial services firms that developed the financial resources and technical skills needed.

Driven by increased competition and growing pressure on the profitability of conventional international lending, a number of commercial and investment banks have succeeded in developing capabilities in a broad range of banking functions, thus enabling them to offer comprehensive financial support and advice through the life of a major project. The financial services industry's increasing sophistication and flexibility in designing financings for such projects has greatly facilitated the strategic thrust by energy companies, real estate developers, and others into international activities.

While project financings reached a high point with the soaring energy prices of the 1970s, they declined rapidly thereafter with the significant drop in energy and minerals prices, tighter credit conditions, and the onset of the LDC debt crisis during the first half of the 1980s. The number of new projects dropped by 66 percent from 1981 to 1986, and the value of these projects declined by 33 percent during the same period. Most financial institutions active in project finance greatly reduced or shut down their energy and engineering groups during this period, reassigning expensive and highly skilled individuals or eliminating their positions altogether. Project financing structures, as discussed in this chapter, nevertheless have significant enduring value, and in the late 1980s they made a reappearance in applications to electric power generation, tunnels, bridges and other infrastructure projects, as well as in real estate ventures. This included

191

a number of new adaptations of the basic technique, such as the build, operate, transfer (BOT) model.

BACKGROUND

Modern project financing appears to have been largely an American invention. It can be traced to bank financing of independent oil companies during the 1930s, particularly in Oklahoma and Texas. Few of the "wildcatters" who dominated the oil business at the time had the financial resources to bring new discoveries into production or had strong enough balance sheets for ordinary unsecured bank borrowing on anything but a very limited scale. Secured borrowing was likewise precluded, since the principal "assets" to be financed were usually a hole in the ground and some associated equipment and supplies with questionable resale value. Yet it was clear that the hydrocarbon resources in the ground represented a prospective value as a future revenue stream that could become the basis for attractive lending opportunities. Bank loans could be serviced from the proceeds of the future sale of the resource without necessarily looking exclusively to either the operating company's balance sheet or to production assets for credit support.

Called "production payment financing," this approach in effect mortgaged the resource in the ground, with financial institutions betting (1) that it was actually present in sufficient quantity, (2) that it could be lifted economically, and (3) that it could be sold at a price that lived up to a set of initial expectations, all within reasonable margins for error. Given the nature of large-scale energy projects such as offshore oil and natural gas ventures as well as terminals, pipelines, and other facilities that rely upon throughput charges for cash flows, the rapid development of "project financing" on much the same basis since World War II has been assured on an international scale.

The concepts underlying project financing were later extended to other ventures such as power plants, tunnels, bridges, pipelines, office buildings, and telecommunications facilities for which resources in the ground could not be mortgaged. Here, the future receipts of the project were regarded as the primary means for the underlying loans. A survey of project financings in the 1970s and 1980s revealed that energy projects were the largest users, constituting 40 percent of all project financings during the period, followed by power plants (20 percent), minerals mining (16 percent), transportation (14 percent) and other activities (10 percent).[1]

STRUCTURAL ASPECTS OF PROJECT FINANCING

A fairly standard approach to structuring a project financing, is for the sponsors to establish a vehicle company in which they are principal shareholders (for example, in the petroleum industry the sponsors might be BP, Shell and Exxon). The vehicle company tends to have relatively thin capitalization in relation to the financial needs of the project. Each sponsor holds a sufficiently small share of the equity in the joint venture so that for legal and accounting purposes the vehicle company cannot be construed as a subsidiary.

Funding of the project is then routed through the vehicle company. Ideally, a record of such financing does not appear on the sponsors' balance sheets at all. If it does, it is only as a footnoted contingent liability. Similarly, the assets acquired in the course of undertaking the project appear on the financial statements of the vehicle company alone.

The purpose of project financing is to preserve the sponsors' own credit standing and future access to financial resources. However, evolving accounting practices seem to require greater disclosure of corporate involvement in project financing, thus possibly constraining this advantage by highlighting contingent claims on the firm.

Vehicle companies may take a variety of forms, particularly if the project involves multiple sponsors. The presence of multiple sponsors might be appropriate for several reasons: (1) if the project exceeds the financial, technical, or human resources of a single company, (2) if the need for risk sharing clearly exists, (3) if a large project yields significantly greater economies of scale than several smaller ones, (4) if the resource itself is jointly owned, (5) if the sponsors are complementary in terms of their capabilities, or (6) if the country where the project is located mandates a joint venture with local interests.

In the case of multiple sponsors, either a separate corporate entity, partnership construction trust, or contractual joint venture may be created. Each entity may have a number of subforms and different managerial, legal, tax, and credit implications. Each may exist through the life of the project or for specific shorter time periods. Figure 9–1 depicts the project structure used in the case of the $1.1 billion Maui offshore natural gas project in New Zealand. The project began in 1974 and will operate well into the twenty-first century. Maui Development Company Ltd. (MDC) is the vehicle company for the project.

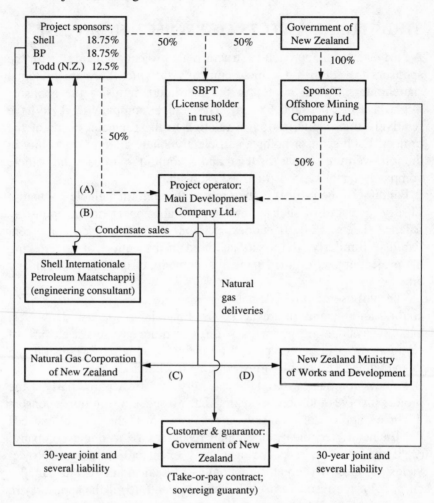

(A) Contract covering design, construction, and operation of offshore production and onshore treatment facilities.
(B) Contract covering onshore and offshore engineering services/consulting.
(C) Contract covering construction of offshore gas transmission system.
(D) Contract covering construction of onshore gas transmission system.

Figure 9–1.   Example of Project Structure: Maui Gas (N. Z.) Project Stage I.

Financial Design

Once the vehicle company has been established, the financing of a project must be "engineered." The financial design process must take into account the risks involved, the various prospective sources of financing, accounting and tax regulations, the possibility of recourse to the various parties, the different entities having an interest in the project, and similar factors. Financial design may be assigned to a financial advisor—possibly an investment or merchant bank. The advisor must have the necessary technical expertise, contacts, track record, and innovative thinking necessary to help stitch together the highly complex financial undertakings required, each of which may have one or more unique characteristics.

Working closely with sponsors' financial staffs, the advisor must pay careful attention to potential sources of finance worldwide, must understand opportunities for laying off risks and achieving leverage targets, and must be able to aid in, identifying project risks and support arrangements, contingencies, foreign exchange aspects, and related facets of the deal. The objective is to minimize the cost and exposure to risk of the sponsor, while making it attractive to prospective lenders and investors. Individual lenders, including local banks in host countries and smaller banks in third countries, may be receptive to particular deals at various times. Attractive "windows" for parts of a financing package are often open only for brief periods of time.

Supplementary financial advisors may be brought in for their special expertise and contacts to arrange official export credits, to resolve legal and tax issues involved in accessing national capital markets, and to coordinate with multilateral development agencies.

The evolving and sometimes conflicting relationship between sponsors and their vehicle company is illustrated by the A$11.9 billion Woodside natural gas project (see Figure 9–2). When the domestic phase of the project had been successfully completed, with financing requirements of A$2.1 billion, some of the sponsors feared that the vehicle company would not be able to arrange the A$9.8 billion funding needed for the second stage, the liquefied natural gas (LNG) export phase, and thus meet commitments and performance obligations over the life of the project. The alleged deficiency, in the view of some of the sponsors, could have deterred Japanese customers from signing long-term LNG sales contracts.

Shell Development and BHP Petroleum, each of which had held an 8.3% share in the domestic phase of the project as well as a minority stake (21.35%) in the main shareholding company, Woodside Petroleum Proprietary Ltd.—which in turn held a 50% share in the project—arranged for a majority takeover of Woodside in June 1985. Their intention was to obtain fresh capital through an earnings dilution

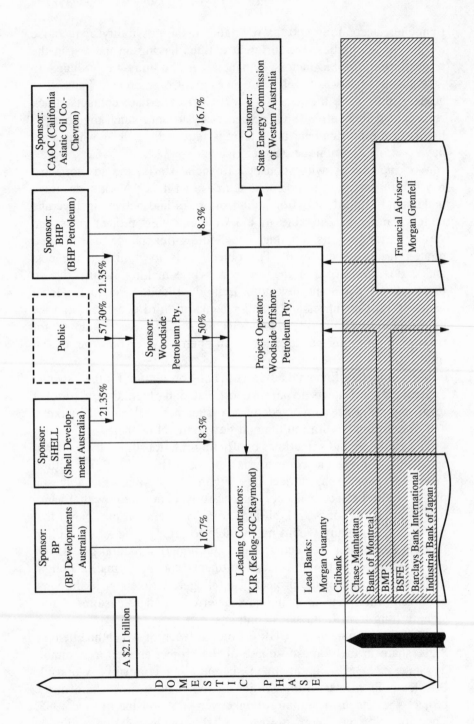

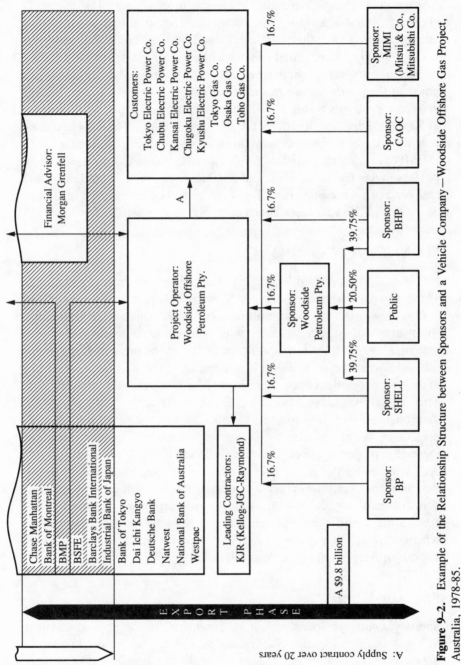

Figure 9–2. Example of the Relationship Structure between Sponsors and a Vehicle Company — Woodside Offshore Gas Project, Australia, 1978-85.

197

that would accompany a rights issue and to gain control of the project itself. Woodside vigorously but unsuccessfully fought the takeover attempt, convinced that sufficient fund raising could be achieved without a rights issue. Fund raising without a rights issue could be accomplished by reinvesting revenues derived from the domestic gas phase of the project, from recourse and nonrecourse loans from banks, and from proceeds resulting from the reduction of Woodside's original 50% participation (to 16.7%) in the export phase. The 33.4% reduction in Woodside's share was taken over by Japan Australia LNG (MIMI) Proprietary—Mitsui & Co. and Mitsubishi Co. as new equity holders of 16.7% each. Shell and BHP added 8.3% each in late 1984. Deliveries of liquefied natural gas to Japan began in 1989 in accordance with a 20-year sales contract signed in August 1985.

FINANCING COMPONENTS

It is useful to identify the principal components of project financing. These usually differ considerably from one project to the next. Generally, however, they use multiple sources of funds. These include short-term and long-term debt, with medium-term lenders often replacing short-term lenders upon completion of the project. Repayment schedules may be quite flexible, including some automatic resetting of debt service under various conditions (e.g., delays and cost overruns). This permits sponsors to develop financial strategy in other parts of their business with less concern for possible unanticipated project cash needs. In order to obtain the most favorable financial arrangements for projects, all conceivable sources of funds must be tapped. As one observer put it: "It is essential that the financial officers know the credit market thoroughly and design the financing to fit existing demand and supply conditions. It's important to know lenders around the world—their preferences, needs and idiosyncrasies—and what one lender is prepared to do that others won't."[2] An analysis of various project financing options follows.

Sponsor Loans

Sponsor loans are loans and advances made by the sponsor-owners of the vehicle company. Such loans would appear on the sponsors' balance sheets, compromising the off–balance sheet intent of project financing. Sponsor-owned captive finance companies, however, can be used to achieve the same objective. The captive finance company, with limited equity investment by the sponsor, can borrow and lend on its own account without altering the financial profile of the parent corporation and can permit greater financial leveraging.

Supplier Credits

Energy projects in particular are highly capital intensive. Much of their total outlays involve machinery and equipment—drilling platforms, steel pipe, draglines, pumps, engines and compressors, communications equipment, and so on. A variety of countries have suppliers who can provide the needed equipment on competitive terms, and their governments may vigorously promote such exports.

Concessionary terms include long maturities, fixed interest rates well below market levels, and attractive insurance cover for lenders. It is advantageous to shop for the most attractive (subsidized) *supplier credit arrangements*—financing provided either directly by governmental export credit agencies or by banks benefiting from government credit subsidies and guarantees.

Such loans can be quite lucrative for commercial banks, especially in Europe, where government export credit agencies assure that banks receive substantially above-market risk-adjusted spreads on approved deals. This means that some banks will provide related loans to the same project at preferential rates if they are guaranteed a piece of the export credit package. In addition to the benefits of below-market fixed interest rates and longer maturities, such credits sometimes are linked to government grants, soft loans, and similar forms of foreign aid to the country where the project is situated. Thus, this component of project financing takes advantage of intense export competition among supplier countries.

A number of potential sources of supplier credits may be approached by project sponsors and their advisors to secure the best possible financing terms for equipment of engineering services. Concessionary credits and/or loan guarantees can be obtained from the Export-Import Bank in the United States, Hermes in West Germany, COFACE in France, the Export Credit Guarantee Department (ECGD) in the United Kingdom, and comparable agencies elsewhere.

For example, in the energy industry an export credit of $650 million was assembled in 1981 by the Nederlandsche Credietverzekering Maatschappij NV credit agency in favor of a Dutch-led joint venture set up to construct an 1,800-kilometer gas pipeline across Argentina. Nacap, a wholly owned subsidiary of the Dutch civil engineering company Royal Boskalis Westminster NV, held a 70% share in the COGASCO Joint Venture (the other two partners, TESCA and PAMAR, were Argentine companies). The entire project was worth $875 million, with three-quarters covered by export credits. The remaining financing was obtained on the Euromarket via a syndicated credit and from individual banks. The financing was nonrecourse with the risks borne by the lenders, who enjoyed a $1\frac{3}{4}\%$ spread over LIBOR on the syndicated Eurocredit (see Figure 9–3).

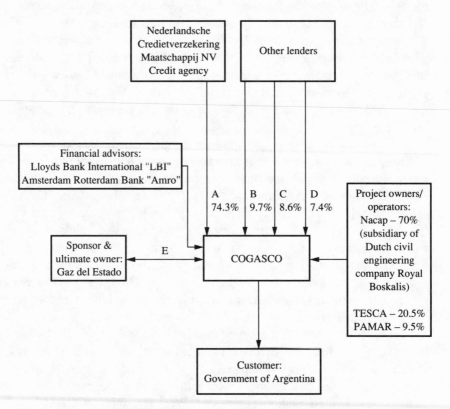

A – Export credit of $650 million including 95% insurance cover
B – Euroloan of $85 million
C – Syndicated standby facility of $75 million
D – Syndicated short-term loan of $65 million
E – Contract covering tariff payment for gas supplied by owners of pipeline

Figure 9–3. Example of a Financing Structure—Cogasco Gas Pipeline Project, Argentina, 1981.

One interesting aspect of this project was the role of the Argentine government, which wanted to avoid increased external indebtedness and involvement in issuing state guarantees. Argentina was aiming at a deal in which the contractors would design and build the pipeline and subsequently own and operate it for a certain period of time. During this period the sponsor and ultimate owner, Gaz del Estado, would pay an agreed charge for the entities of gas supplied. The idea materialized in the form of the Nacap Consortium, which is scheduled to turn over the pipeline to the state in 1996.[3]

Large-scale projects will obviously vary widely in terms of the percentage of total cost accounted for by capital equipment and services eligible for supplier credits. If capital equipment and construction services are to be provided domestically by vendors in the country where the project is located, the prospects for financing through supplier credits will naturally be less.

Customer Credits

Customers can also be an attractive source of financing, especially when a project is specifically designed to provide raw materials or energy to a particular buyer (e.g., an electric utility, steel company, trading house, government procurement agency). For instance, the Kreditanstalt fuer Wiederaufbau (KFW) in West Germany is charged with securing supplies of basic materials for German industry, and it has made 10- to 15-year fixed interest loans available for minerals projects worldwide.

The motivation of the German Government to secure copper supplies, for example, can be seen in the OK Tedi mining project in Papua New Guinea (PNG). German industry retained marketing rights on 50% of the project's output. In turn, the KFW became involved in the project and provided a $100 million loan for development of the mine. Other lenders were the export credit agencies of Australia, Austria, the United Kingdom, and Canada, and commercial banks (led by Citicorp). A further significant portion of the loan package under an Overseas Private Investment Corporation (OPIC) guarantee was financed by U.S. institutional investors (see Figure 9–4).

Security for KFW loans was provided by the German shareholder, Kupferexplorationsgesellschaft (KE).[4] The remaining shareholders in the project and consortium partners BHP (Broken Hill Proprietary Co., Ltd. of Australia) and Amoco (Standard Oil of Indiana) underwrote other commercial obligations. The PNG government held a 20%

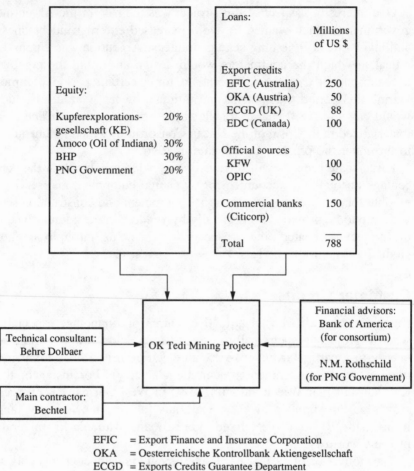

Loans:

	Millions of US $
Export credits	
EFIC (Australia)	250
OKA (Austria)	50
ECGD (UK)	88
EDC (Canada)	100
Official sources	
KFW	100
OPIC	50
Commercial banks (Citicorp)	150
Total	788

Equity:

Kupferexplorations-gesellschaft (KE)	20%
Amoco (Oil of Indiana)	30%
BHP	30%
PNG Government	20%

Technical consultant: Behre Dolbaer

OK Tedi Mining Project

Financial advisors:
Bank of America (for consortium)

N.M. Rothschild (for PNG Government)

Main contractor: Bechtel

EFIC	= Export Finance and Insurance Corporation
OKA	= Oesterreichische Kontrollbank Aktiengesellschaft
ECGD	= Exports Credits Guarantee Department
EDC	= Export Development Corporation
KFW	= Kreditanstalt fuer Wiederaufbau
OPIC	= Overseas Private Investment Corporation

For tax reasons under the German law, the PNG government agreed to transfer 5% of its share to the German companies so that their project share would officially reach 25%. The German companies covenanted to vote the 5% transferred shares in accordance with government directions and pass through all dividends directly to the government.

Figure 9–4. Example of a Financing Structure—OK Tedi Mining Project, Papua New Guinea, 1980–81. (*Source:* W.S. Pintz, *OK Tedi Evolution at a Third World Mining Project*, London: Mining Books Ltd., 1984; reprinted by permission.)

equity stake in the project. It gained access to the equivalent of US $12 million (denominated in European currency units) through the European Investment Bank's (EIB) mining fund to finance part of its equity contribution. Under the terms of the aid agreement with the

European community, the PNG government became eligible to borrow substantial additional funds on top of the basic loan at concessionary rates (20-year term at 2% fixed interest). Also, a portion of the KFW loans was refinanced through the EIB.

Again, the motive behind these advantageous financial arrangements was primarily political. The German government was even willing to underwrite exploration risks in granting loans to the KE investment group for up to 60% of its total exploration cost. These loans were to be repaid only if the project was developed; otherwise, they would turn into an outright grant.

The Overseas Mineral Resources Corporation in Japan has likewise provided equity capital for joint ventures abroad. U.S. utilities have sometimes subsidized exploration and development of energy resources through advance payments, and private German and Japanese buyers of metals have either been willing to provide direct financing or to help secure support from government sources. Individual firms, trading companies, and minerals consortia have made sizeable loans against future resource deliveries in order to assure themselves of reliable supplies.

Advance payments by sponsors may also be used for this purpose—in effect serving as loans to the vehicle company to be repaid in the form of shipments after the facility becomes operational. The absence of customer credits—perhaps due to financial limitations or lack of agreement on price concessions—may sometimes be partially offset by loans from indigenous sources in the country where the project is located, giving other prospective lenders an indication of the project's importance.

Insurance Companies, Pension Funds, and Bonded Debt

Insurance companies and pension funds, traditional sources of long-term financing in many countries, would appear to be ideal participants in project financing packages, because the gestation periods on large-scale ventures are often very long. The relatively stable and predictable cash flows of such nonbank institutions would seem to allow them to finance at much longer maturities than commercial banks, for example. However, insurance companies and pension funds generally demand commensurately higher interest rates as well as exceedingly strict security arrangements or guarantees. And in many countries, including the United States, they are severely restricted in their lending abroad. This could require a supplementary guarantee from their home government, or it may negate their participation altogether.

Lack of investor interest in anything but conventional government and corporate debt all but precludes the international bond markets as a source of financing for projects until they are up and running with a proven track record. Purely domestic public debt markets are usually equally inaccessible, although private placements can sometimes be used to good advantage—particularly in conjunction with bank financing.

Lease Financing

Another potentially useful source of project finance is leasing, which may have important legal, tax, and accounting advantages. A leasing company (perhaps bank owned) typically holds title to mobile equipment used on a project, claims depreciation for tax purposes, and leases it to the project operator, who in turn may be able to claim lease payments as an expense for tax purposes. The leasing company may also pass some of its tax benefits on to the operator in the form of lower rentals. The lessor, in turn, may finance the equipment through long-term borrowing secured by the equipment itself, often at relatively favorable rates of interest.

Commercial Bank Loans

Lending by commercial banks comprises a critical part of the typical project financing package, generally in the short and medium maturities priced on a floating-rate basis. Bank loans usually cover the critical earlier years of a project and traditionally have involved full recourse to sponsors or third-party guarantors. As noted earlier, they may also be serviced by production payments on a nonrecourse basis if appropriate guarantees can be provided and if the issue of legal claim to the minerals in the ground can be satisfactorily resolved. Bank loans are often arranged on a syndicated basis, which means that multiple banks must be convinced of the soundness of the loan and the project. Successful bank financing depends in part on the "fit"between the term over which loans are needed and the repayment requirements specified by lenders. For many projects, financial needs may extend well beyond conventional bank lending terms, sometimes limiting this form of financing to shorter periods in the construction or initial operating stages.

Equity

While a central aspect of project financing is the undercapitalization of the vehicle company, equity capital can nevertheless cover a significant part of total project cost. Sponsors may inject cash into the project, particularly in the very early planning and start-up stages, or they may contribute to the engineering labor force, know-how, or administration. In addition, third parties, particularly potential customers, may be prepared to provide substantial equity capital to a project on a minority participation basis. In a few cases, such as Eurotunnel, a major public equity offering may be undertaken to form the basis for large-scale debt financing.

Financial Profile

Other potential sources of project funds may include wealthy individuals (domestic and foreign), central banks or monetary authorities, and investment management firms. Participation forms may include common or preferred stock, notes and debentures, convertible debentures, trade credit, and commercial paper. Straight or unsecured loans, often enhanced by warrants, conversion rights, or rights to other securities are also potential sources. Local-currency financing may be secured from indigenous banks, particularly for working capital purposes, or possibly on a longer-term basis from local insurance companies or other sources of term financing. Often one form of financing, such as subordinated loans, will make participation more attractive to one or more other sources of funding. Certainly, the financial "mix" or "profile" of a project will tend to differ substantially at various points in its life.

An example of such a financial profile, and specifically the role of equity finance, is the COMINAK Uranium Development Project in Niger. The joint venture was developed in the mid-1970s by Japanese, French, Spanish, and Niger interests holding 25%, 34%, 10%, and 31%, respectively, of the equity capital of 3.5 billion CFA francs.

A Japanese investment company, Overseas Uranium Resources Development Corporation (OURD), had been established for this project and held a ¥5.4 billion equity position. OURD shareholding

Electric companies	Trading Companies
The Tokyo Electric Co., Inc.	Mitsui & Co., Ltd.
The Chubu Electric Co., Inc.	Mitsubishi Corp.
The Kansai Electric Power Co., Ltd.	Sumitomo Shoji Kaisha, Ltd.
Chugoku Electric Power Co., Inc.	Nissho-Iwai Co., Ltd.
Hokuriku Electric Power Co., Inc.	C. Ito & Co., Ltd.
Tohoku Electric Power Co., Inc.	Marubeni Corp.
Shikoku Electric Power Co., Inc.	
Kyushu Electric Power Co., Inc.	
The Hokkaido Electric Power Co., Inc.	*Manufacturers*
	Hitachi, Ltd.
Mining Companies	Tokyo Shibaura Electric Co., Ltd.
	Mitsubishi Heavy Industries, Ltd.
Mitsui Mining & Smelting Co., Ltd.	Sumitomo Electric Industries, Ltd.
Toho Zinc Co., Ltd.	The Furukawa Electric Co., Ltd.
Mitsubishi Metal Corp.	Fuji Electric Co., Ltd.
Nippon Mining Co., Ltd.	
Sumitomo Metal Mining Co., Ltd.	
The Dowa Co., Ltd.	The Industrial Bank of Japan, Ltd.
Furukawa Co., Ltd.	
Nittetsu Mining Co., Ltd.	
Mitsui Mining Co., Ltd.	*Mr. Yoshiteru Suzuki (Chairman of the*
Mitsubishi Mining & Cement Co., Ltd.	*Dowa Co., Ltd.)*

Figure 9–5. Shareholders of OURD, COMINAK Project Niger, 1974. (*Source:* Hidea Ishihara, "Financing for Energy Resources Development Projects: Japanese Experience, *Revue l'Energie Le Financement des Investissenents Energetiques* [Energy Investment Finance], August–September; 1980, p. 220; reprinted by permission)

consisted of 32 companies—9 electric power companies (36.7%), 10 mining companies (28%), 6 trading companies (20.6%), 6 electric machinery manufacturers (6.9%), and 1 bank (4.8%)—and 1 individual (4.4%)—the chairman of Dowa Co. Ltd., itself a shareholder in the project (see Figure 9–5). Most of the companies involved were themselves directly or indirectly interested in the final product, uranium. OURD absorbed roughly half of the project's output.

Japanese debt financing for exploration and development (representing 70% of total project funding) was provided by the Japanese Export-Import Bank as well as private banks. The funds were subsequently re-lent to the joint venture company, COMINAK (see Figure 9–6).

As illustrated in this example, corporations involved in major projects often do not have the strong financial capacity of major international mineral or oil companies. Hence, the participation of a large number of companies as equity holders is often necessary.[5]

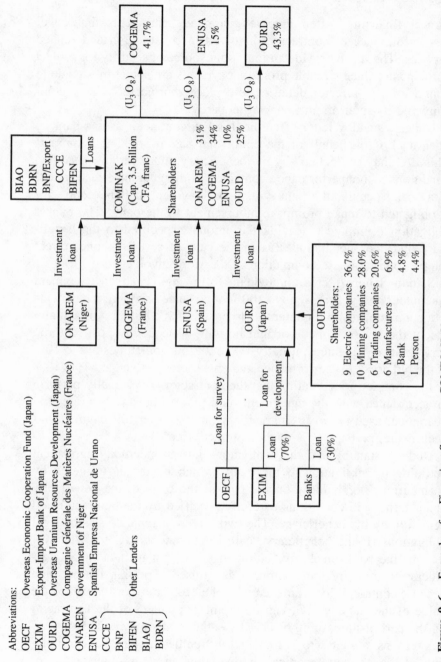

Abbreviations:

OECF   Overseas Economic Cooperation Fund (Japan)
EXIM   Export-Import Bank of Japan
OURD   Overseas Uranium Resources Development (Japan)
COGEMA Compagnie Générale des Matières Nucléaires (France)
ONAREN Government of Niger
ENUSA   Spanish Empresa Nacional de Urano
CCCE
BNP   Other Lenders
BIFEN
BIAO/
BDRN

Figure 9–6. Example of a Financing Structure—COMINAK Uranium Development Project, Niger 1974/75. (*Source:* Hidea Ishihara, "Financing for Energy Resources Development Projects Japanese Experience, *Revue l'Energie Le Financement des Investissements Energetiques* [Energy Investment Finance], August–September; 1980, p. 220; reprinted by permission)

207

Standby Letters of Credit and Guarantee Facilities

Project financings often involve guarantee instruments that cover the performance of contractors involved in construction and related services. These can provide an important source of security for project participants, since sizeable progress payments are sometimes made to contractors. Contractor default could place a project's vehicle company and its sponsors in financial jeopardy.

Under a standby letter of credit (L/C), a contractor asks a bank to open an L/C on behalf of the entity that has awarded the contract. This L/C may be "called" by the beneficiary under certain, specified conditions of nonperformance contained in the guarantee instrument. If a "call" occurs, the bank will make payment and the contractor is obligated to make prompt reimbursement to the bank. The bank's obligation is limited to paying the amounts specified to the beneficiary and does not include (as in the case of a surety bond) direct intervention to assure completion of the work involved.

Standby letters of credit include the following: (1) advance payment guarantee, posted against up to 100% of advance or progress payments to a contractor; (2) bid guarantee, to ensure that a bidder will actually accept the award if made or that he will subsequently post required performance guarantees, usually 1% to 2% but sometimes 5% to 10% of the bid price; (3) performance guarantee, often valued at 5% to 10% of the contract price, stating that the contractor will actually perform in accordance with the agreement; and (4) maintenance or retention guarantee, used to cover contractor warranties after full payment has been made, perhaps 10% of the contract price.

Under a standby L/C the contractor signs an indemnity agreement outlining his obligation to the bank, which in turn is triggered by an incurrence of liability on the part of the bank to the beneficiary under terms and conditions carefully specified by the contractor and agreed to by the beneficiary. The two represent separate sets of legal obligations. If the beneficiary "calls" the standby L/C for whatever reason, the bank must pay, although it will not incur a loss unless indemnification by the contractor is refused. For this reason, and because contractor losses in the event of a "call" may vastly exceed the value of the standby L/C, careful credit assessment of the contractor on the part of the issuing bank is essential. Calls may occur for various reasons: a contractor's financial difficulties may prevent completion of the project; technical or operating problems may occur; or the beneficiary may act in an arbitrary or fraudulent manner. The latter possibility reinforces the need to specify conditions of default, possibly including independent certification, since the bank's obligation is unconditional.

In order to backstop its position, a bank issuing a standby L/C or other type of guarantee may require a lien on the contractor's assets, other security interest, cash margins, or certain covenants related to debt and coverage tests. The guarantee instrument may also be structured to diminish over time, while the project draws to completion and the risks involved decrease commensurately. Banks' fees for standby letters of credit or other guarantee instruments can be substantial and are paid by the contractor, presumably to be passed forward to the extent possible in the contract price.

Foreign Exchange Considerations

Finally, foreign exchange considerations can assume a major role in project financings since cash needs, financial obligations, and resource sales will often be denominated in different currencies. The risks involved may be addressed in the short term by means of currency swaps or borrowings in the currencies needed; in the long term, they may be addressed by financing in the appropriate currencies, swaps, long-dated forward contracts, and local-currency financings. Because of the extended duration of project financing, the foreign exchange aspects can be exceedingly complex, testing the ingenuity of the financial advisors and banks involved.

COFINANCING

The World Bank, the regional development banks in Asia, Latin America, and Africa, and other intergovernmental institutions have traditionally been in the business of project financing. They are often able to provide attractive terms because of direct agency financing by participating national governments or because the agency is able to fund itself in the long term on domestic or international markets on a favorable basis. Particularly large projects in developing countries that exceed conventional financing capabilities may be able to proceed under a cofinancing arrangement with international institutions, based on agreements with the host country government.

Cofinancing can take the form of *joint financing,* in which all lenders share responsibility for the entire project, or *parallel financing,* in which each lender finances a separate part of the project. The

Table 9–1. World Bank Lending Operations by Major Purpose
(as of June 30, 1985)

	IBRD Loans [a]	Percentage of Total
Agriculture and rural development	23,411.20	20.73%
Development finance companies	10,432.00	9.24%
Education	4,203.90	3.72%
Energy		
Oil, gas, and coal	5,506.00	4.88%
Power	20,492.50	18.15%
Industry		
Iron and steel	1,388.80	1.23%
Mining, other extractive	1,117.20	0.99%
Other industries	4,873.00	4.32%
Nonproject	6,932.40	6.14%
Population, health, nutrition	542.20	0.48%
Small-scale enterprises	2,727.80	2.42%
Technical assistance	200.60	0.18%
Telecommunications	1,828.20	1.62%
Tourism	363.60	0.32%
Transportation	20,580.80	18.23%
Urban development	2,901.10	2.57%
Water supply and sewage	5,420.50	4.80%
Total	112,921.80	100.00%

a. In millions of dollars.

SOURCE: *World Bank Annual Report*, 1985.

World Bank has a long history of bringing other lenders and investors in on large-scale natural resources ventures for which it has taken a leadership role.

In recent years, however, only about 7% of World Bank global lending has gone into natural resources projects. As Table 9–1 shows, most of the funding went into agricultural and rural development, power, and transportation projects. With respect to the World Bank's cofinancing activities, the share attributable to natural resources projects is higher. From 1975 to 1984 it represented between 10% and 15% of World Bank cofinancing. Slightly under half of the financing for World Bank projects came from colenders—that is, official institutions, export credit agencies, and commercial banks.

Cofinancing from official sources was concentrated on projects in low-income developing countries. Since 1975 about two-thirds of World Bank resources have gone to countries with a per capita GNP of under $1,000. As far as export credit agencies are concerned, cofinancing mainly went into the wealthier developing countries. Commercial bank lending follows the same pattern, and the tendency is even more pronounced. More than 95% of private cofinancing has been concentrated on the higher-income developing countries. Only one-third of World Bank cofinancing has gone into the low-income group of developing countries. However, this is partly offset if cofinancing from the International Development Agency, a World Bank affiliate, is included. In absolute terms, overall World Bank cofinancing amounted to $4.5 billion in 1984, for example. However, the relative amount of cofinancing—only about 1% of the total stock of World Bank loans outstanding to developing countries—remains small.

Cofinancing is clearly desirable for projects in which the resources of the borrower, the World Bank, and other immediately related sources of finance are insufficient to cover necessary outlays. It "stretches" World Bank resources over a broader portfolio of projects without significantly diluting its degree of responsibility or the care taken in project appraisal. At the same time, it gives colenders additional assurances of the quality of projects and the prospect of reduced sovereign risk attributable to the World Bank's presence.

How World Bank Cofinancing Operates

In evaluating the financial requirements of a project likely to require cofinancing, the World Bank looks first to prospective sources of long-term, fixed-rate financing. Most often these are found among official bilateral or multilateral institutions or official export credit agencies, and generally they are tied to purchases in a particular country. Funding is then sought from commercial sources to fill remaining gaps. In the case of a typical electric power project, for example, the Bank reviews a specific portion of the borrower's investment program and agrees to finance certain subprojects within it. Funds from private lenders are then sought to help finance other subprojects closely related to those financed by the Bank.

Generally, the Bank's resources can only be used to finance the foreign exchange costs of goods and services identified in advance, and only those expenditures that are made after approval of the loan by the Bank's executive directors. Hence, borrowers often find that commercial financing is required to cover expenditures that may not qualify for World Bank assistance, such as start-up costs, other imported goods and services, local procurement, and working capital needs. In addition to the use of private cofinancing to complete the financing plan of a project as defined by the Bank, there have cases in which cofinancing was sought to help fund investment programs that are complementary to, but not included in, Bank-assisted projects.

When negotiating the Bank's loan, borrowers generally have to make two decisions: (1) whether to approach commercial lenders for cofinancing and (2) whether to take advantage of the formal World Bank cofinancing arrangements (i.e., whether there is a perceived benefit from the World Bank's involvement with prospective private financial sources). If the Bank and borrower agree that the participation of commercial lenders is appropriate, the Bank advises the borrower that it is willing to consider entering into formal cofinancing arrangements.

It is common practice for borrowers at this point to test the reaction of international financial markets through informal discussions with bankers. Such discussions involve the possible terms and conditions of private sector financing that would be supported by a formal association with the World Bank compared with similar but nonassociated loans. This advantage may take several forms. For example, a commercial bank may agree to a longer amortization schedule than it would without a formal World Bank link. Borrowers may also benefit from resulting contacts with a larger number of banks in different financial markets, from an increase in the amounts that individual banks are willing to lend as a result of the World Bank's presence, or from less stringent legal documentation. And although interest rates and fees depend on market conditions, competition among commercial banks for cofinancing opportunities has tended to ensure that the borrowers obtain the finest available pricing.

The World Bank and Private Sector Lenders

Under the World Bank's cofinancing program, borrowers are ultimately responsible for selecting the private sector lenders brought into a deal. However, the Bank does provide assistance by making cofinancing opportunities widely known to potential lenders and often provides borrowers with names of banks in the major capital markets that have in the past shown an interest in cofinancing. At the request of borrowers, the Bank also takes the initiative in establishing contacts with prospective private sector lenders. The purpose of such assistance is to ensure that borrowers make a reasonable effort to explore the prospects for commercial financing with a representative sample of banks before reaching a decision. The Bank encourages private sector lenders and borrowers to establish early and direct contact whenever a cofinancing opportunity has been identified.

Timing in the selection of private sector lenders need not coincide with the processing of a World Bank loan, and in certain cases the borrower will request a commitment from private sector lenders only shortly before the deal is submitted to the executive directors for approval. World Bank management does not request approval unless there is a reasonable assurance that the project's financing plan will be successfully completed. In many cases, commercial sources of funds are not needed until the later stages of a project, sometimes as long as a year or more after the approval of the World Bank loan.

The terms and conditions of the commercial loans under cofinancing are negotiated directly between the private sector lender and the borrower, just as the World Bank negotiates, independently of colenders, the terms and conditions of its own commitments directly with the borrower. Once drafts of the loan documentation pertaining to each lender become available, the World Bank and the private sector lenders agree on any cross-reference clauses to be included, as well as provisions to be incorporated in the text of the memorandum of agreement. The World Bank reserves the right to approve clauses in the loan agreement between the commercial bank and the borrower that affect its own rights, such as the cross-default clause.

To date, all World Bank borrowers that have secured cofinancing from private sources have chosen to borrow in the Euromarket, usually on a syndicated basis. The lead banks, acting on the borrower's mandate, assume full responsibility for arranging and managing the loans, although, at the request of the borrower, the World Bank's cofinancing staff has occasionally helped to identify potential syndicate participants. The applicable loan agreements have followed established Euroloan precedent with respect to terms and conditions, again negotiated directly between the private sector lenders and the borrower. Since the disbursement procedures of commercial banks differ substantially from those of the World Bank, they are handled separately and independently. Although it is common practice to agree upon periodic staged disbursements over a fixed period, loans are frequently drawn down in a lump sum soon after signing. Similarly, payment of interest and principal to colenders are set independently of the World Bank loan.[6]

A longer-term benefit related to World Bank cofinancing activities involves introducing borrowers in developing countries to new commercial bank lenders, thus assisting them in securing continued access to international capital markets. At the same time, commercial banks emphasizing the financing of specific projects, as opposed to country lending, have found new clients in developing countries.

World Bank projects for which private cofinancing has been arranged have historically been concentrated in the industrial and utility sectors. Projects in these two sectors account for more than half of the cofinancing undertaken, both in numbers of projects and amounts raised. More recently, however, cofinancing has been directed to projects in other sectors as well—a shift very much in line with the World Bank's evolving lending policy. Although World Bank cofinancing with private sources has grown quite rapidly and has become more diversified, the number and scale of these operations have not so far been particularly large when compared with the volume of all project lending by private banks. For those projects benefiting from the Bank's cofinancing program, the share of private banks has been about 73% of World Bank funds for the same projects.

RISK ASSESSMENT AND RISK MANAGEMENT IN PROJECT FINANCE

As we have seen, project financing is intended to design financial structures to be serviced from future cash flows, often with limited recourse to the project's sponsors. Financing that is structured in this way limits the burden placed on sponsors' balance sheets and diminishes future borrowing capacity and creditworthiness less than other modes of financing. Lenders and investors rely on the project's expected revenue stream and often carry a share of the technical, commercial, and political risks. Thus, evaluation of risk and the application of risk-limiting techniques is critical in project financing because of the heavy reliance on the project itself to provide effective debt service. There are at least nine distinct types of risks lenders face in project financing.

Resource risk involves the possibility that the oil, gas, or minerals in the ground, which represent the basis for debt service in natural resource and energy projects, are not there in the required quality or quantity.

Input or throughput risk concerns nonextractive projects such as power plants or pipelines, in which the basic viability of the project depends on the availability and price of energy, raw materials, or other resources under the original terms. In the case of tunnels, bridges, and similar projects, the risk is that supply or demand factors may result in a traffic shortfall, leading to a revenue deficiency.

Technical risk relates to the engineering characteristics of the project itself. A project may turn into an outright failure for technical reasons or may result in substantial cost overruns, requiring significant additional capital infusions.

Timing risk focuses on the possibility that delays, from whatever source, will stretch out the period of construction before the cash flows that support the financing actually begin. Such delays (especially in an inflationary period) can be the source of substantial cost overruns and can raise interest charges considerably. Even relatively short delays may lead to extensive escalation of construction costs. For example, six major natural resource projects examined during the late 1970s ended up (on average) 107% above their initial cost estimates.[7] Delays occurring in liquefied natural gas (LNG) projects, for example, tend to have a greater impact on the financial situation than delays in oil field projects, where intermediate cash flows can be generated as the project is developed in stages. Generally, LNG projects only become operational once the last piece of equipment from the offshore production and collection facilities to the onshore liquefaction plant and the transportation network is in place.

Completion risk (sometimes called *precompletion risk*) combines technical and timing risks. Completion problems include: errors in engineering and design; construction delays due to strikes, weather, or late delivery of equipment and supplies; unanticipated topological problems; new and untested construction techniques under prevailing conditions; and cost escalation due to a serious lack of skilled labor.

In practice, the lenders have traditionally been willing to rely on cash flows from projects only after they have become operational, requiring the sponsors to provide financial supports and guarantees before loans become strictly nonrecourse. More recently, there has been a greater willingness on the part of lenders to accept, under appropriate circumstances, a range of precompletion risks that previously the sponsors alone had to carry.

In the early 1960s, several nonrecourse project financing deals appeared in the minerals industry. Freeport Minerals, for example, undertook a $120 million copper project in Indonesia and a $305 million nickel mining venture in Australia, with equity investments of less than 25% and totally nonrecourse loans—albeit with substantial customer financing and full support of U.S. lenders by the Export-Import Bank and the Overseas Private Insurance Corporation. Another example was the Oaky Creek coal project of Mount Isa Mines Ltd. (MIM) in Australia. For this project banks lent $345 million without a project completion guarantee and without comprehensive sales contracts to cover the project's output over the life of the loans—and with MIM able to abandon the project at small cost if things went badly.

By the late 1970s and early 1980s, nonrecourse loans were being arranged for petroleum projects in which, for a price, the borrowers did not have to guarantee completion. For example, Marathon Oil omitted the traditional completion guarantees in a $100 million, 10-bank syndicated loan for the Kinsale Head natural gas field in the Irish Sea in 1977 and another $200 million loan in 1981. It organized yet another $650 million nonrecourse financing for a $2 billion project in the Brae (North Sea) field. The estimated cost was $\frac{1}{4}$% to $\frac{3}{8}$% over the full-recourse alternative, with the sponsors free to walk away from the project if it became uneconomical according to a set of agreed criteria. Of course, the contractual debt service involved was significantly smaller than the estimated project cash flows in order to provide the banks with an acceptable margin of safety. The funds raised by Elf Aquitaine and Total for the Alwyn North Field (North Sea) in 1984 involved margins of $\frac{3}{4}$% over LIBOR, excess reserves of 25%, and a complete offloading of the resource risk.

In the 1981 Woodside natural gas project mentioned earlier, there was no completion guarantee for the company's 50% share of the development costs, but there was a guarantee by Shell Australia and Broken Hill Proprietary of a standby facility of at least $345 million if additional funding was needed. Bankers at the time considered Woodside the deal that revolutionized energy-related lending, since it was essentially the first time banks were prepared to assume all of the project completion risks from the outset. Similarly, Atlantic Richfield in 1981 obtained a $950 million loan secured only by its 45% interest in the Kuparu (Alaska) oil field, estimated at 330 million barrels of recoverable reserves.

Market risk concerns future demand for the product or service supplied by a given project. Prices for many raw materials are naturally volatile, and they also may be subject to significant long-term (secular) shifts over the extensive period of time that faces the financing. What happens, for example, when demand for the customer's own output undergoes a severe and prolonged recession? In addition, some products and services such as natural gas, transportation, and electric power are highly dependent on local or regional market developments and may easily encounter a demand shortfall. This problem may be complicated by difficulties in storing or finding alternative uses for certain resources (e.g., natural gas). In assessing market risk, demand forecasts clearly hinge on such factors as price and income elasticities, competition, exchange rates, availability of substitutes, governmental policies, political developments, and environmental concerns.

Operating risk focuses on the long period of time that projects and their financing generally involves. During this time, costs may change or labor, transportation, or other critical elements may be disrupted by external sources or management incompetence. Operating problems also include poor engineering or design work, unexpectedly high maintenance costs due to corrosion or wear, price increases on energy equipment and materials, exchange rate movements, the inability to meet output targets or quality specifications, and other factors.

The Greenville nickel-cobalt project in Queensland, Australia, for example, encountered serious problems after energy costs rose dramatically and fundamentally altered the economics of latrite nickel processing. The fuel component of operating costs rose from 10% to over 50% during the 1970s. The results included four debt reschedulings, a massive overhang of unamortized debt and deferred interest, and loans written down on the part of most of the banks involved.[8] A study of 17 new ventures in the 1960s and early 1970s found that over half of them encountered serious cash flow problems that required a restructuring of debt service arrangements, although in only one case was there a loss to lenders.[9]

An important source of operating risk is the quality and stability of the local labor pool, particularly in developing countries. This risk often can be reduced by training programs, astute labor relations, and tapping external labor sources. Prospective operating expenses and their variability, project location, complexity of environmental problems, and similar factors may also influence perceived operating risks. The best assurance to lenders is a proven track record under similar circumstances on the part of the project operator. Management-related sources of operating risk are of direct concern to sponsors and operators if the project is to be completed and operate as planned. Project logistics, links to subcontractors, labor relations, and environmental conflicts are often of major concern here.

Force majeure risk involves acts of God, such as earthquakes, hurricanes, or other weather-related calamities, warfare, and other uncontrollable events that may lead to failure, escalated costs, delayed completion, or disrupted operations. Provisions to take on force majeure risk are usually accepted by lenders in project financings—generally for a limited duration only.

Political risk involves the political conditions that surround a project during the period covered by a financing. Many of the loans in Australian project finance during the 1970s could be attributed not only to that country's wealth of natural resources, but also to a modest perceived level of country risk (as compared with alternative sites in developing countries). Terrorist acts, labor disruptions, tax changes, newly imposed pollution controls, invasions from abroad, and similar events arising from the political environment fall under this general heading. So do expropriation or nationalization, imposition of exchange controls, changes in royalties or depletion allowances, pressures for indigenization of equity or human resources—some of which may be imposed retroactively.

A major contentious issue illustrating the role of political problems arose in Papua New Guinea (PNG) in 1974 between Rio Tinto Zinc's Australian subsidiary and the PNG government over a copper mining project on the island of Bougainville. Bougainville Copper Ltd. (BCL), in which the PNG government held a 20.2% share, realized an enormous profit of over £100 million in the first year of operation, causing several factions in the PNG government to demand outright control of the project and an 80% profit tax. They considered the mining concession agreement signed in 1967 with the Australian government, at that time acting as administrator of the territory of Papua New Guinea on behalf of the United Nations, to be one-sided and heavily in the company's favor. The rise in copper prices in world markets during the 1970s had not been foreseen at the time.

Conzinc Riotinto renegotiated the investment agreement in 1974 with the PNG government so as not to place the entire project in jeopardy. In the intervening years political unrest in the territory (e.g., domestic eruption of tribal warfare, sectionalism, violent strikes and riots), caused substantial damage to the mine.

Issues related to country problems should be covered in standard assessments of country risk carried out independently by project lenders and investors. However, a given project may have a risk profile that is quite different from that of the country as a whole. A project may be politically sensitive in a country that is otherwise characterized by a very low degree of assessed risk. The specific kind of natural resources involved, project location, employment of nationals, the nature of the target markets and downstream uses, and shifting government and interest group priorities may dictate a project risk profile that may be a cause for lender concern. This deviation of "project-specific risk" from conventional country risk often requires complex analysis.

Variance in Expected Returns

As with any type of business risks, those related to project financing hinge on the variance in the expected returns to the lenders and investors. Some of these risks are related to short-term exposures and will be eliminated early in the life of the project or are incurred and eliminated during comparatively brief periods as the project moves ahead. Others involve relatively long-term exposures that are characterized by a rather high degree of variance in expected returns. Moreover, for some lenders, variance in expected returns is not symmetrical (they can only lose, never gain), while for investors variance in expected returns describes the chance of gain as well as loss that may be attributed to some of the sources of project risk. Finally, it is important to note that, within the framework of a given project, exposure to risk does not lend itself to diversification—unlike cross-border lending to countries, where some local borrowers may fare quite differently than others in response to changed country conditions.

In essence, lenders have to decide which of these risks are "bankable" and which must be covered by any of the available contractual arrangements involving either project sponsors or third parties (e.g., customers, governments, or international organizations). This decision depends on prior experience, technical expertise, financial innovation, and the perceived degree of control over a wide range of variables. Such perspectives, of course, differ among participants in project financings—a complex deal can yield several different views on who is really carrying the risks involved. Lenders' perceptions can also be self-reinforcing, leading to a "herd mentality" and an erosion of independence in evaluating project risks.

Willingness to Assume Risks

For banks, assumption of a major share of completion, operating, and market risk in various projects during the 1970s and 1980s clearly stemmed from competitive pressures among the major players in international project financing. It was also a product of increased inhouse sophistication and technical competence in evaluating project risks, and increased familiarity (1) with specific types of energy projects, (2) with political and economic conditions in those areas of the world most active in the development of new projects, and (3) with the competence and reliability of individual sponsors with whom a sustained coincidence of interest must exist over the life of the project. These dimensions form the basis for barriers to entry and profitability in project financing.

A bank's willingness to assume project risks is dependent on the specific project or sponsor. For example, lenders might be fairly comfortable evaluating the risks associated with a new production platform in the North Sea if they have arranged similar deals in the past. In the case of the Woodside project cited previously, the proven reserves at prospective market prices were considered well in excess of the required capital outlays and debt-servicing projections, the output being sold in Western Australia and later in Japan. In the case of Shell and BHP, the projects' sponsors represented highly regarded and experienced operators in the energy field.

The Frigg Natural Gas Project

A spectacular instance of just how things can go wrong in project financings is the Frigg natural gas project in the North Sea, jointly owned by British and Norwegian interests. Between 1972 and 1977, when the first gas was delivered to British Gas Corporation, the cost of the project rose from a budgeted $1 billion to $4 billion, and it faced a gamut of political and technical disasters that put it in jeopardy on more than one occasion.

The first political problems arose when the U.S. Export-Import Bank turned down a request for export credits covering the second project phase, following the Watergate affair and the subsequent changes in the U.S. government. The Frigg project was saved by the concessionary credits provided by European export credit agencies. Both the Norwegian Exportfinans and British Export Credit Guarantee Department granted the partners in Frigg export financing for installations in their respective territorial waters. The Norwegians, using creative legal reasoning, agreed to consider the entire North Sea a special zone eligible for export credits. Prior to the start of financial negotiations, Norway and Britain had already made some geographical adjustments and redrawn the median line dividing their territorial waters. Had this not been the case, borrowings on the basis of the initial distribution of natural resources would have entailed further technical, legal, and political problems.

The 1973 oil crisis had a negative impact on the project because it shocked the Eurocredit and Eurobonds markets and accelerated cost inflation associated with most of the required capital outlays. Moreover, serious problems occurred throughout the construction phase. These ranged from industrial disputes and strikes in the United Kingdom to management errors due to lack of experience in estimating time and funds necessary for the offshore work. In addition, uncertainty about changes in British tax law prevented the conclusion of a lease finance agreement which would have permitted greater off–balance sheet financing. As a result, costs escalated beyond all projections and financing requirements grew commensurately. At the same time, financial markets were under strain and the projected profitability of the project was declining sharply. As a crowning blow, a major technical disaster occurred. The first drilling platform and the ballast tanks collapsed and sank. A U.S. regional bank and a Norwegian bank abandoned the project at this stage. In their view, the credibility of the engineering was seriously flawed.

What eventually saved the Frigg project was the rapid increase in oil prices in the 1970s. Frigg's gas price had an escalation formula linked to the price of oil. Moreover, in 1976 stability returned to the Euromarket and sources of funding once more became plentiful.[10]

Evaluation and Mitigation of Project-Related Risks

As noted, some of the sources of risk to lenders and investors in project financing relate only to completion of a project, while others are longer term and concern project operation. Evaluating and reducing both completion and operating risks require expertise and ingenuity.

Financial management of these risks generally relies on various guarantees. These may be *direct* (full and unqualified commitment on the part of the guarantor), *limited* (in terms of amount or duration), or *contingent* (involving relatively unlikely events that lenders may feel the need to be covered for to secure their participation). Guarantees may be *implied* as an obligation of the guarantor or *indirect* via performance of some related activities that will, in effect, make the lender whole in the event of problems.

Resource risk facing lenders is normally evaluated by independent technical studies. The sponsoring firm or consortium will have made its own evaluation of the available quantity and quality of the resources to be recovered. This information will be carefully assessed by the major lenders' in-house technical experts and confirmed by outside consultants with cost of any further independent evaluation of natural resource reserves borne by the vehicle company or its sponsors. Project financings will almost always involve multiple financial institutions. The technical assessment of available resources must be convincing to the lead institutions and to the other participants. This procedure has the added advantage of independent verification of the viability of the project.

Similarly, the sponsor's own evaluation of the technical problems involved in completing a project needs to be assessed in-house and possibly by engineering consultants or other outside experts. The track record of the sponsors in successfully undertaking comparable projects elsewhere is of great importance. Projects involving new technologies or particularly adverse conditions (climatic, topological) tend to multiply the risks incurred.

Limiting Exposure to Completion Risk

Lenders often require completion guarantees from project sponsors, which unconditionally warrant that performance will be as specified (quantity, quality, timing, and minimum period of operation) and that any and all cost overruns will be covered by the sponsors. Sponsors are typically asked, in advance, to agree to specific tests of physical and/or economic completion, with lender recourse lapsing only after these tests have been satisfactorily met. Cost-sharing arrangements may oblige sponsors to carry a specific pro rata share of all project outlays, including debt-servicing payments.

Other ways of reducing completion risk include penalty clauses, performance bonds and guarantees (e.g., standby letters of credit covering contractors on the project), and completion guarantees issued by the sponsors themselves or other banks. These warrant that construction will be finished on schedule and that there will be no cost overruns. Technical criteria relating to performance of the facility upon completion are often employed to ensure that things work as they should. Guarantors, in turn, may syndicate the guarantee or protect themselves by means of bonds or insurance covering individual contractors and others involved in the construction phase of a project.

Sponsors may also provide "comfort letters," sometimes called "letters of moral intent" or "keepwells," promising to supervise and maintain an active interest in the vehicle company throughout the precompletion and operating phases of the project without issuing a formal guarantee. Such documents, even when tightly worded, cannot be viewed as de facto guarantees by project lenders.

Throughput Guarantees

Supply or throughput risk on major resource-related projects (e.g., pipelines) can, where applicable, be handled by obtaining guarantees from the suppliers of raw materials or energy sources, specifying the required throughput amounts and prices to be charged. In payments for the use of such facilities, there often is a "hell-or-high-water" clause that anchors the absolute, unconditional nature of the obligation irrespective of nonperformance by the other party.

The throughput concept, developed domestically in the United States, was applied in the $6.7 billion Ekofisk oil/gas field complex in the Norwegian sector of the North Sea. As Figure 9–7 shows, the six consortium partners entered into a throughput and deficiency agree-

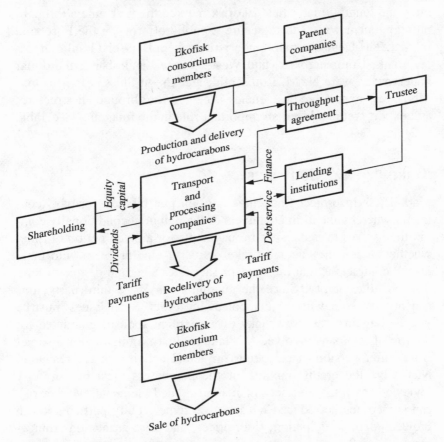

Figure 9–7. Example of throughput guarantees—Ekofisk Oil/Gas Project, North Sea, 1970. (*Source:* G. McKechnie, ed., *Energy Finance*, London: Euromoney Publications, 1983, p. 13; reprinted by permission)

ment with four transport and processing companies, which had been established to own and operate the relevant facilities. The borrowing companies then assigned their rights under the agreement to a common trustee for the benefit of the lenders, who thus had recourse to both the partners and the project as well as the parent oil companies. For transport and processing services, the four companies received through-put payments from the consortium members, allowing them to meet all of their operating expenses, service their debt, and pay annual dividends.

Development and execution of the funding program on the Ekofisk project was managed by a finance committee composed of repre-sentatives from each of the six partners. The committee selected financial markets and currencies—largely bond markets in dollars and Deutsche marks—which were advantageous in terms of fixed interest rates and lengthy maturities. Ekofisk marked the first time a through-put agreement was used to secure a public offering in the Eurobond market. The Deutsche mark underwriters were Deutsche Bank, Dresd-ner Bank, Commerzbank, and Westdeutsche Landesbank, the dollar underwriters were N. M. Rothschild, and Credit Suisse First Boston. Moreover, export credit agencies accepted the throughput structure, and export credits played an important role in the financing (see Table 9–2).[11]

"Take-or-Pay" Contracts

Market risk in project financings is often met by "take-or-pay" con-tracts, whereby the ultimate buyers of the output unconditionally com-mit themselves to make specific payments for a given period of time, whether or not they actually take delivery. One problem with take-or-pay contracts is that the sponsor sacrifices a certain degree of con-trol over the facility. Since the guarantor may be a third party, this can involve somewhat higher borrowing costs. Such issues must be weighed against the drawbacks of an explicit sponsor guarantee for the life of the loans involved. A "take-and-pay" obligation is a some-what softer version that depends on actual delivery of the resource. Naturally, the credit standing of the purchasers must be carefully reviewed, as must a variety of market-related elements. Market risk can sometimes be reduced by direct customer equity participation in projects, debt participation, floor prices, and price-escalation arrange-ments.

As an example, a take-or-pay contract subject to availability of liquefied natural gas (LNG) was concluded in 1973 between five

Japanese utility companies (Chubu Electric, Kansai Electric, Kyushu Electric, Nippon Steel, and Osaka Gas) and Pertamina, Indonesia's state-owned oil and gas company. The Arun and Badak gas fields, located on land near the Indonesian coast, were discovered in 1971–72 by Mobil Oil Indonesia and the Huffco Group.[12] In this project, Pertamina, which was not involved in the gas field development, took over the key roles of exclusive promoter of LNG sales, borrower of funds, interlocutor with the Indonesian government, and transporter of the gas. Mobil and Huffco entered into production-sharing (P/S) agreements with Pertamina on a 35:65 basis. Mobil developed and operated the Arun field, and the Huffco group did the same for the Badak field. Under the agreement, costs were first borne by Mobil and the Huffco Group and then recovered from the natural gas proceeds. The P/S contractors made their share of LNG available to Pertamina, for exclusive sale to Japanese buyers (see Figure 9–8). PT Arun and PT Badak were set up for liquefaction of the natural gas under equity participation of the various interested companies. Operating expenses of PT Arun and PT Badak, as not-for-profit companies, were covered by Pertamina and by Mobil and the Huffco Group. Under a separate transport agreement concluded between Pertamina and Burmast East Shipping Corporation, Burmast provided and operated the LNG carriers necessary to transport the product form Indonesia to Japan. Arun and Badak were structured as independent projects, although their output was sold under a single sales contract with the Japanese buyers.

Responsibility for funding the project was split between the P/S contractors, responsible for gas field financing, and Pertamina, responsible for the gas liquefaction facility. Financing for the LNG facilities (approximately $1.1 billion) consisted of two kinds of loans: (1) yen credits equivalent to $200 million supplied to the Indonesian government by a Japanese government agency (OECF), then re-lent to Pertamina by the government and (2) a $898 million loan to the Japan Indonesia LNG Co., Ltd. (JILCO) by the Exim Bank Syndicate, consisting of the Export-Import Bank of Japan and 16 other banks, funds that were then re-lent to Pertamina. JILCO had been set up as an investment, financing, and liaison company by the 5 Japanese customers, 7 trading companies, 16 banks, 2 utilities, and Far East Oil Trading Co. (FEO), a Japanese/Indonesian company involved in sales of Indonesian crude oil to Japan.

The financial risk of the import credit (the loan from the Exim Bank Syndicate to JILCO) was carried in part (40%) by the Japanese utilities, which provided a guarantee to the Exim cofinancing syndicate.

Table 9–2. Historical Summary of Ekofisk-related Debt

	Bank loans[a]	Lead bank	Bonds	Export credits[a]	Total[a]
1970	$75	Citibank/Rothschild (F)			$75
1971				Eximbank–3190 $56-25 (F)	
				BNP Suppliers Fir 151-85 (F)	
				IMI NW 15-24 Lire 2,561 (F)	$91-443
1972	$50	Citibank/Rothschild (F)		Eksportfinans NKr 114 (F)	$72-179
1973	$150	Chase (F)			
	$600	Citibank/Société Générale (T)			$750
1974	$230	Citibank/Société Générale (T)		Exim–4688 $67-95 (F)	
	DM 125	Commerzbank (T)		BNP–Buyers Fir 490 (F)	
				Exim–4689 $126-9 (T)	
				BNP–Buyers Fir 50 (T)	
				Barclays ECGD £10 (T)	$618.367
1975	DM 120	Deutsche Bank (T)		IMI–NW 88 Lire 3,687 (F)	
	$275	Citibank/Société Générale (T)		Williams & Glyn's £30 (F)	
	DM 400	Deutsche Bank (T)		Barclays ECGD £5 (T)	$593-621

Year				Bonds					
1976	Dil 1-50	Mees and Hope	(T)			Williams & Glyn's	£22-8	(F)	
	Dil 1-50	AMRO	(T)	DM 100 M 8½% Bonds	(T)				
				$50 M 9¼% Bonds	(T)				
				DM 100 M 8% Bonds	(T)				
				DM 150 M 7¼%	(T)				$304-268
1977	$75	Citibank/Société Générale	(T)	$50 M 8½% Bonds	(T)				
	$300	Citibank/Société Générale	(T)	DM 100 M 7% Bonds	(T)				
	£45	Commerzbank	(T)	DM 200 M 6% Bonds	(T)				$653-807
1978	$60	Deutsche Bank	(T)			BNP	Fir 150	(F)	
	£60	International Westminster	(T)						$213-333
1979	$75	Commerzbank	(T)						$195
	£60	Barclays	(T)						
1983	$200	Citibank	(T)						$200

a. In millions.
(F) Field development
(T) Transport system
SOURCE: G. McKechnie, *Energy Finance*, Euromoney Publications, 1983, p. 14; reprinted by permission.

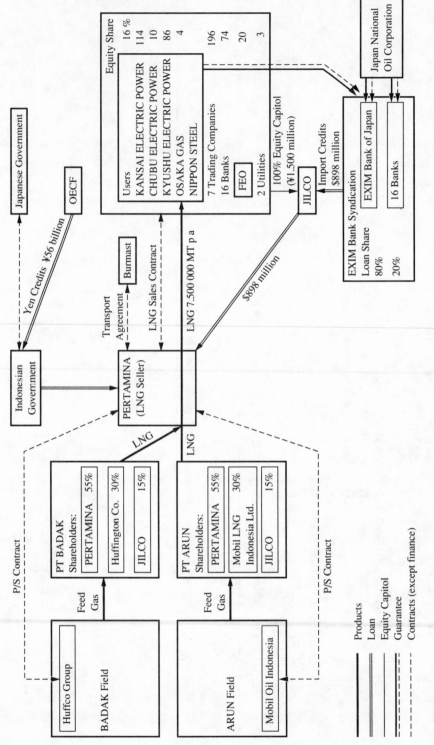
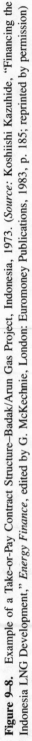

Figure 9–8. Example of a Take-or-Pay Contract Structure–Badak/Arun Gas Project, Indonesia, 1973. (*Source:* Koshiishi Kazuhide, "Financing the Indonesia LNG Development," *Energy Finance*, edited by G. McKechnie, London: Euromoney Publications, 1983, p. 185; reprinted by permission)

Japan National Oil Corporation (JNOC) guaranteed the other 60% of the loans. The guarantors were prepared to assume the associated risks because the entire output of the plant was to be exported to Japan, which had urgent need for the gas because of the country's energy diversification policy following the 1973 oil crisis.

JILCO, in turn, had to look primarily to Pertamina for repayment of its loan. The Indonesian government did not provide a guarantee, and liquefaction facilities were not available as security. JILCO had only the security that a certain percentage of LNG sales proceeds would be transferred directly into an escrow account in the United States for disbursement of principal and interest due on the loan. Reliability of the cash flow was enhanced because the operators were highly respected for their knowledge and experience.

Other Options to Reduce Risk

Unlike the Badak/Arun project, it may also be possible in project financings to obtain "deficiency guarantees" covering an entire venture, either from the sponsors or from the government of the country where the project is located—or perhaps the home country governments of the sponsors. Some guarantees cover losses of principal and interest suffered by lenders after any collateral has been liquidated in the event of default. In the case of a government's sovereign guarantee, country risk assessment will determine its true value.

Collateral in offshore project financings can take many forms: (1) a lender's mortgage over the borrower's interest in the license or project facilities; (2) assignment of the lender's interests in the various agreements and contracts; (3) assignment of insurance proceeds; (4) assignment of revenues received, such as liens on accounts receivable; (5) liens on petroleum inventories; (6) contingent claims on related bank accounts; and (7) a pledge of shares of the borrower.[13]

In addition, sponsors may be required not to reduce their financial interest in a venture below a specified level. Sellers of equipment to the project may also be willing to provide certain guarantees, or this function may be taken up by government agencies in the exporting country. The existence of a complex of guarantees, of course, provides support for project financing only to the extent that the guarantors are able and willing to meet their obligations; hence, each guarantor must be subject to careful credit analysis. Even after all guarantees are taken into account, the underlying soundness of the project itself still tends to be the determining factor.

Political risks in project financing can be dealt with in a variety of ways, including purchase of political risk insurance, participation of influential banks from a number of different countries (particularly from major trading partners or creditors of the host country), or participation of regional development banks or the World Bank. Sometimes the country's needs for continued balance-of-payments loans, including rollovers of maturing debt, may give banks sufficient implied leverage to constrain adverse political moves.

A central function in project financing is to identify and quantify the various categories of risks and to structure the deal to allocate these risks acceptably among the various participants. As financial institutions develop a better understanding of the risks in particular types of projects, they seem increasingly prepared to accept a larger share of total project risks, which means less onerous covenants and guarantees for project sponsors. A reputable sponsor with a good record should be able to negotiate over a range of risks that bankers would not have accepted early in the history of project finance. The fundamental challenge facing financial advisors on major projects is to put together a financing package that will align the interests of all parties, given the financing sources available, the risks, and the options available for reducing these risks.

The Build, Operate, Transfer Model

Given the scarcity of public financings for infrastructure projects in many countries in the late 1980s, a new technique, the build, operate, transfer (BOT) model, made its appearance. Essentially, BOT takes what is conventionally defined as a public sector infrastructure project, under a concession granted by the government, and applies private capital to develop the project and to operate it. After the project has operated for a period of time at a profit and the investors have received an acceptable return, the facility is transferred to the government. The technique actually originated with the development and financing of rail systems in various parts of the British empire in the nineteenth century. The most prominent modern example is the rail tunnel between France and the United Kingdom (Eurotunnel).

Essentially, equity is raised from private sources or through a public share offering by a sponsorship consortium for a special-purpose vehicle company. The sponsors may be contractors seeking engineering and construction work, operating companies, equipment manufacturers, suppliers, or customers, usually with the active support (but not direct participation) of the public sector. The equity serves as an incentive for the contractor and operator to perform on time and within budget, since each has a significant stake in the venture, and provides cushioning and comfort to lenders in terms if the project's economic viability. A pure BOT project would raise debt financing purely on its own merits, although in many cases government guarantees are involved. Eurotunnel is an exception, although here the project's importance to France and the United Kingdom and indeed the European Community as a whole could be take as a source of some comfort for lenders.

A pure BOT example is the third Dartford tunnel under the Thames River in the United Kingdom that links two stretches of the M 25 motorway circling London and benefits from virtually guaranteed toll income. In this case, a vehicle company was created by a consortium and nominally capitalized at £1,000; the remainder of the capital was raised in the form of subordinated loan stock (essentially preferred shares) paying a specified margin over British government securities (gilts). A syndicated bank loan led by Bank of America priced at a margin over LIBOR covered the remainder of the funding. The contractors, covered by performance bonds, considered equity to be superfluous in this case, and the capital was written off at an early stage. The vehicle company will operate the Dartford Crossing project for 20 years, following which the facility will revert to the British government. The estimate was that the loan stock would be paid off in 15 years, providing an acceptable cushion to the investors.

Other types of transportation projects, such as a proposed North-South highway in Malaysia, may not be as suitable for BOT structures because of uncertainties as to the cash flow streams and public pressure to keep tolls down. On the other hand, the small number of reliable offtakers in cogeneration plants makes them very suitable for BOT structures. Even in electric power projects, however, guarantees with respect to volume and price of offtake, cost of fuels, and noninsurable risks are often required of the government. BOT techniques have also been used in real estate projects, such as the Messeturm in Frankfurt, the tallest building in continental Europe.

Designing BOT structures is not cheap—putting together the Dartford Crossing project cost the sponsors several million pounds; the higher quality the risk assessment, the higher the costs incurred by the sponsors who have no guarantee that the project will actually proceed.

ADVANTAGES AND COSTS OF PROJECT FINANCING

The growth of project financing is obviously linked to material advantages over more traditional forms of lending to accomplish the same objectives. First, to be economically viable, projects must often be so large that they outstrip the financial capabilities of the firms involved, even in the joint ventures. North Sea oil development, the Alaska pipeline, and Eurotunnel are perhaps the most well-known examples of project financings. With all possible supports for the loan captured in the financing package, the project itself must in the end be capable of justifying a significant share of the debt incurred.

Second, we have noted that project financings are largely off–balance sheet activities as far as the sponsoring companies are concerned, except perhaps as footnotes related to long-term debt. Full guarantees, nevertheless, must be captured in financial statements as contingent liabilities, although completion guarantees might be omitted on the grounds that they are merely normal parts of doing business. Raters of corporate creditworthiness have traditionally ignored off-balance-sheet obligations, either partially or fully, unless they exceed 5% to 10% of assets. Such obligations for the most part also fall outside loan indentures on existing corporate debt. Hence, sponsors' borrowing capacity is enhanced in the view of prospective lenders. This permits a far higher degree of de facto leveraging of their capital than would otherwise be possible without incurring commensurate downside risks.

As one study notes, "Investment bankers use the term 'lender psychology' to suggest that lending institutions are locked in by traditional debt-equity ratios in the particular industry. By setting up the project as a separate borrowing entity, however, the sponsor can better demonstrate its prospects and debt servicing capacity."[14] If successful, ventures structured along project financing lines can have an extraordinarily positive effect on the sponsors' profitability picture.

Third, project financing may permit a greater degree of bank risk reduction through loan portfolio diversification than alternative forms of financing. In some ways, project financing may indeed be superior to sovereign lending. The project itself may generate independent export revenues or reduce import expenditures, or it may have favorable effects on the external debt-servicing capacity of the host economy. Projects may also provide an unusually good indication of a country's long-range economic outlook and the quality of its economic management. And, of course, external participants and guarantors tend to substantially reduce the risks and increase creditor leverage. For all of these reasons, the importance of project financing can be expected to grow in the future, especially within the overall framework of lending to developing countries.

Costs of Project Financing versus Other Forms of Financing

Project financing costs can be expected to exceed the costs of comparable financings undertaken directly by project sponsors. Involvement of multiple lenders and other parties tied together by a complex structure of undertakings absorbs a substantial amount of time and effort that can translate into equally substantial legal, management, and financing fees. The incremental costs clearly depend on the extent of the work involved and may reach $1\frac{1}{2}\%$ or more of the amount of the financing. In addition, it has already been stressed that interest spreads on substantially nonrecourse financings will tend to reflect the incremental risks accepted by lenders, with borrowing costs potentially well above the sponsors' corporate borrowing rates. Where such risks are shifted through insurance, the associated premiums will add to overall financing costs, while other forms of risk transfer (e.g., off-take contracts or consumer financing) may involve substantial price concessions. It is also to be expected that state-owned energy and resources companies will sometimes shun project financing, as government-guaranteed or imputed government-backed financing is less costly for them.

Clearly, it is possible for costs of project financing to become prohibitively high, forcing a return to more conventional arrangements—especially in the case of smaller deals and projects that are closely integrated with the sponsors' own operations. Nevertheless, in a growing number of large-scale natural resource projects, there may be no alternative.

COMPETITION AMONG FINANCIAL INSTITUTIONS

From a profitability point of view, project financing offers potentially attractive opportunities to certain financial institutions. The global presence of large international banks provides an important information advantage in obtaining leadership positions in project financings and in evaluating risks and assembling the financial resources necessary to carry them out.

Financial "packaging" is the essence of project financing, and economic returns to advisors and others that can be attributed to this function—actually returns on proprietary information and financial innovation—can be very substantial. However, project sponsors and their advisors sometimes find it possible to "unbundle" the project financing package to secure different services—loans, foreign exchange contracts, standby letters of credit, and lease financing—from a variety of different competitive suppliers.

An institution serving as financial advisor on a project can work closely with sponsors, governments, international agencies, suppliers, customers, other advisors, and guarantors to establish contracts that may prove useful in generating future business. This is a high-profile activity, and the advisor is called upon to use a great deal of ingenuity. The advisor must be able to satisfy borrower needs for suitably structured financing at the lowest possible cost and be able to satisfy respective lenders, each having quite distinct interests and objectives of the inherent soundness of the project. Usually advisors must design a financial plan that can be presented to lenders as a unified, consistent whole to minimize disagreements, negotiations, and delays.

Success in project financing gets around quickly—but so does failure. The most lucrative part of project financing clearly is fee income, which on a complex financing arrangement can be sizeable. Since to some extent it is unrelated to lending, it can have a very positive impact on overall returns on assets. A lead institution in a project financing will generally participate directly in a financial package. It may also be called upon to lead manage one or more syndicated loans or bond or equity issues, thereby tapping into profits from that source as well. Additional returns may come from funding profits, foreign exchange business, interest rate swaps, and other sources.

The profitability of project financing to international commercial or investment banks, and to the limited number of other banks able to participate effectively, is tied to its complexity and its risks and returns. Relatively few financial institutions seem to have the necessary legal, accounting, tax, financial, and technical skills, either at their head offices or at strategically located regional offices, to become major players. When this constraint is combined with the need for capable syndicate leadership, close sponsor contact, and large-scale financing power in various maturities, it is not surprising that the number of major participants is limited. Even during the 1960s and 1970s, a good deal of project lending appears to have been undertaken by bankers anxious to enter the field without fully recognizing the risks involved in limited-recourse lending.

As a result of the high barriers to entry, project financing has emerged as something of an oligopolistic market. It is dominated by those few major banks with the financial and technical resources and the experience and expertise to evaluate the risks and devise suitable financing packages. Because of their reputation and power in the market, the leadership in most project financings is likely to involve at least one of the major players. In an informal manner, other banks may rely on the 10 to 12 international banks that constitute the top tier in project financing, in the same way that smaller banks may look first to the lead manager and then to the borrower in making a decision to participate in a loan syndication or in lending to a sovereign borrower. Such reliance, without adequate recourse, is clearly unhealthy, and may well lead to a suboptimal allocation of financial resources in project financings worldwide.

Project financing techniques and large-scale capital-intensive ventures are clearly inseparable. The latter could not be carried out with the same degree of effectiveness and efficiency without access to global financial markets and the economic discipline imposed on such ventures by the funding approaches developed in project financing. Lending techniques are brought to bear to assure that all risks and returns are carefully weighed by a large number of parties and that the risks are borne by participants best able to cope with them in the light of perceived returns. To be sure, losses will be incurred from time to time, but future perceptions will be altered accordingly and carry with them correspondingly altered terms and conditions.

SUMMARY

Few types of financial transactions are as complex or as rational in their structure as project finance—the financing of large-scale ventures in the areas of oil and gas, industrial facilities, and infrastructure investments. Project finance almost always involves sophisticated players in all of its dimensions. Sponsoring companies or governmental agencies tend to be as familiar, or more so, and the financial institutions called in often find themselves operating in a buyer's market.

In some cases, sponsors have sufficient in-house expertise to be able to unbundle the financial requirements of a project in order to cut costs to themselves and erode returns to the financial institutions involved. In other cases, financial advisors are brought in from among the investment banks to help structure the project. In virtually all cases, the engineering and technical, legal, and financial structures must be combined into a viable credit profile that usually involves considerable ingenuity and represents "financial engineering" in one of its most advanced forms.

No less complex is the assessment of the risks involved in project financing—particularly in separating the various types of risk, pricing them, measuring exposures, and finding ways to lay them off. Of particular concern is the assessment of risks and returns on the part of participating financial institutions that are asked to take on exposure but have no independent way of assessing the risks. Project finance remains an excellent example of an international financial service that adds substantial value to borrower/issuer and lender/investor, with substantial gains left on the table for the institutions involved in the deal.

NOTES

1. J. L. Gabriel, "Le Financement sans Recourse des Projects Industriels," Concept for Conference on Project Finance, Paris, 1981.
2. Larry Wynant, "Essential Elements of Project Financing," *Harvard Business Review*, May/June, 1980, p. 169.
3. O. Curtin, "The Risk Explosion in Energy Financing," *Euromoney*, January 1982, pp. 42–43. See also *The Wall Street Journal*, March 12, 1980, p. 147.
4. KE investment group was originally set up in 1975 by Metallgesellschaft AG (a copper processor), Kabel and Metallwerke Gutehoffnungshuette AG (fabricators), Siemens AG (users), and Degussa AG. Deutsche Gesellschaft fuer wirtschaftliche Zusammenarbeit later replaced Kabel and Metallwerke and Siemens as shareholders.
5. Hidea Ishihara, "Financing for Energy Resources Development Projects: Japanese Experience," *Revue de l'Energie: Le Financement des Investissements Energetiques* [Energy Investment Finance], August–September 1980, pp. 202–10.
6. World Bank, Bank News Release No. 83/7, 12 August 1982, and "The New Co-financing Initiatives of the World Bank," outline of the presentation of Mr. B. Snoy, World Bank, at the seminar on "Co-financing of Development Projects," Luxembourg, September 20, 1984.
7. R. Radez, "Opportunities in Project Financing," *The Banker*, August 1978, pp. 12–14.
8. Larry Wynant, "Essential Elements of Project Financing," *Harvard Business Review*, May/June 1980, p. 169.

9. Grover R. Castle, "Project Financing—Guidelines for the Commercial Banker," *Journal of Commercial Bank Lending*, April 1975, pp. 22–30.
10. Andre Gester, "The Financing of Frigg," *Revue de l'Energie: Le Financement des Investissements Energetiques* [Energy Investment Finance], August–September, 1980, pp. 47–50.
11. G. McKechnie, ed., *Energy Finance*, (London: Euromoney Publications, 1983).
12. The Huffco Group consisted of Roy M. Huffington, Golden Eagle Inc., Union Texas, Superior Oil, Universe Tankships, and Virginia International.
13. Uwe H. Jahnke and P. Gordon Webb, "Security Consideration in Norwegian Offshore Project Finance," *Noroil*, November 1983, pp. 41–47.
14. Larry Wynant, "Essential Elements of Project Financing," *Harvard Business Review*, June 1980, p. 1972.

SELECTED REFERENCES

Barnett, Matthew.   "Project Finance Develops New Risks." *Euromoney*, October 1986.

Barnett, Matthew.   "Putting Your Equity on the Line." *Euromoney*, October 1987.

Castle, Grover R.   "Project Financing—Guidelines for the Commercial Bank." *Journal of Commercial Bank Lending*, April 1975.

Derechio, Stefan D.   "Co-Financing Between International Agencies and the Private Sector." *Euromoney*, March 1976.

Ishihara, Hidea.   "Financing for Energy Resources Development Projects: Japanese Experience," *Revue de l'Energie: Le Financement des Investissements Energetiques* [Energy Investment Finance], August–September 1980.

Koshiishi, Kazuhide.   "Financing the Indonesian LNG Developments." *In Energy Finance*, edited by G. McKechnie. London: Euromoney Publications, 1983.

Lal, Deepak.   *Methods of Project Analysis: A Review*. Baltimore: Johns Hopkins Press, 1974.

McKechnie, G., ed.   *Energy Finance*. London: Euromoney Publications, 1983.

Mikesell, R. F.   *New Patterns of World Mineral Development*. Washington, DC: British-North American Committee, 1979.

Nevitt, Peter.   *Project Financing*. London: Euromoney Publications, 1979.

Pouliquen, Louis.   *Risk Analysis in Project Appraisal*. Baltimore: Johns Hopkins Press, 1979.

Radetzki, M., and Zorn, S.   *Financing Mining Prospects in Developing Countries*. London: Mining Journal Books Ltd., 1979.

Reutlinger, Shlomo.   *Techniques for Project Appraisal Under Uncertainty.*
Baltimore: Johns Hopkins Press, 1980.

Sassoon, David.   "Financing the Mining Sector: The Bank's Role." *Finance
and Development*, September 1975.

"Second Thoughts About Project Risks." *The Banker*, September 1982.

World Bank.   *Co-Financing*. Washington, D.C.: World Bank Special Publication, 1980.

World Bank.   *Prospective on Cofinancing with Commercial Bank Loans and
Export Credits*. Washington, D.C.: The World Bank Advisory Unit on
Cofinancing, 1985.

Wynant, Larry.   "Essential Elements in Project Financing." *Harvard Business Review*, June 1980.

10

Legal Dimensions of Global Commercial Banking

The law is an integral aspect of international banking. Most fundamentally, lending relationships with borrowers and funding relationships with depositors and holders of bank debt are contractual; hence, they are governed by a set of legal principles and obligations anchored in written agreements. These are intended to protect each side from possible loss attributable to departures by the other side from the terms of the financial relationship. Examples include failure to pay interest or principal on time, actions affecting the value of the security underlying a loan, failure to honor a depositor's legitimate demand for payment, and the like. On a purely national level, these issues are complicated enough. On an international level, involving multiple legal systems, courts of law, traditions, and public policies, they take on even greater degrees of complexity.

In this chapter, we will focus on the legal aspects of cross-border lending and lending-type transactions (e.g., Euronote facilities), and we will examine financial instruments that embody standard legal clauses (e.g., floating-rate securities). We will begin with a discussion of international loan agreements and then consider several problem situations involving legal remedies to illustrate what happens when things don't go as planned. Regulatory issues concerning the operations of foreign banks are discussed in Chapter 24.

FUNCTIONS OF A LOAN AGREEMENT

A loan agreement must be a clear and unambiguous record of what has been agreed upon by all those who are party to the agreement covering the facility. Its objective is to provide for every possible contingency and, since the obligation of all parties ought to be clearly understood at the outset, there should theoretically be no need for eventual litigation, arbitration, or other form of dispute-settlement procedures.

The first function of a loan agreement is to identify and describe the position (lender, borrower, agent) of the various parties to a facility, defining their rights and obligations and the remedies available in the event that there is any material departure from its terms. It must also state those terms—the principal sum, currency of denomination, maturity, rate of interest, drawdown and repayment schedules, etc. The conditions that are required to be met by the borrower fall into two categories: (1) *conditions precedent* (or "closing conditions" as they are sometimes called), which must be satisfied before the facility can be finalized, and (2) *continuing conditions*, which the borrower is required to meet throughout the life of the facility.

Conditions Precedent

Before a loan agreement is actually consummated and the principal sum is transferred to the borrower, the lender will require proof of both the borrower's authority to borrow and of the authorization of the individual signatories to the agreement. The borrower's representatives must furnish proof of compliance with any relevant statutory or regulatory requirements and with the borrower's articles of association. They must also be able to attest to the accuracy of the financial information provided to the lender and confirm that there has been no materially adverse change since its preparation and no material legal action pending that could alter any of the factors on which the decision to lend was based.

Continuing Conditions

Continuing conditions deal with the operation of the loan agreement, the calculation and method of payment of interest and principal, the compliance with various covenants, and the continued sound financial condition of the borrower. They should also define the circumstances under which the agreement can be terminated prematurely, either as a result of the loan being recalled by a lender not in a position to continue lending or because the borrower is in violation of the agreement. When such a development occurs, it is important that it be provided for in the agreement. The need for clarity is particularly important in the case of syndicated facilities because there often are many parties involved and the rights and obligations of all of them, as well as the agent, must be clearly defined and fully understood.

In any loan agreement, there is always a tradeoff between legal purity and operating practicalities. A loan agreement is fundamentally designed to avoid the need for litigation. It must be legally watertight, but too much "legalese" will interfere with the operation of the agreement and may even precipitate misunderstanding, unnecessary complexity, and ultimate litigation—the very thing the agreement is intended to avoid. Figure 10–1 presents a short form, single-bank Eurodollar, loan agreement for a hypothetical bank named "Metropolitan Bank." Similar, albeit amplified, terms would be found in a typical syndicated Eurocurrency credit.

(Text continues on page 252.)

FIGURE 10–1.   SHORT-FORM EUROLOAN AGREEMENT

The following short-form sample loan agreement involving a corporate borrower and guarantor within the same group of companies is to be used only as a reference for officers of the bank with regard to reference for officers of the bank with regard to *minimal* documentary requirements for a single-bank Eurodollar loan. Requirements may vary considerably depending on the country and status of the borrower, the type of the credit facility, and the nature of the guarantor. This draft contains no financial covenants which would typically be required by application of Metropolitan Bank's current credit policy to the Borrower. *All* documentation for actual transactions on which outside counsel is not used must be referred to Metropolitan Bank's internal bank counsel for comment and approval *prior to* negotiation with client. THIS DOCUMENT IS NOT FOR RELEASE TO CLIENTS OF THE BANK.

_____ ("the Lender") is pleased to offer you, _____ ("the Borrower"), a loan facility in the aggregate principal amount of US $ _____ ("the Facility") to be guaranteed by _____ ("the Guarantor") under which we will make advances (each "an Advance") to you for the purpose of _____ on the following terms and conditions:

1. *Availability*

    (A) The Facility will only be available to the Borrower upon receipt by the Lender of each of the following in the form and substance satisfactory to it:

Figure 10-1. (cont.)

(i) the enclosed copy of this agreement with the form of acceptance attached hereto duly signed by the Borrower and notarized by a notary public (the agreement thereby constituted being hereinafter referred to as "the Agreement");

(ii) the guarantee ("the Guarantee"), in the form previously agreed between the Lender, the Borrower, and the Guarantor respectively, duly executed by the Guarantor;

(iii) copies, in each case certified a true and up-to-date copy by a director of the Borrower and the Guarantor respectively, of the Memorandum and Articles of Association of the Borrower and the Guarantor;

(iv) a copy, certified a true copy by a director of the Borrower, of resolutions, which remain in full force and effect, of the board of directors of the Borrower, authorizing the acceptance of the Facility on the terms and subject to the conditions hereof and the performance of the Agreement in accordance with its terms, a named director to countersign and deliver this copy of resolutions;

(v) a copy, certified a true copy by a director of the Guarantor, of resolutions, which remain in full force and effect, of the board of directors of the Guarantor authorizing the execution, delivery to the Lender and performance according to its terms of the Guarantee, delivery to the Lender of such Guarantee to be made by a named director of the Guarantor;

(vi) a certificate of a director of each of the Borrower and the Guarantor, respectively, setting out the incumbency and signatures of the persons authorized to sign the Agreement and the Guarantee and any documents to be delivered pursuant thereto;

(vii) evidence satisfactory to the Lender that all governmental or other consents required in relation to the Agreement or the Guarantee and the performance thereof have been obtained and are in full force and effect; and

(viii) evidence that _____ and _____ have each agreed to act as the agent of the Borrower and the Guarantor for the service of process in New York.

(B) When the conditions in Clause 1(A) have been satisfied, the Lender will at the request of the Borrower make an Advance to the Borrower on any day on which banks are open for business in New York and dealings in dollars are carried out in the London Interbank Market (each a "business day"), which is or precedes the day three months from the date hereof (the "Termination Date") if, but only if, (i) the Lender has received at least five business days earlier a request from the Borrower for such Advance, each such request specifying the amount (which shall be at an amount or integral multiple of US $500,000 and less than or equal to the amount of the undrawn Facility), the proposed date of drawing ("the Drawdown Date") of the relevant Advance and, in the case of the first Advance, the duration of its initial Interest Period (as hereafter defined); (ii) deposits in U.S. dollars in the relevant amount for the relevant period are available to the Lender in the London Interbank Market for value on the proposed Drawdown Date; (iii) the representations set out in Clause 7 are true on the Drawdown Date; and (iv) no event has occurred which is or may become (with the passage of time or the giving of notice or both) one of those events mentioned in Clause 9 hereof.

2. *Interest Periods*

   (A) The period for which an Advance is outstanding shall be divided into successive periods (each an "Interest Period") each (other than the first) starting on the last day of the previous such period.

   (B) Subject as hereinafter provided, the duration of each Interest Period relating to an Advance shall be three months or six months as the Borrower may elect by not less than five business days written notice prior to the first day of such period provided that (i) any Interest Period which begins during or at the same time as any other Interest Period shall end at the same time as that other Interest Period, (ii) any Interest Period which would otherwise extend beyond a date for the repayment of principal under Clause 4(A) or would end prior to but in the same calendar month as such date shall be of such duration that it shall end on such date, and (iii) if no such notice is received, such duration shall be three months.

Figure 10-1. (cont.)

(C) Where two or more Interest Periods end at the same time, the Advances relating thereto shall then be consolidated and thereafter shall constitute and be referred to as one "Advance."

3. *Interest*

   (A) On the last day of each Interest Period the Borrower shall pay to the Lender interest on the Advance to which such Interest Period relates.

   (B) The rate of interest applicable to an Advance during an Interest Period shall be the rate per annum, which is the sum of _____ percent ___% (the "Margin") and the rate per annum determined by the Lender to be the rate at which it was offering US dollar deposits of an amount equal to the amount of that Advance and for a period comparable to such Interest Period to price banks in the London Interbank Market at or about 11:00 a.m. Greenwich Mean Time two business days before the beginning of that Interest Period.

   (C) The Borrower shall pay to the Lender a commitment fee at the rate of _____ of one percent ___(%) per annum on the daily undrawn amount of the Facility during the period beginning on the date hereof and ending on the Termination Date, such commission to be payable on the Termination Date.

4. *Repayment*

   (A) The Borrower shall repay the aggregate amount of all Advances outstanding on the Termination Date by _____ equal installments, one such installment being payable on the last day of each successive period of _____ months from the date hereof up to and including the day _____ months from the date hereof.

   (B) If at any time it is unlawful for the Lender to make, fund, or allow to remain outstanding all or any of the Advances made or to be made by it under the Agreement, the Facility shall be reduced to zero and, if the Lender so requires, the Borrower shall, on such date as may be specified by the Lender, repay each Advance (together with accrued interest thereon and any other sum then due hereunder).

5. *Increased Costs*

If by reason of the introduction of or any change in the interpretation or administration of any law or regulation or compliance with any request, direction, or requirement (whether or not having the force of law) from any competent governmental or other fiscal, monetary, or other authority there shall be any increase in the cost to the Lender of making, funding, or maintaining any Advance made or to be made under the Agreement, or there shall be imposed on the Lender any reserve or special deposit requirement in respect of loans made or deposits taken by it, then the Borrower shall from time to time forthwith upon demand pay to the Lender such amount as it certifies to be necessary to compensate it for such increased cost or, as the case may be, such portion thereof is in the opinion of the Lender attributable to its making, funding, or maintaining Advances hereunder.

6. *Taxes*

All payments to be made by the Borrower under the Agreement shall be made free and clear of and without any deduction or withholding for or on account of (i) any set-off or counterclaim or (ii) other than as required by law, and taxes, levies, imports, duties, or other charges of similar nature ("Taxes"). If at any time, the Borrower is required by any applicable law, to make any deduction or withholding from any such payment or the Lender is required to pay any sum on account of Taxes (other than tax on its overall net income) on or in relation to such payment, the sum due from the Borrower in respect of which such deduction, withholding, or payment fails to be made shall be increased to the extent necessary to ensure that, after the making of such deduction, withholding, or payment, the Lender receives and retains a net sum equal to the sum which it would have received and retained had no such deduction, withholding, or payment been required to be made. The Borrower shall within 30 days of having made any such deduction or withholding deliver to the Lender a receipt issued by the applicable authority evidencing the deduction or withholding of all sums required to be so deducted or withheld.

7. *Representations and Warranties*

(A) The Borrower represents and warrants to the Lender that:

Figure 10-1. (cont.)

    (i) the Borrower and the Guarantor are each companies incorporated with limited liability in the country of _____ having the power and having taken all corporate and other action to enable them: (a) to enter into the Agreement and the Guarantee respectively, (b) to exercise their respective rights and perform their respective obligations thereunder, (c) to ensure that such obligations are legal, valid, and binding, and (d) to make the Agreement and the Guarantee admissible in evidence in the Country of _____;

    (ii) the execution, delivery, and performance of the Agreement and the Guarantee will not cause the Borrower or the Guarantor or any of their respective subsidiaries (the Borrower and the Guarantor together with their respective subsidiaries being hereinafter referred to as "the Group") to be in breach of or default under any agreement binding on any member of the Group, and will not result in the existence of or oblige any member of the Group to create any encumbrance over any of its revenues or assets;

    (iii) no material litigation before, by, or of any court or governmental authority has been commenced or threatened against any member of the Group or any of its assets;

    (iv) the consolidated financial statements of the Group for the financial year ended 31 December 19 ___ ("the Original Statements") were prepared in accordance with generally accepted accounting principles of the United States of America and present fairly the Group's financial position at such date and there has been no material adverse change in the business, assets, or condition of the Group since that date; and

    (v) none of the events mentioned in Clause 9 has occurred.

8. *Covenants*

    (A) The Borrower shall:

        (i) within ninety days after the end of each of the Group's financial years and within sixty days after the end of the first of each of its financial half-years deliver to the Lender copies of the Group's consolidated financial statements (including balance sheet, income statement, and statement of changes in financial position) in respect to such financial year prepared on a basis consistent with the Original Statements and, in the case of yearly statements, audited by auditors acceptable to the Lender;

(ii) from time to time on request deliver to the Lender such other information relating to the business, assets, and financial condition of the Group as the Lender may require.

(B) The Borrower shall not and shall procure that no other member of the Group shall without the prior written consent of the Lender create, assume, incur, or suffer to exist or permit to be created, assumed, incurred, or suffered to exist any mortgage, charge, pledge, lien, or other encumbrance over all or any of its present or future revenues or assets.

(iii) [other covenants such as maintenance of minimum debt equity and debt service ratios, dividend payout restrictions, maintenance of existing management and ownership, limiting lines of business, etc.]

9. *Default*

If:

(i) the Borrower fails to pay any sum due from it under the Agreement at the time, in the currency, and in the manner specified herein; or

(ii) any representation or statement made by the Borrower or the Guarantor in the Agreement or, as the case may be, the Guarantee or any notice or other document delivered pursuant thereto is or proves to have been incorrect or misleading when made or deemed made or at any time thereafter; or

(iii) the Borrower or the Guarantor fails duly to perform any obligation expressed to be assumed by it in the Agreement or the Guarantee, as the case may be, and such default (if capable of remedy) is not remedied within thirty days after the Lender has given notice thereof to the Borrower or the Guarantor, as the case may be; or

Figure 10-1. (cont.)

(iv) any other indebtedness of the Borrower or any other member of the Group becomes due and payable prior to its specified maturity or any creditor or creditors of any member of the Group become entitled to declare any indebtedness of such member due and payable prior to its specified maturity; or

(v) any member of the Group is unable, or admits in writing its inability, to pay its debts as they fall due or declares a general moratorium on the payment of indebtedness or commences negotiations with any one or more of its creditors with a view to the general readjustment or rescheduling of its indebtedness or makes a general assignment for the benefit of its creditors; or

(vi) the Guarantee shall cease for any reason to be binding on and enforceable against the Guarantor in all respects in accordance with its terms; or

(vii) any member of the Group takes any corporate action or other steps are taken or legal proceedings are started for its winding up, dissolution, or reorganization or for the appointment of a receiver, trustee, or similar officer of it or of any or all of its revenues and assets; or

(viii) the Borrower ceases to be a subsidiary of the Guarantor; or

(ix) any governmental consent, approval, or undertaking granted to or at any time required by the Borrower or the Guarantor in connection with the Agreement or the Guarantee is revoked or restricted in any material way and such revocation or restriction is not canceled or otherwise remedied to the satisfaction of the Lender within thirty days of its imposition; or

(x) at any time it becomes unlawful for the Borrower to perform any or all of its obligations under the Agreement or the Guarantor to perform any or all of its obligations under the Guarantee; or

(xi) any circumstances arise which give reasonable grounds in the opinion of the Lender for the belief that the Borrower or Guarantor may not (or may be unable to) perform its perform its obligations under the Agreement or under the Guarantee, as the case may be;

then and in any such case and at any time thereafter the Lender may take either or both of the following actions:

(a) by written notice to the Borrower, declare all amounts outstanding under the Facility to be immediately due and payable, whereupon the same shall become so payable together with accrued interest thereon and any other sums then owed by the Borrower under the Agreement; and/or

(b) by written notice to the Borrower, declare that the Facility shall be canceled, whereupon the same shall be canceled and the Borrower shall not be able to draw any further Advances.

10. *Default Interest and Indemnity*

(A) The period beginning on the due date for payment of any sum due and payable under the Agreement and ending on the date upon which the Borrower's obligation to pay such sum is discharged shall be divided into successive periods, each of which (other than the first) shall start on the last day of the preceding such period and the duration of each of which shall be selected by the Lender; during each such period (as well after as before judgment) the outstanding balance of the unpaid sum shall bear interest at the rate per annum which is the sum of _____ percent (__ %), the Margin and the rate at which the Lender was offering to prime banks in the London Interbank Market deposits in dollars in the amount of the unpaid sum for such period at or about 11:00 a.m. Greenwich Mean Time two business days before the first day of such period provided that if any unpaid sum is of principal of an Advance repayable during an Interest Period pursuant to Clause 9 of the Agreement, the first such period applicable thereto shall be of a duration equal to the unexpired portion of that Interest Period and the rate of interest applicable to such unpaid sum during the unexpired portion of that Interest Period shall be that applicable to it immediately before it fell due plus _____ percent (__ %). Interest accruing under this subclause shall be due and payable at the end of each period by reference to which it is calculated.

(B) The Borrower shall indemnify the Lender on demand against any claim, cost, loss, or expense (including fund-

Figure 10-1. (cont.)

ing costs) incurred by it as a result of the occurrence of any event mentioned in Clause 9 of the Agreement or by reason of the receipt or recovery of any part of an Advance during an Interest Period relating thereto, the loss in the latter case being the excess of (i) the amount of additional interest which would have been recoverable if that sum had been received or recovered on the last day of such Interest Period over (ii) the amount that could have been received (in the opinion of the Lender) by depositing in the London Interbank Market two business days after its receipt such amount for the remainder of that Interest Period.

(C) Any sum which the Borrower fails to pay when due shall (for the purposes of this Clause and Clause 5 hereof) be treated as an advance and accordingly in this clause the term "Advance" includes any sum which the Borrower fails to pay when due, and the term "Interest Period" in relation to any such unpaid sum includes such period for which a rate of interest is determined under subclause (A) of this clause.

11.   *Set-Off*

The Borrower authorizes the Lender to apply any account of the Borrower with the Lender in satisfaction of any sum due and payable from the Borrower under the Agreement but unpaid; for this purpose the Lender is authorized to purchase with the monies standing to the credit of any such account such other currencies as may be necessary to effect such application.

12.   *Costs and Expenses*

The Borrower shall on demand reimburse the Lender for all costs, fees, and other expenses incurred by it in connection with the negotiation, preparation, and execution of the Agreement and the Guarantee and the preservation and enforcement of its rights thereunder, shall pay all stamp, registration, and other taxes and duties to which the Agreement or the Guarantee is or at any time may be subject and shall indemnify the Lender against any liabilities, costs, claims, and expenses resulting from any failure to pay or any delay in paying any such tax or duty.

13. *Payments*

(A) All payments to be made by the Borrower under the Agreement shall be made in the lawful currency of the United States of America which is both the currency of payment and of account and all payments so made shall (i) be made to the Lender in U.S. dollars and in same day funds (or in such other funds as may for the time being be customary for the settlement of international banking transactions in U.S. dollars) by 11:00 a.m. (New York Time) on the day for payment account number _____ at Metropolitan Bank of New York, 1 Metrobank Plaza, New York, New York 10006 (CHIPS number _____).

(B) If any payment to be made hereunder would otherwise fail to be made on a nonbusiness day it shall be made on the next succeeding calendar business day unless such day would fall in the next succeeding calendar month in which case such payment shall be made on the immediately preceding business day.

(C) Interest and the commitment fee shall accrue from day to day and be calculated on the basis of a year of 360 days for the actual number of days elapsed.

14. *Notices*

(A) Any communication to be made hereunder shall be made in writing but, unless otherwise stated, may be made by telex or letter, and any such communication or document to be delivered by one party to the other pursuant to this Agreement shall (unless the addressee has given 15 days' prior notification to the addressor of a change of address) be made or delivered to the following addresses:

For the Lender

_____

_____

For the Borrower

_____

_____

For the Guarantor

_____

_____

Figure 10-1. (cont.)

Each communication shall be deemed to have been made when received unless the date of receipt is a nonbusiness day in which case the same shall be deemed to have been made or delivered at the opening of business on the next succeeding business day.

(B) Each communication and document made or delivered by one party to the other pursuant to the Agreement shall be in the English language unless the original of any document is not in the English language, in which case such document shall be accompanied by an English translation thereof certified as accurate by the Borrower.

15. *Applicable Law and Jurisdiction*

(A) The Agreement shall be governed by and construed in accordance with the Laws of the State of New York.

(B) The Borrower agrees that any legal action or proceedings arising out of or in connection with the Agreement may be brought in the Courts of the State of New York or the Courts of the United States of America in New York, irrevocably submits to the jurisdiction of each such court, and agrees that any writ, judgment, or other notice of legal process shall be sufficiently served on it in connection with proceedings in England if delivered to _____, London and in New York if delivered to _____, New York.

_____

for and on behalf of Metropolitan Bank as Lender

_____

for and on behalf of _____ as Borrower

Dated _____, 19_____

Substance versus Form

Fundamentally, there is no difference between international and domestic lending—the principles are the same. The lender's paramount consideration is timely repayment, consistent with the terms of the loan agreement, while the borrower is concerned that the operating and financial constraints imposed by the lender do not jeopardize managerial flexibility. It is important, therefore, to devise a *workable* agreement. While it might on occasion be possible for a lender in a particularly strong position to elicit a very restrictive agreement from the borrower, there is the risk that such restriction might precipitate a technical default or even a financial collapse in the future. Even the best securities or guarantees are of little value if the borrower is insolvent. We thus have a tradeoff between overly restrictive covenants, which give the lender a great deal of control over the borrower's operations, and too few covenants, which allow the borrower a relatively free hand but may in turn ultimately lead to serious difficulty in debt service.

A good lending facility is not made because the loan agreement is technically flawless and legally impeccable, it is made because the lender exercised good credit judgment when making the original decision to lend. No matter how restrictive the covenants are or how comprehensive the clauses contained in the loan agreement are, there will likely be trouble if the credit decision is not sound. The more restrictive covenants will often end up being modified or relaxed to accommodate the borrower. More generally, covenants and liens define the operating and financial parameters bearing on the borrower: thus they act as an early warning system, alerting the lender to potential trouble. Ultimately, the lender's security lies in the continued viability of the borrower, not in the attachment of assets and liquidation. Default is a last resort and a very costly alternative to both parties. Therefore, it is a matter of mutual interest that the terms of the loan agreement be maintained; this, more than its specific terms or conditions, is probably the lender's best security.

MAJOR CLAUSES AND PROVISIONS

There are a number of provisions common to international loan agreements that form the core of the legal dimensions of international lending.

Covenants

Affirmative and negative covenants place restraints on the borrower's activities for the duration of the loan. In addition, they permit the lender to monitor performance and to influence the future conduct of the borrower in a manner that is deemed to reduce the risk that the loan will not be repaid. Covenants accomplish this in a number of different ways: (1) by forcing the borrower to comply with applicable legal requirements; (2) by restricting excessive leveraging (e.g., restrictions on additional debt or leases); (3) by preventing the borrower from preferring other creditors (lien covenants) over the lender; (4) by maintaining the assets of the borrower (e.g., restrictions on dividends and the maintenance of net worth); and (5) by requiring the borrower to retain adequate liquidity (e.g., working capital covenants).

Financial Covenants

These enable the lender to monitor the performance of the borrower by establishing operating parameters at the outset that define reasonable operating performance. They act as an early warning system and, if violated, give the lender an opportunity to review the situation and take the appropriate action to ensure the continued integrity of the loan. In some cases, this could mean accelerating the maturity of the loan.

Financial covenants have not been so widely accepted in European countries, where banks typically exercise greater control over the affairs of the borrower without the necessity for contractual policy controls. While they have not gained universal acceptance internationally, there are many cases in which the principles have been assimilated into international lending practices. To the extent that management has control over the financial condition of the firm, financial covenants serve the positive function of disciplining and directing financial policy. On the other hand, a financial covenant could provide a nervous lender with an excuse to accelerate the loan—a move more likely to precipitate rather than prevent financial collapse and ultimate insolvency.

Most financial covenants are couched in terms of certain minimum acceptable financial ratios such as debt ratios, working capital ratios, dividend ratios, and net worth ratios. They are also likely to require that the borrower supply certain financial and other information to enable the bank to monitor performance on an ongoing basis throughout the life of the loan. The most important of these financial covenants relate to the borrower's overall indebtedness. Prime-quality borrowers will encounter relatively few debt covenants, while lenders are more likely to impose limits on the future indebtedness of smaller or more risky borrowers. A debt covenant may provide for a maximum amount of allowable debt, perhaps broken down by class or maturity or expressed in ratio form (e.g., as a fraction of equity or current assets).

Lien Covenants

The purpose of lien covenants is to protect the unsecured or under-secured creditor who relies on the general and continued creditworthiness of the borrower as a going concern, rather than specific collateralized assets. They are intended to preserve the assets and revenues of the borrower, so that in the event of an adverse change in circumstances funds are available to settle the claims of all creditors rather than be appropriated in favor of higher-ranking classes of debt. Conventional lien covenants usually provide that the borrower agrees not to grant any liens or encumbrances on any assets except as specified—exceptions will usually relate to obligations arising in the ordinary course of business that the borrower is unable to avoid, such as taxes, worker's compensation, social insurance, or liens already in existence when the loan agreement is signed.

There are two alternatives to the conventional lien covenant. The first is the *pari passu* clause, which is simply an undertaking by the borrower that the indebtedness being incurred will rank "equally and ratably" with all other indebtedness of the borrower. The second is the *negative pledge* clause.

Negative Pledge. The negative pledge clause in loan agreements restricts the borrower from granting security interests in favor of other creditors. In its simplest form, it forbids any secured borrowing unless the lending bank is secured "equally and ratably" or "pari passu." Its purpose is to maintain the position of the lending bank relative to all other lenders and to prevent the borrower from assigning any priority among creditors that might subordinate a bank's loan in the event of financial difficulties or default. Unsecured lending would obviously be very unattractive if the assets and earnings of the borrower were preferentially assigned to a secured lender. Although few banks enter into a loan agreement expecting repayment from the liquidation of assets, this is nevertheless a possibility that must not be overlooked. Therefore, a situation in which a borrower's assets are pledged is intended to provide a pool of assets that are available to settle the claims of unsecured creditors collectively, without regard for any preferences or distinctions among them.

In practice, a negative pledge is often qualified in various ways—for example, to exclude secured lending already in existence or to permit a certain amount or type of secured borrowing. Another variation prevailing in the Euromarket involves restrictions on the sale of assets or a major portion of the business. However, from the lender's view-point, the negative pledge clause offers protection only insofar as the bank has a right to receive future collateral. It does not limit the amount of future debt that can be secured. The lender's interest could therefore become so diluted that it no longer offers any substantive protection. From a borrower's viewpoint, the main disadvantage of the negative pledge is that there is an obligation to allow existing creditors to share in any future security interest granted, a factor that could cause problems in obtaining new funds.

Negative pledges are rarely comprehensive because of various trans-actions that may not constitute "security" in law but have the same economic and commercial effect. Examples of such arrangements are leasing, hire purchase, sale and leaseback, and factoring. Because most of these arrangements are accepted commercial practice, it is of-ten virtually impossible to distinguish between a routine transaction involving such an arrangement and an evasive financial move on the part of the borrower.

The weakness of negative pledges is particularly evident with sovereign loans because of the unwillingness of governments to accept restrictive wording. The purpose of a negative pledge in the case of a sovereign credit is to prevent a government from discriminating in favor of a particular lender by pledging foreign currency reserves or other official assets as security, when such assets might otherwise be available to meet its external debt. In practice, there are a number of ways that a sovereign borrower who is so disposed can circumvent the spirit of a particular negative pledge without violating the letter of the agreement.

Changed Circumstances

This standard clause in international loan agreements provides for possible future changes in any country's laws or regulations that have the effect of making the loan illegal, requiring that under such circumstances the borrower must repay the loan. Where a syndicated loan is involved, the clause normally only provides for repayment to those banks affected by the legal or regulatory change involved.

Although it has become conventional practice to include this clause in loan agreements, there is some doubt about its necessity. In the first place, if a loan becomes illegal, the agreement itself is no longer valid. Moreover, the clause has a retroactive impact, and it is conceivable that the banks could find themselves compelled to cancel a loan under one clause yet be unable to do so under another clause in the same agreement that stipulates the date of earliest repayment.

A second aspect of the changed-circumstances clause addresses the issue of increased costs bearing upon the lender to maintain or fund a loan as a result of changes in reserve requirements or taxes (other than income taxes). Under this provision the borrower, once informed of these additional costs, can choose to either absorb them or repay the entire loan. Although once again rarely invoked, this clause has now become standard practice in Eurofacilities, where spreads are often too thin to allow the lender to absorb such extra costs.

Misrepresentation

Representations and warranties are basically statements of common understanding reached among the parties to a loan agreement and are the legal and financial assessment that form the foundation of the lender's evaluation and final decision to extend credit to the borrower. These assessments are extended beyond what is known to be fact and into certain assumptions that serve as a basis for assigning risk to the borrower. If certain facts are unknown or unable to be verified, or if the lender is uncertain about some particular condition involving the borrower, the borrower may be required to make specific representations pertaining to such facts and conditions. The borrower therefore assumes certain risks that his representation will not in fact hold true. Such representations may nevertheless serve as alternatives to clauses relating to events or conditions of default or conditions precedent to the final obligation to lend.

Until the facility is actually signed, the accuracy of the lender's representations is a condition precedent. Afterward, a breach of representation or warranty by the borrower will bring the facility into technical default, and the lender will have the right to accelerate the maturity of the debt or seek available legal remedies to enforce the terms of the agreement. A deliberate or negligent misrepresentation by one party may entitle the other to recover damages or losses resulting from reliance on that misrepresentation.

A misrepresentation clearly is a reflection on the integrity of the misrepresenting party and one that can have wider repercussions. Therefore, it is important that both parties to a loan fully understand the exact nature of the representations made. A commonly cited example of a misrepresentation pitfall occurs when a borrower certifies that his firm conducts business in compliance with all applicable laws and regulations. In practical terms, it is almost impossible for a major firm to be absolutely certain of meeting this requirement even at the national level. Violation of some minor local regulation could technically be considered a misrepresentation, even though it may have no bearing whatsoever on the financial condition of the borrower or his ability to service the debt.

Unrepresentative Cost

If the cost of money to the lender or to certain banks in a syndicated transaction ceases to be adequately represented by the interest rate or spread associated with the facility, the lender is entitled under this clause either to establish a new rate mechanism or to be repaid. The unrepresentative-cost clause is obviously designed mainly to protect smaller banks, who sometimes have to pay a premium to obtain funds relative to the larger banks, although it may be unclear whether this is sufficient grounds for a smaller bank to nullify its commitments to the syndicate. This clause cannot compensate for an individual failure, and it relates only to factors affecting broad financial conditions. From the borrower's viewpoint, the clause might be important when a lending syndicate comprised of a number of small banks is involved, or when the majority of the banks are from a weak country or countries that might be similarly affected by having their ability to fund themselves somehow compromised by changing market conditions.

Events of Default

One of the most sensitive areas of any loan agreement is that which sets out the events of default. These are events or circumstances that will permit the bank to declare the loan immediately due and payable and will terminate the bank's commitment to extend credit under the terms of the agreement. Lenders will obviously tend to favor strict events of default that give them the discretion either to accelerate or to waive that right in the event of problems with the loan. Borrowers, on the other hand, are wary of nervous or oversensitive lenders invoking their right to accelerate based on a trivial or immaterial technical default resulting from a simple mistake or omission.

Typical events of default that will be found in most loan agreements include failure to pay interest and principal when due, breach of a representation and warranty, violation or nonperformance of a covenant, cross-default to some other debt of the borrower, as well as events of an obviously more serious nature (e.g., bankruptcy or expropriation). Other events are somewhat more controversial and often the subject of heated negotiation. In particular, the "material adverse change" clause permits the lender to declare a default when there has been a material adverse change in the financial condition, operations, or assets of the borrower, or a change in prevailing political or economic conditions in the country of the borrower. The problem with such a clause is in the interpretation of what constitutes a material adverse change. Many borrowers contend that the clause can be used as an "out" by the careless or imprudent lender whose analysis of the credit is somewhat less than circumspect. Lenders view the clause as a form of insurance or comfort, given that the future is always uncertain. Experience has tended to support lenders' claims that the clause will only be invoked in extreme circumstances, when the collection of the loan is seriously at risk.

Violation of certain covenants, especially financial covenants, may give rise to an automatic default if such covenants are considered fundamental to the basic credit decision or if the possibility of correction is limited. However, automatic events of default can also have an adverse effect on lenders if they trigger cross-default provisions among other credit agreements outstanding with the borrower. Certain less significant or critical events of default will sometimes be subject to a grace period or notice of requirement. In such instances, violations of covenants become events of default only after notice has been given by the bank to the borrower and after a grace period lapses without the default being corrected.

Cross-default

In its simplest form, the cross-default clause provides that if the borrower defaults under any other loan agreement (thus enabling those creditors to demand payment or renegotiate their position), it also constitutes an automatic default under the loan agreement covering a particular transaction. The cross-default provision can also be broadened to include events that will ultimately lead to default if not corrected or will lead to a situation in which sufficient conditions for declaring default exist, even though one or more other lenders have chosen to waive that right. The cross-default clause gives all banks the same opportunity to negotiate with the borrower and protect their respective positions, rather than be forced to wait until formal default can be declared under their particular loan agreements, even though such an outcome is seen as inevitable.

Cross-default clauses that give a bank the right to accelerate repayment of a loan if any other lenders *could have* declared a default have become a rather controversial issue. In effect, such a provision makes available to all lenders the highest restraints negotiated by any lender to the same borrower. Therefore, it is important that lenders be aware of how other financing agreements to a particular borrower are cross-referenced. A bank could find itself working to improve its loan and keep a borrower from default, only to have another bank with a weaker agreement force the borrower into default by means of a strong cross-default clause. From the borrower's point of view as well, technical default could enable a bank to demand that its loan be immediately due and payable, even though it is in no real danger under an agreement to which it was not a party, and even though the party in default has chosen to waive the right.

On the other hand, a cross-default clause can be an effective early warning system, allowing a bank to review its position and make its decision accordingly. Because one lender has chosen not to accelerate repayment of its loan does not mean that its reasons for doing so are necessarily applicable to all other lenders with loans outstanding to that borrower. Needless to say, cross-default clauses can also act as a powerful deterrent to a borrower contemplating a default on a particular loan or against a particular lender or group of lenders.

Creditor Remedies

A well-drafted loan agreement will allow the lender to exercise various remedies upon the occurrence and continuance of certain events of default. The most dramatic of these remedies, as noted, is the right to terminate the lending commitment and declare the outstanding loan immediately due and payable. But the right to accelerate payment in this manner is not the only remedy available to the bank, and in practice it is rarely used, except as a last resort, because it is likely to trigger acceleration by the borrower's other creditors and could even precipitate bankruptcy on the part of the borrower.

There are several less drastic remedies available to the lender that do not require acceleration of the loan. First, the bank would have the right to set off deposits of the borrower against the borrower's obligation to repay the loan, either by virtue of a specific provision within the loan agreement or based on statute or common law. Second, provided the borrower has not declared bankruptcy, the bank would normally be able to obtain judgment for the principal sum due; it would then have remedies available under the legal system for the enforcement of the judgment. The bank may also be able to resort to legal proceedings to enforce certain provisions of the loan agreement. In fact, the most frequent result of an event of default is a renegotiation of the loan agreement by the bank and the borrower, along with a renegotiation of the borrower's other credit relationships. Although rarely invoked, the right to accelerate strengthens the bank's negotiating position substantially and serves as a powerful incentive for the borrower to remain in compliance.

Specifically, when the borrower is a foreign sovereign—that is, a foreign state, its agency, or instrumentality—the bank lender is likely to have special problems in exercising adequate remedies. There are certain legal and practical limitations on the bank's contractual right to terminate the agreement and accelerate the loan. Most typical default provisions make it clear that an event of default not only must have occurred, but must also be continuing at the time this right is exercised. Once the condition of default is rectified, the lender could lose that right and the agreement would become valid once again. Of course, once the agreement has been terminated or the loan maturity accelerated, it is too late to rectify the event of default. Although the New York courts have generally enforced termination and acceleration provisions in accordance with the terms of their loan agreements, they have also pointed out that the equitable principle of good faith can be applied to prevent termination or acceleration in appropriate cases. The principle is designed to provide equitable relief to a borrower who is technically in default as a result of a trivial or wholly immaterial breach of the terms or provisions of the loan agreement. To terminate or to accelerate the loan in such a case would be unjustified and entirely out of proportion with the source of the problem. However, the ultimate limitation on the lender's right to accelerate is a practical one. To do so would be to invite all other creditors to do likewise, to substantially increase the risk of multiple lawsuits against the borrower, and, in the case of sovereign borrowers, to risk unforeseen political repercussions.

The Right of Set-Off

Among the remedies available to a bank lender with respect to default by a borrower, one of the most useful and effective measures is the right to set off the amount of the loan outstanding against the deposits of the borrower placed with the bank. In legal terms, the right of set-off is generally defined as the right of one party unilaterally to extinguish mutual obligations prior to any judicial determination of that party's rights. In banking terms, it is simply the right of a bank lender to charge its deposit obligations against the depositor's loan obligations to the bank.

A bank's right of set-off is usually subject to certain conditions. Under New York law, the offsetting obligations must have matured or must be due—a term loan is deemed to be "due" when accelerated. This condition, however, may be modified by contract or statute. Another condition of set-off is that the obligations to be set off must be "mutual"—that is, between the same parties acting in the same capacities. This condition is intended to protect the rights of innocent third parties. Problems can arise in the case of sovereign lending, when a bank will typically lend to one government entity against deposits held by the bank in the name of some other government entity—usually the central bank—of the same country.

In a case of default by a sovereign borrower, the courts will be called upon to decide whether all or some government entities should be considered part of one legal entity for the purposes of set-off and other remedies. There seems to be no general rule governing this particular issue, and the courts have tended to apply the *one-entity theory* based on the facts and *entities* in each case. If a government creates a separate and distinct legal entity to engage in commercial activities, the courts will not ordinarily consider the government and the entity as one and the same. The bank lending to a foreign state and requiring the support of a government instrumentality should thus obtain the express guarantee or similar obligation direct from that government instrumentality.

In the Iranian crisis of the 1970s, the one-entity view became known as the "Big Mullah" theory. The U.S. banks claimed that all Iranian entities were deemed to have passed under the control of the revolutionary government, thus giving them the right to set off all Iranian deposits and other assets against defaulting loans, without regard for strict mutuality between the parties.

The Iranian crisis also raised another very important issue with respect to set-offs concerning international loan agreements. The location of the deposits determines the law under which the set-off issue is decided. A substantial portion of Iranian deposits were booked in the London branches of U.S. banks, while the loans were usually booked outside London (e.g., Nassau) for tax reasons. The Iranians had set out to challenge the legality of the freeze on their deposits in American banks outside the United States and their right of set-off. The final settlement of the hostage crisis was resolved outside of the courts, leaving undecided a number of issues regarding a bank's right to set off outstanding debt obligations against bank deposits.

Sovereign Immunity

The involvement of governments and their agencies in international borrowing and in guaranteeing lending facilities, either directly or through participation in international trade and commerce, has grown significantly over the years. In the U.S. capital market and the Euromarkets alike, foreign governments and quasi-governmental agencies and organizations engage in substantial financing and guarantees. Sovereign states and state-owned entities have been among the most frequent and largest borrowers in the international markets. Therefore, the issue of sovereign immunity has assumed commensurately increased importance; it is the basis under which legal remedies are available to the lender in the event of a breach of the loan agreement.

Sovereign states have traditionally been immune from suit or seizure of assets outside their national political frontiers and sometimes within them as well. However, as states have become increasingly involved in ordinary commercial activities, the maintenance of sovereign immunity has resulted in substantial injustice to the private sector. Most commercially significant jurisdictions now hold that a sovereign that descends to the marketplace must accept the sanctions of the marketplace.

In the United States, under the Foreign Sovereign Immunities Act of 1976, sovereign immunity rulings are decided exclusively by the courts and are limited to contracts of a governmental rather than a commercial nature. The act also provides that a foreign government or its instrumentality can explicitly or implicitly waive its immunity from suit. Such waivers are effective irrespective of any subsequent attempt to revoke them (unless the waiver is interpreted as revocable). Under the provisions of the act, foreign governmental borrowings from U.S. commercial banks are considered "commercial" in nature; sovereign immunity, therefore, is not applicable.

Until 1978 the courts in the United Kingdom adhered to the absolute theory of sovereign immunity, granting foreign governments immunity from suit. Moreover, a waiver of any immunity prior to the commencement of proceedings against the borrower was deemed to be ineffective. Obviously, a government being sued could not be relied upon to waive its immunity. English law was out of step with the United States and other jurisdictions in this respect. With the increased involvement of governments in commercial transactions, London was running the risk of losing its preeminent position as a Euro–lending center unless the law was changed. This change occurred with the passage of the State Immunity Act of 1978. A sovereign state now automatically waives its immunity from suit when it submits to the jurisdiction of the English courts. A further waiver of immunity from execution of attachment orders on its assets is also required.

Legislation in both the United States and the United Kingdom has adopted the same principle of restrictive immunity, although there are some significant differences in the implementation of that general doctrine. In general, however, these differences will only be material when a borrower is either unprepared to or does not have the constitutional power to submit to the jurisdiction of foreign courts or to grant explicit waivers.

But while international lenders are now more likely to obtain judgments against foreign government debtors, either on the basis of an advance waiver of sovereign immunity or on the basis that the facility represented a commercial transaction, the lender's real concern is still the execution of that judgment. A defaulting government will likely have few external assets, and as long as there is a possibility of a judgment being entered against it, those assets are unlikely to be held in the United States. The 1976 Foreign Sovereign Immunities Act sanctions waivers only with respect to property "used for a commercial activity in the United States," although many loan agreements contain clauses that explicitly waive the foreign government's immunity from execution over all its property, not merely its commercial property. If the courts decide that such an explicit waiver is ineffective with respect to noncommercial property, it is unclear where the distinction between commercial and noncommercial assets will be drawn.

The dollar remains the principal currency for international trade, and a significant portion of foreign central bank reserves are invested in the U.S. capital markets. If foreign central banks believed that the distinction between commercial and noncommercial assets might subject their U.S. holdings to increased risk of attachment or execution, they might be less likely to maintain assets in the United States. This would have obvious adverse repercussions on U.S. international payments and the government's ability to manage the public debt. This issue was resolved by a special exemption clause incorporated in the 1976 act. In effect, this clause stipulates that the property of a central bank is not commercial in nature when used for central banking functions. However, when a foreign central bank acts as an agent of the state or carries on non-central-banking activities, it will be subject to the general provisions of the act and will not be granted explicit immunity.

Governing Law and Jurisdiction

The purpose of a loan agreement is to document the mutual understanding reached between the parties and to clearly define their rights and obligations under the agreement. A carefully drafted agreement seeks to eliminate ambiguity and reduce the possibility of an uncertain or unexpected outcome. In the event of a dispute, the agreement should be interpreted in a consistent and predictable manner. However, an international agreement could involve the laws of more than one country, and could therefore be subject to different interpretations under different legal jurisdictions. In order to increase the degree of certainty and predictability, nearly every international loan agreement contains a clause that specifies the law under which the contract will be governed. It is generally accepted that the governing law chosen must have some natural link with the contract itself. Typical connecting factors are the place where the loan agreement is negotiated or signed, the place where one of the parties is located, the place where the loan is funded (e.g., London), or the place where payments are to be made.

A bank will normally insist that the law of the country or state in which it is located (e.g., the law of the state of New York) should be applicable, since it provides the most familiar legal environment. Alternatively, it might settle on some other jurisdiction (e.g., the law of England) that has a developed body of commercial law and a reputable legal system that can be relied upon to deliver a relatively impartial and unbiased decision, consistent with established legal precedent.

In multilender, syndicated Eurocurrency transactions, it is common to see the laws of New York and/or England selected. There is in both cases a substantial body of law and precedent in dealing with complex financial and commercial matters that should render an efficient and equitable outcome. Regardless of the jurisdiction settled upon, it is important from the lender's standpoint that the agreement be consistent with the laws of either party's home jurisdiction or of any other jurisdiction under which the lender might be likely to seek a remedy for nonperformance.

The governing-law clause has occasionally become a sensitive issue, particularly with sovereign borrowers from the developing countries, whose governments often strive for greater political acceptance and frequently require the designation of their domestic law to govern the transaction. In refusing to accept the law of that country, it could be held that, by implication, banks are casting aspersions on the integrity of the government and its legal system. It is virtually impossible for a bank to enforce a claim against such a government under its own legal jurisdiction or many others. The lending bank often has an edge in bargaining power before the loan is made, although the lender is in a weak position and in need of the greatest protection once the loan has been disbursed. At that time it has performed its part of the bargain and has only rights under the agreement, primarily the right to receive payments of interest and principal. The borrower, on the other hand, has only obligations, the most pressing of which is the repayment of interest and principal as it falls due. It is, therefore, most important to the lender to establish jurisdiction under a governing law that will offer fair and impartial judgment and an enforceable claim.

There have been cases in which a borrowing country has not been prepared to compromise its sovereignty by submission to a foreign law, and the lender has been unwilling to accept the application of the law of the borrowing country. Such an impasse is sometimes overcome by simply omitting any selection of governing law altogether and leaving the matter to be inferred. If no choice is made, there are ways to ascertain which law applies. The courts will usually look first to see whether there is any evidence in the loan agreement itself showing a clear intent to apply the laws of a particular country. Many jurisdictions will regard submission to the courts of their country or arbitration there as being evidence of a tacit choice of that country's laws. Other possible factors are the language (more likely a factor of market convenience if the agreement is in the United Kingdom, rather than an inference in favor of English law) and terminology used or references to a particular country's statutes.

If no tacit choice is apparent, the rules of many jurisdictions follow the *center-of-gravity theory*—they apply the law with which the contract is more closely connected. This judgment is likely to be based on factors such as currency of payment of interest and principal, location of parties to the agreement, location of funding, or where the agreement is negotiated and signed. This is considered a more flexible view, in contrast to other inflexible rules (e.g., rigid presumption), that assign governing law based on nationality or the law of place of contracting or performance.

In the United States the classical doctrines of rigid presumption and the center-of-gravity approach have been eroded by a number of more flexible approaches.

Forum Selection

The purpose of an express forum-selection clause is to confer jurisdiction on external courts that otherwise would not be called upon to decide an action on a loan agreement. This provides an additional forum outside the home country of the borrower and gives the lender the option of bringing an action locally, or in the external forum. Because many international borrowers have worldwide assets, the absence of a local judgment is not necessarily fatal. To be effective, the terms of a loan agreement must ultimately be enforceable, and the threat of judicial enforcement is a most important weapon in their arsenal, even though it is viewed as a last resort by many lenders.

An enforceable action is of little use if the borrower is insolvent, and creditors are naturally reluctant to institute proceedings that will trigger similar action by other creditors. There has been ample evidence to suggest that defaults are more likely to result in an agreed rescheduling of the debt and often in an infusion of new funds to assist the borrower. Therefore, the power to obtain judgment is viewed by many as predominantly a measure to balance the inequality of bargaining power that generally favors an insolvent debtor and to give some credibility to the default negotiations.

The choice of the external forum is influenced by a mixture of legal and economic considerations; however, from the lender's viewpoint, the most important consideration is generally to protect the insulation that is provided by the choice of an external governing law. Without this insulation, the only available forum for enforcement would be the courts of the borrower's country, and there is a risk that they might either ignore the governing law altogether or apply it only to the extent that it is consistent with local laws.

Borrower's objections are often based on the presumption that the external forum is not in fact independent, since in most cases it is the forum of the lender. In the case of sovereign borrowers, these objections are often based on political considerations, and considerations of national prestige, rather than legal factors. It is more unlikely that the local courts would be permitted to hear an action against a sovereign or its agency or instrumentality. The lender, therefore, relies on external enforcement and the judiciary in those countries, (e.g., the United States and the United Kingdom) that are prepared to grant express waivers of immunity from enforcement, thereby allowing attachment of assets that come within their jurisdiction.

Although they are theoretically separate, it is desirable that legal forum selection should follow the governing law in order to confer greater predictability. The courts of the governing-law country, being most familiar with their own law and precedent, are more likely to arrive at an expected result than a court that is asked to adjudicate on the basis of a foreign governing law. In determining the appropriate forum, it is important to select a judiciary that is experienced in international lending disputes, without undue bias in favor of local interests and with commercially oriented court procedures. These characteristics will most likely be found in countries with a reputable legal system and a developed body of commercial law and established legal precedent. Thus, although theoretically separate, the choice of governing law and the choice of external forum are likely to be closely related.

Special Legal Problems

Syndicated Transactions

After securing the borrower's mandate, the lead manager on a syndication will normally send out an information memorandum, prepared in conjunction with the borrower, to banks that have expressed an interest in the loan. The information memorandum will virtually always include a disclaimer clause that will disavow any liability on the part of the bank for the accuracy of the information. The soliciting of loan participants in this way gives rise to two major legal questions: Is the information memorandum a regulated prospectus?; and is the lead manager responsible for any inaccurate or incomplete statements in the information memorandum? Some countries have introduced legislation regulating prospectuses inviting public subscription for securities. But in general the offering memorandum will be exempt because it is not a public invitation. It is, rather, a private offering that is circulated among sophisticated lenders who do not require protective legislation. With regard to the second question, liability for an information memorandum will rest primarily with the borrower. Experience shows that most actions alleging misrepresentation are brought by injured lenders only when the borrower is insolvent and, in such a case, they are forced to look elsewhere to settle their claim. The Colocotronis case discussed in the "Problem Cases" section of this chapter is a good example. In this case several U.S. regional banks alleged that they were induced to participate in a syndication by untrue and incomplete representations by the lead bank.

Once the terms of the agreement have been negotiated by the lead bank and the borrower, the documentation is usually forwarded to the syndicate members for their comments. The lead manager will generally be able to avoid liability, provided that syndicate members are given access and adequate time to review the loan documentation, that they are advised to seek independent legal counsel, and that a specific exculpation clause is inserted into the loan agreement expressly limiting the lead manager's liability.

The syndicate will appoint one of their members as their agent to carry out certain functions on their behalf (see Chapter 5). The relationship of the agent with respect to the syndicate and the borrower is sometimes ambiguous, and the scope of the duties placed upon the agent by law is rather unclear. The delegation of power to the agent by the syndicate is effected by a specific clause in the loan agreement, which expressly limits the power of the agency and confines the duties to those specifically described. The objective is to protect the syndicate against unauthorized actions outside of those powers specified and to include certain onerous duties on the part of the agent that may be implied by law. This divestment of authority is binding for the duration of the loan; normally a syndicate could not, even by unanimous declaration, withdraw the authority they have vested in the agent unless the latter is in breach of duty or has explicitly consented.

Project Financings

Project loans rely on the anticipated cash flow of the project for repayment, rather than relying on the general creditworthiness of the borrower (see Chapter 9). Many projects are so large and complex that they require the financial support and expertise of a group of companies. Rather than relying on a loose joint venture, the project sponsors, and probably the local government, are likely to favor the local incorporation of a separate entity to manage the project. As well as offering certain local tax advantages, a project company will enable the sponsors to isolate the project risks by vesting ownership of the assets in a single company and avoiding consolidation of the project liabilities in their own accounts. From the lender's viewpoint, a project company makes it easier to obtain a security over assets since they are vested in a single entity; this reduces problems arising from fragmented ownership and managerial control. The most significant disadvantage of a project company is the increased political risk resulting from reliance on local jurisdiction and the increased risk of expropriation associated with a locally incorporated company.

The essence of project finance is to identify and evaluate all the risks involved and spread those risks among the parties involved. The documentation associated with a project financing will therefore include a wide variety of contractual forms and support guarantees designed to reduce these risks to the greatest extent possible. In practice, however, litigation as a means of enforcement is considered only as a last alternative and, in practice, is probably more important as a source of bargaining power than as a means to secure effective legal remedies.

Contracts do allow the lenders to claim damages resulting from a sponsor's breach, although under most contracts it would be a claim for damages that are unliquidated and unascertained, with a wholly uncertain result depending on the nature of the particular contract under which damages are claimed. These problems associated with damages cannot usually be resolved by seeking a court order for specific performance. Specific performance is at the discretion of the court and will not be available if the court considers damages to be adequate, if such an order would be impractical, or if the court is not in a position to supervise the order due to the location of the project.

Ship and Aircraft Financing

The most accepted form of security in many asset-based financings (see Chapter 7) is for the lender to take out a mortgage. In the case of ship financing, shipowners may set up separate companies for each ship in their fleet to isolate the financial risks associated with each ship. The shipowning company will guarantee the loan to the borrowing company and secure the guarantee by a mortgage on its ship. If the ship is under charter, the bank will take an assignment of earnings as the source of repayment of the debt. The security is also likely to comprise an assignment of insurances to cover total or partial loss of the bank's security.

The 1958 Geneva Convention on the High Seas required participating states to grant nationality (subject to certain conditions designed to ensure a genuine link between ship and state), to register all ships that so qualify, and to exercise jurisdiction and control over administrative, technical, and social matters. The eligibility of a ship for registration on a national register is of great importance to a mortgagee since, if the vessel does not in fact qualify, registration may be struck out of the documentation along with the registered mortgage.

Most countries of registry base eligibility for national registration on the nationality of the ownership of the vessel. This is fairly straightforward in the case of individuals; however, with a locally incorporated company, it is often more difficult to determine true nationality.

Not all countries are signatories of the 1958 Geneva Convention. The most notable exceptions are Panama, Liberia, and Honduras, which do not require any "genuine link" and will accept ships on their register that are owned directly by foreign nationals — giving rise to the term "flags of convenience." Since it is difficult for a state to exercise control over the activities of foreign nationals located outside their jurisdiction, they are not in a position to monitor or enforce compliance with accepted international conventions governing the construction and operation of ships. This laissez-faire approach toward regulation and an absence of operating restrictions has an associated cost savings that has attracted many shipowners to fly a "flag of convenience" in preference to national registration.

The enforcement or acceleration of a shipping loan tends to be a very expensive and difficult process, primarily because the circumstances giving rise to such an action are usually the result of a shipowner's insolvency, which means that other creditors will be similarly affected and will seek to enforce their own claims against the ship. Competing claims may be subject to dispute, leading to lengthy litigation before the vessel can be sold to realize the various claims. In periods of overcapacity in the industry — when the number of failures is likely to be highest — the parties to a dispute could find they are arguing over claims to an asset whose realizable value is diminishing at an alarming rate. In some cases, a bank may have to pay off the seizing creditors to obtain release of the ship, in order to proceed to a jurisdiction more favorable to its particular interest.

Ship mortgages are the predecessors of the registered aircraft mortgage, and although legislators have incorporated some refinements and improvements, the techniques of financing and the documentation are similar in many respects. The major differences are (1) many aircraft are owned by nationalized airlines, who can borrow on their own account, and (2) spare parts are important in aircraft financing — especially engines, which are a substantial portion of total cost and hence of the security. In the United States, where private airlines are the rule, title financing is common. In most of these transactions, the financier retains or takes title or ownership to the assets but gives possession to the debtor.

The Geneva Convention of 1958 was an undertaking among a large number of countries. Although not binding on nonmember states, it has achieved wide acceptance. Perhaps the most important principle adopted was the recognition that a mortgage should be tested according to the law of the relevant flag.

Other Secured Financing

Secured lending has not had an important role in international finance, mainly because of the difficulty in monitoring security interests internationally and because international borrowers generally have a very good credit standing. The only areas in which a security has become standard are shipping and project loans. The purpose of security is to enable the lender to sell the security in the event of default and use the proceeds to pay out the loan ahead of other creditors. In the case of a ship loan, there is clearly a saleable asset; however, since it is a movable asset, problems of attachment could arise. Project assets often are not marketable because of their nature; however, control over the assets and being in a position to operate the project may be just as important as the ability to realize the assets by sale.

Security law differs substantially from country to country, and each type of property attracts its own rules, making generalizations difficult. Registration has become mandatory in most jurisdictions, raising the possibility of adverse extraterritorial effects not foreseen by the lender. The basic purpose of registration is to publicize the security so that other lenders are not deceived into granting excess credit on the basis of the apparent absolute and unencumbered ownership of assets.

PROBLEM CASES

It is difficult to describe the legal dimensions of international banking without some practical examples of what can happen if things go awry. The Iranian default is discussed here as an example of problems encountered by banks in the case of a sovereign debtor, and the Colocotronis ship financing case illustrates in a similar way the legal entanglements triggered by a private debtor default.

The Iran Case

Iran had long been a favorite among the major lenders in the world's capital markets. The Shah was a stable ruler in an otherwise unstable area of the world; his government enjoyed the continued support of successive U.S. administrations and the benefits of vast oil export revenues. But the Shah's commitment to the industrialization and modernization of his ancient monarchy meant Iran also became a heavy international borrower—the bulk of which was financed by loan syndicates led by the large United States money center banks and mostly arranged through their London branches. Given the traditionally close relationship between the United States and its most important ally in the Gulf region, the correspondingly close relationship with U.S. money-center banks is not surprising. But participation in Iranian credits also extended to the major Japanese and European banks, as well as to a large number of U.S. regional banks.

The events that followed the Shah's departure early in 1979 are now well documented. It was initially thought that as long as Iran maintained the flow of oil exports it would be in a position to service its external obligations; therefore, it was thought that its massive debt was in no immediate danger of rescheduling or default. This view, of course, failed to recognize the strength or the depth of the revolutionary tide sweeping the country. The situation continued to deteriorate, and the economic infrastructure of the country began to erode as revolutionary forces progressively gained control. Ten days after the U.S. embassy was occupied by radical Muslim "students" and its staff taken hostage, the then Finance Minister Abdulhassan Bani-sadr delivered a speech that appeared to indicate that his government planned to repudiate all international loans arranged under the Shah's regime and to shift deposits out of U.S. financial institutions. The Carter administration reacted swiftly; in an effort to hang on to a major bargaining lever, the president announced a freeze on all Iranian assets held in the United States. Although widely interpreted as a purely political action, the move was also taken to prevent possible pressure on the dollar and U.S. banks as a result of the withdrawal of Iranian assets and to make funds available to settle the claims of American lenders in the event of the threatened Iranian default on outstanding loan obligations.

These events triggered a chain of events that eventually had widespread repercussions throughout the world financial community.

Just prior to the Carter freeze order, the Khomeini government instructed the Chase Manhattan Bank, the agent on a $500 million syndicated loan to the imperial government of Iran, to draw on Iranian assets in London to meet an interest installment. Chase maintained that payment was held up by the freeze, and it was unable to execute the order in time. The loan, therefore, was technically in default. Chase hastily polled the 10 other members of the syndicate (6 of whom were American banks) on the matter of default. The voting went along country lines, and the loan was declared in default— immediately due and payable. This action triggered the cross-default clauses, which are common in most syndicated loan agreements, and brought Iran into technical default on virtually all of its international borrowings. The scramble for Iranian assets then began. U.S. banks moved quickly to protect their interests by making use of the right of set-off and attaching Iranian assets wherever they could be found— taking a rather broad interpretation of assets belonging to the defaulting sovereign now known as the "Big Mullah" theory—maintaining that all governmental and quasi-governmental assets held abroad were the property of the sovereign.

The speed with which the U.S. banks moved to declare Iran in default represented a major deviation from normal banking practice. Obviously, it was motivated more by political considerations associated with the unprecedented hostage-taking and embassy seizure than by careful financial deliberations. Indeed, Iran was a most unusual case of default—its financial assets were well in excess of $10 billion in November 1979, which far outweighed its obligations to foreign commercial lenders. Normally, when a borrower fails to meet a payment, the lead bank will at the very least arrange a meeting of lenders with the borrower to try to save the situation. All possible alternatives will be considered, with a declaration of default being the last resort. In the Iranian case, the U.S. banks involved were motivated by a revulsion at the events in Tehran, sharing the helpless sense of frustration over the Ayatollah's hostile acts aimed directly at American national sovereignty and centuries of diplomatic tradition.

The American banks were given an edge to their sword by the application of the Carter freeze order to their overseas branches, permitting Iranian balances there to be set off against outstanding loans. The $4 billion in Iranian balances held with the overseas branches of U.S. banks exceeded net liabilities so, overall, the U.S. banks had a net surplus. Non-U.S. banks involved in lending to Iran were not in as fortunate a position and felt victimized by a "political dispute" between the United States and Iran that was now being waged on a financial front.

There may also have been some justification to their claim that Chase did not fully acquaint its syndicate partners with the circumstances regarding Iran's default and why the interest due had not been paid. Iran had argued that failure to make the interest payment was due to "force majeure," although it is unlikely that the agreement with the Chase-led syndicate included such a provision. Many non-American bankers feared that the speed and the motives behind the U.S. action in declaring Iran in default, their alacrity in attaching assets, and the spate of lawsuits that followed upset the generally accepted code of conduct among international bankers and caused permanent damage to the global banking system. Some U.S. bankers also felt that the episode might jeopardize their future leadership position in syndicated lending and in their ability to attract deposits that might conceivably be subject to similar action. The counterargument was that the U.S. embassy seizure and the taking of hostages were such unprecedented and provocative actions that the United States had no choice, short of a declaration of war, but to use any other available weapons. According to this view, the whole episode could be considered a one-of-a-kind, historical curiosity that would not be repeated and would leave no lasting imprint on international banking.

The move to set off deposits against loans did touch on a number of contentious legal issues. First, the practice of combining or offsetting customer accounts is a long-established one, but only when both the loan and the offsetting deposit are due and payable. Thus, only a small portion of total deposits that were on call would normally be available to be set off. Second, the right to set off only applies when the debtor and creditor are the same legal entity. In the Iran case, most of the deposits were in the name of Bank Markazi, the central bank, while most of the borrowing was done by various public sector institutions. This is where the U.S. banks came up with the "Big Mullah" theory, claiming that Iran should be viewed as a single entity. This enabled them to justify offsetting Iranian assets against liabilities, irrespective of the particular debtor or creditor relationship involved. Third, there was the problem that setting off across international boundaries being legally recognized by the English and other national courts. A substantial portion of Iranian deposits were booked in the London branches of U.S. banks, while the loans are usually booked elsewhere for tax reasons.

In the final analysis, most of these issues were not resolved by the courts. Under the agreement worked out in 1981 to free the 52 American hostages, $3.7 billion was made available out of the frozen assets to repay the outstanding syndicated bank loans. A further $1.4 billion was transferred to an Algerian-controlled escrow account to settle the claims of individual banks with nonsyndicated loans. An international tribunal was established in The Hague to hear the claims of corporations or individuals against Iran. In agreeing to such a tribunal, Iran clearly waived sovereign immunity, which might have prevented private claimants from suing its government. To settle the residual legal claims, a further $4 billion was also transferred to the escrow account on the understanding that the balance in the account would not be permitted to fall below $500 million and would be untouched by Iran while there were still claims outstanding. All remaining assets were returned to Iran.

The banks, therefore, came out of the Iranian ordeal surprisingly well—the only unresolved issue was related to the amount of interest payable on the frozen assets, and this was to be decided by the international arbitration panel. Although they may have had difficulty defending the legality of various set-offs, it should be explained once again that the banks were in a strong position at the time the freeze was instituted and default was declared. In November 1979 they held $6.2 billion in Iranian deposits, including more than $4 billion in overseas branches against outstanding loans of $3.7 billion. The Iranian crisis and the resulting litigation ultimately had a significant impact on the structure of international lending to governments and the terms and conditions of loan agreements.

The Iranian crisis also raised some very serious questions concerning the increasing use of "standby" letters of credit, which are used to guarantee various types of obligations across a variety of business settings. A number of U.S. corporations that had entered into contracts with agencies of the Shah's government were required to take out standby letters of credit as guarantees of good performance or as security for the return of unearned downpayments. In the Shah's fall from power, these companies found themselves exposed to unanticipated and often unreasonable demands. It was feared that the new regime, being no longer concerned about long-term relations with U.S. companies, would demand payment without regard for performance. This fear drove many contractors into court where they sought limited injunctions, requiring the banks issuing the standby letters of credit to give the contractors an appropriate period of notice before paying on an Iranian demand or, in the case of the more drastic injunctions, absolutely forbidding payment. Up until the November 14, 1979 freeze on Iranian assets, those contractors who sought limited injunctions were generally successful, while those that sought outright injunctions against payment consistently failed to obtain relief. It was not until the freeze, which independently blocked payment by the issuing bank on their standby letter of credit in favor of Iran, that contractors were able to successfully prevent payment by U.S. banks.

In the aftermath of the Iranian experience, the problems of obtaining meaningful relief in an international transaction, especially when the beneficiary is a foreign sovereign, are now more clearly appreciated. In such a situation, it becomes correspondingly more important for the account party or contractors to attempt to minimize the beneficiary's ability to obtain payment on the standby letter of credit without regard to the status of the underlying contract. The American companies clearly learned this lesson with Iran, and their experience will be reflected in future dealings with sovereign governments.

The Colocotronis Case

The Colocotronis Group was a Greek shipping company that had grown rapidly during the late 1960s from a one-vessel operation to a 50-vessel fleet, including a number of supertankers. This rapid growth was closely related to the booming tanker markets prior to the Arab-Israeli war in 1973 and the wide availability and heavy use of bank finance. The Colocotronis Group was managed in a manner that is common for such organizations. Each vessel is registered to a separate and distinct Panamanian or Liberian company; there is really no holding company in the accepted sense of a parent corporate entity with significant assets and cash flows. Management, crewing, and other administrative considerations are carried out in London or Piraeus by organizations whose only apparent connection with the flag-of-convenience shipowning company is a management contract.

The European-American Banking Corporation (EAB), a consortium bank headquartered in New York and owned by six major European banks, made a number of loans to the Colocotronis Group. These loans were actually made to Panamanian companies for the purchase or construction of vessels to be owned by those companies as their respective sole assets. Each loan was generally secured by a Greek first-preferred ship mortgage on a single vessel, by an assignment of charter hire and insurance covering the vessel, and by the personal guarantees of the members of the Colocotronis family. Thus, even before it was purchased, a vessel would already be committed to a specific time charter, ensuring that it would produce income—an arrangement that worked very well during the boom years of the 1960s, given a shortage of tanker capacity and ready availability of time charters.

During the 1960s, EAB had made most of the loans to Colocotronis direct for its own book. Eventually, it chose to reduce its actual loan exposure, and formed an arrangement with smaller, mostly regional U.S. banks selling them participation in the Colocotronis loans. Banks involved in participation loans do not individually negotiate terms with the borrower; rather, the lead bank makes the loan and then sells shares in the rights and obligations arising under it to the other participating banks. Participation agreements have some important legal and procedural differences from the more common form of syndications, but the general principles governing relationships between the borrower and the lending banks are the same.

At the time EAB was reducing its own exposure through loan participations, the bottom was falling out of the international shipping industry and the operations of the Colocotronis Group were seriously affected. The group's weakened financial condition became increasingly serious, and it began defaulting on repayment of interest and principal on the loans arranged by EAB. Seven U.S. regional banks individually filed suit against EAB, charging that they had been induced to participate in the loans as a result of the EAB's concealing the true financial condition of the Colocotronis Group and misrepresenting the arrangements for securing repayment.

The case illustrates a number of the difficult aspects of multibank financing. At the core of the regional banks' suit was the contention that the EAB was a "sophisticated" bank with special skills and expertise in ship financing and syndication. It had a long and close relationship with the Colocotronis Group, and it was this relationship upon which the participating banks relied to a very large extent in making their loan decisions. EAB had sole responsibility for determining pricing and other loan terms and had prepared and distributed the initial circular, including financial data. The participating banks, on the other hand, had little information about the borrowing company other than what EAB had provided them, and they were not able to examine the loan documentation until after the loans had actually been made.

The complaints alleged three kinds of failings by EAB: (1) breach of terms of the participation agreements, (2) failure to fulfill fiduciary and other duties on behalf of the participant banks—in effect failing to properly establish the creditworthiness of the borrower, and (3) misrepresentations and omissions of material facts relating to the borrower's financial position, the collateral security, and the risks associated with the loan.

The case clearly raised the issue of individual bank responsibility in lending its own money. But more important from the point of view of loan syndication and participation lending was the question of whether a lead bank could be held liable to other participating lenders for knowingly or unknowingly misrepresenting a borrower's credit standing, general financial condition, or other relevant information. The question is connected to the other very important issue presented by the case—that is, whether loan participation shares are securities for purposes of U.S. federal securities laws. The individual suits against EAB were all predicated on alleged violations of the disclosure requirements under the Securities and Exchange Act of 1933. Securities laws require sellers or purchasers of securities to adequately disclose all relevant information in their possession. This is particularly important in international lending, since syndicate members often have very little direct knowledge or information on the borrower. Were securities laws to be held applicable to this type of arrangement, smaller banks would be less uneasy over this important source of potential liability.

The success of the financial intermediation process performed by banks relies to a significant degree on good working relations between banks in the system. An incident like the Colocotronis case strains these relations and adds to the effective cost of lending. For smaller banks, the decision to join a syndicate is often based largely on the informational memorandum, which serves as the lead bank's principal document for interesting other banks in taking part in a loan. They may not have the resources or the expertise to investigate independently such proposals in any detail, and thus they rely on the judgment of the lead banks. Lead banks have traditionally waived any liability by simply incorporating a broad disclaimer in the information memorandum. A typical disclaimer tells lenders that the lead bank does not vouch for the "accuracy and completeness" of the document and disavows any responsibility to lenders relying upon it. Should lead banks actually be held liable for the integrity of the information provided to potential colenders, the result would almost certainly be fewer syndications and the exclusion of smaller banks from participation, leaving international term lending to the large international banks.

In the Colocotronis case, the seven separate suits brought by U.S. banks against EAB were all settled out of court, so that many of the issues raised by the action have yet to be tested. However, it did cause banks and their legal counsel to review and revise their thinking about structuring multibank financings and the role and status of the various parties to the agreement. Rather than risk bank participations being deemed securities issued by the lead bank, it is now more common for each bank to receive a note or other debt instrument directly from the borrower. The actual structure of syndicates has also become more important. If the lead bank possesses broad discretion over management of the loan, the participation shares are more likely to be deemed securities than if it has powers equal to or only nominally greater than those held by participants. An even more direct result of the Colocotronis case is the increasingly widespread use of protective clauses, which disclaim responsibility for the creditworthiness of the borrower, by managers and lead banks in loan and participation agreements. In particular, the "Colocotronis memorial clause" affirms the responsibility of each lending bank for making its own independent appraisal of the credit without reliance on the lead bank.

SUMMARY

Clearly, legal considerations are an integral part of all bank lending. When cross-border flows necessarily involve the legal system and courts of more than one country, the need for a comprehensive and comprehensible agreement among all parties is even more critical. The fundamental purpose of loan agreements and the body of commercial law is to protect each side from the adverse consequences of a departure from the terms of financial relationship. The objective of a well-drafted loan agreement is to avoid the necessity of going to court to seek a remedy, since each party's obligations are clearly documented and well understood. Such an agreement will raise the degree of certainty (and therefore reduce the risk), even in the event of an uncertain outcome, since it should anticipate and provide for all possible contingencies. In the same way, the determination and agreement of the appropriate legal jurisdiction is important in order to confer a greater degree of predictability on the outcome of a dispute. A reputable legal system is more likely to produce a predictable outcome based on the courts' interpretation of the law in previous decisions.

Given all of the foregoing discussion on the importance of the legal aspects of banking, it is appropriate to conclude with a note of qualification. Even though the legal considerations associated with international banking facilities are more numerous and complex than the domestic counterpart, they should not camouflage the fundamental consideration. Whether the transaction is domestic or international, the ultimate success of the loan will depend on the credit judgment. No amount of legal documentation will compensate for a poor credit judgment. It is important that bankers and their legal counsel recognize this fact and assign their priorities accordingly.

SELECTED REFERENCES

Friesen, Connie M. *International Bank Supervision*. London: Euromoney Publications, 1986.

Hendrie, Anne, ed. *Banking in the EEC, 1988 Structures and Sources of Finance*. London: *Financial Times*, 1988.

Huber, Steven K. *Bank Officer's Handbook of Government Regulation*. Boston: Gorham & Lamont, 1984

McDonald, Robert. *International Syndicated Loans*. London: Euromoney Publications, 1982.

11

Retail Financial Services Abroad

The competitive changes that have taken place in the banking environment have forced many banks to reconsider areas of commercial banking that had previously lost their attractiveness to the main players in the market.

First, the dramatic decline in sovereign and corporate lending opportunities was due to the LDC debt problems and the decline in corporate borrowing—in many cases, corporations were funding a much larger percentage of their growth internally and increasing disintermediation and securitization of debt of all types.

Second, technological development has dramatically changed the economics of retail banking. Its primary effects have been to drive down the high costs associated with dealing with billions of individual transactions and to offer faster, more accurate, and more responsive information and processing systems. These developments have allowed banks to become more aware of changes in the retail market, thereby enabling them to identify the different subsegments that make up that market, to improve their marketing skills, and to assess more clearly the profitability and risks associated with different retail products and various segments of the market.

Third, the pace of deregulation, while clearly more rapid in some markets than in others, has allowed banks to widen the range of services they offer their customers and price the goods according to their costs and market demand. In addition, it has opened up new possibilities for cross-selling products to customers.

Fourth, there has been a general increase in the level of economic welfare of retail banking clients both in terms of income and assets—a movement of asset formation from a predominantly corporate environment toward households. Capturing fiduciary control of as much of this increased income and assets as possible, and maximizing fee income through selling financial products and services have become primary objectives.

All in all, banks have increasingly come to realize that individuals provide a cheaper and more reliable source of funds for banks. Also, spreads on retail lending are significantly wider than those on corporate lending, although this has been set off to some extent by the higher level of bad debts among retail clients. Many banks have made a strategic reassessment of the economics of certain aspects of retail, mass-market banking versus wholesale banking. These reassessments found that it was no longer clear whether wholesale banking was the source of the most lucrative business. They also determined that the rapid advances in processing and information technologies had reduced the costs and improved the achievable quality of retail transactions.

RETAIL AND BRANCH BANKING

Retail banking can be looked upon as that part of commercial banking concerned with the activities of individual customers, generally in large numbers. In the United States and Europe retail lending has grown at a faster pace than overall bank lending. Between 1981 and 1988 the overall level of bank lending in the United States increased at about 11.4% annually, while lending to individuals increased by 15.7% annually. In 1988, 60% of U.K. bank lending was to individuals and households. The activities of most commercial banks prior to the 1980s consisted of borrowing money at a low (often no) rate of interest on customer deposits, lending money out at market rates to sovereigns and corporations, and engaging in the processing and transactions processing. With gross spreads compressed as a result of deregulation and increased competition, as well as disintermediation and securitization, spreads on retail transactions became increasingly attractive.

While branch banking was at one time seen as a source of cheap deposits, it has increasingly become a valuable source of high margin lending and fee and commission income. The high levels of cash left on deposit free of interest or left in low-interest saving accounts in the past are typically sufficient to cover the cost of running branch networks and money transfer networks. This became less important as market-related interest began to be paid on deposits. The economics of running large branch networks became less attractive, and this put more pressure on banks to reduce their operating costs or increase revenues, or both. In any case, retail money is a more stable source of funds than wholesale funding, which tends to reduce the risk-adjusted cost of funds to the bank.

The increase in interest in retail banking on the part of the international commercial banks has been very impressive in some cases. In 1985 Citicorp had already reached the goal it had set 10 years previously— that is, to have retail activities account for 20% to 30% of the corporation's net income. The retail banking activities of Chase Manhattan, a bank better known for its correspondent and institutional banking, accounted for 33% of net income in 1987.

The Market

Retail banking is concerned with the financial needs of consumers, who have undergone major changes over the years.

Demographics

The age profiles of the major economies have been subject to significant changes. A demographic breakdown of the consumer base is important due to the different spending and saving characteristics of each age segment. The baby boomers born in the years immediately after World War II reached the high-income, high-spending part of their lives in the mid-1980s, providing a very attractive market for retail lending.

Financial behavior has also been influenced by family structure. The most significant changes are the rise of the two-income households and the single-parent family structures. In the United States, for example, 66% of women between the ages of 25 and 54 work. One-quarter of all married women are in professional or managerial posts. Two-income households tend to have more money and less time and are thus less interest-sensitive and more convenience-sensitive.

Household Wealth and Debt

Real incomes have increased 1.2% annually in the U.K. and 3.2% in Japan since 1975 (in the United States, Germany, and France they have increased somewhere between those two rates). Just as there has been an increase in the wealth of consumers in many countries, there has also been an increase in their debt obligations, especially for U.S. consumers.

Financial Preferences

Consumers now tend to be more active in managing assets, liabilities, and liquidity than in earlier periods. Many can be classified as aggressive users of debt. Thus, for example, Americans owed 23% more at the end of 1985 than at the beginning of the year, while the figure for Britain was 20%. While much of this borrowing was due to the fact that the postwar baby boomers were in their prime borrowing age—spurred on by negative real interest rates in the late 1970s—it was also catalyzed by a significant change in attitudes toward household debt. Even in Japan, borrowing has become a sign of status.

Figure 11-1 shows forms of household assets in the United States, Japan, Britain, and West Germany in 1980 and 1987. Although there has been an increase in the level of household borrowing in the United States, assets have been growing faster than liabilities. Wealth has tended to shift more rapidly among the same group of people, and banks have moved from a role of redistributing funds among population groups to shuffling it around within the same groups.

While the predominant trend in wholesale banking in many countries has been toward disintermediation, the trend in retail banking has been toward increasing financial intermediation. Thus, 65% of British adults had checking accounts in 1987, 93% of the French, about 80% of Americans, and nearly all Germans. Credit and bank cards have become ubiquitous in many countries, with the average American adult holding six or seven cards.

Although consumers have become more interest rate sensitive, they are not especially so. Studies carried out in the United States estimate that it would take a change in interest rate on the order of 100 to 300 basis points for a consumer to change his or her bank account. Clients are perhaps most price-sensitive in the area of bank fees.

Regulation

The banking industry has been one of the most protected industries in the world. Due to the negative externalities associated with banking failures, the importance of the stability of the monetary system, and the fiduciary nature of many banking activities, banks' activities have received three main types of protection—on price, on product, and on market.

The banking industry's cost of funds has often been kept artificially low through deposit rate ceilings. Their product scope has been narrowly defined, with other competitors being denied access. Geographically, the industry was often constrained; in the United States the constraint was enforced on a regional basis. All such constraints had serious repercussions on the development of the market. Interest rate regulations motivated consumers to find higher yielding assets elsewhere. Regulations on nonbanks providing banking ser-

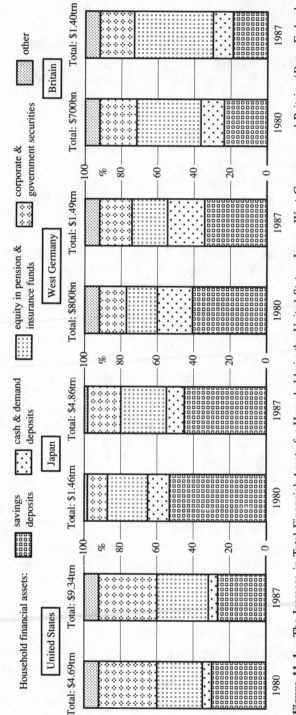

Figure 11–1. The Increase in Total Financial Assets for Households in the United States, Japan, West Germany, and Britain. (*Data:* Federal Reserve, Bank of Japan, Deutsche Bundesbank and U.K. Central Statistical Office.)

vices also restricted banks from providing nonbank services, and geographical constraints stifled the natural spread and development of the industry.

Competitive Dynamics

The competitive posture of banks for retail business changed considerably. Higher levels of competition, both from banks and from nonbanks, drove down returns on consumer lending, which caused some banks to take on more marginal credits with a resulting higher level of writeoffs. Deregulation of deposit interest rate ceilings triggered the movement of consumers into higher-yielding financial assets. A rapid pace of technological innovation in banking required significant front-end investments. Competition from outsiders for the means-of-payment function traditionally controlled by the banks intensified. And the client base developed an increased financial sophistication. As in most aspects of the banking industry, buyers of retail banking services face a wide array of institutions trying to service their financial needs. It is not only the commercial banks that have discovered the potentials of retail lending; there has been an increase in competition from the so-called nonbank banks and from many large corporations as well. The range of new competitors includes retailers, manufacturers, security houses, life insurance companies, and savings institutions.

Barriers to Entry

With the increasing levels of deregulation in the market, banks are losing their monopoly position over retail banking activities as barriers to entry fall rapidly. Indeed, the term "retail banking" is not homogeneous with respect to market definition; instead, it is composed of a large number of smaller strategic businesses each with a very different competitive environment requiring quite distinct strategies for success. For this reason, it is difficult or impossible to put forward an all-purpose viable strategy. A vital consideration for banks is how to build their own barriers to entry. It is widely felt that the payments system is the heart of the financial system, so it will be important for banks to retain control of access to the payments and clearings systems in order to impede nonbanks from challenging them in this respect. In particular, large retailers using flexible credit cards represent a competitive threat.

Automation and Electronic Banking

Automation has simplified the banks' bookkeeping function and has enabled them to handle larger volumes of transactions. Automating the processing of payments has accelerated transactions and reduced the costs dramatically. Automation has also brought advantages directly to the client. With the onset of automated teller machines (ATMs), customers no longer even need to visit the banks; in some cases, the transfer of funds and related routine transactions can even be done from a terminal in the home. It has enabled a much wider arena of products and services to be made available to the consumer. Most notably, the exponential growth in plastic credit is due to technological advances.

Automation has also allowed for the more efficient transfer of information within the organization, enabling the bank to market selectively and more profitably. In this respect, the advancement of technology has been an absolute necessity for banks to generate the necessary information to work out the profitability of different products and market segments. In 1984 Salomon Brothers estimated that only 10 of America's top 40 banks have any idea of the profitability of their different products and different segments. Banks will need to generate large-scale, flexible, on-line systems to generate the necessary information. In this respect, a critical issue is how the information is broken down for management use. It will be vitally important for those banks who want to be major players to reduce their internal operating costs and to improve their market and management accountancy systems. The large banks seem to be attending to the twin poles of the middle-market customer and the affluent, high-net-worth client.

RETAIL FINANCIAL SERVICES

Table 11–1 provides an inventory of financial services supplied to individuals. This inventory is divided into five broad categories.

The first services are those that appear on the liability side of the bank's balance sheet—demand and savings accounts as well as customer balances linked to money market interest rates (e.g., retail certificates of deposit). The services, from the point of view of the customer, are valued in terms of quality (convenience, timeliness and accuracy of account statements, and transaction efficiency) as well as cost—the latter reflected in fees charges on deposit and payments

Table 11–1. Inventory of Retail Financial Services

Liability-side Services
Current account
Savings account
Money market account

Asset-side Services
Auto loans
Mortgage lending
Big-ticket consumer-durables lending
Credit card loans
    Bank cards
    Travel and entertainment cards
Personal loans

Investment Management
Mutual funds/unit trusts
Pension plans
Individual portfolio management
Stockbrokerage
Fixed-income securities sales
Personal financial risk management

Insurance
Whole life
Term life
Auto
Home
Health
Casualty

Other Consumer Services
Travelers' checks
Retail forex
Travel agency
Real estate brokerage
Estate agency
Travel and entertainment cards
Debit cards
Money transfer
Mortgage servicing
Custody/lock-box
Tax planning
Estate planning

services as well as interest paid in comparison with market rates that represent potential alternatives to the customer. Liability-related and transactions services are handled in widely divergent ways internationally—in some countries most consumer transactions are conducted in cash, others are highly check-oriented, still others rely heavily on bank transfers.

For banks, liability-related consumer services are the source of potentially significant fee income as well as relatively low-cost, stable funding. Foreign-based banks find this attractive in order to do local-currency lending—the alternative being to borrow in the local money market, which is generally dominated by local bank competitors.

On the other hand, consumer deposits are also high cost in nature. Thousands of transactions have to be processed, many of them very small. Contact points with the customer have to be numerous and convenient, often involving high real estate expenses. Deposit and transactions services are labor-intensive as well.

Fortunately, technology has provided an answer to several of these problems, taking the cost out of transactions processing as well as significantly lowering the cost of the customer interface using automated teller machines (ATMs), computer banking, electronic funds point-of-sale terminals (EFPOSTs), and electronic funds transmission for both payments and customer deposits. The ability to get the transactions costs out of liability-related consumer services is likely to continue to grow, with further improvements in information and processing technologies. The hardware can be bought. It is in the applications software that the product differentiation and the barriers to entry are created, as well as the scope for technology transfer internationally among markets where a bank wants to be active in local-currency retail funding.

Consumer transactions that appear on the asset side of the bank's balance sheet are listed next. In the absence of interest rate ceilings and usury laws, the spreads between interest rates charges on consumer transactions and funding costs can be very sizeable indeed in many markets. Such transactions include loans to finance big-ticket consumer items (e.g., automobiles, boats, and other consumer durables) and secured and unsecured personal loans and credit card overdrafts, some of which lend themselves to securitization. They also include first and second mortgage lending and home-equity transactions. This business lends itself to differentiation in terms of product quality and is extremely cost-sensitive for the most part, requiring direct contact with large numbers of customers and heavy transactions processing. Consequently, retail outlets and their associated costs are generally unavoidable, more so than in the case of deposit and transaction services since the scope for automation is more limited. Nevertheless, automated lending is possible to some extent on a preapproved or revolving basis.

Consumer lending is also sensitive to credit risks, and default rates tend to differ substantially across countries. However, since there are large numbers of relatively small transactions, it is possible to develop a strong actuarial risk base, which makes it possible to get a reasonable fix on the prospects for bad debt losses.

Again, it is possible to transfer marketing, risk assessment, account management, and processing technologies internationally at relatively low cost in consumer lending. This has made it possible for some banks to gain a strong consumer franchise in foreign markets— Citibank, Barclays, and National Westminster, for example.

The third category is investment management services marketed to consumers abroad. This includes mutual funds (called unit trusts in some countries), pension plans, and portfolio management for individuals. It also includes stockbrokerage services and sales of fixed-income securities to individuals and families. Helping consumers to manage risks related to interest rates, inflation, recession, and other economic shocks is another such service. Wealthy clients provide attractive opportunities in this area (see Chapter 12). But mass-market clients are also buyers of money management services, a fiduciary business that can be highly profitable.

Portfolio management for the mass market is not a very labor-intensive business. It is relatively easy to determine relative performance, which can make funds under management quite volatile. It can also be highly automated, with telephone and computer links to the customer handling a significant share of routing account inquiries, funds transfers among accounts, and the like. Besides portfolio performance and charges, the quality and timeliness of statements and transactions accuracy are important qualitative variables.

Because such services are relatively new in some markets, it is possible for foreign-based players to gain a viable foothold (as Fidelity Investor Services has shown in the United Kingdom and other European markets). Product technology can be highly innovative (e.g., financial planning using laptop computers in the home of the client), but it can also be abused by charlatans (as Investor Overseas Services, operating at the retail level throughout Europe from a base in Geneva, demonstrated during the 1960s).

The fourth category is insurance—life insurance and property and casualty insurance. In some markets, insurance and retail banking services can be effectively cross-marketed—termed "Allfinanz" in the German context. Many banks in the United Kingdom, France, and Germany, for example, have either gone directly into the insurance business or affiliated with local insurance companies. Table 11–2 indicates the extent to which that has occurred in some prominent cases during the late 1980s in Europe. In other markets, such as the United States and Japan, the two industries are kept separate by regulation.

Insurance is attractive to banks because it provides a relatively predictable flow of funds that can be used to complement normal banking liabilities or to structure more efficient asset portfolios. The direct profits from insurance underwriting are also attractive. On the other hand, the insurance business requires quite different actuarial and sales skills and is often compensated differently using commission structures. These differences may limit the ability of banks to compete effectively with insurance companies. Only banks that solve these problems effectively at home have any prospects at all of competing in this segment of retail financial services—often against extremely stiff and entrenched competition—in foreign markets.

The fifth category is a combination of other consumer financial services, ranging from travelers' checks, travel and entertainment cards, bank credit and debit cards, retail foreign exchange at airports and retail bank outlets, domestic and international money transfer, safekeeping and lock box services, real estate, tax and estate planning, and even travel services. It is unlikely that these services would provide banks with a viable business base in their home countries, much less abroad. Exceptions are those services that can be grafted onto a general retail banking business (e.g., foreign exchange and lock box services) and two major exceptions—credit cards and travelers' checks. Foreign-based issuers of travelers' checks, most notably American Express but also including Citibank, Fuji, Barclays, and a few others, have taken a large share of the global market. The same is true of credit card networks, notably American Express, Diners Club (Citibank), MasterCard, and Visa.

In all such cases, prompt replacement in case of loss and widespread point-of-sale acceptance must be assured. The near-universal accept-

Table 11–2. Examples of Banking-Insurance Linkages

Banking Products	Insurance Products	Arenas
Bank für Gemeinwirtschaft	Aachener & Muenchener Royal Insurance (20%)	Germany
Deutsche Bank	Own (Allfinanz)	Germany
Dresdner Bank	Allianz	Germany
Banque Nationale de Paris	UAP	France
Lavoro	Own (Life)	Italy
San Paolo di Torino	Guardian Royal Exchange Baltica Hambros Salomon Brothers	Italy Denmark U.K. U.S.
Verenigde Sparbank	AMEV	Holland
Most Spanish Majors	Own	Spain
Santander	Metropolitan Life	Spain
Hispano-Americano	Aetna Life & Casualty	Spain
Banco Popular	Allianz	Spain
PaineWebber	Yasuda Mutual	U.S.–Japan
Shearson Lehman Deutsche Bank Crédit Lyonnais	Nippon Life	U.S.–Japan Germany–Japan France–Japan
Lloyds Bank	Abbey Life (57.6%) Black Horse Life (Own)	U.K.
Midland	Commercial Union	U.K.
Trustee Savings Bank	Own	U.K.
NatWest	Own	U.K.
Barclays	Own	U.K. – Europe

ability of travelers' checks and broad acceptance of travel and entertainment (T&E) cards and credit cards implies the creation of global networks of banks or other institutions to provide service locally. This also implies the sharing of returns with these institutions. Travelers' checks are sold locally through franchised outlets, for which the customer will normally pay a 1% selling commission, while interest-free balances (float) accrue to the issuing institution. T&E cards, with debit balances payable monthly, are issued on a proprietary basis by individual institutions such as American Express, against an annual fee paid by the client as well as commissions paid by the establishments accepting the card for payment. Credit cards work the same way, often with lower fees and commissions, except that balances do not have to be settled monthly—if the client fails to pay in full, a revolving credit line is automatically activated and the client has the option to pay in monthly installments. Debit cards may be issued either by a single bank or by a bank consortium (e.g., Carte Bleue in France), and any charges are automatically debited to the account of the cardholder. Finally, there are check cards (e.g., Eurocard) that permit the client to pay for merchandise or services or to obtain cash at banks.

Cards have five basic functions—payment convenience, passive extension of credit (as when credit card balances are settled monthly), active extension of credit (as when the customer activates his or her credit line by not paying monthly balances in full), access to cash, and protection from loss and theft. These functions can be added or subtracted from a card product—the American Express green card has all these features except active credit extension, while the gold card includes a revolving personal credit line made available by a participating local bank (not American Express). A wide variety of additional features can be added—enhanced loss protection and card registration, "smart" features through use of a microelectronic chip imbedded in the card, cash machines at airports and rail terminals to dispense currency notes and travelers' checks, and the like.

Global networking is the key to success in the card business, due to the critical importance of acceptability. With the introduction of microelectronics and its application to new processes and products, there has been rapid growth in the scope for networking in the financial services industry in general. In some cases the emergent networks may involve only a pair of financial institutions, as in traditional correspondent banking relationships; in other cases, complex webs of banks and other financial or nonfinancial firms have been formed in a single network, as in credit card systems.

These credit card networks, which are sometimes termed "shell organizations," are characterized by business structures that seem to defy identification. Their boundaries are elusive, and their corporate autonomy remains enigmatic. Interesting questions emerge as these networks are studied. Which institutions have established links with which others? What are their strategic, operational, and organizational characteristics? What motivates their decision to enter into a joint venture? To what extent have environmental factors such as deregulation, globalization, and technical diffusion been responsible for financial firms relinquishing autonomy? What are the implications for competitive structure, conduct, and performance in retail financial services? What are the apparent economies of scale and of scope that result? To what extent have credit card networks been developed indigenously in various countries or imported from abroad? To what extent has participation been considered a defensive as opposed to a reactive move on the part of the institutions participating in them?

Questions can also be raised on the composition of the shell organizations themselves. There are not only the usual issues pertaining to geographic boundaries, number of firms involved, or the legal/contractual foundations of such organizations, but there are also interesting issues concerning the structure of financial services shells in the credit card business as networks. Are they simple (involving one product, service, or resource-sharing arrangement), or are they multiplex (involving a multitude of sharing arrangements)? Are they geographically dense, or does their density revolve around other factors such as strategic groups or size of firms? These are important issues if the performance of financial institutions in international retail services is to be understood.

Delivery Systems

Banks that have penetrated into retail banking abroad tend to fit into one of four categories: (1) banks that have followed the flag and have remained in a developing country after the departure of the colonial powers; (2) a small group of banks that were grandfathered—that is, they had foreign offices in various countries before any protective barriers favoring indigenous banks were laid down; (3) banks that have bought foreign banks; and (4) a large number of banks that have adopted a niche strategy in foreign markets.

Table 11–3 lists a number of issues that are critical to understanding the ability to deliver retail financial services, which are by nature highly local, on an international or even global scale.

The first issue is the problem of market segmentation. Mass-market products and those targeted at specific market segments (e.g., Finns living in Sweden, the New York Puerto Rican community, certain

---

Table 11–3. Delivering Retail Financial Services Internationally

Client Segmentation
  Mass market
  High net worth
  High net income (affluent)
  Profession-based market segments
  Other segmentation criteria

Points of Sale
  Over the counter
    Specialized
    Joint (cross-selling)
  Door to door
  Mail
  Personal computer and videotex

Economies-of-scale Characteristics

Economies-of-scope Characteristics

Cross-selling Potential

Market Penetration Vehicles
  On-the-ground greenfield
  Acquisitions
  Intercountry penetration (e.g., via mail or personal computer)
  Joint ventures and strategic alliances

Sources of Competitive Advantage
  Physical capital (e.g., installed distribution outlets)
  Financial capital
  Human resources
  Product technology
  Risk management technology
  Process technology
  Marketing/management know-how
  Franchise

---

professions) are by definition highly local. For foreign-based institutions to compete, they must offer better service (using almost entirely local resources), product differentiation, or lower price. Being "international" counts for nothing. Nevertheless, product differentiation can be accomplished, as NatWest USA has shown in catering to upper-income customers in the New York area, as Citibank has demonstrated by dealing with consumer finance in Germany though an affiliate called Kundenkreditbank (KKB), and as Chinese-owned Hong Kong banks have shown by targeting Chinese communities in London, New York, and elsewhere. But it is not easy, and the burden of proof rests invariably with the foreign institution. Local consumer banking abroad is by its very nature an uphill battle.

Product differentiation can also be achieved through distribution channels, and here a critical marketing question is whether financial services are "bought" or "sold." Payments services are typically "bought" in that the client actively seeks out banks to provide these services for a very clear need. Life insurance, on the other hand, is typically "sold" (like encyclopedias) in that the product can be complex and there may be no immediate perceived need. This means that selling over the counter, as in a bank, may be appropriate for some products while direct-mail selling, door-to-door selling by commissioned salespeople, or selling by personal computer or videotex may be best suited for others.

Marketing know-how is critical in retail financial services. What works in one country may, with some modification, also work in another, and marketing technologies are relatively easy to transfer internationally. Institutions such as Citibank in the United States, Allied Dunbar in Britain, and Compagnie Bancaire in France all have particular marketing approaches for various products; in many cases, these strategies are not easy to emulate but do lend themselves to international transfer.

Retail financial services are also highly cost-sensitive, and that means high levels of application of information and processing technology are necessary. The secret tends to be in the software, which differentiates cost structures among institutions using basically the same hardware and permits them to offer the same product at lower cost or lower losses.

Besides selecting promising products, client segments, and delivery systems, distribution economics in retail financial services are also highly sensitive to economies of scale and economies of scope. There is evidence that scale economies are more important in retail transactions than in other financial services because of the large transactions volumes involved, by definition. The existence of scope economies are clear when multiple products are pushed through the same relatively fixed-cost delivery systems, but they are less clear in terms of cross-selling potential and the "financial supermarket." Whether customers are willing to pay a higher all-in price for buying banking services, insurance, and mutual funds from the same institution instead of separately from a bank, an insurance company, and a stockbroker remains an open question in many markets. Whether the same individual can sell an array of (often complex) financial services as effectively as product specialists is also a debatable issue.

Table 11–3 also indicates some of the sources of competitive advantage in retail financial services (examples of the expansion and costs of automation, which are necessary to secure a competitive advantage, are shown in Figures 11–2 and 11-3), and alternatives for penetrating international markets are also shown. Clearly, physical capital in the form of point-of-sale outlets is critical in many cases, although independent agents selling on commission and direct-mail sales can reduce this requirement. Financial resources are obvious, both for credit extension and investment purposes. The latter is far more important, since finance for relending can be bought on the market at vastly lower interest rates than can be earned on retail financial transactions. Financial capital is critical for building up the ability to distribute and differentiate products and manage the attendant risks. If management is willing to invest and has the staying power to ride out the initial lean years, the capital required to be a serious player in retail financial services may still be a barrier to entry but in many cases it can be leveraged internationally.

Entry into national markets and international distribution of retail financial services is a closely related problem. The options are to proceed *de novo*, to buy a local bank or other financial services firm, to sell into another country from home (e.g., by mail or traveling salespeople), or to create joint ventures and strategic alliances. The first two are expensive—*de novo* requires creation of branch networks, and sellers of local financial institutions are not unaware of their value to foreign-based players and will charge accordingly. In cross-country selling it is not easy to overcome consumer risk aversion, and memories of horror stories (e.g., Investor Overseas Services) remain. It may also not be practical, although in Europe it may be facilitated by the financial liberalization implied in the European Community initiatives of 1992 and in North America by the free trade arrangement between Canada and the United States.

Joint ventures and strategic alliances may be more viable in the retail sector than in some other sectors of financial services. For example, banks in two or more countries can agree to honor the checks and credit cards for each other's customers in order to provide banking services to tourists and business people. Such initiatives include a 1989 arrangement between the Royal Bank of Scotland and Banco Santander of Spain. Another example involves a relationship developed in late 1986 between Citicorp and Dai-Ichi Kangyo Ltd. (DKB) of Japan. The customers of each bank are now able to use the ATMs in the other's home country, and the two banks act as each other's agents in consumer loans and home mortgages (allowing

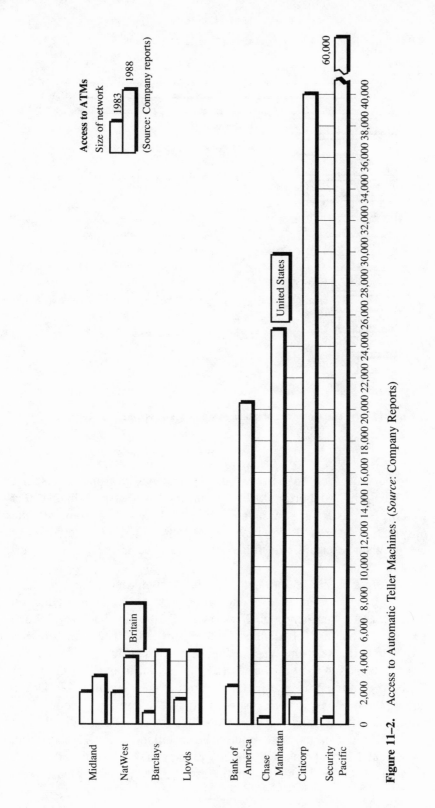

Figure 11–2. Access to Automatic Teller Machines. (*Source:* Company Reports)

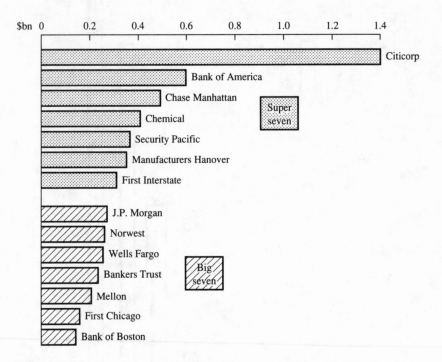

Figure 11–3.   The Cost of Computer Systems, 1987. (*Data*: McKinsey & Company, Inc.)

customers of each to borrow quickly and easily from the other), with Dai-Ichi "supporting" (distributing and processing charges for) Citicorp's MasterCard in Japan. Each bank is able to tap into the information base and expertise of the other. The arrangement has helped each to establish a full-service presence in the other's country.

Citicorp's presence in Japan had been composed of a consumer finance company, an investment banking presence, loan production offices, and a seat (through Vickers da Costa) on the Tokyo Stock Exchange, but no full-fledged banking affiliate. The link to DKB provided Citibank with access to Japanese retail customers, who could use the bank's ATMs in the United States, and provided ATMs for Citicorp customers to use in Japan. Both banks' retail networks are among the broadest in their respective markets; however, the need for bilingual software and the expense of hardware, along with the fact of small client bases, had limited the installation of ATMs by both DKB and Citibank in each other's markets. The collaborative link eliminated this problem. Under the arrangement, Citicorp customers in Japan now have full access to all of DKB's 862 ATMs and 621 cash-dispensing machines (1988) as well as (for an additional charge) ATMs maintained by other Japanese banks belonging to the DKB network. This permits Citibank to compete in the Japanese retail market, while DKB acquires similar capabilities in those U.S. markets in which Citibank operates at the retail level.

Of course, strategic alliances are most prevalent in truly international retail businesses like bank cards, which require networks to operate effectively and shell organizations to run them. The theory underlying shell organizations involves the "resource-dependence" paradigm, the key argument of which is that organizations cannot muster all the resources internally and must resort to interfirm relationships with important environmental actors to achieve competitive viability. Here it is important to make a distinction between horizontal and vertical relationships. Credit card services involve the creation of alternative ways of delivering banking services, but they typically link together competing organizations (i.e., they involve horizontal relationships). At the same time, credit card service strengthens an individual firm's competitive position in providing what is increasingly called a "commodity" service. Financial organizations may form shell organizations because management sees this as a way to reduce competitive uncertainty.

GLOBAL RETAIL BANKING?

Do most retail banking services really lend themselves to globalization? Most retail services are really local in nature, and it is unclear what foreign-based institutions bring to the table. Whatever it is, it must be sufficiently superior in quality or lower in cost to convince mass-market customers to defect from their local institutions. Given the absence of patents, copyrights, and other statutory entry barriers in the financial services industry, sustaining such a basis for competitive advantage—assuming it can be achieved in the first place—is not easy in local markets around the world. Foreign-based institutions, in short, must win a local franchise against entrenched local competition that may be quick to react to encroachments on what it regards as its turf.

Failures in international retail banking are perhaps more common than successes. Chase Manhattan failed with a retail banking venture in Germany in the 1970s called Familienbank and pulled out of a number of other European retail markets. Efforts by Chemical Bank,

Manufacturers Hanover Trust Company, and BankAmerica also failed. Many of the banks attempting to penetrate the retail sector in Australia (see Chapter 27) suffered a similar fate, as did Lloyds Bank, Barclays Bank, and Midland Bank (acquiring Crocker National Bank in California only to sell it later to Wells Fargo at significant financial and reputation cost to itself) in the United States market—against which the NatWest USA case stands as a successful counterexample. Nor does it seem that failure in one foreign market precludes success in another. For example, Lloyds Bank achieved a market share of 20% in New Zealand, but only 2% in California during the mid-1980s.

Of course, banks can try, as Citicorp has done, to progressively build a global consumer financial services franchise. In mid-1989 Citicorp had 8 million household customers in 40 countries, and 20 million customers in the United States. It sells personal financial services through Kundenkreditbank in Germany, makes automobile loans in Spain, and mortgage loans in Taiwan. In 1988 the bank achieved a return on equity of 20% from its international retail business, and targets for 1991–93 were set at over $1 billion from consumer banking worldwide (compared with total bank earnings of $1.9 billion in 1988). The Citicorp strategy is based on the view that retail financial needs are relatively generic and can be relatively easily tailored to the specifics of local demand patterns around the world. It also considers its product, processing, marketing, and risk management know-how to be transferable internationally at tolerable cost and believes that its name can eventually be built into global recognition.

Citicorp's entry strategies run the gamut from greenfield in the United Kingdom, Hong Kong (21 branches in 1989), and Panama (9 branches) to acquisitions such as the 1974 purchase of KKB in Germany (291 branches), the 1985 purchase of Compagnie Generale de Banque in France (12 branches), and the 1983 acquisition of Banco de Levante in Spain (renamed Citicorp España) from the government (20 branches). In the KKB case, a successful operation was left intact and actively built up; in the Spanish case, the bank was fundamentally restructured; and in France an initial corporate banking focus was later shifted to retail—with indifferent initial success against powerful local competitors. In all three cases the key to competitive performance was seen to be innovative consumer products and superior service. Whether the bank can pull off a true global retail banking franchise or one that does so in at least the principal markets, or whether it "cherry-picks" in niches and countries that are particularly subject to local market inefficiencies, remains to be seen.

SUMMARY

Retail banking is one sector of the financial services industry that does not lend itself uniformly well to internationalization. Some activities are naturally international and lend themselves superbly well to globalization, such as travelers' checks and "plastic." Others are highly idiosyncratic and local—Herr Mueller behaves differently from Monsieur Meunier, who behaves differently from Mr. Miller in terms of what he expects his bank to do for him—and this requires a great deal of adaptation of competitive advantages in products and processes. Indeed, the key success factors in retail banking may in the end be more related to awareness of the market than to technology and systems.

Nonetheless, it is clear that international and even global niches exist in specific retail services, such as mortgage and consumer lending, stockbrokerage and mutual funds, and family financial planning. The jury is still out on whether there is a role for truly global retail financial services players.

SELECTED REFERENCES

Channon, Derek F. *Bank Strategic Management and Marketing*. New York: John Wiley & Sons, 1986.

Coulbeck, Neil. *The Multinational Banking Industry*. New York: New York University Press, 1984.

Hempel, George H., Coleman, Alan B., and Simonson, Donald G. *Bank Management*. New York: John Wiley & Sons, 1986.

Stevenson, Merrill, "A Survey of International Banking." *The Economist*, March 22. 1986.

12

International Private Banking Services

A notable characteristic of banking today is the unprecedented level of competition facing all players in the market, which has forced many institutions into a reappraisal of existing client bases and an attempt to penetrate new and attractive ones. One such segment of major interest comprises wealthy or *high net worth* (HNW) individuals and families served by so-called private banking services.

THE NATURE OF PRIVATE BANKING

Since the late eighteenth century, international private banking has been the particular domain of Swiss banks of unlimited liability status engaged in fiduciary activities. Recently, competition has increased considerably. In the late 1970s a number of American banks, in particular, established "private banking" departments to cater specifically to the needs of their wealthy clientele. According to one observer, these clients had previously been served on a more ad hoc basis.[1] The concept was developed by banks such as J. P. Morgan, Chase Manhattan, and Citicorp and rapidly became a generic description of HNW targeting in financial services. It was the first real attempt to segment the consumer market. Private banking has come to mean different things in different banks. According to one Swedish banker, private banking is "a counselling service for affluent people."[2] A general definition would include all mainstream services a bank can legally provide specifically for HNW individuals.

Why has international private banking, which for years had been viewed by other banking sectors with near derision, enjoyed newly found interest and credibility, and why have the HNW clients become so valuable?

With competition reducing the margins on lending and central bank concerns about capital adequacy, banks have had to review carefully all new on–balance sheet activity, with many deciding to emphasize off–balance sheet and other fee-generating services. Simultaneously, there has been an attempt to reduce dependence on commoditylike bank lending and to move into higher value-added financial services. This has involved a reappraisal of the profitability of retail banking — in particular, private banking. Banks have been forced to consider the profit potential of individual clients.

The HNW client base offered a number of attractions. In terms of competitive analysis, it appeared underbanked. This was especially so in view of the increasing demographic importance of the wealthy in the main industrialized countries. The baby boomers were entering their thirties and forties, a time when income level and wealth base tends to increase significantly. In addition, national income had been growing at between 1 percent and 3 percent for several years in real terms, and falling inflation had stimulated equity markets throughout the world, increasing both individuals' wealth and their awareness of financial assets. Notwithstanding the rapid rise in HNW individual banking competition in recent years, bankers still believe that the market retains vast potential. Citibank has estimated that there are 8 million affluent people worldwide with investible wealth of $7 trillion. This would mean more than $50 billion in bank fees if the whole market were tapped. Due to the highly personal nature of private banking, HNW clients generally prefer to stay with a particular bank, if possible. This may result in lower price elasticity of demand, facilitating product cross-selling and enabling institutions to compete on qualitative variables instead of pricing alone. In addition, the cost structures of many banking activities allow economies of scale in transactions processing and portfolio management activities.

The range of private banking services is extraordinarily wide — from having meals arranged for clients in prison or hospitals (as some Swiss banks have been known to do) to traditional fiduciary activities to arranging personal lines of credit, secured loans on yacht purchases, leveraged buyouts, and tax shelter financing. The essential factor, however, is to offer a truly personal service — a point exemplified by a statue unveiled outside the private banking offices of a large money center bank in New York supposedly depicting a banker walking his client's dog.

Private banking services, being provided explicitly for wealthy individuals, may be broken down through reference to the balance sheet of a HNW client:

Assets	Liabilities and Net Worth
Cash	Personal Loans
Financial Assets	Business Loans
Real Personal Assets	
Business Assets	Net Worth

Private banking services ultimately affect the client's net worth, by focusing on either the asset or liability side of the balance sheet or on a combination of both. But the common factor is that they affect the structure of that balance sheet and, in a dynamic sense, its composition over time.

Wealth and the Wealthy

For a financial institution developing its private banking business, an understanding of the nature of wealth and of the HNW client characteristics is vital to deciding which specific segment of the potential client base to target and what services to offer. How can one define wealth, and who are the wealthy?

Wealth can be discussed in terms of command over economic resources. It may be either financial (currency, bank balances, stocks, bonds) or real (commodities, precious stones, objets d'art, real estate). It may be considered on a liquidity/yield continuum ranging from highly liquid but low-yielding assets (e.g., currency) to higher-yielding but low-liquidity assets (e.g., real estate, antiques). Command over economic resources depends on an individual's claim on risk-adjusted economic returns expected in the future. The market value of a portfolio of assets will depend upon the expected returns and risks associated with that portfolio. The risk of an asset derives from the variance of its expected returns; the risk of a portfolio results from the covariance in the returns of all the assets contained therein. The ability to measure wealth at any given time will depend on the existence of a market for the particular asset and the ability to "mark to market."

According to one observer, such a definition of wealth is a purely economic measure; it does not necessarily equate with an individual's own assessment of his or her personal worth in a broader context, which is affected by many other factors. People vary, for example, in the marginal satisfaction they gain from higher wealth levels; they differ in their reaction to risk; they are influenced by social, political, religious, and philosophical attitudes to wealth. All of these factors color their vision of the value of what they have, and they are highly relevant for the private banker seeking to understand his or her client and the marketplace.[3]

Wealth can be generated legitimately or illegitimately. Legitimate wealth is the product of economic rents in the provision of goods and services to society. *Economic rents* are returns to labor and capital above the normal returns that would be earned in a competitive marketplace, either past or present. In that sense the individual wealth accumulated, from the provision of superior products or services or superior cost effectiveness, can be considered prima facie evidence of economic contribution in a market-oriented system.

Wealth can, however, also be amassed at the expense of the rest of society through such illegitimate means as extortion, prostitution, racketeering, insider trading, gun running, and drug trafficking. Such activities cost society twice over—first through noncontribution and social damage and second by causing otherwise productive resources to be diverted to anticrime measures.

The specific income-generating activities of the wealthy provide a useful method of categorizing these clients according to the source of their assets—which in turn affects their attitudes and banking requirements. We distinguish five main groups: corporate, entrepreneurial, and family (which are socially legitimate) and political and criminal (which are socially illegitimate).

1. *Corporate wealth* is generated through service within a corporation in the form of salaries, bonuses, stock options, and severance payments. This form of wealth is increasingly common, particularly in the United States and Western Europe where the corporate culture is strong.
2. *Entrepreneurial wealth* is accumulated throughout an individual's lifetime by owning or co-owning a business enterprise. It is particularly pervasive in the United States and Asia due to their respective patterns of economic development. To a large extent,

entrepreneurial wealth is paper wealth. In the case of private companies, this wealth may be realized when the enterprise goes public.

3. *Family (inherited) wealth* involves the transfer of wealth from one generation to another; therefore, it is highly dependent upon national fiscal and economic policies. "Old" wealth is probably more pervasive in Europe than elsewhere. It can arise from any of the other sources of wealth specified here.

4. *Political wealth* can usually be attributed to corruption in political office at varying levels within national or regional governing administrations. The sources include misappropriation of public funds, bribery, extortion, political contributions, kickbacks, and financial holdings benefiting from government contracts. Although functionaries within government usually receive limited official compensation, the power residing in their hands often makes it relatively easy to siphon off funds. This form of wealth may be more pervasive in developing countries than in the United States, Japan, and Western Europe.

5. *Criminal wealth* derives from organized crime and other illegal activities. Illegal organizations thrive on every continent, ranging from the Italian and American Mafiosi to Chinese Tongs and Japanese Yakuza to the Latin American drug syndicates. This type of wealth can be expected to occur in most societies, but there is reason to believe that it is more pervasive in developed countries due to greater scope for illegal activities and greater organizational abilities of criminals.

While it is dangerous to generalize, it may be reasonable to argue that the more reliance societies place on the operation of free markets and transparent, democratic politics, the more important entrepreneurial and corporate wealth will be and the less important political and criminal wealth will be. This is because fewer distortions tend to exist in free and open systems. Political corruption and criminal activities arise in part from market distortions.

Determinants of Wealth Distribution

The matter of wealth distribution, both on a national and international scale, is of basic importance for private banking. Wealth distribution is primarily an empirical question, although three conceptual factors are of interest as well.

1. *Per capita income.* Although wealth is a "stock" measure and income is a "flow" measure, since wealth is based on past or current resource inputs into the economy—and since capital, along with labor, natural resources, and productivity determines national income and output—higher-income countries should harbor greater wealth concentrations than poorer ones.
2. *Market distribution mechanisms.* The distribution of property rights as well as those of capital ownership, education levels, and other sources of earning power will differ significantly from one country to another. In these circumstances, markets for goods and services, capital, natural resources, and human resources may generate markedly different distributions of wealth and income between countries, even when economic size and per capita income are comparable.
3. *Government policies.* These tend to result from a confluence of historical, religious, cultural, and sociological factors that generate a political concept of a "fair" distribution of income and wealth—and, more importantly, the extent to which free markets are permitted to determine that distribution. This political concept will, in turn, determine national policy with respect to taxation, wealth and income transfers, nationalization, expropriation, and other policy measures affecting the wealthy.

These three factors, analyzed together, explain to a large extent the geographical distribution of wealth within different countries—not only where wealth may be found but where it is privately held rather than institutionalized.

There are plenty of "wealthy" societies where wealthy individuals are few and far between, while others have them in abundance (e.g., Sweden versus Switzerland). This is of paramount importance to the private banker. If wealth accumulation is heavily taxed or heavily institutionalized (for example, in the form of pension funds or union assets), it is of little interest. Rather, it is the disposable or discretionary element of wealth and income that matters. It is in those societies where markets are allowed to determine income and wealth levels that HNW individuals and families can emerge.

The social and political "climate" for wealth is also relevant. We noted earlier that legitimate wealth accumulation is evidence of economic contribution. But this is in a capitalist context. In some societies wealth may instead be considered evidence of exploitation and economic parasitism. Even without going that far, views on the "worth" of wealth will vary enormously. What does it bring in terms of kudos, power, and worry? These variables will affect an individual's attitude to wealth accumulation, which in turn is likely to influence his or her economic performance.

Two last points deserve mention. First, the extent to which there is a functioning black market in a country is important. Second, international mobility of capital and transfer of income should be considered. Capital can be expected to be responsive to governmental shifts in policy, and to prospective future risks and returns associated with financial and real assets. Capital flight, resulting from ill-conceived national economic policies and international economic shocks, is of great importance to private banking.

While factors such as these will be among the principal determinants of the geographic distribution of wealth, supply-side developments also drive world wealth allocation, the most notable recent case being the two oil shocks of the 1970s. This was particularly important because at the time the Middle East had little experience managing wealth and because the national economic infrastructures initially had difficulty absorbing the volume of funds generated. Middle Easterners were besieged by offers for help from hordes of private bankers especially from the United States, Switzerland, and the United Kingdom, with the latter's merchant banks succeeding in attracting a high proportion of the net investible funds.

Wealth Allocation

What does the HNW client seek from private banking services? He or she is faced with the question of how to effectively manage wealth. At its broadest level this is an exercise in balance sheet management, the overall objective of which is to maximize net expected returns subject to a risk constraint—or minimize risk subject to a total return target. Other objectives include a desired level of confidentiality, tax minimization, and estate allocation. Reaching these objectives will require a number of critical decisions on asset allocation. If the objectives are mutually inconsistent, the client will need help to make and execute those decisions. The basic choices may be divided into five main categories:

1. *Investment/consumption.* In what proportion should the client's wealth be divided between current consumption and asset accumu-

lation? This will obviously depend on individual time preferences and the opportunity cost of consumption. The higher the expected real after-tax return on assets, the higher the opportunity cost of consumption. So that an optimum consumption/investment pattern can be achieved, the fact that a measure of consumption can take place simultaneously with real investment also must be taken into account. The German Expressionist painting hanging in the dining room, for example, provides the owner with both intrinsic and status benefits, even as it may make good sense from an investment perspective.

2. *Domestic/international*. How much wealth should be committed to home country interests and how much to investments in political jurisdictions abroad? This will depend on the relative attractions and risks associated with various asset markets and the value of confidentiality.

3. *Onshore/offshore*. How much wealth should be allocated within domestic or foreign national jurisdictions, and how much should be allocated to "offshore" havens? Taxes, security, and secrecy will again play a role here. Domestic economic policy will also be of considerable importance.

4. *Real/financial assets*. This choice will be influenced to a considerable extent by macroeconomic environments. For example, the expected level of domestic inflation is a crucial determinant. In periods when inflation exceeds the rate of interest, individuals tend to leverage themselves as much as possible, since funds borrowed today are repaid in discounted real terms. Preservation of the real value of wealth will be of paramount importance. Real assets and financial assets denominated in stable currencies will tend to be favored over domestic financial assets, and there is typically a rise in demand for gold, property, and objets d'art. As noted earlier, assets are often notable for their low levels of liquidity and imperfect markets. If they have to be sold quickly, substantial discounts must be accepted. Therefore, the investor's attitude toward liquidity risk, the investor's future cash flow requirements, and the investor's need for "precautionary funds" will be major factors in determining any real/financial asset split.

The political environment also has an important bearing on this particular choice. Preferential taxation for individuals investing in private enterprise, for example, may encourage wider stock ownership. Tax relief on mortgage interest may increase investment in real property. Governments in many countries have from time to time

offered preferential treatment to public rather than private investment in order to fund fiscal deficits. Sometimes the incentives are reversed, with governments encouraging privatization
or attempting to increase the attractiveness of venture capital.
5. *The economics of financial intermediation.* How much of his or her
wealth should the HNW client place with financial intermediaries,
and on what terms should this be done? At one extreme, the client
may seek minimum involvement from a financial institution. At
the other, he or she may entrust a large share of assets to an individual agent (e.g., a bank's trust department) acting in a fiduciary
capacity. This may give rise to principal-agent problems, including
the agent's correct interpretation of the principal's wishes, and to
dangers of agent self-enrichment at the expense of the principal.
Alternatively, the HNW client may commit his or her wealth to
multiple investment managers in order to impose the discipline of
competition. A certain degree of intermediation is inevitable, particularly when investments are in financial assets such as futures,
options, equity and preferred shares, bonds, and warrants, and
when a strict regulatory structure governs transactions and neces-
sitates the involvement of agents. In addition, the very high dealing costs associated with purely disintermediated investment reduce
its attractiveness. Financial intermediation provides the following
advantages to a wealthy individual:
a. *Risk-shifting.* This falls into two categories depending on the
nature of risk pooling involved. One alternative is for the investor
to place his or her funds at the disposal of the financial institution, which then invests them. The individual has no control
over the allocation of the funds or the levels of risk borne by
the bank and thus is exposed to the risk of the bank itself (bank
intermediation). The second alternative is for funds to be channeled to specific direct or portfolio investments, with the financial institution reacting to the individual's own risk preferences
in the allocation process. In this case, the HNW client bears the
risk of the investment (investment intermediation).

Bank intermediation may be considered a lower-value-added,
commodity-type service to private clients, while investment intermediation represents a higher-value, interactive, and personal
service. In general, the former will be characterized by inter-
est-margin income to the financial institution; the latter will be
characterized by fee income.

b. *The value of information.* To maximize (within a cost constraint) the HNW client's often complex objectives requires expert advice and help. Banks provide expertise in two key areas—products and markets—for clients who frequently have little interest in or effort to spare for such things.

The proliferation and increasing complexity of new financial instruments make it even more difficult for an individual to stay abreast of developments. At the same time, given its broad network of daily contacts in the financial market, resulting from a broad range of trading functions, a financial institution is likely to have a more comprehensive knowledge of market sentiment and a more soundly based view of future developments than most individuals. It will also receive critical new information more quickly than an outsider.

c. *Market power.* The larger the financial institution and the greater the volume of transactions it carries out in a particular market, the greater its firepower to obtain better prices. The rationale for grouping together small securities deals into block orders has been exemplified by the rapid growth in recent years of mutual funds and unit trusts. The net price achieved will also be affected by the commission structure of the markets in question. For example, New York and London have negotiated commissions; Tokyo and Zurich retain fixed commissions. Where commissions are negotiated, larger dealers benefit, since they have the market power to achieve more advantageous rates. The extent to which a financial institution will pass on any benefits to the client will naturally depend on how important that client is and how much leverage he or she has.

d. *Time considerations.* The effective management of wealth is exceedingly time consuming. Individuals in the wealth-building phase of their lives, in particular, typically work under severe time constraints. Therefore, they expect a prompt response to their requests at any time and will want to deal with someone with the authority and ability to make quick decisions. Other private banking clients devoting time to charitable or other pursuits have similarly limited time for investment decisions. This has forced the decentralization of private banking, with the allocation of more authority to officers. Clients with significant time constraints also tend to be more price inelastic.

INDIVIDUAL OBJECTIVES

We have considered the main decisions required for private wealth allocation as separate and distinct. They are, of course, highly inter-related and tend to be resolved intuitively and simultaneously. The results are aimed at maximizing the individual's objective function, which we have defined as a combination of preferences across a number of variables among which time, yield, security, confidentiality, and service level are paramount. Each of these plays a distinctive role.

1. *Yield*. The traditional private banking client in Europe was concerned with wealth preservation in the face of antagonistic government policies and fickle market dynamics. These clients demanded the utmost in discretion from their private bankers with whom they maintained lifelong relationships initiated invariably by personal recommendations. Yield was not an issue.

   Today, however, a new and growing breed of active and sophisticated HNW client is emerging. Aware of the opportunity cost of funds and often exposed to high marginal tax rates, they consider net yield to be far more relevant than the security traditionally sought by HNW clients. They tend to prefer gains to accrue in capital appreciation rather than in interest or dividend income, and they can be expected to have a much more elastic response to changes in total rate of return.

2. *Security*. The world today is arguably a more stable place than it has ever been. The probability of revolution, war, and gross confiscatory taxation is dropping in Europe, North America, the Far East, and, arguably, even in Latin America and Africa. Nevertheless, a large segment of the private banking market remains highly security conscious. Such clients are generally prepared to trade off yield for stability and safety.

3. *Confidentiality*. Secrecy is a major factor differentiating international from domestic private banking. Clearly, with every government in the world subject to international pressure, "secure" funds against which another country makes legal claim can rapidly become insecure if their presence is advertised to those who have leverage over the authority regulating the custodian private banker (the confidentiality issue will be further discussed later in this chapter).

4. *Service level*. While some of the tales of personal services provided for private banking clients are undoubtedly apocryphal, the "fringe

benefits" offered to HNW clients may well influence their choice of and loyalty to a particular financial institution. Such benefits may save time, reduce anxiety, increase efficiency, or make the whole wealth management process more convenient. Personal service is a way for banks to show full commitment to clients accustomed to high levels of personal services in their daily lives.

The essence of private banking is to identify accurately each client's unique objective function and to have the flexibility and expertise to satisfy it as fully as possible in a highly competitive marketplace.

DOMESTIC PRIVATE BANKING

Domestic private banking consists of all domestic banking services provided explicitly for wealthy residents. It should be viewed as an extension of the concept of "personal banking" or a broadening of the concept of "trust banking." It is primarily concerned with credit extension, tax minimization, and investment management.

The concept of domestic private banking is perhaps most developed in the United States, which has large amounts of private wealth and social attitudes that tend to be highly positive—with social success generally accompanying economic success. In recent years, nearly all of the major banking players have committed themselves to compete in this market in one form or another. For example, Citibank was offering private banking at 22 locations across the country in 1989, Chase Manhattan had opened several specialist trust companies, J. P. Morgan had assembled all private banking services into one cohesive group, and Bank of America had set up 15 private banking offices and attracted more than 20,000 customers in under two years.

The prime difference between financial institutions competing for this business is the wealth cut-off point for private banking clients. In 1989 J. P. Morgan reportedly maintained a minimum requirement of $10,000 in balances for checking accounts and $5 million for custodial and/or investment management accounts. Chase was more flexible— the minimum requirement of $500,000 in investible assets could be dropped if an individual appeared to have "potential." Similarly, at Chemical Bank, which considered its strength as lying "in the middle market, dealing with entrepreneurs", exceptions to its $1 million net worth rule would be made for the "right" client. Citicorp had dropped specific requirements for net worth and income but did require that each customer generate $6,000 in fees annually. Indeed, one study indicated that many private banks expect at least $10,000 in fees per household per year.

Other financial institutions have positioned themselves at the not-so-wealthy end of the market. For example, in 1989 Union Bank in Los Angeles had an income limit of $75,000 on their clients and charged one fee that covered all banking activities for their 6,000 private banking customers—intending to spread their low-fee system to other markets in the United States. There are also many small niche players in the field that focus on fee-generating private banking business. This is indicative of the general move away from typical commercial lending and the growing awareness of the need for meaningful market segmentation into distinct client categories. Private banking is at the leading edge of this transition.

The Client Base

The client base for domestic private banking services consists of resident wealthy individuals. Again, they may be divided into two groups with differing risk, liquidity, and credit needs—that is, the active and the passive investors. The latter are defined as traditional risk-averse individuals whose predominant use of financial resources is for consumption purposes. Taxes are paid mainly on income and real property. Bank performance is primarily measured against rates of return on assets under management and the deposit rates. It has been estimated in 1987 that this segment was only profitable, in terms of fees generated, when net worth exceeded $1 million, which limited the potential market to 1 percent to 3 percent of the U.S. population.

Active investors, on the other hand, represent a less traditional customer base for the larger banks, their needs having in the past been served by smaller institutions. As many as 20 percent of such clients do not maintain bank accounts at all, while those that do mainly use them for transaction purposes. They tend to be more risk oriented than the passive client and are much more financially sophisticated. They are profit motivated rather than income motivated, they pay taxes through nontraditional means, and generally they use their financial assets to increase their wealth.

American banks compete aggressively for new private banking customers. They are particularly anxious to attract active investors and the lending possibilities and asset management potential those investors could generate. They are also interested in individuals in the wealth-building phase of their lives, the so-called seed corn client. By helping them in the early stages, a bank may keep them later on. And there is a move to pursue the high-income individual—high current income being recognized as strongly related to future wealth accumulation.

The large U.S. banks were at first slow to exploit the active investor, losing ground in the 1970s to many small independent banks, but they have firmly reentered the battle—often with client segmentation focused on professionals. A survey of the characteristics of the wealthy in the United States suggested that although only 2 percent of the sample were employed in commercial and investment banking, real estate, and insurance, they accounted for over 30 percent of the highest-income groups. Lawyers, accountants, and other professionals accounted for a disproportionate share of the high-income subgroups, with their greatest concentration in the second-highest group. A 1984 Federal Reserve study indicated that some 10 percent of U.S. households in 1982 were estimated to have incomes of more than $50,000, a figure roughly similar to 1969 and 1976. However, this 10 percent held 33 percent of all U.S. income, as compared with 29 percent in 1969 and 32 percent in 1976.

Products and Services

Many commercial banks are attempting to become one-stop financial supermarkets for the wealthy, offering the entire gamut of financial services from loans and deposits on the banking side to investment management on the trust side.

Deposit-Related Activities

With the removal of constraints on the payment of interest on deposits in the United States, a proliferation of deposit and checking accounts has become available to wealthy individuals—NOW and super-NOW accounts, money market accounts, savings accounts, IRAs, checking accounts, money market CDs, purchases of commercial paper, bankers' acceptances, and Treasury bills. They vary in yield and liquidity characteristics and in flexibility, with deposit accounts particularly attractive to the passive investor concerned about combining liquidity with yield.

Credit Extension and Personal Lending Activities

The need to borrow is particularly prevalent among entrepreneurial HNW individuals. This client, who is in the wealth-creating phase of life, will tend to be illiquid and will rely on the private banker to find a way to structure a deal around an existing asset base. The skills necessary for this function fall into three main categories: (1) creativity in constructing a nontraditional deal, and the ability to analyze a loan request and understand the reality of personal financial statements by identifying outside sources of repayment and collateral beyond the assets financed by the loan; (2) valuation skills, to accurately appraise and evaluate the market for a range of assets from fine art to thoroughbreds; and (3) organizational and administrative skills to give the client quick responses to requests.

Corporate Lending Activities

The overlap between the personal and corporate needs of the wealthy is particularly interesting for banks. It allows them to penetrate more deeply into the individual's finances and to provide a range of corporate banking activities in addition to the personal financial services. These include bankers' acceptances, letters of credit, revolving lines of credit, and term loans. In many cases, the lending activities will be undertaken as an adjunct to the financial advisory service provided by the banker. Due to the links between the corporate and personal sides, familiarity with the individual's attitudes toward risk and the client's requirements regarding currency, maturity, and liquidity gives a significant advantage to an institution already servicing a wealthy client's private needs. In addition, the intense nature of the relationship can provide bankers with a good feel for the client's business and the chance to observe the evolution of the company's earnings and risk profile over time. This can substantially reduce the risk associated with bank financing.

Investment Management

Services provided vary between and within institutions depending on the type of client served and the size of funds available for investment. At U.S. Trust Company, for example, accounts over $10 million in 1989 were offered an individually managed portfolio. For those under $1 million, a family of nine in-house mutual funds was available. Due to economies of scale in portfolio management, smaller accounts will often be pooled, with many banks offering a variety of funds across a broad range of investments. The bank may also provide real estate services; custodian accounts; investments in precious metals, currencies, commodities, and artwork; and advice on the establishment of estates, trusts, and corporations. The bank will advise on the acceptable level of personal leverage and the most prudent structure for borrowings. Tax advice is another key private banking function that can have real value. Changes in the tax structure as well as changes in the client's circumstances will mean that the optimal structure of an individual's balance sheet will also have to change.

For many banks, investment management activities were originally handled by the trust department. More recently, they have increasingly been extended into the mainstream, enabling the bank to tailor investment vehicles to clients in a more comprehensive and personal way.

Specific Personal Services

For a business in which quality of service is of paramount importance and the fiduciary nature of the relationship is critical, private bankers provide a range of "friendly" activities atypical to mainstream banking. These tend to be requested in response to particular client problems and time constraints.

Strategic Considerations and Competitive Dynamics

The small relative size and the attractiveness of the market has resulted in fierce competition in private banking. One estimate suggests that no single player has more than a 2 percent or 3 percent market share in the United States.

Institutions compete in different ways—there are advertising campaigns, toll-free numbers, attempts to influence intermediaries (e.g., attorneys and accountants), and referrals from other sections of a bank. Whatever the "surface" tactics for attracting clients, the key to profitable private banking is maximizing the net present value of the bank-client relationship across all product offerings.

A number of services are bundled together into a single package, which can make sense strategically for several reasons. When functions are bundled, it is much more difficult to evaluate the price/return relationship of each one, allowing the bank to extract higher returns. It is also possible that the client may be more price inelastic with respect to the purchase of the bundled services than with respect to each of the services separately. Similarly, when services have traditionally been bundled together, the client has no opportunity to easily acquire a market valuation for each component separately. While other parts of banking have been subject to a general unbundling of services as a result of a proliferation of new financial products and techniques, this has been less true of private banking.

Due to the existence of economies of scope, a bank can often provide two services more economically than two banks each providing a single service. This represents an important rationale for cross-selling of banking products. Since the fiduciary nature of the relationship gives the bank access to client-specific information, it has a competitive advantage in servicing the client and will not face the same search costs as other banks.

In order to perform effectively, private bankers in competitive markets must engage in more meaningful market segmentation than before. The simplistic distinction between "haves" and "have-nots" must be developed into a far more sophisticated analysis that incorporates the differing characteristics, needs, and financial-sourcing habits of specific customer groups. This can help an organization focus its resources more accurately in order to target its product line, its distribution system, and its promotional efforts to particular market segments more successfully than its competitors.

Marketing is vital in order to persuade customers to stay with a given bank even when their wealth and portfolio preferences change. However, the most important component of any private banking effort is the quality of the bankers. It is not easy for a private client to share confidences with his or her banker, so a low turnover in bank staff is particularly important. This provides the bank with an opportunity to compete on more qualitative variables than on yield or pricing. Still, many banks turning to private banking for the first time face serious strategic problems as they attempt to integrate this rather unusual business sector with their other activities.

Given the tendency for HNW clients to prefer to stay with the private banker they know, it is not surprising that the predominant competitive focus in domestic markets such as the United States is to find new clients rather than to poach existing ones from other financial institutions. The prime drive is to acquire seed corn clients. Nevertheless, there are some client segments that appear to be more yield conscious and therefore more mobile. Banks often try a strategy of attracting such clients with high promotional yields that decline over time. Success depends on what the client's yield elasticity really is and whether the client can be persuaded to stay as a result of quality service.

INTERNATIONAL PRIVATE BANKING

International private banking (IPB) is distinct from its purely domestic counterpart in that it consists of banking services provided primarily for wealthy nonresidents. It also differs in the priorities of clients—safety and secrecy have historically tended to outweigh investment performance as criteria. There are, of course, many different points along the spectrum, but the primary objective of IPB clients is to maintain and increase their wealth in an environment safe from the potential scrutiny of certain third parties.

Secrecy

For some people, just having assets offshore is satisfactory. For others, the guarantee of banking secrecy is a prerequisite. There are a number of locales throughout the world that specialize in the provision of confidentiality. A country provides banks with the ability to sell secrecy through an appropriately structured regulatory system and/or built-in secrecy protection. Success, therefore, is highly dependent upon domestic banking laws. Although Switzerland automatically comes to mind in this context, it is hardly unique. Luxembourg, Austria, Panama, and the Cayman Islands are among many countries that have strict secrecy provisions imbedded in their banking statutes. However, Switzerland is quite different in that not only is breach of banking secrecy a criminal offense, but there is a 200-year tradition of conservative and reliable asset management and quality personal service to back it up.

There are indications, however, that the quality of secrecy is on the decline worldwide as a private banking criterion. It is not only national secrecy provisions that count, but also international attitudes toward financial secrecy and the kinds of pressure that international authorities can and do bring to bear on foreign jurisdictions. Due to the pervasive powers of national authorities in the United States and elsewhere, their growing determination to use these powers to combat criminal uses of secrecy as well as tax evasion, and their increasing willingness to share information, it is becoming more difficult to guarantee total secrecy. The primary driving force is governments' acknowledgment that financial secrecy facilitates criminal activities and that one of the best ways to attack these activities is to increase the cost and reduce the opportunities to launder money. For example, one observer notes that in 1986 some SFR7.66 billion flowed into Swiss banks from the Bahamas, around SFR6.08 billion came from the Cayman Islands, and another SFR8.9 billion entered from Panama. It seems reasonable to assume that not all such enormous sums can possibly relate to legitimate business. In the crackdown, of course, legitimate private banking clients may well be caught in the middle.

Moreover, there seems to be a growing disparity between the quality of financial secrecy offered in the up-market or value-added offshore centers like Switzerland (where it may be declining) and those of lesser standing. This is probably because the former have more to lose from being "tainted" and are at the same time more vulnerable to outside pressure due to their own banks' large presence internationally. Switzerland's actions in the Ferdinand Marcos affair in 1987 are indicative—the Swiss National Bank froze assets before it had even received an official request from the new Philippine government, thereby unnerving investors and banks alike and revealing the Swiss National Bank's keen awareness of the importance of world public opinion.

Informal estimates suggest that approximately $1 trillion in fiduciary accounts were under management in the world in 1988, with 33 percent residing in Switzerland, 50 percent in the United States, and the balance elsewhere. More than perhaps any other banking activity, international private banking is arena specific, with different financial institutions offering their services in different arenas. This is largely because the activities of private banks are disproportionately dependent upon the regulatory protection offered locally.

The IPB Client Base

The core IPB client base is the security-seeking HNW individual or family who wishes to hold funds offshore in a form that will maintain its value but that is hidden from exposure to national regulatory and political authorities. They may have a variety of reasons for the need for offshore banking—most of which, it has been suggested, can be traced to either fear or greed. A primary concern is to have funds in a safe haven in case of emergency (e.g., to facilitate temporary residence abroad or even permanent emigration). People wish to protect their wealth from political uncertainty, taxation, expropriation, arbitrary exchange controls, adverse inheritance laws, and the like. Consequently, HNW clients resident in different geographic regions tend to favor different private banking arenas. U.S. clients are inclined to keep their money at home or in nearby Caribbean havens. Latin

Americans look to Miami, Panama, and, to a lesser extent, New York. Far East clients have mainly used Hong Kong, while those from the Middle East have tended toward Europe, primarily London and Switzerland.

The needs and attitudes of clients affect the range of services offered by private bankers. While the European or American client, for example, may well be happy to leave money with professional money managers, a less-sophisticated client from another country may be hesitant to grant anyone discretion over his or her funds and will consequently be unimpressed by banks' trust activities. This client will also tend to prefer deposit accounts and will avoid gold and commodities whose prices can fluctuate dramatically.

Even given the common secrecy component, HNW clients using IPB services have varying risk/returns attitudes with respect to different elements of their portfolio. For schematic purposes, one can split a portfolio into three categories: sacred, safe, and speculative. These terms are obviously subjective—an entirely safe portfolio for one individual may for another be entirely speculative.

The wealth can be arranged across a risk continuum ranging from perceived total security (in which the client is effectively yield inelastic and the objective is to maintain the real or nominal value of wealth) to targeting on high yields with little exposure to risk. This suggests two main categories—stability-seeking money and yield-seeking money. Institutions that attempt to service both groups may encounter real delivery problems in attempting to supply them.

Products and Services

There are essentially four types of services that comprise the IPB business.

1. *Transactions Activities.* A major role for the financial institution serving the HNW client with a significant component of wealth offshore is to ensure that funds are where they are needed when they are needed. This is all the more difficult since in many cases HNW clients are not permitted to hold foreign currency under exchange control regimes imposed by their national authorities, and any transactions involving offshore currency will, of necessity, have to be done abroad. In many developing countries, all foreign mail can be opened randomly by the authorities, and great care must be taken by private bankers to ensure total efficiency and discretion.

One bank error could cost a client an entire fortune, a career, or worse. This exposure to risk, combined with the personal nature of many of the transactions (e.g., mortgage and credit card payments) render the IPB client highly service oriented. The IPB business, even more perhaps than its domestic counterpart, is closely linked to personalities. When top names leave a bank, they usually take a number of clients with them.

2. *Credit Extension.* Although few banks actually extend credit to IPB clients in the traditional sense of the term, some institutions will lend clients certain small amounts that are backed by assets, typically no more than 40 percent of the value of the portfolio under management, and generally for short time periods. Banks generally will not provide unsecured loans as part of their IPB business, although some institutions will provide trade financing and other forms of transactional or corporate lending activities. These include:

   a. *Lending against promissory notes.* The client requests a loan backed by his or her deposits.

   b. *Letters of credit.* IPB clients often need to import goods in the course of the business. This type of service is provided by many banks when backed by deposits.

   c. *Overdrafts.* Overdraft facilities usually involve less documentation than promissory notes but are again only given when backed by deposits.

   d. *Credit card loans.* Many banks offer their own credit card services, while others act as references for their clients. The most popular cards worldwide are the American Express Gold Card and the corresponding credit-linked Visa and MasterCard products.

3. *Asset or Portfolio Management.* Fiduciary activities for HNW clients dominate the product range. As noted, the objective is to build a portfolio appropriate to each client's needs by managing effectively the interrelationship between risk, return, liquidity, and confidentiality, all of which are interdependent and among which difficult tradeoffs often have to be made. IPB provides clients with access to financial, real, and speculative assets, given that their clients have complex financial objective functions encompassing a variety of financial products in a number of currencies and across a range of locations. Thus, a broad range of portfolios may be available to satisfy a given individual's specific requirements.

4. *Personal Services.* The personal services provided for IPB clients are as wide ranging as those provided for clients of domestic private

banking operations. A key difference between these and transactions-related activities is that the latter services are typically paid for explicitly, while the former are part of the "extended product" of an IPB relationship.

Location Criteria

We have noted that HNW clients from certain geographic areas tend to use particular IPB arenas. There are three main factors affecting the attraction of specific IPB locales.

First, geographical location will determine the convenience of managing transactions. Communications and transportation are important, as are time zones that can limit the amount of time available each day to control an account. A balance will also have to be struck between the HNW client's residence and the location of the client's business interests. In some cases, the client places funds offshore, sets up business abroad, and then finally emigrates.

A second issue involves matters related to country risk. Individuals will have less real control over their assets when those assets are offshore, a problem compounded by the fact that such locales may be associated with unstable governments. HNW clients may be paying for secrecy in part by accepting higher levels of country risk.

For those who find such a price too high, the United States can offer significant attractions, both from a geopolitical and sociopolitical point of view. The likelihood of expropriation of private wealth, economic collapse, or political instability is slight, although taxation may be a problem with respect to certain types of assets. Consequently, HNW clients are still tempted to use banks and trusts in tax havens. Government policy plays an important role as well. In 1979, for example, the United States took retaliatory action against Iran by freezing Iranian assets; in 1986 similar actions were taken against Libya, raising concerns among some HNW clients.

There also exists information risk. The HNW client is buying confidentiality, but there is always the possibility that the client's affairs will not remain totally secret—that third parties, be they national authorities or unscrupulous bank employees, will somehow gain access to the details of a client's financial affairs. At the other end of the scale, it may be that the HNW client is denied full information on his or her own assets, due to the need for total discretion in such matters in order to avoid the prying eyes of home country authorities.

The third factor involves financial and yield concerns. Although the client's primary motivation may be security, many IPB customers are becoming increasingly yield conscious. The net yield characteristics of a location, the overall level of financial sophistication, and the integrity and efficiency of the local banking sector and of the individual banks themselves will all be of relevance in the HNW client's decision.

The IPB Arenas

The three main IPB arenas are Switzerland, the United States, and the United Kingdom. The institutions providing IPB services differ in each case. In Switzerland the primary players are the traditional private banks, the large universal banks, and the foreign banks; in the United States it is the large commercial banks; and in the United Kingdom the primary providers are the classic British merchant banks.

Switzerland

Switzerland has had a highly developed banking and financial system for over 200 years. The integrity of its financial institutions, the existence of secrecy statutes since 1934, and its inherent political, economic, and social stability have made it a highly attractive offshore banking center for private funds management. The only comprehensive data on funds managed are maintained by the Swiss Banking Commission, which publishes nothing. Market rumor suggests that a conservative figure for funds under management is approximately SFR600 billion; the 24 private banks manage perhaps SFR100 billion of this amount. Corroborating that conservative estimate, a study by McKinsey concluded that the total Swiss private banking market totals SFR1.3 trillion to SFR1.5 trillion. With only one-quarter to one-third of those funds owned by Swiss nationals, Switzerland is the worldwide leader in IPB, accounting for about one-half of the world total. Assuming that Swiss banks earn 0.6 percent to 1.2 percent per year on trust portfolios through a plethora of transactions fees (unlike the United States and Britain, the Swiss do not use a flat fee of 1 percent of the portfolios under management), the sector is worth U.S.$3 billion to U.S. $10 billion per year to Switzerland.

Traditional Swiss private banks are similar to proprietorships or partnerships in that the owners (partners/shareholders) have unlimited liability. The main advantage in remaining private is that the principals avoid double taxation—they are subject only to taxation as owners of the assets of the company. Private bankers also like to point out that their own capital is permanently at risk, which suggests more conservative and attentive management. As there are no requirements for disclosure of private banking activities, traditional private banks can be more discreet than their publicly owned limited liability counterparts. However, certain institutions, although still referred to as private banks, have now dropped their unlimited liability status in order to gain access to capital and securities markets to pay off owning members no longer interested in banking and meet the needs of business expansion.

Today, the most important Swiss participants in HNW individual banking are the three universal banks—Credit Suisse, Swiss Bank Corporation, and Union Bank of Switzerland. They differ from the traditional Swiss private banks in their size and in the fact that they are publicly held with limited liability. They are thought to manage more than 50 percent of the funds in Switzerland, which also gives them substantial placing power in the domestic and international securities markets.

Foreign banks in Switzerland competing for IPB business were initially attracted by the country's wholesale banking market and only later turned their attention to private banking. The result is that many of them are now fighting to make up for previous neglect of this market.

The main activities of the Swiss private banks are asset management and transactions-related activities. Due to their unlimited liability status, they tend not to extend credit to their private banking clients—although they will lend small amounts backed by assets under management for personal needs. The universal banks are more flexible in this respect and will serve some private banking clients' corporate financial needs as well. Most of the Swiss banks expect large amounts of funds to manage. Private client balances with the universal banks start at SFR 200,000, but the average is around SFR 500,000. Below-average sums are normally only accepted on a special client's recommendation, or in the case of attractive future prospects, and will be placed in a grouped portfolio. The consensus is that individually tailored portfolio management is not viable for accounts under SFR 350,000 to SFR 500,000. The level of discretionary power given to banks varies, and it is likely to change as HNW clients become more financially sophisticated.

There has been significant consolidation in the Swiss market over the years. There were 260 private banks in Switzerland at the turn of the century, but this number declined to 49 in the 1960s due, in part, to the rise of the large universal banks. At the end of 1984 it was estimated that this figure had declined again to 24, and it has continued to fall despite an annual growth potential of over 10 percent for the market as a whole.

Over a period of two centuries, the Swiss banks have established a formidable reputation for conservative banking, skilled international asset management, discretion, reliability, and highly personalized service. This reputation acts as an important barrier to successful entry for newcomers in a world where the "personal touch" plays such a vital role and where the most important way of increasing the client base is through referrals. Moreover, family wealth tends to figure highly as a source of Swiss private banking business—indeed, a good deal of European wealth moved to Switzerland during World War II and has remained there. Importantly, staff turnover is very low, and an employee of a Swiss private bank is expected to spend his or her entire career with that bank. This provides a desirable degree of continuity that permits a client to retain the same portfolio manager. These factors combine to give the established Swiss private and universal banks a major advantage over their foreign competitors. Private client business depends more than any other banking service on building relationships. That takes time, and the "outsiders" are years behind.

Even so, the Swiss private banks face problems. The competitive environment is changing. It is becoming more difficult to attract and retain the right caliber of personnel, because the limitation on numbers of partners makes it hard to share rewards with top employees. Some clients are becoming more aware of the opportunity cost of money and more yield elastic—the level of service is no longer necessarily more important than portfolio performance, and the incidence of account switching is increasing. There has always been a certain degree of switching between the larger universal banks and the private banks, with investors attracted to Switzerland by the universal banks and then drawn to the private banks by their higher levels of service, personalized treatment, and reputedly lower levels of transactions and statement errors. But competition between the private banks themselves seems to be growing less "gentlemanly."

The Swiss private banking units of foreign banks have their own strengths as well. Citicorp and J. P. Morgan, for example, have a global organization to offer their clients, placing them on a different plane than many local competitors. If clients want to buy bonds in Europe, stocks in Singapore, and real estate in California, there is a worldwide network at their disposal matched only by the Swiss universal banks. With the decline in the value of secrecy and the rise in performance orientation of clients, the traditional advantages of private banks are declining as sources of competitive performance. Lloyds, the British clearing bank, has also followed this strategy with the opening of its IPB office in Geneva in 1988.[3]

The most widely reported example of the interplay of Swiss and international competition in the HNW individual banking market in Switzerland concerns the Lebanese-born Edmond Safra, founder of the Geneva-based Trade Development Bank. American Express spearheaded its attack on the Swiss market with the purchase from Mr. Safra of the highly successful Trade Development Bank in 1983. As part of the purchase agreement and following his departure from American Express, Mr. Safra promised not to engage in private banking in Switzerland for three years. After the end of that time, Mr. Safra came back with his new vehicle, Safra-Republic Holdings, 49 percent of which was owned by Republic Bank of New York (Mr. Safra owned 33 percent of the Republic Bank). By March 1989, pursuing an ultra-conservative investment management policy of maximizing bank liquidity at the expense of returns, Safra-Republic had over $3.1 billion in private banking accounts. Clearly Safra's personal contacts and undisputable Swiss-style discretion and commitment to providing good service helped his rise, but that rapid rise itself reflects the changing character of the Swiss market.[4]

Swiss banks can no longer trade on security and reputation alone. They must compete on returns and, at the same time, extend their traditional client base. This involves attracting institutions (e.g., pension funds and insurance companies) as well as HNW clients, a move that will place severe demands on their resources and organizations as they try to transfer from service-driven to performance-driven products. Institutional investors are very yield conscious and, unlike HNW clients, not as willing to sacrifice total returns for secrecy, security, or stability. It will be difficult for Swiss private banking to provide internationally competitive yields and simultaneously maintain traditional levels of flexibility and customization. This could lead to polarization between those providing high levels of personal attention and less competitive yields and those providing higher yields and less service.

The problem of Swiss-based investment performance may be a serious one. In London and New York, money managers are familiar with the range of sophisticated capital markets and hedging instruments that can dramatically alter a portfolio's risk/return profiles. In Switzerland a futures and options exchange (SOFFEX) was not introduced until 1987. There is also a lack of skilled money managers and computer specialists. At the same time, Swiss private banks must build up their capital bases. And while much of their income has traditionally come from brokers' commissions, this is bound to end with the introduction of screen dealing, negotiated commissions, and Swiss banking deregulation.

With characteristic discretion, Switzerland's answer to London's Big Bang (as revealed in a 1989 Cartel Commission Report) will be to phase out the fixed "conventions" (or fees) of foreign exchange, brokering, and other banking services over a period of years expected to take until 1991. The result is likely to be an end to the much-maligned Swiss banking cartel and changes in the way HNW individual banking customers are charged. More competition is likely to result.

The Swiss private banks have also been comfortable as members of the dominant bank syndicate in the domestic capital market; however, when the syndicate structure eventually breaks up, they will have to fend for themselves. Historically, French residents have formed a large part of their client base, but the French banks themselves as well as foreign banks in France are making significant efforts to attract private banking clients. The Swiss IPB arena is becoming wide open.

The United States

The United States is regarded by many wealthy individuals as the safest haven of all for their funds and business interests—and indeed, in some cases, for themselves. Banks that have followed the evolution whereby HNW clients move funds from their home countries, set up business, and finally emigrate to the United States can adapt their range of services accordingly to help the client at each stage. The importance of the dollar as an international medium of exchange and the relatively low level of political risk (despite the lack of secrecy) are both attractions.

The major U.S. locations for IPB services are New York and Miami. New York has particular appeal as a thriving international financial capital, with one of the largest and most liquid equity markets in the world. Miami has drawn a large amount of wealth from Latin America due to its favorable location and strong Hispanic community. In New York the main IPB participants are the large money center banks, led by J. P. Morgan managing $17 billion of private money. Along with U.S. Trust Company Bank of New York-Irving Trust, and Republic National Bank, J. P. Morgan tends to concentrate on domestic clients. Citibank and Chase Manhattan are the major exceptions to this national focus, with far more extensive international banking operations than their domestic counterparts. Some of the larger financial services companies, such as Merrill Lynch and American Express, also offer IPB services. The money center banks invariably have an IPB presence in Miami as well, along with a large number of smaller, more specialist banks, regional banks, and foreign banks. Other IPB centers include Houston and Los Angeles.

The main IPB activities include transactions services, provision of checking accounts, and dollar loans. Checking accounts are a vital product given the importance of the Latin clientele. Minimum balances vary from one bank to another, but tend to be in the range of $1,000 to 5,000. There are higher requirements but these are generally compensated by more flexibility with respect to withdrawals, interest rates, linked services, and related functions. Dollar loans have a particular attraction for many IPB clients, since they often provide a valid obligation against which to request foreign currency from the home country's central bank. Banks will generally charge large spreads for this service. For funds management, IPB accounts are normally over $250,000; accounts of less than $100,000 are viewed as only marginally profitable. In keeping with the desire to remain clear of illegitimate wealth, banks generally prefer new clients to come with solid references.

To provide any meaningful degree of secrecy, the U.S. banks have to enact business through offshore locales, using the following vehicles:

1. *Trusts.* In trust agreement, a private contract is drawn up between the client and trustee in which the legal title is transferred to the trustee, who remains bound by law to administer the vehicle according to the trust directives. The trust provides security, privacy, and control over assets, and it minimizes taxes.
2. *Private Investment Companies.* Private investment companies are incorporated to hold, manage, and invest the assets of the owner. As the assets are held in a company name, the owner's identity is shielded. In the case of a limited company, the owner is liable only for the amount that remains unpaid on its shares.

3. *Offshore Trust and Insurance Companies*. This vehicle is a hybrid of the first two. It allows the owner more confidentiality, particularly after death when it is not subject to court probate and public disclosure.

Few data are available on the competitive dynamics of the IPB market in the United States. It appears, however, that competition is increasingly focused on attracting money that is already offshore from other financial institutions. The U.S. market, which is highly dependent upon the Latin American investor, has suffered as many of the client's home countries have imposed more rigorous exchange controls in the wake of massive capital outflows resulting from overvalued exchange rates and political/economic instability during the height of the debt crisis. The migration abroad of between $125 billion and $400 billion of Latin American money, a telling vote of nonconfidence against domestic economic policies, was one of the key factors precipitating the debt crisis.

The U.S. banks have provided the Swiss private banking institutions with serious competition in the international arena. They have a clear "people advantage." They believe the Swiss lack the versatility, innovativeness, and expertise necessary for an all-around international private banking service. In addition, the U.S. banks are more performance oriented and more aggressive marketers, which gives them a strong head start in some markets. Then there are specific strengths relating to each bank's particular circumstances and experience. Citibank, for example, has the benefit of a global network that provides it with a large referral base and enables it to meet a variety of client needs. On the other hand, the large organizational structures make it difficult for the U.S. institutions to be as flexible and as personal as some of their Swiss competitors.

United Kingdom

Although London, home to the Eurodebt and Euroequity markets, is arguably the financial capital of the world, its private banking industry and clientele have traditionally been domestic. At C. Hoare & Company, an unlimited liability bank partnership of the Hoare family members since 1672, customers can maintain a current account at the bank's head office and single branch without fees if they have a deposit of over £750. Only 500 of the bank's 10,000 customers use investment services. What are the advantages to this style of private banking? Says director Henry Hoare: "The advantages of banking with us may only be perceived once in a lifetime, when you need a quick, intelligent response to a proposition."

The predominant British providers of IPB services are the merchant banks. Their asset management activities are focused essentially on institutions; however, several, including Robert Fleming, S. G. Warburg, Morgan Grenfell, Kleinwort Benson, and Schroders, also provide services for private clients. Most of the accepting houses do as well, but for many the volume of business is insignificant, particularly in relation to their other activities. In most cases, the asset management activities are undertaken in separately capitalized subsidiaries.

Institutional asset management is a completely different product from private funds management. As noted, it is a far more yield-elastic business. Fund managers must produce competitive returns, or money is moved. IPB business in the United Kingdom, therefore, is best viewed as an adjunct to the merchant banks' institutional fund management activities, although quite different levels of service tend to be offered to the private banking client.

It would be wrong, however, to conclude that the HNW client has been unimportant to London institutions—for example, an estimated 80 percent of all Eurobonds end up in the hands of individual investors. The minimum amount required for a U.K. private banking account differs from one bank to another. Many accept £100,000 minimum—Kleinwort Benson requires £200,000 and Morgan Grenfell £400,000. Merchant bankers either manage the client's funds on a discretionary basis (as they do their own and those of institutional clients) in order to maximize risk-adjusted returns, or they can simply concentrate on sales of financial assets to HNW clients.

The British clearing banks, like the American commercial banks, have recently made competitive inroads into private banking, although the problem remains to maintain a clear distinction between branch and private banking. National Westminster has recently been successful with its private banking subsidiary, Coutts & Company. Barclays has also enjoyed some success in private banking, and there were rumors that the bank planned to revive Martins, the oldest bank in the United Kingdom before its merger with Barclays in 1968. The allure of old money remains important in HNW individual banking.

The London merchant banks clearly have competitive advantages, particularly over the Swiss, when it comes to attracting yield-sensitive capital. They have access to the most modern financial techniques, they can provide their clients with high-quality and detailed advice due to their large research teams, and their trading and market-making activities afford them a good feel for the market's expectations. London has also attracted the private banking activities of various foreign players, including U.S. commercial and investment banks, continental European banks, and Japanese institutions.

INTERNATIONAL COMPETITIVE DYNAMICS

IPB clients pay for services in two ways—through real costs and opportunity costs. The former relates to the explicit fees paid, the latter concerns yields foregone by having money managed in a particular arena with a particular level of service and degree of confidentiality. Since the primary concern for many IPB clients remains security, they tend to be willing to incur greater opportunity costs than other clients, and each location varies in the costs its institutions tend to exact.

The Swiss banks charge a variety of fees. These consist of government charges as well as bank charges, fees for brokerage, custody, dividend collection, and asset management. The client may also be charged market rates, even though banks themselves may have executed deals at substantially lower prices. Switzerland has the highest level of fees and probably the lowest real yields among the major private banking arenas, making costs of doing business very high in both real and opportunity cost terms. Nevertheless, when one considers that in some developing countries assets are depreciating by 40 percent or 50 percent a year, the opportunity cost concept perhaps seems less relevant.

The fee structure in London is considerably lower than in Switzerland, and returns are more competitive. There have been few performance-related fees, but they are expected to become more prevalent over time. In the United States the predominant source of private banking earnings is deposit income (e.g., from the sale of CDs as well as straight bank deposits). One New York bank estimates that about 90 percent of its IPB earnings are deposit based; in domestic private banking, the figure is 60 percent, with the remaining 40 percent attributable to more complex asset management services.

REGULATION AND IPB STRATEGY

Sellers of IPB services, no less than other banking services, must work within the complex and diverse regulatory structure that characterizes the international banking arena. Each private banking vehicle will be constrained by a set of regulations specifically relevant to its location and organizational form. Therefore, one must view the regulatory structure in terms of the financial institution itself as well as the arena in which it operates.

For commercial banks the regulatory structure relates primarily to capital adequacy and the level of on–balance sheet and off–balance sheet activities. If they are not engaged in securities underwriting and distribution, there is no danger that they will force upon IPB client accounts the stocks or bonds they cannot profitably sell elsewhere. In contrast, a major issue for merchant and universal banks is precisely the problem of conflict of interest. For the Swiss private banks the main regulatory issue is secrecy. In terms of location the Swiss clearly have the most favorable IPB regulatory climate. In the United States and United Kingdom, many IPB accounts have to be administered through offshore havens—in effect using brass-plate operations merely to take advantage of the legal and regulatory environment in order to satisfy client needs.

Private banking is a worldwide business involving three major groups of contenders. At one end of the spectrum are the Swiss private banks, with their lower yields and higher secrecy and service levels; at the other end are the London merchant banks, far more competitive on returns but lacking secrecy and the personal touch. The most obvious approach for individual institutions is to specialize in what each does best, especially given the cultural difficulties of attempting to manage both yield-seeking and stability-seeking funds within the same institution. Even the Swiss private banks have had to establish branches in London, where the competitive environment and lack of withholding taxes allows them to achieve rates of return expected by their more performance-oriented clients. Still, there exists the possibility of trying to cater to both types of private banking client, a strategy that the large U.S. banks with multiple private banking sites seem to be following.

To what extent can an individual institution succeed in broadening its private banking services in order to attract—and, more important-ly, to keep—the existing clients of other players? "Attracting" has traditionally been the more difficult part, due to the HNW client's preference for a personal and long-term relationship. But with the growing breed of performance-oriented HNW clients, "keep-ing" them will pose problems as well. There is evidence of an increasing incidence of both intrasectoral private banking competi-tion (i.e., rivalry within the same product segment) and intersectoral private banking competition (rivalry between product segments). The danger in the case of the intrasectoral competition is that it will increasingly focus on the price variable, due to the difficulty of differentiating between the same product offered by different financial institutions. The intersectoral competitive dynamics will depend on the perceived level of product and institutional substitutability. For some HNW clients, London merchant banks and U.S. commercial banks may be interchangeable; for others, they may not be.

A second strategy for developing a strong IPB base involves attracting new HNW clients rather than clients already being served by other financial institutions. This is particularly appealing in view of the fact that the distribution of wealthy individuals can change very rapidly. The current battle is focused on the Far East, where the large U.S. commercial banks, the U.K. merchant banks, and the Swiss banks are all competing actively for new business. The distinction between the "brash," aggressive style of the U.S. banks, with their mass marketing and mass mailing, and the traditional, conservative approach of the Swiss banks, the epitome of discretion, is clearly evident in the field.

The Asian market is a particularly vital one due to the nature of IPB. It is a region where client penetration usually comes from satisfied customers and word of mouth and where people can become rich very quickly, so that a seed corn targeting can be highly effective. In Hong Kong, for example, Chase Manhattan has focused on this sector of the market with its Golden Circle account. Each customer is assigned a personal account manager trained in tax planning, financial instruments, and banking law. It requires HK$200,000 for deposit accounts and HK$5 million for investment management. It also offers real estate investment services and credit lines for those thinking of U.S. residential or commercial real estate purchases of $4 million or more. Between 1983 and 1987, assets handled by Chase's Hong Kong unit rose from zero to $600 million.

The specific services offered in each IPB market depend not only on the chosen target segment, but also on an institution's inherent strengths. American Express Bank, for example, can offer its clients 80 offices worldwide and private banking centers in 8 locations, and it can offer to stockholders the services of Shearson Lehman Hutton, a group asset management center in London, and a chain of real estate firms in the United Kingdom. A private banking client receives a "premier services" card entitling him or her to 24-hour assistance with travel plans, medical needs, and other services.[5]

SUMMARY

The HNW client is likely to remain an important element in global banking for the foreseeable future, although the pattern of wealth ownership will probably shift steadily from inherited wealth to that created by the current generation. The passing of property rights from one generation to another is constantly subject to fiscal and political challenge. At the same time, newly created wealth appears ever more acceptable alongside market-oriented economic policies. Economic structures are becoming increasingly competitive, which simultaneously diminishes the chances of successive generations successfully retaining the wealth earned by their forebears and increases the chances that the newly wealthy will be sharper-thinking and more international in outlook. Private banking players will have to adapt to these changes, remembering that their fate ultimately will be sealed by the quality of the human resources they are able to attract to what essentially remains a "people business."

NOTES

1. Mark Kindley, "Do You Sincerely Want to be This Rich?" *Euromoney*, November 1987.
2. Richard Evans, "Sometimes Eccentric, Always Profitable," *Euromoney*, November 1987.
3. "Money Talks, Wealth Whispers," *The Economist*, June 24, 1989.
4. Richard Evans, "Private Change is Client-Driven," *Euromoney*, November 1988.
5. Pauline Loong, "Spectacular Growth in Hong Kong," *Euromoney*, November 1987.

SELECTED REFERENCES

Costella, Evelyn. "Why Banking Secrecy Is Not Enough." *Euromoney*, June 1985.

Davis, Glenn, et al. "Special Report: Private Banking in Asia." *Asian Business*, October 1985.

Kolbenschlag, Michael. "From Gettys To Yuppies." *Euromoney*, June 1985.

McDermott, Anthony. "Private Banking in Switzerland: Banking Finance and Investment." *Financial Times Supplement*, December 20, 1985.

McGruder, Barnewall M., and Rogowski, R. "Pursuing the Active Investor in Private Banking." *The Banker*, July/August 1985.

Prickett, F. Daniel. "Banking On A Segmented Market." *The Banker*, March-April 1985.

Studer, Margaret. "Hardy Band Of Swiss Private Banks Mixes Tradition, High Technology." *Wall Street Journal Europe*, January 30, 1985.

Stevenson, Merril. "A Survey Of International Banking." *The Economist*, March 22-28, 1986.

Walter, Ingo. *The Secret Monkey Market* (New York: Harper & Row, 1990).

13

Money Market and Foreign Exchange Dealing

The previous chapters have dealt principally with asset management in international commercial banking—the risks, returns, market conditions, and determinants of competitive performance. Of course, there is a liability side to a bank's global balance sheet, and it also involves risks, returns, market conditions, and competition. It must be managed as well, and over the years liability management has gained significantly in international banking importance. Assets must be funded—where and how they are funded has a great deal to do with profitability and exposure to risk of banks as financial institutions. In fact, risk management of assets, liabilities, swaps, and foreign exchange positions as well as exposure to contingent claims (e.g., options) are essentially inseparable facets of international banking. The domain of *international treasury management* focuses on foreign exchange, liabilities, short-term assets, and off–balance sheet exposures. It is a high-powered, fast-paced set of activities not recommended for amateurs. Essentially, the main objectives of international treasury management are managing a bank's exposure to risk, funding a bank's global loan portfolio, and securing its liquidity position through the management of short-term assets and liabilities in a world of volatile interest rates and exchange rates.

ASSET AND LIABILITY MANAGEMENT

We can start with a conventional bank balance sheet. The typical *asset* side comprises cash, interbank deposits, loans, various marketable debt instruments, and, in some countries, equity holdings, each with its own yield and liquidity characteristics. The typical *liability* side comprises customer demand and time deposits, interbank deposits, long-term debt, and bank capital, each displaying certain cost and maturity characteristics.

The classic view of banking as financial intermediation is (1) to transform relatively short-term liabilities into longer-term assets, thereby meeting the maturity needs of both borrowers and lenders, (2) to reduce exposure to risk through portfolio diversification, and (3) to improve financial allocation through greater levels of expertise—all within accepted limits of banking prudence. Earnings come primarily from the difference (spread) in the respective returns derived from a bank's assets and the costs associated with its liabilities. If longer-term interest rates consistently exceed short-term rates in a stable interest rate environment, the maturity transformation process alone should ensure bank earnings, as should risk diversification and the application of its banking expertise in asset selection.

If government regulations limit bank interest payable on demand and time deposits and forbid issuance of long-term bank debt, then profit maximization becomes largely a matter of *asset* management—maximizing the return on assets subject to an acceptable level of risk. Liquidity considerations can be handled on the asset side through reserves and by holding short-term financial instruments that can be sold either in the money market or to the central bank if the need arises. The implicit assumption is that the overall size of the bank's balance sheet is fixed—or at least not under day-to-day control of the bank itself—and that management's problem is basically maximizing the risk-adjusted return on assets.

Suppose, on the other hand, that banks have considerable or even total freedom regarding what they pay for deposits and what kinds of financial instruments they may issue in order to attract funds. Regulation is limited to reserve requirements, capital-based lending limits, capital ratios, and similar broad-gauge asset controls. In this case, a bank is free to attract funds in any manner it sees fit, and the size of its balance sheet is limited only by its capital position and its ability to achieve higher returns on its assets than it has to pay on its liabilities. Assuming it has attractive asset-side opportunities that exceed its traditional sources of funds, it can always "purchase" the necessary liabilities in the marketplace.

The bank now faces a far more diverse set of highly interest-sensitive funding possibilities, as well as the task of liability management alongside asset management. The problem is to minimize the cost of funds subject to acceptable risks—a portfolio problem on the liability side that is quite similar to the traditional portfolio problem on the asset side. The two problems are virtually inseparable and have to be managed together.

Financial innovation, changing financial markets, and financial deregulation have together propelled liability management to a position of prominence in international banking—perhaps beginning with the issuance of negotiable certificates of deposits (CDs) by major U.S. banks in 1961, advanced by the growth of the Euromarkets in the years following, and anchored in the development of fierce competition from nonbank financial institutions in more recent times. There are also a wide variety of off–balance sheet and transactional items (see Table 13–1), which may or may not give rise to exposure management problems of various kinds.

Balance sheet and off–balance sheet business growth today tends to be limited only by capital adequacy and legal constraints, as long as marginal returns on the asset side exceed marginal costs on the liability side and both are appropriately adjusted for risk. Asset and liability management, therefore, have become full partners in the business of international banking.

Domestically, the "raw material" of bank liability management consists in the U.S. domestic market of Federal Reserve funds (*Fed funds*), securities repurchase agreements (*repos*), CDs, and debentures, each having particular interest costs and maturity attributes. This raw material differs from country to country, as does the scope for active liability management in individual national financial markets. Internationally, the principal "purchased" funds are Euro-CDs and interbank Eurocurrency deposits. Interbank deposits in the Euromarket range in maturity from overnight to 3, 6, or 12 months, although significantly longer deposits are available, especially to the major established banks.

Funding possibilities in the internal money markets of different countries are highly variable. In some, regulations may prohibit deposit taking or other types of funding by foreign-based bank branches or affiliates. In others, indigenous banks may have a hammerlock on customer deposits and can make life difficult for their foreign competitors if they are the principal source of interbank deposits. In still others, central banks may pursue erratic monetary policies, abruptly altering the availability of funds in the local money market. Particularly if a foreign-based bank's involvement in a country is limited to finance companies, merchant banks, or similar forms of banking organization without a sizeable customer deposit base (or the right to borrow from the local central bank), the bank may be potentially vulnerable to funding risks and may be forced to rely on Euromarket funding or on parent support. However, in the absence of governmen-

Table 13–1.   Summary of Off-Balance Sheet Activities

Contingent Claims	Financial Services

Loan commitments
Overdraft facilities
Credit lines
Backup lines for commercial paper
Standby lines of credit
Revolving lines of credit
Reciprocal deposit agreements
Repurchase agreements
Note issuance facilities

Guarantees
Acceptances
Assets sales with recourse
Standby letters of credit
Documentary or commercial letters of credit
Warranties and indemnities
Endorsements
Financial support to affiliates or subsidiaries

Swap and hedging transactions
Forward foreign exchange contracts
Currency swaps
Currency futures
Currency options
Cross-currency swaps
Interest rate swaps
Cross-currency interest rate swaps
Interest rate options
Interest rate caps, floors, and collars

Investment banking activities
Securities underwriting
Securities dealership/distribution
Gold and commodities trading
Market-making in securities

Loan-related services
Loan origination
Loan servicing
Loan pass-throughs
Asset sales without recourse
Sales of loan participations
Agent for syndicated loans

Trust and advisory services
Portfolio management
Investment advisory services
Arranging mergers and acquisitions
Tax and financial planning
Trust and estate management
Management of pension plans
Trusteeships for unit trust, pension
   plans, and debentures
Safekeeping of securities
Offshore financial services

Brokerage/agency services
Share and bond brokerage
Mutual fund (unit trust) brokerage
General insurance brokering
Life insurance brokering
Real estate agency
Travel agency

Payment services
Data processing
Network arrangements
Clearing house services
Credit/debit cards
Point-of-sale systems
Home banking
Cash management systems

Export/import services
Correspondent banking services
Trade advice
Export insurance services
Countertrade exchanges

tal controls, domestic and international funding sources have become essentially unified, with ample scope for liability management activities ranging across national money markets and the Euromarkets.

Internationalization, of course, means that exchange rate considerations must be added to interest rate considerations on both the asset and liability sides of bank balance sheets as sources of risks and returns. And so the liability management and foreign exchange activities of international banks are generally combined under the heading of "treasury management." This involves high-pressure, minute-by-minute adjustment of the bank's liability profile to align it with its asset mix, its expectations as to future interest rates and exchange rates, and management's attitude toward risk. The day-to-day activities that form the core of this process cut across assets and liabilities and, as such, can in themselves generate gains and losses for the bank—the net returns from bank trading or positioning activities.

Dealing in Interest-sensitive Assets and Liabilities

Suppose a bank decides to match the maturity structure of its assets precisely by the maturity structure of its liabilities. For long-term assets, the bank enters financial markets and seeks long-term funds; the same is done for each bracket of the maturity spectrum. Because of risk differentials and information asymmetries, lending rates may still exceed the bank's own borrowing rates, including traditional customer deposits, and so the bank may well turn out to be profitable. However, securitization, competition among banks, and better-infomed, more financially sophisticated clients will tend to compress this "matched spread" and cause profits to erode.

Suppose an upward-sloping yield curve prevails in the market—that is, interest rates are higher for successively longer-term maturities. The bank can now enhance its profits by "mismatching" its book, or *gapping*. Instead of matching its assets and liabilities at each stage of the maturity scale, the bank concentrates its borrowing increasingly in the shorter maturities and its lending in the longer maturities— that is, its liabilities will exceed its assets at the short end, and its assets will exceed its liabilities at the long end. As a result, it can enhance its overall profitability by reducing its funding costs in relation to its overall *interest earnings*. This is the classic *maturity transformation* function of banks and other financial intermediaries, and the bank reaps an additional return for undertaking this role. There are commensurate liquidity risks, since short-term liabilities must be rolled over periodically to fund the longer-term assets and since the availability and cost of short-term liabilities depends on market conditions prevailing at the time.

Of course, interest rates are volatile, and expectations about their future are formed both within the bank itself and in the marketplace. If interest rates generally are expected to rise, a bank will want to shorten its asset maturities and lengthen its liability maturities. As existing assets mature, they should be replaced with short-term ones to avoid being locked into low current yields, while maturing liabilities should be replaced with longer-term ones to lock in current low-cost funds. If the bank expects interest rates to fall, management will want to do the reverse—lengthen asset maturities to lock in high yields, yet shorten liability maturities to take advantage of the lower funding costs expected in the months ahead. The extent and direction of maturity mismatching, therefore, will depend fundamentally on interest rate expectations.

Unfortunately, actual interest rate movement does not always follow a bank's expectations. Furthermore, all other market participants are forming their own expectations about future interest rates. A bank's assets are someone else's liabilities, while its liabilities are someone else's assets. In bank asset and liability management, therefore, a profitable bank must not only be right about interest rate movement much of the time, it also must be right sooner and act faster in order to beat the other participants to the punch before the market as a whole has moved and the opportunity for profit has evaporated.

It is easy to see, in the context of interest rate instability, how asset and liability management are really two sides of the same coin. Expectations that push a bank's asset mix in one direction will push its liability mix in the other.

Figure 13–1 summarizes the process of maturity mismatching. The horizontal axis shows the interest rate on an annual percentage-equivalent basis, and the vertical axis shows asset and liability maturities in months. OY is a yield curve facing a bank at a particular point in time. In this case, it indicates that the yield on long maturities is consistently higher than on short ones, with the most significant yield differences among individual maturities appearing at the short end. With this as given, a bank on the liability side will usually have some zero-yield deposits in customer and idle balances, very short-term interbank deposits, time deposits, and possibly some longer-term debt issues, as well as capital, with the weighted-average liability mix represented by point L. On the asset side, the bank will have some

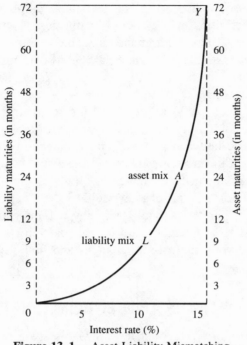

Figure 13–1.   Asset-Liability Mismatching.

zero-yield assets in required reserves and accounts with other banks and a broad range of maturities in loans outstanding—the weighted-average asset mix being represented by point *A*.

If no mismatching is undertaken, points *A* and *L* would be essentially identical in terms of maturities, but *A* would be slightly to the right of *L* (a matched spread of perhaps 1 or 2 percent) to indicate the effect of risk, expertise, transactions costs, and other considerations mentioned earlier. To the extent that mismatching occurs, points *A* and *L* will differ. In this example, the average liability maturity is 9 months and the average interest cost is 10 percent, while average asset maturity is 24 months at a yield of 14 percent, giving an average interest spread of 4 percent—obviously a much better result. If assets are priced off a floating-rate base, then the "maturity" factor at the beginning of each interest period would be 24 months, even though the loan itself may be for 5 or 8 years, because the interest rate repricing is limited to the two-year period.

Clearly, the shape of the yield curve will dictate the appropriate direction and strategy of mismatching, with a greater emphasis on floating-rate assets placing a great deal more emphasis on treasury management activities in the shorter maturities. A bank that has a large retail deposit base, commands sizeable compensating balances from corporate customers, or has a particularly strong "name" in the money markets may be able to push point L to the left, thereby widening its gross interest margin. Similarly, a bank that can negotiate better interest rates on loans or is willing to assume greater credit risk can push point A to the right. Gross profitability will depend on the difference between points A and L on the horizontal (interest rate) axis, which in turn depends on (1) the shape of the yield curve, (2) the extent of maturity mismatching, and (3) the ability to lower the costs of funds and raise asset yields in the various markets in which the bank operates. A bank's strategy will depend heavily on its attitude toward risk. Greater maturity mismatching involves greater risk (associated with interest-rate changes and liquidity, as discussed below).

FUNDING OPTIONS AND EUROMARKET DEALING

Customer deposits may account for a sizeable share of a bank's total deposits and, being partly interest free, are naturally highly desirable. Besides being low cost, they can also be a relatively stable source of funds. A significant retail banking activity at the national level can tap that particular source of funds, albeit at relatively high cost. Corporate deposits, representing working capital and possibly compensating balances on lending facilities, depend on the relationship a bank (or its parent) and the client have built up over the years and the value of the services provided to the client by the bank. Banks with a particular industry or sector specialization sometimes have an inside track for deposit business with relevant firms. High net worth individuals are sometimes cultivated as another distinct source of deposits (see Chapter 12). Central banks may also be a good source of funding as a manifestation of their reserve management activities, again depending on a bank's relationships and activities at the national and regional level.

Whatever funds a bank cannot raise through customer deposits in order to support its assets it must "buy" in the open market. Banks that are "long" or "short" funds, based on their asset commitments and liability management strategies, will naturally do a great deal of business with each other—whether in domestic money markets or in the Euromarkets. The transactions involved may consist of three types of deposits: (1) *clean deposits*, which are unsecured, unconditional placements for fixed periods of time between banks whose creditworthines is deemed mutually satisfactory; (2) *secured deposits*, which are secured against collateral of equal or greater value; and (3) *negotiable deposits*, which take the form of marketable certificates that can be sold by the lender on the open market (should it be necessary to do so for liquidity reasons prior to maturity) and that carries either a fixed or variable interest rate.

The vast majority of interbank transactions in the Euromarket consist of clean deposits in short maturities, with Euro-CDs also strongly represented. The latter may be issued to nonbank clients as well. The negotiability feature gives the holder a liquidity advantage over ordinary time deposits, and so a bank will generally be able to obtain such funds at a small discount to prevailing interbank deposit rates for the same maturities. These funds can then be placed even in the interbank market at a spread sufficient to make a profit.

In the major Euromarket centers, such as London, the key interest rate attached to purchases (borrowing) of funds between banks is called the *interbank offered rate*, which is always specified as to placements in particular currencies. For example, a three-month placement in U.S. dollars between two banks in London may be done at "three-month Eurodollar LIBOR"—the *London Interbank Offered Rate*—discussed in earlier chapters as the base rate for various types of lending facilities and published daily by the Bank of England.

Banks that are market makers, or *dealing banks*, in interbank placements must be prepared to quote both *bid* (borrowing) and *offered* (lending) rates. In London, the former is published daily as the *London Interbank Bid Rate* (LIBID), the rate at which a dealing bank is prepared to borrow, or "buy," funds. A dealing bank—one that is known to be in the market both to sell and to buy funds—receiving a call from another bank, a potential *counterparty* on an interbank transaction, will not know whether that bank is on the buying or selling side of the market. But it can hazard a guess, and will want to adjust its bid or offered quote accordingly. In this way, certain banks that are particularly prominent, that are favored by particular customers, or that happen upon an unsophisticated counterparty may be able to obtain interbank placements well below LIBOR, thereby lowering their overall funding costs.

The opposite may also be true. A bank may be considered potentially risky by the market because it is a new entrant or has problems with credit quality, because it is a special-purpose bank not normally in the market, or because it has potential liquidity problems in particular currencies. Such a bank may only be able to attract interbank funds by paying a premium over LIBOR. This is called "tiering," and it can seriously increase funding costs for the weaker participants in the interbank market (particularly at times of market turmoil). This can put them at a competitive disadvantage against the larger or more prominent banks that continue to fund themselves at or below LIBOR.

Just as gapping is a major source of bank profit along the entire range of asset and liability maturities on a bank's balance sheet, so maturity mismatching to enlarge profits is heavily practiced in Euromarket dealing activities as well. For example, a dealing bank may be able to place a six-month deposit with another bank at LIBOR and fund it with another six-month placement from a second bank at its own bid rate—its profit being the bid-offer spread. Alternatively, the bank may be able to fund the same six-month placement with a three-month deposit at lower initial interest cost, in the hope that it can roll it over favorably at maturity for another three-month deposit. If it is correct, gapping will lower the cost of funding the loan and commensurately increase the spread. Or the loan might be funded by a succession of one-month or one-week or even shorter-term deposits. Again, it all depends on what the bank thinks will happen to interest rates—expectations that will alter its short-term asset and liability mix. Correct anticipation and quick action bring dealing profit. Being wrong, indecisive, or slow will not make for a long and successful career in the business.

Euromarket dealing activities have taken on even greater importance, with floating-rate medium-term bank facilities and securities priced at a negotiated spread over, say, six-month LIBOR. For funding purposes, we have already noted that it is the six-month rollover date that is relevant, not the final maturity of the loan or security. Thus, long-term interest rate risk has been effectively eliminated, but this has placed a far greater burden (and profit opportunity) on short-term treasury management.

It is exceedingly important that an international bank be active on both the buying and selling sides of interbank lending in the Euromarket, even though the spread between bought and sold funds may be exceedingly narrow at times. The bank should be perceived as making a "contribution" to the market by those banks that are large net suppliers of funds. As part of its liquidity management, a bank will want to allocate a certain percentage of its short-term assets to interbank placements. The need is to get "inside" (wholesale) and not "outside" (retail) prices. But besides this, an image of prominence and acceptance in the Euromarket involves sizeable, consistent, and reliable activity in every aspect of that market.

DEALING IN FOREIGN EXCHANGE

So far, our discussion of the dealing function as it concerns the Euromarkets is not much different from similar money market activities domestically, except perhaps for a substantial lack of regulation. However, Euromarket dealing has always been closely linked to dealing in foreign exchange. In fact, as international financial integration moves ahead, dealing on domestic money markets, Euromarkets, and foreign exchange markets is becoming increasingly inseparable.

Table 13–2 gives the foreign exchange dealing profits for the thirteen major U.S. players from 1979 to 1988. The consistent profitability of every institution listed is striking, yet there are enormous differences in profits among the players and the year-to-year variation in profits coinciding with the degree of exchange rate volatility.

Like Eurocurrency dealing, foreign exchange operations of international banks are conducted largely on an interbank basis. A bank will maintain deposit accounts in a series of foreign currencies either with its own branches abroad or with correspondent banks. These "nostro accounts" represent a pool of funds in each currency that the bank can draw upon to honor its foreign exchange contracts in that currency or replenish by buying foreign exchange. A bank will have to decide the optimum balances to be left in nostro accounts, which it will naturally want to keep as low as possible to minimize loss of interest and exposure to possible exchange rate movements. In a simple case, if orders to buy a certain currency on a particular day exceed orders to sell, the bank will have to enter the foreign exchange market and buy that currency, usually from other banks, in order to restock its nostro accounts. The opposite holds if sell orders exceed buy orders.

Foreign exchange traders in a bank will receive buy and sell orders for *spot* foreign exchange (immediate delivery) settled two business days after the trade from its nonbank customers and from other banks. It will also receive orders from the same set of counterparties for *forward* purchases or sales of foreign exchange to be delivered at a specified future date (e.g., 30, 60, or 90 days ahead). Extended forward contracts beyond such conventional terms are called "long-dated forwards."

Whether for spot or forward exchange contracts, a dealing bank will always quote buying and selling rates, both of which will be set by competitive market forces and represent firm commitments on the part

Table 13–2. Foreign Exchange Trading Income of Major U.S. Banks [a]

	1979	1980	1981	1982	1983	1984	1985	1986	1987	1988
American Express International Bank [b]	27.3	35.0	28.0	38.0	32.0	43.0	54.0	60.0	94.0	114.0
Bank of America	90.2	101.0	112.2	113.8	102.4	101.4	150.1	141.0	140.0	122.0
Bankers Trust [c]	16.6	22.8	30.8	46.2	27.8	67.7	107.5	57.4	512.8	153.9
Chase Manhattan Bank	77.0	96.5	123.4	130.5	116.7	119.5	173.4	223.2	232.3	249.7
Chemical Bank	9.9	34.8	39.5	55.5	40.4	60.6	101.5	103.2	152.8	143.2
Citibank [d]	113.6	175.0	265.0	241.0	274.0	258.0	358.0	412.0	453.0	616.0
Continental Illinois	11.3	31.0	34.3	19.5	24.4	20.0	26.0	24.4	28.4	20.9
First Chicago	11.2	21.8	28.0	27.2	35.5	25.5	47.2	94.0	118.6	148.6
Irving Trust [e]	10.0	16.9	11.6	16.1	12.6	15.9	30.4	30.8	50.7	30.9
Manufacturers Hanover	16.1	15.1	28.6	30.0	27.1	34.2	45.8	36.3	62.7	103.0
Marine Midland	11.0	20.7	32.4	27.0	18.8	17.8	26.2	10.2	38.2	5.0
J. P. Morgan & Co.	35.9	62.8	106.0	57.0	74.3	29.5	172.6	229.6	251.2	186.8
Republic New York Corp.	4.9	12.9	7.9	11.5	8.1	12.5	25.3	34.2	39.2	35.4

a. In millions of dollars, exclusive of translation income.

b. Figures for 1982 to 1984 include "Foreign Currency Transactions Gains."

c. 1987 figures are adjusted downward by $80 million due to revaluation of open options.

d. Includes translation gains and losses.

e. 1988 figure is only for first three quarters prior to merging with Bank of New York.

SOURCE: Annual Reports/10Ks.

of the bank. The buying rate will be slightly lower than the selling rate (in local currency), the difference being a source of gross foreign exchange trading gains. Naturally, the spread will be somewhat wider on smaller trades (retail) than on larger ones (wholesale) in order to reflect competitive and cost differentials. A bank that does not deal in a particular currency (e.g., an American bank in Australian dollars) can simply find another bank that does and can carry the transaction through on an interbank basis, which will mean an additional cost to its customer.

An international bank is naturally susceptible to foreign exchange risk. Its exposure in a particular currency consists of (1) any capital investments it may have in that country in the form of branches or affiliates; (2) the difference between "buy" and "sell" contracts it has entered into with respect to that currency in both spot and forward foreign exchange transactions at any given time; (3) the difference between interest receivable and interest payable in that country; (4) the net balance of all other payables and receivables denominated in that currency, such as fees, taxes, and dividends; and (5) balances held in its nostro accounts. All such exposures must be carefully tracked on a daily basis, a desired level of exposure (long or short position) must be decided by management, and cumulative foreign exchange transactions must be structured to achieve that optimum.

Trading profit in foreign exchange comes from differences in buying and selling rates during the course of a day (or longer). If traders think a particular currency will strengthen during the course of a day, they will buy that currency quickly, either for spot or forward delivery, hoping to sell it later at a higher price. If they perceive differences in exchange rates among counterparties in the same or different geographic centers (e.g., New York and London), they will move to take advantage of the arbitrage opportunities provided, if the time zones permit, a practice that is sometimes called "jobbing." Toward the end of the trading day, any excess exposure in a particular currency will have to be *closed out* unless overnight developments, in the opinion of management, justify a *long* (balances plus receivables exceed payables) or *short* (payables exceed balances plus receivables) *open position*.

If a long open position is held, traders naturally expect the currency to rise, so they can sell out their position later at a profit. A short open position means that traders expect the currency to fall, so that they can buy foreign exchange cover later at a lower price to honor the bank's obligations. A *square* position simply means that a bank has fully covered its foreign exchange exposure at a particular point in time.

In fact, of course, the foreign exchange markets, Eurocurrency markets, and national money markets are inexorably linked from the standpoint of a bank's international treasury management. For one thing, funding a bank's asset portfolio may mean attracting deposits denominated in various currencies in order to secure reduced funding costs, thus involving potential foreign exchange risk for the bank. This, however, can always be covered (at a price) through offsetting foreign exchange contracts. Traders can also engage in *covered interest arbitrage*—buying term funds in one currency, selling them in another, and entering into spot and forward exchange contracts simultaneously to cover foreign exchange risk on the transaction. If the interest-equivalent cost of hedging is less than the nominal yield spread on the bought and sold funds, a sure (riskless) profit can be made.

In practice, therefore, the price of foreign currencies and the price of credit, both having the potential to vary over time and over space, define the dealing function in international banking. Foreign exchange and money market dealers need to be in constant touch with each other on developments in their respective markets—and on expectations as to future interest rate and exchange rate movements—if a bank's dealing function is to be a contributive part of the organization.

Besides dealing currencies on a cash basis either for spot or forward delivery to the counterparty, banks also are involved in a number of derivative products that are linked to the underlying foreign exchange market. These include *foreign exchange futures*—that is, blocks of foreign currencies that can be bought and sold for fixed settlement dates on organized exchanges in Chicago, New York, London, and elsewhere. Forex futures are not perfect substitutes for interbank forward transactions due to the differing needs of buyers and sellers, the organization of the market, margin requirements, and other factors—although futures and forward rates are obviously closely linked. Given customer requirements as well as arbitrage, positioning and hedging opportunities, major commercial and investment banks find it desirable to have a presence in forex futures markets as well.

The same is true of *forex options*—that is, the right to buy (call) or sell (put) a fixed amount of foreign exchange at a fixed rate (strike price) with a fixed future expiration date (European option) or anytime up to that date (American option). A forex future is an obligation, while a *forex option* is an asset that can be taken up if the strike price is better than the current market price (in the money), or it can be allowed to lapse if it is not (out of the money).

Options can be purchased, at a higher price than forex futures or forwards, by banks or their clients as a hedging vehicle to insure against adverse exchange rate change. Options can be sold (written) by banks or their clients, betting that they will end up out of the money for counterparties, or options can be traded against a spread with substantially greater leverage than in underlying cash transactions. They can also be embedded in various kinds of financial instruments such as multicurrency bonds, for example.

Finally, there are *forex swaps* arranged for clients, as discussed in greater detail in Chapter 15. Table 13–3 ranks how individual banks have fared in the foreign exchange business and how they are regarded by their interbank counterparties.

Profits and the Dealing Functions

There has always been a good deal of argument about the extent to which an international bank should look to its dealing department as a profit center. On the one hand, it could be argued that its primary

Table 13–3. Interbank Performance in Foreign Exchange, 1989

London		New York	
1.	Midland	1.	Citibank
2.	Barclays	2.	Chemical
3.	Lloyds	3.	Chase
4.	Chemical	4.	Morgan Guaranty
5.	NatWest	5.	Bankers Trust
6.	Citibank	6.	Crédit Suisse
7.	Amex	7.	Irving Trust
8.	Royal Bank of Scotland	8.	Manufacturers Hanover
9.	Hambros	9.	NatWest
10.	Standard Chartered	10.	Amex
Frankfurt		**Tokyo**	
1.	Deutsche	1.	Bank of Tokyo
2.	Dresdner	2.	Dai-Ichi Kangyo Bank
3.	Commerzbank	3.	Sumitomo Bank
4.	BHF	4.	Sanwa Bank
5.	DG Bank	5.	Mitsubishi Bank
6.	Bayerische Vereinsbank	6.	IBJ
7.	Citibank	7.	Citibank
8.	Hessische Landesbank	8.	Morgan Guaranty
9.	Security Pacific	9.	Fuji Bank
10.	Morgan Guaranty	10.	Irving Trust

SOURCE: *Euromoney*, October 1989, p. 321.

roles are (1) to satisfy the needs of bank customers with respect to the money and foreign exchange markets and (2) to supply the funding needs of the bank with minimum exposure to risk. On the other hand, it is possible to do more that just meet the funding needs. Sizeable funding and foreign exchange profits are indeed possible—assuming a bank is willing to take the associated risks—as a result of interest rate and exchange rate volatility.

It is probably safe to say that any competitive international bank today will have an aggressive and well-developed dealing function and will serve as a market maker in national and international money markets and in the foreign exchange markets. For one thing, we have seen that active gapping can significantly enhance effective interest spreads. Since much of the interest rate risk has been taken out of the long asset maturities, with lending facilities being priced at contractual spreads over LIBOR or some other floating base rate, greater emphasis is placed on "funding profits" through gapping in the shorter maturities and foreign exchange operations. Furthermore, how can an international bank provide sound advice to its major clients, many of whom face similar risks in foreign exchange and interest-sensitive money markets, if it is not among the active participants in those markets? Float (transactions in process of settlement), commissions, and trading profits are further sources of income from the dealing function.

Of course, dealers themselves are the critical element. They must be bright, quick, decisive, ambitious, honest, and capable of developing an intuitive "feel" for the market and for the probable impact of unanticipated information ("news") on these markets. They also must be kept motivated, with trading profit and losses clearly ascribed to dealer performance and with compensation levels tailored accordingly. Unless they are given some leeway to test their judgment against that of the market, a bank's dealing function and its value to the organization as a whole will quickly deteriorate. Individualism notwithstanding, a dealer must also be a good team player and must be able to disseminate information rapidly, build an effective consensus, and accept the trading constraints that have been laid down by management. Like so much of international banking, dealing is a "people business."

Nevertheless, international banks must strike a balance between looking to the dealing function as an explicit source of profit and as a cost center, the primary role of which is to service the rest of the bank and its customers. Emphasizing the former means that traders will naturally aim for greater returns by taking greater risks, raising the possibility of large trading losses and possibly even bank failure. Excessive emphasis on the latter threatens the vitality of the trading function and motivation of the traders themselves, and ultimately it may prove damaging to the bank's competitive positioning in this market.

Client Contact

Besides other banks, principal counterparties in foreign exchange, money market dealing, currency swaps, options, and futures are central banks and multinational corporations. A central bank will intervene in national money markets to influence the money supply and interest rates—for example, by selling short-term money market instruments in selected maturities to bring about tighter credit conditions. Besides their value as a source of deposits, banks need to continually monitor such activities, along with statements by central bank and other government officials and the money supply figures themselves, in order to gauge which way interest rates—and possibly exchange rates—will go.

Central banks will also be active in the foreign exchange markets, possibly selling foreign currencies in order to bolster the domestic currency or buying them to moderate upward pressure on the home currency's value. Some such trades are ultimately designed to influence exchange rates. Others aim to test the market sentiment, check on the competence of market participants, or remain simply an active participant in the market. Dealers' abilities to sort out central bank motivations, and maintain contact with the responsible officials, may provide valuable leads on a day-to-day basis about the prospective direction and magnitude of exchange rate and interest rate movements.

Multinational corporate clients (MNCs) will also be in regular contact with the dealing function of international banks. With large cash flows and balances denominated in a variety of different currencies, MNCs are faced with many of the same problems relating to interest rate and exchange rate movements as are bank dealers. The MNC treasurer may want to hedge foreign currency receivables against exchange risk, obtain cover for balance sheet exposure, undertake short-term Euromarket borrowing, or engage in a variety of currency swaps, options, and futures transactions—all potential sources of interest income, commissions, fees, or funding or hedging possibilities for the bank.

Its MNC counterparties often are highly sophisticated and have access to the same information on global economic and political developments; thus, they can communicate with dealers on terms not much different from dealers at other banks.

At the same time, an international bank's expertise in sheer numbers of dealers and presence in multiple markets does provide an important information and transactions cost advantage and makes it a source of useful advice to corporate treasurers. Based on information and "interpretation" advantages, many international banks have formed international money management groups, foreign exchange advisory services, international financial management consultancy teams, and similar "clusters" of expertise to draw on their institutional comparative advantage in this regard. Such groups work closely with traders — so much so that they are often an explicit part of the bank's treasury function. However, they must be made up of individuals with diverse capabilities, as distinguished from pure traders, who can diagnose a company's problems, interact effectively with managers, and make presentations that make sense to nonbankers. Such groups form an important link in the relationships between banks and companies doing business internationally, with the rewards coming in the form of fees, balances, or collateral business that helps to further establish banking relationships.

Like corporate treasurers, central bank managers have problems with international money management as well. The foreign exchange reserves of central banks must be invested in a mix of assets to provide a desired combination of yield and liquidity characteristics. Various types of hedging must be undertaken virtually continuously. Similarly, their external borrowing strategy must be carefully matched to prevailing market conditions. In both respects, central banks value regular contacts with and advice from international banks, which in turn have sometimes established central bank services groups. Again, the need to stay plugged in to international financial and foreign exchange markets virtually dictates that this function be lodged within a bank's treasury operations. The returns to the banks include central bank balances, foreign exchange and hedging business, and the chance to help meet possible future borrowing requirements. Table 13–4 lists the market share rankings of international banks dealing with clients on foreign exchange transactions.

RISKS AND RISK MANAGEMENT

Banks, in their day-to-day money activities, are exposed to a variety of risks. They have developed appropriate safeguards intended to

Table 13–4. Market Share Rankings of International Bank Dealing in Foreign Exchange (1987–1989)

Rank				Estimated market share (%)		
1989	1988	1987	Bank	1989	1988	1987
1	1	1	Citibank	6.1	5.1	8.3
2	2	3	Barclays	4.2	4.1	3.3
3	5	4	Chase Manhattan	3.2	2.9	3.1
4	4	2	Chemical	3.0	3.3	3.4
5	3	9	Royal Bank of Canada	2.9	3.5	1.4
5	–	4	Morgan Guaranty	2.1	–	2.2
7	–	13	National Westminster	1.9	–	1.1
8	9	14	Lloyds	1.6	1.8	1.0
9	16	8	Westpac	1.6	1.1	1.6
10	11	–	National Australia	1.6	1.5	–
11	13	–	Bank of Tokyo	1.4	1.4	–
12	8	–	Commonwealth Bank of Australia	1.4	2.1	–
13	–	10	Bankers Trust	1.2	–	1.2
14	10	–	Dai-Ichi Kangyo Bank	1.1	1.8	–
15	–	12	Midland	0.9	–	1.1
16	–	20	Goldman Sachs	0.9	–	0.6
17	–	19	Standard Chartered	0.9	–	0.6
18	–	6	Bank of America	0.9	–	2.0
19	18	15	Security Pacific	0.8	1.0	0.9
20	6	18	ANZ	0.8	2.2	0.6
			Total market share for top 20 banks	38.3	40.8 [a]	36.7 [a]

a. These totals include banks featured in the Top 20 rankings in 1988 and 1987 but not named in this table.

SOURCE: *Euromoney*, May 1989, Pg. 79; reprinted by permission.

limit that exposure, and they seek reduced dealing risk through diversification and careful analysis of the creditworthiness of counterparties. There are two polar approaches to the range of problems associated with risk management—centralization and decentralization.

The centralized approach, which Chase Manhattan Bank seems to favor, involves heavy investment in systems that strive to enable central managers to make bankwide portfolio decisions designed to minimize exposures created by dealing in global markets. If the systems work as planned, they prevent large positions from being built up in several units without the compounding implications of those positions being appreciated. They allow concerted position taking (if the bank's top management so wishes) and enable a single trading book in each instrument to be passed around the world.

Citibank is usually seen as applying the decentralized approach. This approach gives each trading room considerable leeway in setting its positioning strategies within trading limits. The advantage that this approach seeks to gain at the loss of bank unity and central control is to more highly motivate the traders in each location. In fact, no bank can afford to adopt either one of the polar extremes in its entirety. The question is how to trade off the benefits of the opposite poles to confront effectively the problems associated with risk management.

Fraud

Dealers almost always live under severe pressure in the marketplace and handle transactions of enormous amounts every day. To a degree, dealers are gamblers who play individual and collective hunches. They may be tempted to take bribes or kickbacks for doing a certain deal, usually by being in cahoots with a particular counterparty and doing transactions on terms less than optimal for their own bank. A dealer may also be in league with dealers at other banks for purposes of outright larceny. Or the dealer may have erred in a particular transaction and may try to hide the mistake, quite possibly compounding it. In all such cases, especially if there is collusion between the dealer and the bank's operations area or even its management, the losses can be serious indeed. The 1970s and 1980s saw a number of several major criminal cases emerge in international banking specifically linked to fraud in the dealing function, the largest of which was a $250 million fraud perpetrated against Volkswagen AG by crooked employees and brokers.

Banks can limit their exposure to the risk of fraud by carefully selecting, training, and supervising dealers; by limiting positions dealers are permitted to take; by performing periodic internal and external audits, including surprise visits from auditors; and by carefully separating the operations function from the dealing function.

Operations

Given the importance of time in money and forex dealing, bank operations are vitally important and problems in this area can seriously disrupt a bank's dealing activities. Even a short delay in transfer of funds can fundamentally alter the profit/loss profile of a particular deal. Inefficiency can quickly erode a bank's position in the market; similarly, a bank constantly runs the risk of dealing with other banks whose own operations (or those of their correspondents) are less than fully competent. Experience and reputation in a market in which news travels fast, coupled in extreme cases with refusal to complete a transaction until full confirmation of a deal is in hand, can limit exposure to operational risks in money and foreign exchange dealing.

Creditworthiness

Dealing activities assume that counterparties are able to make good on forex contracts or repay purchased funds and complete options, futures, and swap transactions. Of course, the risk in interbank deposits is that the counterparty bank will fail before the loan comes due. In foreign exchange dealing, the risk is that the counterparty will be unable to honor the contract on the settlement day and that the bank will have to reenter the market and cover itself, possibly at a less favorable exchange rate. Furthermore, when the settlement day rolls around, a bank may fail in one time zone before its counterparty has received the funds contracted for in another, possibly resulting in full loss of the principal amount. Such events usually send shock waves through bank dealing rooms worldwide.

Since foreign exchange lines and interbank deposits are unsecured, periodic financial analysis of banks that are counterparties in money and foreign exchange dealing activities is critical—that is, analysis of their capital structure, size, credit ratings, managerial competence, and other factors (see Chapter 5). Based on this analysis, a bank will normally set *dealing limits* for redeposits, foreign exchange lines, swaps, and other transactions.

We have already mentioned that placements with banks not among the premier institutions may involve a practice known as tiering, which usually tends to be a no-win situation. For example, less highly regarded banks may be forced to pay a premium over LIBOR in times of Euromarket stress in order to meet liquidity needs. Yet the very fact that they are paying such premiums could be interpreted to indicate their possible lack of creditworthiness, thus leading to possible further funding difficulties or intensified tiering down the road. For this reason, banks have often exhibited great aversion to paying premiums on interbank deposits, preferring instead to limit their own growth to that permitted by funding possibilities on full market terms.

Certainly the most significant shock affecting international treasury activities since the origin of the the Euromarkets occurred in 1974. Growth of the market and the number of participants had been enormous. Mismatching of maturities in some banks went beyond reasonably prudent standards. Aggressive lending policies eroded margins. Financial analysis and personal acquaintances among counterparties in interbank placements was sometimes perfunctory or even nonexistent. Exchange rate volatility and the promise of trading profits led to the temptation to relax dealing limits; these limits were often poorly enforced and sometimes were absent altogether. It was a go-go environment that left the system ripe for a crisis and that magnified the effect of that crisis when it did occur.

Bankhaus I.D. Herstatt failed in June 1974, with a foreign exchange exposure of some $200 million that it was unable to cover. The resultant losses forced the German authorities to close the bank during the day. Its forward foreign exchange contracts were canceled, and banks had to scramble for cover in the market. To make matters worse, settlements due on that day for which banks had delivered Deutschemarks in the morning expecting dollar cover in New York later in the day were never made—the bank had been closed in Germany before the New York market opened. In the eventual settlement that was negotiated, creditors had to swallow 20 percent of their exposures as outright losses. Intraday risk on spot foreign exchange transactions had become a reality.

At about the same time, the Franklin National Bank, which was one of the top-20 banks in the United States at the time, had $3.8 billion in foreign exchange contracts outstanding at the end of 1973. Errors in forecasting exchange rates, especially the French franc, led to the discovery in May 1974 of $40 million in foreign exchange losses. In early October 1974 the U.S. Comptroller of the Currency declared the bank insolvent, and its assets were acquired by the European-American Bank and Trust Company. Foreign exchange speculation by inexperienced and imprudent management had caused the then largest banking collapse in U.S. history.

The result was a Euromarket crisis of major proportions. Rumors of doom for other market participants—particularly those without a major dollar funding base and some of the smaller and newer banks—spread like wildfire. Many were unable to roll over their liabilities. Some had to liquidate large amounts of assets or had to look to their parent banks or shareholders for support by transferring illiquid assets to them.

Funding risks in the Euromarket became much more apparent as a result of the 1974 crisis. The consequences included: much greater caution, financial analysis, and personal knowledge in interbank placements; the beginnings of central bank moves to make parent banks responsible for their affiliates' liabilities; greater control over foreign exchange exposure; and recognition of certain risks (e.g., intraday risk) previously considered unimportant.

Liquidity

In their dealing activities, international banks will periodically be "long" or "short" funds. Neither should present major problems if money markets are working properly. Long positions can be handled by placements or redeposits in the interbank markets, while short positions can be taken care of by buying funds in the market—both can be accomplished at prevailing interest rates. Problems arise, however, when serious market disruptions occur. Imposition of financial controls by governments, major interest rate or exchange rate movements or expectations, or loss of confidence due to certain events (e.g., bank failures) may make it difficult for banks to secure funds. A bank may have to pay a premium or look to affiliated banks, or even its home or government, for support.

For example, Japanese bankers facing liquidity problems in the 1974 Euromarket crisis were bailed out in part by large Saudi Arabian deposits arranged by the Japanese Ministry of Finance, an embarrassment that led to severe restrictions and tightened supervision of their Euromarket activities. The possibility of tiering or one-way markets and their consequences for trading activities is always present.

Transfer Problems

As discussed in detail in Chapter 19, entities to which a bank is exposed in cross-border dealings usually carry with them exposure to "country risk" as well. A foreign bank may be unable to repay interbank placements if its government imposes exchange controls or shuts down all foreign exchange dealings in a time of national balances-of-payments emergency. The counterpart bank may be fully able to repay but cannot do so because of transfer problems. Even when its own government guarantees repayment, there may be difficulties.

In 1977, for example, Turkey encouraged interbank placements with local banks at extremely favorable interest rates, with a full government guarantee of the convertible lira deposits involved—a golden opportunity for dealers. Of course, the scheme represented a desperation move to attract short-term funding for a deteriorating balance-of-payments situation, and the government convertibility guarantee ultimately proved worthless. What started out as attractive short-term interbank placements ended up as long-term loans to Turkey. Clearly, banks searching for dealing profits had been "sucked in" to a situation they would probably have stayed clear of had the issue been one of long-term lending.

Banks can also run afoul of existing national exchange control regulations, either inadvertently or deliberately, which may involve commercial liability, fines, and loss of operating privileges. Since the existence of exchange controls usually involves significant profit opportunities if the regulations can be evaded, the temptations and the penalties assume greater importance in some cases than they otherwise might.

A good example of this problem involved Citibank's dealings in the Philippines during the final days of the Marcos regime in 1985. The bank was dealing Eurodeposits out of an international banking facility in Manila, paying slightly higher rates than were being dealt for comparable deposits out of Hong Kong or London. Given the deteriorating Philippine financial situation, the central bank ordered banks to suspend all payments to foreign creditors until further notice. The freeze included Citibank's Eurodeposits. Counterparty banks demanded payment by Citibank elsewhere. Citibank refused, arguing that depositors took Philippine risk and got paid for it, and that it could not legally honor the claims until permitted to do so by local authorities. Although accounts were eventually settled, a lawsuit was filed against Citibank by Wells Fargo on behalf of banks whose depositors were frozen. Wells Fargo won the lawsuit. However, the presence of country risk in interbank dealing was emphasized once again.

Limits

The principal technique of controlling risk in international bank dealing is the use of *limits*, based on appropriate economic, financial, managerial, size, and profitability criteria. Within the trading function itself, however, there are a variety of limits that must be applied in order to ensure conformity with risk constraints and sound banking practice.

Limits on the amount of deposit dealing are established in the form of *undisclosed* (to the counterparty), *uncommitted* (by the lender) *internal guidance lines* that determine one bank's policy on size and maturity of placements with another. Since a bank may have lines with hundreds of others, the analysis and decisions setting these limits represent a formidable overall task. Their size is generally established as a percentage of borrower net worth, with some absolute dollar and maturity limits applied in some cases. Personal relationships, dealing reciprocity, credit analysis, relationships, and market standing are other factors that influence deposit-dealing relationships.

Maintenance of confidence in a bank's soundness is critical to successful treasury operations. For this reason, for example, new Euromarket entrants must start slowly, developing close personal links with other market participants, using its parent's relationships fully, and projecting an image of financial responsibility. Gradually, foreign exchange lines and placements will be developed, with careful attention to diversification both among other banks and between banks and other sources of deposits. Attention must also be paid to the external *perception* of its maturity mix of assets and liabilities, particularly the adequacy of liquid assets and backup lines, and the possibility of securing long-term floating-rate liabilities.

Trading limits are allocated to individual traders and set the level to which they can commit the bank in interbank placements and foreign exchange transactions. Besides the traders themselves, approval limits will apply to others in the trading function. Unauthorized trading is a major source of risk encountered by banks in treasury management.

Open-position limits set maximum short or long positions that a bank is willing to hold at the end of the trading day. A *daylight limit* may be used, in addition, to set the maximum open position that may be held at any one time during the trading day, and *override limits* may be used to provide a certain degree of discretion for trading-room managers if market conditions seem to warrant going beyond established open-position limits. *Gap limits* constrain open positions for different maturities, and generally are smaller for successively longer forward exchange contracts and for currencies with a relatively limited market. Gap limits may also apply to interbank placements — for example, to prevent excessive buying of funds in the short end to finance excessive selling in the long end, thereby elevating the bank's exposure to interest rate risk.

Settlement limits are, in effect, sublimits on the amount of foreign exchange business or interbank placements that can be done with a particular counterparty, as established in the corresponding *dealing limits* imposed on it by the bank. It may not be wise, for example, to have more than 20 percent of a bank's total interbank placements due from Bank X or to have more than 10 percent of foreign exchange dealings with Bank Y coming due on a particular settlement day — both to limit exposure in the event of bank failure and to constrain the cost of possible operations errors or delays in funds transfer. At the same time, *maturity limits*, expressed as periods of time, may also be used to define how far into the future a bank is willing to go in trading with a given counterparty in view of the possibility that its financial condition may change in the meantime.

It is conceivable that the sheer volume of trading that a bank undertakes in a given period outstrips its own operations capabilities, leading to increased costs and more frequent errors. It is also possible that a high volume of trading causes a bank to run into the trading limits that its principal counterparties have set for it, possibly resulting in increased costs of funds. Traders may be moved to overtrade in order to gain prestige in the market, or there may be other reasons for overtrading. To guard against such problems, an *overtrading limit* may be set to restrict the total number of trades per day or to "cap" the total value of the bank's forward exchange contracts outstanding. Such a limit can also serve as a useful trigger for management's reexamination of the overall size of its trading operation.

Various other trading limits are the product of specific institutional factors. They may be aimed at defining conditions under which certain trades may be undertaken in the longer maturities, the conditions under which currencies may be traded, how much can be left overnight in nostro accounts with correspondents, how options are to be treated, and how long a position (if any) may be taken against the local currency. The latter, which are called *parking limits*, are generally in response to policies of local monetary authorities.

In order to constrain the risks to which a bank is exposed in its dealing activities—in time, by counterparty, through market changes, and by currency—dealers and their managers are guided by a network of limits that may not be exceeded without explicit authorization by management. Changes in any of the underlying variables and market conditions, bank strategy and size, audit reports, expectations of future developments, even the dealing room cast of characters may call for a review of the relevant limits, which, in fact, constitute a set of dynamic constraints within which the bank strives to optimize the contribution of the dealing function to overall profitability.

Standby Facilities

It is conceivable that a bank may have difficulty purchasing funds in particular currencies to support assets of long maturities or to obtain foreign exchange cover. For this reason, many banks have negotiated *standby lines* with other banks that have a strong base in these currencies. These represent unconditional, backup borrowing facilities that can be called upon in the event that the bank runs into trouble purchasing funds in the respective currencies on the open market.

In its home money market, a bank may go to its central bank for this purpose, which acts as a lender of last resort by providing facilities for emergency liquidity. The Federal Reserve's discount window performs this function in the United States, the Bundesbank's Lombard-kredit does so in Germany, and so on. The Euromarkets, however, have no explicit lender of last resort, and so standby lines are used in part to perform this function. In addition, an overseas branch of a major bank may also be able to look to its parent for support should the need arise.

SUMMARY

Today's banking environment consists of relatively free international capital flows, essentially unregulated Euromarkets, and floating exchange rates. The treasury operations in this environment together with unstable interest rates represent in large measure an integrated whole. Interest rates are linked between national financial markets and are linked between the national markets and the Euromarkets. In turn, exchange rates are linked to interest rates. Both are volatile, with significant opportunities for gains and losses in trading and in asset and liability management. For this reason, the treasury operations of most international banks have been increasingly integrated (both geographically and between foreign exchange and money market activities), maximizing the flow of information and access to arbitrage and funding opportunities.

The point is to make the most effective use of the bank's balance sheet. This requires a sophisticated management information system and some sort of centralized asset and liability management group within an international bank charged with deciding on funding strategy, asset planning, maturity mix, arbitrage policy, foreign exchange exposure policy, liquidity issues, and related questions. All of these considerations are predicated on building a consensus as to where interest rates and exchange rates are going and the various sources of risk in international financial markets.

SELECTED REFERENCES

Citicorp. *Managing the Liability Side of the Balance Sheet*. New York: Citicorp, 1979.

Davis, Steven I. "Running a Mismatched Book." *Euromoney*, June 1973.

Davis, Steven I. *The Euro-Bank*, 2nd ed. London: Macmillan, 1980, Chapter 4.

Davis, Steven I. *The Management Function in International Banking*. London: Macmillan, 1979, Chapter 7.

Guttentag, Jack, and Herring, Richard. "Financial Disorder and International Banking." Mimeographed. Philadelphia, PA: University of Pennsylvania, 1981.

Hudson, Nigel R. L. *Money and Exchange Dealing in International Banking*. London: Macmillan, 1979.

Silber, William L. *Commercial Bank Liability Management*. Washington, DC: Association of Reserve City Bankers, 1977.

Wilson, Neil. "Curiouser and curiouser . . . ." *The Banker*. April 1989.

Investment Banking Services

14

Eurobonds and Other International Debt Issues

International financial markets are nothing new. Residents of one country have invested their money in securities issued by residents of another country for a long time—usually when there were shortages of good investment opportunities in their own country and when, for one reason or another, money was piling up. There were great waves of foreign investment in the nineteenth century (a lot of which flowed into the United States) and in the 1920s (when even Latin American governments issued large volumes of bonds). But the greatest wave of all began in 1963 when the Eurobond market first came to life.[1]

Prior to 1963, the method used to raise long-term capital from international sources was to float a bond issue in some other country, denominated in the currency of that country and issued in accordance with the standard procedures of the bond market there, usually at a premium interest rate reflecting the exotic nature of the borrower and/or the possibilities of collection difficulties. Such issues are and have long been called "foreign bonds." Today when foreigners issue dollar-denominated bonds registered with the U.S. Securities and Exchange Commission (SEC), they are called "Yankee bonds"; those registered with the Japanese Ministry of Finance and denominated in yen are "Samurai bonds"; those involving sterling issues in the United Kingdom are called "Bulldog bonds"; and so on. Despite these distinctions, however, they are all foreign bonds.

The total annual volume of foreign bonds averaged $2.6 billion from 1964 to 1974. After the removal of U.S. capital market controls in 1974, volume jumped sharply, averaging about $16 billion annually for the rest of the 1970s. In the 1980s, foreign bonds, which are subject to all market regulations of the host country, accounted for an average of $27.6 billion of new issues each year.

The Eurobond market, by contrast, became the preferred international market for most issuers after 1980. Though it operated mainly in U.S. dollars, it also produced issues denominated in: Deutsche marks; Dutch guilders; British sterling; Japanese yen; Australian, New Zealand, and Canadian dollars; and other currencies from time to time. (Swiss franc issues were not permitted, however, nor generally were those in French francs or Italian lira.)

Between 1964 and 1974 the total annual volume of Eurobond new issues averaged about $2.3 billion, and from 1974 through 1979 it averaged $11 billion. However, from 1980 to 1986 the average annual new-issue volume soared to $79.2 billion, with almost $190 billion being issued in 1986 alone—almost five times the volume of new issues of foreign bonds in that year. In 1987, this pattern of growth was broken. Total Eurobond volume declined by 26 percent, to $140 billion, largely because of a shift in investor preference to nondollar securities, which kept U.S. issuers at home. A rebound began in early 1988 as the dollar firmed and investors were attracted to dollar-denominated securities again.

Eurobond volume is impressive even in comparison to the U.S. corporate bond market (which consists of everything in the bond market except U.S. government and agency securities and municipal bonds). Figure 14–1 compares the Eurobond and foreign bond

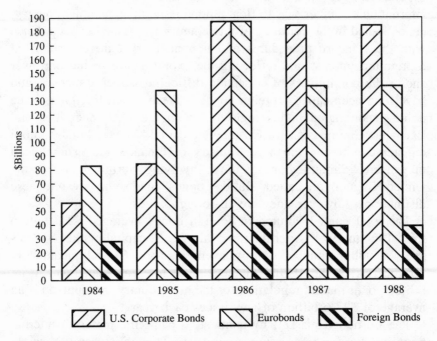

Figure 14–1. Bond New-Issue Markets. (*Source*: Federal Reserve Bulletin, Morgan Guaranty Trust Co.)

markets with the U.S. corporate bond markets for the period from 1983 to 1988.

This chapter begins with a brief history of the international bond market and describes how it evolved into its present form. It identifies and contrasts the principal investors in the market and shows how certain unique structural features of the market have developed in order to meet the requirements of the different types of investors. The chapter also explores who the issuers have been and the different types of offerings that an issuer can make. It explains the role played by interest rate and currency swaps in the Eurobond market, new-issue procedures, the interdealer "grey market" for Eurobonds, and underwriter's stabilization practices. It also discusses prospects for the emerging intra-European capital market in the 1990s and explores evolving competitive practices and the profitability of the Eurobond for its participants.

EVOLUTION OF THE MARKET

Eurobonds originally were fixed-rate, unsecured promissory notes that were denominated in U.S. dollars and issued by a corporation or government entity. Not being registered with the SEC, these bonds could not be sold in the United States. Instead, they were sold to non-U.S. residents who wished to invest in U.S. dollar-denominated securities. Issuers were paid the proceeds of the bonds in the form of a dollar deposit in a European bank or a European branch of a U.S. bank (Eurodollar accounts).

The Euromarket began with the build-up of Eurodollars resulting from a continuing run of U.S. balance-of-payments deficits in the early 1960s. These were the days of the fixed exchange rate system in which the noncommunist world's currencies were linked to the U.S. dollar and the dollar was pegged to gold. Countries often defended their exchange rates by the imposition of foreign exchange and/or capital controls. In 1963, in an attempt to stem the outflow of dollars, the United States imposed an interest equalization tax, intended to deter foreign governments and corporations from borrowing in the U.S. capital markets. Later, controls imposed by the Commerce Department's Office of Foreign Direct Investment required U.S. companies investing abroad to raise the money outside of the United States. So a supply of borrowers—Europeans who could no longer borrow in the United States and domestic companies who now had to borrow outside the United States—met with a supply of funds. These came in the form of Eurodollars that were owned by international investors whose financial affairs were managed by banks in Switzerland, Luxembourg, Belgium, France, and, to some extent, in the United Kingdom.

Initial bond issues were small but well received. The first Eurobond is generally thought to be a $15 million issue for Autostrade, the Italian toll road authority, guaranteed by an Italian government agency. The issue was managed by S. G. Warburg and comanaged by banks in Belgium, Germany, the Netherlands, and Luxembourg. It was underwritten according to the U.S. underwriting method, in which the issue is announced, syndicated, and marketed before it is priced and underwritten, and sold throughout Europe. The Autostrade issue became the prototype for many other issues by various European entities, mainly government-related credits. U.S. investment banks with sales offices throughout Europe became active participants in the market, having sharpened their selling skills by distributing foreign bonds issued in the United States by European governments and agencies to investors elsewhere in Europe.[2]

U.S. corporate bonds were held in high esteem by investors, and when they and their bankers volunteered responsible standards of disclosure and investor protection these were accepted without question. Totally outside the legal jurisdiction of any single country, the market began to function as a self-regulated structure involving participants from a dozen or more countries. Interest rates to investors were higher than in the United States, and the costs to issuers were a great deal higher—the market was not very efficient in the beginning, and participants had to distribute $25 to $50 million worth of bond issues in units of 100 bonds or less.

The U.S. Commerce Department regulations through the Office of Foreign Direct Investment that forced U.S. companies to finance their overseas investments abroad, despite the fact that such issues at that time involved higher costs, resulted in substantial use of the market by U.S. companies. From 1968 to 1973, thanks largely to these regulations, U.S. companies floated 271 issues raising approximately $7 billion and accounting for about one-third of the entire Eurobond market over that period. European issuers, also not allowed to finance in the lower-cost markets in the United States, were forced to raise their growing requirements for capital in the Euromarkets. This somewhat artificially induced volume of new issues helped the market get off to a good start.

By 1971 the world financial system installed at the 1944 Bretton Woods Conference was no longer able to cope with the pressure brought on the dollar by the U.S. balance-of-payments deficits, and the fixed exchange rate system broke down. The United States closed the gold window and floated the dollar. This meant that market-driven movements in exchange rates would, over time, adjust balance-of-payments disequilibria, and there was no further need for such capital controls as the interest equalization tax and regulations of the Office of Foreign Direct Investment, both of which were abolished in 1974. But the pool of Eurodollars did not dissipate. With the U.S. gold window closed, central banks could not draw off excess dollars for conversion into gold. Moreover, in the aftermath of the first oil shock of October 1973, the trade surpluses of the OPEC countries became a primary source of Eurodollar balances. The Eurobond market then began in earnest, as liquidity built up and trading in Eurodollars and other instruments flourished. These conditions, began to attract European and multinational institutional (as opposed to individual) investors to the market in a significant way.

These new investors included European pension and insurance funds of U.S. and other companies, bank trust departments, investment companies, financial institutions (e.g., the World Bank and central banks of various countries), and, increasingly after 1973, Middle East funds managed by Western financial institutions. After the election of Margaret Thatcher in 1979 and the subsequent removal of British foreign exchange controls, U.K. investors also began to enter the market, although modestly at first.

THE EUROBOND BOOM, 1981–1985

By 1980 institutional participation in the market was at such a high level that an infrastructure began to develop to support it. Purveyors of such services as *bond brokerage* (arranging for the sale and purchase of bonds between dealers), *when issued trading*, or *grey market trading*, (i.e., buying and selling of primary securities prior to the actual offer date), and bond market research began to arrive in London like waves of an assault force. More capital was committed, and more traders and salespeople were hired; it became important to many banks to be "seen" in the right issues. Some of this was nonsense, but it expanded the market nevertheless. After Ronald Reagan's election and Paul Volcker's reappointment, the dollar turned from a scorned and underappreciated currency to a much-admired and overvalued one, which also led the Eurobond market to soar. The dollar became one of the world's strongest currencies; however, unlike strong currencies in the past, it yielded very high rates of interest, so the demand for Eurobonds rose to a point where European investors would pay more for a U.S. corporate obligation than American investors would.

This enthusiasm for Eurobonds was spurred by competition and by the expectation that total investment profits would include attractive foreign exchange gains, but it was also greatly influenced by the fact that investors could buy Eurobonds of top-grade U.S. companies free of withholding taxes on interest (because the bonds were issued by offshore subsidiaries guaranteed by their parents), but they couldn't buy U.S. Treasury securities on the same basis. So, high-grade corporate bonds became the substitutes for U.S. government securities in the eyes of investors (as represented by the large continental banks). In the end, a kind of competitive bidding occurred between investors to get the top names; and the retail investors, as might be expected, won out—that is, they bid the highest prices, or the lowest interest yields, for the bonds. Thus, from 1980 to 1985 it was quite common for U.S. companies rated AA or better to be able to borrow 5- to 10-year money more cheaply in Europe than in the United States, and in some cases, more cheaply than the U.S. Treasury could. This condition resulted in a surge of Euroissues. In 1982, for example, several U.S. investment banks found that they had sold more corporate bonds at new issue in London than they had in New York—a fact many firms found hard to believe (and few would duplicate in the years to follow).

This feeding frenzy, however, occurred at a time when U.S. nominal interest rates were declining and the dollar was rising. Treasury securities were certainly not unavailable in the United States, as the growing fiscal deficit brought the government to market more and more often, if not crowding U.S. companies out then perhaps arguably nudging them toward Europe. It was not important whether an issuer was known as a multinational corporation—many companies that were entirely domestic, including some U.S. public utilities and even savings and loan associations, came in. And the investors began to include insurance companies from Birmingham, bond funds from Lyon, pension fund managers in Melbourne, and agricultural cooperatives in Osaka. Some of these investors had only recently been allowed to invest overseas by their home governments, which were following patterns elsewhere and dismantling overseas investment regulations.

The active participation in the Eurobond market of U.S. and foreign corporations caused securities industry regulators at the SEC to consider ways to alter the regulatory stance in the United States so as to increase the competitive appeal of U.S. capital markets. Among other considerations, the SEC noticed that many U.S. issuers preferred the Euromarket because no delay was involved in approaching the market. In the United States several weeks would elapse while a registration statement was reviewed by the staff of the SEC. In highly volatile markets instant market access was very important—it was available in Europe but not in the U.S. market. The SEC dealt with this situation by announcing its proposed Rule 415 providing for "'shelf registrations," under which a registration statement could be filed and reviewed in advance of a company's needs, thus permitting the company to come to market without further delay afterward. Rule 415 was operated on a trial basis initially and formally adopted in 1984. With its adoption, U.S. capital market activities were materially changed. Longstanding client relationships could be displaced by a better idea from a different underwriter; and the Euromarket "bought deal," in which lead underwriters bought issues directly from clients without having a syndicate in place, was soon imported into the United States.

Despite the rise in the institutional sector of the market, the Eurobond market still retained a very significant participation by retail investors. Although no precise data exist as to the extent of this participation, certain Swiss banks have estimated that 40 to 60 percent of all Eurobonds ultimately find their way into Swiss-managed accounts of individuals, and most are held there until maturity. By contrast, less than 5 percent of U.S. corporate bonds are ever bought by individuals. Naturally, some Eurobond issues appeal more to individuals than to institutions, but most issues are pitched to attract investment by both. Institutions, however, do trade actively in the secondary market. They are also more aware of markets around the world. Institutions are willing to invest in domestic U.S. securities despite withholding taxes (which were removed in 1984) and the nonavailability of bearer certificates, and they are much sharper buyers than individuals. Individual investors are also less sophisticated than institutions in managing foreign exchange risk—for example, they tend to avoid dollar issues, at times when the dollar is weakening and they can switch into issues denominated in Swiss francs or Deutsche marks.

Although Eurodollar bond issues have been floated throughout the past 25 years during times of both a strong and a weak dollar, the bulk of market activity has remained in dollars even during times when the currency has been weak. The foreign exchange situation has always had a significant effect on the Eurobond market; of course, this is not the case in the U.S. domestic bond market. Figure 14–2 illustrates how

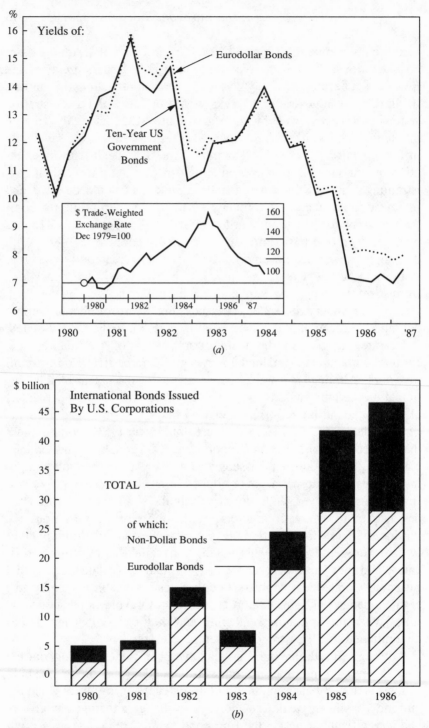

Figure 14–2. When Eurobonds Are Cheaper, Americans Borrow. (*Source*: *The Economist*, May 16, 1987. ©1987 The Economist Newspaper Ltd. All rights reserved.)

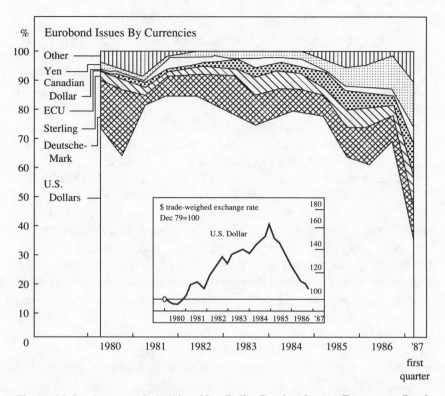

Figure 14–3. Investors Switch into Non-Dollar Bonds. (*Source*: Euromoney Bondware: Bank of England; from *The Economist*, May 16, 1987 ©The Economist Newspaper Ltd. All rights reserved.)

the volume and cost of funds of dollar issues by U.S. corporations have varied with changing exchange rates. Figure 14–3 shows how the market for nondollar issues increases during periods of a weak dollar—as best demonstrated in 1987, when only 40 percent of all new Eurobond issues were dollar denominated.

THE WORLD'S ONLY UNREGULATED CAPITAL MARKET

The Eurobond market is virtually unregulated. However, it is subject to self-imposed standards of practice. Eurobonds are typically listed on the London Stock Exchange or Luxembourg Stock Exchange in order to attract investors, and each stock exchange has its own specific disclosure requirements. The issues themselves are typically subject to U.K. law, and the Association of International Bond Dealers (AIBD) set minimum trading standards.

These standards differ from legal requirements. Whereas individual firms may be regulated by their national authorities, there are no legal requirements on the issuer or on bankers to provide for investor protection, orderly markets, or courts of law in which to deal with disputes or abuses. There have been no financial regulations that apply to the market, such as queuing, capital requirements, or margin rules. However, the Financial Services Act, passed by the British Parliament in 1987, provides for certain capital and other requirements for all Eurobond market participants using London as a base.

The market has been self-regulated, and as such it has performed remarkably well. The emphasis has always been on doing what works in such a manner that permits doing it again.

Different things work for different participants, however, and this has given many banks, investment banks, and brokers the chance to operate in the market with certain competitive advantages. Swiss and other continental banks have the advantage of being able to "encourage" their customers to purchase Eurobonds which they bring to the market, and for which they can charge full fees although they will not expect to see the bonds trade at par in the immediate aftermarket. U.S., Japanese, and British investment and merchant banks have the advantage of influential relations with issuers and with institutional investors, who may only buy new issues at prices reflecting discounts from the market but who will certainly be the source of follow on trading business afterward. Other participants appear from time to time— for example, merchant banks owned by U.S. commercial banks have been key participants in floating rate markets and in swaps. Japanese firms have benefited not only by a steady flow of Japanese issuers in the market but also by the huge appetite for Eurobonds on the part of financial institutions in Japan.

A MAJOR SOURCE OF INNOVATION

The absence of regulation, the lack of barriers to competition, and the variety of players have made the Eurobond market a hothouse for innovation. Many of the best ideas to influence the U.S. bond markets had their origin in the Eurobond market. The Section 415 underwriting rules introduced by the SEC in 1984, which provide virtually immediate access by companies to the U.S. bond market, is one such example. The bought deal, the zero coupon bond, the floating-rate note, currency option bonds, and convertible put bonds are just some of the successful innovations in Europe that have been copied in New York. Of course, not all of these new ideas were universally applicable; however, they greatly extended the range of financing and investing alternatives, which attracted more participants to the U.S. bond markets on the issuing and the investing sides.

The greater penetration by financial institutions of the international markets has led many of them to adopt aggressive trading strategies that involve U.S. treasuries and the financial futures markets and to substantially increase their investment in U.S. and other equity as well as equity-related securities. London is the largest market for American securities outside the United States; however, Tokyo has recently appeared as a strong challenger to London, although Tokyo still has a way to go.

RETAIL AND INSTITUTIONAL INVESTORS

The Eurobond market today is broad and complex, with various different and changing components that tend to be defined by investor types or their location. A *retail investor* is a private individual who usually entrusts his or her money to a bank, which invests it according to some general instructions. The typical retail investor in Europe is described by the market as a "Belgian dentist," although in recent years retail investors have grown to include wealthy individuals from all over the world whose money is invested for them anonymously by European banks. Swiss banks are the best known and largest institutions managing retail investment accounts, but they have their equivalents in all the other European countries. They charge relatively high fees for their services and do not have an outstanding reputation for investment performance, since their true function is to preserve capital and confidentiality. Swiss banks alone have several hundred billion dollars of customer funds in their custody. A very high percentage of these funds is invested outside Switzerland. Portfolio managers have a strong preference for "household" issuer names because their cautious and conservative customers insist on dealing only with well-known companies or governments. However, the portfolio managers do have more than a little discretion in handling their customers' accounts, and so they also participate in the occasional special or less well-known situation—especially if the issue is being managed by the bank.

In recent years wealthy Japanese individuals have also become bond market participants, particularly in zero coupon issues where— under the Japanese tax code—they do not have to pay taxes on the imputed interest. Japanese demand for zero coupon Eurobonds became so strong that the Japanese Ministry of Finance imposed a regulation restricting the percentage of any issue that could be sold into Japan. Japanese individuals invest in Eurobonds mainly through Japanese securities firms. The role of these firms in the Euromarket has expanded enormously, reflecting the strong demand for Eurobonds of all types in Japan.

The institutional sector of the Eurobond market is not too different from its counterpart in the United States. London has long been a center for professional money managers (e.g., those who manage corporate funds, pension funds, and private wealth). Other European financial institutions invest their own funds, and they all have a trading and performance orientation that is similar to practices in the United States (though not quite as intensive). Recently, large Japanese insurance companies, trust banks, and other institutions have begun to participate in the market. Because of their size, the funds available for investment, and their practice of acting more or less in the same way at the same time, Japanese institutions had a very large impact on the market from 1985 to 1989. Japanese investors are very sensitive to quality, to the "prestige" of issues, and to their competitive performance.

On the whole, both institutional and individual investors have a heavy bias in favor of the better-quality names. There have been times when a Baa-rated issue has done well, but this occurs much less frequently than in the United States. Still, there are some who predict that with the right sales effort, a Euro junk bond market might emerge. So far it has not done so.

The growing international acquisition of U.S. Treasury securities has largely been confined to institutional investors. Before the withholding tax was removed in 1984, these investors either would reclaim the tax or would trade out of their position before having to pay it. Institutions are willing to provide the technical declarations that the treasury requires to avoid the U.S. "backup" withholding tax, which was exposed when the foreign withholding tax was removed, and so their participation continues to grow. However, for the most part, European retail investors continue to avoid purchasing treasuries because their banks do not as yet wish to make the required disclosure to the U.S. Treasury (that the holder is not a U.S. citizen) to be exempt from the backup withholding tax. The banks, mainly the Swiss banks, do not want to do this because they feel it opens them up to the possibility of being investigated by the Internal Revenue Service in the future, which could create conflicts with Swiss bank secrecy laws.

TWO-TIERED PRICING

The distinction between Eurobond investors who are buyers of treasuries and those who are not is important because it helps to explain a two-tiered pricing structure in the Eurobond market for U.S. companies. With the Swiss sector avoiding treasuries, it does not use the treasury market as a benchmark for pricing new issues. Top-quality sovereign or industrial paper becomes the benchmark for them; therefore, they may be prepared to buy issues by well-known companies at a higher price—or lower yield—than an institutional investor.

The Swiss and other continental banks handling retail investors also require a comparatively large amount of underwriting compensation to distribute Eurobonds to their clients. Whereas a seven-year bond issue could easily be underwritten in the United States (where 95% of bond investors are institutions) at a gross underwriting commission of 0.65%, a Swiss underwriter will require a commission of 1.875%. As the Swiss will often account for a substantial amount, if not the majority, of the distribution of a Eurobond issue, their requirements are carefully attended to. The Swiss explain that they incur substantial expense in distributing a large volume of Eurobonds to thousands of individual accounts through hundreds of portfolio managers and that they only charge their customers the stated commission on the transaction—therefore, the stated commission must be ample.

If one sector of the market is more aggressive than others it can create difficulties in pricing new issues, especially when all sectors are needed to make the issue a success. The market dealt with this problem until 1989 by the longstanding practice of not requiring underwriters to sell issues at a fixed price during the underwriting period, as is the practice in the United States. The Swiss bank acting as an underwriter will charge a customer the full selling commission provided, but a U.S. firm probably will have to offer an institutional investor a rebate of the larger part of the selling commission as an inducement to take the bonds. So on most new issues, in which both institutional and retail investors are involved, there is one set of pricing arrangements for the retail customer and another for the institutional customer. Needless to say, the Swiss like this system and are not eager to change it because they can get their customers to accept a lower yield than might actually be available in the market, and the banks can pocket the full selling concession (which is usually around 1% to 1.25% of the principal amount). Table 14–1 illustrates how two-tiered pricing is accomplished.

Table 14–1.   Two-Tiered Pricing in the Eurobond Market

	Bond Offered to Customer by Swiss Bank	Bond Offered to Institutional Investor
Coupon	9.25%	9.25%
Gross spread	1.875%	1.875%
Cost of funds to issuer	9.53%	9.53%
Price bought by investor	100.00%	98.375%
Yield to investor	9.25%	9.48%
Spread retained by banker	1.875%	0.25%

In this example an issuer has agreed to sell some new Eurobonds to a group of underwriters at terms that provide a net cost of funds to the issuer of 9.53%. The Swiss bank applies its usual underwriting spread of 1.875% to this rate to obtain the bond's coupon—in this case, 9.25%. The bank then places the bond with its clients at 100%, the 1.875% spread being retained by the bank to assist in defraying the expenses of its portfolio managers and as profit. By contrast, 9.25% bonds offered to institutional investors at par will be rejected by the buyers because the yield on the investment is below market rates. The institutional investor is fully acquainted with market rates, although the clients of the Swiss Bank may not be. The institutional investor says it will only purchase the 9.25% bonds being offered at a price of 98.375% at which they will yield 9.49%, a level considered to be on the market. As the underwriter bought these bonds for 98.125%, a profit of only 0.25% was realized.

EUROBOND ISSUERS

Over the years Eurobond issuers have included a wide variety of borrowers. Corporations and banks from the United States, Canada, Europe, Japan, and Australia that relied on the market for floating-rate and medium-term fixed-rate funding were the principal users of the Eurobond market during its most active period from 1980 to 1986. European governments—particularly Scandinavian and French government agencies, which did not have well-developed capital markets in their own countries—were also very active users of the market. Canadian provinces too often found better terms for dollar financing in Europe than in the United States, and they became major users of the market.

In the corporate sector, the market has been dominated by U.S. and Japanese issuers, although major corporations from other countries have also found ready access to the market. Developing countries have not been well accepted as issuers. Figure 14–4 shows the composition of Eurobond issuers from 1980 to 1986.

European Issuers

European issuers have been the most active issuers in the Eurobond market since 1980. Although the capacity of domestic capital markets in Europe has been increasing, these markets are mainly taken up with government, mortgage, and bank securities. From 1980 to 1986, 43 percent of all Eurobond issues were offered by European issuers, most often by banks and government entities. Such financings have often been denominated in European currency units (ECUs) or otherwise swapped into home country currencies.

Non-U.S. issuers have been attracted to the market because of its easy access and simple documentation, but also because they often felt the Euromarket valued the issuer more highly than the U.S. market did and that lower rates would be available. Sometimes this was true, especially for five- to seven-year issues, but often it was not, especially for longer maturities. Prior to 1984 one of the largest difficulties in a U.S. issue was having to wait a month or so for SEC authorization to sell an issue in the United States. Considerable expensive disclosure of information was also required. Most issuers preferred to avoid these obstacles and instead used the Eurobond market. Access to the U.S. market has been made much easier by SEC rule 144a, which went into effect in early 1990. It permits foreign securities to be sold to institutional investors in the United States without the securities having to be registered with the SEC.

U.S. Issuers

From 1981 to 1985 the net effect of the two-tiered pricing system, the strong preference for dollar investments at the time, and the tailoring of maturities and other features to suit the international

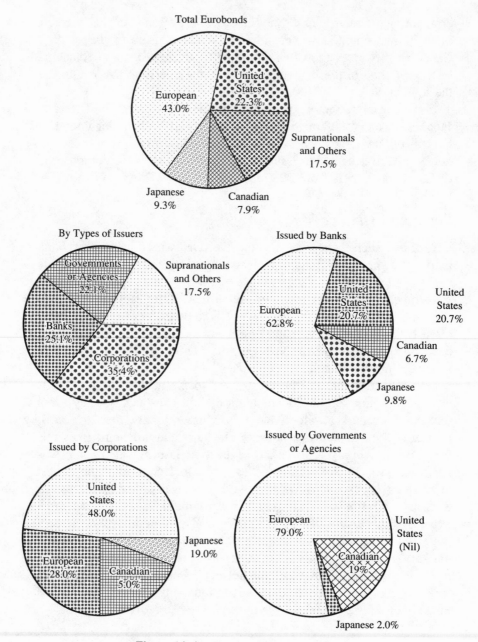

Figure 14–4.   Eurobond Issuers, 1980–86.

investor resulted in a somewhat lower level of interest rates being available in the Eurobond market for prime U.S. issuers than the same issuer would experience in the U.S. domestic market. For the most part, the difference was about .10% to .20% during 1985. Before the removal of the U.S. withholding tax in 1984, the difference was somewhat greater. Such differences naturally increased the number of new issues of Eurobonds by U.S. companies during this period.

Following the substantial weakening of the dollar beginning in 1985, the system has gone into reverse, with the retail sector appearing to require a higher interest rate than the institutional sector. This has led generally to a pricing disadvantage for most top-grade U.S. issuers, as compared to the cost of financing available domestically. Also, institutional investors participate in arbitrage transactions, often through swaps, which tend to close the gaps that periodically open between the two markets.

Nevertheless, despite the fact that the comparative advantage of one market or the other may change over time, U.S. companies have become very acclimated to the Eurobond market. In 1983 to 1985 many U.S. companies that are large issuers of debt used the Eurobond market more often than the U.S. domestic market; in the ensuing period, many of these companies continued to utilize the Euromarkets for nondollar bond issues or dollar issues with equity or other special features, but they returned onshore for most of their U.S. dollar bond issues.

Japanese Issuers

Japanese companies, by comparison, face a highly regulated and expensive corporate bond market in Tokyo and, as a result, have made heavy use of the Euromarket as compared to their domestic alternative. From 1981 to 1989 Japanese corporations floated more than 1000 issues of straight and convertible bonds, and bonds with equity purchase warrants, in the Eurobond market totaling more than $100 billion. For most Japanese publicly owned companies the Euromarket offers cheaper and/or more convenient financing than the markets in Japan do. Eurobond issues are extremely easy to put together and to sell—especially during the past few years since Japanese investors have been permitted to acquire Japanese Eurobonds without classifying them as "foreign investments," which makes these investments especially attractive to some institutions still subject to regulation of eligible investments.

Many Japanese banks and government agencies have issued straight debt bonds denominated in dollars and other currencies and swapped them into yen obligations to lower their effective yen financing costs. Some have swapped fixed-rate bonds into floating-rate obligations to fund loan portfolios. A great many opportunistic financings of this type have been arranged over the past several years, but the greatest volume of Japanese Eurobond financing has occurred in the area of equity-related securities (i.e., issues convertible into common stock or accompanied by stock purchase warrants). Such issues are very attractive to the companies issuing them due to the high value of the equity component, which has permitted a lowering of the interest coupon to exceptionally low levels. One dollar-denominated issue for Toyota, for example, had an interest coupon of 1 percent.

After 1986, when the market in Japanese warrant-bonds became especially active, it became common practice for Japanese companies to issue large amounts of securities through Japanese securities firms in London, which would resell 70 to 80 percent of the issues to investors in Japan. The warrants were bought by Japanese stock investors who could thus increase the amount of margin used in accumulating shares. Most of the bonds, stripped of their warrants, were sold to Japanese banks who packaged them with other such bonds and swapped the deep discount interest income into floating-rate asscts to replace bank loans being repaid by their increasingly cash-rich Japanese customers.

The issuing companies did not need the money for their businesses, but they found the financing opportunity too good to pass up. Most of them engaged in a form of arbitrage called "zaitech" in Japan in which money raised in such ways was reinvested in securities at a substantial profit. The attraction of this business to the Japanese, as reflected by the growth in Japanese issuances of convertible and warrant bonds, is shown in Table 14–2. In 1989 alone total volume of such securities issue by Japanese companies exceeded $70 billion, or 32 percent of all Eurobond new issues for the year.

This exercise in excess liquidity was played out in London because it is beyond the reach of strict rules governing the use and cost of the Japanese capital market. Two effects resulted: (1) Japanese securities firms rose to become the leading underwriters for the entire Eurobond market, displacing all European and U.S. houses, and (2) Japanese authorities began to consider steps that would bring the Japanese new-issuance business back to Japan.

Over the past 20 years the leading underwriting firms for Eurobonds

Table 14–2. Japanese Equity Bond Issues, 1984–1989 [a]

Type of Issue	1984	1985	1986	1987	1988	1989 (est.)
Convertible bonds	$5,275	$5,431	$2,450	$6,759	$6,800	$7,000
Warrant bonds	1,819	2,845	11,473	21,276	31,200	63,000
Total	7,094	8,276	13,923	28,035	38,000	70,000
As % of total foreign and domestic Japanese equity issues.	46.8%	46.1%	42.5%	23.3%	25.3%	n.a.

a. In millions of dollars.
SOURCE: Goldman, Sachs & Co.

have changed several times. Although some firms have been active in the markets throughout the period, others enjoy periods of special activity during which their natural client base is making extra heavy use of the market. The period since 1986 has been one dominated by Japanese issuers, and the underwriting league tables reflect this activity (see Table 14–3).

Japanese authorities traditionally have taken an exceptionally protective posture with respect to what sort of corporate debt issues were permitted to be sold to unsophisticated Japanese investors. Most companies are required to offer collateral to investors and to pay fees to "commission banks" that act as trustees for the issue. A lengthy registration period is involved, which makes the market appear to be extremely old-fashioned to most Japanese companies. As a result, borrowers have fled the world's most abundant capital market to use an unregulated market in Europe. To recapture the market, Japanese officials of the Ministry of Finance have begun to liberalize the new-issue process in Japan. Shelf registrations, similar to the U.S. SEC Rule 415, are now permitted. Further liberalization is expected with respect to eligibility to issue unsecured bonds, and, at the end of 1989, consideration was being given to making warrants and other securities flowing back to Japan be registered. Though the issuance of equity-related bonds by Japanese companies will no doubt continue for some time, in due course Japanese capital market conditions will be forced to approximate Euromarket conditions. This is an example of "regulatory arbitrage," in which market or regulatory practices of one area come to change the market practices of another area.

Table 14–3.   Top Euromarket Underwriters
of 1989 (Non-U.S. debt and equity)

Manager	Amount [a]	Percent of Market
Nomura Securities	$33.36	15.4
Yamaichi Securities	16.96	7.8
Daiwa Securities	16.82	7.7
Nikko Securities	15.31	7.1
Deutsche Bank	10.23	4.7
CS First Boston	9.65	4.4
J. P. Morgan	7.64	3.5
Morgan Stanley	7.06	3.3
Banque Paribas	6.68	3.1
Merrill Lynch	6.55	3.0
SUBTOTALS	$130.26	60.0%
INDUSTRY TOTALS	$217.18	100.0%

a. In billions of dollars.

SOURCE: Securities Data Co. Reprinted by permission of *The Wall Street Journal*,©Dow Jones and Company, Inc., 1990. All rights reserved worldwide.

Note: This data appeared in *The Wall Street Journal*, Jan 2, 1990.

EUROBONDS WITH SWAPS

It is clear that the U.S. and the international markets are already very closely linked, not just in terms of the relationship between domestic and Eurodollar interest rates, but also through the newer forms of linkage that the interest rate and currency swap markets provide. During the 1980s a system for swapping interest rate and foreign currency obligations among debt obligors around the world developed (see Chapter 15 for a full discussion of this subject). It is now possible for a company that owes floating-rate debt to swap the interest portion of the debt with another company that has a fixed-rate obligation; in fact, there is a large volume of this type of business. Thus, without actually doing a financing, a company can switch its future interest rate exposure from fixed to floating or vice versa, which is a very useful tool for managing financial liabilities. It is also useful for managing assets; for example, a pension fund investor can swap a contract to receive fixed interest payments for a contract to receive a floating rate of interest. Some use swaps more aggressively than that. For instance, a Japanese bank may issue a Eurobond at a very low fixed interest rate and swap it with an issuer such as Potomac Electric Power Company, which can fund a floating-rate obligation cheaply by issuing commercial paper. The Japanese want to generate floating-rate funding at a rate below LIBOR, which it does by offering its attractively priced fixed-rate obligation to Potomac Electric at a premium. Potomac Electric can afford this because at the time it cannot borrow in Europe on as fine terms as the Japanese bank. In any case, it makes a small profit on the difference between the LIBOR it will be receiving and its funding cost in commercial paper. This profit offsets the premium paid for the low-cost fixed-rate obligation. With such techniques, companies can alter the whole structure of their liabilities on very short notice, or they can use them to lower their costs of funds.

Swaps can also be used to exchange foreign currency obligations, sometimes in very unusual ways. In 1985, for example, Walt Disney Corporation did an ECU bond issue. This was swapped with a French government agency for a yen obligation that it had. Disney ended up with a low-cost yen obligation that it will repay out of its yen royalty income from Tokyo Disney World®, and the French switched out of a yen loan into an obligation that it preferred in managing its own foreign exchange exposure.

One can now create "synthetic" dollar assets or liabilities through nondollar bond issues combined with an appropriate currency swap, or synthetic fixed-rate securities can be credited by combining a float-ing-rate note with an interest rate swap. The search for lower-cost liabilities and higher-yielding assets is extensive on the part of corpo-rations and financial institutions, so that the spreads between true and synthetic paper are narrowing as the arbitrage transactions take place in the markets involved in these varied and numerous transactions. It is generally recognized by investment bankers that approximately 70 percent of all Eurobond transactions in 1986 to 1989 involved swaps of one sort or another.

NEW-ISSUE PROCEDURES

National bond markets have fairly orderly new-issue procedures that reflect regulatory requirements and traditional underwriting practices. Because it lacks regulatory requirements, the Eurobond market operates somewhat differently from the U.S. corporate bond market, which it most closely resembles.

In the United States, securities issues must be filed with the SEC, which must declare issues "effective" before they can be sold to the public. To be declared effective, issues must meet disclosure and procedural requirements. In the past the SEC would routinely take a few weeks to review filings placed with it. Today, some companies are eligible for accelerated review and others can file shelf registration statements that, when effective, will provide an issuer with the means to come to market at any time on very short notice. Issuers distribute securities through investment bankers, acting as underwriters, who usually will syndicate issues with others. The issue, when ready to be launched, will be priced, and a gross underwriting spread will be established by negotiation between the issuer and the lead underwriter.

Thereafter, the issue will be allocated among underwriters by the lead underwriter. The underwriters will begin to sell the issue to investors, virtually all of whom are experienced institutional investors who know the markets and all the underwriters intimately. All sales to investors, by terms of the agreements between underwriters, must be at the fixed offering price until such time as the lead underwriter "releases" the issue for free trading at whatever price the market may command.

In the United States, issues may be brought as "bought deals," in which one or a few underwriters purchase the entire issue (which may or may not subsequently be syndicated), or they may be done through the more traditional practice in which the issue is purchased from the company by the entire syndicate following pricing negotiations. Bought deals may be awarded to the lowest bidder following a competitive process, or they may be awarded without competition if the issuer likes the proposal made to it and wants to avoid taking any risk that the market may move against it before the issue is priced.

In the Eurobond market there are a number of different practices. There are no requirements for filing an issue with any regulatory bodies except for the listing requirements of the London or Luxembourg stock exchanges. In earlier years most issues were "mandated" by a corporation to a particular lead manager who would form a syndicate, test the market, and then agree on price and gross spread with the issuer. Today, most issues are bought deals that are mandated to the underwriter offering the best net cost of funds in the currency that is ultimately desired by the issuer.

A EUROBOND PRICING EXAMPLE

A company may inform those who ask that it is "thinking about" raising $100 million with a maturity of five to seven years. It may actually communicate this message to three or four underwriters within the first day or two. Each underwriter will discuss the situation internally and try to come up with the best idea it can. For example, an issuance of ordinary seven-year notes, with perhaps three years of interest payments only and three years of noncallability, (a "plain vanilla" issue), is estimated to sell in the market to knowledgeable investors at, say, an annual yield of 9.25%. Annual coupons are a traditional practice in the Eurobond market. They were originally offered in place of the semiannual coupons, common in the United States, as an accommodation to Swiss banks and their customers.[3]

Normally, a gross spread of 1.875% would apply to a seven year issue. The underwriter would be willing to purchase the issue from the company at a coupon and offering price to investors such that the investors would receive a yield of 9.25%. To achieve this, the underwriter could select a coupon of 9.25% at an offering price of 98.125% (i.e., 100% minus the 1.875% underwriting discount) or a cost-of-funds bid of 9.63%.[4] The bonds would be reoffered to investors at 100%, for a yield of 9.25%.

However, if an underwriter offered the company a cost-of-funds bid of 9.63% in a competitive situation, there would almost certainly be a lower bidder. A competitor, might offer to lower the coupon to 9% (at the same 1.875% gross spread), which would reduce the cost-of-funds to 9.38%. This underwriter would reoffer the bonds at 98.75%, or at a "discount" of 1.25%, which will give clients their 9.25% yield and allow the underwriter to retain 0.625% of the 1.875% gross spread as the "effective" commission (1.875% minus 1.25% =0.625%). The 1.875% stated gross spread is fictional as far as institutional distributors are concerned because it is almost always discounted (through the practice of reoffering bonds at prices below the stated offering price).

Underwriters putting syndicates together do not want to lose the potential support of the continental banks, so the market has accepted the practice of applying a large stated gross spread to all Eurobond issues, with the understanding that one price will be offered to retail investors (through the continental banks) and that a discounted price will be offered to institutional investors (through U.S. and other institutional distributors).

The gross spread is made up of a *management fee* (divided among the lead and comanagers of the issue with the lead manager receiving a *praecipium,* or special portion of the management fee for itself), an *underwriting fee* and a *selling concession.* In the case of a gross spread of 1.875%, the breakdown might be .25%; .25%; 1.375%, respectively. By offering the bonds in the preceding example to institutions at 98.75%, an underwriter will have given up almost all of the selling concession; this leaves only the difference (.125%) plus a share of the management and underwriting fees (against which all expenses of the issue are applied) for the underwriter's compensation. Despite the fact that syndication of this issue could only offer prospects a little better than break-even to the syndicate members, syndication can almost certainly be accomplished by inviting other underwriters eager to appear as comanagers of Eurobond issues or to gain (or improve) a relationship with the issuer.

A more aggressive competitor may decide to offer the borrower a coupon of 8.875%, with the same 1.875% gross spread for a cost-of-funds of 9.25%. But to give the institutional investor a yield of 9.25%, the underwriter will have to reoffer bonds at 98.125% — which represents a discount equal to the entire gross spread. Such a deal (usually called a "kamikaze" offering by other underwriters) might still be done by syndicating with especially eager continental banks or Japanese banks, or others willing to appear in the issue or capable of selling to retail investors. The lead manager may be arranging the deal for competitive purposes or to generate a transaction that would involve a swap, for which an additional fee would be earned. However, if this underwriter is an institutional house without direct access to retail investors in Switzerland or Japan, then care must be taken so as not to so underprice the issue that the underwriter's portion cannot be sold except at a loss. Care must also be taken so that the underwriter does not have to stabilize the issue extensively in the grey market (this is more fully discussed later in the chapter).

Still another bidder might be a large commercial bank that was willing to offer an interest rate or currency swap at below-market rates in order to lower the borrower's cost of funds even further. The bank, for example, might suggest that the borrower offer a seven-year Swiss franc–denominated bond issue at the market rate of 4.75%, together with currency and interest rate swaps into fixed-rate dollars, which would enable the borrower to realize a net cost of funds of, say, 9.24%. The Swiss franc–dollar currency swap may be quoted at a rate that would make the swap appear to be subsidized by the bank.

However, the bank may very well be able to make some money on the swap—to which it would add the comparatively high gross spread of the Swiss franc bond issue (and related fees) plus the prestige of winning an important piece of business. In such cases, the subsidy, if any, is soon forgotten.

Finally, another bidder may offer a low-cost interest rate swap together with a seven-year Eurodollar bond at a fixed-rate cost of funds of 9.38% (a coupon of 9% and a gross spread of 1.875%). The terms of the swap can be made sufficiently attractive against LIBOR to provide below-market floating-rate financing, say .20% below LIBOR. Assuming that the issuer does not need the funds immediately, the proceeds can be inventoried (e.g., by buying an appropriate maturity CD at LIBOR) and the 20 basis points can be taken as profit. Upon using the funds, or at some later date, the issuer may wish to switch back into a fixed-rate financing (by reversing the interest rate swap, possibly at some cost).

It should be clear from these examples (which are summarized in Table 14–4) that issuers, especially those with well-known names who stay in touch with the market, will very often be able to generate a range of financing possibilities in the Eurobond market in which the highest-cost alternative will be no worse than paying the rate required to attract institutional investors.

Once an issuer selects one of the available offers, it will usually confirm and accept the terms proposed on the telephone. If so, the transaction becomes a bought deal—the underwriter has agreed to purchase the issue outright. There are no outs for syndication, investigation into the issuer's business, documentation, or market changes. The underwriter is the sole owner of the entire issue. In other cases, the issuer will mandate an underwriter to proceed with the transaction, subject to a rather precise understanding as to when the issue will be priced and underwritten.

Either way, the underwriter's next step is to arrange for a syndicate of other underwriters to share the risk. It may be that the issuer has imposed on the transactions a group of "co–lead managers" of the issuer's own selection. Such co–lead managers are functionally the same as "comanagers" in U.S. transactions—that is, they share in the management fee portion of the gross spread and appear prominently at the top of the list of underwriters alongside the lead manager, or "book running manager" in U.S. terms. A lead manager will usually not propose or initiate the inclusions of co–lead managers for competitive reasons. However, the lead manager will look for coman-

Table 14-4. Cost-of-Funds Comparison for Various Eurobond New-Issue Proposals

Issue Terms	Institutional Issue Trading at Par	Aggressive Pricing for Institutions	"Kamikaze-Priced" Issue	Swiss Franc Issue With Currency Swap	Aggressive Eurobond with Interest bond Rate Swap
Size	$100 million	$100 million	$100 million	SF 150 million	$100 million
Coupon (%)	$9\frac{1}{4}$	9	$8\frac{7}{8}$	$4\frac{1}{2}$	9
Gross spread (%)	1.875	1.875	1.875	2.66	1.875
Proceeds to issuer (%)	98.125	98.125	98.125	97.34	98.125
Issue cost of funds (%)	9.63	9.38	9.25	4.95	9.38
Fixed-rate equivalent after swap(s)				9.24[a]	9.18[c]
Final cost-of-funds	9.63	9.38	9.25	9.24	9.18
Bond selling price (%)	100	98.75	98.125	100	98.75

	Priced to Trade at par	Will trade Inside Gross Spread	Will trade Outside Gross Spread	Currency Swap Appears "subsidized"	Interest Rate Swap Appears "subsidized"
Investor yield to maturity (%)	9.25	9.25	9.25	4.50	9.25
Retained selling commission (%)	1.375	0.125	-0.5	0.41 [b]	0.125
Probable grey market bid	-0.25	-1.5	-2.0	n.a.	-1.5
Remarks					

a. Two swaps are involved (1) a Swiss-franc fixed-rate to dollar fixed-rate currency swap and (2) a fixed-rate dollar to floating-rate dollar interest rate swap. Between the two swaps it is assumed that an improvement in cost of funds over the fixed-rate dollar cost equivalent (9.38) of .14% can be obtained, which produces the 9.24 cost of funds realized by the issuer.

b. The (2.66%) gross spread is divided into management and underwriting (2.25%) and selling (41%), all of which is retained.

c. Only one swap, fixed rate to LIBOR is involved. For seven years the quoted swap market might show "T+92 bid," which would produce a fixed rate of 9.38 vs. LIBOR. In this case, however, the bidder might offer T+118, which would provide an income of 9.53 vs. a payout obligation of LIBOR. The issuer picks up .15% from the fixed-rate differential. A further pick up .05% may also be possible by funding the LIBOR obligation in the U.S. commercial paper market, resulting in a net savings of .20%.

agers. They are functionally about the same as U.S. "special bracket" underwriters, which rank just ahead of traditional "major bracket" underwriters. In Eurobond issues large numbers of comanagers have become common; it is not unusual to have 8 to 12 comanagers. The lead manager will try to lay off as much as 90 percent of the underwriting risk of the issue, keeping about 10 percent. Some issues are completely syndicated among the managers; however, in most cases a general underwriting group, representing about 50 percent of the underwriting, is invited. If an issue is too underpriced, the lead manager may not be able to fully syndicate the issue. This will increase the lead manager's underwriting by the amount of any shortfall.

THE GREY MARKET

Once syndication has begun on an issue and its terms are known, it will appear in the *grey market*. This is an informal, unauthorized, electronic quotation service that is provided to the market by certain bond brokers over information networks, such as Reuters. On one or more Reuters' "pages" there will appear a list of all of the latest issues that have been announced, together with a brief summary of their terms and indicative bid and asked quotations, expressed as a percentage discount from the offering price or as a percentage of the principal amount (in cases where the prices are above par). All market participants and most institutional investors stay tuned into the grey market pages continuously (see Figure 14–5).

For example, a seven-year issue with a coupon of 9% and a stated price of par might be quoted at "less 1.50% bid, less 1.25% offered," which means that the broker expects to be able to purchase bonds, from underwriters who cannot find buyers for their bonds, at 98.5% (100% less 1.5%), or the broker expects to sell them to other underwriters at 98.75% (less 1.25%). In a transaction such as this, the selling concession would have been 1.375%, indicating that the broker would be willing to try (on a best-efforts basis) to take over an underwriter's unsold bonds at no profit to the underwriter and sell them to the lead manager or another dealer at 98.75% (a yield of 9.25%).

In the Eurobond market an issue that left .125% in selling concession after discounts to customers would be considered a reasonably successful deal. Often, as a result of aggressive bidding by prospective lead managers, deals open in the grey market at levels that reflect discounts of more than the entire gross spread (e.g., less 2%, etc.).

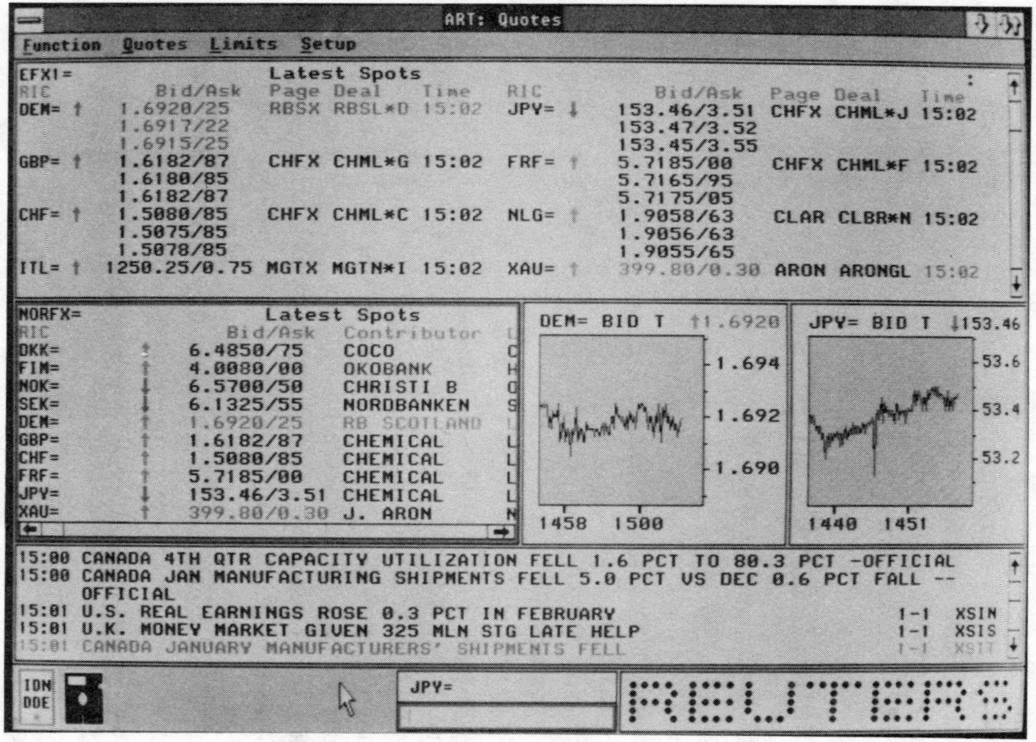

Figure 14–5. The Reuter Money 2000 Service, launched April 4, 1990, brings together on a single color screen rates contributed by banks and brokers in 82 countries and quotations for all leading instruments in the major financial and options markets. Reuters news coverage is also available. The above photo is a typical Money 2000 screen format showing foreign exchange "tiles" (top and middle left), two real-time "tick" graphs (middle right), and real-time money news headlines (bottom).

Such issues are considered unsuccessful, especially by the comanagers, who do not share in any swap-related or other collateral fees and who are usually allocated their full underwriting subscription of bonds to either sell at a loss or to carry as inventory until such time as they can sell them. Hot issues (e.g., equity-linked issues or other issues with special features), however, can trade to a premium in the grey market. These are rarely allocated generously to comanagers, who repeatedly stand to lose on the unsuccessful issues and not gain much on the successful ones.

FIXED-PRICE UNDERWRITINGS

During the latter part of 1989, the market for new issues on straight Eurobonds was very unstable and very competitive. The outlook for both interest rates and exchange rates were uncertain, and demand for straight Eurobonds was soft. At the same time, underwriting capacity in the market was large, as banks and investment banks attempted to demonstrate their global capabilities. During this period, the profitability of Eurobonds for underwriters eroded away to practically nothing.

In order to stem this erosion and to restore discipline to the market, some leading underwriters proposed bringing issues on a "fixed-price" basis—that is, on the same basis as bonds in the United States. They agreed that a spread of 0.25% to 0.375% should be retained by the underwriters and that no underwriter would sell bonds at lower prices than was needed to assure this spread. The new method of underwriting was accepted by some Swiss banks, which had long opposed any reduction in the large spreads they charge their clients for Eurobonds, in the interest of restoring order to the market. Twenty or so issues were brought in this manner during the second half of 1989—some were successful in maintaining price discipline, others were less so. Most observers believe that the new system is a function of the difficult market conditions and that in another bull market for Eurobonds the discipline will be very difficult to maintain. At the same time, however, others feel that new or different methods for underwriting Eurobond issues need to be developed that offer greater protection to underwriters.

Usually, overly competitive situations such as these are resolved by departures from the market of some banks or a unilateral reduction by others of resources committed to serving the market. Other methods have been attempted also, such as a greater effort to place securities on an "off-market," or private placement basis, or through simultaneous offerings in several markets.

STABILIZATION

Comanagers (and other underwriters) finding themselves being allocated bonds in poorly priced issues may decide that they do not wish to retain the market risk of holding the bonds in inventory; therefore, they elect to sell the bonds in the market. The easiest market to access is the grey market. If the issue is tightly priced (as in the preceding example) and the comanager has no demand from customers, the comanager will call a bond broker to arrange a sale of bonds on a confidential basis. This way the issuer and the lead manager will not be able to know for sure that the comanager was unable to sell the bonds. The bond broker will immediately ask the lead manager of the issue to buy the bonds back at the grey market price. If the lead manager wishes to stabilize the issue around the grey market level, he will purchase the bonds. Depending upon the lead manager's response, the bond broker may adjust his quotes.

Such lead manager's stabilization purchases, in effect, are for his own account, not for the account of the whole syndicate, because stabilization losses can only be charged to the syndicate up to the amount of the underwriting commission. This is because in a variable-price underwriting, stabilization prices will vary and further profits or losses may occur, which may be substantial. It becomes difficult for the lead manager to separate transactions made for his own account (i.e., regarding his own bonds) and those of the syndicate. Accordingly, if any stabilization is to occur, it will be performed by the lead manager acting on his own and at his own risk.

It is often in the interest of the lead manager to stabilize issues—it prevents the grey market from collapsing to levels below the full amount of the gross spread, and it buys time for the marketwide sales effort to take effect. If the stabilization effort is persuasive, the issue will respond; if not, it will drop in price, which is most injurious to the manager holding the largest amount of bonds—usually the lead manager. If the issue is clearly mispriced, however, the lead manager may be better off to attempt to hedge the issue as early as possible (e.g., by selling treasuries or, preferably, a similar Eurobond issued by another company) and then let the market manage on its own without accumulating additional bonds through stabilization. If the cost of financing the inventory of bonds is less than the income received on them, some participants are willing to carry the unsold bonds for as long as several months, until they can be sold off at higher prices when opportunities present themselves. Sometimes they can only liquidate such positions at a loss—often a large loss.

Lead managers utilize a number of tactics to influence the market to take up the bonds. Sometimes comanagers are selected because of their willingness to hold bonds over the distribution period or because they agree not to "dump" the bonds on the market. Since the market is anonymous, this is hard to enforce. Sometimes vigorous efforts are made during the night before the pricing of the issue to "preplace" a large portion of it in Japan, before the grey market has quoted a price on it. Sometimes bonds are offered to investors together with swaps or other inducements, including an offer to buy back other Eurobonds from the investor. Sometimes lead managers will sell overallocated bonds short to other underwriters and cover these sales with bonds purchased in stabilization transactions. And sometimes lead managers will appear to allow the grey market quotes to drop sharply, only to then underallocate bonds to comanagers and other underwriters, which forces them to buy bonds in the market to cover their short sales into the grey market. There are many skills that a lead manager must master in order to be effective at the job and to reduce the risk of worsening an already tight pricing situation by mishandling the complex job of managing the syndicate.

These various practices have provided much room for abuses and practices that many lead managers, especially those with captive placement capability, regard as injurious to the market as a whole. Periodically, continental bank managers complain about the predatory behavior of the bond brokers and their principal customers—aggressive U.S., Japanese, and other firms without ability to place issues with in-house funds under management. In early 1989, after a lengthy period in which the profitability of the Eurobond new-issue business had been under pressure, several leading Euromarket figures announced that their firms would no longer quote prices on new issues to bond brokers and would request that members of syndicates arranged by them also not do so. This action would prevent market participants from dumping bonds allocated to them, or bonds they never owned, in the secondary market—thus lowering the price of the newly issued bonds. Although several firms agreed to cooperate with the market leaders in this regard, most recall that such steps have been taken before and that they have not been effective for long. Such lack of market discipline is clearly one of the costs of a self-regulated market without enforcement powers.

FOREIGN BONDS SINCE 1986

The annual volume of new issues of foreign bonds increased from a level of $39.4 billion in 1986 to $40.2 billion in 1987 and to about

Table 14–5. Foreign Bond Issues, 1984–1988 [a]

Type of Issue	1984	1985	1986	1987	1988
Swiss franc bonds	$12,626	$14.954	$23,213	$24,301	$28,000
U.S. dollar bonds	5,487	4,655	6,782	7,416	8,500
Japanese yen bonds	4,628	6,379	5,223	4,071	5,800
Other bonds	5,212	5,037	4,141	4,465	4,700
Total foreign bonds	27,953	31,025	39,359	40,253	48,000

a. In millions of dollars.

SOURCE: Morgan Guaranty Trust Co.

$48 billion in 1988. Swiss franc–denominated foreign bonds (Swiss franc Eurobonds not being permitted by the Swiss National Bank) continued to dominate all such issues. Indeed, during 1987 Swiss issues accounted for 65 percent of all foreign bond new issues, over $23.9 billion in value, rising to about $28 billion in 1988. Yankee bonds (dollar denominated) increased to $7.4 billion in 1987, from $6.8 billion in 1986, and to about $8.5 billion in 1988. Samurai bonds (i.e., yen-denominated foreign bonds) decreased by 22 percent to $4.1 billion in 1987, but returned to about $5.8 billion in 1988 (see Table 14–5).

Because there is no Euro–Swiss franc bond market, all transactions in that currency must be accomplished in the Swiss national market. This market in the past has been subject to strong traditional practices that govern underwriting arrangements, which are dominated by the three largest banks. Recently, however, these underwriting practices have been changed to permit non-Swiss banks to lead issues in Switzerland and to participate more extensively as comanagers and in the allocation of bonds for sale. With the weakening of the dollar, international investors (especially retail investors) have shown a strong preference for bonds denominated in Swiss and German currencies. In 1985, for example, when the dollar reached its peak, only $15 billion worth of Swiss franc—denominated foreign bonds were issued.

Although, Samurai bonds (yen denominated) issued in the domestic Japanese market declined sharply in 1987, Euroyen-denominated new issues increased substantially. Japanese authorities have gradually removed controls that effect the volume of Euroyen new issues in accordance with a government policy to permit the "internationalization" of the yen. The Euroyen bond market is more efficient and convenient for issuers than the more cumbersome domestic yen bond market, and, accordingly, most of the international new issue activity in yen during 1986 and 1987 took place in the Euromarket. To balance this situation, and in recognition of the unusual demand for Japanese Euro warrant bonds, Japanese government authorities began to take steps to reduce the interest rate controls and queuing (sequenced market access) and other controls and approvals necessary in order to allow domestic yen issues to be completed more quickly and competitively. In 1988 shelf registration procedures were inaugurated in Japan, although these are still more cumbersome than prevailing Euromarket requirements.

Deregulation of various national capital markets, partly attributable to the prospect's business being lost to the Euromarkets, has been continuous for several years. Will such deregulation continue so as to obviate the need for the Euromarket?

This subject has received much attention. Those who believe the Euromarket will wane with the rising importance of deregulated national markets consider that issuers prefer domestic markets when they are competitive and that international investors prefer them as well because of greater secondary market liquidity. Those who are doubtful that the Euromarket is on its last legs believe, to the contrary, that there will always be enough regulation in most national markets to be able to reward those who attempt to escape it. They also believe that in a world of very diverse internationally minded investors, bargains will be offered from time to time to attract business into the unregulated and untaxed arena of international bond and capital markets.

EVOLUTION OF THE INTRA-EUROPEAN NEW-ISSUES MARKET

As of the end of 1987, the total volume of all intra-European capital market financing by European corporations had grown to levels equal to approximately 76 percent of comparable corporate financing activity in the United States and to 81 percent of the level of activity in Japan. This volume of financing indicates that the consolidated European markets have achieved a comparatively mature state of development in relation to the world's two other principal capital markets (see Table 14–6).

The consolidated European markets data include financing issues by European corporations in the Eurobond markets, plus the volume of

Table 14–6. Volume of Capital Market Financing by Regional Corporations in Their Respective Regional Markets, 1987 [a]

	United States			Europe			Japan		
	Financial	Nonfinancial	Total	Financial	Nonfinancial	Total	Financial	Nonfinancial	Total
Equities	$25.3	$28.1	$53.4	$13.8	$75.8 [c]	$ 89.6	$ 14.0	$ 28.5	$ 42.5
Bonds [d]	143.2	220.1	363.3	170.1	31.5	201.6	227.9 [b]	103.1	331.0
Total [e]	168.5	248.2	416.7	183.9	107.3	291.2	291.9	131.6	373.5
Gross national product		4,700			5,300			2,400	
Financing per dollar of gross national product	0.036	0.053	0.089	0.035	0.020	0.055	0.101	0.055	0.156

a. In billions of dollars of proceeds at yearly average exchange ratio.

b. Includes discount notes issued by banks, many of which can be considered short term.

c. Total gross shares old through public distributions, including privatization issues.

d. Includes private placements where reported, as well as local government and revenue bonds.

e. Issues by domestic firms outside their home regions are excluded, for example, US corporate issues of Eurobonds. However, the totals include European corporate sales of Euro-issues and foreign issues estimated at $35.7 billion in 1987.

SOURCE: OECD, October 1988 (based on data supplied by central banking authorities)

domestic capital market issues and issues in other European national markets.

Domestic capital markets have been especially active for new issues of debt securities in Germany, France, and Italy and for equity securities in France and the United Kingdom, where large privatization programs have occurred in 1986 and afterwards. Altogether, domestic new issues totaled $240 billion in 1987. To this amount, European corporations (including public sector incorporated entities) added a further $50 billion of new issue financing in the Eurobond and equity markets, and from issues floated in the domestic markets of other European countries (see Table 14–7). The total of all European capital market issues, including privatization issues, in 1987 was $291 billion—$201 billion in debt and $90 billion in equity issues. European nonfinancial corporations accounted for 38.1% of all European issues in 1987, although they accounted for 46% of all Euromarket and foreign market issues.

By comparison, corporate new issues of securities in the United States in 1987 totaled $381 billion, of which 53% were issued by nonfinancial corporations. In Japan, corporate new issues totaled $359 billion, of which about 35% was issued by nonfinancial corporations. The overall amount of capital market new-issue activity in the three regions, on a per-dollar-of-GNP basis, shows a reasonable degree of similarity. There is a substantial difference between them, however, as regards nonfinancial corporate use of capital markets for new issues. European nonfinancial corporations appear to be lagging behind their counterparts in the United States and Japan by a ratio of about 1 to 1.7, as shown in Table 14–6.

In Europe the long tradition of reliance by nonfinancial corporations on their banks, and the relatively poorly developed capital markets of several countries, have prevented companies from gaining experience with securities transactions. This condition has gradually changed as a result of the rapid development of the Euromarkets and of the market in Switzerland and because of the effects of privatization sales by several European countries. From 1985 to 1987 intra-European debt and equity issues by European nonfinancial corporations exceeding $265 billion were sold (see Tables 14–7 and 14–8).

The market for debt and equity issues in Europe has developed substantially since the early 1980s. It appears to have achieved a level of activity sufficient to supply competitively the capital requirements of Europe. Industry, in turn, has begun to decrease its reliance upon

Table 14–7. Capital Market Financing by All European Companies, 1985–1988 [a]

	Total Debt Issues				Total Equity Issues				Total Issues			
	Euro-Bonds	Foreign Bonds	Domestic Bonds	Total Bonds	Euro-Equities	Foreign Equities	Domestic Equities	Total Equities	Euro-Issues	Foreign Issues	Domestic Issues	Total Issues
1985												
No. of issues	340	93			45	6			385	99		
Volume	$33,588	$3,478	$110,432	$147,498	$3,253	$156	$29,233	$32,642	$36,841	$3,634	$139,665	$180,140
Average issue size	99	37			72	26			96	37		
1986												
No. of issues	449	95			107	17			556	112		
Volume	49,465	4,582	142,509	196,556	13,943	2,297	57,570	73,810	64,408	6,879	200,079	270,366
Average issue size	110	48			130	135			114	61		
1987												
No. of issues	337	165			109	26			446	191		
Volume	29,239	6,465	165,845	201,549	11,924	3,377	74,306	89,607	41,463	9,842	240,151	291,156
Average issue size	87	39			109	130			92	52		
1988												
No. of issues	511	208			43	11			554	219		
Volume	53,931	9,401	n.a.		5,911	740	n.a.		59,852	10,141	n.a.	
Average issue size	106	45			138	67			108	46		

a. In millions of dollars of proceeds at current exchange rates.

SOURCE: Euro and Foreign bond data, Securities Data Co.; domestic data, OECD

Table 14-8. Capital Market Financing by European Nonfinancial Corporations, 1985–1988 [a]

	Nonfinancial Debt Issues			Nonfinancial Equity Issues			Total Nonfinancial Issues			
	Euro and Foreign	Domestic Bonds	Total Bonds	Euro and Foreign	Domestic	Total Equities	Euro and Foreign	Domestic	Total Issues	Nonfinancial as a Percentage of Total Issues
1985	$11,779	$12,249	$24,028	$ 2,660	$23,610	$26,270	$14,439	$35,859	$ 50,298	27.9%
1986	25,314	19,122	44,436	13,112	45,886	58,998	38,426	65,008	103,434	38.3
1987	13,576	23,894	37,470	9,872	64,113	73,986	23,449	88,007	111,456	38.3
1988	31,996	n.a.		6,351	n.a.		38,347	n.a.		n.a.

a. In millions of dollars of proceeds at average exchange rates.

SOURCE: Euro and foreign data, Securities Data Co.; domestic data, OECD.

Table 14–9. Volume of Nondomestic European Capital Market
Issues by All European Corporations, by Currency of Issue [a]

	European Currencies	ECUs	Other Currencies	European and ECUs as a Percent of Total
1985	$12,707	$3,004	$24,764	38.8%
1986	33,982	2,531	33,773	51.6%
1987	36,984	2,681	11,339	77.8%
1988	46,567	5,489	17,937	74.4%
Total	130,240	13,705	87,813	62.1%

a. In millions of dollars of proceeds at current exchange rates.
SOURCE: Securities Data Co.

the banking system and markets abroad for its requirements for funds. Only comparatively small amounts of financing were done by European companies from 1985 to 1988 in the United States or Japan.

It is also no longer necessary for European corporations to rely upon financings denominated in non-European currencies when financing outside of their own markets. In 1988, 74 percent of all European corporate Eurobond and foreign financing was denominated in ECUs, as compared to only 39 percent in 1985 (see Table 14–9).

COMPETITION IN EUROPEAN BOND MARKETS

In the United States the six leading underwriters of corporate bonds together represented 76 percent of the market in 1986, a figure that has not changed very much over the last 10 years. In the Eurobond market it is necessary to combine the market shares of the top 21 firms to exceed 75 percent of the market. Among the top six firms in the United States in 1986, four were among the top six in 1978. Among the top six Eurobond underwriters in 1986, only one was among the top six in 1978.

As markets change to reflect investor preferences—for dollars over other currencies, for fixed over floating rate, or straight debt over equity-related securities—the competitive picture changes and different institutions emerge as having the greatest comparative advantage. Firms that have built a strong distribution and trading capability and strong investment banking capabilities in various markets will probably do best over the long run. Certainly, however, the Eurobond market is not one that can be dominated by any single firm, or small group of firms, over any length of time. The vigorous competitive action of the unregulated, innovation-oriented market will keep it that way.

All banks and investment banks seeking to compete in the international market must come to terms with three basic factors: (1) the new-issue business for investment grade bonds has become global; (2) globalization has made the business extremely competitive, and realized underwriting profits have declined accordingly, and (3) firms must regard new issues, secondary market-making and trading, hedging, swaps, and arbitrage related to bonds as one integrated business.

That the business has become global is no surprise today. Borrowers, when discussing possible financings with their bankers, want to know what is the cheapest way to raise funds from whatever source. A competitor, for example, who does not operate in the United States and/or the Eurodollar bond markets, the Swiss franc market, or in Japan will be at a significant disadvantage as compared to a firm that is active in all of these markets. Becoming involved in these markets entails a substantial threshold of cost, personnel, and supervision without which a firm is, in effect, only an occasional participant in the global debt markets.

That the business has become less attractive is also no surprise. Profits, once ample (during the boom period of the early 1980s), have crumbled, at least in the (non-Japanese) dollar sector, where spreads are low and positioning requirements are high. These unattractive and dangerous economics have been sufficient to cause many marginal players to withdraw from the business and have frightened away others who might have been formidable competitors. Perhaps some degree of competitive equilibrium is returning to the markets after an apparent absence of several years.

On the other hand, two types of firms have fared comparatively well in the Eurobond sector in recent years: (1) those with the mobility to move into more attractive markets (e.g., the Japanese warrant-bond market and the domestic Swiss franc bond market) and (2) those with the ability to bundle together all of their various businesses that relate to bond new issues (e.g., hedging, swaps, secondary market activity) and to look at their combined profits instead of incremental new-issue profits alone. Most of the profits today are earned by introducing original ideas or innovative transactions and by good steady performance in the global secondary bond markets. Hedging and swapping fees also contribute to gross income.

PROFITABILITY

The profitability of issues in the Eurobond market will vary considerably, depending upon what role the firm is playing, what type of issue is involved, and how well (or poorly) priced an issue is relative to the market. The lead manager is in the best position to earn or to lose the most. Co–lead managers and comanagers are essentially at the mercy of the lead manager. Underwriters usually have such modest exposures as not to be greatly affected one way or the other.

Equity-related issues, if correctly priced, tend to be the most profitable—these have mainly been Japanese issues in recent years, which have been extremely profitable for their lead managers during a time when other Eurobond issues have been comparatively unprofitable. Next in terms of profitability are bonds with innovative or special features or those in nondollar denominations. The "plain vanilla" seven-year Eurodollar bond, won in a highly competitive bidding, will often be unprofitable to the lead manager unless a captive investor is found who will pay the full gross spread on the issue or unless the market rises immediately after the offering due to a decline in interest rates.

Secondary market trading in Eurobonds can be an attractive business for those firms equipped with a full complement of sales and trading personnel, research, and other support—and adequate capital to support inventory positions—although the business has become increasingly competitive as more firms gear up to compete in the secondary market. Secondary market trading spreads average about .25% in the Eurodollar bond market, which is about the same as in the United States.

Most firms believe that for a Eurobond business to be profitable the banker must be in the new-issue flow as lead or co–lead manager sufficiently often so as to have some influence in the market. Such influence will enable an underwriter to capture a certain amount of profitable new-issue business and to have a preferred position in the secondary market, having sold bonds to customers who later decide to sell or swap them back. The Eurobond business also generates additional income from hedging, interest rate and currency swaps tied to specific transactions, foreign exchange, and financial futures.

Some new products have been very profitable to their originators until they have been turned into commodities by other firms copying the idea. Zero coupon bonds, floating-rate notes, warrant issues, perpetual notes, and various securitized issues are examples of successful products that became ordinary over time, after which subsequent issues were less profitable for their originators. With obsolescence affecting products quickly, a premium is placed on innovation and new ideas.

COMPETING FOR EUROPEAN NEW ISSUES AFTER 1992

Banks and financial corporations in Europe have for many years been shrewd and aggressive seekers of low-cost funds. These were quick to learn of the newer financing techniques that began to flood the market in the early 1980s. Often they would underwrite their own issues or arrange syndicates for such issues from among other banks with whom they enjoyed profitable reciprocal business arrangements. However, they also subscribed to the principal that any other bank or investment bank bringing an attractive new idea would be rewarded with the lead managership for the issue. Thus, competition based on performance and innovation developed. With it developed the financial management skills of the banks' lending and client relationship officers, who after 1980 were themselves increasingly having to compete.

Attracted by these offerings, many European corporations broke away from their traditional, exclusive "hausbank" relationships in order to open themselves up to ideas, proposals, and solicitations from other banks. These corporations have become customers of the globalized market for finance, where a menu of possibilities is always available for treasurers to select from. Some of the larger corporations have issued securities in the U.S. market or in Japan, but most prefer the greater European market. In this market European companies feel they are known and appreciated and can expect to be treated well. As they grow into world-class enterprises, they will consider financing in other areas. But until then, they and most of the rest of the nonfinancial corporations in Europe will be content with the new-found wonders of their internal intra-European market.

THE INTRA-EUROPEAN MARKET

A loosely integrated, three-market structure of Eurosecurities, foreign bonds and equities, and domestic issues is already in place. As a consequence of the changes and the competitive energies associated with the Europe 1992 initiatives, these markets can be expected to converge into a single European capital market comprised of institutional investors (e.g., pension funds, insurance companies, and investment companies) and a retail sector consisting primarily of the portfolio managers of continental banks that manage private funds. There will be no reason for the traditional three-market construction to continue, subject to how the regulatory issues regarding prospectus disclosure and other matters are resolved.

It is probable that financial institutions will become active traders of their portfolios as they endeavor to compete for funds to manage. Many of these institutions will seek to demonstrate higher returns based on their superior performance as investment managers. Such has been the pattern in the U.S. market, and it is increasingly becoming the case in the United Kingdom subsequent to deregulation. As these institutions begin to compete with each other on the basis of their financial management skills, their skills will improve and they will become customers for the newest investment ideas and the latest thoughts and strategies for beating the averages. Thus, the relative impact of Euromarket institutional investors in the markets should become much greater.

The retail market, traditionally insulated by tax avoidance factors necessitating bearer securities and bank secrecy, is not likely to alter greatly in the near term. Some of the funds on deposit with continental banks will continue to value anonymity and the preservation of capital over investment performance. Other customers of such banks, perhaps the next generation of owners of the accounts, may elect to be more open in their investment activities in order to obtain a higher return, greater liquidity, and mobility. British, Dutch, or German mutual funds may attract some of this business. Some may flow into brokerage accounts of U.S., British, or Japanese brokers who offer sophisticated and varied investment opportunities including venture capital, risk arbitrage, asset-backed securities, and many other products emanating from London, Tokyo, or New York. Certainly, in the environment promised by the free movement of capital in Europe, many competitors will be establishing themselves to affect a diversion of the retail business from the banks into active trading accounts with their firms.

Thus, the new-issue markets in Europe should be both deeper and more varied. A broader spectrum of investors can be expected to develop, which will in time lead to filling in the gaps that have existed in the Euromarkets and most European domestic markets for some time. The gaps are represented by the lack of interest and activity in European markets for maturities over 10 years, securities backed by mortgages or real estate assets (some of which have been issued in the Euromarkets and in the U.K. domestic market but without high levels of acceptance), or for "non-investment-grade" securities (i.e., "junk bonds").

Further, as developments discussed here occur and the gaps are closed, additional market support services will be developed, such as bond rating services (some Eurobond issues are already rated by the U.S. rating agencies), improved custody and clearing procedures, and improved methods for financing securities inventories (e.g., through repurchase agreements). These services will assist the market in increasing new-issue volumes.

THE EFFECT OF EUROMARKET COMPETITION ON INVESTMENT BANKERS

The underwriting business in Europe has been characterized by several distinctions between it and similar markets in the United States and Japan. Of course, the Eurobond market is an unregulated (or more correctly, self-regulated), highly competitive market in which any bank or securities firm from any country is free to compete. The Euromarket has traditionally favored those competitors with substantial captive placing power, such as the large Swiss banks, which have had the predominant influence on the market since its beginning in the early 1960s. Other bankers, however, have been able to survive (and occasionally prosper) by securing lead managerships of issues originated by companies from their own countries or as a result of innovation in either a product or a technique used by the market. U.S. firms fared very well during the early 1980s by managing issues for American companies. Japanese firms have benefited substantially from the large flow of Japanese Eurobond issues since then.

As the market evolves, particularly with the increasing importance of institutional investors in the Euromarket, the comparative advantage of the Swiss banks should recede to some extent. Those firms with well-developed skills in servicing institutional investors should, as in the United States, rise in importance in the market hierarchy. However, because of their continuing activity in managing substantial sums of private wealth, the continental banks can be expected to remain powerful forces in the Euromarkets with continuing influence in areas of market structure and pricing.

The extremely changeable character of the Eurobond market has caused the profitability of the principal participants to ebb and flow over time. Such variability of returns has discouraged many participants from developing their Euromarket capabilities to their fullest. In recent years, however, the integration of the Euromarket into the global market for debt and equity securities has meant that any investment bank seeking to compete on a global basis has had to become proficient in the Euromarkets, and has had to maintain that proficiency even through unprofitable periods, in order to be successful. Expertise in the markets and its products can be protected from losses by securing a respectable market share of the new-issue business, by perfecting the science (or art) of hedging, by building distribution capabilities that ensure the ability to sell all underwritten securities quickly, by knowing how to construct and package synthetic securities that will add to a firm's distributive capacity and profits, and by managing the extensive direct costs of Euromarket activities skillfully so as to minimize expenses.

National debt markets historically have been the preserve of national firms. In recent years, however, deregulation in the United Kingdom, Germany, Switzerland, and France has led to increased roles in national markets by international firms. These firms do not as yet have much business with national companies in the national markets, but some have managed to do international issues for them. Perhaps national market issues will be next.

As deregulation has occurred in financial markets throughout Europe and further changes in the 1990s appear to be inevitable, some observers have come to believe that national capital market activity will displace the Euromarkets, which will no longer be needed—the financing business that was generated in the past in the Euromarkets because of exchange controls and other regulations will no longer have to be done outside the home market.

We do not agree. After 25 years of activity, the Euromarket has become the single most important market for corporate issues in Europe. It is also the most technically developed market in Europe. But in any case, the free flow of capital in Europe should lead instead toward a single, integrated Euromarket rather than back to the fragmented collection of separate markets that existed before. Further, institutional investors will operate within Europe as a whole in seeking the most interesting opportunities. If they should want Deutsche mark investments, they would go to Germany to get them. If they want dollar investments, however, they do not have to go to the United States to get them—the U.S. balance-of-payments deficit assures them of a supply of Eurodollar investments in Europe. Borrowers and bankers will tap into the pool, as they always have, and build a market in various currencies around it. Access to the market, we assume, will continue to be free and unregulated. Given a choice, most participants will prefer an unregulated market to a regulated one.

In any case, the retail sector, still the major part of the Euromarket, will prefer to remain beyond the view of tax collectors or other authorities that it has always sought to avoid. Much more likely than decline and collapse of the Euromarket is the emergence of a new intra-European financial marketplace that is built upon and encompasses the Euromarket of today. In time, the distinctions between national markets and the Euromarkets will fade, and nonnational competitors will compete, on a performance basis, for the business of national companies and periodically will win assignments.

It is also likely, we believe, for a substantial increase in the overall level of Eurocapital market activity to occur as a result of corporate restructuring. Active capital markets are necessary to effect such restructurings. Funds must be raised by buyers and reinvested by sellers. New types of financial structures will be developed to suit transactions being put together in Europe. New types of securities, possibly including Eurojunk bonds may emerge. A centralized capital market that draws from all over Europe, from the national markets as well as from the Euromarkets, will be the most efficient way to marshal capital resources. It seems logical to expect the markets to evolve in this way in an essentially deregulated environment. Of course, we do not yet know the extent to which the concurrent development of regulatory matters may affect our expectations.

To be effective in vying for European new-issue business, the competing banks will have to be aggressive, innovative, and efficient. They will have to have staying power to develop their franchises in the newly liberated areas and to weather the storms of unprofitability when they come. As the market consolidates into a large regional market, certain competitors will emerge as market leaders and a process of concentration of market share is likely to emerge, as it has done in the United States.

SUMMARY

The international bond market has experienced phenomenal growth for over a quarter of a century, primarily in the Eurobond sector. As an unregulated market bringing together high-quality issuers and a widely diverse and changing body of investors from all over the world, the market is historically unique. The Eurobond houses, based in London but coming from all corners of the world, compete to offer issuers rapid access to low-cost funds. Their success has furthered international financial integration and has contributed to the drive for deregulation. In the future, developments related to the creation of a common "internal" market by the European countries should cause capital market activity in Europe to expand greatly. Such increased activity may further diminish the differences between onshore and offshore debt financing as it increases the worldwide selection of debt instruments.

NOTES

1. For a brief but interesting history of international bond markets see: F. G. Fisher, *International Bonds* (Euromoney Publications, 1981), pp. 15–27.
2. One of the U.S. firms that was very active in selling U.S. securities through offices in Europe was White Weld & Co., Inc. Subsequently, White Weld's European operations were separately incorporated as White Weld Ltd., which formed a joint venture with Credit Suisse, a prominent Swiss bank. The joint venture, called Credit Suisse White Weld, specialized in Eurobonds. It was recapitalized into a new company, Credit Suisse First Boston, in 1978 when White Weld & Co. was sold to Merrill Lynch. In 1989 Credit Suisse First Boston and First Boston Corporation were merged into a new company, CS-First Boston.
3. Yields and costs of funds for Eurobonds are often expressed in terms of semiannual coupon equivalents for the benefit of those issuers whose alternative financing sources are expressed in semiannual terms. An annual coupon yield of 9.25% would have a semiannual equivalent of 9.05%.
4. This and subsequent prices and yields are calculated with the aid of a bond calculator such that price = the sum of discounted coupon and principal payments where the yield is the discount rate. Here, $98.125 = 9.25/1.0963 + 9.25/1.0963 + \cdots + 9.25/1.0963 + 109.25/1.0963$.

SELECTED REFERENCES

Aliber, Robert Z. ed. *The Handbook of International Financial Management.* New York: Richard D. Irwin, Inc., 1989.

Altman, Edward I. ed. *Handbook of Financial Markets and Institutions.* 6th ed. New York: Wiley, 1987.

Evans, Garry. "How to Stop the Eurobond Market From Committing Suicide." *Euromoney,* May 1988, pp. 46–58.

Fisher, F. G. *International Bonds.* Euromoney Publications, 1981.

Friedman, Jeffry A. *Banking on the World*. New York: Harper & Row, 1987.

Grant, Charles. "Euromarkets." *The Economist,* May 16, 1987.

Hakin, Jonathan. "The World is Their Oyster." *The Economist,* March 16, 1985.

Hayes III, Samuel L., and Hubbard, Philip H. *Investment Banking: A Tale of Three Cities*. Cambridge, MA: Harvard Business School Press, 1990.

Levich, Richard M. "Financial Innovations in International Financial Markets." Working Paper Series, National Bureau of Economic Research, Inc., 1987.

Securities and Exchange Commission. *Internationalization of the Securities Markets*. Report of the Staff of the U.S. Securities and Exchange Commission to the Senate Committee on Banking, Housing and Urban Affairs and the House Committee on Energy and Commerce, July 17, 1987.

Smith, Roy C. *The Global Bankers*. New York: E.P. Dutton, 1989.

Walter, Ingo, and Smith, Roy C. *Investment Banking in Europe*. Oxford: Basil Blackwell, 1989.

15

Swaps and Synthetic Securities

Few events have stimulated international capital market activity as much as has the development of interest rate and currency swaps. Prior to 1980, swaps scarcely existed. By 1988 they had become so much a part of the international financial scene that it has been widely accepted that Eurobond transactions involving swaps are responsible at times for more than half of all new issues. In mid-1988 over $1 trillion worth of swaps were outstanding according to the International Swap Dealers Association (see Table 15–1).

Swaps constitute valid and binding agreements between participants to exchange one future flow of interest (and sometimes principal) payments for another. Swaps, however, do not appear on anyone's balance sheet, nor have they traditionally been subject to banks' reserve requirements. They are considered "contingent liabilities." Swaps are enormously accommodating; they enable parties to change their financial assets and liabilities at will, to make a fixed interest payment obligation into a variable one, or to change a dollar payment obligation into a Deutsche mark one. They are so accommodating that borrowers from all around the world use them, and in doing so borrowers explore the previously unknown territory of "synthetic" securities.

THE ORIGIN OF SWAPS

In the early years of the international capital markets, around the mid-1960s, foreign exchange controls that blocked or impeded the flow of funds across borders were abundant. In the days of fixed exchange rates, the conventional method of preventing funds from exiting or entering one's country was to surround it with a ring of exchange controls.

For example, a British pension fund manager wanting to invest in the U.S. equity market would either have to sell an existing overseas

Table 15–1.   Estimate Volume of Swaps[a]

Type of Swap	1982	1983	1984	1985	1986	1987	1988
Currency	$ 3	$ 5	$ 19	$ 50	$100	$150	$175
Interest Rate	2	30	90	175	190	388	568
Total	5	35	109	225	290	538	743

a. National amounts in billions of dollars.

SOURCES: International Swap Dealers Assn., Bank of England, Salomon Brothers, *The Economist*.

holding to pay for the new investment or purchase international "investment currency" to do so. Investment currency was rigged to be more expensive than domestic currency—it was the same as buying dollars for the U.S. investment at a premium or paying a higher rate for the dollars than otherwise prevailed. Similarly, if a U.S. company wanted to make a capital investment in its manufacturing facility in Manchester, it was under considerable pressure from U.S. authorities (finally legalized) to finance the investment with funds borrowed outside the United States even if that should mean (as it did until the late 1970s) that the cost of financing would be greater than what was available to the company domestically.

Parallel Loans

To accommodate the requirements of both parties mentioned here, the *back-to-back* or *parallel loan* was devised. The U.S. firm would lend an agreed amount of dollars to a U.S. affiliate of the British pension fund, and in a separate but parallel transaction, the U.K. pension fund would lend the same amount in sterling to a U.K. affiliate of the American company. Two loan agreements were required, both containing substantially the same terms and conditions, often including provisions for "topping up," or reducing the amount of one loan as an offset to the changed market value of the other. The loans did provide substantial value to each party, but the cost of arranging and executing them consumed a large portion of this value, especially when the principal amounts were small, which was often the case. Credit considerations were complex, even though the loans provided for a mutual offset in the case of default, and agreement on interest rates was often difficult to achieve when the maturities involved exceeded the one- to two-year periods for which forward foreign exchange rates could reliably be obtained.

Banks were often asked to stand in the middle, to ease questions of counterpart credit exposure, though such arrangements added further to the cost of the transactions. Accountants ruled that because of the offsetting provisions, the loans would not have to be included on the face of the companies' financial statements, which provided an advantage that direct borrowing from a foreign bank would not. After a time, much of the process was made easier by the familiarity of the participants and the standardization of some of the procedures, but the overall volume of parallel loans was very modest by current standards.

TYPES OF SWAPS

After the collapse of the Bretton Woods fixed exchange rate system and the adoption of floating exchange rates, controls governing the international transfer of funds became obsolete and began to be removed. The U.S. regulations were rescinded in 1974, the British government abolished exchange controls in 1979, and other countries followed suit thereafter. Parallel loans were no longer necessary, and immediately went into decline.

Currency Swaps

In August 1981 a significant transaction took place in which IBM and the World Bank agreed to exchange the future liabilities associated with borrowings in the Swiss franc and U.S. dollar bond markets, respectively. IBM is perceived in Switzerland as one of the two or three best "names" from the United States and is able to borrow Swiss francs in the Swiss market on extremely favorable terms, compared to all other foreign borrowers (i.e., at about the same rate as the Swiss government). The World Bank, having used the Swiss market several times in recent years and being involved with third world loans, was not regarded quite so favorably by the Swiss and, therefore, was required to pay a significantly higher rate than the best U.S. credits— about 20 basis points above the Swiss government rate. On the other hand, the World Bank, like IBM, carried an AAA rating and was well respected as a credit in the U.S. dollar markets because of the backing of the U.S., German, Japanese, and other governments. The World Bank could borrow in the United States at rates only narrowly higher (e.g., 40 basis points) than U.S. treasuries, but IBM would have had to pay a slightly higher rate than this.

So, if each borrowed in the market in which its "comparative advantage" was the greatest (i.e., if IBM borrowed Swiss francs and the World Bank borrowed dollars), both borrowings would be at rates superior to the available alternatives. If they swapped the liabilities each had incurred, then the World Bank could "create" Swiss francs at a bargain rate, saving perhaps 10 basis points on the transaction. Assume the World Bank had been able to borrow at a 5-basis-point advantage over IBM in dollars. If IBM relends its Swiss francs to the World Bank at 10 basis points higher than it incurred, then the World Bank gains a net 10-basis-point advantage over its alternative Swiss franc borrowing cost. IBM gains a net 15-basis-point advantage by combining the World Bank's 5-basis-point advantage in dollars with the 10 basis points that it kept for itself on the Swiss franc financing.

Each party had swapped its funding obligation for a different obligation (see Figure 15–1). The first currency swaps using public bond markets had taken place. Each party, by swapping its own obligation, had changed its liabilities into something quite different. The World

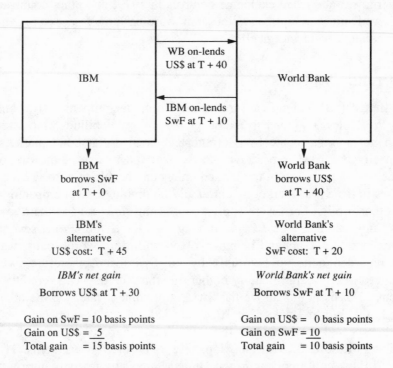

SwF basis points do not exactly equate to US$ basis points on a one-on-one basis.

Figure 15–1. The First Currency Swap, August 1981.

Bank had created a "synthetic" Swiss franc security for itself that had all of the properties of the real thing, and IBM had done the same in dollars. After these transactions, the activity in currency swaps began to increase rapidly.

Another stimulus to currency swaps, once the financial intermediary community became attuned to them, was caused by local market borrowing restrictions and withholding taxes. For example, in 1985 swaps involving the New Zealand dollar were common. The currency carried a high nominal interest rate and was strengthening against the U.S. dollar. Overseas investors that might wish to invest in New Zealand dollar bonds, however, encountered a 15 percent withholding tax. So it was arranged that U.S. and other corporations would issue Euro-New Zealand dollar bonds, at interest rates considerably below local market rate in New Zealand (but above 85 percent of those rates), and swap the coupons into U.S. dollars at a substantial savings— which was made possible by the New Zealand dollar borrowing rate differential. Similar programs involved the Euro-Australian dollar, the Euro-Canadian dollar, and the Euroyen. After a period of such activity, local government authorities were forced to reconsider the effectiveness of the controls that they have had in place.

In the period preceding the IBM–World Bank currency swap, it was possible to arrange for foreign exchange purchases and sales in the forward markets, although these markets did not always operate beyond one- to two-year maturities. Forward transactions involved contracts requiring that a specified principal amount of a particular currency be bought or sold at some specified time in the future. The value of the principal amount of the contract was discounted to the present at the relevant discount rate to determine its spot market value, but the forward market contracts only dealt with principal amounts. In currency swaps, payments of both principal and interest are required. (In interest rate swaps, no swapping of principal amount is required as the same amount of "notional" principal in the same currency is involved; therefore, the swap needs only to pertain to the payments of interest.)

Interest Rate Swaps

Having observed currency swaps develop, some bankers began to think of ways to apply the same idea to transactions involving short- and long-term dollar borrowings. They were encouraged by the existence of different credit risk premiums in the fixed-rate and floating-rate term debt markets. For example, a weaker credit such as a BBB-rated industrial company would have to pay as much as 70 basis points more than an AAA-rated bank for a five-year bond issue, but it would have to pay only 30 basis points more for a five-year bank loan based on LIBOR. So the BBB company could maximize its comparative advantage by borrowing from its bank and swapping the floating-rate interest payment obligation with, say, a Japanese bank for a stream of fixed-rate interest payments that the Japanese bank has incurred through the issuance of Eurobonds. The Japanese bank would pass on its fixed-rate obligation to the BBB company at, say, its cost of funds plus 50 basis points. The BBB company is now able to create a synthetic five-year fixed-rate borrowing at 20 basis points less than its alternative cost of funds. The Japanese bank assumes the BBB company's floating-rate obligation to pay LIBOR plus 30 basis points, but it reduces this by the 50 basis point spread that it made in the fixed-rate bond swap, resulting in a net cost of funds of LIBOR minus 20 basis points (see Figure 15–2). In this way, an interest rate swap was created. Many more followed, with further modifications and improvements. Documentation became standardized, "user friendly," and transferable. A secondary market in swaps developed. New applications were introduced rapidly as

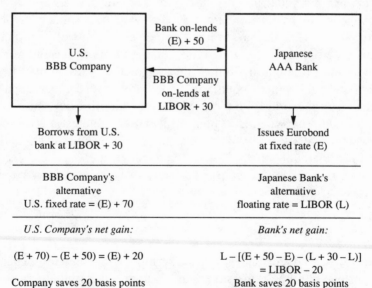

Figure 15–2.   An Early Interest Rate Swap.

volume built up and the number of participants and intermediaries increased sharply.

Two basic types of interest rate swaps have become common since 1981—*coupon swaps* of fixed-rate to floating-rate swaps, such as the previous example, and *basis swaps* in which floating-rate obligations indexed to different reference rates are exchanged. An example of the latter is a swap between a rate indexed to U.S. treasuries and one indexed to LIBOR. Basis swaps include exchange of rate obligations indexed to the same reference but for different maturities (e.g., 30-day LIBOR versus 90-day LIBOR).

Interest rate swaps are accounted for in terms of their *notional* value, or the principal amount that would be swapped if such were required. The notional value of swaps are often counted twice (or more) when volume data are compiled. An end user, such as the BBB company, may wish to initiate a $100 million swap, and a bank or investment bank, acting as an intermediary, may arrange it with a Japanese bank. The intermediary may have to stand in the middle if the Japanese bank is not comfortable with the BBB company's credit. When the swap is complete, the BBB company and the Japanese bank have what they wanted. One swap occurred, but the intermediary will count two, one for each client. If the swap is subsequently sold in the secondary market, it will be counted again, twice. As a result, the number of swaps actually being employed by end users is considerably less than the volume of swaps reported by dealers.

Through the end of 1982, the interest rate swap market had operated in mainly an international context. During 1983, however, a large volume of swaps developed between exclusively domestic U.S. counterparties. Top-quality borrowers, such as Student Loan Marketing Association, would issue fixed-rate securities to swap them into floating-rate obligations to fund its essentially floating-rate loan portfolio at a lower cost.

Then a major new use for interest rate swaps was found in the distressed U.S. savings and loan industry. These organizations had fallen into great difficulty as a result of financing fixed-rate home mortgages from the proceeds of floating-rate deposits. When interest rates soared in the late 1970s, many savings and loan institutions suffered heavy losses. As rates began to decline again in the early 1980s, some savings and loans sold fixed-rate debt securities, collateralized by mortgages, to pay down variable-rate liabilities. Others simply swapped their existing floating-rate obligations into fixed-rate obligations, again offering existing mortgages as collateral.

RISKS OF SWAPS

The principal risk associated with a swap occurs when a counterparty's obligation, which establishes certain economic advantages, has to be replaced, because of counterparty failure, prior to maturity. If the BBB company defaults on its obligation to exchange payments with the Japanese bank, which has funded its commitment with a fixed-rate Eurobond, the Japanese bank finds itself with a sudden reversal of its funding—from LIBOR minus 20 basis points to a fixed rate. If the Japanese bank has used the swap to fund a floating-rate loan to a Japanese client, it no longer has a locked-in spread on the loan over its cost of funding. Instead, it has what might be a substantially different interest rate differential on the loan, plus an unhedged exposure to the future movement of fixed-rates versus LIBOR.

The Japanese bank has some choices to make. It can call the Eurobond (if that is possible), which involves paying a call premium and other expenses, or it can hedge the interest rate exposure that now exists for the remaining life of the Eurobond, also at some expense. It can replace the defaulted swap with another at whatever rates then apply, or it can live with the mismatch. Thus, the simplest measure of the risk to a party engaging in an interest rate swap is the cost of replacing the swap in the market. If interest rates have changed since the original swap, then the replacement cost (i.e., the market value of the swap) will be different. In this respect, a swap's replacement may result in a cost or a profit. If a profit is possible, then it may be realized in the market by selling the swap and replacing it with another one at lower cost.

The replacement cost of an interest rate swap, however, can never come close to its notional value. The risk exposure of swaps, therefore, is small in relation to notional values. According to the International Swap Dealers Association, the writeoffs on the more than $1 trillion worth of swaps outstanding in mid-1988 have so far been less than $35 million.

The replacement cost of a currency swap, even if it does not approach its full notional value, will be different from that of an interest rate swap, because the exchange of principal payments are also involved. How interest rate and currency swaps are to be valued for regulatory purposes is discussed in the following section. It is possible that certain accounting and tax issues (which, if changed, could impose an adverse economic effect upon a swap holder or counterparty) constitute another aspect of risk associated with swaps.

SWAPS AS BRIDGES BETWEEN MARKETS

Swaps are a means of integrating markets that would otherwise remain substantially independent of one another. In the early days of the Eurodollar bond market, substantial differentials existed between its rates and other terms of borrowings and those of the domestic dollar bond market. The European investor base was quite different and greatly influenced by such factors as exchange rates, tax factors, and the need for anonymity. In recent years the Eurodollar and U.S. dollar bond markets have become substantially more integrated. The original distinguishing factors remain important, but investors have less leverage over borrowers now than they had previously because borrowers enjoy greater flexibility. Among these alternatives are interest rate and currency swaps, which permit the creation of synthetic securities in which the interest rate is set in the most favorable market.

Interest rate swaps link short-term and long-term rates, or capital market rates and bank lending rates. When the spreads between the rates available become great enough, they attract enough business to reduce them. In any case, however, the demand for "plain vanilla" interest rate swaps is sufficiently large that market makers in interest rate swaps now quote very narrow bid/asked spreads (e.g., spreads of 5 to 10 basis points for five-year LIBOR swaps against 30-day treasuries).

In the same way, currency swaps link long-term dollar and non-dollar rates. More accurately, perhaps, it could be said that currency swaps link dollar bond market borrowing conditions with those of various nondollar bond markets.

Figure 15–3 is a schematic showing linkages between capital markets that are one result of swaps. The swap market has become very efficient in scouring the world's capital markets on a 24-hour-a-day basis to locate swapping possibilities that provide added values to participants and in quickly communicating these possibilities to clients. Once a transaction is completed, the market is aware of it immediately, and any new aspects of the deal are quickly assimilated. A few more transactions of the same type occur bearing the higher fees or other costs, reflective of the innovation. Then, usually after a relatively short period, the spreads close, the advantages disappear, and the market goes looking for the next opportunity. Such speed and efficiency is made possible by competitive forces, by excellent telecommunications facilities, and by a major increase in the market sensitivities and technical competence of both the bankers and their

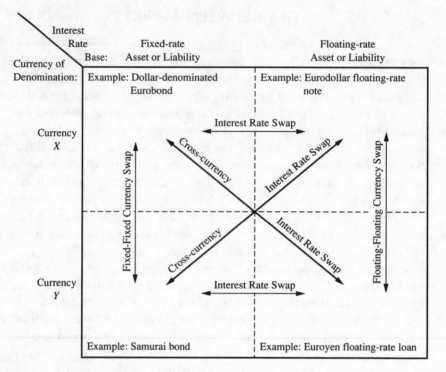

Figure 15–3. Swaps Effect Linkages between Markets.

clients. The more rapidly and efficiently markets work, the more efficient the linkages.

THE USERS OF SWAPS

The widespread availability and simplicity of swaps have attracted a variety of worldwide users who enter into swap contracts for a wide range of reasons. The more active the market, the more innovative it has become. New applications involving swaps appear continuously. The result has been a substantial broadening of the range of opportunities available to both borrowers and investors.

The effect of such an enlarged financial menu has been to globalize the palate of virtually all capital market users. Each borrower preparing a financing must check several different markets to be sure that the optimal course has been selected. Not only must prospective borrowers determine what the rates, terms, and conditions of a transaction would be in their own domestic market, they must also check the comparable opportunities in the Eurobond markets and all of the synthetic possibilities that can offer competitive alternatives. Clearly, the ability to monitor, understand, and execute such a wide variety of different financings requires a substantial upgrading in the financial skills of the borrower's treasury department personnel. It has also required that investment and commercial bankers form global capital market groups, which specialize in watching all the world's markets and in creating opportunities for their clients to consider.

As an example, consider a frequent financer, such as General Electric Capital Corporation (GE), which in the course of a single year will routinely borrow several billions of dollars. The financial staff of GE will daily receive calls and telexes from dozens of bankers suggesting different types of financings. All domestic markets will be covered, together with the Eurobond market, which will often contain a special "bargain," such as an offer to issue warrants to purchase additional debt or equity securities at terms that would value the warrants more highly than they would be in the United States. There would also be opportunities to issue nondollar Eurobonds denominated in yen, or Australian, Canadian, or New Zealand dollars, Swiss francs, each to be swapped back into U.S. dollars for the desired maturity. From this profusion of opportunities, GE must select the choice that serves it best, knowing that during the course of the year it will be doing many additional financings and will want to balance its use of any single market appropriately. GE benefits by spreading its total financing needs across all of the world's capital markets, which ensures that it is achieving the lowest cost of financing possible. However, this requires a financial staff that is the equal of those in the banks and investment banks that serve them. The more competent the staff becomes, the less it needs pure advice and the more it looks for the best among many possible transactions.

As corporate financial staffs become more attuned to global opportunities, they quite naturally become more opportunistic as well. They become aware of the spreads in markets created by differential financing opportunities. If GE can offer warrants in Europe to purchase General Electric shares in the future at a price per warrant that is higher than the price of a comparable warrant in the United States, then there is a high probability that GE could purchase a hedge in the United States, (i.e., purchase calls on General Electric shares at the exercise price per share provided for in the warrant) to cover the issuance of the warranted shares at a lower price than it received for the warrants. If so, GE can pocket the difference or apply it to reducing the overall cost of the financing to which the warrants were attached.

Other companies with high debt ratings but a small requirement for new financing might decide to utilize their "excess" debt capacity to benefit from arbitrage profits. Such a company might issue a fixed-rate dollar Eurobond at an attractive rate relative to its alternative in the United States and swap the issue into a floating-rate obligation carrying a net interest rate of, say, LIBOR minus 25 basis points. The proceeds from the original financing might then be used to purchase a floating-rate obligation from, say a Japanese bank, at LIBOR plus 10 basis points, a resulting spread of 35 basis points. Naturally, companies do not participate in interest rate arbitrage to the point where it might interfere with their own borrowing requirements; however, should an unexpected requirement arise, the swaps can always be reversed—although usually at spreads different from those originally undertaken, which therefore may result in an additional cost to the company. To be as opportunistic as most companies would wish usually involves some participation in financial arbitrage. Not only does it help to reduce overall financing costs of the company from the arbitrage profits, it also keeps the staff actively involved in the markets on a regular basis. This helps them develop their market skills and keeps them continually abreast of optimal financing possibilities for the company.

There are many other uses for swaps in creating alternative financing-investing possibilities (see Figure 15–4). Banks, of course, are themselves very active users of swaps as a means to lower their cost of funds to improve lending profits and manage their funding gaps. Japanese banks, among others, have been very active issuers of their own fixed-rate notes that have been swapped into low-cost floating-rate obligations. They, and most other major international banks, have also been very active in providing swaps to their clients (which usually are written as a direct funding liability of the bank). If the kingdom of Sweden floats a yen-denominated bond issue in Tokyo, it might subsequently decide to escape its exposure to a rising yen by swapping the yen into fixed-rate (or floating-rate) dollars. A Japanese bank may decide to take over the yen obligation as part of its own long-term funding for yen loans, offering dollars that it has secured in the Eurodollar market.

Alternatively, a bank might retain the newly created exposure together with a counterpart swap as part of a portfolio of "matched swaps," which it treats as an off–balance sheet revenue-producing asset. The bank usually will manage such a portfolio actively, buying and selling extant swaps at prices it considers attractive while adding to the portfolio new swaps that it has created. Many banks like to create swaps for their transaction value more than they like to retain them as a portfolio investment. Thus, originating banks are able to

For Investors	**For Borrowers**
Objective: High Yield $ Investment	Objective: Low Cost $ Financing
— Fixed-Rate in U.S. Dollars or Eurodollars	— Fixed-rate in U.S. Dollars or Eurodollars
— Floating Rate $ & Interest Rate Swap – Bank loans – Commercial paper – Floating-rate notes	— Floating rate $ & Interest Rate Swap – Bank loans – Commercial paper – Floating-rate notes
— Fixed-Rate Foreign Currency Borrowing – FCB with Currency Swap – Swiss franc bonds – Yen bonds – U.K. sterling bonds – Deutsche mark bonds	— Fixed-Rate Foreign Currency Borrowing – FCB with Currency Swap – Swiss franc bonds – Yen bonds – U.K. sterling bonds – Deutsche mark bonds

Figure 15–4.   Swaps Create Alternative Financing and Investing Possibilities.

sell swaps to nonoriginators in much the same way as they sell bank loans. Many companies have also found various types of swap transactions to be useful for tax planning purposes.

Finally, managers of large investment portfolios are also swap users. A bond portfolio manager may find it is more advantageous to swap the future payments from a German government Deutsche mark bond for the future payments from a U.S. treasury bond than it is to buy the treasury bond outright. Likewise, the portfolio manager likes the liquidity of a portfolio of money market securities but wants to fix rates before a market change and, therefore, enters into an interest rate swap to do so. Asset managers are less advanced in their use of swaps than liability managers, but many believe they will catch up quickly once they become accustomed to handling the wide range of opportunities that swapping provides.

FORWARD SWAPS AND CAPS

As the market for swap transactions developed, comparable developments were occurring in the comparatively new field of financial futures and options. Financial futures became available in many different currencies and instruments and came to be traded on futures exchanges in London, Singapore, and Tokyo and other locations, in addition to the futures markets in the United States. Through sophisticated usage of financial and foreign exchange futures contracts, new ways of hedging against interest rate and foreign exchange exposures were developed. Ultimately, these resulted in the ability of dealers to sell options on hedged positions, which they carried on their own books.

Soon, markets were being made in option contracts in which purchasers could, in effect, acquire insurance against future risk exposures. The ability to price options that one was selling to others became crucial to the dealer's operation. Whereas the premium could be collected at the outset, the actual result of the contract would not be known for some time, often for several months or even years. If the dealer had misjudged the value of the options sold at the beginning of the year, it might not become apparent until nearly the end of the year, although after a time the development of an active secondary market in various types of options helped. Gradually, the financial market environment became much more sensitive to and aware of sophisticated hedging devices and strategies, many of which were based on the improving understanding in the market of the many uses and values of swaps, futures, and options transactions used in various combinations. Options on swaps are called *swaptions* and hedging programs to fix maximum interest rate levels are called *caps* (see Table 15–2). Some of the more recent swap market innovations are detailed in the following sections.

Forward Swap

This is a swap in which the payment accruals commence at some specified time in the future. It can be used to fix funding costs in the future, (e.g., after the construction phase of a real estate project has been completed). There are many other uses as well, as illustrated by Figures 15–5 and 15–6, which illustrate a forward swap used in conjunction with the issuance of a callable bond to provide the issuer with greater flexibility and a lower overall financing cost.

In this case, a French bank issued 7.5 percent yen bonds in 1984. The bonds, callable in 1989, matured in 1992. Upon issuance of the yen bonds, the French bank entered into a currency swap in which it would receive yen and pay European currency units (ECUs). After

Table 15–2.   Nominal Volume of Swaptions and Caps

	1988 Transactions	Outstanding at Dec. 31, 1988
Swaptions	$ 31 billion	$ 37 billion
Caps, floors & collars	172 billion	290 billion

SOURCE: International Swap Dealers Association.

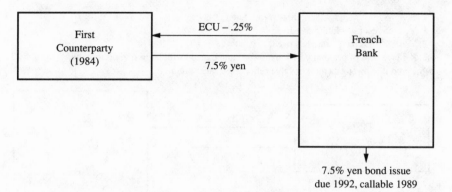

7.5% yen bond issue
due 1992, callable 1989

Forward Swap I Consists of:

1. Fixed-rate yen / Fixed-rate dollar swap
2. Fixed-rate dollars / Floating-rate LIBOR dollar swap
3. Floating-rate LIBOR dollar / ECU swap

Effects of Forward Swap I:

1. Yen in-flow extinguishes yen interest payment on bonds.
2. Favorable yen rate obtained on bonds is swapped for favorable rate on ECU financing.
3. French bank ends with more favorable ECU financing (i.e., ECU .25%) than available to it in ECU market.

Figure 15–5. A Forward Swap Transaction—Part I.

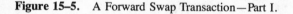

three years, the yen had strengthened substantially against the ECU, and yen interest rates had declined. The value of the yen/ECU swap had appreciated, and the French bank wanted to realize this value in some way. It chose to do so by entering into a second swap, a four-year forward ECU/yen swap that would become effective in 1989, at which time the French bank would call the yen bonds if it did not wish to continue its ECU funding in yen. The original swap, which matures in 1992, would remain outstanding, but it would be reversed after 1989 by the second swap coming into effect. The net result would be a four-year positive cash flow (i.e., 1989 to 1992), or immunity for the French bank, resulting from the differential in the rates required for the second swap as compared to those required for the first one.

Because of advantageous tax and accounting treatments (in the United States and some other countries), forward swaps are the preferred means to hedge interest rate risk for hedge periods exceeding six months.

Caps and Floors

Caps and floors involve the purchase of a series of options on short-term interest rate indexes, which enables purchasers to fix the upper

Three Years Later, 1987:
1. Yen interest rates fall to 5% area.
2. Yen/ECU exchange rate has risen.
3. Replacement of original yen/dollar swap can be made with large savings to bank.
4. Yen/dollar swap has market value reflecting a large premium.

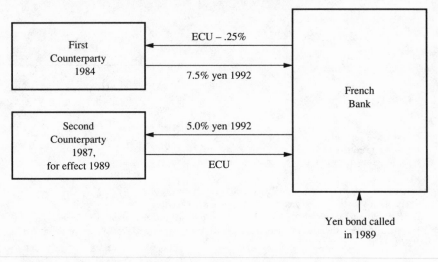

Effects of Forward Swap II:
1. Replaces 7.5% interest on yen bond with 5% interest as of call date in 1989.
2. ECU interest rate received in 1989 is .25% greater than ECU rate paid in Swap I.
3. Savings from yen and ECU payment differentials for the remaining four years of Swap I will be realized.

Figure 15–6.   A Forward Swap Transaction—Part II.

or lower interest rate to which they would be exposed. In combination with other instruments, almost any kind of desired asset or liability exposure to interest rates can be created.

Collars

A combination of a cap and a floor in a single transaction to limit both upside and downside risk is a *collar*.

Callable/Puttable Swaps

Customized swaps can be created by the addition of call or put features. In a callable swap, called a "swaption," which is made up by combining a regular interest rate swap and an option (at some additional cost for the option premium) on a reverse of such a swap, a hedge can be established at the outset of a swap transaction involving, for example, a callable Eurobond issue for which the call feature is deemed to have high value.

Contingent Swap

This is in essence an option on a swap with particular characteristics that could be exercised if, for example, bond purchase warrants attached to a Eurobond issue to lower its cost should be exercised.

In these and similar cases involving combinations of swaps with other instruments, the desired customized package can be purchased from swap dealers who create them by taking counterpart, or "mirrored," positions, on their own books.

Repackaged Securities

There have been recent occasions when a particular issue of floating-rate securities has gone awry in the secondary market, because of credit deterioration or regulatory concerns that have affected the market, and the issue has traded at unusually depressed prices. On such occasions, bankers have stepped forward with the intention to tender for the floating-rate securities and sell them to a newly formed trust. The trust would enter into an interest rate swap with a substantial counterparty, making the trust an obligor of fixed-rate payments, which are backed by assets and cash flow of the trust. The bankers would then sell the fixed-rate obligation of the trust in the bond market. Thus, the swap made it possible to remove the securities from the distressed floating-rate note market and move them into the more healthy fixed-rate bond market.

A MATURE INDUSTRY?

Although swaps only developed into a market as recently as 1981 or so, there are many signs that the rapid growth in the market since that time has quickly resulted in the maturing of the swaps market into a market of considerable infrastructure, with high volume, high levels of competition, low growth, and low profitability. As we have seen, a huge volume in swaps has been created, with a large portion of this volume being in the hands of dealers. An active secondary market has developed that permits swaps to be sold or transferred to others, voluntarily terminated or nullified by entering into reversing transactions. A self-regulatory body, the International Swap Dealers Association, has made many useful contributions in the area of regulatory matters and in the standardization of documentation and transferability for swaps and caps. Spot, futures, and options all exist for swaps. Swaps markets have also become thoroughly globalized, and competition has emerged from banks and other financial institutions from all over the world. Many users of swaps have become devotees, and they have helped to encourage competition among dealers, which in turn has resulted in a lowering of commissions on swaps.

Many observers believe that substantial future growth will occur as more end users from among both asset and liability managers discover the benefits of swaps for interest rate and currency hedging and as new users from other sectors (e.g., real estate, mortgage finance, international government, investment management, and corporate sectors) become involved in the market.

ACCOUNTING AND TAX ISSUES

There are many types of swaps, and the accounting procedures used for these can differ. In general, however, the central accounting issue concerning swaps is that of their disclosure. Both interest rate and currency swaps do not have to be disclosed in financial statements in the United States and other countries unless individually or together they are considered to be material to the financial position of the company as a whole, in which case they must be described in the footnotes to the financial statements. At present, most accountants in the United States do not consider swap exposures (i.e., their market value or replacement cost) to be material. So for financial reporting purposes, swaps are considered off–balance sheet items in most cases. More supplementary information may be required in the future. In July 1989 the U.S. Financial Accounting Standards Board issued an exposure draft calling for additonal disclosures for swaps of information concerning credit exposure, market risks, and liquidity of the instruments among other matters.

For income statement purposes, swap payments typically are reported as adjustments to interest expense, with gains, losses, or lump sum payments being amortized over the life of the original transaction.

For tax purposes, swap payments are treated in most countries as ordinary income or expense, with gains, losses, and lump sum payments being taken as adjustments to income in the period incurred.

REGULATORY ISSUES INVOLVING SWAPS

For many years central banking authorities have exchanged information on bank capital requirements and supervisory matters. By the early 1980s, following a decade of rapid expansion of banking assets and off–balance sheet exposures, it became clear to these authorities that bank capital ratios were being eroded all around the world. A committee of bank supervisors was formed under the auspices of the Bank for International Settlements (BIS) involving representatives of the 12 leading banking nations (the Group of Ten countries plus Switzerland and Luxembourg) to look into the question of bank capital adequacy. The committee, formally known as the Basel Committee on Banking Regulations and Supervisory Practices. In December 1987 the BIS published the work of the committee as a consultative paper entitled "Proposals for International Convergence of Capital Measurement and Capital Standards." A precursor of the BIS paper was an accord on bank capital requirements reached by the U.S. Federal Reserve Board and the Bank of England in March 1987. The BIS proposals, which reflected a number of modifications to the U.S.-U.K. accord, were to be discussed by banking authorities for six months and then, subject to further amendment, adopted by all participating countries in June 1988 for implementation over a phase-in period of five years.

As discussed more fully in Chapter 23, the Basel proposals were aimed at "strengthening the stability of the international banking system and removing a source of competitive inequality for banks arising from differences in supervisory arrangements among countries." One element of the Basel proposals concerned a weighting system for relating capital to banking risks, including off–balance sheet exposures.

The latter would include procedures for calculating the "credit equivalent amounts" of interest rate and currency swaps as well as certain forward market transactions.

The credit equivalent amounts, as finally adopted by the committee and against which capital must be reserved, are to be calculated by adding together the current exposure of a contract and the potential future exposure. The Basel proposals did not reach a final consensus on valuing the current exposure of swaps, but it was agreed that bank regulators could use discretion, relying on either the marked-to-market or replacement cost method in doing so. In calculating the marked-to-market exposure of a swap contract, only positive exposure counts — that is, if the swap is "in the money" (i.e., in the current market, the swap has a positive value), it cannot be used to offset current exposure of "out of the money" swaps (i.e., in the current market, the swap has a negative value). Potential future exposure is determined by multiplying the notional value of the contract by a risk factor as follows:

Remaining Maturity	Interest Rate Swap Contracts	Currency Swap Contracts
Less than 1 year	-0-	1.0%
1 year and over	0.5%	5.0%

The difference in the risk factors reflects maturities and the structural differences between interest rate and currency swaps, the latter involving principal payments and cross-currency foreign exchange exposure.

In January 1988 the Federal Reserve Board issued for comment a joint interagency proposal (revised and adopted in March 1988) for implementing the Basel proposals in the United States. The method for calculating the credit equivalent exposure of swaps was set forth as described in Table 15–3.

Table 15–3. Examples of Capital Requirements against Swap Expenses

1. A three year, fixed/floating interest rate swap with a notional principal of $10,000,000 and current market value of $200,000

> Potential Exposure = .015 × $10,000,000 = $150,000
> +
> Current Exposure = $200,000
> ───
> Credit Equivalent Exposure = $350,000

2. A three-year, fixed/floating interest rate swap with a notional principal of $10,000,000 and current market value of − $250,000.

> Potential Exposure = .015 × $10,000,000 = $150,000
> +
> Current Exposure   =   − $250,000
> ───
> Credit Equivalent Exposure =   0

3. A 120-day forward foreign exchange position with a notional principal of $5,000,000 and a current replacement cost of $100,000.

> Potential Exposure = .01 × $5,000,000 = $50,000
> +
> Replacement Cost = $100,000 $100,000
> ───
> Credit Equivalent Exposure = $150,000

4. A seven-year cross-currency floating/floating interest rate swap with a notional principal of $20,000,000 and a current replacement cost of − $1,300,000.

> Potential Exposure = .05 × $20,000,000 = $1,000,000
> +
> Replacement Cost   = − $1,300,000   0
> ───
> Credit Equivalent Exposure = $1,000,000

SOURCE: Board of Governors, Federal Reserve System.

The Federal Reserve's proposals only apply to U.S. banks and bank holding companies. Neither they nor the Basel proposals as yet apply to nonbank financial institutions (e.g., investment banks, insurance companies, or financial or commercial corporations) in the United States or in other countries.

The net effect of the capital standards is to increase the amount of capital that banks must have to maintain their swap portfolios. Some observers note that the measures will not fall evenly on the banks— that German, French, and Japanese banks may have to reserve greater amounts of capital to maintain their portfolios than others would. Nonbank participants also have a substantial advantage over banks in being able to carry swaps without capital reserves, although it may only be a matter of time before securities regulatory authorities are required to impose the same rules. Table 15–4 is an extract from the 1988 financial statements of J. P. Morgan, Inc., which illustrates the effect of these reporting requirements on a U.S. bank.

COMPETING IN SWAPS AND SYNTHETICS

There are many different competitors in the market for swaps and synthetic securities. These include banks, investment banks, finance companies, and insurance companies from the United States, the United Kingdom, continental Europe, and Japan. Essentially there are two groups of competitors: swap arrangers (or brokers) and swap providers. Swap arrangers act as agents for clients. Swap providers act as principals, taking the swap onto their own books, at least temporarily.

In the early days of the market, investment bankers tended to act as agents, and commercial banks acted as principals. Competitive pressure, however, quickly drove a number of investment banks to "position" swaps that they were trying to arrange in order to complete a particular, fast-moving deal. Thus, if First Boston was trying to arrange for a seven-year interest rate swap for Alcoa, it might decide to wrap up the business by taking the First Boston exposure on its own books (together with an interest rate hedge), with the intention of selling it or matching it with another swap later on. In time, First Boston might sell the package of (a) Alcoa's obligation to First Boston, and (b) its obligation to Alcoa (together called a "matched swap") to another bank or party acting as principal. Or First Boston might repackage the swap by selling one obligation, with or without a match, and keeping the other for its own portfolio to be matched with another obligation more advantageously.

Table 15–4.   A Financial Statement Accounts for Swaps

The total combined risk-adjusted assets and off–balance sheet exposures of J. P. Morgan & Co., Incorporated at December 31, 1988, excluding the assets and off–balance sheet exposures of J. P. Morgan Securities Inc., were approximately $61.9 billion as follows:

Dollars in millions	Contract Amount	Credit Conversion Factor	Credit Equivalent Amount	Risk Weight	Risk-Adjusted Balance
A. Total risk-adjusted assets, per previous table:					$38,760
B. Commitments and contingencies: Financial Guarantees and standby letters of credit	$ 3,793	100%	$ 3,793	20–100%	2,417
Nonfinancial guarantees	4,827	50%	2,414	100%	2,414
Other letters of credit	135	20%	27	20–100%	17
Commitments to purchase: securities, assets sold with recourse, and securities lending indemnifications	5,571	50–100%	5,296	0–100%	1,832
Commitments to extend credit:					
One year or less	1,424	0%	—	0%	—
Over one year	26,385	50%	13,193	20–100%	$12,546

	Contract or Notional Amount	Current Exposure	Potential Exposure	Credit Equivalent Amount	Risk Weight	Risk-Adjusted Balance
C. Foreign currency contracts: *(including currency swaps)*	$156,642	$7,142	$3,230	10,372	0–50%	$3,273
D. Interest rate: *contracts (including interest rate swaps)*	109,936	1,578	319	1,897	0–50%	601
Total risk-adjusted assets and off–balance sheet exposures						61,860

By skillful management of its matched book of swaps, First Boston could earn revenues, could stay on top of the market in swaps so as to compete more vigorously, and could offer its clients swaps as principal so as to minimize the risk of the business being done with another party. Disadvantages include substantial administrative costs associated with keeping track of all the swaps passing through First Boston's hands, and risks associated with swap counterparty failure and the possibility of swaps requiring an allocation of regulatory capital in the future.

Many of the major U.S. investment banks operate in the swaps business as principals, and virtually all of the international commercial banks do so as well.

For those acting only as agents, it can be more difficult to be competitive. Each transaction is essentially two transactions, both of which are open to competitive offers until the deal is agreed to. Such agents must be very skillful at knowing who the takers of particular swaps are at a given moment, and they often must rely on a few principals with limited origination capability to "bank" deals for them. On the other hand, agents do not spend time fine tuning portfolios or quoting rates to the market. They tend to look for deals in which the swap is part of a package of several transactions that is offered to a client as a whole, such as an issue of Swiss franc bonds, a Swiss franc to U.S. dollar fixed-rate swap, and a fixed-rate to floating-rate swap to yield a sub-LIBOR financing that can be reinvested to capture an arbitrage profit. One or more of the swaps in such a transaction might have to be acquired in the wholesale, interdealer swap market, but even if this is so, the overall profit on the transaction should still be attractive. Also, some agents feel that granting positioning authority to their swaps departments may result in a strong temptation to become the lowest-rate bidder in competitive situations, which may build up market share but in the long run could be adverse to profits.

Both types of participants recognize that to be effective competitors, firms must enlarge upon the linkages that exist between the swaps desk and other financing departments of the firm. The global capital markets department is in daily contact with a large number of potential bond issuers. The fixed income department is in daily contact with a large number of asset managers. The type of transaction to be selected by such issuers or investors may involve one or more swaps. To quote a deal to the client requires hands-on attention of the swaps desk and a very short response time.

Swaps in many ways have become commodities applicable to transactions involving corporate finance, mortgage and real estate finance, project finance, asset management, foreign exchange, and virtually all other areas of a firm's business that involve the assembling of sophisticated financial packages. Maximizing the value of these interdepartmental linkages provides a substantial competitive capacity and broadens the scope of transactions for which swaps are or could become applicable.

Finally, swap market participants will have to adjust to the new capital requirements for swaps resulting from the Basel proposals and whatever competitive imbalances result from them. Competitors, on the whole, may wish to discontinue booking swaps for a while; thus, market liquidity may suffer temporarily. In time, larger fees or trading spreads will reflect the capital requirements. There may also be a reshuffling of swaps on to the more formidable balance sheets (including those of the larger nonbanking financial institutions such as General Electric or Prudential Insurance, both of which are active in the swap market), which may be able to charge a premium for carrying them.

The swap markets are still in an early stage of development. More end users are attracted to the market every year. More intermediaries are learning how to use swaps to help them provide more efficient services to their clients. The market will continue to welcome new ideas and further applications for swaps. As in virtually all financial services today, competition is extensive and favors those who are able to create value for their clients, to manage their own exposures efficiently, and to keep abreast of and contribute to the fast-moving technology of the market.

SUMMARY

Unknown before 1980, swaps and their family of related transactions have become a large and important part of the global financial landscape today. They are useful to issuers of securities and to investors. They enable participants to bridge (and thus aid in integrating) financial markets across maturities, currencies, and forms of payment. Through swaps, a multitude of derivitive products and synthetic securities can be created. Swaps are comparatively cheap, quick to arrange, involve standardized and simple documentation, and expose their participants only to modest risk levels in relation to the nominal amounts involved, which nonetheless must now be accounted for by banks under the current capital adequacy rules.

SELECTED REFERENCES

Antl, Boris, ed. *Euromoney Swap Finance*. London: Euromoney Publications, 1986.

Bank for International Settlements. *Innovations in International Finance*. Basel, Switzerland: BIS, 1987.

Bank for International Settlements. "Proposals for International Convergence of Capital Measurement and Capital Standards." 1987.

McDougall, Rosamund. "Switch or Shrink." *The Banker*, March 1988.

Pitman, Joanne. "Swooping On Swaps." *Euromoney*, January 1988.

Platt, Gordon. "Swap Dealers Adopt Standard Document for Rate Cap Market," *The Journal of Commerce*, March 6, 1989.

Stillit, Daniel. "Swap Finance." *Euromoney Corporate Finance*, August 1987.

16

International Equity Securities

International transactions in equity securities have expanded enormously, as reflected in the substantial increase in cross-border transactions in secondary markets and by new issues offered to investors under one of several different "globalized" distribution techniques. This market phenomenon is the result of the convergence of many factors, which has led toward the integration of capital markets around the world—factors such as the opening up of national markets through various deregulatory processes, the substantial improvements in financial information gathering and dissemination technology, and the growing involvement of major financial institutions as investors and as providers of services to the markets.

International equity transactions include issuing, purchasing, and selling equities to investors in markets outside the issuer's domestic market. To the extent that these activities require multiple listings on stock exchanges in different parts of the world, international equity transactions face administrative and regulatory difficulties greater than Eurobonds. As rapidly as the volume in international equity transactions has grown, only modest progress has been realized in terms of the integration of the different stock markets of the world. Considerable differences continue to exist in the methods the markets use to value shares and in the area of commissions, trading practices, new-issue regulation, and settlement procedures. For many of these, a long time will be required before (or if) common ground can be reached. In other cases, some movement toward an international standard is clearly in evidence. Precedents occurring in one market will be observed by others and emulated as appropriate. The abolition of fixed commission rates by the New York Stock Exchange in May 1975 ("Mayday") generated a number of changes in equity markets not only in New York, but in London, Toronto, Zurich, Tokyo, and Sydney as well. In less than a decade many of the principles established by the actions of Mayday were adopted in these other markets.

There are three types of international equity transactions: (1) those in which investors and issuers (e.g., from the United States) tap equity market resources in other countries to enhance the market liquidity that is available domestically; (2) those in which international markets are used (e.g., by Europeans) because the domestic market is insufficient to meet the requirements of domestic participants; and (3) those in which the international markets are employed (e.g., by Japanese) as a way to avoid domestic market restrictions and entanglements. As in the case of the Eurobond market, the lack of regulation and the presence of a large, highly diversified, and very liquid pool of international investment funds has caused equity markets to evolve and develop internationally in such a way as to provide something for everyone.

This process has begun, but it is a long way from being finished. Much of what is now happening in international equity markets was just invented. Not all of it will survive future innovations. Almost everything that is happening, however, contributes to a foundation for a more highly integrated international market in the future. For these reasons, this is a uniquely instructive time to observe how a new market operating in a free international environment is formed— or perhaps how it forms itself.

Unlike the Eurobond market, which (notwithstanding London or Luxembourg stock exchange listings) can be said to be extranational (i.e., having an existence separate from specific countries), the international equity market is more multinational. New issues are simultaneously offered in specific national markets in different parts of the world. Thus, the international equities market is not a clone of the Eurobond market (though on occasion it travels down the same path), but it has proven to be equally resourceful in adapting itself to new and varied requirements of its principal users.

As in the case of the Eurobond market, this free market adaptation is watched by domestic regulators and, as a result, is likely to play back into national markets some of its more successful experiences. For example, discussions have been underway between the securities regulatory authorities of the United States, the United Kingdom, and Canada regarding common new issue prospectus requirements. Undoubtedly, future discussion will help to standardize new issues requirements for other countries (e.g., shareholder voting entitlements and various trading regulations and procedures, including rules preventing insider trading).

EVOLUTION OF THE INTERNATIONAL EQUITY MARKETS

Participation in international equity investments is a comparatively new development for U.S. and Japanese investors, but it is not for Europeans. For many years the most international of all investors were the Swiss banks, who managed money on behalf of their many overseas customers. There was very little to invest in in Switzerland, so they were always looking for suitable investment opportunities abroad. During the 1960s and 1970s Swiss banks were the principal foreign investors in U.S. stocks. Subsequently, they became substantial investors in Japanese stocks as well. Similar to the Swiss banks, which for many years had attracted foreign "safekeeping" funds, were banks and investment companies in Holland, Belgium, and Luxembourg—countries where few good investment opportunities existed.

The British have also had a long history of overseas portfolio investment. Up until 1979, however, Britain had been subject to foreign exchange controls that required that a premium be paid for foreign currency to be used for investment outside the country. Most other countries in Europe have had similar foreign exchange regulations, though most have now been abolished. Once the foreign exchange controls were lifted in the United Kingdom, a substantial increase in overseas investment, mostly into the United States and Japan, took place. Institutional investors in the United Kingdom have greatly increased their activities abroad and now hold and trade substantial volumes of international securities of all types. More recently, U.S. and Japanese institutional investors also entered into active programs for investing in international equities. As a result, the international pool of funds participating in equities has greatly increased.

Over the years, U.S. investment managers have been forced by competitive pressures to improve investment performance. To do this, many felt it was important to diversify holdings into stocks in other markets where not only the market performance would be counted but also foreign exchange gains or losses would too. As more and more foreign opportunities were presented to U.S. investors, they learned more about investing abroad and began in the early 1980s to do so extensively.

Until the 1980s Japanese institutional investors were subject to foreign exchange controls that limited their investment abroad. Therefore, they had not learned much about foreign markets, nor were they familiar with particular stocks and how these were valued. After the controls were eased, Japanese foreign portfolio investors mainly concentrated their activities in the bond markets, principally buying U.S. treasuries.

By 1986, however, when foreign exchange losses were eating into the returns that Japanese investors were earning on dollar-denominated bond investments, they began to shift to the equity markets. They were attracted to foreign equities by the prospect of larger capital gains and because of their low valuation and high yields compared to Japanese equities, which had risen to exceptional price levels.

Among new participants in international equities markets over the years have been pension funds, many of which have continued to enjoy a substantial inflow of funds each year and thus find their overall investment funds growing rapidly. Not only have total pension assets grown, but there has also been a substantial increase in the percentage of total assets invested in foreign securities. This has been true for pension funds in countries all over the world, as Table 16–1 illustrates.

Japanese pension funds have been growing very rapidly as the country adjusts to demographic problems of an aging population that has not had sufficient pension plans in the past. Pension assets in Japan have grown by more than 20 percent per year since 1980.[1] An increasing amount of this money, which is managed by insurance companies and trust banks, is invested in international equities. Japanese investors, who purchased only about $1 billion of U.S. equities in 1980, were expected to acquire more than $20 billion in 1987. However, the market crash of October 19, 1987 not only slowed their

Table 16–1. Foreign Investment as a Percentage of Total Pension Fund Assets

	1986[a]	1990[a]
United States	4%	8%
Canada	9	10
Japan	10	10
West Germany	4	10
France	2	4
United Kingdom	20	25
Netherlands	10	10
Australia	15	15
Switzerland	5	15

a. Estimate

SOURCE: InterSec Research Corporation and Salomon Brothers Inc.

purchases considerably, but also resulted in substantial net sales during the fourth quarter of 1987. This resulted in purchases for the full year of only $12 billion. Purchases resumed in 1988.

U.S. pension funds have also become very active as international investors as their exposure to foreign shares increased from about $22.5 billion at the end of 1985 to about $41.5 billion by the end of 1987. These investments were made while U.S. private pension funds were net sellers of U.S. equities, having sold (net of purchases) more than $47 billion from 1985 to 1987.[2]

Corporations have also become involved in equity markets in the United States and Japan—in the United States through mergers and acquisitions and corporate repurchase of shares, and in Japan by increasing intercorporate investments in shares of customers and suppliers and by special investment trusts. The corporate involvement has contributed greatly to the upward price movements in both markets, thus perhaps helping to attract further foreign investment.

Advances in information and communications technology have been essential to the growth in the international equities markets. Market information of all types is now available internationally, through newspapers, screens, and contact with brokers. Securities can also be traded internationally with a high degree of reliance on a trouble-free delivery, which had not always been the case. The computerization of the international marketplace has made possible a level of expansion that probably could not otherwise have occurred. With this has come a large increase in the number of trained professionals who provide the many services needed to sustain a growing market—that is, investment research information, trading and positioning capabilities, hedging, operations, and settlement facilities.

During the period of this great expansion of the international equities market, investment conditions have been extremely favorable. Stock markets in virtually all countries powered their way to all-time highs. These market rises, sustained for several years and touching so many separate markets, led to an unusually high level of enthusiasm for equity investments, including those abroad, until it was sharply curtailed by the worldwide market collapse in October 1987. By the end of the 1989 most markets, the Japanese in particular, had recovered their earlier losses, and international activity was revived. With the market support infrastructure in place, the free access to world markets intact, and the mentality of investment managers to look abroad for better performance opportunities still in force, it is unlikely that even fairly sharp price reversals will deter the growing participation in international equities for long. Indeed, many investors realized several months after the collapse in Oct. 1987 that the performance of funds that had remained invested in various international markets was superior to the performance of funds that repatriated foreign investments at the time, as many did.

Furthermore, the bull markets and the exposure to international opportunities has caused U.S. money managers to recognize that the U.S. market represents less than 30 percent of the world's total market capitalization of exchange-listed shares today and that a great many previously unknown investment opportunities are available (see Figure 16–1).

One should note, however, that in the United States, unlike almost all other countries, a substantial over-the-counter equity securities market exists that accounts for approximately 40 percent of all share

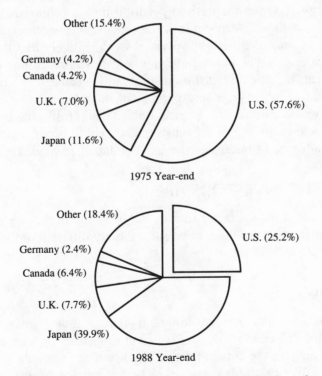

Figure 16–1. World Share of Market Capitalization of Exchange-Listed Shares (Source: Goldman, Sachs & Co., FT–Acuaries World Indicies; used by permission).

trades and virtually all trades in convertible securities. The market capitalization of over-the-counter stocks is not included in the world comparative data for exchange-listed companies that appears in this chapter.

Foreign equity investment is a two-way street for most countries. In the United States net foreign portfolio investment in U.S. equities increased to approximately $175 billion at the end of 1987, at a time when net U.S. investment in non-U.S. equities increased to approximately $60 billion.[3] In the United Kingdom, both foreign investment in U.K. stocks and U.K. investments in foreign stocks are also rising. In Japan high levels of foreign investment were subject to some profit taking during 1986 and 1987, but Japanese investment in overseas equities is rising rapidly.

Throughout the world institutional investors are adjusting their portfolios, sometimes for the first time, to achieve the mix between domestic and international equities that they will be comfortable with for the future. When the desired portfolio mix is achieved, notwithstanding year-to-year adjustments, the volume of international equity transactions may stabilize; however, it is more likely that the result will be a high level of trading in international portfolios (typical of performance-oriented institutional money management practices elsewhere). If so, a large and permanent international trading environment would come into existence. Such a market, like the Eurobond market, is to the world of debt instruments, could become equivalent in size and style of trading to the U.S. or Japanese market.

WHO THE INVESTORS ARE

A brief look at the characteristics of the investors in the international equities market shows them to be substantially different in the United States, Europe, and Japan.

U.S. Investors

Institutional investors account for about 40 percent of share ownership in the United States but about 70 percent of share trading, over 50 percent being in the form of large block trades. Accordingly, they are very active portfolio managers. The business of managing funds for others is extremely competitive and performance oriented in the United States, more so than anywhere else in the world. As a result, many investment managers have developed specialties. Some have specialized in investing in foreign stocks, though as a group there are probably not more than 20 to 25 such managers who have been active overseas investors for more than the last 10 years. In recent years, however, most major investors have realized that higher net returns have been available in many overseas market than were available in the United States, and, as a result, they have quickly turned themselves into international investors. (See Table 16–2 for a comparison of price performance returns on stocks from different countries and regions from 1982 to 1988). Today, approximately 200 U.S. institutional investors could be classified as active international equity investors. This number should increase as public funds and others as yet uncommitted to international investment become involved.

Many U.S. institutional investors have opened offices or set up subsidiaries abroad to manage their foreign investments more closely. These investors operate out of London, Geneva, Zurich, Tokyo, and other cities to combine local research coverage with good market sensitivity and execution. Other investors manage overseas investments from their U.S. offices, combining occasional visits abroad with research provided by U.S. brokers and foreign brokers covering them at home. Still others have engaged overseas investment managers (frequently those from the United Kingdom) to manage a portion of their funds to be invested abroad. In covering U.S. investors in international equities, brokers must be somewhat ubiquitous, covering the head office, the various field offices, analysts as well as portfolio managers, and sometimes covering the foreign firm that is managing the U.S. investor's funds.

U.S. institutions have long encouraged competition and better service among brokers. They have brought this with them as they have expanded their activity in international markets. They negotiate hard for lower commissions in markets where they can, or they trade on a negotiated-rate basis off the market in markets where they cannot obtain lower commissions. In Japan, for example, a U.S. institution might trade over the counter in London in order to avoid payment of Japanese commissions. Such actions add to pressure on the local exchanges to fully deregulate commission rates.

U.S. institititutions also seek international brokers who will service their requirements for block trades. As block trading in international securities increases, the U.S. institutions become role models for institutional investors in other countries, who in turn are served by the international brokers that have been "trained" by doing business with the U.S. institutions. Indeed, the heightened propensity to trade

Table 16–2. Ranked Price Performance by Currency, Compound Growth Rate, 1982–1988

Country	US$	Local Currency	£	Yen	DM	Relative to World	World except Japan
Mexico	47.1%	131.1%	44.6%	31.1%	39.3%	21.3%	29.4%
Japan	40.5	26.6	38.1	25.3	33.1	15.9	23.6
Spain	32.0	30.1	29.8	17.7	25.0	8.8	16.1
Ireland	29.4	27.9	27.2	15.4	22.6	6.7	13.8
France	29.3	27.1	27.1	15.3	22.4	6.6	13.7
Italy	29.3	28.4	27.1	15.2	22.4	6.6	13.7
Belgium	28.6	23.7	26.4	14.6	21.7	6.0	13.1
Sweden	23.2	19.6	21.1	9.8	16.6	1.6	8.3
Norway	22.8	21.4	20.7	9.4	16.3	1.2	8.0
Denmark	22.1	18.1	20.0	8.8	15.6	0.6	7.4
Netherlands	21.8	16.4	19.7	8.5	15.3	0.4	7.1
Austria	20.5	14.8	18.5	7.4	14.1	-0.6	6.0
Hong Kong	20.1	23.9	18.1	7.0	13.7	-1.0	5.6
West Germany	19.8	14.2	17.8	6.8	13.5	-1.2	5.4
Australia	18.7	21.5	16.7	5.8	12.4	-2.1	4.4
United Kingdom	17.5	15.4	15.5	4.8	11.3	-3.1	3.4
New Zealand	16.3	19.3	14.3	3.6	10.1	-4.1	2.3
Switzerland	12.5	7.3	10.6	0.2	6.5	-7.3	-1.1

United States	11.3	11.3	9.4	-0.8	5.4	-8.2	-2.1
Canada	10.1	9.6	8.3	-1.8	4.3	-9.2	-3.1
Singapore	7.3	5.9	5.5	-4.4	1.6	-11.6	-5.6
Malaysia	2.3	5.1	0.6	-8.8	-3.1	-15.6	-10.0
South Africa	-3.3	15.4	-4.9	-13.8	-8.4	-20.3	-14.9
Europe	20.6	17.5	18.5	7.5	14.2	-0.6	6.0
Pacific Basin	38.1	26.1	35.8	23.1	30.8	13.9	21.5
Europe & Pacific	31.3	23.2	29.0	17.0	24.3	8.2	15.5
North America	11.2	11.2	9.3	-0.9	5.3	-8.3	-2.2
Europe except United Kingdom	23.2	18.9	21.1	9.8	16.7	1.6	8.4
Pacific except Japan	15.9	17.9	14.0	3.3	9.8	-4.4	2.0
World except United States	29.3	22.4	27.1	15.3	22.5	6.6	13.8
World except United Kingdom	21.6	17.5	19.6	8.4	15.2	0.3	7.0
World except South Africa	21.6	17.4	19.5	8.4	15.1	0.2	6.9
Japan	13.7	13.0	11.8	1.3	7.7	-6.3	0.0
World	21.3	17.4	19.2	8.1	14.8	0.0	6.7

SOURCE: Goldman, Sachs & Co, *Anatomy of World Markets*, October 1989.

more actively, and to force brokers to compete more actively for business, is clearly visible among U.K. institutional investors following London's Big Bang and in all the other countries in which substantial deregulation of securities markets and trading practices have occurred.

The activity of the U.S. investors in foreign markets has drawn many U.S. brokers into the business. The international research, trading, and sales specialists now employed by U.S. brokers serving the U.S. institutional investor community have grown significantly, both in numbers and in quality. Of course, the brokers do not confine their marketing of investment services for the U.K. market, for example, to U.S. investors. They also offer them to U.K. investors and those in other parts of the world. As the number of stocks covered in research increases and the number for which international trading markets are made increases, so does the penetration of the worldwide investor community by the U.S. investment firms (and others) providing the best-quality services. Gradually such competitive penetration will raise the standards of investment services available to all investors, and this can be expected to further raise trading and competitive activity.

U.S. institutional participation has done more than add to the funds flows for international equities. It has also contributed significantly to the increasing trading activity in equity securities by helping to bring more efficient U.S. practices to major investors in other countries.

European Investors

Figures are not available to tell us what percentage of the shares of European companies are owned by institutional investors, but one could guess that it would probably be over 50 percent. Individual share ownership is comparatively small in most European countries, where large banks, insurance companies, and investment trusts are the principal investors. These investors, however, have not been very active as traders, nor have they had especially active equity markets to trade in until very recent years. Several events during the 1980s changed the situation. First, privatization programs, begun in Britain in 1981 but soon adopted by most of the other countries, resulted by the end of the decade in nearly $100 billion of new equity securities being placed on the market in Europe. Second, deregulation of stock market rules, commissions, and competitive structures occurred throughout the continent, again following the British. Third, the general air of investor confidence inherent in the bull market of the 1980s permeated markets in Europe and increased both local and foreign investor demand for shares. Despite the market setbacks in October 1987 and again in October 1989, several successful privatization and other new issues were completed in Europe. Many more are planned for the next few years.

As a result of the these developments, the European role in world market trading activity has grown considerably during the past few years. Indeed, in 1988 Europe as a whole accounted for about as much of world trading volume of exchange-listed shares as the United States did (see Table 16–3). An active market in new issues in Europe during 1989 (which saw further privatizations in new issues in the United Kingdom, Spain, and Holland and a $900 million issue for Euro Disneyland) contrasted with the U.S. new issue market, which was substantially below levels reached during the preceding three years.

European equity investors, as in the case of investors in Eurobonds, can be divided into retail and institutional categories, with the retail group being mainly those individuals who invest through large continental banks. These banks, through their many branches, collect orders for brokerage transactions and for funds to be managed on a discretionary basis. Banks retain a large number of employed portfolio managers for this purpose. These will be supported by the bank's own research viewpoint and central guidance. Execution of orders

Table 16–3. Proportion of 1988 World Trading Volume of Exchange Listed Shares by Region

Region/Country		1982	1984	1986	1988
Japan		16.0%	21.1%	30.0%	41.7%
USA		62.2	56.2	43.2	25.4
Europe		18.2	19.0	22.9	23.4
of which,	U.K.	7.1	7.3	8.4	8.9
	Germany	1.8	2.6	4.8	6.5
	Switzerland	6.0	4.9	4.0	3.6
	France	1.0	1.0	1.1	1.4
	Italy	0.3	0.3	1.4	0.6
	Holland	1.1	1.9	1.9	1.2
	Spain	0.1	0.1	0.4	0.4
	Other	0.8	0.9	0.9	0.8

SOURCE: Goldman, Sachs & Co., *Anatomy of World Markets*, October 1989.

is often done by each branch, but it can also be centralized. Retail investors are especially sensitive to currency movements and to name recognition.

Institutional investors (e.g., investment managers, insurance companies, pension funds, and banks) subscribe to local practices when investing in their own countries, but when investing internationally they tend to behave similarly to U.S. institutional investors. These investors have shown a preference for U.S. and Japanese stocks over the years, though they have also become active participants in the large new issues of European corporations that have come to market.

Japanese Investors

In Japan approximately 70 percent of shares are owned by Japanese corporations or institutional investors, and 5 percent are owned by foreign institutional investors. Share ownership by individual investors has declined over the past decade, partly because individuals are disinvesting from the market (as they are in the United States) and also because of the extraordinary amount of new investment in stocks made by institutional investors (espcially pension funds) and corporations. Much of this new money going into the market is the result of "excess liquidity" in Japan during the period from 1984 until 1989. Excess liquidity is the increase in money supply less the GNP growth for the year. From 1984–1989 Japanese excess liquidity averaged 4.5%, an unusually large amount even for Japan, which has enjoyed a high savings rate for many years. By comparison, from 1980 to 1984 excess liqudity averaged 0.6%.

Many corporations and institutions invest in other corporations with which special relationships exist. Such cross holdings of shares are estimated to account for approximately 30 percent of all outstanding shares of common stock in Japan. Cross holdings are rarely, if ever, traded, and as a result there has been an apparent shortage of shares available for the high levels of demand that have existed for them. Corporations and institutions, however, have increasingly been investing their surplus funds in shares of companies for investment purposes only. Corporations in particular have preferrred to make such investments through tax-advantaged special investment funds called "Tokkin" and in special fund trust accounts. At year-end 1985, the value of assets on Tokkin and fund trust accounts was $60.4 billion; by year-end 1989, the amount had increased to $283 billion. (See Table 16–4 for a profile of the changing Japanese stock market investor.)

Table 16—4. Net Purchases (Sales) by Investor Group of Japanese Equity Securities 1981–1989[a]

Period	Individuals			Financial Institutions	Industrial Corporations	Investment Trusts	Foreigners
	Total	Cash Transactions	On Margin				
1981	¥ (425)	na		¥ 417	¥ 288	¥ (95)	¥ 110
1982	(330)	na		423	84	18	182
1983	(862)	¥ (1417)	¥ 555	769	28	(69)	726
1984	(55)	(1228)	1173	1479	320	325	(1922)
1985	(943)	(1586)	643	1825	284	468	(869)
1986	(1782)	(3109)	1327	4568	754	1057	(3787)
1987	(1304)	(3350)	2043	6289	1154	1824	(7193)
1988	(3350)	(5451)	1784	4711	606	1589	46

a. In billion of Yen.

SOURCE: Goldman, Sachs & Co., "Investment Research Japan", January 1990.

Approximately 50 percent of the secondary market trading that occurs in Japanese shares, however, include trades with individual or foreign investors. For the most part, individual investors are exempt from capital gains taxes. Many of the investors in Japanese shares are housewives (who tend to be the family money managers), and as a result nearly half of the sales representatives of the large brokerage firms are women who call on customers in their neighborhoods.

Japanese institutional and retail investors have not until recently been active in foreign stock markets. This is because of the extensive range of high-performance investment opportunities in Japan, unfamiliarity with foreign shares, and regulatory restrictions. However, as the Japanese market rose to price levels reflecting a marketwide average price/earnings ratio of about 70 (1986) with negligible dividend yields, many investors began to look at the U.S. and European markets, which naturally appeared quite cheap to them. This casting of the eye abroad was aided by the actions of aggressive Japanese securities firms who undertake to sell large blocks of foreign shares accumulated through underwritings abroad to retail investors throughout Japan.

Institutions in Japan that purchase foreign equities include investment companies (managed mainly by the principal Japanese securities companies), insurance companies, and trust banks, which manage corporate and individual pension funds. Apart from the investment companies, the most active institutions to invest in foreign shares in recent years have been the trust banks, and the Tokkins. These accounts reportedly have rapidly increased their investments in foreign equity securities. Japanese investors, being latecomers to the international equities markets, have only a negligible proportion of their funds in overseas equities. However, this has begun to change as investors have become more familiar with foreign markets. Japan's net investment in foreign equities, and foreigners' net investments in Japanese equities, are shown in Table 16–5.

DIFFERENCES IN VALUATION

While it may be true that each national market values its equity securities in terms of similar views about how to determine what a future stream of dividends might be worth when capitalized at a locally suitable discount rate, it is also true that very great differences can exist between markets that are not explained by factors in the formula.

Table 16–5. Japanese Capital Flows[a], 1981–88

Year	Long-Term Capital Outflow	Foreign Net Purchases of Japanese		Japanese Net Purchases of Non-Japanese		Current Account Surplus
		Equities	Bonds	Equities	Bonds	
1981	$ 9,672	$ 3,519	$ 5,772	$ 240	$ 5,808	$ 4,770
1982	14,969	1,613	4,861	151	6,076	6,850
1983	17,700	4,120	2,068	659	12,507	20,799
1984	49,651	(7,249)	3,456	50	26,773	35,003
1985	64,542	(3,111)	4,525	993	53,479	49,169
1986	131,461	(19,415)	(2,109)	7,048	93,024	85,845
1987	136,532	(48,500)	6,675	16,874	73,257	87,015
1988	130,930	1,844	(21,628)	4,125	85,812	79,631

a. In millions of dollars.

SOURCE: Bank of Japan

In the United States experienced financial institutions employing what they consider to be the most sophisticated tools for valuing securities tend to set prices. In Japan fund managers with a large cash flow to invest and enthusiastic individual investors tend to follow the advice of stockbrokers who can create a kind of herd instinct that can move the market more than careful attention to market valuation formulae. In Europe local markets may be so inactive in particular stocks that they appear undervalued by Americans looking for bargain investments that they believe in the long run will reflect true values. Many people feel they cannot apply their own valuation procedures to equities that are mainly traded in another country. Instead, one must understand the market as locals do and go with the flow. Why else would a foreigner buy a Japanese bank stock at 40 times earnings hoping it would rise to 80 times earnings?

On the other hand, as the markets become more closely linked (and as foreign trading becomes as important as any other domestic source of trading), pricing mechanisms ought to converge. In many respects they have begun to do so.

Local investors, who were not trading oriented, were not buying European shares. U.S. and London based institutional investors were, and offered prices to local institutions that they did not expect to get for large blocks. Europeans sold into a rising market created in part by foreigners, who became a larger factor in valuing the shares. The "bargains" disappeared after a while, but so did some of the excessive concentration of local shareholdings. Local notions of valuation were altered by the foreign purchases.

Table 16–6 shows various data regarding foreign involvement in certain European stock exchanges. It would appear that those exchanges with high foreign involvement ought to have fewer price anomalies than those with low foreign involvment, such as Japan. With more experience in these markets, more data can be obtained that might explain differences in valuation between markets somewhat better.

Valuation differences in different markets for stocks in the same industries are not only the result of local factors. Frequently adjustments must be made to place the companies on a comparable valuation basis. For example, in Japan price-to-earnings ratios are very much higher than in the United States. However, in order to understand how much higher, one must make certain accounting and other adjustments to the financial statements of the Japanese company to

Table 16–6. International Involvement in European Stock Exchanges

	Foreign companies listed as % of total (main market)	Foreign investors' % of total turnover (by country)	Stock-exchange members with foreign capital as % of all members
Amsterdam	50	50	16
Frankfurt	48	9	11[a]
Paris	32	44	16
London	24	21	41[b]
SEAQ Intl	100[c]	48	86
Milan	0	23	0
Madrid	0	25	4

a. Member banks

b. As of March 1989

c. 180 of the equities quoted on SEAQ International are listed on London's International Stock Exchange; trading in those shares is also included in London figures. All its market-makers are also members of the International Stock Exchange

SOURCES: Federation of Stock Exchanges in the EC, Salomon Brothers, national stock exchanges; *The Economist*, December 16, 1989. ©1989 The Economist Newspaper Ltd. All rights reserved.

make the two comparable; otherwise the analyst has the problem of comparing apples and oranges.

First, one might attempt to assess the market value of shareholdings in other companies held by the company being valued. Generally, such holdings are carried on the books of the company at the share's par value when issued (virtually nothing), though today these shares would be worth many millions of dollars. The same may be true for Japanese landholdings not essential for the business.

Second, one wants to be sure that the financial data being reviewed are the company's consolidated financial statements—in Japan by tradition the market records price/earnings (p/e) ratios on a parent-company-only (unconsolidated) basis. Consolidation may increase earnings by 20 percent or more (and thereby lower the p/e accordingly).

Next, there are certain accounting adjustments, for depreciation, reserves for employee severance, number of shares outstanding, and other items that need to be taken into account. When all of these adjustments are made to conform with U.S. Generally Accepted Accounting Principles, the p/e ratios of the U.S. and the Japanese company will have converged substantially. In fact, prior to about 1980, on a fully adjusted basis, Japanese p/e ratios were lower than those of U.S. companies. During the 1980s, the adjusted Japanese ratios exceeded U.S. ratios; however by the end of the 1980s the two were converging again. Similar (but not all of the same) adjustments should be made when attempting to value European as well as Japanese companies from a U.S. valuation viewpoint.

INTERNATIONAL NEW ISSUES

Through the end of 1987 the U.S. domestic market continued to be the world's largest market for new issues of equity securities. Over 1,000 issues of common stock and convertible debentures, aggregating approximately $57 billion, were offered in the United States during 1986. Since then the new-issue volume in the United States has declined to $37 billion in 1988 and to $21 billion for the first 10 months of 1989.

By contrast, the equity new-issue volume was considerably larger in Europe and Japan in 1989. In Europe, largely because of continuing privatization programs, the aggregate new-issue volume in the various national markets and in the Euroequity market (of approximately $75 billion) substantially exceeded the new-issue volume in the United States. In Japan new issues of common stock, convertible debentures, and straight bonds with warrants (including those issued in the Eurobond market) exceeded $120 billion. The Japanese market has been affected by large privitization programs during preceding years (NTT and Japan Air Lines), a steady stream of warranted-Eurobond issues (see Chapter 15), and several large issues—of approximately $1 billion each for banks building up their stated capital—and other corporations funding large overseas investments.

Based on 1987 published data, Japanese corporations accounted for approximately 45 percent of the world's equity new issues, European corporations 35 percent, and U.S. corporations 20 percent. Based on preliminary indications, 1989 data will show the U.S. share to have declined to about 10 percent.

International issues of two types tend to be offered in the United States: (1) issues sold by foreign companies to establish or improve markets for their shares in the United States or to obtain a higher share price than would have been available in the home market; and (2) issues that were part of larger offering schemes originating in Europe, in which the U.S. piece, or tranche, is marketed as part of a global offering. In addition, international new issues can be made outside the United States. These are neither registered with the SEC nor made available for sale in the United States. Such offerings often include Euroequity issues and national market issues (e.g., privatizations) that are sold globally but do not include U.S. tranche.

The U.S. market is attractive to large corporations seeking broader distribution of their shares. Most of the foreign volume in the United States during the past few years is accounted for by issues of shares in the form of *American Depository Receipts* (*ADRs*) of such large companies as British Telecom, British Gas, British Steel, Philips NV, British Airways, Barclays Bank, Telefonica, and British Petroleum. ADRs are negotiable certificates, issued by a U.S. bank in evidence of shares of a foreign issue placed in custody with a depository in the country of issue. Holders of ADRs can exchange them on demand for the underlying share with the depository.

The United States requires that new issues of securities to be offered to the public be registered with the SEC. Many foreign companies are very reluctant to go through this process, which is extremely expensive and time consuming for a company that has not previously been registered. As long as approximately the same pricing and terms are available in the home market or European equity market, such companies often prefer to issue their securities outside the United States. In recent years other non-U.S. companies have made efforts to educate investors in the United States about their shares, with the understanding that in due course the company would become a "reporting company" that files annual reports with the SEC in a form similar to what is required for a public offering registration statement. Despite the aversion to registration with the SEC, the benefits of having shares trade actively in the United States appear to be drawing a number of the larger multinational companies toward becoming reporting companies.

However, the U.S. market is less important to non-U.S. issuers than it was a few years ago. As the Euroequity market has developed ($23 billion of new issues in 1987, followed by a sharp decline in 1988 and a recovery to about $12 billion estimated for 1989) those issuers seeking sales outside their home markets have alternatives they did not have before. A large issue for a major European bank, for example, can be done entirely within Europe—partly in the home market and partly through various Euroequity tranches (e.g., a Swiss tranche, a U.K. tranche, and German tranche, etc.). A large European equity issue might not have been possible a few years ago without tapping the U.S. and Japanese markets. Now such issues are commonplace, and their appearances in the U.S. market are diminishing. In 1989, there were only 20 ADR new issues in the United States, aggregating $2.6 billion.

This decreasing participation in the U.S. market is partly caused by the requirement for foreign companies to register with the SEC if they want their shares to be actively traded in the United States, requirements that involve expense, extensive restating of financial statements, additional disclosure, and exposure to litigation. It is also partly caused by greater willingness of European investors to acquire shares of European companies, which presumably they know better and are more comfortable with. This decrease is also partly due to the fact that the preponderance of international equity portfolio managers are located in Europe. As *The Economist* reports, approximately "$180 billion of foreign equities are held in Britain, $120 billion in Switzerland, $60 billion in America and $40 billion in Japan—according to best guesses."[5]

For the U.S. equity market to become joined with the European market (in the way, for example, that the British market is joined with it) will require some changes in the SEC reporting requirements for foreign issuers, and will require some patience while the international equity investment skills build up in the United States. The SEC reporting requirements have been the subject of discussions for years, and some headway has been achieved in reducing the difficulties to be faced by foreign companies in the U.S. market. However, there remain sufficient difficulties to dissuade all but the most determined foreign multinational companies from accessing the market. Some discussion has occurred along the lines of permitting home country disclosure to satisfy host country disclosure requirements, but the SEC has so far been concerned that all home countries do not offer the same degree of investor protection as the United States does, protection that it does not wish to diminish in order to attract more foreign issuers. Although the matter is difficult, it is likely that some accommodation will be reached in the next few years as the U.S. market becomes more closely integrated with the rapidly developing markets in Europe.

The Japanese equity market remains substantially unjoined with any other market. Japanese investment in U.S. and other international equities, although growing, remains quite modest in relation to Japanese resources and to the investment commitments of investors from the other regions. The Japanese market has been expanding continuously for several years, much to the disbelief of foreign observers.

The Japanese market is the only major market in the world in which domestic portfolio performance would not have been improved during the 1980s by substantial diversification into foreign equities. It is likely, however, that the Japanese market will conform more closely to world market patterns during the 1990s if its excess liquidity and savings rate continue to diminish and market prices begin to reflect price/earnings ratios that are more in keeping with those in the United States and Europe. As these conditions occur, the Japanese market will begin to be drawn more closely into the international environment for equity securities.

WHO THE ISSUERS ARE

Issuers of equity securities in the international market are beginning to become an extremely diverse group. Before 1980, issuers would have been confined to large multinational corporations from one of the principal developed countries. Today there are many different types of issuers from many different countries—large and not-so-large corporations, banks, and special consortia (e.g., Eurotunnel or EuroDisney World). Issuers come from all of the European Community countries, plus the rest of western Europe, Israel, the United States, and Canada. They also come from Japan (mainly in the form of convertible debentures or Eurobonds with warrants), Hong Kong, Korea, Singapore, Malaysia, Australia, and New Zealand. In addition a number of country funds specializing in securities from a particular country have been launched for investment in Korea, Malaysia, Thailand, Taiwan, India, Mexico, Brazil, and various European countries.

Some of the more noteworthy international issues include shares of Japanese subsidiaries of non-Japanese companies in the Tokyo market, issues of shares of U.S. subsidiaries of Japanese companies in the U.S. market, and an initial public offering of an American company (Mrs. Fields' Cookies) in the London market.

DISTRIBUTION METHODS

The practice is developing for large issues, in which a particular distribution of shares is desired, to organize simultaneous, coordinated distributions of shares in several national markets. The large British privatizations utilized this practice, which was originally developed in 1984, for the issue of $1 billion worth of Texaco Euro–convertible debentures.

In the first British privatization distributed internationally—British Telecom in 1984—U.S., Canadian, European, and Japanese tranches were employed. For the subsequent and much larger issue of British Gas in 1986, similar tranches were employed. Subsequent to the British Telecom issue, the practice of using separate international tranches spread to U.S. issuers. This method of distributing shares was quite widely accepted by U.S. companies seeking a more visible participation by non-U.S. investors. Indeed, today U.S. corporations seeking to sell new stock issues almost always insist on some portion of the issue being targeted for an international tranche that is closely coordinated with, but technically separate from, the main U.S. offering.

During 1987, 20.75 million shares of Philips NV (valued at approximately $500 million) were placed around the world through simultaneous offerings in the United States, the Netherlands, the United Kingdom, Switzerland, West Germany, Japan, and the "rest of the world." The largest tranche, accounting for 5.75 million shares, was sold in the United States through a registered public offering. Later in the year, a combined offering of 42.5 million shares of Barclays Bank plc (valued at $393 million) was offered simultaneously through separate issues in the United States and Japan. Other issues have since followed these early global syndication pioneers.

The largest such international distribution was the sale of 2.2 billion shares of The British Petroleum Company in October 1987. The transaction, which was underwritten according to the British method (see the following section) on October 15, for subscription prior to October 28, was divided equally between the domestic U.K. market and the U.K. institutional markets and markets outside of the United Kingdom. The crash on October 19 occurred during the subscription period, causing the offering to be almost completely unsubscribed. The underwriters were left with the entire issue. Four U.S. underwriters had committed between them to underwrite $1 billion of the BP shares in partly paid form to be sold in the United States. Between them the U.S. underwriters shared losses totaling more than $250 million after taxes. In time the issue was distributed, and the market for BP shares returned to normal. The issue had been a disaster, but the international syndicate held and did its job, despite extreme duress.

Multiple tranche issues have produced some conflicting views as to how well the practice works. In essence, these views are those of American firms and those of European (mainly international continental) banks. The American firms prefer a flexible tranche populated with powerful international underwriters, to which shares are allocated in accordance with hard demand for the shares as indicated by each syndicate member. On the assumption that the best sales effort is the most competitive one, no geographical restrictions are observed (other than those required by law). Thus, if the Merrill Lynch office in Frankfurt received large orders for the shares, which Merrill Lynch would reflect to the syndicate manager, then Merrill Lynch would be allocated shares accordingly. If Dresdner Bank had only modest demand from its portfolio managers, then Dresdner Bank might not be allocated any shares. The German market is presumed to be covered by those doing business in Germany, whether German or not. Tight control of share allocations tends to ensure that shares get into the hands of investors who want them on the first try—that is, shares do not have to be redistributed in the secondary markets in order to get to the highest-priced investor. American firms use this method of distribution within the United States to ensure tightly priced deals with firm aftermarkets.

According to this view of the syndicate function, multiple tranches are not necessary; indeed they may only serve to loosen up distribution within the separate tranches. Most U.S. syndicate managers, however, when organizing European syndicates for U.S. issuers will insist on a single "book running" manager for both the U.S. and the international tranches. They will, in essence, treat the smaller European syndicate as if it were a part of the U.S. syndicate and allocate shares to its members strictly in accordance with demand. Otherwise, there is the danger that European syndicate members that have only weak demand from customers may try to sell the shares into the grey market in Europe, or to another dealer who probably would sell them back into the U.S. market where a fixed-price offering is underway.

The European view is quite different. They like separate tranches separated by "ring fences" because this method enforces market discipline, (underwriters must restrict sales within their tranche), provides a lot of focus and attention to the issue within each tranche, and relies on what European banks do best, which is to underwrite shares that their clients are invited to subscribe for with the bank being prepared to "sit on" any unsold portion for an indefinite time. Large corporate issues and privatizations can work very successfully through such a system (e.g., Daimler-Benz, the British and French privatization issues, etc.). However, if an issue is not fully subscribed or is uninspired, then a great run to dump shares into the home market can occur, which can have extremely severe consequences for the issue.

The large sale ($2.36 billion) of Fiat during 1986 was an example of how multiple-tranche European-style issues can go wrong. It can be expected that underwriters from each different area that might be represented by a tranche will argue that a tranche in their particular area makes great sense, even if other tranches do not.

In order to secure high participation by investors in any tranche, it is usually necessary to structure the distribution in that area as a public offering, which requires registration of offering documents with national authorities. The United States and Japan have the strictest rules governing the registration of securities, though both markets can be approached on "private placement" bases, in which sales efforts are restricted to qualified (i.e., sophisticated, usually institutional) investors. American firms have developed the argument that the most practicable yet fully global distribution is achieved through an offering that is registered with the SEC, with a syndicate led by a U.S. firm that includes major international banks and securities firms from around the world and with vigorous marketing efforts to be conducted in Europe and Japan, and the United States. However, share allocation should be determined on the basis of solid demand. It is perhaps not surprising that European and Japanese firms have their own version of the optional global distribution method.

UNDERWRITING

In the United States underwriting procedures are designed to obtain the highest price for the seller of the securities being offered. This is done by forming a syndicate of securities firms that will agree to purchase the shares from the seller and resell the shares immediately to investors. The price is not fixed until just before the offering is made to the public, after a period during which sales personnel from the underwriting firms have marketed the issue to their customers and developed a "feel" for the price level needed to sell the shares without a big price run up in the aftermarket. A successful issue is one in which the entire issue moves into investors' hands at the offering price and the issue opens at a premium of no more than about 10 percent. The underwriting syndicate in such an issue is only exposed to a minimal holding period between the purchase and the confirmation of sales with customers. Of course, if the issue is mispriced or the market changes before the distribution is complete, underwriters can suffer losses. They are compensated for this risk, however, and most underwriters are comfortable with it.

The Euromarket uses U.S. underwriting procedures for the most part. Important differences exist in the lack of a fixed offering price to investors and in certain legal aspects, but the principles and objectives are similar. International equity markets can be volatile, and underwriters have suffered losses on a number of issues.

In the United Kingdom, and in many other parts of Europe, an older system of underwriting is used, which many people refer to as the "British underwriting method." In this system the announcement of the transaction and the offering price occur at the same time. Also at the time of announcement the issue is underwritten by one or more merchant banks acting as "underwriters," a term borrowed from the insurance industry where it originated. The underwriters, in effect, write an insurance policy for the issue to the effect that when the subscription period is ended any shares not subscribed for will be purchased by the underwriters at the same subscription price that the other subscribers paid. Thus, in exchange for a small insurance premium (called an underwriting fee), the issuer of the shares will know for sure that the shares have been sold at the agreed price. As soon as the underwriting is agreed, the underwriters contact "subunderwriters" with whom they wish to lay off some or all of their insurance risk. The subunderwriters are usually long-term securities investors e.g., a pension fund) who can afford to hold on if the market sags under the weight of the offering. Subunderwriters are "reinsurers," and indeed they operate much the same way by agreeing to all reasonable deals during the course of a year, expecting to make a profit, on balance, just for standing by.

Before the announcement of the issue, pricing is agreed between the issuer and the underwriters. Usually the subscription price reflects a modest (5 percent to 10 percent) discount from the last sale price as an incentive to the market to subscribe. There is also an underwriting fee, which must be shared with subunderwriters. After the announcement, the subscription period will remain open for about two weeks, during which time investors subscribe for the issue, in writing, through a bank or broker. In the case of a new issue of shares by a company in the United Kingdom and some other countries, existing shareholders are deemed to hold "preemptive rights" to purchase any new share issue before a nonshareholder may purchase shares. To the extent that the subscription price reflects a discount from the last sale price, that discount is equivalent to a dividend to the existing shareholder. Shareholders do not have preemptive rights in the case of the sale of existing shares by one shareholder to the market, as in the case in privatizations.

When the subscription period is over, the underwriters count up the number of subscriptions, and prorate them if the issue is oversubscribed, or allocate any unsubscribed shares to the underwriters if it is not. If the issue is substantially undersubscribed, then the market will expect the subunderwriters to be selling the shares and the stock price will drop.

Apart from arranging the subunderwriting syndicate, brokers have little to do in the process. Nor do the underwriters, including the lead merchant bank handling the issue, have much to do with marketing. This system recognizes that the main institutional investors in the market will be the likely buyers. As an incentive to get them in, they are paid an underwriting fee for using their capital to prop up the issue while individual and other investors go through the subscription process. The definition of a successful issue is one that is fully subscribed; in fact, some believe the more oversubscribed the issue the more successful it is. Unfortunately, such oversubscription tends to result in a sharp rise in the stock price when it is free to trade (or put another way, the subscription price tends to be set sufficiently low to be sure that oversubscription occurs). On the other hand, if the issue is undersubscribed, the underwriters can sustain substantial losses, as the British Petroleum issue more than amply demonstrated.

The British method is still in use in many parts of Europe, although the recent success of several very large U.K. privatization issues has resulted in some modest tinkering with the program—mainly by circulating a preliminary prospectus (a "pathfinder" in their terms) without a price to feel out the market first. It is probable that the many changes in the U.K. market that occurred as a result of Big Bang and the failure of the British Petroleum and several other underwritings during 1987 will lead to further changes in the British underwriting method in the future.

SECONDARY TRADING

Secondary trading in international stocks has been conducted in most financial centers for many years. Sometimes the international shares have been listed on principal exchanges. Often they have not been; instead they have been the object of small over-the-counter activity by firms specializing in international stocks. For years, the principal activity was foreign stock arbitrage (e.g., one would buy an ADR of a Dutch stock and simultaneously sell the number of underlying shares represented by the ADR in Amsterdam). To do this profitably, one must be a master of the details involved. The purchase in dollars after commissions must cost less than the proceeds of the sale of the shares after commissions, transfer expenses, and the foreign exchange costs of converting back into dollars. Such arbitrage activities have kept prices of international shares around the world in line with their home market values.

The next development was to provide market-making services to customers interested in buying foreign securities that were not available on exchanges. For example, a U.S. pension fund might want to buy shares in Fujitsu Ltd., which is not listed on any U.S. exchange or in NASDAQ, but for which ADRs are available. The pension fund might call a Japanese broker based in New York who could say, "We will take your order and purchase Fujitsu shares overnight. We will confirm tomorrow and tell you at what dollar price the order was executed. We will then deposit the shares with the agent bank in Japan and have ADRs put into your account." Alternatively, the pension fund might call a U.S. market maker in Fujitsu and be told: "We will sell you Fujitsu dollar ADRs right now for x." The U.S. broker who does not have Fujitsu ADRs in inventory will try to buy them in the New York market or trade with a Japanese broker overnight to get the shares to deliver to the pension fund. The market maker's price will reflect these various uncertainties. The volume in international equities has built up considerably over time, and pricing has been tightened up accordingly.

In recent years several further developments have improved secondary trading in international stocks. U.S. and other firms now make over-the-counter markets in listed U.S. shares in London in the morning before the New York Stock Exchange opens. This has improved liquidity in U.S. shares for European investors to some extent.

With foreign membership now available in the London, Tokyo, and New York stock exchanges, it is possible for participating firms to be active market makers in U.S., British, and Japanese stocks around the clock. Such firms are able to balance orders from around the world, not just from their home market.

Institutional investors are increasingly placing portions of the funds under their management into international stocks. Many such investments are done actively and require selection from among many different stocks in the same industry. Such choices require research and information from many sources. Other investments are passive—that is, they are made according to a system for indexing. Several indexes now exist, as does the capability for program and large block trading in non-U.S. equities.

The commitment to dealing in international equities by major firms is very substantial and is reflected in the number of personnel that have been added in research, trading, sales coverage, systems, and foreign exchange by major U.S., British, and Japanese firms. A very large increase in market infrastructure has occurred, which not only makes improved services possible but also provides competitive energy in the market as all of these new employees seek to advance their careers.

The improvement in market information in international shares is also very important. More foreign stocks are now traded on the New York Stock Exchange and in the highly efficient NASDAQ System. In London many foreign shares are listed in London and now traded in its market system, SEAQ, which is similar to NASDAQ. In Tokyo many foreign shares are listed on the Tokyo Stock Exchange with quite a few others in preparation. It is now possible to receive by phone a reliable quote on virtually any stock whose home market is one of the major financial centers. Quotes are also available for securities from many other countries on very short notice.

Also, there are the changes created by Big Bang—that is, the reconstitution of the London Stock Exchange. These may be the most significant and far-reaching changes that have yet occurred to international equity markets. Since October 1986 London has given up all of its longstanding securities market practices and has adopted in their place procedures that are almost identical to those in use in the United States. Not only will these steps make the London market more efficient, they will make it much more compatible with the U.S. market. Big Bang stands as a monumental example to other Europeans who will in time need to conform their national securities markets to international standards and practices. It will perhaps not be long before the U.S. and British electronic markets are merged (in terms of trading activity). With this may also come a further merging of market practices, regulation, and infrastructure, which will lead to a dominant English-speaking financial marketplace that others will wish to join. As it spreads, so will the prospects for equity market integration around the world.

COMPETING IN INTERNATIONAL EQUITIES

The global market for equity securities is vast and involves many powerful competitors. No single firm will be successful in commanding a significant share of all the national markets for equities. However, the rapidly growing cross-border trading activity in international equities is more concentrated, and participants in this market segment are capable of significant improvements in market share. Of course, they could be displaced by more effective competitors.

Secondary market activity in international shares within one's own country is perhaps the place where competitors must begin to develop their strengths. U.S. brokerages must become proficient in offering U.S. shares to international investors and in offering international shares to U.S. investors, principally institutions. British firms must do the same in London, and Japanese firms must do so in Tokyo. In each case, a firm is competing not only with its traditional domestic competitors, but also against the biggest and best of the foreign firms. Once successful in dealing in international securities with one's own clients, an ambitious firm can then attempt to compete abroad for the international business of nonclients.

Comparative Advantages

Firms have quite different comparative advantage profiles in the international equities business. U.S. firms are especially keyed to institutional investors, including European institutional investors. Many U.K. and European firms are substantial money managers and know about the markets because of their experience as investors. There are a great many money managers in the international arena, however, and only a small percentage are able to use their placing power and influence to command lead managerships of international equity new issues. Some, such as the major Swiss Banks and certain U.K. merchant banks, do manage to project their influence in the market into underwriting positions.

Other firms will attempt to cover retail demand for international investments, including the demand for international or specific national investment company shares. Some firms prefer to be more specialized—for example, concentrating on global banking or insurance. However, to be a successful competitor, a firm must be recognized as possessing "placing power"—the more the better. Those firms that can place international issues will be invited into or will be able to lead underwriting groups for new issues. They will also be able to profit from trading opportunities related to international equities.

Institutional Emphasis

Most firms agree that when operating abroad they must emphasize institutional business, despite the lower commissions, because it is the only way to build up trading volume quickly, which provides the firm with customer activity and keeps it "in the market," knowing what is going on. Institutional business is very competitive, especially in the United States and the United Kingdom.

To succeed in institutional business, a firm must offer three basic services—sales coverage, research, and trading. All of these can be expensive, yet if they are better than the competition's services, business will soon follow. Traditionally, firms would offer research and trading support to institutions from all over the world, but only in home country shares. Japanese brokers did not sell Dutch stocks, and U.S. firms did not promote German banks shares. Each participant stuck to what it knew best.

Research in International Equities

Such tidiness is no longer in effect. The U.S. broker, in an attempt to reclaim from U.S. investors a share of the commission volume on foreign stocks lost over the years, now not only will have to make trading markets in New York in a worldwide spectrum of issues (e.g., in BMW, Daimler-Benz, Fiat, Toyota, etc.), it will also have to start having research "ideas" on these stocks for their customers. Before long, the firm finds itself conducting macroeconomic research on several international economies, and following dozens of large-capitalization non-U.S. companies. At first, the firm's clients doubt the international capacity of the firm, but if the quality of the firm's research is as good as it can be, the research will soon gain a good reputation and will be sought out. Commission business usually follows. This process is very expensive, and it can take years to achieve a reputation for across-the-board excellence in research. When the process succeeds, however, it provides the firm with a strong international reputation for competence that enables it to attract a significant share of the market.

Trading and Market Making

Researchers must trade in the securities they recommend, but traders do not have to offer research in the securities they trade. Some firms prefer to compete only as market makers in international equity securities. There has been an active over-the-counter market in New York in international stocks for years. Recently, this business has expanded greatly, especially as institutional investors have become more active in international shares. Market makers have become members of the London and the Tokyo stock exchanges to round out their ability to trade in European and Japanese stocks, and more non-U.S. firms have become members of the New York Stock Exchange to improve their ability to execute U.S. orders for their non-U.S. clients.

Like large commitments to international research, these foreign exchange memberships are expensive, not only due to the cost of the stock exchange seats, but also because a firm must become subject to capital and reporting regulations of the other exchanges and commit substantial resources to back-office operations. In addition, the management time involved in getting established and in building local business can be considerable. Also, a firm must have have a fairly substantial volume in the shares traded on these exchanges to operate profitably. In New York and London commission rates are fully negotiable, and in Tokyo, where they are not, large-order discounts are common. Again, however, the firms that successfully pursue strategies of international trading will end up with the strongest franchises and the largest market shares.

New Issues

Some firms have preferred to compete in the international equities business by emphasizing new issues and underwritings, rather than becoming quite so committed to the secondary markets. Firms with an effective corporate marketing capability, or with a special ability to place issues with funds under the firm's own management, have often succeeded in gaining mandates to lead manage public offerings of international equity issues. Such issues, however, do have to be priced competitively and distributed skillfully. Secondary market making and research coverage has to be provided for, even if by different firms than the lead manager. It is possible, by virtue of the relationship between banker and client, for firms without developed capabilities in research or trading and without convincing placing power to win mandates. But it is much more difficult to do so than in the past. Large international equity issues can be extremely profitable for lead managers; as a result, there is always keen competition for almost every management appointment. Most of the managerships are won by firms with the ability to demonstrate across-the-board qualifications. Comanagerships and other lesser positions, however, are still made available quite often to firms that have fewer demonstrable qualifications but a longer and closer relationship with the issuer.

CONTINUING TRENDS AND ISSUES FOR THE FUTURE

A great deal has happened in a very short time to the international equities market, and much is happening yet. International activity in equity markets gives every indication of being a permanent and growing feature of the investment business.

As international ownership increases, there is reason to believe that valuation will converge toward a loose sort of international standard.

New methods of international distribution are being tried. In time, perhaps a common practice will evolve. If so, it will have to be one that makes room for all those market participants capable and desirous of a role. The greatest competitive energy, however, appears to be behind the traditional U.S. notion of hard-working brokers developing clients who respond to service and put in orders, as opposed to portfolio managers who wait for clients to ask for advice or to have something done.

The demand for services to professional investors will rise to U.S. levels in newly liberated Britain, and institutions on the continent will watch closely to see how things work out. As U.S. practices become the norm in London, British institutions will become much more active traders (as indeed they have already done), and their portfolios will become more aggressively managed. New standards of investment performance will be adopted, which will create more competition and more services and will result in more liquid markets for British equities—and perhaps for all other European equities, which may find the bulk of their trading activity gravitating to London. British companies and, in time, other European companies will become more active issuers of equity securities of various types. Ultimately, Japan will also be included in the embrace.

Until Big Bang, equity markets outside the United States were locked into an old-fashioned, highly national environment that lacked competition and opportunity. Prior to Mayday in 1975, markets in the United States were similarly constrained. Since Big Bang, there have been important liberalizations in other equity markets, notably

Canada, Australia, and Japan. It appears inevitable that much further change lies ahead, as in many ways the process of conversion from national to international markets has just begun.

SUMMARY

In equities, as in international bonds, issuers tap international markets to increase the pool of available funds, lower costs of raising capital, expand their investor base, and/or avoid domestic regulatory complications. Investors move to international markets to improve portfolio performance. Both groups' interests have been furthered by the erosion of regulatory barriers—exchange controls, limits on ownership, limits on participation in domestic markets, and obstructive listing and trading practices.

Particularly in Japan, which now boasts the largest domestic equity capitalization in the world, deregulation has allowed an outflow of investing capital seeking diversification and higher returns. The institutional investors of the United States, home to the world's most-sophisticated equity markets, have made their impact on developing European equity markets by demanding the same high standards of research, trading, and brokering as they enjoy at home. Investors throughout the world, having been offered proof of the efficiency of international diversification in the wake of the October 1987 crash, are unlikely to return willingly to domestic markets.

While governments and stock market regulatory agencies have made some progress in standardizing procedures, full integration is a long way off. Issuers are discouraged from the otherwise attractive U.S. market by the stringent listing requirements of the SEC. Recent high volumes of new issues by Japanese issuers of Eurobonds with warrants—positioned to attract Japanese investors—clearly circumvent onerous regulatory requirements of the domestic market. Europeans and Americans continue to differ over new-issue procedures for international equities, with Americans favoring a single international syndicate and the Europeans favoring multiple syndicates with exclusive national markets. The pricing conventions in the secondary market continue to exhibit national divergences, the most striking being the high Japanese price/earnings ratios bid up by a large individual (rather than institutional) investing public.

But the emergence of a single world market is already discernible. The large investment houses, committed to supporting globalization of institutional investment, stand prepared to make markets 24 hours a day in selected stocks traded in New York, Tokyo, and London. That infrastructure, built during the bull market of the early 1980s, will now be consolidated. It will be well positioned to continue to serve its clients, taking advantage of further deregulatory progress.

NOTES

1. Inter Sec Research Corp., March 1988.
2. Steven Einhorn and Patricia Sangkuan, "Equities—Supply and Demand," *Portfolio Strategy*. New York: Goldman, Sachs & Co., March 1988.
3. Michael Sesit, "Japanese Investors Wrest from the British No. 1 Rank as Net Foreign Buyers," *The Wall Street Journal*, April 8, 1988, p. 00.
4. Walter, Ingo and Smith, Roy C. *Investment Banking in Europe*. Oxford: Basil Blackwell, 1990, p. 26.
5. *The Economist*, "Euroequities and the London Money Mill," December 16, 1989.

SELECTED REFERENCES

Bush, Janet, et. al. "A Glum 100 Days." *Financial Times*, (London), January 27, 1988.

Einhorn, Steven, and Sangkuan, Patricia. "Equities—Supply and Demand." *Portfolio Strategy*. New York: Goldman, Sachs & Co., March 1988.

Elliot, Charles, and Akers, Nicholas. *Japan Investment Strategy Highlights, February/March 1988*. New York: Goldman, Sachs & Co., 1988.

Jones, Rosamund. "Annual Global Equity Report." *Euromoney*, May 1987.

Kamijo, Toshiaki. "Securities Markets and Investment Banking in Japan." *Investment Banking Handbook*, edited by J. Peter Williamson. New York: John Wiley and Son, Inc., 1988

Schwartz, Robert A. *Equity Markets*. New York: Harper and Row, 1988.

Securities Markets in Japan, 1987. Tokyo: Japan Securities Research Institute, 1986.

Sesit, Michael "Japanese Investors Wrest From British No. 1 Rank as Net Foreign Buyers," *The Wall Street Journal*, April 8, 1988.

Troughton, Helen. *Japanese Finance, The Impact of Deregulation*. London: Euromoney Publications, 1986.

Viner, Aron. *Inside Japanese Financial Markets*. Homewood, IL: Dow Jones-Irwin, 1988.

Walter, Ingo. *Global Competition in Financial Services*. Cambridge, MA: Ballinger Publishing Co., 1988.

Walter, Ingo, and Smith, Roy C. *Investment Banking in Europe*. Oxford: Basil Blackwell Ltd., 1990.

17

Mergers, Acquisitions, and Financial Advisory Services

In addition to raising capital for corporations through the issuance of new debt or equity securities or bank loans, corporate financial services include the giving of advice on a variety of complex matters that a corporation must deal with in order to evaluate or accomplish particular transactions. Such transactions are usually ones that require specialized knowledge of the markets involved and often require a network of contacts and extensive knowledge of local practices that a corporation itself is unlikely to possess to the degree necessary to ensure success. Advisory services are provided by both commercial banks and investment banks, although they have been a speciality of investment banks for a long time—since they usually involve the valuation of new or unusual securities by the market.

Advisory services are provided on an agency basis for a fee that tends to reflect the value added by the banker in the transaction. Typically, a small retainer fee is agreed upon, which is payable regardless of the outcome of the transaction, with the main part of the fee being dependent upon the completion of the transaction and usually based on an agreed percentage of its value. Among such financial advisory services are those involving mergers, acquisitions, and divestitures; recapitalizations; leveraged buyouts; creative "financial engineering" for new facilities or projects; and real estate finance.

Advisory services follow the markets for the transactions they involve. International advisory services provide advice on mergers, restructurings, and other financial matters applied to cross-border transactions or to those services that are carried out in another country.

This chapter mainly is concerned with how financial advisory services are conducted on an international basis. Certainly, the recent movement that has globalized financial markets has had its effect on related financial advisory services as well. Large-scale mergers, restructurings, and investment projects are now conducted in a global environment in which new international participants, for or against one's own interests, can easily become involved.

The international dimension to the mergers and acquisition business is not confined to the comparatively small number of important cross-border and non-U.S. transactions that occur every year. It also involves many transactions that are never completed or are completed differently. For example Hoffmann La Roche, the large Swiss pharmaceutical firm, did not succeed in acquiring the American Sterling Drug Co. in early 1988; Eastman Kodak did. But Hoffmann La Roche was a participant in the transaction anyway—as a potential buyer that actually stepped forward to make an unsolicited bid. For every large transaction, there are potential bidders beyond the border—whether they come forward or not. Those who advise in the business have to know who these bidders are, what they are thinking, and what their telephone numbers are—they have to be in touch. And being in touch, the advisors learn new things about the foreign companies and vice versa. Soon the advisers find themselves with a new client, and the circle expands.

THE MARKET FOR INTERNATIONAL MERGER ADVISORY SERVICES

The United States and the United Kingdom represent the largest markets for financial advisory services, and their investment and merchant banks represent the greatest repository of financial advisory know-how. This is partly because of the large volume of merger and acquisition (M&A) transactions that occur in these countries, but also it is because the underlying capital markets are active in many innovative ways that have not as yet caught on in the national capital markets of other countries. We can expect other financial centers in time to assimilate, in one form or another, the practices of corporate reorganizing and restructuring that are common in Britain and America.

The Intra-European Market

The market for M&A services within Europe differs considerably from the United Kingdom, where M&A activity has been active along U.S. lines for many years, and continental Europe, where it has not been. Corporations in the United Kingdom have been able to benefit from a well-developed market for corporate control since the 1950s. A comparatively large number of publicly owned corporations exist in

Britain, and these have been, and continue to be, mainly owned by financial institutions. Share markets in Britain, as compared to the rest of Europe, are active, and prices of shares are held to be fair representations of the value of corporations. Takeover transactions are governed by the Takeover Panel, a self-regulatory organization that is authorized to determine the rules of fair play. The International Stock Exchange in London also has regulations that apply to takeovers. Next to the U.S. market, the British market is the largest in the world for M&A transactions.

On the continent, different conditions exist. There are far fewer publicly owned companies in each of the continental countries than in Britain. Instead, there are more privately owned enterprises, partnerships, and closely held companies. Despite the fact that there are many large, world-class continental European corporations, most companies are considerably smaller in size than those traded in the London market. In France, for example, about 900 companies are listed on the Bourse, and these comprise a market capitalization equal to about 30 percent of the French GNP—a percentage that is about the same in Germany, Italy, and Spain. In the United Kingdom the market capitalization of companies is approximately 90 percent of the GNP. In the United States, which has a very large number of small, listed companies, it is about 50 percent.[1]

Accordingly, the environment on the continent for M&A transactions is quite different from that of the United Kingdom. Information is not as readily available, transactions tend to be negotiated face to face by controlling parties, stakeholdings and corporate alliances are common, hostile activity is scorned, and sophisticated tactical and financial maneuvers are regarded with suspicion. Notwithstanding these traditions and attitudes, however, conditions are changing in the M&A business on the continent, and larger numbers of transactions have been completed in recent years.

European Restructuring and 1992

One reason for the increase in continental M&A activity since 1983 has been the growing recognition of the need for industrial restructuring in Europe. This powerful economic drive has superseded traditional concerns in a number of countries, and the increasing liquidity of European capital markets has made nontraditional alternatives possible. No longer must an entrepreneur look for a friendly bank or competitor to buy all or part of his or her holdings upon retirement. The entrepreneur can now sell shares at a decent price in the open market or hire an investment banker to find a wealthy stranger to buy the company. No longer must an industry suffering structural difficulties be forced to hold on to businesses that no longer fit. It can now dispose of them in the market. And, of course, no longer must a healthy company seeking to expand across European borders build up new businesses in other countries step by step. It can now purchase a complete business from someone else at a market price.

Consequently, it is likely that the market for corporate control and related M&A services will continue to grow rapidly throughout all of Europe—the European Economic Community (EC) countries and the non-EC European countries as well. Several factors shape this outlook.

First, the emerging internal market in the 1990s will require larger, more competitive enterprises able to reap significant economies of scale and economies of scope, particularly in such industries as transportation, information technology, telecommunications, financial services, food products, consumer electronics, and pharmaceuticals. Like the waves of M&A activity that have from time to time rolled over the United States—driven by underlying industry economics—global competitive shifts, and the perceived need to diversify will likely cause large amounts of industrial restructuring in Europe during the 1990s.

The greater are managements' convictions about the specific competitive impact of the EC-1992 initiatives, the more aggressive will be their drive to develop a market presence throughout the EC that is competitively viable on a global basis. For many, the conviction that their objectives can only be achieved in the short term through acquisition activity will be powerful. Consequently, as has been the case in the United States and the United Kingdom, a determination to pursue acquisitions despite objections of the target company will introduce, to a much greater extent than previously, predatory actions on the part of acquirers. Unless opposed by public policy—which, although much more relaxed on the matter of hostile offers than in the past, is still a very complex area and differs widely from country to country—the hostile takeover attempt can be expected to become much more common in the Europe of the 1990s.

Second, acquisitions of brand names and manufacturing facilities in an internal market for highly competitive products may be a cheaper alternative than *de novo* investments in Europe, as has been true in the United States.

Third, the growing concentration of shareholdings in institutional portfolios subject to a progressively higher performance orientation serves to increase the emphasis on realizing underlying equity values. More competition among investment managers, more liquidity, and more room to maneuver will require all financial managers to become more performance oriented than they have been in the past. Thus, investment managers should be more inclined than in the past to favor takeovers and short-term returns in preference to maintaining long-term holdings out of loyalty or inertia. This change has already occurred to a significant degree in the United Kingdom. Such shifts in continental European investor behavior are likely to occur—although perhaps not to the extent, for example, as has developed in the United States, where performance orientation appears to be at a maximum.

Fourth, ample financing continues to be available from banks anxious to earn large fees and spreads on M&A transactions. Under the Bank for International Settlements risk-based capital adequacy standards, which lump all corporate lending into one category, M&A loans are advantageous for most banks. These banks can earn significantly increased spreads in takeover financings without any increased charge against capital than they can earn for a straight loan to an AAA corporation such as Unilever. In addition to the banks, liquidity is available for M&A financings from investment funds that purchase high-yield bonds and "mezzanine" debt issues (i.e., quasi-equity) of acquiring corporations. Such funds have been widely sold to private, institutional, and corporate investors in the United States and in Europe.

Finally, sufficient M&A "technology" is in place, both home-grown in Europe as well as that developed in the United States and adapted to European conditions, to facilitate such transactions. The nature of this technology is discussed below.

Among the constraints holding back M&A activity in the EC are limited and often fragmented public shareholdings—that is, heavy concentrations of voting stock in the hands of management or by parties friendly to management (e.g., banks or investment companies). Because of national differences among the EC countries concerning the ways in which the market for corporate control is regulated, and the unpredictability of national or EC antitrust intervention, risk arbitrage markets in Europe have not fully developed. Until new and transparent EC-wide regulations covering antitrust considerations and takeover behavior on the part of principals (and those connected with them) are promulgated, the various markets will remain fragmented and comparatively inefficient. On the other hand, once the new regulations are agreed upon, as is anticipated, the markets should become integrated and comparatively efficient, enabling risk arbitrage activities to flourish and, in general, easing the process of M&A completion considerably.

Perhaps the most salient difference between the M&A business as it has evolved in the United States and the United Kingdom, as compared to continental Europe, is the availability of information. The information base necessary to undertake M&A transactions is much less developed in continental Europe. In the United States and the United Kingdom firms interested in acquisitions and investment banks can have at their disposal in a very short time a broad array of information about target companies, their industries, financial resources, regulatory issues, and other data necessary to make bids. In much of continental Europe such data are very difficult and expensive to obtain; they are incomplete, misleading, or nonexistent. Much information must be inferred and obtained through contacts, and this lack of transparency has a major impact on both the volume and character of European M&A transactions. As European financial markets become liberalized and more highly performance oriented, however, this situation is likely to change, albeit gradually.

STRUCTURE AND EVOLUTION OF INTERNATIONAL M&A DEAL FLOW

Between 1982 and 1988 the pattern of worldwide M&A activity—broadly defined to include mergers, acquisitions, tender offers, purchases of stakes, divestitures, and leveraged buyouts (LBOs)—has changed considerably. Transactions in the United States appear to have peaked, while both American cross-border transactions and transactions entirely outside the United States have grown much faster and appear to be continuing to grow.

Table 17–1 shows combined M&A activities on a worldwide basis from 1982 to 1988. During this period, approximately 13,500 transactions involving mergers, tender offers, purchases of stakes, divestitures, and LBOs with a market value of $1.5 trillion were completed. Of these transactions, approximately two-thirds were transactions between U.S. companies. Nearly $300 billion worth of transactions, or 20 percent, were entirely outside the United States—that is, only non-U.S. companies (or non-U.S. subsidiaries of American compa-

Table 17–1. Volume of Completed International Mergers and Acquisitions, 1982–88

Year	Domestic U.S.[a]		Cross-Border (U.S.)[b]						Outside U.S.[c]	
			Buyer from U.S.		Seller from U.S.		Total Cross-Border			
	No.	Value[d]	No.	Value[d]	No.	Value[d]	No.	Value[d]	No.	Value[d]
1982	879	$ 52,260	32	$ 866	52	$ 2,985	84	$ 3,851	71	$ 5,629
1983	1,396	81,080	57	2,920	79	6,564	136	9,484	163	21,848
1984	1,690	143,915	47	2,720	104	17,138	151	19,858	168	18,023
1985	1,689	199,616	50	2,201	83	7,061	133	9,262	298	42,188
1986	1,828	195,489	57	2,871	176	31,837	233	34,708	294	45,846
1987	1,595	169,697	79	14,474	194	47,336	273	61,810	566	104,941
1988	1,120	160,038	48	5,035	221	59,683	269	64,719	578	55,515
Total										
1982–88	10,197	1,002,094	370	31,087	909	172,606	1,279	203,693	2,138	293,990

a. Completed mergers, tender mergers, tender offers, purchases of stakes, divestitures, and LBOs in U.S. companies by U.S. companies.

b. Completed mergers, tender mergers, tender offers, purchases of stakes, divestitures, and LBOs in which either the buyer or the seller is a U.S. company and the counterpart is a non-U.S. company. Transactions involving divestitures are recorded by the nationality of the division being bought or sold.

c. Completed mergers, tender mergers, tender offers, purchases of stakes, divestitures, and LBOs in which both participants are non-U.S. companies.

d. In millions of dollars at current exchange rates.

SOURCE: Ingo Walter and Roy C. Smith, *Investment Banking in Europe: Restructuring for the 1990's* (Oxford: Basil Blackwater, 1989). Data from Securities Data Corporation (1989).

nies) were involved—and $204 billion worth of transactions, or 14 percent, were cross-border transactions (U.S. parent companies acted as buyers and sellers with non-U.S. counterparts).

The predominance of U.S.-to-U.S. transactions obscures important changes that have been occurring outside the United States. The value of U.S. domestic transactions in 1988 was $160 billion. This represents nearly a threefold increase over the volume of such transactions in 1982, but it indicates a 20 percent decline from the peak level of activity in 1985, when $200 billion in transactions were completed. U.S. cross-border transactions have grown much more rapidly. Transactions in which U.S. corporations were sellers to non-U.S. buyers were approximately twenty times larger in 1988 than in 1982. U.S. buyer transactions were five times larger in 1988 than in 1982 and represented a decline from a much larger volume in 1987. Finally, deals completed outside the United States grew tenfold between 1982 and 1988—or twentyfold if the much higher 1987 volume is considered. Apparently, the 1988 volume was reduced by dislocations following the market crash of October 1987 and perhaps by uncertainties following insider trading and M&A scandals in the United Kingdom and elsewhere in Europe.

Cross-Border Transactions

During 1987 and 1988 cross-border transactions accounted for 28 percent of all M&A transactions involving U.S. corporations; 85 percent of these deals were inward investments, most of which involved European buyers. Clearly, European corporations were not interested only in the EC internal market. For many years they had recognized the importance of deploying more of their business activities into the United States, where the domestic economy had been expanding rapidly, the dollar had declined sharply after 1985, and fears of possible protectionism interrupting market access through imports were rising. Table 17–2 provides a list of some of the major foreign acquisitions in the United States during the 1980s. The dominance of European corporations as acquirers is evident.

Cross-border transactions often precipitate additional subsidiary transactions. For example, in 1986 Unilever, an Anglo-Dutch company that is one of the world's largest distributors of consumer products, acquired Chesebrough-Pond Inc., a U.S. company, in a transaction valued at $3.2 billion. Almost immediately thereafter, Unilever divested itself of three of Chesebrough's subsidiaries, Stauffer Chemical Company, Prince Manufacturing Co. (maker of the famous tennis racquets), and Bass Shoe Company—for a total of about $2 billion. The original purchase of Chesebrough was financed initially by the issuance of commercial paper in the U.S. market. Advice was given to Unilever by its financial advisor, Goldman Sachs, on all of these transactions.

U.S. cross-border transactions have included numerous large transactions in which European corporations acquired the outstanding minority interests in their majority-owned U.S. subsidiaries. In 1970 British Petroleum(BP) exchanged certain Alaskan oil production interests for an increasing share in the Standard Oil Company of Ohio (Sohio), which reached 53 percent in 1978. In 1987 BP decided to acquire the remaining 47 percent through a $7.9 billion tender offer to shareholders. Similar acquisitions of minority interests have been undertaken by Royal Dutch Shell, N.V. Philips Gloeilampenfabrieken (the large Dutch electronics concern), and Britain's Midland Bank plc (which acquired the 43 percent interest in Crocker National Bank that it did not own prior to selling the whole of Crocker to Wells Fargo in 1986). In addition, of course, smaller acquisition transactions took place, many of which involved U.S. companies that were for sale, looking with their advisors to expand the list of possible U.S. buyers to include appropriate international names.

Divestitures of companies that no longer suited their foreign owners also occurred. For example, BAT Industries, the large British-based tobacco, retailing, and insurance concern, acquired Gimbel's in 1973 and sold it in 1986; Imperial Group, another U.K. tobacco company, acquired Howard Johnson's in 1980 and sold it in 1985. The international aspects of M&A business involve the buying and selling of companies big and small.

Cross-border transactions have also involved a number of Japanese and other Asian corporations. Japanese corporations, on the whole, appear to have preferred making direct investments in the United States or Europe through the construction of new facilities, rather than through the purchase of businesses. Frequently, such projects have involved imaginative low-cost leasing or other financing schemes that were arranged by U.S. financial advisors. Other transactions, however, have involved purchasing facilities, or lines of business from U.S. companies, and converting them to Japanese manufacturing methods. On other occasions, Japanese companies have purchased

Table 17–2. Major Acquisitions of U.S. Companies by Foreign Companies, 1981–88

Year	U.S. Company Acquired	Size of Transaction[a]	Foreign Company Acquirer	Country of Acquirer
1981	Conoco Energy Inc.	$ 913	Dome Energy Ltd.	Canada
1981	Texasgulf Inc	5,100	Elf Aquitaine	France
1981	Crocker National Corp.	820	Midland Bank Ltd.	U.K.
1981	Santa Fe International Corp.	2,552	Kuwait Petroleum Corp.	Kuwait
1984	Shell Oil Co. Inc	5,670	Royal Dutch Shell	Netherlands
1984	Carnation Co.	3,025	Nestle SA	Switzerland
1985	SCM Corp.	925	Hanson Trust	U.K.
1986	Genstar Corp.	1,850	Imasco Ltd.	Canada
1986	Big Three Ind. Inc.	1,070	Air Liquide SA	France
1986	USX Corp.	754	Bell Resources	Australia
1986	Allied Stores	3,600	Campeau Corp.	Canada
1987	Standard Oil Co.	7,900	British Petroleum	U.K.
1987	Texaco Inc.	1,053	Robert Holmes a Court	Australia
1987	Kidde Inc.	1,761	Hanson Trust	U.K.
1987	Marine Midland Banks	1,567	Hongkong Shanghai Bank	Hong Kong
1987	Manpower Inc.	1,340	Blue Arrow	U.K.

Year	Target	Amount[a]	Acquirer	Country
1987	First Jersey National Corp.	821	National Westminster Bank	U.K.
1987	G. Heileman Brewing Co.	1,260	Bond Holding Corp.	Australia
1987	North American Philips Corp.	1,800	Philips N.V.	Netherlands
1987	Staley Continental Inc.	1,500	Tate & Lyle	U.K.
1987	Consumer Electronics (GE)	1,000	Thomson SA	France
1987	Stauffer Chemical	1,923	ICI Ltd.	U.K.
1987	CBS Records	2,000	SONY Ltd.	Japan
1988	Farmers Group Inc.	5,200	BAT Industries	U.K.
1988	Federated Department Stores	6,750	Campeau Corp.	Canada
1988	Firestone Tire & Rubber	2,670	Bridgestone Ltd.	Japan
1988	Intermedics Inc.	800	Sulzer Brothers	Switzerland
1988	Macmillan Inc.	2,640	Maxwell Communications	U.K.
1988	Triangle Publications	3,000	News Corp.	Australia
1988	Gould Inc.	1,150	Nippon Mining Co.	Japan
1988	Pillsbury Co.	5,850	Grand Metropolitan	U.K.
1988	First Boston Inc.	1,100	Credit Suisse First Boston	Switzerland
1988	Triangle Industries Inc.	3,960	Pechiney SA	France

a. In millions of dollars.

SOURCE: Ingo Walter and Roy C. Smith, *Investment Banking in Europe: Restructuring for the 1990s* (Oxford: Basil Blackwell, 1989)

minority stakes in U.S. companies, particularly in the steel industry, as a basis for securing a source of production in the United States. Some Japanese companies, particularly banks and trading companies, but also such industrial corporations as Bridgestone (a tire manufacturer) and Sony have acquired 100 percent interests in large U.S. corporations. On one noteworthy occasion, a Japanese company (Dai Nippon Ink) acquired a U.S. company (Reichhold Chemicals Co.) in 1987 through a hostile takeover bid.

Other applications of cross-border financial advisory services occur when a company is seeking to achieve a particular domestic objective but finds (usually through the assistance of an advisor) that an international transaction can best achieve the intended results. In 1985 Dunlop, a troubled rubber products company in the United Kingdom, was the target of a hostile takeover bid from BTR, another British company, at a price that Dunlop considered exceptionally low. Dunlop decided, on the advice of its U.S. investment banker, to attempt an LBO of its U.S. subsidiary, thereby revealing the substantial hidden value contained in that subsidiary. Once this was done, BTR was forced to substantially increase the price that it bid for Dunlop.

Non-U.S. Transactions

Of the transactions entirely outside the United States between 1982 and 1988, approximately 58 percent have been intra-European deals, and the United Kingdom accounted for the majority of those transactions. Approximately 22 percent have been intra-Canadian, 7.4 percent intra-Australian, and 3.4 percent intra-Asian (see Table 17–3). Transactions not involving U.S. corporations have grown to approximately 26% of the worldwide total in 1987 and 1988, up from about 9% in 1982. Non-U.S. and U.S. cross-border transactions (i.e., international transactions from the point of view of U.S. investment bankers) have grown from 16% of worldwide transactions in 1982 to 47% in 1987 to 1988 (see Table 17–1).

As recently as 1985, 87 percent of all European M&A transactions consisted of mergers, tender offers, tender mergers, and purchases of stakes in companies. Shortly thereafter, however, divestiture activity increased sharply, and European LBOs became significant. In 1987 and 1988, 271 divestitures valued at more than $30 billion took place, in addition to 18 LBOs of publicly held companies valued at $2.4 billion. These divestitures and LBOs accounted for more than 28

Table 17–3. M&A Transactions Involving Non-U.S. Corporations, 1983–88

Nationality of Buyers		Nationality of Sellers			
		Europe	Canada	Australia	Asia
Europe	No.	1,202	38	12	9
	Value[a]	$171,256	$ 4,824	$ 852	$ 657
Canada	No.	26	553	3	2
	Value[a]	$ 3,445	$65,043	$ 94	$ 38
Australia	No.	33	10	105	6
	Value[a]	$ 4,344	$ 2,491	$21,814	$1,632
Asia	No.	24	6	0	72
	Value[a]	$ 2,196	$ 1,087	$ 0	$9,922

a. In millions of dollars.

SOURCE: Ingo Walter and Roy C. Smith, *Investment Banking in Europe: Restructuring for the 1990s* (Oxford: Basil Blackwell, 1989).

percent of total transactions in those two years. Total European M&A transactions of all types grew from $26.5 billion in 1985 to $71.3 billion in 1987, before declining to $42.8 billion in 1988 (see Table 17–4).

Relatively few European M&A deals represented very large transactions, with the average transaction in 1987–88 valued at about $120 million. Most European M&A deals have been for less than $50 million.

Table 17–5 presents a more detailed summary analysis of data for both European domestic and cross-border transactions exceeding $50 million in value and involving mergers, acquisitions, stakes, and divestitures. For these transactions the seller firm is located in one of the 12 EC countries. The data cover the years from 1983, two years before the 1992 initiative was announced by release of the EC White Paper, through 1988. Transactions are classified according to the regional origin of the buyer firm undertaking the transaction — Europe, Canada, the Middle East, the United States, Asia, Australia and New Zealand, and South Africa. From 1983 to 1988 505 total transactions worth over $150 billion were undertaken involving EC targets: 81% (78% in terms of value) were intra-European; 5% (3%) involved principals from Asia, Australia, and New Zealand; 2% (2%)

Table 17–4. M&A Transactions For European Corporations[a]

Year	Mergers & Aquisitions[b]		Divestitures		LBOs		Total Transactions	
	No.	Value[c]	No.	Value[c]	No.	Value[c]	No.	Value[c]
1985	140	$23,204	49	$ 2,849	2	$ 407	191	$26,460
1986	151	19,557	74	10,130	5	76	230	29,763
1987	267	56,166	141	13,550	10	1,609	418	71,325
1988	335	24,750	130	17,332	8	752	473	42,834

a. Data include all completed transactions in which seller company was European.

b. M & A data include all completed transactions involving mergers, tender offers, tender mergers, and purchases of stakes.

c. In millions of dollars at current exchange rate.

SOURCE: Ingo Walter and Roy C. Smith, *Investment Banking in Europe: Restructuring for the 1990s* (Oxford: Basil Blackwell, 1989).

Table 17–5. European Mergers, Acquisitions, Stakes, and Divestitures Valued at $50 Million or More, Cumulative Data for 1983 to 1988 (European Sellers)

Location of Buyer Firm

	M & As		Stakes		Divestitures		Total	
	No.	Value[a]	No.	Value[a]	No.	Value[a]	No.	Value[a]
Europe	102	$33,722.1	156	$39,559.2	151	$43,729.1	409	$117,010.4
Middle East	—	—	8	15,187.2	2	250.0	10	15,437.2
United States	9	1,926.2	17	3,542.8	21	4,275.8	47	9,744.8
Australia & New Zealand	2	312.2	10	2,304.1	5	747.3	17	3,363.6
Canada	2	469.9	8	1,473.7	1	328.0	11	2,271.6
Asia	—	—	5	1,012.2	4	500.5	9	1,512.7
South Africa	—	—	1	710.0	1	81.7	2	791.7
Total	115	36,430.4	205	63,789.2	185	49,912.4	505	150,132.0

a. In millions of dollars at current exchange rates.

SOURCE: Ingo Walter and Roy C. Smith, *Investment Banking in Europe: Restructuring for the 1990s* (Oxford: Basil Blackwell, 1989).

were from Canada; 2% (10%) were from the Middle East; and 9% (6%) were from the United States. The transactions in the Middle East were disproportionately large (mainly the Kuwait Investment Office stake in BP), and U.S. transactions were smaller than average.

Based on type of transaction, 23% (24% by value) of the deals during this period (1983 to 1988) involved acquisitions, 41% (42%) involved stakes, and 37% (33%) involved divestitures. For the entire period, 38% (34%) of intra-European transactions represented stakes, compared with 36% (36%) for principals based in the United States. Thus, the data do not confirm the idea that European firms have given substantially more precedence to the acquisition of stakes in Europe than American firms have done.

Nevertheless, the high proportion of stake acquisitions in Europe, as compared to the United States, indicates a uniquely European modus operandi. European companies appear to favor stakes for several reasons: (1) forging an alliance for a common purpose—offensive or defensive—without giving up independence appeals to these companies, (2) a gradual commitment to a final arrangement is wiser, cheaper, and reversible, and (3) in many situations a substantial minority stakeholding can assure *de facto* control of a company. In the United States, by comparison, acquirers are motivated by tax, accounting and legal reasons to prefer 100 percent ownership; however, American companies often recognize that when in Rome, Brussels, Lyon, or Dusseldorf it may be best to abide by local customs, at least for a while.

Some academic observers have suggested that lengthy European liaisons and courtships may lead to full mergers that prove to be more beneficial from static and/or dynamic economic perspectives than some of the more impulsive, opportunistic U.S. acquisitions that appear so often to fail in delivering expected benefits. This may be the case. There are many reasons, such as those mentioned above, for preferring a minority stake to a 100 percent purchase. In many situations the seller of the stake wants above all to preserve a status quo, which is in fact economically inefficient. Hence, the matter may not be one that can yet be resolved—certainly not from the data available so far.

Table 17–6 presents annual data for transactions involving European sellers from 1985 to 1988. Over this period, the total volume of transactions valued at $50 million or more increased by 66 percent from \$17.3 billion in 1985 to \$56.0 billion in 1987 and then declined to \$28.7 billion in 1988—compared with \$15.2 billion in 1983 and \$10.2 billion in 1984. Whereas the value of intra-European transactions dominated during the post-1985 period, those involving non-European principals grew far more rapidly, although from a much smaller base. In 1985, 93.6 percent of the value of transactions were intra-European; by 1988 this percentage declined to 84.7 percent. There was also a major change in the types of transactions from year to year.

Besides source and type of transaction, the data have also been broken down by Standard Industrial Classification (SIC) codes identifying the primary business of firms on both sides of each transaction. Table 17–7 indicates the flow of large European M&A deals by major industry category (1) of the firm undertaking the transaction and (2) of the target. Industries most heavily involved as principals included food products, oil and gas, chemicals, banks, and electronics and electrical equipment; those most heavily involved as targets included oil and gas, food products, chemicals, banks, and transportation equipment.

The data show that an active and rapidly growing EC market for corporate control has developed since 1983—a market that promises to have a significant catalytic impact on the further economic restructuring of Europe, especially as remaining institutional and regulatory obstacles are eased. The industry segments subject to restructuring through M&A transactions in the EC are similar to those subject to M&A activity in the United States. This is not surprising, as the underlying economic forces affecting these industries are similar on both sides of the Atlantic.

THE ROLE OF FINANCIAL ADVISORS

It is natural, of course, to expect leading financial firms to be in the business of providing advice and executing transactions in their own countries on behalf of foreign companies. They are selected because they have the knowledge of local markets, practices, and personalities that will be required to complete the transaction. The same is true when an American company wishes to obtain advice in a foreign market. In Germany, for example, a U.S. company might seek the advice of a German bank to complete a transaction. It might also, however, retain a U.S. banker whose investment banking skills and

Table 17–6. Annual M&A Transactions Valued at $50 Million or More That Involve European Seller Companies

Year and Type of Transaction	Buyer Company from:													
	Europe		Canada		Middle East		United States		Asia		Australia New Zealand		Total	
	#	$a	#	$a	#	$a	#	$a	#	$a	#	$a	#	$a
1985														
Aquisition	18	7,655.4	–	–	–	–	–	–	–	–	–	–	18	7,655.4
Stake	27	6,875.0	–	–	2	435.0	–	–	–	–	1	87.2	30	7,397.2
Divestiture	12	1,678.2	1	328	1	50.0	3	215.0	–	–	–	–	17	2,271.2
Total	57	16,208.6	1	328	3	485.0	3	215.0	–	–	1	87.2	65	17,323.8
1986														
Aquisition	14	4,978.9	–	–	–	–	4	592.7	–	–	–	–	18	5,571.6
Stake	25	8,395.6	7	743.7	–	–	–	–	2	407.0	1	309.0	35	9,855.3
Divestiture	21	8,579.9	–	–	1	81.7	3	213.8	–	–	1	190.5	26	9,065.9
Total	60	21,954.4	7	743.7	1	81.7	7	806.5	2	407.0	2	499.5	79	24,492.9

494

1987

Aquisition	32	9,438.5	1	343.0	–		2	547.5	–		1	61.0	29	10,390.0
Stake	26	12,406.1	1	730.0	2	14,915.6	6	1,748.0	2	461.2	7	1,308.9	69	31,569.8
Divestiture	55	12,307.3	–	–	–	–	5	974.0	2	280.5	2	431.0	64	13,992.8
Total	130	34,151.8	2	1,073.0	3	14,915.6	13	3,269.5	4	741.7	10	1,800.9	162	55,952.6

1988

Aquisition	32	6,363.0	1	126.9	–	–	1	182.0	–	–	–	–	34	6,671.9
Stake	26	6,810.4	–	–	1	196.0	6	786.9	–	–	1	599.0	33	8,392.3
Divestiture	43	11,102.5	–	–	–	–	7	2,375.0	–	–	2	125.8	52	13,603.3
Total	101	24,275.9	1	126.9	1	196.0	14	3,343.9	–	–	3	724.8	120	28,667.5

a. In millions of dollars at current exchange rates.

SOURCE: Ingo Walter and Roy C. Smith, *Investment Banking in Europe: Restructuring for the 1990s* (Oxford: Basil Blackwell, 1989).

Table 17–7. Large European M&A Transactions by Industry, 1983–88

By Industry of Purchaser

SIC[a]	Description	No.	Value[b]
67	Holding companies	166	$66,358.0
20	Food products	26	12,403.3
13	Oil and gas	23	8,342.3
28	Chemicals	23	8,269.4
63	Insurance carriers	20	4,057.0
36	Electronic and electric equipment (excluding computers)	17	3,893.4
37	Transport equipment	11	3,608.7
27	Printing and publishing	11	3,278.4
35	Industrial and commercial machinery and computer equipment	9	3,257.8
61	Nondepository credit institutions	13	3,210.4
26	Paper and allied products	7	2,991.6
62	Security and commodity brokers, dealers, exchanges, and services	8	2,357.2
65	Real estate	11	2,094.5
49	Electric, gas, and sanitary services	7	1,983.4
86	Membership organizations	5	1,779.8
50	Wholesale trade, durables	12	1,753.8
58	Eating and drinking places	4	1,733.2
48	Communications	8	1,685.5
32	Stone, clay, glass, and concrete products	10	1,552.9
34	Fabricated metal products, excluding machinery and transport equipment	8	1,423.9
59	Miscellaneous retail	7	1,413.6
51	Wholesale trade—Nondurables	8	1,361.0
53	General merchandise stores	3	1,340.5
10	Metal mining	8	1,140.4
70	Hotels, rooming houses, camps and other lodging	10	1,126.4
60	Depository institutions	2	1,050.0
44	Water transportation	6	1,042.4
22	Textile mill products	3	1,019.8

By Industry of Target

SIC[a]	Description	No.	Value[b]
13	Oil and Gas	32	$32,995.6
20	Food	32	13,701.9
28	Chemicals	38	11,179.7
60	Depository institutions	39	10,170.3
37	Transportation equipment	17	9,749.3

a. The table shows only those two-digit SIC categories whose members participated in transactions of an aggregate value exceeding $1 billion.

b. In millions of dollars at current exchange rate.

SOURCE: Ingo Walter and Roy C. Smith, *Investment Banking in Europe: Restructuring for the 1990s* (Oxford: Basil Blackwell, 1989).

Table 17–7. (cont.)

By Industry of Target

SIC[a]	Description	No.	Value[b]
27	Printing and publishing	32	$6,492.7
63	Insurance carriers	20	6,196.4
36	Electronic and electric equipment (excluding computers)	23	4,914.3
89	Miscellaneous services	12	4,885.9
48	Communications	19	4,819.8
33	Primary motel industries	8	3,271.7
53	General merchandise stores	10	2,941.3
64	Insurance agents	7	2,610.3
67	Holding companies	15	2,473.5
26	Paper and allied products	13	2.210.7
35	Industrial and commercial machinery and computer equipment	10	2,173.2
62	Security and commodity brokers, dealers, exchanges, and services	13	2,112.6
32	Stone, clay, glass, and concrete products	11	2,075.8
51	Wholesale trade—nondurables	10	1,890.6
70	Hotels, rooming houses, camps, and other lodging	15	1,884.9
61	Nondepository credit institutions	13	1,775.0
10	Metal mining	12	1,753.8
57	Home furniture, furnishings, and equipment stores	6	1,538.0
47	Transportation services	6	1,183.7
65	Real estate	8	1,176.0

Major Intraindustry Transactions

Target SIC	Principal SIC		No.	Value
13	10	Oil and gas—Metal mining	2	$249.5
10	10	Metal mining	4	328.4
22	22	Textile mill products	3	444.8
67	67	Holding companies	6	743.0
64	64	Insurance agents, services, and brokers	3	896.6
47	47	Transportation services	6	1,183.7
48	48	Communications	7	1,617.8
63	63	Insurance carriers	11	2,130.1
60	67	Depository institutions— Holding companies	10	2,489.0
37	37	Transportation equipment	6	2,879.6
27	27	Printing and publishing	15	3,091.8
60	60	Depository institutions	17	3,978.7
28	28	Chemicals	14	5,928.8
13	13	Oil and gas	19	8,259.0
20	20	Food products	20	9,734.4

international knowledge will help the company to interpret the advice of the German banker. The reverse is perhaps also true; when German companies seek U.S. advice, they may also retain a German bank to help understand it.

What is new in recent years, as a result of the globalization of financial markets and the worldwide presence of major financial services firms, is the movement of international firms into the business of providing indigenous financial advice. An example is the growing involvement of U.S. investment banks in the intra-U.K. M&A business, which had long been the exclusive preserve of British merchant banks.

There are several reasons why the U.S. firms became involved in this activity. As their London operations and their senior British staff expanded, so did their knowledge of the U.K. merger market, the companies involved, and the relationships they enjoyed with them (many were companies that the U.S. firm had done business with in the past). Also, many U.S. firms began to become familiar with U.K. merger transactions as a result of purchasing stocks of U.K. companies subject to takeover bids (i.e., participating in risk or merger arbitrage) and in following such companies in their research departments for the benefit of U.S. investor clients.

Perhaps most important, however, is the fact that the merger business, like capital markets, has become globalized. Networks and procedures now existed to enable buyers and sellers of companies to participate in a single marketplace for corporate control. And the agents and brokers who are capable of providing advice and guidance to their clients seeking to use the marketplace are the bankers with the infrastructure, the trained personnel, and the contacts with the worldwide corporate community.

For some years U.S. companies looking to be sold sought to include international companies in the bidding. This is now happening in the U.K. For example, if a U.K. company is to be sold voluntarily, or otherwise is attempting to escape the unwelcome embrace of a U.K raider, it is common practice to look for alternatives in the United States and elsewhere. These alternatives can include selling the company either to a group of investors seeking to buy the company with a substantial amount of borrowed capital as a financial investment (i.e., an LBO) or to a friendly corporate purchaser, a "white knight." To find an international LBO opportunity or a white knight, one must be able to access potential participants in the United States and the rest of the world quickly, efficiently, and confidentially. U.S. firms have this capability. After a slow beginning, it has become fairly common to see U.S. investment banks working alongside British merchant banks in raid defenses in the United Kingdom.

Some U.S. firms have become involved in giving advice to European companies acting as purchasers of other European companies, in order to help these companies be better able to anticipate the evasive moves of their targets. In some cases, a European company may even invite a U.S. firm to join its team of otherwise all-U.K. investors, because the European company is impressed by the U.S. firm's abilities to value companies for the global merger market and its tactical and structural ideas.

Table 17–8 shows summaries of league tables for several categories of international M&A activity for 1988.

DEVELOPMENT OF M&A SERVICES

Few sources of revenue are more attractive to investment and all other types of bankers than merger and other high value-added fees. A loan involves a commitment of a bank's capital and offers the risk of nonrepayment. A bond or equity issue requires the bank's underwriting commitment and exposes it to market risk. A swap involves booking a contingent asset or liability. But advisory fees are earned exclusively as a result of putting the firm's skills and knowledge to work, not as a result of committing the firm's capital, which is increasingly the case in other parts of the international banking and securities business. And the fees, commensurate with the added value of the service, are considerable. On transactions of several hundred million dollars, fees might average 1% to $1\frac{1}{2}$% of the purchase price.

The experience of a number of U.S. firms in Europe and elsewhere has encouraged many to embark upon efforts to enter the indigenous business for merger and other financial advice in other countries. It takes several years to develop a strong franchise in a particular market, but the potential rewards encourage many to undertake the effort to build up local capabilities. Not all markets are equally penetrable by foreigners, nor do mergers and related transactions—or those involving a comparable degree of financial sophistication—represent equally attractive opportunities in all countries. However, many observers believe that as Europe experiences gradual envelopment in greater

Table 17–8. International M & A Advisors for 1988

Ranking	By Total Value of All Deals Worldwide			By Total Value of Cross-Border Activity			By Total Value of Intra-European Activity		
	Advisor	Value[a]	No.	Advisor	Value[a]	No.	Advisor	Value[a]	No.
1	Morgan Stanley	$86,003	121	First Boston	$34,421	34	S. G. Warburg	$18,315	75
2	Goldman Sachs	84,891	167	Goldman Sachs	31,356	46	Goldman Sachs	17,749	22
3	First Boston	71,236	142	Schroder Group	20,907	58	Schroder Group	17,210	103
4	Shearson Lehman	63,059	223	Morgan Stanley	20,568	29	Lazards	16,789	66
5	Merrill Lynch	52,476	134	Shearson Lehman	17,971	57	Morgan Grenfell	15,947	105
6	Wasserstein-Perella	38,926	25	Wasserstein-Perella	16,130	12	Kleinwort Benson	14,825	84
7	Salomon Bros.	38,142	138	Lazards	12,806	23	County NatWest	12,772	76
8	Drexel Burnham	36,258	165	S. G. Warburg	12,734	31	First Boston	11,119	11
9	Schroder Group	36,234	156	Security Pacific	8,655	23	Samuel Montagu	9,711	72
10	S. G. Warburg	27,275	99	County NatWest	8,540	26	Shearson Lehman	9,232	26
11	Security Pacific	21,201	106	Merrill Lynch	7,753	24	N. M. Rothschild	8,816	63
12	Baring Bros.	21,082	60	Salomon Bros.	5,692	36	Salomon Bros.	8,056	14
13	Kleinwort Benson	21,081	98	Samuel Montagu	4,863	21	Security Pacific	7,372	37
14	Kidder Peabody	17,910	70	Kleinwort Benson	4,790	22	Baring Bros.	7,258	39
15	Lazards	17,126	69	Morgan Grenfell	4,634	48	Morgan Stanley	6,878	16

a. In millions of dollars.

SOURCE: Ingo Walter and Roy C. Smith, *Investment Banking in Europe: Restructuring for the 1990s* (Oxford: Basil Blackwell, 1989).

amounts of necessary corporate restructuring, it will, in turn, create a broad new market for financial advisory services of virtually all types. Ultimately, this phenomenon can be expected to spread to Japan, where it will undoubtedly change its shape somewhat to conform to unique Japanese cultural considerations, which eschew outright takeover activity.

The great activity in the area of mergers, recapitalizations, and specialized financings in the United States and the United Kingdom over the past decade or so has caused financial service firms to place a very high importance on finding a suitable place for themselves in this growing and lucrative segment of the investment banking business. Many new competitors have entered the field, including investment bankers that specialize in investing as principals in takeover or LBO situations; small firms of specialized advisors have also entered the field. Commercial banks have also set up M&A departments and have developed special capabilities in leveraged and related transactions. All participants in the mergers business now have to recognize the considerable strategic implications resulting from the globalization of mergers, restructuring, and financial advisory services.

The basic distinction among M&A services is whether the service is offered to the buyer of a company or to a seller and, especially in the case of the latter, whether the sale is voluntary or involuntary. In each country local practices governing mergers and acquisitions differ very considerably. For example, in the United States legal considerations and tactics are of paramount importance; there is a wide range of maneuvers open to both sides, and the pursuit and defense of companies can be quite aggressive. In most other countries aggressive legal actions are much less common and the room for tactical maneuvering is less, but still the quality of the advice received by the company attempting to capture or escape the other will have much to do with the outcome.

Seller Representation

When advising a seller, whether a victim of a raid, a corporation seeking to divest a subsidiary, or a family hoping to sell the inherited business to "nice people," the role of the advisor is to provide objective and experienced counsel and to assist the client in coping with the pyschological trauma involved. There is almost always pyschological trauma involved—buying and selling companies creates emotional involvement and anxiety on the part of those directly affected by the outcome. However, spending the time with a client to explain what lies ahead and what realistically can be expected often helps to lessen trauma that might otherwise be experienced later in the transaction.

A seller's advisor will perform the following tasks in the course of the assignment:

1. Analyze a list of possible buyers, including all names of possible buyers furnished by the client, to determine the most likely buyers and their abilities to obtain financing for the transaction.
2. Explain how particular buyers would go about making an evaluation of the company and what the impact of the acquisition would be on the financial statements and stock price of the buyer.
3. Determine the value of the company based on a thorough understanding of the company's business, a review of current market data, and the banker's own experience, and advise the client what the probable selling price range is.
4. Prepare materials that describe the company, based on information supplied by it; these materials should emphasize the points of value to a buyer but should also be fair and objective in all respects.
5. Contact potential buyers at decision-making levels and serve as the exclusive contact person for buyers.
6. Control the process of distributing information to prospective buyers and providing opportunities for such buyers to ask questions about the business, to meet with management, and so forth.
7. Control the bidding process so as to create an auctionlike situation aimed at getting the highest price for the seller (or to maximize any other factors that may be important to the seller).
8. Advise on the structure of the transaction so as to get the maximum advantage for both sides.
9. Ensure that all important nonfinancial terms are settled at an early stage, and see that postagreement documentation flows smoothly.

This process is fairly straightforward. For larger-sized transactions, a number of international names will be included on the list of prospective buyers. It will be up to the banker to make contacts at the appropriate level. Adding non-U.S. multinational corporations to the prospective buyer lists, which ultimately results in closer contact between the banker and the foreign multinational, may result in a future business relationship with the foreign company. For this reason and for competitive reasons as well (sellers tend to select bankers they believe can reach a broad spectrum of prospective buyers), most U.S. investment bankers have begun to develop a wide-ranging network of international M&A players.

Raid Defense

When defending a company against a raid, the banker, in addition to complying with all the regulatory and legal requirements of the country involved, must assist the client in evaluating the company's and the shareholders' alternatives. Once a hostile takeover effort has begun, it is very difficult to escape without either selling to another company instead (a white knight) or undergoing a substantial reorganization or recapitalization. In all cases, the banker will look to international participants and markets to find a way to enhance the value of the client's shares.

Buyer Representation

When representing a buyer, the banker faces a more complex series of problems. The first of these is the necessity to make an assessment that the buyer is serious and will be prepared to move forward when all is ready. Second, the banker must have no real or apparent conflict of interest in representing the buyer in the specific transaction. The banker could already be pledged to another client for the particular target, or the target could be a company that the banker is close to or already representing in some other capacity. Third, the banker may discover that the client does not have a single company in mind, but perhaps several. Or the client may want the banker to come up with "ideas" for acquisitions, which the banker may not be in a good position to do.

Many bankers are willing, even eager, to conduct buyer searches for their clients. Frequently, these searches, especially for international companies, do not result in a completed transaction. They are often the subject of miscommunication between the banker and the client, and sometimes disappointment or ill feelings result. On other occasions, the assignment cements a relationship that survives the early stages of the transaction and ultimately is able to bear fruit. Investment bankers are not at their best offering what are essentially management consultancy services; however they are at their best in carrying out the execution of transactions that clients have already decided to undertake — (e. g., valuing securities, assessing merger market values for companies, and piloting their clients through a complex tactical operation to complete the transaction at a fair price).

Many international corporations do not fully understand how to use investment bankers and frequently do not take their advice because they are not comfortable with it. Frequently, under such circumstances, the transaction contemplated by the international company fails. Many international corporations dislike the idea of a competitive auction process to acquire a particular target. They would prefer direct, one-on-one negotiations; but the seller and the seller's banker know that more aggressive bidding is likely to come as a result of competition. The international buyer may balk at these procedures or bid too low to win. Their approach should be to obtain the advice necessary to win the bidding, not necessarily the advice that they prefer to hear. Usually, however, when an international company has been through the process unsuccessfully once, it adapts and does much better the next time.

When representing a buyer, a banker will perform the following tasks:

1. Conduct a thorough review of the target and all of its subsidiaries based on all publicly available information.
2. Advise as to the probable price range necessary to acquire the target, bearing in mind the advice that would be given to the target if the target had asked the banker to sell the company.
3. Advise as to the likelihood of the target's receptiveness to an invitation to enter into discussions aimed at a merger.
4. Advise on how the target will react when apprised of the client's interest, what it will consider to be its options, and what actions it is likely to take.
5. Evaluate each of those options in detail. Play the role of the seller's advisor in the circumstances. Devise tactics accordingly.
6. Prepare recommendations on the financial structure of the transaction and how the buyer should best proceed to arrange financing for the transaction.
7. Advise on the initial approach to the target, the value to be suggested, and steps for following up.
8. Function as a liason between the client and the target or the target's bankers.
9. Advise on the changing tactical situation and the responses to communications from the target.

10. Arrange the purchase of shares through a tender offer.
11. Assist in arranging long-term financing for the transaction and in selling assets that are not to be retained.

There are many other steps and functions that occur. However, much of what goes on in an acquisition situation is in response to moves undertaken by the other side. It is essential that good communications and mutual understanding exist between banker and client in order to be able to respond to the changing circumstances in the most timely and effective way.

Over the years sellers have learned that they receive a higher net price for their shares by playing hard to get. No one accepts a first, or even a second, unsolicited offer. Tactics are employed to maximize the public visibility of the transaction with the hope of attracting additional suitors. To persuade prospective buyers that they must increase their bid, the defender must be credible. If the buyer senses a lack of credibility regarding the seller's wish to be acquired or the viability of the seller's alternatives, the bid will not be raised— indeed, it may be lowered.

Even companies that know the buyer well and might like to be acquired will still impose an auction process on a sale of the company in order to protect shareholders' interests. In this context, there are no longer any more friendly, easy deals. European and Japanese buyers of U.S. companies have had to adapt to a tougher, more abrasive environment when seeking acquisitions. Of course, many have already done so and perhaps will apply their new-found toughness to future transactions in other areas.

It is perhaps predictable that as M&A activity and tactics spread across the Atlantic and the English Channel, and perhaps someday across the Pacific, much of the rough and tumble of the U.S. market, with its heavy emphasis on aggressive legal maneuvering, will travel with it. The surprise effort to acquire control of the Societe Generalé, the dominant industrial and financial concern in Belgium, by Carlo de Benedetti, an aggressive Italian financier, and his large cohort of mixed international investors in early 1988 is an early indication that this is happening already. De Benedetti's incorporated acquisition vehicle for this vigorously opposed transaction was named "Europe 1992," in anticipation no doubt of further adventures of this kind in the future.

The effort by de Benedetti demonstrated that Belgium had far fewer real barriers to takeover than had been assumed; even if "the right people" owned a corporation, this was not enough to prevent takeovers. Recently in the United Kingdom, the Monopolies Commission has taken a lenient view of international acquisitions. In Holland the significant barriers that have prevented takeovers are being partially dismantled. At the same time that Mr. de Benedetti was attracting attention to the comparative ease with which a prominent establishment corporation could be shaken up, the Amsterdam Stock Exchange announced the beginning of a program to gradually dismantle antitakeover defenses available to hitherto well-insulated Dutch companies. This rule change, made in anticipation of the environment of the 1990s, would prevent the issuance of preferred shares without the approval of common stockholders and would disallow nonvoting shares.

OTHER FINANCIAL ADVISORY SERVICES

Most banks offer additional advisory services:

1. *Swaps.* Advice is given on how to manage liabilities for companies and other banks. This entails the structuring of swaps and the use of options and futures in various currencies. Typically, banks offer these services with the intention of being paid through fees and commissions associated with execution (see Chapter 15).
2. *Share Ownership.* More international companies are undertaking programs designed to promote ownership of their securities by investors in capital markets around the world. As a result, bankers arrange listings on international stock exchanges and of unregistered "private placements" of debt and equity securities of companies with institutional investors in the United States, Japan, and Europe (See Chapter 13).
3. *LBOs.* More international companies are showing interest in LBOs by management (called "management buyouts" in the United Kingdom) assisted by investor groups. So far this activity has been restricted mainly to management buyouts of subsidiaries that parent companies have agreed to sell; however, many observers believe a speading of this activity will continue into continental Europe and elsewhere.
4. *Project Finance and Financial Engineering.* Japanese corporations continue to make large direct investments in factories and other facilities in the United States, which can be financed in various creative ways (e.g., through the sale of adjustable rate preferred

stock, private placements, lease arrangements, commercial paper, and municipal revenue bonds). Such transactions present opportunities for the company's Japanese banks and for U.S. bankers able to come up with and to communicate high value-added financing ideas to the Japanese.

5. *Real Estate.* Many Japanese investors and European institutions have become active investors in both debt and equity positions in U.S. commercial real estate. For those bankers active in real estate finance, many opportunities are created, and many more are expected to be as real estate transactions of the sort conducted in the United States begin to appear in Europe, and in Japan.

COMPETING IN INTERNATIONAL FINANCIAL ADVISORY SERVICES

The market for international advisory services is broad, and, because of its globalized character, it is often indistinguishable from the market of financial advisory services conducted at home. Competing successfully in this market has more to do with basic competence in financial advisory work than it does with its international overlay, but at the same time, without international capabilities, even a firm with a strong reputation in the field may lose business to those who operate on a global basis.

This would be the point of view of an American investment bank that is active in the M&A business. For such a firm, cross-border transactions are not separated from those that occur in the United States, and the distinction between "domestic" and "international" mergers has begun to fade. The U.S. firm, however, would view the offering of merger advisory services to the indigenous market in another country (e.g., Australia) as a separate international business.

A German bank, on the other hand, having had little opportunity to participate in the world-wide M&A activity that involves German companies, might look at domestic and international mergers differently from the American firm. So would the Japanese banker, for whom international mergers are rare indeed and domestic ones are even rarer.

This does not mean that only U.S. and British firms will be able to compete in the international merger advisory business of the future, but they do have the advantage of being firmly in place at the game's beginning. Those continental European and Japanese firms who want to become involved will find various ways to do so. They can acquire firms with an existing franchise in the merger field, or they can acquire or create a jointly owned international firm (e.g., CS, First Boston) that can operate independently from its parents in the more freewheeling markets of London and New York. They also can hire experienced professionals to conduct the mergers business for them. Perhaps renowned merger "stars," like those leaving investment banks in New York to set out on their own, will be induced to align themselves with Daiwa Securities, Amro Bank, or Banco di Roma. Several have already lined up with other large international firms. European houses have set up shop in the United States before with their eyes on the high value-added investment banking business. Lazard Freres formed an American partnership around 1900. Today it is a small but extremely potent firm in the M&A business. The European Rothschild firms have a U.S. affiliate, Rothschild, Inc., that is headed by an American who is a well-known former takeover lawyer. The affiliate has been quite active in representing European firms seeking to buy companies in the United States.

Developing a Strategy

To compete in the top bracket of the world M&A market every participant must develop a strategy for the business that is consistent with the rest of the firm's business and is one that the firm can gain strong support for throughout its organization. A prospective entrant, be it a domestic commercial bank, a foreign bank, or an investment bank not in the business, must address three fundamental issues:

1. Mergers and acquisitions are essentially an aggressive and highly visible, if not controversial, activity. Can the rest of the firm's business, which may depend heavily on close, longstanding client relationships, survive the transition? Will clients draw back from the relationship if they fear that the firm might align itself with another client planning an unwelcome approach?
2. Costs, both out of pocket and contingent, are considerable. Is the firm prepared to pay the cost of fielding a world-class team of merger specialists, which not only requires highly paid executives but also a sizeable support staff and expensive international facilities? Is it prepared for the next step too—that is, is it prepared to take equity and junk bond positions in client transactions for its

own account? Is the firm prepared to accept the consequences of failure and exposure to considerable litigation?

3. Is the firm prepared to grant the M&A team the autonomy that it needs to act quickly and aggressively? Will the firm allow the M&A team a kind of relationship priority with chief executives and other top executives of client companies?

Many players will feel the future rewards are worth the trouble and the money. Others will try to find a niche that does not require such a heavy commitment. Perhaps they can avoid unfriendly deals or focus on helping clients with smaller, domestic transactions. Other banks will find the unexpected problems of the M&A business to be significant, and they may lose enthusiasm for being in the forefront of the business.

In most of the world commercial banking is essentially a relationship business in which loyalty is expected and rewarded. Banks as lenders have loan portfolios to maintain, and to do so requires them to maintain credit information about their clients, some of which is highly confidential. Banks must guard carefully against breaches of the "Chinese Wall" that separates information retained in one part of the bank from being used by another. They must also guard against developing conflicts of interest, which can occur when one client wants to acquire another who does not wish to be acquired.

Commercial banks, and perhaps some European universal banks, may also discover that their particular comparative advantages in the global competition for financial services, (i.e., a large capital base and a large, widespread organization) are not necessarily helpful in the area of merger-related services. Capital is not important in an advisory business, and their large calling organizations may not have good access to chief executives.

Many banks will decide that they are better off in the business of lending to their clients, especially when they need acquisition financing, than in competing in a business they may not be especially good at or have the stomach for. Other banks will disagree, feeling that the future of wholesale banking is unattractive and that they must develop competence in the M&A field, with its many related transactions, in order to retain a prominent position in domestic and international financial services for the 1990s and beyond. Such banks obviously look at mergers and related services as part of a general restructuring of the banking industry—one from which they are not precluded from participation by regulation.

ORGANIZING FINANCIAL ADVISORY SERVICES

Most investment and merchant banks group their advisory services into three basic functional groups:

1. Mergers and acquisitions and related transactions (which usually involve or are closely tied in with LBOs, "bridge financings," and other principal investment activities)
2. Capital market services (which will include swaps and related activities, whether conducted as principal or as agent)
3. Project and/or "private" financing activities (which specialize in large, financial engineering endeavors for a fee)

These three services may not be linked directly, but they are linked indirectly. Mergers have to be financed, and advisors must review a lot of information on what financial options participants have. LBOs start out as mergers or divestitures and end up as financial engineering projects, which require market information on a variety of sophisticated financial methods that can involve swaps, hedges, "synthetic" securities, and junk bonds. Firms that possess strength in all three advisory areas, and are capable of effecting close coordination between them, will find themselves with a competitive advantage over firms without comparably interlinked capabilities.

Any complex advisory assignment involves a large team effort. Relationship officers, execution specialists, experts in many different related activities, capital market and foreign exchange specialists, legal and accounting advisors, and sometimes the firm's own capital commitment apparatus are called upon to see a transaction through to a successful conclusion. As in an operating room in a hospital, when the team works well together the chances for success are maximized; when a part of the team does not fit in well, the probability of success drops sharply. The wise patient selects doctors carefully but is equally attentive to the team that supports them.

MARKETING

Marketing advisory services can be difficult unless one's firm is a market leader, in which case marketing is not difficult. There is a high level of concentration in the M&A and financial advisory businesses. Companies tend to seek out those with the greatest experience or most aggressive reputation, at the expense of other firms who may know the company better but who are not as well regarded in the advisory area. The "star" system that characterizes Wall Street and London tends to reinforce this behavior. Nevertheless, for those firms seeking to improve their penetration of the market for advisory services, all is not lost. Stars come and go; new ones are created all the time. Technology and the broadening international scope of the field of play make for new opportunities.

Effective marketing of financial advisory services requires focus, credibility, and frequent contact with clients. Many clients may honor the existing relationship with the firm and want to use it for merger advisory work as long as they can be convinced that the services offered are as good as those offered by anyone else. Indeed, many firms are suspicious of those firms that are highly identified with mergers and their attendant controversies. Foreign firms, in particular, want to be advised by someone they trust. To persuade clients that the firm is ready and able to advise it in complex mergers and other advisory assignments, the firm first must have resolved at least the following three matters:

1. The marketing message must clearly reflect the firm's strategy as to where and how it wishes to compete.
2. The firm must have developed a first-class execution capability that is totally consistent with the firm's strategy.
3. The firm must have painstakingly taken the time to convert, upgrade (if necessary), and train its worldwide calling organization in the marketing message and in what should be done to deliver it to the right people in the right companies. Then, the message must be repeated over and over again until it is accepted. "This is what our bank does, this is why you can believe we are good at what we do, and this is how we can work together."

DANGERS AND PITFALLS

A strategy that is well tailored to the bank's own circumstances, an effective and credible execution capability, and a well-coordinated marketing effort will surely produce results in time. There are many things that can go wrong, however, and many will. Top management must be prepared to stand by the commitment to be in the advisory business despite setbacks and occasional embarrassments. This is often easier said than done. Some of the other difficulties that must be faced are listed below.

Autonomy versus Control

The firm must find the balance between freedom for well-informed professionals to pursue transactions aggressively and reliable assurance that the system is under control— that is, the young tigers are not overlooking legal, regulatory, or ethical considerations in their quest for success.

Not Controlling the Client

Clients like things to be done their way, but often they are wrong, stubborn, or misinformed. Under such circumstances they must be controllable—that is, the advisor must be able to get the client to sit down and understand the issue correctly. An uncontrollable client at the very least can be embarrassing or can tie the firm to an unpromising player in the game, perhaps at the cost of having to refuse another. At worst, such a client can get the firm involved in ugly litigation and risk its reputation.

Fee Cutting

In a free market fees are there to be cut. If cutting them makes it easier to land an assignment, then they tend to get cut. The newcomer, however, will realize that the reason why merger fees have remained where they are for so long is because they are, in the end, reflective of value (or the expectation of such value) created by the efforts of the advisor for the client. The major clients know this or, in due course, are persuaded of it. Drug companies charge a lot for their proprietary compounds, far more than the value of the raw materials and labor that go into them. They have produced, at great expense over a great many years, a substance of high value to the user. Cut-rate drugs, surgeons, lawyers, or financial advisors are not always looked upon as the most valuable or reliable. Banks seeking to gain entry to the mergers business will invest heavily in the capability to participate in it. Markets of the future are not predictable; mergers activity may decline. Fee cutting to get into the game may be difficult to reverse once established; in any case, it may remove some of the economic incentive for entering the business in the first place.

Internal Discord

There are many opportunities for internal discord within a firm active in providing merger and related high value-added services. Young, aggressive professionals with insufficient regard for their seniors are a constant problem, especially when they are earning higher salaries and bonuses than the seniors. The lack of access to a client's chief executives, the need for restricting information to a need-to-know basis, and the inability to reach members of the merger squad, or have them attend meetings with other clients, are constant irritations. These are balanced by the complaints of the advisory group that the firm is stodgy, bureaucratic, and overly conservative in terms of clients that it will take on and transactions it will do for them. The only resolution is good leadership of the unit and an understanding and acceptance of the firm's goal's by everyone involved.

SUMMARY

For the U.S. and U.K. investment banks, providing international advisory services has been a natural extension of providing the same services domestically. Whether the client is a buyer, a reluctant seller, or a willing target, tapping the international market for better terms than can be accessed domestically is often advisable and sometimes imperative in today's business environment. Banks with a strong local M&A team and an international presence—primarily U.S. investment houses—have been well positioned to take advantage of this aspect of globalization.

The European and Japanese environments have lacked the free-wheeling capital markets and strict legal framework that have fostered the U.S. M&A business. As globalization continues, however, homogenization of environments will be approached. The evolving environment will have more of the U.S. characteristics than the European or Japanese and will be characterized by a profitable internationalized M&A business.

As an activity generating substantial fees but requiring no direct commitment of the bank's capital, M&A business and related advisory work are irresistible to many. However, newcomers should be warned that M&A activities may not coexist easily with relationship banking in the same firm. Managing the M&A department is highly challenging. One must control the customer without alienating him and must control the team without stifling it. One must maintain the delivery networks and the firm's image, knowing which deals to pursue and how to pursue them and knowing which to decline. All demand skills specific to the M&A business increasingly projected into an international dimension.

NOTE

1. Michel Fleuriet, "Mergers and Acquisitions: The French Experience," mimeographed (Paris: Chase Manhattan S.A., 1989).

SELECTED REFERENCES

Altany, David.   "Foreign Investors: Allies or Aggressors." *Industry Week,* February 1, 1988.

Brooks, John.   *The Takeover Game,* New York: E. P. Dutton, 1987.

Evans, Garry, et al.   "M&A for Richer, for Poorer." *Euromoney,* August 1987.

Gray, Frank.   "Britain Buys Back the Colonies." *Business Month,* November 1987.

Mergers & Acquisitions, Various issues 1987–1988.

Smith, Roy C.   *The Money Wars.* New York: E. P. Dutton, 1990.

Walter, Ingo, and Smith, Roy C.   *Investment Banking in Europe: Restructuring in the 1990s.* Oxford: Basil Blackwell, 1989.

18

International Investment Management

In the late nineteenth century, Britain, the Japan of the day, had accumulated substantial excess savings as a result of its world pre-eminence as a manufacturer and an exporter. The United States was, in the eyes of many British investors, the land of the future, the Japan of tomorrow. The United States had big plans—for railways that now connected the two sea coasts, for industry, and for farming and raw materials extraction. British capital poured into the United States to participate in these remarkable and comparatively inexpensive (in terms of the value of the pound) investment opportunities. The British were not alone; American opportunity was not a secret. French, German, Dutch, Swiss, and other Europeans also joined in, resulting in a substantial flow of investment capital from Europe to the United States. The investments were made by wealthy individuals, families, and investment partnerships made up of such persons. There were no institutional investors of note at the time, and corporations were not players as such, since business investments tended to be made by their owners directly as individuals.

INTERNATIONAL MONEY MANAGERS

Individual investors had investment advisors who assisted them in managing their money. These advisors were often bankers or lawyers of their acquaintance who knew their way around the City of London and the other European financial capitals. These advisors would be supplied with information about investment opportunities by brokers or promoters, whose job it was to place new issues of securities. Many of the bankers and brokers had offices or affiliations in New York, Philadelphia, and Boston and were a steady source of new investment ideas.[1] Investment performance was difficult to measure— whether one made money or not, and got in on the really good deals that one's friends were offered tended to be the crude yardstick by which success was measured.

Investing in America was good speculation, but it was not really safe. One could not send one's "core capital" to New York to rest in an unregulated bank deposit or to invest in government securities of a country with such an unstable financial history. When political changes and upheavals came, as they often did in Europe during the latter part of the nineteenth century, families wanted a safe haven for their core capital that would be outside the political and fiscal reach of whatever new government was in power in their home countries. Many funds found their way into neutral, stable, remote Switzerland, where for many years its thrifty and tidy inhabitants had offered safe, secure, and confidential banking services.

This periodic migration of capital into the Alps continued as the reputation of the Swiss for competence and confidentiality grew and spread. Latin Americans, Asians, Middle Easterners, middle Europeans, and investors from all over the rest of the world were attracted to Zurich, Geneva, or Lugano, where their affairs would be handled reliably and graciously. During the 1920s and 1930s further political and economic upheavals sent additional funds to Switzerland. After Hitler's rise to power, Switzerland found it expedient to offer secret bank accounts to Jewish clients and others. After the war, the Swiss continued to attract funds from all around the world, especially from those countries where political or economic instability was high or where new wealth was accumulated without a commensurate structure for investing it (e.g., in Iran and the other oil-producing countries).

During the 1920s, the United States continued to grow and enjoy boom times, while most of the European economies were barely getting by. Spurred by its capital-raising experiences during World War I and its lively economy, the New York securities markets bubbled with activity. More funds flowed into the country for investment in the stock market, which was climbing to new heights. At the same time, U.S. funds were being invested in foreign securities (other than war loans) for the first time. Bonds were floated in New York by issuers from Scandinavia, Austria, Japan, Russia, China, Colombia, the Philippines, Brazil, and other countries. Although some were bought by individuals, most were bought by banks and other institutional investors who were just beginning to appear on the financial scene.[2] After the stock market crash of 1929, the Great Depression and World War II, U.S. institutions had lost much of their earlier interest in foreign securities, except for those of the highest quality.

They had more than enough opportunities in the domestic market, especially in the 1960s when many insurance companies and pension funds began to invest heavily in U.S. common stocks.

As the U.S. institutional investor became an increasingly important, and then dominant, factor in U.S. securities markets, the professional standards of investment management began to rise. Prudence was essential, but institutional investors could still be prudential and provide exceptional performance if their managers were trained in the most modern practices of investment management and were motivated. The performance-oriented, professional money manager appeared on the scene; soon thereafter, theories of portfolio diversification, risk/return optimization measures, and aggressive, hands-on portfolio management were put into practice. Such practices stimulated securities markets, especially the stock market, in the late 1960s and attracted substantial portfolio investment to New York from money managers in Europe—especially from Switzerland and the United Kingdom, although the latter still suffered the weight of exchange controls at the time.

Throughout much of the 1970s the U.S. markets struggled with high inflation and difficult securities markets. Europeans remained invested, but more because they felt they had to be than because their profits were so high. The dollar declined, bonds lost value in the soaring interest rate environment, and the Dow Jones industrial average had hardly increased at all during the 10-year interval ending in 1980. International investors were not totally disheartened by the dull performance in the United States, however, because they had discovered Japan.

Beginning in the early 1970s Japan's stock market attracted huge investments from European portfolios—whose Swiss, British, Dutch, French, and German managers recognized it as the America of the future. They studied the Japanese economy and stock market carefully, though no doubt without really understanding it, and committed large amounts to Japanese stocks, which were almost immediately profitable. Some American investors, institutional and individual, joined the party, but most Americans still believed that the greatest opportunities remained in the United States (if only the blasted stock market would behave). They felt the Japanese market was too unfamiliar for them to be able to apply their portfolio management practices. By the time many of the U.S. portfolio managers had learned what they needed to know about Japan, the Reagan bull market was on the run at home.

Europeans (especially the quick-acting British and Dutch managers) switched a large portion of their funds back into the United States to catch this market phenomenon, which was accompanied by the additional bonanza, from their point of view, of a soaring dollar. U.S. investments became irresistible, at least until the dollar peaked in late 1985 and began its sharp decline. By this time U.S. investors realized that nondollar investments could be very profitable, especially when they were made in markets that were outperforming the U.S. market. U.S. investors began to look seriously again, for the first time since the 1920s, at foreign stocks. A few U.S. money managers had been significant investors in foreign securities for several years, but by the mid-1980s many more had joined them. By 1989 the 50 largest international managers in the United States accounted for more than $60 billion of international assets under management. Twenty-one of these managers had international accounts exceeding $1 billion (see Table 18–1).

Table 18–1.   Top 50 Managers Ranked by Combined International and Global Account Assets (as of March 31, 1989)

	U.S. $ Millions
1. State Street Bank	5,584
2. Capital Guardian	3,455
3. First Chicago	2,933
4. Batterymarch	2,552
5. J. P. Morgan	2,449
6. Morgan Grenfelt	2,404
7. Baring Int'l	2,383
8. Templeton Int'l	2,249
9. GE Investments	2,174
10. Rowe Price-Fleming	2,115
11. Grantham, Mayo	2,111
12. Wells Fargo	1,954
13. Schroder Capital	1,900
14. WorldInvest	1,648
15. Warburg Investment	1,533
16. Nomura Capital	1,529
17. Chase Investors	1,227
18. PCM Int'l	1,217
19. Oechsle Int'l	1,084
20. TCW Global	1,012
21. Fidelity Int'l	1,000
22. N.M. Rothschild Int'l	971
23. Bankers Trust	922
24. Dimensional Fund	885
25. Boston Int'l	826
26. Alliance Capital	804

Table 18–1. (cont.)

27.	Scudder, Stevens	791
28.	Posthorn Global	708
29.	Mercator Asset[a]	700
30.	Discount Corp./N.Y.	650
31.	IDS Int'l	624
32.	Julius Baer	623
33.	Mellon-Pictet Int'l	580
34.	Kemper-Murray	550
35.	Brown Brothers[a]	515
36.	Fiduciary Trust[a]	505
37.	Daiwa Int'l	482
38.	Arnhold/Bleichroeder	480
39.	Hill Samuel/Investment	403
40.	G.T. Capital	394
41.	Phillippe Investment	386
42.	Nikko Capital	380
43.	Capital Research	360
44.	Wellington Mgmt.	349
45.	SBC Portfolio	342
46.	Citicorp Investment	338
47.	Globe Finlay	330
48.	Capital Mgmt., Int'l	297
49.	County NatWest[a]	280
50.	ANB Investment	275
	TOTAL	**60,263**

Manager of Managers

Strategic Investment Partners	755
Frank Russell Trust	325
John Hancock Financial	15

a. as of Dec. 31, 1988

Ranking is based on U.S., institutional, discretionary, tax-exempt assets managed.

SOURCE: *Pensions and Investment Age*. June 26, 1989. p. 18.

Whose Money Is Being Managed?

Pension Funds

A number of events have shaped the U.S. institutional investor. Most important was the growth of pension funds, following the passage of the Employees Retirement Investment Security Act (ERISA) in 1974, which provided that underfunded corporate pension accounts be fully funded and that trustees of pension funds be required to provide "prudent" management of them. The first effect of ERISA was to dramatically increase the amount of money under active management by pension funds. The second result was to encourage the use of modern, professional portfolio management practices, including the practice of investing a substantial portion of fund assets in common stocks. Money managers were hired to manage, at their discretion, portions of the pension funds. Their performance was to be reviewed periodically, and competition among managers was encouraged. Managers considered to be performing less well than others would be dropped, and others would be added in their place. Common performance measures were adopted, such as comparing performance to indexes (e.g., the Dow Jones industrial average or the Standard & Poor's 500).

The need to compete and to exceed performance measures established by fund sponsors led to many changes in the investment management business in the United States. The number of money managers proliferated. Boutiques were formed by those with the hottest records. Traditional pension fund managers, insurance companies, and banks lost business, reorganized themselves, and won some of it back. Money managers began to share the pressure they were under with the brokers who supplied them with services. These services were extended to include high-quality securities research and idea generation (usually about specific stocks to buy or sell, but increasingly on the overall shape of their portfolios), block trading, and low-cost execution services. Brokers, who compete vigorously with one another, responded to the pressure. They hired research professionals so that the portfolio managers could keep their own staffs to a minimum. They cut commissions to the bone, offered up their best ideas, and provided what clients wanted in the way of the latest investment theory (e.g., quantitative analysis, transactions involving options and futures, and program trading to support indexed investments and portfolio insurance).

Amidst all this energy and effort to perfect investment management performance, investment in foreign securities was not overlooked, partly because the pension fund trustees were beginning to allocate portions of their funds to overseas managers to invest in non-U.S. assets. Slowly at first, then with greater conviction, U.S. money managers began to make bold investments in stock markets in Europe, Asia, and Australia. They looked to their brokers to provide them with the same kind of backup support and services for international investments that they provided for domestic investments.

Fund trustees and money managers realized that there were several reasons for them to emphasize foreign investments. For over a decade it had been obvious that the fluctuating dollar and U.S. economic performance periodically created superior investment opportunities outside of the United States. It would be prudent to invest a portion of the funds' assets in other markets to hedge against the underperformance of the U.S. market. (This also meant that a U.S. money manager might be able to outperform U.S. indices by spreading some of the investments into other markets that would do better than the U.S. market.)

Money managers also knew that many portfolios were oriented to invest in selected industries—(e.g., automobiles, chemicals, etc). With so many large foreign companies competing effectively with U.S. companies, it began to make sense to look at an industry on a worldwide basis. For example, a manager with investments in the auto industry might decide to concentrate only on Ford or General Motors in the United States, but to add shares of Nissan, Honda, BMW, or Fiat to the investment portfolio as well.

The trustees and the managers also knew that the boom in stock markets around the world meant there were occasional opportunities to invest in new markets that had room for enormous price appreciation—markets like Italy, Spain, Taiwan, Korea, and so on.

It was not long before the U.S. pension "revolution" spread to other countries. In Europe pension funds grew rapidly, fueled by increasing recognition of the need to fund past service obligations. In the United Kingdom pension fund managers have shown a preference for investments in real estate and common stocks as compared to fixed-income securities, but some have also invested in venture capital, farmland, and fine art. In most European countries exchange controls that restricted the investment of funds abroad have been removed. The lifting of these controls permitted a large volume of British investments to be made outside the country, especially in the United States and in Japan. Today, a typical U.K. pension fund will have 20 to 30 percent of its investments in non-U.K. assets.[3]

The Japanese too have undergone substantial pension reforms in the past 15 years. Before this, Japanese workers faced a retirement age of 55, at which time they were given a lump-sum severance payment based on the duration of employment. The payment was not nearly sufficient to purchase an annuity in an amount needed to support the worker's prospectively long retirement, so the worker was required to save his or her own money for retirement and/or obtain postretirement employment or assistance from other family members to make ends meet. More recently, however, Japanese corporations have adopted pension fund arrangements similar to those in the United States and in Europe, and these funds have grown extremely rapidly as a result of corporate contributions and the steep appreciation of the value of investments in the Japanese equity market.

Public pension funds (for government employees) in the United States have approached international investing very slowly, although these are expected to become more active in the future. In other countries huge investment organizations designed to provide social security and/or other benefits for citizens of the country have emerged. Especially active as international investors are such organizations from Singapore, Kuwait, Abu Dhabi, Saudi Arabia, and Venezuela.

International investments have grown as a percentage of total pension fund assets for the past several years. In some European pension funds, international investments may have reached their optimal level as a percentage of total assets; however, in U.S. and Japanese funds (where the ratio is somewhat below 10 percent), this is much less often the case, and further investment in international securities is expected.

Other Institutional Investors

Apart from pension fund managers and investment management companies, other institutional investors have become active participants in international securities markets. Such investors include insurance companies, savings and loan institutions (or their more healthy equivalents outside the United States), central banks and monetary authorities, religious organizations, and a variety of not-for-profit institutions and foundations from around the world. Many of these institutions manage their own international investments; others retain professional money managers to do it for them.

Corporations also are substantial investors in international securities. Apart from those engaging in merger and acquisitions activity during which shares are acquired (or sold), corporations invest in foreign securities as a way of managing their own cash reserves and of managing arbitrage between markets of various types. They also invest in international securities in order to hedge against the risks of foreign exchange and interest rates. In many countries corporations invest in securities as a way of improving corporate profits or in order to speculate on possible capital gains—especially in Japan, where corporations have been able to invest some of their large cash surpluses in tax-advantaged investment accounts. Such accounts (called "Tokkin") have accumulated large amounts for investment and accordingly have had a significant impact on domestic Japanese markets and, to a lesser extent, on certain foreign markets as well.[4] (See Chapter 16 for further discussion of these investors)

Individuals

Individuals have been substantial investors in overseas securities through accounts that are managed by professional investors. Such investments tend to be in the form of redeemable mutual funds (open end) or shares of investment companies (closed end) or through a personal account with a bank, in which investment discretion is given to the bank.

Investment companies have existed for a long time. Those specializing in general international investments have been common in Europe, especially in the United Kingdom (which offers various tax-advantaged funds based in the Channel Islands) and in Holland. In recent years they have also been widely offered in Japan through Japanese securities firms, and as of mid-1987 they comprised assets of about $160 billion.[5] These funds are managed either by the investment management affiliates of the securities firms, a designated foreign advisor, or some combination of the two.

Also available are funds designed to appeal to particular areas of potential investor interest (e.g., North American growth companies, Japanese and Pacific Basin companies, high technology companies, and foreign exchange investments). Such funds are popular in the United States, where recently a rich array of different "country funds" have been sold, enabling investors to concentrate on investments in specific countries. Among these have been funds aimed at Japan (the first Japan Fund was sold in the United States in 1962), Mexico, Spain, Thailand, Korea, Taiwan, Germany, Italy, and several other countries. Similar funds have also been sold in Europe. Bond funds and various money market funds are also available for international investors.

Private banking accounts for the bulk of individual investments in foreign securities emanating from Europe. Swiss banks are the best known among the continental banks offering private banking services. They feature high degrees of confidentiality, a risk-averse investment bias, and individual client interaction with account managers. Although the large Zurich-based banks (which operate throughout the country) command the largest share of the private banking assets, a large number of smaller *private banks* (meaning banks that are privately owned partnerships or closely held corporations) exist in Switzerland and manage a considerable amount of funds for their individual clients.

All of the universal banks in Europe offer investment management services to their clients. Most of these are oriented to the domestic markets, but the larger banks offer skilled international portfolio managers. In some countries—particularly the United Kingdom, Holland, Belgium, Germany, and France—merchant banks or *banques d'affaires* manage private wealth also.

By the end of 1989 it had become clear that huge pools of investment funds had accumulated around the world from pension funds, governments, investment companies, other institutional investors, and corporations and that an increasing proportion of these funds should be invested outside of the home countries of the funds. Equally, it was clear that different skills and capabilities, requiring different support services from brokers and dealers, were necessary to manage these internationally directed funds competitively. The funds' owners wanted superior investment performance, diversification, and safety in varying degrees. Few of these funds were fully capable of internally managing their international investments, so they turned to outside suppliers of international investment management services.

Who Are International Investment Managers?

U.S. Investment Managers

In the United States there are approximately 200 to 300 institutional investors in international securities, and the number grows steadily. Not all of these investors have committed a substantial portion of the funds that they manage to the international markets, however. Some, of course, have considerably more international investing experience than others. But on the whole, the U.S. institutional investor is less internationally attuned than the European institutional investor.

There are various types of international investment managers in the United States. There are the large investment institutions themselves (e.g., the College Retirement Equity Fund and Prudential Insurance), several investment companies and mutual funds (e.g., Capital Guardian Trust, Templeton International Fund and Fidelity International Fund), and banks (e.g., State Street Bank and Trust, J. P. Morgan Investment Management, and Bankers Trust). There are also specialized money managers (e.g., Scudder Stevens and Clark) who advise on international investment funds, and there are investment bankers and brokers (e.g., Morgan Stanley and Shearson Lehman Hutton) that manage funds for their clients.

These firms compete in the United States for contracts to manage international portions of pension funds and other assets with Swiss banks, Japanese investment managers, merchant banks from the United Kingdom, and others. There are hundreds of non-U.S. investment managers operating in the United States looking to attract part of the lucrative pension fund business. All investment management business is highly competitive in the United States, and management fees are comparatively small (around .75 percent of assets actively managed in equity portfolios and considerably less for fixed-income assets or assets managed according to passive, or indexed, programs).[6] For certain international equity investment programs, however, management fees can be higher than for domestic programs.

Competition in the investment management business in the United States has caused a number of significant changes in the last few years. The pressure on performance and on fees has caused several players long associated with the traditional money management business to leave the high-volume, domestic equity and fixed-income management businesses behind in order to concentrate on the higher-margin businesses of international investment management and private banking. Early in 1988, for example, Citicorp announced that it was selling its $21 billion domestic pension management business. Earlier, Manufacturers Hanover and Bank of America had taken similar steps. Profitability and management compensation and integration issues were apparently at the root of the decisions to sell. At the same time, however, Chemical Bank was reorganizing and reinforcing its investment management business and others were reaffirming their commitment to remain in the game.[7]

In Europe the scene is even more complicated by virtue of numerous different types of competitors populating the landscape. In London several merchant banks and brokers (e.g., S. G. Warburg, Kleinwort Benson, and Cazenove) manage funds that are to be invested abroad. There are also several important investment managers in Edinburgh. Further, a number of insurance companies and banks manage investments for their individual and pension fund clients. Well before Big Bang and the associated stock exchange reforms in late 1986, London had attracted financial firms from all over the world—each of which was seeking to manage funds or execute transactions in all sorts of international securities. In London there is also a steady procession of brokers and other financial firms from the United States, Japan, Australia, Canada, Singapore, India, Hong Kong, and Korea visiting U.K. institutional investors and seeking to attract a portion of their assets to be managed in their home country securities. And there are various Swiss and other European institutions domiciled in London for the purpose of persuading investors to trust their long experience and global investment skills. London is a bazaar of international financial services of all types.

In Japan investment management companies owned by the major securities firms are the principal managers of investment company assets, sometimes with the assistance of a designated advisor upon whose name the fund was marketed to investors. Recently, insurance companies and trust banks have become active investors in international securities, especially U.S. treasury securities and other fixed-income securities. Insurance companies and trust banks are the principal managers of corporate pension fund assets, which have been growing rapidly. Trust banks are active in managing corporate Tokkin funds and fund trusts, a significant amount of which has gone into overseas investments.

Foreign firms operate freely in the Japanese investment management market. They have been permitted, for example, to form joint ventures with Japanese banks for the purpose of overseas investment management, and several have done so. They are also free to manage any accounts they may be able to attract without any partner. As in the other markets, competition for Japanese asset management is very keen. Non-Japanese managers were acting as advisors for or themselves managing nearly $17 billion worth of Japanese institutional and individual assets as of the end of 1987. Among the top ten foreign managers were three U.S. banks—Bankers Trust, Chemical Bank, and J. P. Morgan—which set up Japanese trust subsidiaries.[8] Table 18–2 presents a schedule showing the major international discretionary managers of Japanese overseas investments.

Products and Services

Active Management

Investing in equity securities is an art more than a science, even when the task is not complicated by choices between currencies and markets. International investing is about as complex a task as can be set for any financial professional. One must weigh many factors in deciding how to allocate funds between different markets, while sticking to the basic investment approach that has sold the client on one's particular services.

Some managers believe that patience and a well-reasoned investment strategy is the best approach in the international arena. Managers should pick the main areas of concentration, by markets and by indus-

Table 18–2. Japanese Assets Under Management by Principal Non-Japanese Managers as of December 31, 1986

Non-Japanese Manager	Japanese Relationship	Discretionary or Advisory Assets[a]
Bankers Trust	Sumitomo Bank	$ 2,650
Chemical Bank	direct	1,500
J.P. Morgan	direct	1,000
Credit Suisse	Mitsui Trust	762
Morgan Grenfell	direct	750
Mercury Securities	direct	378
(S.G. Warburg)	New Japan	100
	Nikko	110
	Yamaichi	90
Union Bank of Switzerland	direct	570
Barclays Bank	direct	560
CIGNA	direct	525
Hill Samuel	direct	520
Jardine Fleming	Yasuda Trust	500
Merrill Lynch	Nomura	500
MIM Britania	direct	500
Paribas	direct	400
Wells Fargo	Nikko	300

a. In millions of dollars.

SOURCE: *Pensions and Investment Age*, July 27, 1987.

try segment, and stick with that choice. Truly good investment selections do not have to be changed often. Many savvy portfolio managers who invested in Japanese insurance companies and banks in the early 1970s still hold their original investments almost 20 years later, and their profits have been extraordinary. The investors selected the right market and country (Japan), the right segment of it (financial institutions, then selling at very low price/book value levels), and the right time (relatively early in the Japanese stock market miracle).

Such investors often work against a main theme, such as a long-term optimism, faith in the Pacific Basin, faith in technology, or changes in the way people live. In the international context, however, it is necessary to scan many horizons in order to find the next Japan. For example, could Hong Kong, under Chinese rule after 1997, turn out to be the equity market that will reflect China's ultimate power and influence in the world economy? The best managers answer these questions correctly enough of the time to be able to cover a few mistakes and still look good on the performance charts.

Other investors prefer a more aggressive, trading-oriented approach. These investors look for the next market to experience substantial growth, or they look for opportunistic situations wherever they may appear. A number of such managers were first to discover the Korean, Spanish, and Thai markets, each of which appreciated considerably in the late 1980s. They might also invest in international merger arbitrage situations—for example, by purchasing shares in the Belgian company La Generale after the Italian entrepreneur Carlo de Benedetti had announced his position or by purchasing international equity options and futures contracts to increase portfolio leverage. Though breathtaking, these practices can be very rewarding to those who manage funds according to this approach.

Finally, some managers insist on formula guidelines that impose limitations and constraints on the overall balance of the portfolio. Within these guidelines, portfolio managers may trade as they wish, but the principal investment and safety criteria will be preserved by the guidelines. Such guidelines, as practiced by one very large and success-ful Dutch funds group—the Robeco Group—include limitations on the maximum percentage of the shares outstanding in a single company, the market capitalization of the company, a maximum weighting that any single company investment, or all investments in a single country, may have in the portfolio as a whole. Even large funds find that such guidelines do not seriously restrict the ability of portfolio managers to turn in competitive performances.[9]

Two governing principles of international investment management that are reflected in the management practices described here are the freedom to find the best opportunities, even if these exist outside of one's own country, and the idea that diversification of assets between countries does work. That the juiciest plums may fall in a neighbor's garden is no surprise. However, the principle of diversification was not so universally accepted; diversified assets may be impossible to repatriate in a hurry if one needs to, and diversification into markets that are less liquid than one's home market may be a mistake when difficult times come.

The market crash of October 19, 1987 provided a test of the diversification principle—one that it passed with honors. Perhaps, considering the extent to which communications and globalization of markets have developed, it was not much of a surprise to find all the world's principal stock markets participating, sympathetically and simultaneously, with the market collapse in New York. Markets crashed everywhere in tune with New York; however, they recovered at different paces. By the end of October, the Morgan Stanley Capital International's Europe, Australia, and Far East (EAFE) stock index fell by only 11 percent as compared to a 23 percent decline in the Standard and Poor's 500 index.[10] The EAFE index is heavily weighted to Japan, which shrugged off the crash and soon exceeded precrash highs, but even with Japan weighted less, the diversified international portfolio outperformed a diversified U.S., U.K., German, or Swiss portfolio. Only the Japanese would have done better in exclusively Japanese investments.

Such apparent strength in diversification encourages many active U.S. investment managers to believe that they can outperform the demon performance index, the S & P 500, more easily by maintaining an internationally diversified portfolio.

The principle applies to other managers too. Swiss and German portfolios, for example, have not made such large gains on their investments in foreign stocks; however, compared with losses that they incurred in their home markets in 1987, the foreign stocks have been a help. Diversification has worked for them too.

The advantage that an active, internationally diversified manager has over a passive manager, of either a domestic or an international index fund, is that the active manager can change the diversification weightings to achieve (if the decisions made are right) a superior performance.

Passive Management

Index funds have existed in the United States for a number of years. Most are based on the S&P 500, and many variations and reweightings of the S&P 500 index have been introduced. Many of the pension fund assets in the United States are now being indexed, on the grounds that most active managers fail to exceed the indices and passive management is much less expensive. International indices now exist and passive funds management based on them is being practiced— again, mainly by U.S. pension funds.

The leading indices are the previously mentioned EAFE index, the FT World Actuaries index, and the Frank Russell-Salomon Brothers index. Others are in preparation. All of these indices report on the major companies in the major markets around the world. Price data can be organized in many ways and combined into other indices to provide a tailor-made product.

Indexing has not been confined to the United States, although it is still used there more than anywhere else. Barclays de Zoete Wedd Investment Management and Baring International Management have index funds that they offer to clients. The Baring approach is to use active management to select and weight the countries and to use indexing to invest in stocks from those countries.

As the technology of indexing improves, with managers finding more ways to tailor it to their purposes, and as pension fund sponsors and others express frustration with the performance of funds under management, there is bound to be a substantial increase in the use of indexing for international investments. Such increases prompt many questions. What impact will such indexing and its companion program trading have on equity markets around the world? What regulatory responses will there be in these markets? What effect will the regulatory responses themselves have on the markets? Ultimately, if the markets cannot tolerate program trading they will have to reduce their reliance upon indexing and revert to active management programs.

Private Client Services

Services offered to private clients vary considerably according to the institution providing the services.

In the United States some investment managers accept private accounts for international investment. Normally, there are no services included in the package. The manager invests your money for you, distributes the income and capital gains, and issues a form for tax reporting purposes. If you are satisfied with the results, you remain invested in the fund; if not, you withdraw your funds. Some U.S. banks offer a variety of personal financial services along with money management. These can include certain international courtesies, but they do not constitute much in the way of investment management variations and choices.

Japanese banks, similarly, do not offer individual private international investment services. Their Japanese clients are more inclined to receive these services from the affiliated mutual funds of Japanese securities firms—which themselves do not manage investments.

Private banking services represent a special European product— one that dates back many centuries (see also Chapter 10). Merchant banks and small, exclusive private banks (e.g., Coutts) provide these services in the United Kingdom. There are similar institutions in France (e.g., Banque Worms or Lazard Freres of Paris). A long line of small banks from Germany, the Netherlands, Belgium, Luxembourg, and Austria, as well as the giant banks, offer personalized services. But private banking services are best developed in Switzerland.

Geneva is the capital of Swiss private banking, where several old, prestigious, and successful banking partnerships and corporations (e.g., Pictet and Lombard Odier) carry on businesses begun several generations ago. Many private banks, however, are located in Zurich, Basel, Lugano, and other parts of Switzerland. Their services are highly personal. They are perhaps more geared to the preservation of their client's wealth, and its anonymity, than to its growth. Their relationships with their clients are very close and involve high levels of trust, loyalty, and continuity. Usually a relationship is handled by the same individuals at the bank for years. Banks exercise extreme discretion in preserving the confidentiality of not only the client transactions, but of the very existence of the client's relationship with the bank. Clients may, and often do, use numbered accounts.

It should be clear that clients of such banks receive much in the relationship beyond the management of their money. However, they also may choose between a variety of investment management services. They may ask the bank to manage the investments for them, to manage them in a particular way, or to adhere to certain instructions. They may wish to switch between bonds, deposits, equities, foreign exchange contracts, commodities, and metals. They may prefer to remain invested in Swiss securities or bank deposits, or they may wish to participate in international investments. Clients get what they want. Such individuality of investment selection makes it very difficult to measure investment performance against common standards. Clients monitor whether their assets go up or not, mainly they want to avoid any decrease in their assets. There is a strong bias toward capital preservation.

There is also a willingness to accommodate other banking and nonbanking requirements of clients. For example, a Latin American client may be planning a visit to Paris, Geneva (to visit the bank), and Rome. He may want to go skiing while he is in Switzerland, visit the opera in Paris, and see the Vatican in Rome. For the right client, many private banks would be happy to arrange the visitor's itinerary within Europe, get the tickets, make the appointments, and deliver everything to him along with some cash for his immediate requirements.

Private banking is expensive. Banks usually charge their clients around 1 percent for management services, plus all commissions and expenses. The account reporting frequency and practices of private banking services would not be considered highly advanced in the United States or elsewhere in Europe.

Competing in International Investment Management Services

Sorting out the Segments

The market for international investment management services is extremely broad and diverse. It is made up of many segments and cells according to the type of client being served (institutional, individual), the type of product being offered (active/passive management, funds, private banking services), and the geographical market that is targeted (the United States, Switzerland, Japan). No one firm can cover them all competitively. Each player must chose which ones it does best, which ones it wants to upgrade, and which ones it should discard.

This process is essential if a coherent strategy for the business is to be achieved. The investment management business is such that without a coherent strategy, the product and marketing focus and discipline can be lost, which greatly weakens competitiveness over a period of time.

A large American bank, for example, may have been in the investment management business for many years, going back to the days when the bank's customers could be expected to use the bank for custodial, trust, and estate purposes and for assistance in managing the corporate pension fund. Wealthy individual customers were offered personal attention and a few additional services that gave them peace of mind about their money. Investment management services were usually offered in connection with other services, which were mainly aimed at keeping the customer's money in the bank in interest-free demand deposits.

Today things are different, and the bank's need for and use of investment management services have changed, as has the basis for compensating the bank for the service. Many banks find that investment management has become just another commodity, that it is not sufficiently profitable to justify continuing in the business, and that it creates more than its share of management headaches because the key investment managers are not (and will never be) bankers. Several large banks have disposed of their *domestic* investment management business. Others, however, have taken advantage of the changes in the business to position themselves more favorably and aggressively.

This chapter concerns itself with *international* money management services, which may not be separable from the domestic variety. International investment management services consist of three basic groups of products and services: (1) managing international investments for domestic clients, (2) managing domestic investments for international clients, and (3) managing international investments for international clients. If, for example, a bank has developed a good business in the second category (as many U.S. banks did during the heyday of the petrodollar), it will have to have the product execution capability to manage U.S. investments competitively. If it has sold this "domestic" business, it may no longer have the capability to provide the service. To execute investment management services competitively in the United States, a bank must have many trained and talented specialists on hand with considerable back-office and supplementary support capabilities.

On the other hand, it may be much more difficult to offer international investment management services to domestic clients without a domestic investment management client base to offer the services to and without the basic infrastructure of the domestic business, which, with some modifications, can be used to support the comparatively lower volume of international business.

If the bank decides instead to go after the international business, it may have to do so without the benefit of a large client base or without an international investment management infrastructure in place. For some, this forced fresh start might be an advantage—the bank could invest in all the newest equipment and techniques, hire a prominent manager, and market the services on the strength of its existing franchise. But it takes time to build up enough assets under management to be profitable, particularly if the assets have to be weaned away from institutions where relationships and loyalty are very strong.

Also, when competing in the arena with other international investment managers, the bank will have to take account of (and be prepared to compete with) their different strengths and competitive characteristics. As U.S. institutional investors become more involved internationally, they will market their skills in indexing and quantitative analysis and their abilities to attract and utilize first-rate investment research. U.K. money managers, being more internationally sophisticated, will continue to live on their wits and their abilities to find the next rising market over the horizon, wherever it is, and to market their services on the basis of a truly global expertise. The Swiss and other Europeans offer tempting confidential private banking services to rich Americans, Japanese, Arabs, and Brazilians, emphasizing their long-standing mastery of foreign exchange management. Japanese managers will claim a unique ability to understand the Japanese market and to explain the U.S. and other markets to Japanese investors. To compete with these players, the bank must slot itself into the market in the most advantageous way possible.

Marketing

Many U.S. investment managers have been very successful in marketing their services abroad. For most of these, their capabilities in the United States have been their principal selling point. J. P. Morgan, Bankers Trust, and Chemical Bank have all been very successful in Japan, where they have subsidiaries specializing in investment management. They have attracted substantial sums from Japanese institutions and individuals for investment in the United States. These banks have marketed their U.S. expertise in Europe, the Middle East, and Latin America.

These banks and others, American and European, have attracted substantial U.S. funds for investment outside the United States. The competition is fierce, to be sure, but they appear to be maintaining their share. At the same time, other players are achieving success as well. In a field where so many look alike, even when differentiated by country, the ability of a bank to communicate its approach, record, and major selling points is crucial to success. Until a competitor has shaped exactly what its business is to be and what its own strengths are, its marketing message will be too vague to be effective.

J. P. Morgan can say to customers in Europe and in Japan, "Look, we know the U.S. financial markets as well as anyone, and we are a top money manager. We are also an old and reliable bank that your family has trusted for years, and we have people here in your own country to take care of any problems." Fidelity managers can explain their remarkable performance record, Shearson Lehman Hutton can highlight its unique structure, and Prudential Insurance can extol its stability, and so on. Each has something to say that can be said better or more convincingly through better marketing.

Investment Performance

In the end, the effectiveness of the services will be judged by the quality of the investment performance. For large institutions with the ability to measure competitive performance against an index, providers of services will have to survive the gauntlet every year or so. For managers specializing in this business, special approaches to ensure a good performance will have to be undertaken. For those offering mutual funds or investment company shares, performance also must be good, but by segmenting funds into special sectors, the manager may escape some of the burden of comparison to the S&P 500 or other performance indices.

Investment performance in private banking services may be somewhat less important to customers who value other aspects of their banking relationships; but it is still important. Customers do not usually move some or all of their funds to other managers when they are happy with their performance, but they do when they are not. Customers are becoming more sophisticated, more demanding, and more inclined to take advantage of the large number of banks and brokers competing for their business. Also, private banking fees are high and subject to competition from rate cutters and unbundlers. Performance in private banking is the glue that holds the clients.

SUMMARY

Competitors in investment management must focus much of their attention on the quality of the performance that they are able to offer to clients. Much has changed in the art of investment management over the years, including the variety of securities available for selection by the manager—Korean stocks, German bonds, American options. Stock markets are linked globally as never before and are susceptible to synchronized rises and drops. Diversification across a global range of markets works—it can limit losses and improve performance against indexed measures. New ideas and discoveries appear frequently—some work, some don't. The whole environment of international investing is undergoing major structural change, which creates opportunities for some and hazards for others. To compete, players must be able to function in the new environment and must be able to market and to deliver first-rate services.

NOTES

1. D. C. M. Platt, *Foreign Finance in Continental Europe and the U.S.A., 1815–1870* (London: George Allen and Unwin, 1984) pp. 140–143.
2. Allin Dakin, "Foreign Securities in the American Money Market, 1914–1930," *Harvard Business Review*, January 1932.

3. J. A. Morrell, Baring International Investment Ltd., "International Investment," *Euromoney International Finance Yearbook* (London: Economy Publications, 1987).
4. Goldman, Sachs & Co., "Japan Investment Strategy Highlights," February/March 1988.
5. *Pensions and Investment Age*, July 27, 1987, p. 3.
6. Alliance Capital Management L.P., Prospectus, April 14, 1988.
7. Julie Rohrer, "Are Banks Calling it Quits on Money Management?" *Institutional Investor*, April 1988.
8. *Pensions and Investment Age*, July 27, 1987, p. 3.
9. Nicholaas W. Veer, Robeco Group, "International Equity Funds," *Euromoney International Finance Yearbook* (London: Euromoney Publications, 1987).
10. Margaret Elliot, "Beyond Diversification," *Institutional Investor*, April 1988.

SELECTED REFERENCES

Alliance Capital Management L.P., Prospectus, April 14, 1988.

Beidleman, Carl, ed., *Handbook of International Investing*. Chicago: Probus Publishing Co., 1987.

Chernoff, Joel, and Givant, Marlene. "Western Advisers Tap into $16 Billion from Japanese." *Pensions and Investment Age*, July 27, 1987, p. 3.

Dakin, Allin, "Foreign Securities in the American Money Market, 1914–1930." *Harvard Business Review*, January, 1932.

Einhorn, Steven, and Shangkuan, Patricia. Goldman, Sachs & Co., "Equities: Supply and Demand," *Portfolio Strategy*, March 1988.

Elliot, Charles, and Akers, Nicholas. "Japan Investment Strategy Highlights." *International Research Japan*, February/March 1988.

Elliot, Margaret. "Beyond Diversification." *Institutional Investor*, April 1988, p. 74.

Givant, Marlene. "Different Criteria Apply." *Pensions and Investment Age*, October 27, 1986, p. 3.

Givant, Marlene. "International, Global Assets at $51 Billion." *Pensions and Investment Age*, June 29, 1987, p. 2.

Goldman, Sachs & Co. "World Investment Strategy Highlights." *International Research*, April 1988.

"If Only Japan's Financiers Could Pick Brains as well as Pockets." *The Economist*, September 12, 1987.

Jannson, Solveig. "Indexing Goes Global." *Institutional Investor*, April 1987, p. 42.

Morrell, J. A. "International Investment." *Euromoney International Finance Yearbook*, 1987.

Platt, D. C. M. *Foreign Finance in Continental Europe and the U.S.A 1815–1870*. London: George Allen and Unwin, 1984.

Rohrer, Julie. "Are Banks Calling it Quits on Money Management?" *Institutional Investor*, April 1988.

Veer, Nicholaas. "International Equity Funds," *Euromoney International Finance Yearbook*. London: Euromony Publications, 1987.

IV

Competitive Performance and Strategies

19

Country Risk Exposure and Management

Previous chapters have identified some of the types of risks faced by international commercial and investment banks in their operations—credit risks in lending to foreign companies and banks, various types of risks associated with project financing, risks in dealing with foreign exchange, and funding risks related to balance sheet management and off–balance sheet exposures. By definition, international banking activities cross the political frontiers of sovereign national states—nations that have unique histories and unique futures. Thus, we have yet another source of risk in international banking, country risk, which spills out of the uncertain evolution of national fortunes.

THE NATURE OF COUNTRY RISK

Suppose a New York bank makes a U.S.-dollar loan to a Chilean company whose credit standing has been established as satisfactory. When the time comes to repay the loan, however, the company finds it cannot convert pesos into dollars because the Chilean government has imposed exchange controls as part of a general declaration of economic emergency. In this case, the borrower is willing and able to meet this contractual obligations to the bank, yet country conditions prevent the borrower from doing so. In retrospect, credit risk did not prove to be a problem but transfer risk, a form of country risk, did.

Suppose a Japanese bank participates in a large syndicated Euro-dollar credit to the government of Malaysia for infrastructure financing purposes. In this case, the bank has no credit risk, since it is lending against the full faith and credit of the Malaysian national government. However, it does carry sovereign risk, since future circumstances may be such that the government itself may be unable or unwilling to effect debt service—another form of country risk.

All cross-border lending or investment activities by international banks involve the concept of *country risk*—that is, the possibility that the future flow of returns from these activities may be somehow impaired by economic or political events.

In cross-border lending to individual borrowers in a particular country, the credit risks associated with each borrower are unsystematic risks. A bank can reduce the overall level of risk to which it is exposed in that country by carefully building a diversified portfolio of loans and, by lending to many borrowers, it can ultimately drive the level of unsystematic risk close to zero. However, all the borrowers in this example are located in a single country, so their futures are linked by economic and political events in that country. The bank, therefore, is stuck with a form of *systematic risk* that falls under the country risk rubric. Governments may pursue fiscal, monetary, or foreign exchange policies that impair debt service on the part of multiple borrowers by affecting their profitability, undertaking nationalization or expropriation, impeding access to foreign exchange, or other policy measures. Systematic (country) risk limits our ability to diversify away from unsystematic (credit) risk in the management of a bank's portfolio in a particular country.

We have used two examples of country risk. *Transfer risk* involves the possibility that the borrower may not be able to convert domestic currency into foreign currency. *Sovereign risk* involves loans to governments, their entities, or nongovernmental entities under government guarantee for which there is no credit risk, and yet the government itself may be unable or unwilling to service its debt to foreign creditors. *Foreign exchange risk* associated with the borrower's home currency does not confront the lender directly if a loan is denominated in another currency. However, exchange rate movements can influence individual borrowers' creditworthiness, and factors affecting exchange rates are often closely allied to those affecting country conditions.

Besides cross-border loans, a bank may also have certain direct investments in a particular country. These may take the form of equity shares in local companies, bank branches, joint ventures, or other types of ownership interests—all of which are subject to *direct investment risk*, which is quite different from the other risk categories. Clearly, a country may be economically and politically sound, yet the government may decide to nationalize all foreign ownership interests in local banks as a matter of national policy. Country risk may be low, yet risk associated with the bank's own foreign direct investment may be high under such circumstances. In cases where government places a high priority on the direct participation of foreign banks in the development of a nation's financial system, the reverse may also be true.

Finally, a bank that has a well-diversified portfolio of assets in a particular nation, and yet remains troubled by its exposure to (systematic) country risk, always has the option to diversify still further and distribute its asset holdings across a variety of different countries. This way, country risk becomes unsystematic as far as its overall asset portfolio is concerned, and it can pursue intercountry diversification strategies to further reduce its overall exposure to risk. It simply puts its eggs in different country baskets and assumes that the chances of one basket getting dropped has little to do with the possible fate of the others.

But is this a valid assumption? Are country futures indeed independent? Unfortunately, changes in oil prices, conditions in international financial markets, business cycles, protectionism, and global or regional political events affect many countries at the same time, often in the same direction. Brazil's economic future may be quite independent of South Korea's, but both may simultaneously be affected by a major change in world oil prices or global interest rates. The risk that derives from changes that transcend national political frontiers is *ambient risk*—it is systematic and inherent in the global environment and, for practical purposes, sets a limit on the extent to which international portfolio diversification can succeed in reducing a bank's overall exposure to risk. The only way to reduce risk still further is to move into nonfinancial assets that have traditionally served as hedges in periods of global uncertainty (e.g., gold or real estate) or to buy insurance. Unfortunately, neither is entirely free of ambient risk, and both tend to be rather costly alternatives.

We have defined six types of risk in three broad categories, all of which must be considered in international bank asset management: (1) credit risk and foreign direct investment risk at the narrowest, unsystematic level are both easily subject to diversification; (2) country risk, of which transfer risk, sovereign risk, and exchange risk are components, is systematic as far as individual cross-border loans and investments are concerned, but it can be made unsystematic through international diversification; and (3) ambient risk, which is generally systematic, transcends national frontiers and thus effectively limits risk-reduction through portfolio diversification.

COUNTRY EXPOSURE: DEFINITION
AND MEASUREMENT

A basic prerequisite for effective asset management in international banking is exposure measurement, or tracking. Banks need to know their global exposure to risk along a variety of dimensions. We have already seen in previous chapters that keeping track of a bank's net worldwide position (asset and off–balance sheet transactions) with respect to a particular commercial or financial borrower—or another bank—is fundamental to the maintenance of a sound relationship and the balancing of risk and returns. Similarly, it is prudent for a bank to know its net claims on all of its clients in a particular industry (e.g., petroleum, copper, or air transportation) since worldwide, regional, or national developments at the industry level may affect multiple clients simultaneously. Even groups of borrowers sensitive to certain economic or political conditions (e.g., energy-intensive companies), are candidates for exposure measurement at the national, regional, or global level.

The difference between measurement of a bank's exposure to risk associated with particular firms or industries and its exposure to country risk is that the latter concerns only cross-border financial flows, while the former is concerned with total claims and other exposures, whether cross-border or not. For example, a loan by a bank's Buenos Aires branch to a local company funded by Argentine deposits represents firm and industry risk but not country risk (although the branch does involve foreign direct investment exposure), yet the same loan originated by the bank's Paris office involves all these types of risks.

Figure 19–1 indicates, as a three-dimensional display, the kind of information that might be useful in keeping track of a bank's global exposure. With respect to exposure to country risk, the first category is lending exposure. Every cross-border loan, whether originated by the bank's head office or by offices anywhere else in the world, must be promptly reported and captured in the system. It is often deemed useful to have each cross-border loan reported both by the originating office and by the office directly responsible for the country concerned. Exposures by country should then to be broken down into appropriate maturity categories (e.g., less than one year, one to three years, three to five years, over five years), commitments, and drawdowns or disbursements.

It is also useful to know the extent to which the country has claims on the bank. Prudence forbids these claims from being netted against

Categories	Countries[a]	Regions[a]	Totals[a]
E. TOTAL			
D. LOCAL			
C. COUNTRY EXPOSURE			
B. TRANSFERS			
A. CROSS-BORDER			
Lending exposure:			
Firms			
Industries			
Sectors			
Special-interest classifications			
TOTALS			
Investment exposure:			
Portfolio			
Direct—own			
Direct—other			
TOTALS			
Comparative exposures:			
Home country bank totals [b]			
Global bank totals [b]			

a. Breakdowns by maturity classes, commitments, drawdowns, and redeposits. Indication of limit and sublimits.

b. To the extent that data availabilities permit.

Figure 19–1. Global Exposure-tracking Format.

lending exposure, but it is important to be aware of them (and changes therein). In extreme cases, such claims may be used under the right of set-off, as discussed in Chapter 10.

While keeping track of lending activity by country is an important function of exposure-tracking systems, it can serve other useful purposes as well. Figure 19–1 indicates subtotals by regions, for example, wherein country groups may be captured as needed (e.g., Central America, Southeast Asia, sub-Sahara Africa excluding South

Africa, ASEAN, or non-oil-producing LDCs). At the same time, such a system can track lending by borrower type (e.g., banks, industries, public sector, private sector, or energy-intensive companies) or other classifications of special interest to management. This may include exposure to corporate "families" (e.g., General Motors worldwide) as well. While only cross-border exposure is of interest with respect to country risk, total exposure is relevant when examining risk at the firm and industry levels as well as for planning and budgeting purposes.

The A dimension of Figure 19–1 gives direct cross-border exposure. But suppose a bank loan to the Thai subsidiary of an American company is guaranteed by its parent. In that case, the "country of lending" and the "country of risk" are different — one is Thailand and the other is the United States — and this has to be fully reflected in the exposure data. The general rule is that guarantees serve to transfer country risk, but "comfort letters," provided by corporate parents, for example, do not.

Such transfers are reflected in the B cut of Figure 19–1, with $A + B$ reflecting the bank's total country exposure in cut C. Quite often, as in shipping loans, judgment is required to determine the appropriate allocation of country exposure. Non-cross-border lending is reflected in cut D, with $A + D = E$, total lending by countries, regions, firms, industries, or any other categories deemed useful.

In making its judgments about a country and the lending opportunities, a bank will want to set limits on country exposure that should not be exceeded, usually in the form of overall limits and term sublimits. Limits applied to individual borrowers, industries, or regions can also be incorporated here.

Nonlending exposure, either in the form of off–balance sheet transactions, equity interest in foreign firms, bank affiliates, branches, consortium arrangements, and portfolio investments, may be recorded in an exposure information system as well, generally under cut A, although risk transfer may also be possible under home country investment guarantees.

Finally, it may be interesting to know the cross-border exposure of all banks based in the bank's home country and of all large international banks as a group. Basic statistics, albeit without a great deal of detail, are often collected and published by central banks and the Bank for International Settlements. In this way, a bank can compare its own exposure with some broader aggregates for the international banking community at large.

Certainly the most prominent example of cross-border exposures is re lated to the LDC debt crisis of the 1980s. After 1983, crossborder lending exposures of international banks were made public in the United States and certain other countries, both in absolute terms and related bank capital. The 1988 figures for selected banks are compared with the 1983 statistics in Figure 19–2.

Figure 19–3 represents a sample country exposure reporting format as it might have been structured in the mid-1980s. Each bank's approach is somewhat different, depending on the nature of the bank and its business and the degree of sophistication and effort applied. It is not difficult to imagine that the process of generating such reports is technically difficult, time consuming, and costly. This is true even at the input level.

Periodic exposure reports must then be made available to bank officers, either in printed form or in on-line computer display systems. Even more importantly, they must be fully understood and in fact *used* by those involved in exposure decisions.

VALUATION OF COUNTRY EXPOSURE

A bank is naturally interested in the economic value of its exposure in a particular country and in maximizing the economic value of its global asset portfolio, spread among a host of different countries. Both are a matter of expected returns and possible future variance in those returns reflected in the degree of risk attached to them.

We can express this in the form of a conventional present-value equation such as the following:

$$\mathrm{NPV}_j^o = \sum_{t=0}^{n} \frac{E(F_t) - E(C_t)}{(1 + i_t + t)^t}$$

where NPV_j^0 is the net present value of the future stream of expected returns to the bank related to exposure in a particular country j, $E(F)$ and $E(C_t)$ denote the expected value of that future returns stream and any associated collection costs, respectively, at time t, i_t is the risk-free discount factor representing the bank's cost of funds, and $\frac{\alpha}{t}$ represents a country-risk premium, which depends on the variance in returns on the bank's exposure in country j relative to the variance in returns on its overall asset portfolio and on management's attitude toward risk. Prospective future developments in countries in which

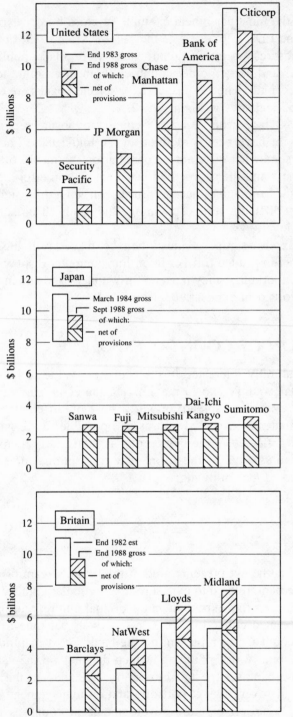

Figure 19–2. Cross-border Lending Exposures of International Banks.

a bank has cross-border exposures will be reflected in the *means* as well as the *variances* of the probability distributions associated with these returns and hence will influence both $E(F_t) - E(C)_t$ and α_t.

It is important, first of all, to develop an accurate picture of the net expected returns side $E(F_t) - E(C_t)$. One important component of returns is, of course, repayment of principal. A second component covers the interest returns, which usually involves either a fixed rate, the spread over LIBOR U.S. prime, or a similar floating base rate of interest.

COUNTRY LIMIT APPROVAL FORM

FOR _____

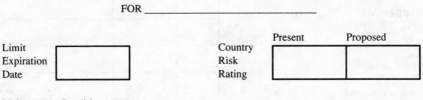

Limit
Expiration
Date

Country
Risk
Rating

Present   Proposed

Maintenance Conditions :

	EXISTING LIMITS	PROPOSED LIMITS
see second page for details		
GROUP I.		
GROUP II.		
AGGREGATE CROSS BORDER COUNTRY LIMIT		

APPROVALS/DATE:

_____   _____

_____   _____

_____   _____

_____   _____

Figure 19–3. Sample Country Exposure Reporting Format.

COUNTRY LIMIT WORKSHEET
U.S.$ MILLIONS

DIVISION/PRODUCT OR TYPE OF BUSINESS	TOTAL LIMIT	OF WHICH LONG TERM	OTHER RESTRICTIONS ON TERM BORROWINGS
LIMITS GROUP I.			
BANKING – Territory			
– Retained Underwriting			
– E&M			
– Shipping			
– Commodities			
– Leasing			
– Other			
TREASURY – Head office			
– Securities Trading Peak			
OTHER			
Accrued Interest			
LIMITS GROUP II.			
BANKING – Interest Rate Swaps			
– Currency Swaps (Risk formula basis)			
– Underwriting limit (peak)			
TREASURY – Swaps (Funding of local currency assets)			
– Swaps (Positional & Other Swaps)			
– FX maximum exposure			
– Long date FX (risk formula)			
– Gross Intercompany liabilities			
AGGREGATE LIMIT			

Figure 19–3.   (cont.)

Another component of returns is the share of commitment, partic- ipation, and management fees agreed upon with the borrower. These may be quite substantial, especially for those involved in organizing and managing syndicated loans. They are generally well in excess of the incremental costs involved in providing the relevant services and— especially as relatively certain and immediate "front-end" payments on syndications and the like—usually add materially to the overall returns of banks engaged in international lending. On occasion, as we have seen in Chapter 5, borrowers unwilling to incur higher published spreads for reasons relating to prestige or future market access may inflate fees in order to adequately compensate international lenders.

Third, we have also seen that banks often lend to a particular borrower on terms that might otherwise be considered unattractive in order to develop or maintain a "relationship." This involves existing and past ties and focuses on the expectation of future earnings from a variety of activities, foreign exchange transactions, deposit balances, advisory services, custody business, and the like. There is ample evidence of the importance of the "relationship" factor in international lending behavior. Banks scramble to get "close to" the borrower, directly and within syndicates, and losers of syndication mandates tend to participate anyway in the loans in order to maintain a relationship with the borrower. Similarly, borrowers can sometimes "encourage" banks to participate in loans that would not otherwise be attractive by suggesting that failure to do so may lead to loss of collateral business or may put pressure on their operations in host countries— thereby requiring the addition to apparent returns, in effect, of an insurance premium against possible future earnings losses elsewhere in the relationship in its present value calculations. Particularly where a relationship with a particular government has been highly profitable in the past and promises to be so in the future, such anticipated "indirect" returns can be an important part of the total country lending programs, and once characterized by their own profile of expected future earnings.

Fourth, a bank's lending to a particular borrower may generate future returns with third parties that might not otherwise materialize. A particular loan to a company or government abroad may create opportunities for future trade financing or letter-of-credit business with home or third-country suppliers, for example. Or a well-structured loan can cement a relationship with a particular domestic or foreign client in a way that promises additional future earnings. Once again, the ultimate returns from this source to the bank may be quite indirect and their evaluation quite speculative.

Finally, there are collection costs. Loans that are delinquent or otherwise "nonperforming" because of conditions in countries where the exposure is lodged often involve sizeable travel, legal, and other expenses. Particularly for bankers that take relatively small participations in major loans, collection costs can loom rather large in relation to expected returns in the event of problems.

It is clear, therefore, that expected returns of principal and interest, fees, and the remaining less tangible earnings components generated by country exposure, as well as expected collection cost form a many-sided, probabilistic picture. Each element has its own time profile and expected value, so that $E(F_t) - E(C_t)$ in our formula is itself a highly complex composite. Each element also has its own measure of variability, so that the associated risk premium α_t is similarly complex. And often there are tradeoffs, as when the terms of loan agreements (legal documentation) are relaxed at the insistence of the borrower, thereby possibly exchanging higher expected returns in some of the aforementioned earnings components for greater risk in others.

Partly for such reasons, as noted in Chapter 21, profit attribution in international banking tends to be extraordinarily difficult, and in most banks it is considered quite imperfect. For such reasons as well, the returns facing individual banks that participate in syndicated transactions may well differ substantially from one to the other, particularly between banks in the management group and the rest, (see Chapter 5).

What about interest rate risk? In the case of floating-rate (e.g., LIBOR-based) loans, a change in interest rates would tend to show up both as a change in i_t and a change in $E(R_t)$, thereby canceling each other out. Of course, in the case of fixed-rate loans, $E(R_t)$ remains constant when i_t changes, thereby causing a corresponding change in the NPV. But even with floating-rate loans, since spreads are fixed either for the life of the loan or for specific periods over the loan's term, there does exist some residual interest rate risk.

Apart from changes in interest rates, what kind of eventualities associated with conditions in countries where a bank has cross-border exposure would tend to influence the real (economic) value of the exposed assets?

First, the borrowing country may ultimately be unwilling or unable to effect debt service. Full scale default on the part of the borrower casues the lending bank to realize accounting losses of principal and/or accrued interest, which the bank must book against earnings, capital, and reserves after recovering what it can. The consequences of nonperformance for the borrower's access to international capital markets and normal channels of credit are such that this event tends to be triggered by unique and relatively rare circumstances.

Second, the borrowing country may be unable to meet its external debt obligations on contractual terms and may be forced to stretch out repayment. By definition, the necessary refinancing or rescheduling under such circumstances cannot be accomplished *at market terms*. It occurs under duress, and so the original lenders are forced to extend further credit in the hope of avoiding accounting losses in the end. This may involve an extension of maturities, a new grace period, negotiation of new facilities, an adjustment in interest spreads, or other modifications. Even if this ultimately results in increased accounting returns, assuming that the lender under free-market conditions would have restructured its portfolio *out of* the exposed assets in question at any point, but cannot do so because it is locked in, the lender actually has incurred an economic loss. The real value of this particular component of the lender's asset portfolio, in effect, has declined. The difference between *economic* and *accounting* shifts in asset values under such circumstances has not always been accepted by bankers, and this may influence their reaction to the causative debt-service problems and lending decisions in the future.

Third, the borrowing country may be perfectly able and willing to service its external debt—successfully avoiding both default and problems leading to reschedulings or forced refinancings—yet something happens that raises the perceived risk associated with the exposed assets from the perspective of the foreign lender. Assassination of the head of state, for example, may mean nothing at all from a debt-service point of view, it may mean eventual debt repudiation and default, or it may result in any number of eventualities in between. Even though neither of our first two types of losses has been incurred by the lender, the value of the lender's assets has declined insofar as they cannot immediately be reallocated in a manner consistent with the lender's new perception of the constellation of relative risks and returns. Some such reallocation may be possible at the margin by running down exposures, beginning with the very short maturities, but it is usually far from the kind of instantaneous adjustment that is needed to avoid a long-term downward revaluation of the bank's portfolio.

Once again, bankers are sometimes reluctant to recognize such shifts and may ignore them in portfolio valuation and decision making.

Yet examples of international lending seem to suggest that markets are in fact responsive to shifts in "risk classes" of countries (e.g., lending to South Korea after the assassination of President Park Chung Hee, Thailand after the Vietnamese invasion of Cambodia, to Mexico after drastic economic measures were imposed in 1982, and to Eastern Europe after the Soviet invasion of Afghanistan). Thus, relative rates of change in (net) new loans become a substitute for market-type portfolio adjustments.

In terms of our equation, a number of country-related events may reduce NVP. Prospective defaults can be viewed as reductions in $E(F_t)$ and as increases in $E(C_t)$, anticipated rescheduling or refinancing losses can be viewed as forced introduction of higher-valued t's that are less than compensated for by negotiated increases in $E(F_t)$; net of $E(C_t)$; and losses from risk-class shifts can be viewed as increases in α_t if, as a result, the country is viewed by the market as being more risky.

Relatively well-defined examples related to the difference between the book values of banks' country exposures and the economic values of certain countries' debt emerged in the latter phases of the LDC debt crisis of the 1980s. The reason was the development of a relatively active secondary market for bank loans in connection with debt-for-equity swaps and other debt conversion transactions. The secondary debt market prices were indicative of the economic value of bank exposures, so that it became possible to see what bank exposures were actually worth—at least notionally (see Table 19–1).

FACTORS AFFECTING COUNTRY RISK

The purpose of country risk assessment is, of course, to get a fix on $E(F_t)$, $E(C_t)$ and α_t. The more certain the bank is about the first two elements, the less "true risk" there remains and the smaller is α_t. The problem facing international banks, therefore, is one of forecasting the future of countries in which they have exposed assets. It represents a strikingly complex task, requiring the construction of a social, political, psychological, historical and economic composite assessment of risk that embodies many factors: structural (supply-side) elements, demand-side elements, monetary elements, external economic and political developments, the quality of the national economic management team, and the domestic political constraints bearing upon decision makers.

A simple view of the problem might begin with an equation such as the following, which represents real flows of goods and services in an economy:

$$Y + M = A + X$$

where Y is output, M is imports, A is domestic absorption (consumption, investment, and public sector spending), and X is exports, all in real terms. Clearly, supply-side changes in Y with unchanged demand will require shifts in imports or exports. Reduced production capabilities at the national level, for example, may mean increased imports or a more limited capacity to export. In a similar way, demand-side shifts affecting A with unchanged supply can be examined. Increased government spending will, for example, have to be met from expanded imports or will deflect export production to meet domestic needs. Monetary variables can affect the picture as well—growth in the domestic money supply, unless offset by changes in exchange rates, will tend to raise A relative to Y and, therefore, will increase M, and/or decrease X.

In order to bring the money side into the picture more explicitly, we can develop an equally simple equation describing international financial flows:

$$VX - VM - DS + FDI + U - K = DR - NBR$$

Here, VX and VM represent the money value of exports and imports, respectively; DS represents debt-service payments to foreigners (usually part of VM in conventional balance-of-payments accounting); FDI are net flows of private and public sector grants such as foreign aid; K is net recorded capital flows undertaken by residents; DR is the change in owned international reserves of the country in question; and NBR is its net borrowing requirement. An overall negative balance on the left side of the equation clearly means that the country will have to increase its foreign borrowing or use up some of its international reserves. Of course, increases in foreign borrowing will mean increases in DS in future time periods.

Tying the two equations together are typical "country scenarios." For example, a government comes under political pressure to increase spending for domestic social purposes. It does so by running a fiscal deficit, which it finances by issuing government bonds. Most of the

Table 19—1. Indicative LDC Debt Prices, August 23, 1989

Country	Indicative Cash Prices		Trading Commentary
	Bid	**Offer**	
Algeria	74.00	75.00	Price unmoved despite recent positive press on country's economic reforms
Argentina	14.50	15.50	Mixed economic signals as inflation breaks 200% despite signs of sensible policies
Bolivia	11.00	12.00	Buybacks fixing price, so predicted price irrelevent.
Brazil	30.00	30.75	Expectations of nonpayment nudge prices below predicted level, so not quite a buy.
Chile	62.50	63.50	Relative price remains high on positive political trends.
Colombia	62.00	64.00	Price relatively higher as financing goes through smoothly.
Costa Rica	15.00	16.00	Slightly softer on supply technicals
Dominican Republic	18.00	20.00	Still following the market.
Ecuador	16.00	17.00	Looks underpriced if faltering political coalition can reunify
Honduras	18.00	20.00	B/O standoff continues.
Ivory Coast	6.00	8.00	No change despite considerable news.
Jamaica	42.00	44.00	Price holds as overall market softens with Manley gaining cautious respect.
Mexico	42.75	43.25	Softens, but less than rest of market as internal economic outlook is positive.
Morocco	45.50	46.50	Little change as awkward bank negotiations continue.
Nicaragua	2.00	3.00	Too-much-rumoured deal hurts itself.

Nigeria	27.25	28.25	Market continues to validate buy signal although sign is now less strong.
Panama	10.00	12.00	New pressures from U.S. keep name cheap.
Peru	4.00	5.00	No change in worst political/economic situation in Latin America.
Phillipines	50.50	51.50	All fundamentals—including base negotiations—point upward while price falls as banks sell.
Poland	37.00	38.00	Price falls faster than market as opposition tests government's resolve.
Senegal	47.00	49.00	Market fall make debt look even more overpriced.
Sudan	1.00	2.00	No comment.
Uruguay	55.00	56.00	Economy looks good, and country has achieved access to voluntary yen market.
Venezuela	37.25	38.25	Still overvalued but less so; bank negotiations could be long and tedious.
Yugoslavia	54.00	56.00	Still looks overpriced with annual inflation nearing 1,000% although BOP still okay.
Zaire	18.00	20.00	Market begins to believe predicted price.
MARKET INDEX: 35.68			Market down sharply as banks increasingly prefer cash to prospective discount bonds

SOURCE: Salomon Brothers, Inc.

557

bonds may end up in the asset portfolio of the central bank, which in turn pays for them by increasing the money supply (central bank liabilities). This tends to put upward pressure on the general price level of the economy, which the government is reluctant to see reflected in a depreciation of its currency. The currency becomes "overvalued," made possible by imposition of exchange controls or central bank intervention in foreign exchange markets. The whole process is likely to show up as an increase in A offset by an increase in M and/or a decrease in X in our first equation—the financial flows appearing in our second equation as a net reduction in the trade balance $(VX - VM)$ financed by a reduction in reserve holdings DR (the central bank's external liabilities). Many such scenarios could obviously be sketched out focusing on a wide variety of internal and external shocks that eventually lead to increased foreign borrowing. If such borrowing is sufficiently large and sustained, it can lead to debt-serving difficulties and economic losses for banks. The problem is to ascertain what each of these scenarios may mean for the different variables we have identified as they evolve over time, particularly DS and NBR. This, together with the underlying political scenarios, is the essence of getting a fix on the expected value and variance of a bank's exposure in a particular country.

In the absence of an efficient market, like stock markets or foreign exchange markets whose data can be analyzed, the delivery of effective country assessment ideally requires the employment of a true "renaissance person"—a person who is exceedingly intelligent, a holder of doctorates from respectable institutions in economics, political science, sociology, psychology, and perhaps a few other fields as well, totally objective, with a great deal of common sense. In addition to being rather well-traveled, he or she should be up-to-date on developments in all countries of interest to the bank (and in other countries that might affect them), and personally acquainted with key policymakers. Obviously, there are few such individuals wandering around these days. And so the question is whether international banks, *as institutions*, can in some way put together all of these qualities using relatively "ordinary" individuals and traditional organization linkages to assemble a superior ability to forecast the future of countries, its bearing on the real value of exposed assets, and its implications for portfolio management. Low-quality estimates of $E(F_t) - E(C_t)$ and α_t yield low-quality portfolio decisions and, ultimately, second-rate performance of a bank in the competitive marketplace. What are the specific components of country analysis, in this context?

National Economic Management

The first question is whether developments in the internal workings of a national economy, both on the supply and demand sides, may seriously threaten a country's ability to service its external debt obligations. We are interested in the linkages between the supply side's ability to produce exports, import-competing goods, and nontraded goods; we are also interested in the qualitative and quantitative dimensions of the labor force, the capital stock, the natural resource base, technology, and entrepreneurship that combine to determine this supply capability. At the same time, we are interested in the contributions of real capital inflows to these supply capabilities made possible by foreign borrowings, foreign direct investment, and other types of financial transfers.

Historical measures of economic performance on the supply side abound, including measures of labor force growth and participation rates, unemployment rates, migration and labor force distributional trends, savings and investment trends, productivity trends, natural resource availability, and the like. The quality, timeliness, and comparability of the relevant data vary widely, but the real problem obviously lies in ascertaining whether the past is likely to be a good guide for the future. Here a great deal of judgment is required in order to identify and project, for example, various types of quantitative or qualitative labor-supply ceilings and possible market disruptions, social and economic infrastructure bottlenecks, capital availability problems, natural resource constraints, and so on. Of primary importance is the evaluation of government policies that will influence domestic savings and investment, capital flight and foreign direct investment, risk-taking and entrepreneurial activity, supply conditions in labor markets, the adequacy of economic and social infrastructure, exploitation and forward processing of natural resources, and the entire underlying complex of incentives and disincentives built into the nation's fiscal and regulatory system. In many cases, such policies are anchored in government planning documents, in which case an evaluation of the degree of realism embodied in these plans may be quite important—government attempts to force the supply side of an economy into a mold that does not fit, but to which a political commitment has been made, can lead to severe domestic and international distortions in the real sector, ballooning of external borrowing, and ultimately, debt-servicing problems.

On the *demand side*, we are interested in factors affecting taxes, government expenditures, transfer payments, and the overall fiscal soundness of the public sector; we are also interested in prospective demand patterns for goods and services from the private and export sectors. Once again, historical data covering consumption spending, government taxation and expenditures, gross national product or gross domestic product and other conventional economic indicators are usually available on a reasonably timely basis to permit an evaluation of the demand picture over a number of years. But forecasts depend in large part on exogenous demand-side shocks that may emanate from the foreign sector, changed expectations, and the ability to predict government demand management and income distribution policies.

In attempting to develop a defensible prognosis of the structural aspects of country futures, therefore, the analyst in an international bank must start from as complete an information base as possible regarding the historical track record of the domestic economy and its current situation and then must try to project both the demand-side and supply-side dimensions. This may not be a particularly serious problem in the short term, since the exogenous and policy elements are relatively fixed. But the sources of error multiply as the forecasting period is extended, and few or none of the important determinants of economic performance can then be considered constant. What will happen to taxes, transfers, government regulations, the use of subsidies and other market distortions, consumption and savings patterns, investment incentives, treatment of foreign-owned firms, and similar factors five or ten years into the future? Everything is up for grabs, and forecasting has to rely in large measure on the basic competence of the nation's policymakers, their receptivity to formal or informal outside advice, and the pattern of social and political constraints under which they operate. Assuming the cast of characters in a country's economic management team remains the same, past experience in domestic policymaking and reactions to outside shocks may not be a bad guide to the future. But this assumption itself is often open to question.

A part of the task of projecting future economic management scenarios—and some would say the most important part—lies in the *monetary sector*. Whereas most good country analyses contain extensive descriptions of the national financial system, the critical factors obviously relate to domestic prices and exchange rates. Useful indicators are the domestic monetary base, the money supply, net domestic credit, and available price indices, together with net foreign official assets and net foreign debt. Monetary disturbances may originate domestically or from the foreign sector (e.g., a large increase in external reserves that becomes monetized). Apart from their inflationary and exchange rate aspects, of course, such disturbances may also influence consumption and savings, capital formation, income distribution, expectations, and the like.

Once again, whereas the mechanisms relating monetary developments to debt-service problems are well understood, and the requisite data usually more readily available than most others, near-term assessments are far easier than formulating a defensible long-range outlook. After all, it is possible to evaluate the relationship of the existing exchange rate to some hypothetical market-determined rate based on a calculated purchasing power parity index and to project this deviation based on relative inflation trends. The larger the degree of projected currency overvaluation, for example, the greater the need for increased external borrowing will tend to be and the greater the likelihood of reserve losses and/or the prospects for a tightening of controls on international trade and payments. Much more difficult is the task of forecasting government responses to problem situations in the monetary sphere (e.g., devaluation, liberalization of controls, domestic monetary stringency, etc.) and particularly the timing of such measures. And in the longer term, the problem once again boils down to the competence of the monetary policymakers and the political pressures bearing upon them—especially with bank exposures often extending out over a decade or more.

The domestic economic management issues involved in country analysis by international banks are summarized in Figure 19–4. Complex as it is, this is still only part of the picture.

External Economic Aspects

Because of the importance of foreign exchange availability in projecting a country's debt-service capabilities, we must also pay a great deal of attention to outside factors affecting its balance of payments and external finance. On the export side, this requires evaluation of both long-term trends and short-term instabilities. Increasing product and market diversification might be a sign of greater export stability and reduced vulnerability to shifting economic and political conditions or of protectionist trends in a country's major markets. Shifts in the ratio of exports to gross national product may signal changing

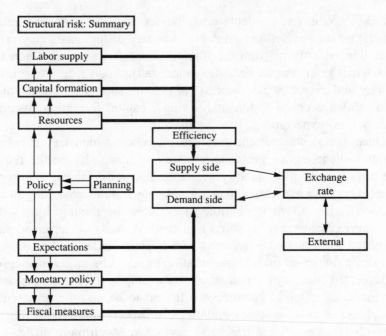

Figure 19–4. Domestic Economic Management Issues Involved in Country Analysis.

future debt-service capabilities, and an analysis of demand and supply elasticities for major export products may indicate possible sources of future instability in export receipts. Domestic export-supply constraints and export-competing demand elements link back into the analysis of structural problems, outlined previously. Export policies set by the national government and by governments of competing exporters may also be important, along with exchange rate policies. In general, we are interested in (1) alignment of a country's exports with its international competitive advantage, (2) diversification of export risk, and (3) home country and third-country policies that might pose a threat to future export earnings.

On the import side as well, concern must focus on both long-term trends and short-term instabilities. The ratio of imports to gross national product, for example, indicates very little by itself, but abrupt and significant shifts in this ratio may be important. The ability of the government to compress imports in times of balance-of-payments trouble may be indicated by measures such as the ratio of food and fuel imports to total imports. Import price volatility, supplier concentration among trading partners, and trends in import-replacement production are among the other measures that can help spot possible problems originating on the import side. Here, as in the case of exports, we are also interested in the policy context—the structure of effective tariff and nontariff protection and its impact of domestic resource allocation and efficiency in production.

We have already noted the importance of foreign direct investment for the supply side of a national economy, in terms of its contribution to aggregate and sectoral capital formation, technology transfer, development of human resources, management and entrepreneurial activity, access to markets, and access to supplies— the traditional multinational corporate "bundle" of services discussed with respect to multinational banks in Chapter 3. Besides the balance-of-payments gains associated with direct investment inflows, induced exports, and import-replacement production, outflows may occur via induced imports of goods and services and profit remittances. Each foreign investment project evidences a more or less unique balance-of-payments profile, in magnitudes as well as in timing. Policies affecting foreign direct investment (e.g., taxation, restrictions on earnings remittances, indigenization pressures, nationalization, and expropriation) may seriously alter this profile and thereby influence country prospects as viewed by international lenders as well. Multinational companies are often extraordinarily sensitive to changes in national policy environments. Because such changes can portend changes in the overall creditworthiness of countries as a whole, shifts in foreign direct investment patterns deserve careful attention. So do capital outflows on the part of domestic residents, which are frequently highly sensitive to the domestic outlook (especially in times of possible discontinuous policy changes). Autonomous private lending by foreigners to domestic residents also warrants close attention.

Finally, it may be important to analyze the magnitude and types of grants and concessional loans that a country receives from abroad and the prospective future development of these flows. The domestic conditions in the donor countries, the donor-recipient relationships, and the economic and political attractiveness of the recipient countries for such transfers is important. Moreover, is there a foreign "lender of last resort?" Countries of strategic or economic importance are obviously prime candidates for future intergovernmental "rescues," which to some extent may backstop private bank lending exposure in severe problem situations and increase the interest of major financial powers in successfully concluding "workout" situations. Figure 19–5 summarizes financial flows and their relationships to the domestic economic picture.

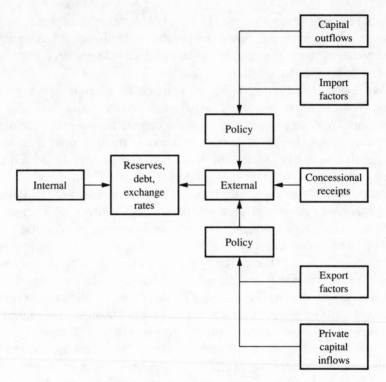

Figure 19–5.   External Stock and Flow Elements.

Liquidity and Debt Aspects

The aforementioned issues usually involve medium- and long-range forecasts of such aggregates as the balance of trade, the current account, and various other "flow" measures. These will naturally be reflected in a country's future international reserve position and in its access to international financial markets for future financing needs. Near-term "liquidity" assessments generally focus on such measures as changes in a country's owned reserves and International Monetary Fund (IMF) position and on ratios (e.g., reserves to monthly imports) intended to indicate in some sense the degree of "cushioning" provided by reserve holdings. The ability to borrow additional sums abroad or to refinance existing debt naturally depends on the projected state of financial markets and assessment of country creditworthiness by international banks and official institutions at the time of need. Indeed, favorable conditions in the financial market and in the country sometimes lead to preemptive borrowing to restructure outstanding debt at market terms and to build up reserves for future use or to improve perceived creditworthiness in the future.

Analysis of the size and structure of country indebtedness and debt-service payments is equally important in this regard. Ratios such as (1) total debt to exports or to gross national product and (2) long-term public debt to exports or to gross national product are used in virtually all country analyses, as are the amount and trends in overall external indebtedness, current versus term debt, and total and short-term claims.

The *debt-service ratio*—that is, debt service payments to exports or "normal" exports—is perhaps the most common. However, by using only exports in the denominator, the debt-service ratio ignores the potentially equivalent contributions of import substitution to a country's debt-service capabilities. And a particular debt-service ratio (say 0.3) may mean entirely different things for different countries as far as creditworthiness is concerned.

Another commonly used indicator is the *cash flow index* (CFI), calculated as follows:

$$\text{CFI} = \frac{R + A + LC + T}{DS}$$

where R represents gross foreign exchange reserves held by the country's central bank; A denotes net foreign assets held by the commercial banks; LC represents undrawn loan facilities committed to the country, including interbank lines; T is the expected current-account balance; and DS represents debt-service obligations for the year ahead. A CFI value of less than 1 would indicate that additional borrowing will be required during the year to meet debt-service obligations. Additionally, the following ratios are commonly used: (1) foreign capital inflows to debt-service payments, (2) exports plus capital inflows and aid receipts to current debt, (3) vital imports plus debt-service payments to exports plus capital inflows and aid receipts (*compressibility ratio*), and (4) the reciprocal of the average maturity of external debt (*rollover ratio*).

The fondness for ratios in country analysis by banks probably carries over partly from the techniques of financial analysis they apply to commercial borrowers, but the similarities clearly can be exaggerated. Countries are not the same as companies. All such ratios must be interpreted cautiously. They have different meanings for different countries and for the same country at different times and stages of development. There are no valid rules of thumb. The skill lies in the interpretation of any ratios used, particularly changes in them, and in the specific context of particular country situations. However, even if a good analyst recognizes the limitations of some of the more pedestrian indicators, they may nevertheless figure heavily and perhaps mechanically into how *other* banks view the situation when a country comes to the market; therefore, these indicators must be monitored carefully.

Figure 19–6 depicts the linkage between internal and external "flow" factors and the associated policies and a country's external "stocks" of reserves and debt. Note that all three elements are closely intertwined. Domestic real or monetary changes may beget trade or payments shifts, or vice versa, and both may affect external borrowing and reserves. Once a country borrows, however, the creditor naturally takes an interest in the goings-on, and as the external debt builds there is more monitoring done and advice given by lenders, public and private alike. This will be discussed further later in this chapter.

Political Aspects

Besides domestic structural and monetary variables and external stock and flow factors, country analysis related to term exposure always requires astute political forecasting. Most closely related to the eco-

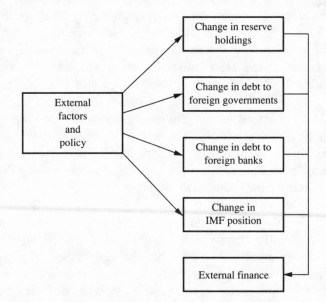

Figure 19–6.   Internal-External Linkages.

nomic variables just reviewed, of course, is the competence or wisdom of the economic managers which, insofar as it relates to the cast
of characters on the stage—the membership of the economic trade—is
basically a political matter. Small casting changes can cause enormous
changes in the quality of the play. There is also the question of whether
the technocrats have a full political mandate to "do what is necessary"
from a debt-service point of view and, ultimately, whether the government itself is firmly enough in the saddle and has the political will
to carry it out. Horror stories in the history of country risk (ranging
from Turkey, Sudan, and Zaire to Jamaica, Peru, and Poland) illustrate the critical importance of evaluating and forecasting the political
"overlay" of national economic policymaking—the degree of resolve,
the power base, and the tools available for implementing sound policy
decisions. Banks that are leaders in country analysis generally place
a great deal of stress on this particular dimension, which requires an
entirely different sort of prognostication and information base than
some of the more mechanical aspects of the problem.

Of particular importance is the extent to which policymakers are
receptive to outside advice. Politicians often find "business as usual" the best way to go—even when it is becoming clear that serious
debt-service problems are just over the horizon—knowing that whatever needs to be done is probably going to be politically painful (tax
increases, monetary restraint, devaluation) and hoping fervently that
"something will turn up." Too often nothing does, and foreign lenders
are moved to offer advice of their own as concern over a country's
debt grows. Sometimes the advice is taken seriously, and the country
makes its way out of the impending problem situation well before it
becomes critical, despite the political costs involved. Sometimes the
country engages outside advisors to help formulate sound economic
plans and policies, improve its image in international financial markets, and perhaps take some of the domestic political heat. In severe
problem cases, however, outside advice is ignored until any additional
borrowing becomes considerably more expensive or less available,
and a crisis looms.

At some point in this scenario (for domestic politicians later rather
than sooner), the country will have to negotiate borrowing facilities
with the IMF. The involvement of the IMF gives a certain degree
of comfort to private banks, and often their own extension of further
credit is conditional on the IMF stamp of approval on a country's
plans. At the same time, it may provide domestic policymakers with
the increased backbone necessary to undertake unpopular but neces-

sary economic measures. Problems can arise if this external pressure
fails to rectify the problem or if the country is not a member of the
IMF. The IMF can play a pivotal role in gradually rescuing countries
from financial distress; unfortunately, this does not always occur soon
enough to save banks from economic losses.

Beyond this, however, there are some rather fundamental political
developments that need to be sorted out, monitored, and forecasted as
well in country evaluations. *Internal* political change in a country may
range from gradual to abrupt, systematic to nonsystematic, and cata-
clysmic to trivial in terms of its importance to international lenders.
For example, political drift to the right or left may mean a great deal
in terms of the internal and external workings of the national economy and the quality of economic management, as the recent history
of countries such as Brazil, France, the United Kingdom, Mexico,
Chile, and Sri Lanka demonstrates. The symptoms can make themselves felt in domestic fiscal and monetary policies, relations with
foreign countries, pressures for nationalization or indigenization of
foreign direct investments, imposition of exchange controls, and the
like. Adverse shifts may result in soaring imports, reduced capacity
to export, drying up of foreign direct investment, capital flight, aid
cutoffs, and problems of access to international capital markets. The
point is that it is necessary to fix on the direction, magnitude, and
timing of political drift, if any, before very much that is sensible can
be said about future macroeconomic scenarios.

A more dramatic version of the same thing relates to violent internal political conflict, which may ultimately produce the type of political "drift" just discussed but, in the meantime, may have serious
direct economic consequences as well. Strikes, terrorism, sabotage,
and popular insurrection may seriously disrupt the workings of the
national economy, with potentially dramatic consequences for a country's balance of payments. Export industries, such as tourism, are
particularly sensitive to such problems. The direct and indirect import
requirements of government anti-insurgency efforts can be significant
as well. It is clearly important to assess the strength of both the insurgency movement and the government in order to forecast the duration
and outcome of such conflict, which (if it results in systemic change)
may even lead to repudiation of external debt. As the Iranian case
in the 1970s shows, such forecasts are as treacherous as they are
critical to the whole process of country analysis. The assassination
of South Korean President Park Chung Hee in 1980 illustrates the
extreme range of possible outcomes of a discrete event of political

violence, from total insignificance to a fundamental political and economic overthrow of the existing order.

External political conflict can also take a variety of forms, ranging from invasion (Afghanistan, Cambodia) and foreign-inspired or foreign-supported insurgency (Zaire, Ethiopia, Morocco, Tunisia) to border tension and perceived external threats (Peru, Israel, Thailand, Taiwan, South Korea). Threats from abroad often require far-reaching domestic resource reallocation in the form of an inflated defense establishment—causing probable adverse trade shifts—and for most countries such threats involve large foreign exchange costs as well. Military hardware, human resources, and infrastructure in an economic sense generally have low or negative productivity in terms of the domestic economy or the balance of payments; thus, they contribute nothing to the basis of effective future debt service. Such distortions alone may have a serious bearing on the risk profile of a country, as viewed by banks from abroad.

These problems reside in both *potential* and *actual* external conflict. The latter simply makes the various distortions worse (to the extent that the costs are not absorbed by foreign political allies). To this must be added the supply-side possibilities of physical and human resource destruction and dislocation, obsolescence, and reconstruction costs if these are not partly offset by reparations or aid receipts. Even if external political conflict is won, there may be derivative internal political upheavals and possibly sizeable costs of occupation (e.g., Vietnam). If the conflict is lost, continued internal resistance and reparations obligations may have a debilitating effect on the home economy (e.g., Kampuchea), quite apart from the possibility of debt repudiation by the successor regime. All such assessments must be undertaken in probabilistic terms, but they are of far more than casual interest in cross-border lending to many countries around the world.

Shifting political alliances, regional political developments, and bilateral relations over such issues as human rights and nuclear proliferation can provide additional sources of political conflict. All are heavily influenced by global, regional, and national political events. Heavy lending exposure in Eastern Europe and China (insofar as a bank is not backstopped by its home government) carries sizeable risks related to future political developments and the possibility of borrower default and cost.

Political forecasting is an art that, despite its central role in plotting the future creditworthiness of countries, remains in its infancy. Indices of political stability developed by political scientists say little that is very reliable about the future or about the ultimate implications for debt service. The more sophisticated projections and information systems detailing possible sources of internal and external political conflict, while useful and necessary, usually leave the critical judgments largely up to the user of the information. There are also problems in the completeness and currency of political information and the inevitable biases embedded in external and in-house information which consensual approach techniques only begin to attack.

To summarize, country analysis is a process that requires careful assessment and weighing of internal economic elements, external trade, and monetary flows, as well as assesments, the impact of each on foreign debt and reserves—all in a political context that is itself often highly complex and difficult to gauge. As Figure 19–7 shows, each element in the analysis is linked to all of the others, and the task is to forecast the future of national politicoeconomic futures with specific reference to the ability and willingness to service external

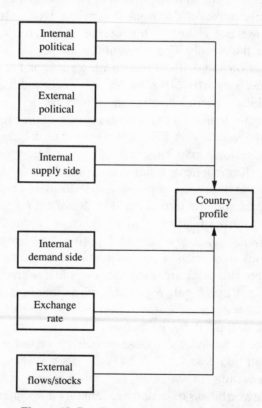

Figure 19–7.   Country Evaluation Summary.

debt. Banks, therefore, are principally concerned with such *base-level* country scenarios, which permit evaluation of the net present value of country lending exposure. The problem becomes significantly more complex, however, if the task is to evaluate *project-specific* country scenarios related to equity investments including the bank's own operations in the country concerned.

Approaches to Country Evaluation

Given the complex of factors affecting the creditworthiness of countries, how should international banks organize and evaluate the necessary flow of information within their own organizational structures and assemble it in a form that is useful from a decision-making point of view?

The kind of analysis one could consider a definitive portrayal of a country's economic and political future, and its implications for creditworthiness, may require writing a book, perhaps several books, about each nation of interest to a bank—a review that is updated every six months or so or whenever there is a significant change in bank interest or country circumstances. Such encyclopedic analyses tend to be useless from a decision-making point of view, even though they would probably give the only conceptually correct and comprehensive overview of all of the critical variables for each country, and the various interrelationships among them—the ifs, ands, and buts that are an inevitable part of any exercise in politicoeconomic forecasting. Banks operate under pressure of time, often severe, and they operate under fiscal and human resource constraints.

Given these realities, what approaches to country analysis suggest themselves? What are the relevant tradeoffs between completeness and accuracy, on the one hand, and usability and feasibility on the other?

Qualitative Assessments

Closest to the custom-tailored, in-depth country analyses just mentioned are purely "descriptive" country studies, which try to cover all of the political and economic bases. They tend to be heavily retrospective and subjective, and they use no standardized formating in order to avoid straightjacketing the discussion. This approach is particularly conducive to political risk evaluation, which tends to be unavoidably "soft." Comparability suffers, but the focus on specific country attributes and prospects is maintained. Updating problems are relatively serious because of the nature of the analysis and the level of detail, and there are great difficulties in distilling the essence of unstructured descriptive studies for use in lending and exposure-setting decisions in international banks.

Structured Country Reviews

The evident shortcomings of this approach are to some extent alleviated in so-called structured country reviews. Using a standard, relatively short format for all countries under consideration, this approach severely cuts back on the narrative and expands the use of data analysis standard ratios, and formal trend assessments. Qualitative elements are retained to the extent possible in an abbreviated format. An effort is made to retain country-specific elements in the analysis, and to enhance usability by means of carefully formated and worded summaries. Responsibility usually rests with overseas or headquarters personnel or with staff country analysts, with each analyst typically following several countries in a particular part of the world. Besides conventional sources of country data, periodic country visits and information flows from bank representatives in the field are supposed to update country files and improve the quality of the analysis. The standard format used in this approach is intended to facilitate cross-country comparisons without loss of significant qualitative country-specific information. Nevertheless, there is sometimes a tendency to deemphasize political risk and to adopt heavily retrospective focus, especially if total reliance is placed on economists.

Country Ratings

Efforts to overcome the weaknesses inherent in essentially qualitative country assessments, and at the same time enhance usability in decision making have produced so-called check-list country rating systems. Using the same information base just discussed, and sometimes backed up by a formal narrative country study, an attempt is made to assign "grades" both to quantitative and qualitative variables. Each grade is then assigned a weight, and one or several weighted summary scores are computed. These are supposed to capture not only the historical evidence, but also the future outlook (as reflected in the score assignment and weighting process) in an effort to facilitate country monitoring, cross-country comparisons, and auditing the performance of the system. Besides weighted country scores, several banks have developed more sophisticated systems to generate composite measures of debt service capacity, political stability, adaptability to external shocks, and the like. Weighted input measures are used to generate composite indicators, which are then sometimes displayed in grid or matrix format. One example is given in Figure 19–8.

Despite their advantages in country comparisons and usability in lending decisions, all rating systems suffer from a variety of ills. Selection of indicators tends to be subjective, and is often not based on coherent underlying modes of politics or economics. Grading of indicators likewise tend to be subjective, as is the assignment of weights. Usually the same indicators and weights are used for all countries examined, which seems to make little sense. Nonquantifiable information is often ignored, which may throw out some country-specific elements that can have a strong bearing on risk. Political-risk grading systems, both as developed in banks and available from advisory services, are even more tenuous in terms of validity. But perhaps the greatest potential problem lies in overreliance upon, and abuse of, such systems in lending decisions. In an area where the use of forecasting in decision-making, especially in the long term, is akin to grasping at straws, this technique in the wrong hands may be particularly dangerous.

Country Evaluation Filters

A still more refined technique of country evaluation involves the use of some form of *multiple discriminate analysis* to differentiate between countries that have in the past encountered external debt problems and those that have not. The objective is to avoid Type I errors (predicting that a country will get into trouble when in fact it does not) and Type II errors (predicting that a country will stay clear of problems when indeed it ends up in the soup). In the first case, a bank may stay away when indeed it should have lent, and in the second case it will go ahead and lend when in fact it should have passed it up. If selected indicators, such as the debt-service ratio or the liquidity ratio, have been found to successfully discriminate between "trouble" and "no-trouble" countries in the past, perhaps they can be used for this purpose in a forecasting context.

Despite their methodological sophistication, neatness, and usability of yes-no results, such filters do have a number of limitations. They provide only partial coverage of the dependent variable of concern—namely, the possibility of a decline in the real economic value of a bank's exposure in a particular country. Empirically, they focus almost exclusively on past debt reschedulings, although several try to broaden this definition somewhat. Most do not even differentiate

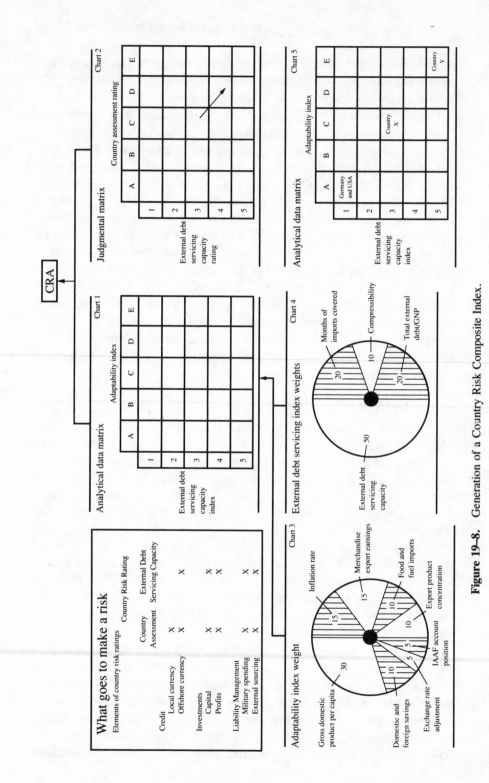

Figure 19–8. Generation of a Country Risk Composite Index.

between voluntary and involuntary reschedulings, which mean quite different things from a lender's point of view. There are also a number of technical limitations to the statistical techniques used, and there are some severe data problems, including unavailability, incompleteness, lateness, lack of comparability, and definitional issues, particularly with respect to country statistics on external debt. Finally, because there are only a few observations of "difficulties" in debt service available in any one year compared with the number of "no-problem" countries, the weights assigned to the former are inordinately large and a single country marginally falling into one or the other category may significantly affect the estimated parameters. In general, the wide economic differences among the countries in which banks have exposed assets, together with sometimes rapid shifts in these countries through time, raise doubts about the advisability of excessive reliance on such filters—or any limited set of indicators—even if statistical performance is reasonably good in evaluating historical experience of sample countries. However, they may indeed be useful for culling countries for close examination by one of the more in-depth techniques described earlier.

Figure 19–9 summarizes the factors to be considered in the form of one particularly well-designed and thoughtfully formated approach used by Swiss Bank Corporation.

Outside Views

Aside from internal country evaluations, a bank may avail itself of outside services that monitor country conditions around the world. A number of political risk services and global country reviews are marketed to banks and corporations by a growing array of firms, all of which profess special methodological expertise, information sources, or analytical competence. Individual consultants, particularly ex–public officials, do the same. Few, however, fully understand the international banking business or have intimate knowledge of individual banks, so that much of their advice is of limited value. On the other hand, outside consultants can provide useful second opinions and serve as a sounding board for internal views. From time to time, there are surveys of bank country ratings that are combined into overall rankings of "what banks think" of individual countries, particularly by *Institutional Investor* magazine (see Table 19–2).

To summarize, Figure 19–10 depicts the kinds of country evaluation systems that are available to international banks in terms of (1) their ability to capture country-specific details that may ultimately lead

Swiss Bank Corporation	Country Risk Monitor
Schweizerischer Bankverein	

	INDICATORS						Estimate	Outlook
DOMESTIC ECONOMY	1. Real GDP Growth %							
	2. Investment / GDP International average = 25%							
	3. Investment Efficiency (1:2) critical level ≤ 0.2							
	4. Inflation %							
	5. Money Supply Growth %							
	6. Real Domestic Credit Creation %							
	7. Fiscal Balance / GDP %							

EXTERNAL ECONOMY	8. Competitiveness (Real Exchange Rate) Index							
	9. Trade Balance (Goods) US $bn							
	10. Exports (Goods + Services) US $bn							
	11. Imports (Goods + Services) US $bn							
	12. Current Account Balance US $bn							
	13. Exports / GDP %							
	14. Export Concentration (high = critical) %							
	15. Imports from Switzerland SFr.m							

DEBT	16. Total External Debt (Public + Private) US $bn							
	17. International Reserves (Excl. Gold) US $bn							
	18. External Debt Service US $bn							
	19. External Debt / Exports critical level ≥ 150%							
	20. External Debt Service / Exports critical level ≥ 25%							
	21. Interest-Adjusted Current Account / Interest Payments %							
	22. International Reserves / Imports critical level ≤ 3 months							

23. Political Risk points 1 —— 10							
24.							
25.							

Remarks: ⬡ : Figure beyond critical level   ⬡ : Figure in critical Change vs. previous year   ⬡ : Figure in critical Change and beyond critical level

Figure 19–9. Swiss Bank Corporation's Country Risk Monitor.

Table 19–2. Institutional Investor's 1989 Country Credit Ratings

Rank			Institutional Investor		
March 1989	Sept. 1988	Country	Credit Rating	Six-Month Change	One-Year Change
1	1	Japan	95.2	0.4	9.6
2	2	Switzerland	94.3	0.4	0.2
3	3	West Germany	93.8	0.7	0.7
4	4	United States	89.8	0.2	−1.2
5	6	Netherlands	87.0	0.3	0.0
	5	United Kingdom	87.0	0.0	0.3
7	7	Canada	85.6	0.1	−0.3
8	8	France	84.8	0.1	−0.1
9	9	Austria	83.1	0.2	−1.0
10	10	Sweden	80.3	0.6	−0.4
11	12	Finland	78.8	0.4	0.2
12	13	Italy	78.2	0.7	0.7
13	14	Belgium	77.9	0.6	0.6
14	15	Taiwan	77.8	1.0	1.6
15	11	Norway	77.4	−1.8	−2.9
16	16	Singapore	75.6	0.8	0.2
17	17	Spain	74.7	1.3	1.2
18	18	Denmark	71.8	0.1	−1.2
19 [a]	19	Australia	69.7	0.5	−0.9
20 [a]	20	Hongkong	69.7	0.6	0.5
21	23	South Korea	66.5	2.8	4.0
22	21	U.S.S.R.	64.9	0.2	−0.5
23	22	New Zealand	63.7	−0.2	−1.5
24	25	Ireland	63.5	1.2	1.1
25	24	China	62.9	−0.4	−1.9
26	26	Saudi Arabia	59.9	−0.5	−0.4
27	29	Portugal	59.6	2.1	3.0
28	28	East Germany	58.7	0.9	0.4
29	27	Kuwait	58.4	−0.6	−0.1
30	31	Thailand	57.3	1.4	1.4
31	30	United Arab Emirates	56.5	−0.7	0.2
32	32	Malaysia	55.8	0.3	1.4
33	33	Bahrain	54.7	0.1	1.0
34	35	Czechloslovakia	54.4	0.3	0.1
35	34	Qatar	54.0	−0.4	−0.3
36	36	Iceland	53.1	0.1	0.4
37	37	Oman	50.7	−0.2	0.5

a. Order determined by actual results before rounding.

(continued)

Table 19–2.   (cont.)

March 1989 (Rank)	Sept. 1988 (Rank)	Country	Institutional Investor Credit Rating	Six-Month Change	One-Year Change
38	39	Greece	48.6	1.4	2.2
39	38	India	47.8	−0.6	−2.1
40	40	Bulgaria	46.5	−0.4	−1.2
41	42	Cypress	44.7	1.6	2.5
42	41	Hungary	44.5	0.5	−2.0
43	43	Indonesia	43.9	1.1	0.8
44	44	Turkey	41.0	−0.1	0.5
45	45	Algeria	39.9	0.8	−2.7
46	47	Papua New Guinea	37.3	−0.4	−0.2
47	46	Colombia	37.1	−0.8	−2.0
48	54	Tunisia	35.5	2.0	2.3
49	52	Barbados	35.2	0.9	1.6
50	49	Venezuela	34.9	−1.0	−0.8
51	50	Israel	34.5	0.0	−0.1
52	51	Jordan	33.4	−1.2	−2.7
53	57	Rumania	32.7	0.3	−0.7
54 [a]	53	Cameroon	32.4	−1.2	−3.6
55 [a]	56	South Africa	32.4	0.0	0.1
56	48	Trinidad & Tobago	31.9	−4.4	−6.5
57	55	Gabon	31.6	−1.7	−2.1
58	61	Chile	31.1	2.2	3.9
59	60	Mauritius	30.7	1.6	3.1
60	58	Pakistan	30.5	−0.5	−0.6
61	59	Kenya	30.1	−0.2	−0.6
62	62	Mexico	29.3	0.5	1.3
63	64	Brazil	29.1	0.7	−0.4
64	63	Uruguay	28.9	0.4	0.5
65	65	Yugoslavia	26.8	−1.3	−2.2
66	73	Morocco	25.8	1.9	1.9
67	66	Paraguay	25.4	−1.4	−2.3
68	70	Zimbabwe	25.0	0.8	2.0
69	67	Ivory Coast	24.8	−0.5	−1.4
70	72	Philippines	24.6	0.6	0.9
71	71	Nepal	24.5	0.5	1.8
72	75	Egypt	24.1	1.1	0.6
73	68	Libya	23.4	−1.6	0.3
74	76	Sri Lanka	22.4	−0.4	−0.7
75	74	Argentina	22.3	−0.9	−2.5
76	81	Iran	21.0	2.1	2.7

Table 19–2. (cont.)

Rank March 1989	Rank Sept. 1988	Country	Institutional Investor Credit Rating	Six-Month Change	One-Year Change
77	69	Panama	20.7	−4.1	−7.9
78	77	Ecuador	19.9	−1.6	−3.3
79	78	Senegal	19.2	−0.1	−0.2
80	80	Nigeria	18.8	−0.4	−1.6
81	79	Syria	18.3	−1.0	0.3
82 [a]	83	Costa Rica	18.1	0.2	0.5
83 [a]	85	Poland	18.1	0.7	0.3
84	84	Bangladesh	17.7	0.2	0.5
85	82	Swaziland	17.6	−0.9	0.8
86	86	Jamaica	17.1	1.1	1.3
87	90	Iraq	15.8	1.0	1.1
88	88	Malawi	15.6	0.5	−0.1
89	87	Dominican Republic	15.2	−0.1	1.0
90	89	Seychelles	14.9	−0.2	1.2
91	93	Guatamala	14.8	0.3	0.8
92	91	Congo	13.4	−1.4	−0.4
93	92	Honduras	13.4	−1.1	0.5
94	95	Peru	11.5	−1.5	−2.6
95	94	Cuba	11.2	−2.2	−1.6
96	97	Liberia	10.6	−0.1	0.5
97	96	Angola	10.2	−0.9	−1.5
98	103	El Salvador	9.9	0.7	1.5
99	102	Bolivia	9.7	0.1	0.9
100 [a]	100	Zambia	9.5	−0.5	−1.3
101 [a]	101	Tanzania	9.5	−0.3	−0.6
102	98	Zaire	9.4	−0.8	−1.2
103	104	Sierra Leone	9.1	0.9	2.1
104	99	Grenada	8.9	−1.3	−0.3
105	106	Ethiopia	7.2	−0.7	−1.5
106 [a]	108	Lebanon	7.0	−0.3	−0.5
107 [a]	105	Haiti	7.0	−0.9	−1.0
108	107	Mozambique	6.7	−0.9	−2.3
109	109	Uganda	5.4	−0.2	0.2
110	110	Sudan	5.2	−0.4	−0.1
111	111	Nicaragua	4.7	−0.4	−0.8
112	112	North Korea	3.6	−0.9	−0.5
Global average rating			38.7	0.0	−0.2

SOURCE: *Institutional Investor*.

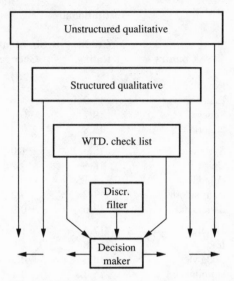

Figure 19–10.   Breadth versus Usability in Country Evaluation Systems.

to losses in the value of bank exposures and (2) the usability of their respective informational outputs in bank decision making. There clearly is a tradeoff. The more comprehensive the analysis, the less usable it is in a banking context. The more mechanical and formal the system, the less country-specific information it tends to capture, which may ultimately be the source of grief for the bank. Reconciling the two components of good country evaluation systems—that is, usability and completeness—is largely a matter of organizational design.

Institutional Design and Country Exposure Decisions

Figure 19–11 represents a simplified schematic of a decision system, one that will vary to some extent among international banks, with the solid lines representing reporting relationships and the dashed lines representing information flows. Information on cross-border exposure of the banks is maintained by a monitoring system at the head office, which receives and consolidates information on the size and tenor of facilities granted, drawdowns, redeposits, and other pertinent elements. As noted earlier, care must be taken that exposure is updated frequently and is correctly measured and allocated in light of third-country guarantees and certain other factors that might be considered to shift the locus of risk.

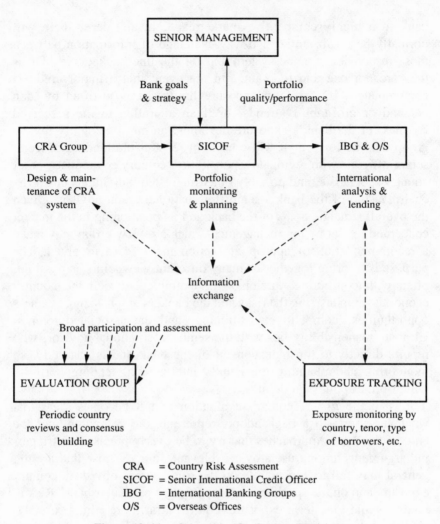

Figure 19–11. Schematic of a Country Decision.

We know that the degree of decentralization of decision making differs substantially among international banks. However, we also know that the need to secure competitive advantages through close client contact, quick response times, and adequate lending authority often leads to greater decentralization with the growth of the bank. This puts a premium on the existence of some type of centralized system that assures that the global asset portfolio, as a whole, is in line with the bank's risk preferences and earnings targets; at the same time, this system should not unduly restrict the activities of the bank in a highly competitive marketplace. In any case, there will normally be a substantial two-way exchange of information between those responsible for the system and for the line bankers, insofar as they are not one and the same. In the event that a major credit is contemplated, if a shift in exposure limits seems justified by loan demand or profitability trends, or if an alteration in the perceived riskiness of the bank's exposure develops, an *ad hoc* country review group may be formed. It will consist of responsible lending officers, senior officials with regional responsibility, country economists, other country specialists, and possibly other interested individuals under the chairmanship of the bank's senior international credit advisor. Given the overall strategic goals of the bank and its positioning in the market concerned, as set by top management, such a review group may make a recommendation of appropriate action in the case involved. The purpose is to bring together as many different viewpoints as possible, often with conflicting opinions—for example between the country economist emphasizing the risks and the bankers emphasizing business opportunities, competitive positioning, and the associated returns. Ultimate responsibility lies with the senior international advisor, who reports directly to top management of the bank and is charged with monitoring and planning the bank's international lending portfolio within broad policy guidelines.

It is in the *use* of country evaluation that it becomes clear that whatever approach a bank adopts represents the beginning, not the end, of the task. Approaches that try to be overly precise risk triggering arguments among users over irrelevant points. Those that are too general may fail to concentrate on the true sources of risk in country exposure and on the specific concerns facing a particular bank. Risk to medium- and long-term exposure requires a far more complex analysis than risk to short-term or special-purpose lending, yet it requires an analysis that is still much simpler than risk to any equity exposure that a bank may have in a particular country.

The twin temptations of "quick and dirty" and "overloaded" country assessments constantly seem to confront international banks. The first approach promises mechanical short cuts and the use of low-priced talent to grind out country ratings at low cost; however, it often appears to succeed only in producing nonsense—there really is no substitute for high-quality analysis, flexibility, judgment, and familiarity. The second approach may rely on well-qualified internal personnel at high cost, yet it may encounter a dangerous narrowing of country expertise, possibly cause dissension in the ranks, and create bottlenecks in the decision-making process.

The conflicting demands of country assessment in international banking, probably means that there is no such thing as an "ideal" country evaluation system. "Appropriate" systems will certainly differ for different banks. The key may reside as much on the human resources side as on the technology side. Training line bankers to use reasonably unsophisticated yet sensible country assessments properly and to be sensitive to changing country risk profiles as they go about their business may contribute more to sound exposure decisions than comparable resources devoted to the design and implementation of more elegant systems. Whether in systems design or in the training function, resources devoted to the assessment of country risk clearly are subject to constraints, and there is some implicit optimum where the incremental costs in country assessment begin to outweigh the economic losses implicit in inefficient international exposure portfolios.

Portfolio Aspects

We have focused in this chapter on the problems of exposure to country risk, what it means from the standpoint of the real value of a bank's assets in a particular country, and the assessment of that risk. Note that our discussion has concentrated exclusively on country-by-country analysis—putting countries individually under the microscope to see what makes them tick and how they are likely to evolve in the future. A favorable conclusion may mean that a bank's exposure limits should be adjusted upward and that business should be actively solicited. A negative conclusion means the reverse.

Recall, though, that international banks are really in the business of managing a global "portfolio" of country exposures, just as they are managing a "portfolio" of loans to companies, individuals, and other entities. This means maximizing returns on the entire portfolio subject to a given risk constraint set by management, or it means minimizing the level of risk to which the bank is exposed with a given target rate of return (i.e., the standard portfolio management problem). One difficulty in managing global portfolios of country exposures is that a country "exposure" cannot easily be sold on a highly efficient market when risk or return perceptions change—it can only be "run down" over time as loans come due, or, in some cases, it can be transferred through loan sales programs or sold on a relatively inefficient secondary loan market. Another problem, as we have seen, is that neither the risks nor the expected net returns are easily measured.

Yet the basic principles of portfolio theory remain valid, since it is trying to maximize returns subject to risk in its *entire* portfolio, not country by country. It may well be, for example, that increasing a bank's exposure in Country X under relatively unfavorable risk return conditions may still make a lot of sense if, by taking on that exposure, the *overall* level of risk of its portfolio decreases through additional diversification. Particularly if the country has little in common with others in the portfolio (low covariances in expected returns), such an outcome may well be possible. Countries like India and China have found receptive markets for their debt during the 1980s in part because few banks had these countries' paper on their books and could benefit significantly from the additional portfolio diversification. After all, it is the risks and returns associated with a bank's *global* asset and liability portfolios that define the value of the bank to its shareholders, although they themselves may hold internationally diversified stock portfolios as well.

To get the best possible fix on the critical $E(F_t) - E(C_t)$ and α_t variables that have been the focus of our discussion, and to achieve integration in a global portfolio context, the exercise of country assessment and exposure setting should be a coherent managerial process that unambiguously focuses a bank's network of information and actively involves individuals with different functions and perspectives. The exercise itself will thus have tangible portfolio benefits all its own, quite apart from its more visible output in the form of defensible country-by-country evaluations. Mechanization and decentralization of the country review process will tend to cut down and perhaps eliminate this benefit; this may help to stifle an environment conducive to sound global portfolio decisions.

Each bank's institutional information flow and decision-making setup has its own profile, depending on such factors as the organization's size and structure. Some banks incorporate country assessments into portfolio decisions quite flexibly and informally, while others seem to rely on rigid and formalized review procedures. In some cases, the review process is closely tied as well to the annual budget cycle and the allocation of lending authority to countries and regions. These again may be quite rigid in some banks, while in others they are relatively easily altered as perceived market and risk conditions change. In some banks, the determination of loan loss provisions is an integral part of the process. It affects the anticipated net profitability of loans by adjusting for risk and presumably permits improved performance evaluation within the bank's organizational framework.

While few international banks fail to maintain adequate cross-border exposure measurement and monitoring, there seems to be far greater variability in the state of the country assessment systems themselves. Some are carefully thought through, while others are largely cosmetic or pseudoscientific. Some are well integrated into the life of the organization, while others seem separate and even isolated. For a time, smaller U.S. banks, particularly when participating in loan syndications, tended to rely on the risk evaluations of the larger money center banks. Besides being unsatisfactory from a regulatory point of view, the appropriate risk/return calculus of the lead banks (where fees and relationship are of critical importance) is not necessarily the same as that of the smaller banks far removed from the borrower. Some banks in Europe and Japan traditionally placed less emphasis on the design of formal approaches to country assessment and incorporating them into international decisions on country exposures or portfolio management, preferring instead to rely more informally on the collective experience and wisdom of senior bank officers.

Whatever the approach, rational portfolio decisions with respect to country exposure management demand that forecasts of country futures be maintained on a comparable basis and be modified in light of covariances arising out of common export markets or sources of supply, conditions in and access to international financial markets, and regional and global political developments. And so it is possible, in terms of Figure 19–11, to envision the consistent application of a portfolio approach, with risk aversion dictated by top management, correctly attributed returns estimated by line bankers, carefully defined risks to these returns estimated by formal or informal approaches to country evaluation, and covariances therein brought into the picture in the setting of exposure limits and term sublimits.

SUMMARY

Whereas country evaluation is itself an exceedingly difficult task, building country assessments into the design of international exposure portfolios that are in some sense "efficient" is even more complicated. Neither the risks nor the returns are clearly definable, and even exposure measurement is a difficult task. Portfolio ideas can contribute importantly in clarifying the risks. It also helps identify dangers inherent in externally imposed evaluations for rational portfolio decisions, particularly when they emanate from the regulatory system. At the same time, the development of informational and interactive networks within international banks as part of the country evaluation process can itself lead to improved international lending decisions that implicitly embody some of the elusive portfolio concepts we have tried to explain in this chapter.

Application of the portfolio concepts we have suggested also help pin down the link between risks and pricing of international loans. Portfolio theory says that it is not the riskiness of any single loan that is important, rather it is the effect of that loan on the riskiness of the overall bank or shareholder portfolio. So, for example, loans by different banks for similar maturities to a single country might well be priced differently, dependent on both the nature of the "indirect" returns accruing to the lending banks and on the structure of their respective international loan portfolios.

SELECTED REFERENCES

Bennett, Paul.   "A Portfolio Approach to Country Exposure Management." *Journal of Banking and Finance*, June 1984.

Ensor, Richard, ed.   *Assessing Country Risk*. London: Euromoney Publications, 1981.

Heffernan, Shelagh.   *Country Risk Assessment*. London: George Allen & Unwin, 1985.

Kobrin, Stephen J.   "Political Risk: A Review and Reconsideration." *Journal of International Business Studies*, Spring/Summer 1979.

Nagy, Pancras   *Country Risk*. London: Euromoney Publications, 1979.

O'Leary, Michael K. and Coplin, William D.   *Political Risk in Thirty Countries*. London: Euromoney Publications, 1981.

Sargen,   Nicholas.   "Use of Economic Indicators and Country Risk Appraisal." *Economic Review*, Federal Reserve Bank of San Francisco, Fall 1977.

Walter, Ingo.   "Country Risk, Portfolio Decisions and International Bank Lending." *Journal of Banking and Finance*, March 1981.

20

Competitive Structure and Strategic Positioning

The previous chapters have discussed the internationalization of the financial services industry and described and categorized "products" of that industry in some detail. What emerges is a complex web of markets, services, and institutions that is not easily subject to analysis.

This chapter presents a coherent model of the industry that focuses on competitive market structure. It not only identifies markets capable of producing supernormal profits, but also specifies the linkages among those markets that are the basis for economies of scale and economies of scope—critical dimensions in the globalization of the financial services industry. This model will be used to analyze sources of national and institutional competitive advantage in this sector and the effects of competitive distortions.

THE C-A-P MODEL

There are three principal dimensions that define the global market for financial services:

1. Client (C-dimension)
2. Arena (A-dimension)
3. Product (P-dimension)

Firms in the global financial services industry have an unusually broad range of choice with respect to each of these dimensions, and different combinations yield different strategic and competitive profiles. Figure 20–1 depicts these dimensions in the form of a matrix comprised of C-A-P cells. Each cell has a distinctive competitive structure based on fundamental economic and public policy considerations.

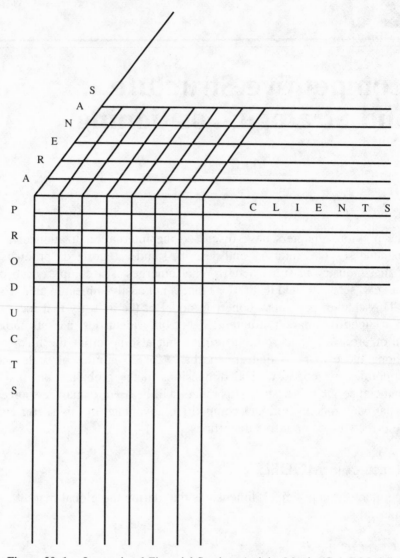

Figure 20–1.   International Financial Services Activity Matrix (C-A-P Model).

Largely as a result of technological change and deregulation, financial institutions confront increasing potential access to each of the dimensions in the global C-A-P opportunity set. Financial deregulation in particular has had an important influence in terms of (1) accessibility of geographic arenas, (2) accessibility of individual client groups by players originating in different parts of the financial services business, and (3) substitutability among financial products in meeting personal, corporate, or public sector financial needs.

Client

As conventionally used, the distinction between generic "wholesale" and "retail" financial services is not particularly helpful in the context of the C-A-P model, and the following categorization of the major client groups may be more appropriate.

1. Sovereign—National states and their instrumentalities.
2. Corporate—Nonfinancial corporations regardless of industry classification, ranging from multinational corporations (MNCs) and parastatals to middle-market and small, privately owned companies.
3. Financial services—Other financial institutions in the same industry subcategory (e.g., correspondent banks) or in other segments of the financial services industry, such as brokerage or insurance.
4. Private—High net worth and high net income individuals.
5. Retail—Mass-market financial services, either sold cross-border or within domestic financial services markets, aimed at individuals and households.

The clients in all these groups can be broken down into narrower segments, each differing with respect to product-related attributes such as currency requirements, liquidity and maturity needs, risk levels, industry categories, overall service requirements, price sensitivity, and timing aspects. Effective market definition and segmentation involves identifying coherent client groups that embody relative uniformity with respect to each of these variables.

ARENA

The international market for financial services can be divided into onshore and offshore arenas with respect to geographic location. The "arena" dimension is different from the standard definition of market "region" in that it encompasses the concepts of regulatory and monetary sovereignty, which are of critical importance in determining international trade in financial services. Each arena is characterized by different risk/return profiles, levels of financial efficiency, regulatory conditions, client needs, and other factors.

As discussed in Chapters 2 and 3, geographic interpenetration on the part of commercial and investment banking institutions with respect to various domestic and offshore markets has become very significant indeed. The A-dimension in Figure 20–1 can be taken into the analysis at the global, regional, national, subregional, and location-specific levels, so that it is not purely country specific. However, the country level of analysis remains paramount due to the importance of national monetary policies, financial regulation, and competition policies — all of which are imposed at the country level. It is only in federal states that the rules of the game are sometimes importantly set at the subnational level.

Product

Financial services offered in the international market have undergone dramatic proliferation. With a clear requirement for product differentiation in the marketplace, firms in the industry have created new instruments and techniques tailored to the needs of their clients.

The range of financial services that can be supplied to the various client segments is evident from previous chapters. Table 20–1 combines the client and product dimensions and links each combination to the underlying type of activity that is being undertaken by the institution concerned.

It is useful to divide the activities of financial institutions into three categories: (1) liability-based activities, (2) asset-based activities, and (3) off–balance sheet activities. There is also a fourth category comprising activities in which the financial institution is acting for its own account on either the asset or the liability side of its balance sheet. This involves arbitrage and positioning and, to a large extent, makes possible the other two types of activities.

In essence, these four activities define the primary services that are sold to clients. These primary services are, however, aggregated into actual banking products. All products that appear in the market, including the most complex innovations, fall into one or more of the following categories.

1. Credit products—Pure credit products are asset-based activities. Although credit products have become a less significant source of returns for many international institutions, they remain the core of much of the business. Credit activities range from straightforward

Table 20–1. Subclassification of International Financial Services

Product	Primary Classification[a]			
	1	**2**	**3**	**4**
Deposit Taking				
Time deposits	L			
Demand deposits	L			
Other	L			
Trading and dealing	(X/L)			
Money Market				X
Securities				X
Foreign exchange				X
Swaps				X
Futures				X
Options				X
Bullion				X
Other				X
Sale of bank securities				
Certificates of deposit	L			
Ordinary shares	L			
Preferred shares	L			
Floating-rate notes	L			
Short- and long-term debt	L			
Lending (Local or foreign currency)				
Sovereign	X	X		
Corporate				
Indigenous majors	X	X		
MNC affiliates	X	X		
Parastatals	X	X		
Indigenous middle market	X	X		
Foreign middle market	X	X		
Correspondent				
Indigenous banks	X	X		
Foreign banks	X	X		
Private				
High net worth	X	X		
High net income	X	X		
Retail	X	X		
Specialized financing activities				
Asset-based financing	X	X		
Equity financing	X	X		

a. The classifications are as follows: 1. Credit products (L = credit extension by counterparties); 2. Financial Engineering products; 3. Risk management products; 4. Market acess products.

(continued)

591

Table 20–1. (cont.)

Product	Primary Classification[a]			
	1	**2**	**3**	**4**
Specialized financing activities (cont.)				
Export financing	X	X		
Project financing	X	X		
Venture capital financing	X	X		
Real estate financing	X	X		
Mergers and acquisitions financing	X	X		
Leveraged buyout financing	X	X		
Securities underwriting				
Sovereign debt				
State debt, revenue, and agency bonds			X	X
Mortgage-backed securities			X	X
Insurance			X	X
Equities			X	X
Other			X	X
Securities distribution				
Domestic				X
Fixed income				X
Equities				X
Other				X
International				X
Fixed income				X
Equities				X
Other				X
Advisory services				
Corporate cash management		X	X	X
Corporate fiscal (tax) planning		X	X	
General corporate financial services		X	X	X
Real estate advisory		X	X	X
Mergers and acquisitions		X	X	
Domestic		X	X	
International		X	X	
Risk management services		X	X	
Interest rate risk		X	X	
Foreign exchange risk		X	X	
Country risk		X	X	
Other		X	X	
International trade advisory services		X	X	X
Trust and estate planning		X	X	
Legal and investment advisory services		X	X	
Tax advisory services		X	X	
General financial advice		X	X	

Table 20–1. (cont.)

Product	Primary Classification[a]			
	1	2	3	4
Consumer services				
Credit cards	X			X
Travelers' checks			X	X
Other consumer services	X		X	X
Asset management services				
Private/retail		X	X	
Fiduciary activities		X	X	
Safekeeping/lock box services		X	X	
Mutual funds		X	X	
Corporate/Correspondent		X	X	
Safekeeping/lock box services		X	X	
Pension fund management		X	X	
Mutual fund management		X	X	
Brokerage				
Money market				X
Eurocurrencies/Foreign exchange				X
Fixed income (government and corporate)				X
Equities				X
Financial futures				X
Options				X
Commodities				X
Gold				X
Insurance				X
Payments mechanism				
Domestic funds transfer				X
International funds transfer				X
Insurance-related services				
Standby letters of credit	X		X	
NIFS, RUFS, and MOFFs	X		X	
Revolving credits	X			
C/P standby facilities	X		X	
Life insurance			X	
Property and casualty			X	
International trade services				
International collections			X	X
Letters of credit business		X	X	X
Bankers' acceptances	X		X	X
Countertrade		X		X
Market intelligence				X

general-purpose term lending to sophisticated and specialized forms (e.g., project finance).

2. Financial engineering products—These comprise the design and delivery of financial services specifically structured to satisfy often complex client objectives at minimum cost. In a world where borrowers, issuers, savers, and investors often have distinctive and complex objectives, financial engineering is perhaps the ultimate form of product differentiation, and it accounts for a great deal of the value-added creation observed in the international capital markets. It can be either "disembodied" or "embodied," depending on whether or not the engineering components are part of specific financial transactions. Purely disembodied financial engineering may take the form of advisory functions that an American investment bank might undertake, based on client-specific information, for a Japan-based multinational manufacturing firm seeking an acquisition in the same industry in the United States. Embodied financial engineering combines this with one or more financial transactions—asset, liability, and off–balance sheet services—sold to the same client as part of a financing package. Other examples include structuring of project financings, leveraged buyouts, complex multicurrency financings, advice on appropriate capital structure, and so forth.

3. Risk management products—Risk bearing has long been recognized as one of the key functions of financial institutions and one of the reasons they tend to be heavily regulated. The main forms of exposure include credit risk, interest rate risk, liquidity risk, foreign exchange risk, country risk, project risk, commodity risk, and technical risk (e.g., in cash transmission areas). Risk management activities fall into two groups: those in which financial institutions themselves assume all or part of the exposure and those in which the institutions provide technology needed to achieve a shifting of risk or themselves take on exposure only on a contingent basis (i.e., an off–balance sheet commitment to buy or sell, borrow or lend). Effective risk reduction through diversification clearly depends on the independence of the various risks represented in the portfolio. Financial institutions provide risk management services that range from simple standby credit lines and forward interest rate agreements to explicit, tightly defined products addressed to a broad range of contingencies.

4. Market access products—Financial institutions can provide value-added services to clients by using their internal networks to transfer

information, funds, or securities from one client or arena to others. Accomplishing this requires both tangible and intangible networks. The former consist of physical assets, such as branches or other outlets covering various clients and arenas. The latter can be looked upon as the institution's access to actual or potential customers in arenas in which it may or may not have a physical presence. State-of-the-art internal operations and systems capabilities drive the competitive positioning of individual players in supplying market-access services internationally.

5. Arbitrage and positioning—Activities that financial institutions engage in for their own account facilitate and, in many cases, make possible the supply of the first four types of financial services to clients internationally.

Arbitrage opportunities occur when the same asset is priced differently in different markets (or market segments), often because of information asymmetries. "Pure" arbitrage takes place when an asset is simultaneously bought and sold. By this definition, financial institutions rarely engage in pure arbitrage. Rather, they engage in "risk arbitrage"—buying an asset in a particular market, holding it for a time (however short), and reselling it in the same or different market. The institution is thus exposed to "differential risk," due to the possibility that the underlying price differential may evaporate or be reversed during the time needed to complete the transaction. Exposure to differential risk depends jointly on the time necessary to complete the transaction and the underlying volatility in the price of the specific asset and the markets in which it is traded.

Positioning is a form of risk arbitrage that has become an integral part of managing international financial institutions during a time of significant exchange rate and interest rate volatility. Interest rate–linked and foreign exchange–linked positioning drives securities, options, and futures trading and dealing.

We can now put the three dimensions together once again in Figure 20–2, which uses two "cells" in the matrix to illustrate the markets for consumer installment lending in Germany (represented by A) and interest rate swaps sold to corporations in Japan (represented by B).

Another illustration can be taken from the global activities of the American Express Company. Figure 20–3 divides the world into broad geographic zones (in this case, the *arena* dimension). It indicates which *products* are actively made available in each *arena* to each broad category of *client*, as of 1989.

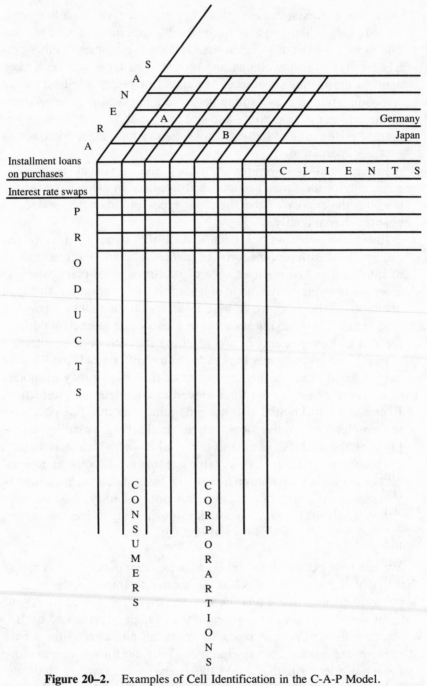

Figure 20–2. Examples of Cell Identification in the C-A-P Model.

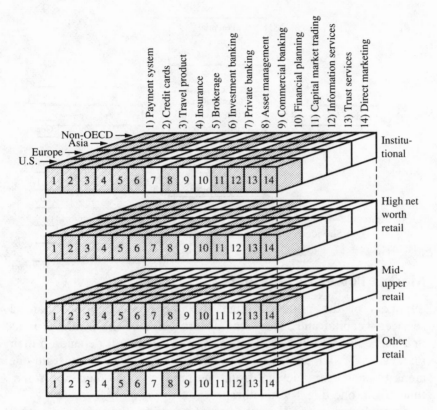

Figure 20–3. Example of Cell Identification in the American Express Model.

CELL CHARACTERISTICS

The inherent attractiveness of each of the cells in Figure 20–1 will depend on the *size and durability* of prospective returns that can be extracted from that cell, adjusted for the perceived risks involved. Each cell has imbedded within it a certain value quotient potentially available to all players. The absolute level of the cell-specific returns depends on the level of demand for a particular financial service, its price and cost, and the price elasticity of demand—which in turn is affected primarily by the existence of product substitutes. The actual returns captured by each institution will depend on its competitive positioning, discussed in the following chapter. Their durability will be based in part on the ability of new players to enter the cell and the development of substitute products over time. Cell characteristics can be analyzed in terms of conventional market structure criteria, as summarized in Figure 20–4.

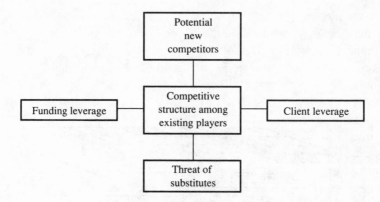

Figure 20–4.   Application of a Competitive Analysis Framework to Financial Services.

Market Power of Suppliers

Suppliers of the principal inputs for the production of financial services—capital and labor—can absorb some of the available rents in a particular C-A-P cell. Their ability to do so will depend on their market power, which can be expected to vary substantially from one arena to another, somewhat from one product to another, and sometimes from one client to another.

First, depositors and purchasers of securities issued by financial institutions demand returns commensurate with the perceived level of risk. This depends heavily on the credit rating of the individual financial institution. To the extent that an institution is perceived as being less creditworthy due to the quality of its assets or its exposure to other types of risk, its market power is eroded as bondholders and depositors demand higher yields for the funds they supply. In this context, the removal of regulations on interest payable with respect to various types of deposit accounts clearly raises the market power of capital suppliers and the cost of liabilities for financial institutions. Moreover, the more financially sophisticated the suppliers of funds become, the more aware they are of alternative opportunities.

To a large extent, the leverage of savers derives from the growing availability of alternative outlets for funds, rather than from individual strategic exercise of market power with respect to financial institutions. Under deregulation, funds are shifted to markets with higher yields, which may then be matched by the affected financial institutions that raise their deposit rates. Certainly, this pattern tends to be the case at the retail level. In the Japanese context, for example, deregulation of interest rates after 1980 gave suppliers of funds to financial institutions considerably greater leverage.

Second, the market for labor facing financial institutions also differs dramatically across many of the C-A-P cells in which they operate. Increases in market power on the part of suppliers of highly skilled labor to financial institutions has occasionally led to dramatic increases in compensation levels, enabling labor to capture some of the returns derived from the cell. The same is true of real estate and other resources upon which financial institutions depend. Again in the Japanese example, there has clearly been a conflict between the need to develop considerable institutionalized financial expertise in the new competitive environment and the traditions of promotions based on seniority and loyalty to a single employer. There are signs, however, that both of these are gradually breaking down.

Market Power of Clients

Buyers of financial services naturally seek to attain highest value-added service at lowest cost. The more successful they are, the narrower the margins and the lower the rents available to the financial institution in a specific C-A-P cell. Especially in international wholesale markets, buyers of financial services are sought after by a large number of institutions competing fiercely for their business. Client groups such as multinational corporations and high net worth individuals have significantly more monopsony power than other client groups for whom competition is markedly less intense. The market power of buyers of financial services can be expected to differ in all three dimensions of the C-A-P matrix—from one client group to another, from one product category to another, and across different arenas.

Availability of Product Substitutes

Product substitutes available to clients in a given cell clearly increase the price elasticity of demand, which in turn determines the price volume vectors that are accessible to the financial institution and, consequently, the overall level of returns. The closer the substitutability among financial services, the higher the price elasticity of demand and the lower the level of returns that are available within a given C-A-P cell. One would expect the degree of product substitutability to differ from one client group to the next and across different arenas.

The most important factor relating to product substitutes in financial services is information and technology content, so that the creation of product substitutes has become one of the most important and pervasive effects of financial innovation. Successful innovations that an institution introduces into a given cell are those embodying a low degree of product or process substitutability over a relatively long duration.

Competitive Structure and Strategic Groups

Clearly, the competitive structure of each C-A-P cell is a major determinant of the excess returns an institution may be able to obtain. To the extent competition takes place on the pricing variable, prospective returns are transferred to clients. Competitive structure is conventionally measured using concentration ratios based on the number of firms, distribution of market share among firms, and similar criteria.

Normally, the addition of players to a particular C-A-P cell would be expected to reduce market concentration, increase the degree of competition, and lead to an erosion of margins and a more rapid pace of financial innovation.

An example of competitive structure can be taken from the Eurobond market (see Chapter 14), which represents an unregulated (or, more correctly, self-regulated), highly competitive market in which any bank or securities firm from any country is free to compete. The Euromarket has historically favored those competitors with substantial captive placing power, such as the large Swiss banks, which have had a major influence on the market since its beginnings in the early 1960s. Other institutions, however, have been able to survive (and periodically prosper) by securing lead managerships of issues originated by companies from their own countries or as a result of innovation in either products or techniques used in the market. American firms fared very well during the early 1980s by managing issues for U.S. companies. Japanese firms have benefited substantially from the large flow of Japanese Eurobond issues during most of the 1980s and particularly during the period from 1985 through 1988.

Table 20–2 presents several alternative measures of the competitive structure of the Eurobond market from 1975 to 1988, including new-issue volumes, the number of firms competing, the Gini coefficient, and the Herfindahl indexes. The Gini coefficients indicate a relatively high degree of market concentration, although the Herfindahl indexes

Table 20–2. Measures of Concentration in the Eurobond Market

Year	Eurobond Volume[a]	Number of Players	Gini Coefficient[b]	Herfindahl Index[c]
1975	8,316	25	.3449	.03002
1976	15,165	25	.4437	.03576
1977	18,087	62	.6443	.04155
1978	12,253	59	.6353	.07350
1979	14,810	63	.5558	.04346
1980	20,558	76	.5996	.03863
1981	27,451	75	.6476	.04521
1982	47,266	75	.6479	.04927
1983	48,980	75	.6703	.07231
1984	79,290	75	.6466	.05242
1985	144,151	75	.6448	.04738
1986	185,272	75	.6224	.03999
1987	141,223	50	.5386	.04659
1988	193,015	50	.5196	.03784

a. In millions of dollars.

b. The Gini coefficient (G) measures market-share distributions ranging from pure monopoly to equal distribution such that $1 > G > 0$, regardless of the number of competitors.

c. The Herfindahl index (H) is the sum of the squares of the market shares and measures *both* the number of competitors *and* the evenness of market-share distribution such that $1 > H > 0$ and H declines as the number of players increases *and* as evenness of market share increases.

SOURCE: Compiled from *Institutional Investor* league table data (various issues), with full credit to lead managers.

show the effects of the large number of players on what has become a highly price-competitive market.

Table 20–3 shows the relevant Herfindahl indexes for the Euro-dollar, Euro-DM, Euroyen, and FRN segments of the Eurobond markets, thereby highlighting the dramatic differences in market structures. The declines in the Euro-DM and Euroyen sectors indicate gradual erosion of the dominant position of the Deutsche Bank and the Big Four Japanese securities houses, respectively, in these sectors.

The extremely changeable character of the Eurobond market has caused the profitability of the principal participants to ebb and flow over time. Figure 20–5 depicts the Euromarkets constancy ratios between 1975 and 1987—firms still active as lead managers of new issues in a given year who had been active in the initial year. The

Table 20–3.   Eurobond Segment Herfindahl Indexes, 1975–1987

Year	Eurobonds Total	Euro-DM Issues	Euroyen Issues	FRN Issues
1975	.03002 (25)[a]	.30250 (5)	–	–
1976	.03576 (25)	.36740 (7)	–	–
1977	.04155 (62)	.25164 (6)	–	–
1978	.07350 (59)	.34132 (7)	–	–
1979	.04346 (63)	.26744 (6)	–	–
1980	.03863 (76)	.41264 (6)	–	.07027 (26)
1981	.04521 (75)	.36676 (6)	–	.07625 (25)
1982	.04927 (75)	.29658 (7)	–	.07342 (27)
1983	.07231 (75)	.29569 (8)	–	.23380 (25)
1984	.05242 (75)	.31550 (7)	–	.10237 (25)
1985	.04738 (75)	.25992 (11)	.26680 (12)	.10143 (25)
1986	.03999 (75)	.25876 (16)	.24398 (25)	.08878 (25)
1987	.04659 (50)	.22026 (17)	.18027 (25)	.05770 (25)
1988	.03784 (50)	.16808 (25)	.11560 (25)	.06735 (25)

a. Numbers in parentheses indicate the number of players.

SOURCE: Compiled from *Institutional Investor* league table data (various issues), with full credit to lead managers.

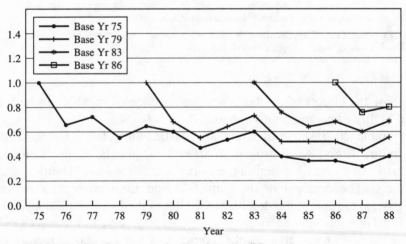

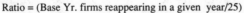

Ratio = (Base Yr. firms reappearing in a given year/25)

Figure 20–5.   Constancy Ratio for the Top 25 Underwriters in the Eurobond Market.

declining ratios are in part attributable to the high variability of Euro-market underwriting returns, which in turn has discouraged many participants from fully developing their new-issue capabilities. The Eurobond market experience has been reflected in several deregulated national markets as well, such as U.K. gilts and equities, and will doubtless be repeated in other EC market segments in the future.

In recent years, however, the integration of the Euromarket into the global market for debt and equity securities has meant that any invest-ment bank seeking to compete on a global basis has had to become proficient in the Euromarkets and has had to maintain that proficiency even through difficult periods in order to be successful. Expertise in the market and its products can be protected from losses by securing a respectable share of the new-issue business, by perfecting the science (or art) of hedging, by building distribution capabilities that ensure the ability to sell all underwritten securities quickly, by knowing how to construct and package synthetic securities that will add to the firm's distributive capacity and profits, and by managing the extensive direct costs of Euromarket activities skillfully.

Returning to the competitive structure of a given cell in the C-A-P model, if new players enter who are from the same basic strategic groups as existing players (e.g., one more investment bank joining a number of other investment banks competing in a given cell), then the expected outcome would be along conventional lines of intensified competition. However, if the new player comes from a completely different strategic perspective (e.g., the finance affiliate of a major oil company penetrating the same market cell for investment bank-ing services), the competitive outcome may be quite different. Cell penetration by a player from a different strategic group may lead to a greater increase in competition than an incremental player from the same strategic group. This is because of potential diversification benefits, scope for cross-subsidization and staying power, and incre-mental horizontal or vertical integration gains that the player from a "foreign" strategic group may be able to capture.

As noted in Chapters 2 and 3, the 1980s saw enormous geographic market interpenetration between Japan, Europe, and the United States. Banks and securities firms home-based in all three areas have devel-oped impressive footholds in the others' markets, leading not only to 24-hour trading in various financial instruments, but also to intensified global competition for all kinds of financial services. This has eroded margins in many types of financial services, in particular because of the activities of competitors emanating from different strategic groups.

The Bank of Tokyo is active in financing international trade in New York; Ford Motor Credit finances car buyers in the United Kingdom; Goldman Sachs, J. P. Morgan Guaranty, and Swiss Bank Corporation are active in the Tokyo capital market; and Yamaichi Securities provides financing in the emerging Euroequity market, to cite just a few examples.

Natural Barriers to Entry and Contestable Markets

The higher the barriers to entry, the lower the threat of new entrants reducing the level of rents available in each C-A-P cell. Natural barriers to entry include capital adequacy, human resources, financial technologies, and economies of scale. They are discussed in detail in the following chapter, which deals with the sources of competitive advantage. Entry barriers also include the role of "contracting costs" avoided by a close relationship between a financial institution and its client, which in turn is engendered by the avoidance of opportunistic behavior by either party.

Not least, the competitive structure of each cell depends on the degree of potential competition. This represents an application of the *contestable markets concept,* which suggests that the existence of potential entrants causes existing players to act as if those entrants were already active in the market. Hence margins, product quality, and the degree of financial innovation in a given cell may exhibit characteristics of intense competition even though the degree of market concentration is quite high.

Price Discrimination and Predation

In penetrating a particular cell or set of cells, it may be to the advantage of a particular player to buy into the market by cross-subsidizing financial services supplied in that cell from returns derived in other cells. This may make sense if the assessed horizontal, vertical, or lateral linkages are sufficiently positive to justify such pricing, either now or in the future. It may also make sense if the cell characteristics are expected to change in future periods, so that an unprofitable presence today is expected to lead to a profitable presence tomorrow. And it may make sense if a player's behavior in buying market share has the potential to drive out competitors and fundamentally alter the structure of the cell in that player's favor. The latter can be termed predatory behavior and is no different from predation in the markets for goods. The institution dumps (or threatens to dump) financial services into the cell, forcing out competitors either as a result of the direct effects of the dumping in the face of more limited staying power or because of the indirect effects, working through expectations. Once competitors have been driven from the market, the institution takes advantage of the reduced degree of competition to widen margins and achieve excess returns.

Conversely, it may also be possible for an institution with significant market power to keep potential competitors out of attractive cells through explicit or implied threats of predatory behavior. It can make it clear to new entrants that it will respond very aggressively to incursions and that they face a long and difficult road to profitability. In this way, new competitors may be discouraged, and the cell characteristics may be kept more monopolistic than would otherwise be the case.

It is important to note that the predatory behavior described here is not consistent with the view of market contestability presented in the previous section. The greater contestability and the credibility of prospective market entry, the less will be the scope for price discrimination and predation.

CELL LINKAGES

Financial institutions clearly will want to allocate their available financial, human, and technological resources to those C-A-P cells that promise to throw off the highest risk-adjusted returns. In order to do this, they will have to appropriately attribute costs, returns, and risks across cells.

But beyond this, the economics of supplying financial services internationally is jointly subject to economies of scale and economies of scope. The existence of both types of economies has strategic implications for players in the industry. Economies of scale suggest an emphasis on *deepening* activities within a cell or across cells in the P-dimension.

Economies of scope suggest an emphasis on *broadening* activities across cells—that is, a player can produce a given level of output in a given cell more cheaply or effectively than institutions that are less active across multiple cells. This depends importantly on the benefits and costs of *linking* cells together in a coherent web of joint products.

The gains from linkages among C-A-P cells depend on the possibility that an institution competing in one cell can move into another cell and can perform in that second cell more effectively than a competitor lacking a presence in the first cell. The existence of economies of scope and scale is a critical factor driving institutional strategy. Where scale economies dominate, the objective will be to maximize throughput of the product within a given C-A-P cell configuration, driving for market penetration. Where scope economies dominate, the drive will be toward aggressive cell proliferation.

Client-Driven Linkages

Client linkages exist when a financial institution serving a particular client or client group can, as a result, supply financial services either to the same client or to another client in the same group more efficiently in the same or different arenas. With respect to a particular client, this linkage is part of the value of the "relationship." With respect to a particular client segment, it will clearly be easier for an institution to engage in business with a new client in the same segment than to move to another client segment. It is possible that client-driven linkages will decline as market segmentation in financial services becomes more intense.

Arena-Driven Linkages

Arena-driven linkages are important when an institution can service a particular client or supply a particular service more efficiently in one arena as a result of having an active presence in another arena. The presence of nonfinancial MNC clients in the same set of arenas as their financial institutions is one important form such linkages can take. By competing across a large number of arenas, a financial institution also has the possibility of decreasing the overall level of risk to which it is exposed, thereby increasing its overall risk-adjusted rate of return.

Product-Driven Linkages

Product-driven linkages exist when an institution can supply a particular financial service in a more competitive manner because it is already producing the same or a similar financial service in different client or arena dimensions. Product specializations would appear to depend upon the degree of uniformity of the resource inputs required and the information and technology commonalities. Thus, certain types of skills embodied in key employees may be applied across different clients and arenas at relatively low marginal cost within a given product category, as may certain types of information about the environment, markets, or client needs.

COMPETITIVE AND COOPERATIVE BEHAVIOR

Whether within cells or across cells, one complication in analyzing the competitive behavior of firms in the financial services industry that does not arise to as great an extent in other industries is the need to cooperate closely with rivals on individual transactions while at the same time competing intensively with them. Examples include securities underwriting and distribution, loan syndication, project finance, and credit card networks.

When should an institution compete and when should it cooperate in order to extract maximum returns from the individual cells in the C-A-P matrix? The diagram in Figure 20–6 can be used to model an

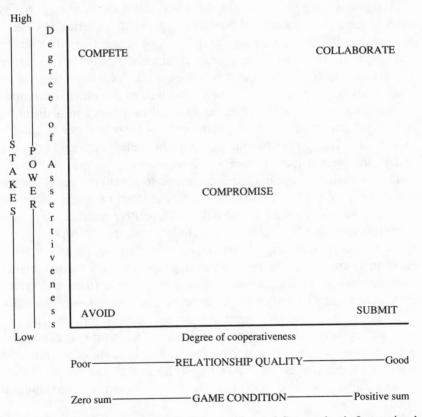

Figure 20–6. A Behavioral Model of Competition and Cooperation in International Financial Services.

institution's behavior with respect to a particular cell or a transaction within that cell.

The vertical axis measures the degree of *assertiveness* the institution will tend to bring against the competition. This is a joint product of the perceived stakes the organization has in the game and its competitive power. The higher the stakes and the greater its power to ride over the competition, the more assertive the institution will want to be. Both stakes *and* power have to be high in order for the assertive mode to make sense.

The horizontal axis measures the extent to which the game is perceived as being *zero sum* (what one gains the other loses) or *positive sum* (both can gain) and the quality of the relationship with other players—usually a cumulative product of past experience. The more the game is viewed as being positive sum and the better the relationship, the more likely it is that the institution will want to cooperate with others.

The grid in Figure 20–6 can be divided into five zones, based on how these four underlying variables appear in a particular case—compete, collaborate, comply, avoid, and compromise. It is likely that one institution will be seen to work closely together with another in a given project in a particular cell even while it is competing vigorously elsewhere, submitting to the dominance of the other institution, or avoiding involvement on the same kind of project in a different cell or a different project in the same cell. A large number of combinations are clearly possible in imposing this behavioral grid onto the underlying market matrix in Figure 20–1.

The evolution of international correspondent banking relationships discussed in Chapter 8 provides an interesting example of cooperative behavior in a fundamentally competitive market structure. Correspondent banking activities include management of local currency accounts, effecting of payments, providing access to the local clearing system, opening and confirming documentary credits arising from international trade transactions, participation in loans and syndicated credits, and custody services in securities business—traditionally paid for largely through correspondent balances. Banks that do not pose a direct threat to their correspondents in their own home markets, either because of their strategic positioning or because of government restrictions, have been in an ideal position to develop correspondent relationships—a classic case of collaboration, in terms of the diagram in Figure 20–6.

Things have changed, however. Improvements in communications and automation have provided direct access for banks to services previously accessible only through correspondents. Disintermediation has altered the value of correspondent banking on the lending side, and high interest rates have raised the cost of correspondent balances. The result has been a significant unbundling of the previously stable correspondent relationship into a less stable and more price-sensitive one centered around a specific set of services that one bank sells to another. Like international finance generally, the drift has been from a relationship-driven to a transactions-driven business. In terms of Figure 20–6, the correspondent banking business has drifted laterally from collaboration in the direction of competition.

In loan syndication and securities underwriting (see Chapters 5 and 14) the same phenomenon can be observed. Although large banks and securities firms are bitter rivals in battling for syndication and underwriting mandates from issuers, they also need to work closely together in providing for effective distribution and market support. Therefore, firms will invite each other into syndicates along reciprocity patterns that develop over time, taking into account relative strengths and weaknesses in distribution to different bank selldown and investor groups.

The acquisition in March 1987 of a 13 percent share in Shearson Lehman Hutton, the investment banking affiliate of American Express, by Nippon Life of Japan provided a good example both of technology and capital acquisition and market interpenetration in a collaborative context.

Nippon Life stood to gain diversification, improved access to international financial markets, and badly needed financial expertise and knowledge of international markets. It also stood to benefit in competing with the large Japanese securities houses, which had increasingly been siphoning off clients directly into financial markets and bypassing the insurance companies—even as the insurance firms were themselves compelled to continue investing through these same securities houses. With Japanese insurance companies increasingly investing rather than lending and increasing their overseas exposures, enhanced portfolio management expertise was needed. Nippon Life stood to gain from possible collaboration with American Express in other areas as well.

Shearson Lehman stood to gain badly needed capital in a period when this consideration became a critical competitive factor in the investment banking industry (becoming the most heavily capitalized of all Wall Street firms); it also stood to gain access to Japanese clients.

And American Express was in a position to improve significantly its access to the Japanese market for charge cards and other financial services and to cross-sell life insurance with its other products in various markets. It agreed not to reduce its holdings in Shearson Lehman Hutton for three years, and it agreed to accept two Nippon Life representatives on the Shearson board and to appoint a Nippon Life "advisor" to its own board.

Another example from the area of international retail banking involves a relationship developed in late 1986 between Citicorp and Dai-Ichi Kangyo Ltd. (DKB) of Japan, discussed in Chapter 11.

A somewhat different example of collaboration was the purchase of a nonvoting share in the Goldman Sachs partnership by Sumitomo Bank of Japan in 1986, presumably with a view toward creating global market power in a combination that neither would be able to achieve alone. Yet Sumitomo clearly did not get all it bargained for in the arrangement. Sumitomo was limited to its 12.5 percent share in the Goldman Sachs capitalization, was prohibited from acquiring shares in any Goldman Sachs affiliate or placing members on the board of any such affiliate, could not send trainees to Goldman Sachs without specific Federal Reserve approval, and could not increase the amount of business conducted with each other—maintaining an arm's length relationship. Besides stringent Federal Reserve restrictions on what sort of collaboration would be allowed, the insider trading scandals of 1986 and 1987 soon enveloped Goldman Sachs as well, potentially reducing the value of the investment.

One of the best examples of a successful cooperative venture in the international financial services industry is Financiere Credit Suisse First Boston (CSFB), now CS–First Boston. Created at a time when both firms were having difficulties developing or even maintaining their market positioning, the formation of CSFB in 1978 provides an excellent example of a positive-sum game in which both parties had high stakes as well as significant power. Credit Suisse, recovering from a financial scandal involving its branch in Chiasso (inflicting a loss of 1.22 billion Swiss francs on the bank), brought to the venture its capitalization, an ability to bear risk, and an ability to place securities in the accounts of institutional and (in particular) individual investors. It had earlier tried a joint venture in London with White Weld & Co., when White Weld was acquired by Merrill Lynch, Credit Suisse bought out the Merrill Lynch share and looked for a new (less dominant) partner. First Boston, at the time suffering market losses at the hands of its major U.S. investment banking rivals, brought to the venture its innovative ideas and deal-making prowess, benefiting from Credit Suisse's financial strength in order to remain a viable independent firm.

Together the two firms probably did far better in the various markets, especially the Eurobond market, than either could have done on its own. Over time, however, even such a world-class collaboration is likely to show strains. First, international financial markets are changing so quickly that the same mode of collaboration cannot be applied consistently. What was a good approach for doing well in the Eurobond market may not be ideally suited for equity transactions. Second, competition in major markets has heated up dramatically, with Japanese securities houses and players from the United States, the United Kingdom, and continental Europe bringing about a serious erosion of margins. Third, there is always the possibility that each partner may itself acquire some of the same kinds of resources the other initially brought to the venture. If, for example, Credit Suisse developed its own technical and deal-making capabilities, while First Boston found it difficult or impossible to acquire the credit standing, capitalization, and placing power of Credit Suisse, one would expect the arrangement to shift from unequivocal collaboration into a gradual assertion of leverage on the part of Credit Suisse and perhaps eventually acquisition of the remaining share in the venture it did not already own. At the same time, one would expect increasing strains within the firm and a gradual deterioration in the quality of the relationship. Regulatory changes, such as repeal of Glass-Steagall in the United States, could also exert pressure on the joint venture. Such factors played a role in the acquisition of effective control by Credit Suisse in 1988.

It is important to remember that the conflict management grid in Figure 20–5 applies only to a single institution evaluating its own situation against a protagonist and using it to derive a normative conflict management strategy. Whether these relationships are stable over time, or whether the outcome will drift into the tension-filled compete zone or the avoid zone (with a joint venture being taken over by one of the partners) or the submit zone (with one partner being taken over by the other) often remains to be seen.

SUMMARY

In order to assess the competitive structure of the international financial services industry, we have introduced a model that permits identification of sources of potential supernormal returns as a product of the competitive structure of markets. Strategic groups, contestable markets, and predatory behavior were introduced as important concepts in the market structure. Intermarket linkages were discussed in terms of their contribution to global economies of scale and economies of scope, as were patterns of collaborative and competitive behavior in those markets.

SELECTED REFERENCES

Aliber, Robert Z.   "International Banking: A Survey." *Journal of Money, Credit and Banking*, November 1984.

Bailey, Elizabeth E., and Friedlander, Ann F.   "Market Structure and Multiproduct Industries." *Journal of Economic Literature*, September 1982.

Bank for International Settlements. *Recent Innovations in International Banking*. Basel: BIS, 1986.

Baumol, William, Panzar, J., and Willig, R.   *Contestable Markets and the Theory of Industry Structure*. New York: Harcourt Brace Jovanovich, 1982.

Caves, Richard.   "Economic Analysis and the Quest for Competitive Advantage." *American Economic Review*, May 1984.

Caves, Richard, and Porter, Michael.   "From Entry Barriers to Mobility Barriers: Conjectural Decisions and Contrived Deterrence to New Competition." *Quarterly Journal of Economics*, May 1977.

Clark, Jeffrey A.   "Economies of Scale and Scope At Depository Financial Institutions: A Review of the Literature." *Federal Reserve Bank of Kansas City Review*, September–October 1988.

Channon, Derek F.   *Bank Strategic Management and Marketing*. New York: John Wiley & Sons, 1986.

Cooper, Kerry, and Fraser, Donald R.   *Bank Deregulation and the New Competition in Financial Services*. Cambridge, MA: Ballinger, 1986.

Cowhey, Peter F.   *Trade in Services: A Case for Open Markets*. Washington, DC: American Enterprise Institute.

Davis, Stephen I.   *Excellence in Banking*. London: Macmillan, 1985.

Fieleke, Norman S.   "The Growth of U.S. Banking Abroad: An Analytical Survey." In *Key Issues in International Banking*. Boston: Federal Reserve Bank of Boston, 1977.

Gladwin, Thomas N., and Walter, Ingo.   *Multinationals Under Fire*. New York: John Wiley & Sons, 1980.

Gray, H. Peter, and Gray, Jean M.   "The Multinational Bank: A Financial MNC?" *Journal of Banking and Finance*, March 1982.

Grubel, Herbert G.   "A Theory of Multinational Banking." *Banca Nazionale del Lavoro Quarterly Review*, December 1977.

Hayes, Samuel, III, Spence, A. M. and Marks, D.v.P.   *Competition in the Investment Banking Industry*. Cambridge, MA: Harvard University Press, 1983.

Newman, H.   "Strategic Groups and the Structure-Performance Relationships." *Review of Economics and Statistics*, August 1978.

Office of Technology Assessment, U.S. Congress. *International Competition in Banking and Financial Services.* Washington, DC: OTA, July 1986. Mimeographed.

Oster, S. "Intraindustry Structure and the Ease of Strategic Change." *Review of Economics and Statistics,* August 1982.

Panzar, John C., and Willig, Robert D. "Economies of Scope." *American Economic Review,* May 1981.

Pastre, Olivier. *Multinationals: Banking and Firm Relationships.* Greenwich, CT: JAI Press, 1981.

Pastre, Olivier. "International Bank-Industry Relations: An Empirical Assessment." *Journal of Banking and Finance,* March 1981.

Pecchioli, R. M. *Internationalization of Banking.* Paris: OECD, 1983.

Porter, Michael E. *Competitive Strategy.* New York: Free Press, 1980.

Sagari, Sylvia B. "The Financial Services Industry: An International Perspective." Dissertation, Ph.D. Graduate School of Business Administration, New York University, 1986.

Teece, David J. "Economies of Scope and the Enterprise." *Journal of Economic Behavior and Organization,* March 1985.

Tschoegl, Adrian E. "Foreign Bank Entry into Japan and California." In *New Theories of the Multinational Enterprise,* edited by Allen M. Rugman, London: Croom Helm, 1982.

Walter, Ingo. *Barriers to Trade in Banking and Financial Services.* London: Trade Policy Research Centre, 1985.

Walter, Ingo, ed. *Deregulating Wall Street.* New York: John Wiley & Sons, 1985.

Walter, Ingo. *Global Competition in Financial Services.* Cambridge, MA: Ballinger, 1988.

21

Determinants of Competitive Performance

Having examined the structure of the global market for financial services in terms of client, arena, and product segments in the previous chapter, and having discussed in detail each of the principal activities of global banking and financial institutions in Parts II and III of this book, we can now discuss the determinants of competitive performance of institutions and the selection of alternative market strategies.

Clearly, the entire C-A-P matrix is potentially open to all players. It is equally clear, however, that the players differ enormously in their exploitation of opportunities available throughout the matrix, both with respect to individual cells and cell groupings. This is a result of different institutions bringing to bear vastly different resource profiles and adopting vastly different organizational strategies.

SOURCES OF INSTITUTIONAL COMPETITIVE ADVANTAGE

One of the striking aspects of the international financial services industry is the high degree of variation in competitive performance among institutions, as measured by earnings. Financial institutions faced with the identical feasibility set, represented by the C-A-P matrix, come away with entirely different results. (See Table 21–1 for some examples using standard performance criteria.)

The ability of financial institutions to exploit profit opportunities within the C-A-P framework depends on a number of key institution-specific attributes. These include the institution's capital base and actuarial risk base, its human resources, information/market access, technology, and the entrepreneurial qualities of its people. The proximate competitive weapons can be listed as follows:

Fixed resources
  Branch and affiliate network
  Information-processing and transmission hardware
Intangible resources
  Technology
    Client specific
    Arena specific
    Product specific
  Systems and procedures
  Placing power
  Franchise
Human resources
  Professional
  Non-professional
Financial resources
  Capital base
  Funding base

How each of these major sources of competitive power interacts with the C-A-P cell structure will be discussed in turn.

Adequacy of the Capital Base

In recent years, financial institutions and their regulators have paid increasing attention to the issue of capital as a source of both competitive power and prudential control. Capital has always played these roles with respect to activities appearing on the balance sheet, such as capital-based lending limits in the case of bank loans, and it is in this area that there has been a perceived deterioration in the general quality of bank assets in various countries, including the United States. With increasing securitization in domestic and international finance, the role of capital has become important as the primary determinant of risk-bearing ability in securities underwriting and dealing, as well as in insurance-related off-balance sheet activities.

Indeed, innovations in both the securities-underwriting business and in merchant-banking transactions requiring extensive commitments of the firm's own capital have given players with large capital bases

Table 21–1. Leading Bank Performance, 1983 ed 1988

	Assets [a]		Shareholder's Equity [a]		Return on Equity [b]		Market Capitalization [a]	
	1983	1988	1983	1988	1983	1988	1983	1988
United States								
Citicorp	134.7	207.7	5.0	8.3	16.1	23.6	4.6	8.3
Chase Manhattan	81.9	97.5	3.1	4.1	12.5	27.4	1.6	2.5
Bank of America	121.2	94.6	4.0	3.4	7.6	19.4	3.1	3.3
J. P. Morgan	58.0	83.9	3.1	5.5	15.3	19.1	2.7	6.3
Security Pacific	40.4	77.9	1.9	3.5	15.4	18.9	1.9	4.1
Japan [c]								
Dai-Ichi Kangyo	108.1	388.6	1.8	7.6	7.1	12.8	4.9	57.0
Sumitomo	94.0	359.7	2.0	8.9	11.4	12.8	4.7	60.6
Fuji	100.6	353.0	2.1	8.5	10.8	13.7	4.7	58.9
Mitsubishi	96.1	338.8	1.9	8.7	8.4	14.3	4.7	55.2
Sanwa	93.0	334.8	1.7	7.8	8.4	13.2	4.7	43.0

Britain

	1987				1987		
Barclays	84.1	189.4	4.2	10.3	10.0	17.0	2.4	8.1
NatWest	86.9	178.5	4.2	10.7	14.5	18.7	2.2	7.0
Midland	76.3	100.8	2.8	5.5	6.6	14.7	1.3	4.1
Lloyds	55.7	93.8	3.3	5.2	13.2	23.5	1.5	4.8

Continental Europe

	1987		1987		1987		
Deutsche	77.2	169.7	2.4	6.7	8.2	5.0	3.3	11.4
Société Générale	86.3	153.0	1.0	3.0	11.4	15.4	na	4.4
Dresdner	59.0	130.8	1.6	4.0	9.8	7.1	1.3	4.9
Paribas	60.5	122.3	0.9	3.3	10.3	10.6	na	4.0
UBS	52.8	111.6 *d*	2.7	6.7 *d*	8.9	7.8 *d*	3.1	9.2

a. Year-end figures in billions of dollars.

b. Year-end figures as a percentage.

c. Figures for end March 1983 and end September 1988.

d. End 1988.

SOURCES: Company reports; Keefe, Bruyette & Woods; Salomon Brothers; UBS-Phillips & Drew; Shearson Lehman Hutton.

a significant competitive advantage. Such innovations as the "bought deal," "merchant banking bridge loans," and leveraged buyouts have meant that only institutions with a large capital base can afford to participate in transactions that involve taking entire blocks of securities onto their books. This requirement and the growing importance of positioning through trading and dealing activities force institutions to hold larger inventories of securities, giving a key competitive advantage to players with a large capital base. Additionally, a large capital base that allows an institution to be a successful player in securities underwriting and dealing also may enable it to undertake mergers and acquisitions activities, private placements, and other value-added financial services for its clients.

Capital adequacy conveys a decided competitive advantage in bringing specific products to specific international markets, in maximizing firepower and reducing costs in funding operations, and in being able to stick with particular clients in good times and bad—thus being considered a reliable financial partner. In addition, regulators in the United States, Japan, Germany, and the United Kingdom have imposed required risk/asset ratios for dealing with off–balance sheet exposure. Institutions are consequently able to increase their asset footings and insurance-related services only by building up their capital base (see Chapter 25).

At the same time, of course, there are reasons why institutions are in general reluctant to increase their primary capital. These concern earnings dilution and the importance of leverage, and some institutions have responded by issuing subordinated debt, perpetual floating-rate notes, and other forms of debt that can be treated as primary capital.

The Institutional Risk Base

Financial institutions fund themselves by creating financial assets held by others. In a deregulated environment, where financial institutions are forced to bid for funds, the perceived quality of an institution is an important determinant of its ability to fund itself at the lowest possible cost. The international debt problems of the 1980s, as well as sectoral problems in real estate, energy, agriculture, and other troubled industries, have called into question the fundamental soundness of the asset structures of certain financial institutions. This in turn has accelerated the pace of disintermediation, with many large corporations and other institutions going straight to the capital markets on the basis of their own credit standing.

The level of institutional risk has become particularly significant in the interbank market, leading to a substantial spread in funding costs between institutions from time to time, particularly in crisis situations. Institutions of lesser perceived quality can be caught in a difficult position if they are forced to pay a premium over the other banks in order to fund themselves in the interbank market. This premium may also be taken as a sign of an impaired credit standing by other institutions. A premier credit rating thus ensures a financial institution substantial advantages on the funding side. This is also true in dealings with corporate and other institutional clients, which are often highly sensitive to the perceived quality of financial services suppliers.

Table 21–2 shows 1987 Moody and Standard & Poor credit ratings for the major international banks (not bank holding companies) and securities houses.

An example of a market dominated by foreign-based banks on the basis of this competitive variable involves standby letters of credit covering municipal securities issues in the United States. State and local government entities issue securities backed by standby letters of credit under which the bank, in return for a fee, will unconditionally cover payments due to bondholders if the issuer is unable to do so. This enhances the marketability of the securities and reduces the municipalities' borrowing costs. The advantage of foreign banks in this market is based on their triple-A credit rating.

In particular, Japanese banks moved aggressively into this market. State and local treasurers were delighted, but U.S. banks found returns severely eroded. Foreign banks, in some cases less encumbered than their U.S. competitors by capital requirements, high funding costs, and managerial focus on quarterly earnings growth, considered the returns acceptable—especially in view of the foothold gained in a new market. And U.S. investment banks involved in underwriting municipal general obligation securities were more than happy to have the L/C part of the deals undertaken by foreign banks rather than by their domestic commercial bank competitors.

Distribution Network

A financial institution's distribution network is the central element in its access to customers, markets, and (in many cases) funds. There are three variables over which it can exercise control.

1. *Geographic spread.* Once a bank has decided to penetrate a given arena it will have to choose the number and form of outlets it needs

Table 21–2.   Comparitive Credit Ratings of Banks, February 1987

Bank	Moody's		S&P	
	Short	Long	Short	Long
Citicorp	P-1	A1	A-1+	AA
Chase Manhattan	P-1	Aa2	A-1+	AA
J. P. Morgan	P-1	Aaa	A-1+	AAA
Bankers Trust	P-1	Aa2	A-1+	AA+
Manufacturers Hanover	P-2	A3	A-1	A+
Chemical	P-1	Aa2	A-1+	AA
Continental Illinois	P-3	Baa3	A-2	BBB
First Chicago	P-1	A2	A-1	A+
BankAmerica	P-3	Baa3	A-3	BBB
Barclays	P-1	Aaa	A-1+	AA+
NatWest	P-1	Aaa	A-1+	AA+
Lloyds	P-1	—	A-1+	—
Midland	P-1	Aa2	A-1	Aa
BNP	P-1	Aaa	A-1	Aa
Societe Generale	—	Aaa	A-1+	AA+
Credit Lyonnais	—	Aaa	A-1+	—
Paribas	—	—	A-1+	AA+
UBS	P-1	Aaa	A-1+	AAA
Credit Suisse	P-1	Aaa	A-1+	AAA
Swiss-Bank Corp.	P-1	Aaa	A-1+	AAA
Deutsche	P-1	Aaa	A-1+	AAA
Commerzbank	—	—	A-1	—
Dresdner	P-1	—	A-1+	—
Dai-Ichi Kangyo	P-1	Aaa	A-1+	—
Sumitomo Bank	P-1	Aaa	A-1+	AA+
Mitsubishi	P-1	Aaa	A-1+	—
Bank of Tokyo	—	Aa1	A-1+	AA
Ind Bank of Japan	P-1	Aaa	A-1+	AAA
Long-Term Credit Bank	P-1	Aaa	A-1+	AA
Salomon Inc.	P-1	Aa3	A-1+	AA-
Merrill-Lynch	P-1	Aa3	A-1+	AA
Daiwa Securities	—	Aa2	—	AA
Nomura Securities	—	—	A-1+	AAA

SOURCE: *The Economist*, March 15, 1987.© The Economist Newspaper Ltd.   All rights reserved.

and their geographic locations. Different arenas will call for different geographic penetration patterns. Thus, investment banks will have few offices in each arena, or none at all, while savings and retail-oriented banks will tend to have several. The choice will depend on the economies associated with the different distribution patterns.

2. *Organization form.* Once the bank has selected its location pattern it must choose the organizational form appropriate for each outlet. A wide range of vehicles is available to penetrate a particular arena, ranging from correspondent banking and representative offices to full branches. Each has a different cost-benefit profile, and the decision will depend on the current level of business, its expected growth, cost, permissibility of each type of vehicle, competition, and related factors.

3. *Specific Location.* Bank offices have traditionally been situated in expensive "high-street" and central city locations. Technological innovations have eliminated the need for this, allowing the outlets to be reduced in number or relocated. These innovations also have implications for the production pattern within different arenas. Many banks have gone over to structures in which most of their activities are centralized, with branches merely serving as sales outlets and back-office activity shifted to lower cost locations.

Hardware

Technological innovation continues to change the banking industry, affecting some parts more than others, and the share of costs accounted for by technology has increased substantially. The size of hardware and related software investments makes the choice and level of technologies an important strategic decision that banks must evaluate carefully. It also gives banks an incentive to maximize volumes in order to reap any technology-related economies of scale that may be available. Technological developments have been most significant in the field of information processing, so the processes that have seen the most far-reaching changes are those that are highly information intensive. New technology allows bankers to have ever-increasing amounts of information at their disposal, and it drastically reduces the time necessary both to transfer information from one application to another and to process transactions.

Quality of Human Resources

While it has long been recognized that financial services basically constitute a "people business," it is only recently that the importance of having truly superior human resources has become apparent to all of the major players. In today's evolving competitive environment, human capital can be viewed as a financial institution's most important asset, and many of the critical capabilities for exploiting competitive opportunities depend directly on the quality of human resources in the organization.

Judgment based on cumulative experience is one central element in the production of a broad range of financial services, rendered necessary because of the complexity of many of the decisions that must be made. In particular, both credit evaluation and risk evaluation depend on the intellectual caliber, experience, and training of the decision maker. These qualities are no less important in the securities business than they are in the more traditional dimensions of banking.

Because of the increase in transactions-driven financial services, individuals increasingly must either make decisions of a highly complex nature very quickly or lose deals. The need for rapid and accurate decision making is particularly evident in the trading function, where traders have to react almost instantly to exploit arbitrage opportunities and where incorrect decisions can mean substantial and unambiguous losses for the firm. Yet swift and accurate decisions are no less important in maintaining relationships with clients, specifically to anticipate client financial requirements and respond to them in a way that adds value—in many cases, this is the root cause of supernormal returns in the financial services industry.

Growing competition and increased complexity have placed a premium on human resource–based advantages. It is reflected both in severe rivalry to attract top-quality people in the labor markets of various financial centers, with compensation levels bid up at an extraordinary rate, and in ferocious competition for talented young graduates. Indeed, some institutions are hiring people from other industries, with recent evidence indicating that successful bankers in the future will often have had experience in another industry. Just as financial assets have varying market values so also do people, and what has emerged is the equivalent of "marking to market" in the human resources area. The international financial services sector thus attracts some of the brightest individuals, and the emerging reward structure in the industry has caused much comment and may indeed not be sustainable.

Beyond devoting very significant time and resources to attracting and retaining superior personnel, firms in the industry invest heavily in training at increasingly high levels of sophistication. The training programs of major institutions are renowned particularly for their high standards. This indicates nothing more than a continuous investment in human capital, as critical in this industry as provision for depreciation and capital investment is in other industries.

Information Asymmetries

If money is "information on the move," then financial services constitute the most information-intensive industry in the international economy. The drive by financial institutions to move beyond commodity-type activities into higher value-added services is augmenting the importance of information-intensive products, both quantitatively and qualitatively. Indeed, *asymmetries* of information among various competitors and their clients contribute a great deal toward explaining differentials in competitive performance. Information is imbedded in specific financial services sold in various arenas to various clients, and all forms of lending and credit-related activities depend on the collection, processing, and evaluation of large amounts of information. Similarly, the assimilation of information about the needs of clients is critical in the development of services addressed to their needs.

There are three special factors regarding information as a determinant of competitive performance. First, information is the only resource that can be used simultaneously in the production of any number of services, and this gives it some unique characteristics. For example, information generated to build an international cash management system for a multinational corporate client can also be used to develop a long-term financial strategy for the same company or perhaps to develop a slightly different international cash management system for another multinational firm.

Second, the half-life of information as a source of competitive advantage may be decreasing. Because of significant market volatility, important types of financial information decay rapidly and actions that may have been warranted at one moment may no longer be appropriate shortly thereafter. The environment consists of many small windows of opportunity.

Third, the growing complexity of the international financial environment and the wide variety of services on offer have made it increasingly difficult for companies and individuals to plan in a straightforward manner. In effect, what clients often need is a means to evaluate the information that is available and some way of distinguishing relevant information from irrelevant. Financial institutions can provide information-related services that help accomplish this.

Client Insight

A special application of information asymmetries has to do with maximizing client-driven linkage effects. Client insight exists when a financial institution has developed a certain base of client-specific knowledge in the course of satisfying that client's financial needs. A transition from relationship-driven banking to transaction-driven banking would imply that either the amount of client insight needed to satisfy its needs is decreasing over time, or that more institutions have the core stock of client-specific information necessary to satisfy their requirements. However, client insight seems to persist as a key to providing differential value added in financial services.

Arena Insight

Just as a financial institution will, over time, generate important client-specific knowledge, it will also generate potentially valuable arena-specific information. The nature of this information will depend on the aggregation level of the arena definition. It is at the national level that much arena-specific information is most relevant, but supranational (regional) and subnational (local) expertise may be important as well. One might argue, for example, that the Japanese firms may have arena-specific insights in the Pacific Rim that could give them an advantage over other players in that particular arena. With suitable adaptation, information and analytical skills derived from dealing in particular arenas can often be transmitted through the organization and used in other arenas as well.

Placing Information

With continued securitization in the financial markets, the ability of underwriters to place securities with individual and institutional investors has become an increasingly important competitive variable, perhaps most clearly exemplified in the Eurobond market. The modern securities industry is essentially about distribution, and firms must focus on the number of securities they will be able to allocate to each investor and the range of investors over whom they may be able to allocate them. Distribution capability depends on the institution's information base regarding portfolio preferences of institutional and individual investors, as well as its own control over portfolios as a result of discretionary trust and investment business. Placing power as a product of information is also important in loan selling and syndication.

Financial Technology and Innovation

Financial innovation depends heavily on information incorporated into value-added services sold to clients. The parts of the international financial services industry that have seen the most far-reaching structural changes are those that appear to be the most knowledge intensive. Information technologies allow financial institutions to have at their disposal increasing amounts of data and reduce the time necessary to transfer data across arenas, client segments, and product applications. With increasing amounts of information hitting institutions at a rapid pace, internal decision and filter systems have come under pressure and new ones have had to be built, as have transaction-driven "back office" systems. Along with management and marketing know-how, these technologies are principally *process* related.

There is an equally important set of *product*-related financial technologies, which to a significant degree are made possible by these advances in financial processes. Technology-intensive financial services may be either embodied or disembodied. Embodied services incorporate technology in a financial transaction and differentiate that transaction from others available in the market. Disembodied technology is provided to clients independent of a specific financial transaction (e.g., in the form of financial advice), although it may subsequently lead to transactions. Returns on financial technology may come through fees or, more commonly, through enhanced returns associated with product differentiation.

Just as manufacturing firms have industry-specific technologies, which can be more or less proprietary depending on the industry concerned, banks have their own industry-specific technologies. "Financial technology" gives rise to economic rents that vary from one arena to another and from one client group to another. In general, there are no intellectual property rights associated with financial technology, and it is therefore almost entirely unprotected by patents or copyrights, with innovations rapidly being transferred from one bank to another, from one arena to another, and from one product group to another. Financial technology consists of four main types: process, product, marketing, and management.

Process

Process technology consists of the systems and procedures within the organization that are intended to facilitate decision making, transfer of information, communications, and transactions throughput. These processes have been internalized over the organization, often through trial and error, and the most efficient processes are the ones that remain. Process technologies can be expected to differ substantially from one organization to another and can account for significant differences in competitive performance. Process knowledge also links different organizational functions, providing for easier coordination, and allows the organization to function more smoothly. Process technology is particularly important in the area of information transfer—if information is to be used efficiently it must be transferred to where it is needed within the organization and must be accurate, relevant, and timely.

Product

Product technologies consist of the know-how necessary to supply financial services. Although this form of technology is almost always nonproprietary, it is an important factor accounting for competitive performance, particularly in leading-edge financial activities discussed in Parts II and III of this book. Like manufactured products, financial services have a product life cycle that dictates the level and duration of excess returns that can be derived from a particular product in a particular market.

Marketing

As competition increases, financial institutions are having to get closer to customers in order to more fully satisfy their needs and provide higher service levels. The ability of a bank to get close to its customer base and to market its services effectively can differ substantially from one institution to another. It is not sufficient to set up a marketing function within the organization. Rather, the whole focus of attention of the organization must be on the market. The ability to introduce this type of thinking, to sustain it, and to make it effective will differ among financial institutions and can provide an important source of competitive advantage.

Management

As in any other industry, the ability to manage an organization both tactically and strategically is an important source of power in the marketplace. Although management skills depend on the level of embodied human capital, they are of a qualitatively different nature than banking-specific technical skills. Management skills tend to be more general and involve a heavy dose of interpersonal abilities.

Whether process- or product-related, marketing- or management-oriented, financial technology permits the innovating firm to open up an "intertemporal gap" between itself and its competitors, reflected either in the cost of delivering financial services or in product differentiation. That gap has both *size* and *duration* implications. It may also be more or less cell-specific within the C-A-P model as per the following taxonomy: (1) client-specific, (2) arena-specific, (3) product-specific, (4) client-/arena-specific, (5) arena-/product-specific, (6) client-/product-specific, and (7) client-/product-/arena-specific. Duration describes the time path (decay) of excess returns that can be extracted from financial innovation in this context, and their discounted present value can be compared with the cost of innovation or technology transfer across clients, arenas, and products.

In general, there appears to be a strong positive relationship between innovation and client specificity in the international financial services industry. There also seems to be a positive relationship between the complexity of the innovation and the imitation lag, perhaps partly offset by a negative relationship between product complexity and success of the innovation, with some innovations being too complex to be put to effective use. In the absence of anything like patent or copyright protection, the imitation lag for financial innovations tends to be relatively short and may be decreasing over time. It is therefore important for an institution to maintain a continuous stream of innovations. In this sense, an institution's most important innovation is its *next* one.

Innovation in this industry can thus be looked on as the introduction of a new process or technique—new in terms of a particular cell—that provides durable returns and adds significant value to the client. The spread of an innovation through the matrix allows the firm to take advantage of its inherent profit potential across the cells. Innovation is particularly important to those players with a substantial presence in the offshore markets, where there are few barriers to competitive behavior and where the relative absence of regulation allows each of the players far more freedom in terms of innovative behavior than are allowed in many onshore markets.

Innovative capabilities—the continuous application of new product and process technologies—are very much a function of the quality of human capital and of investments in the financial equivalent of R&D, which is usually much more market driven, informal, and inductive than industrial R&D. They are also highly sensitive to the "culture" of an organization, its management, the incentives associated with successful innovations versus the penalties of unsuccessful innovation, and the amount of horizontal communication and information transfer that takes place within the organization. Financial institutions compete in the same capital and labor markets, and people move from one institution to another with growing frequency, yet some institutions appear to be consistently more innovative than others.

Franchise

A financial institution's "franchise" is probably its most important asset. Though it is also the most intangible of assets, it clearly distinguishes the more successful competitors in the financial services industry from the rest. A franchise can arise from a number of different sources. It is generally related to a specific expertise—expertise valued by the market—that an institution has developed. It results from the institution's "standing" in the market, a synergistic combination of all competitive attributes in which the whole is greater than the sum of the parts. Franchise is a function of past performance projected over future transactions. In commodity-type activities especially there is little to differentiate one institution from another, and franchise becomes an all-important performance variable. A bank's franchise can be either product-specific or industry-specific, an important consideration with respect to the strategy that the bank should follow.

Franchise value is thus reflected in the market, driven by the perceived quality of the firm's services but also by the quality and quantity of it's public relations and advertising activities. Some banking services are more dependent on advertising than others. For many institutions, advertising and public relations are relatively new activities that, in keeping with a market orientation, are becoming increasingly important—as reflected in growing advertising expenditures. Still, some banking services are quite independent of advertising and are driven largely by past performance. In such cases—securities underwriting, for example—one failure is more significant than many successes, and a single bad deal can cause a bank to lose an enormous amount of face in markets that have very long memories.

An institution's franchise is thus its most intangible asset, yet one that clearly distinguishes *ex post* the most successful competitors in the international financial services industry from the rest. It is generally linked to a specific type of competence and expertise that the market values and that the institution has developed over time. One can argue that Morgan Guaranty or Citicorp have developed strong franchises in various areas of international finance over the years, franchises that are of great value when seeking new business.

The franchise concept has been used to explain a variety of competitive phenomena and appears to be related to an institution's standing

Table 21–3. Alignment of Competitive and Product Dimensions in International Financial Services

Financial Services	Competitive Resources [a]						
	A	B	C	D	E	F	G
Funding	1					3	1
Lending	3	3	2				
Financing	3	3	2				2
Credit Activities	1	2	2		2	2	
Trading	3	3	3		2		
Broking	2	2	3	2		1	
Advisory services		3	3		1	2	3
Asset management services		3	3		1	3	1
Underwriting	3	2	2		2	3	3
Distribution			1	3			
Payments activities			3		3		
Insurance services	3	2	2				
International trade services		2	2		2	1	

a. The competitive resources codes are as follows:
A—Adequacy of capital base; B—Quality of human capital; C—Information; D—placing power; E—technology; F—innovative capability; G—franchise; 1—principal factor; 2—important factor; 3—contributing factor.

in the market as a result of a synergistic combination of all the above attributes—where the whole is greater than the sum of the parts. The franchise imbedded in the value of the firm is thus a product of its past performance, projected into the future.

An attempt to match the principal competitive resources of international financial institutions with the principal product groups is presented in Table 21–3.

RESOURCE LINKAGES

As discussed in the previous chapter, if economies of scale and scope are important, a bank with a presence in two cells within the C-A-P matrix will be able to produce its output more economically than two banks with a presence in each. Economies of scope arise from inputs that are shared or utilized jointly without complete "congestion" and are created primarily through subaddivity of the cost function.

Each of the competitive resources available to financial institutions, as identified above, will have varying degrees of cell specificity ranging from fixed assets, which are arena-specific, to know-how, which may be non–cell specific. A bank will have positive resource linkages when its competitive performance in one cell is augmented by its presence in another cell within the matrix. The ability of financial institutions to exploit proprietary know-how by transferring it throughout the matrix at low marginal costs is a key factor accounting for resource linkages. Resource linkages can be examined from static or dynamic points of view and can again be broken down into client, product and arena linkages, each arising from different sources. *Static* linkages relate to the economies of scope that drive competitive performance within a given cell configuration, and *dynamic* linkages relate to the different expansion paths open to the institution.

Static linkages are associated with the transfer or exploitation of a financial institution's resources among the different cells in which the bank has a presence; these linkages are static in the sense that they relate only to movements within the bank's present cell structure. One can analyze the effects of static linkages on the production of financial services in terms of a standard production function. The inputs into all services are capital, labor, information, technology, and entrepreneurship or innovation. Banks must explicitly examine these static linkages as a key factor driving competitive performance in the international financial services industry.

Labor

In service industries, and particularly in financial services, the extent to which a firm has preferential access to high-quality human capital will have a major bearing on competitive advantage in the marketplace. There are significant positive linkages that affect labor relating to both the arena and the product dimensions. Banks with a broad international network are in a better position to attract high-quality human capital, since they can offer more interesting and stimulating situations. Thus, banks with a geographically diverse presence would tend to have higher quality personnel, all else equal. Similarly, in the large and competitive financial centers such as New York and London the quality of professional employees will tend to be significantly superior to those in protected or otherwise noncompetitive markets.

Banks with a presence in the more competitive financial centers should in general find it easier to attract top-quality bankers that will bring fresh, new approaches and techniques and enhance the firm's culture and delivery systems. These techniques can then be transferred within the organization to other arenas after a certain period of time.

Equally, banks that offer a broad range of products and services can be expected to provide more intellectually stimulating and varied work to their employees. Those active in state-of-the-art financial engineering will be able to give their employees opportunities to become involved in new, interesting financing activities. To the extent that these elements will attract higher-caliber bankers these institutions will have significant static resource linkages, giving them competitive advantages in the labor market.

Technology

One of the key rationales for the existence of multiproduct, multinational manufacturing and financial institutions is the ability to transfer product, process, marketing, and management know-how within the organization at low marginal costs. This transfer of technology is particularly important in the case of financial institutions, where the technology is nonprotected and can be transferred easily from one bank to another as well as within the same bank.

The majority of product innovations are not really innovations as such but are rather existing products transferred from one cell to another within the matrix. For example, options and futures have long existed in the commodities markets and subsequently were transferred to financial assets. Banks that have a specific product expertise can often transfer some product characteristics to other cells, thereby increasing the value added or reducing the risk facing the client. Product-technology transfer can be across clients, across arenas, or across products.

Likewise, banks can transfer new processes throughout the organization's cell framework at low marginal costs. Processes developed in one country can easily be transferred to another, and those developed for one market segment can be applied to others as well.

As marketing has become one of the most important functions within financial institutions, the transfer of marketing skills and know-how between cells is significant. Thus, a bank that has developed particular marketing skills within a particular developing country may be better able to engage in marketing in other developing countries within the C-A-P matrix.

Management know-how is a factor that already distinguishes the major players from the rest, and it will become an increasingly vital factor for success in the financial services industry. Though both tactical and strategic management are important, strategic management is clearly the more important of the two. The major forms of cross-matrix linkage in this area may well arise from learning by doing. In large organizations with a wide range of products, clients, and arenas, management has the opportunity to be exposed to a wide variety of situations. The experience gained can be transferred across the matrix, deepening the range of management experience and expertise available in the firm.

Although innovative capabilities are very much a function of the quality of the human capital, entrepreneurship is a factor of increasing importance in the international financial services industry and therefore can be treated separately as a source of static linkages. It is difficult to pinpoint the actual source of entrepreneurial capabilities, but we know that some institutions are consistently more entrepreneurial than others. Entrepreneurship is cell specific, and the spread of innovation throughout the matrix in an entrepreneurial way allows different players to take advantage of the inherent profit potential.

Entrepreneurial conduct has been particularly prevalent in the offshore markets because of the lack of barriers to competitive behavior. The unregulated nature of these markets allows each of the players a wide range of freedom in terms of entrepreneurship in innovation that differentiates one institution from its competitors. Because the imitation lag for most innovations is short, it is important for an institution to continuously generate innovations.

Again, imitation lag can be increased by increasing product complexity. However, there is a tradeoff between product complexity and the success of the innovation—some innovations will be too complex for effective use.

It would appear that innovative behavior is a function of both embodied human capital and the corporate culture of the organization. The natural intelligence and creativity of the individual can be enhanced or reduced depending on the level of overall product expertise and training, management's overall attitude toward innovation, the incentives to successful innovation versus the penalties of failure, and the amount of horizontal communication and information transfer that take place within the institution.

Dynamic Linkages

Dynamic linkages allow the financial institution to move to new cells within the matrix. Every firm faces both financial and organizational costs when moving to another cell. The presence of dynamic linkages means that a firm will face lower costs in making such a move. These costs can be looked upon as a form of "resistance" to expansion that the firm faces, which will be reduced in the presence of dynamic linkages. These linkages have provided the rationale for much of the multinational development of banking and financial institutions, and allow them to increase the range of products they can offer clients as well as the range of clients they can profitably serve. Without the presence of dynamic linkages there would be no economic rationale for the existence of multiproduct financial firms.

Risk Reduction

Just as a bank will be able to take advantage of risk reduction from static linkages so also risk reduction will operate in a dynamic sense. The diversification effect will be twofold: (1) By competing in a large number of arenas a bank has the possibility of decreasing the overall risk level to which it is exposed or increasing the overall risk-adjusted rate of return on its capital; (2) With the rapid pace of technological change, banks have had to adopt a much more strategic attitude toward technology. Considering that most technology in this industry was created on an ad hoc basis to solve particular problems, financial institutions can easily become dependent on a particular technology and confront the risk of technological obsolescence. By moving into new cells within the matrix, they can diversify the technological base and reduce that dependence.

The existence of *dynamic product linkages* will depend on the homogeneity of bank input requirements across different product categories. A bank's ability to compete in any particular cell will depend primarily on those attributes, identified earlier, that are necessary to produce different financial products in that cell. Dynamic product linkages exist between product cells that depend on the same inputs as those that are necessary to produce the bank's present product range. Thus, a bank will find it easier to move into new products that depend on similar competences and resources for their success.

For example, a bank that is heavily involved in trading activities and has therefore acquired extensive experience with the relevant information systems and technologies will be better able to become active in other financial services that are also highly systems intensive. This is in keeping with the idea of "related diversification" that strategic planners focus on in the manufacturing industry.

Dynamic client linkages depend on the degree of homogeneity of demand for financial services across client groups. Banks will find it easier to serve new client group when the new group requires the same products that the bank is already providing for its existing client base. For example, a bank engaged in asset management for high net worth individuals will be better able to service certain corporate clients with asset management needs than clients with needs for international trade services. Scope economies are proportionate to the degree of homogeneity of bank input requirements across clients product needs.

Even if the new client group does not have exactly the same product needs, if its demand pattern depends on inputs that the bank has available, because of its present cell configuration, the bank will have the ability to exploit a dynamic client linkage. It will be better able to move to service a new client if the banking needs of that client depend upon the same configuration of inputs as did the old client.

Dynamic arena linkages are attributable to the existence of client-specific information, with financial institutions better able to perform in new arenas when their domestic client base is present there as well. The presence of domestic nonfinancial institutions' affiliates in foreign environments is clearly a prime motivating force in the multi-nationalization of banking. The increasing complexity of the financial services means banks increasingly need to be close to the corporate customer in order to tailor their services to particular client needs. Decisions and transactions can therefore be made more quickly and more efficiently than through traditional correspondent banking links or through links from the bank's home office. The ability to access information and personal contacts between banks and nonfinancial corporate clients at low marginal costs provides an important source of competitive advantage to the banks' foreign branches in dealing with the client firm's affiliate abroad, because this information can be incorporated at low marginal cost in the design of new products for clients.

Banks develop skills from dealing in particular arenas, many of which can be transmitted through the organization and used in other arenas. The more similar conditions are from one arena to another, the higher the level of dynamic arena linkages that are likely to exist.

The expansion path that a bank chooses will depend on the different dynamic linkages that are perceived to exist and the presence of economies of scale and economies of scope. Where scale economies are prevalent the drive should be to maximize the product throughput within a given cell configuration—maximizing penetration and engaging in cross-selling of scale-sensitive products to as large an extent as possible. In the case of scope economies, the objective tends to be cell proliferation. Indeed, the existence of dynamic linkages provides one of the most enduring rationales for a financial institution to increase its cell distribution. Banks engage in *related expansion* when they grow along one of the variable dimensions of their present cell configuration—that is, focusing on their present client group, their present product range, or their present arena while simultaneously changing the other variables. Banks will face weaker resistance lines when they engage in related expansion and consequently will often attempt to sell all of their products to all of their clients in every arena where they are present. *Unrelated expansion* occurs when a bank changes all of the variables at once—for example, when it engages in the production of a new product for a new client group in a new arena. A bank's decision to engage in unrelated expansion will obviously depend on the level of economic rents in a given cell, as well as on the existence of dynamic linkages between cells.

STRATEGIC TARGETING

A firm in the financial services industry thus faces a given C-A-P cell configuration and set of linkages at a point in time, alongside a particular institutional capability profile. Some of the cells have already been accessed, and some form a feasibility set for possible further development. The firm's expansion path—and the desired cell configuration of its business—depend on the level of perceived risk-adjusted economic rents associated with the feasibility set of cells, the resistance lines impeding access to those cells, and the assessed value of intercell linkages. Successful players must therefore identify (1) the specific sources of their competitive advantage; (2) those cells where this competitive advantage can be applied, adds value, and is sustainable; and (3) the competitive potential inherent in the cell linkages. Application of a competitive-structure framework, such as the one presented here, will help identify the cells and cell clusters where significant returns based on market power are likely to exist, and (equally important) where they are likely to be durable.

Given the size of the matrix presented in Figure 20–1 in the previous chapter and the complexity of the linkages that exist among the individual cells, it becomes clear how wide the range of strategic options is that faces a financial institution in the global environment. Consequently, it is not surprising that an examination of individual organizations' international structures and their development through time often appears somewhat haphazard, lacking in consistency or coherence. This is the result of management actions under conditions of *bounded rationality* when faced with the task of determining expansion paths; in effect, management confronts an enormous opportunity set, of which it is usually familiar with only a small part. Therefore, it appears to operate much of the time by a process of trial and error—trying various options under the best available information, assessing results to the extent that this is possible, and trying again. It is therefore not surprising that many institutions appear *ex post* to have a relatively ambiguous strategic positioning in the global market for financial services.

Strategic Selection

In order to maximize performance in the international financial services industry, a firm has to go through some sort of strategic process to seek an optimal expansion path within the C-A-P matrix, which may involve either deepening penetration of individual cells or incursions into new cells. These decisions obviously depend on the perceived cost and risk versus benefits of opportunities that present themselves or that are sought out.

The process itself, in stylized form, will look something like this:

1. Development of a consensus on the future macroenvironment (e.g., interest rate and exchange rate stability, disequilibria, real-sector shocks, etc.) that could affect markets and products globally or represent sources of covariance in returns and hence systematic risk.
2. Inspection of existing cell-based activities in terms of market structure, risk and return, linkage effects, and impact on overall competitive performance, and identification of each in terms of its product-, client-, or arena-driven characteristics.
3. Assessment of the feasibility set of additional cell-based activities in terms of market structure, risk and return, linkage effects, and prospective impact on overall competitive performance, as well as product-, client-, or arena-driven characteristics.
4. Breakdown of the relevant product, client, and arena variables into components that identify key competitive factors.
5. Development of an inventory of organizational resources and prospective access to incremental resources.
6. Identification of strategic options involving possible deepening or broadening of cell activities, acquisitions, or divestitures, and their impact on economies of scale and scope, as well as actuarial risk base.

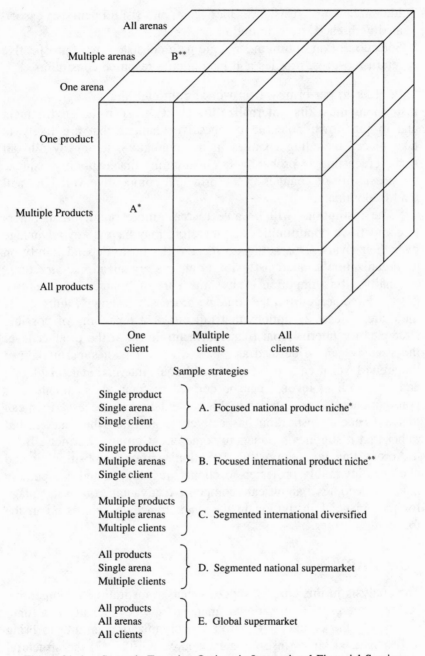

Figure labels on cube:

All arenas
Multiple arenas   B**
One arena

One product

Multiple Products   A*

All products

One client   Multiple clients   All clients

Sample strategies

Single product
Single arena   } A. Focused national product niche*
Single client

Single product
Multiple arenas   } B. Focused international product niche**
Single client

Multiple products
Multiple arenas   } C. Segmented international diversified
Multiple clients

All products
Single arena   } D. Segmented national supermarket
Multiple clients

All products
All arenas   } E. Global supermarket
All clients

Figure 21–1. Strategic Targeting Options in International Financial Services.

7. Identification of resistance lines, cost, and risk dimensions associated with each strategic option.
8. Selection of an optimum strategic path consistent with prospective returns/cost/risk profiles and institutional resource constraints.

In order to perform well in working through the strategic process, institutions must first internalize the ability to scan the environment and to pin down potential competitive changes that are likely to take place, including changes in the regulatory setting. While all such forecasting is probabilistic, institutions that explicitly analyze the possibility of changes in the principal competitive variables will tend to dominate.

Some institutions will be able to react more rapidly than others to competitive opportunities and therefore may have a key advantage over their rivals. This ability to react will tend to depend jointly on an organization's inherent flexibility and its organizational structure.

Finally, it is important that some sort of coherent competitive positioning emerge from the strategic process. As shown Figure 21–1, there are at least 27 options that fall out of a taxonomy of possible strategies for international financial institutions. At the product level the strategy can be defined as niche, diversified, or supermarket; at the arena level it can be defined as national, international, or global; and at the client level it can be defined as focused, segmented, or nonsegmented. Segmentation in this context does not necessarily mean that a financial institution has actively segmented the market, but rather that it supplies products to some client groups, but not all.

Across this taxonomy, an institution's strategic positioning and clarity is invariably projected to clients, regulators, and competitors alike. It becomes a significant competitive advantage or disadvantage for the financial institution in the marketplace, as discussed in the following chapter.

SUMMARY

The analysis in this chapter suggests that an institution's competitive performance in the international financial services industry is a function of (1) the competitive power the organization is able to bring to bear, based on its institutional resource profile, (2) the structural characteristics of the various cells in which it chooses to compete, (3) the lateral, horizontal, and vertical integration gains associated with cell linkages, and (4) economies of scale and of scope potentially available from transactions within and across cells. These dimensions jointly determine the returns that can be extracted from each cell and from the market as a whole. The goals of strategic positioning in this industry involve attending to each of these dimensions, including the institution's relative strengths and weaknesses, to creating and projecting an unambiguous strategic profile.

SELECTED REFERENCES

Aliber, Robert Z. "International Banking: A Survey." *Journal of Money, Credit and Banking,* November 1984.

Bailey, Elizabeth E., and Friedlander, Ann F. "Market Structure and Multiproduct Industries." *Journal of Economic Literature,* September 1982.

Baumol, William, Panzar, J., and Willig, R. *Contestable Markets and the Theory of Industry Structure.* New York: Harcourt Brace Jovanovich, 1982.

Bertrand, Olivier and Noyelle, Thierry. "Changing Technology, Skills and Skill Formation: The Policy Implications of the OECD/CERI Comparative Study of Financial Service Forms." OECD, Paris, 1986. Mimeographed.

Bloch, Ernest. *Inside Investment Banking.* Homewood, IL: Dow Jones-Irwin, 1986.

Boston Consulting Group. *The Future of Wholesale Banking.* Rolling Meadows, IL: Bank Administration Institute, 1986.

Caves, Richard. "Economic Analysis and the Quest for Competitive Advantage." *American Economic Review,* May 1984.

Caves, Richard, and Porter, Michael. "From Entry Barriers to Mobility Barriers: Conjectural Decisions and Contrived Deterrence to New Competition." *Quarterly Journal of Economics,* May 1977.

Cooper, Kerry, and Fraser, Donald R. *Bank Deregulation and the New Competition in Financial Services.* Cambridge, MA: Ballinger, 1986.

Crane, Dwight B., and Hayes, Samuel L. III. "The New Competition in World Banking." *Harvard Business Review,* July–August 1982.

Davis, Stephen I. *Excellence in Banking.* London: Macmillan, 1985.

Dunning, John H. *International Production and the Multinational Enterprise.* London: George Allen & Unwin, 1981.

Galbraith, Craig S., and Kay, Neil M. "Towards a Theory of the Multinational Firm." *Journal of Economic Behavior and Organization,* March 1986.

Gray, H. Peter, and Gray, Jean M. "The Multinational Bank: A Financial MNC?" *Journal of Banking and Finance,* March 1982.

Grubel, Herbert G. "A Theory of Multinational Banking." *Banca Nazionale del Lavoro Quarterly Review,* December 1977.

Grubel, Herbert G. "There is No Direct International Trade in Services." *American Economic Review,* Papers and Proceedings, March 1987.

Hayes, Samuel III, Spence, A. M., and Marks, D. v. P. *Competition in the Investment Banking Industry.* Cambridge, MA: Harvard University Press, 1983.

Kallberg, Jarl S., and Saunders, Anthony. *Direct Sources of Competitiveness in Banking Services.* Salomon Brothers Center for the Study of Financial Institutions, New York, 1986. Mimeographed.

Mathur, Shiv Sahai. "How Firms Compete: A New Classification of Generic Strategies." Centre for the Study of Financial Institutions, The City University Business School, Working Paper no. 81, July 1986. Mimeographed.

McKenzie, George W. *Economics of the Eurodollar Market.* London: Macmillan, 1976.

Miles, R. E., and Snow, C. C. *Organization Strategy, Structure and Processes.* New York: McGraw-Hill, 1978.

Miles, R. H., and Cameron, K. S. *Coffin Nails and Corporate Strategy.* Englewood Cliffs, NJ: Prentice-Hall, 1982.

Morgan Guaranty Trust Company, "America's Banking Market Goes International." *Morgan Economic Quarterly,* June 1986.

Neu, C. R. "International Trade in Banking Services." Paper presented at the NBER/CEPS conference on European–U.S. Trade Relations, Brussels, June 1986. Mimeographed.

Newman, H. "Strategic Groups and the Structure-Performance Relationships." *Review of Economics and Statistics,* August 1978.

Office of Technology Assessment, U.S. Congress. *International Competition in Banking and Financial Services.* Washington, DC: OTA, July 1986. Mimeographed.

Panzar, John C., and Willig, Robert D. "Economies of Scope." *American Economic Review,* May 1981.

Pastré, Olivier. *Multinationals: Banking and Firm Relationships.* Greenwich, CT: JAI Press, 1981.

Pastré, Olivier. "International Bank-Industry Relations: An Empirical Assessment." *Journal of Banking and Finance,* March 1981.

Pecchioli, R. M. *Internationalization of Banking.* Paris: OECD, 1983.

Porter, Michael E. *Competitive Strategy.* New York: Free Press, 1980.

Sagari, Sylvia B. "The Financial Services Industry: An International Perspective." Ph.D. diss. Graduate School of Business Administration, New York University, 1986.

Swoboda, Alexandre K. "International Banking: Current Issues in Perspective." *Journal of Banking and Finance,* September 1982.

Teece, David J. "Economies of Scope and the Enterprise." *Journal of Economic Behavior and Organization,* March 1985.

Tschoegl, Adrian E. "Size, Growth and Transnationality Among the World's Largest Banks." *Journal of Business,* 56, no. 2 (1985).

Walter, Ingo. *Barriers to Trade in Banking and Financial Services.* London: Trade Policy Research Centre, 1985.

Walter, Ingo. *Global Competition in Financial Services*. Cambridge, MA: Ballinger-Harper & Row, 1988.

Walter, Ingo, and Smith, Roy C. *Investment Banking in Europe: Restructuring for the 1990s*. Oxford: Basil Blackwell, 1989.

Yannopoulos, George N. "The Growth of Transnational Banking." In *The Growth of International Business,* edited by Mark Casson. London: George Allen & Unwin, 1983.

22

Strategy Formulation and Implementation

The formulation and implementation of effective competitive strategies are challenges of the first magnitude that face all international banking institutions. A great many factors are involved, and each bank will emerge with a somewhat different recipe for success. As discussed in the previous chapter, individual strategies are affected both by market and competitive conditions and by those characteristics of the institution that are unique to it. Many judgments are made as to the weighting of particular considerations and the priority given to them. At best, it is a difficult and complex task in need of continuous updating. Even an effective strategy may take years to show results. Ineffective strategies produce either no results when some are needed or, worse, unwanted results. Over the long term, those with effective strategies become competitive and survive, and those without do not. After all, to quote baseball great Casey Stengel, "If you don't know where you're going, you might end up someplace else."

In this chapter we will look at some of the more important determinants of global strategy formulation for financial service concerns. These include (1) a good understanding of the major developments in the market for global financial services over the past 15 years or so; (2) an appreciation of the strategic implications of these developments; (3) some idea as to how these play on individual institutions, given their particular strengths and weaknesses, goals and ambitions; and (4) how the strategy formulation process works.

MAJOR DEVELOPMENTS IN FINANCIAL MARKETS

Table 22–1 reviews once again a number of the important developments that have had major significance in financial services markets over the past 15 years. Many of these have been discussed elsewhere

Table 22–1.   Major Developments in Financial Services Markets, (1975–1990)

- Extensive Institutionalization of Markets
- Worldwide Deregulation
- Increased Transactional and Performance Orientation
- Extensive Restructuring of Companies and Portfolios
- Globalization or Integration of Markets
- Securitization of Illiquid Assets
- Growth in Assets and Capital Requirements of Financial Firms
- Widespread Dependence on Computers and Telecommunications
- Emergence of New Forms of Risk Taking (e.g., "Merchant Banking")

in this book, and by now most of them will be quite familiar to the reader. Accordingly, only brief comments on each should be necessary to place it in its proper strategic context.

The institutionalization of financial markets is a worldwide development that reflects the rapidly growing size and importance of pension funds, insurance companies, investment companies of various types, banks, and other professional investors in the United States, Europe, Japan and other parts of Asia, and Australia. These professional investors are increasingly sophisticated, demanding, and performance oriented. They have developed an appetite for trading that has encouraged the introduction of many new types of securities and investment ideas. A premium has been placed by these investors on high-grade research, market liquidity, and on trading capabilities offered by their suppliers of services.

Deregulation of several different types has also had a major effect on financial markets. With the abandonment of the gold-based fixed exchange rate system in 1971, exchange controls were no longer necessary in the developed economies and gradually these came to be repealed, releasing capital to flow overseas in search of investment opportunities that were unavailable at home. In time, this free flow of investment capital resulted in the formation of a large, global investment pool with greatly increased liquidity and competition. Deregulation cleared away two other important pathways for financial institutions, the removal of internal market barriers, such as occurred with the restructuring of the London Stock Exchange (Big Bang), and the loosening of rules preventing the participation by foreign firms in domestic markets. The bottom-line effect of nearly two decades of deregulation has been increased market liquidity and performance and greatly increased competition.

Heightened transactional and performance orientations of all market participants have been clear results of the foregoing. Not only are users of financial services placing increasing pressure on their suppliers, they too are under competitive pressure. Boards of directors of financial institutions are continually changing their "portfolios" of money managers. A manager who is seen to underperform relative to others is dismissed and replaced by another. Banking business of all types is increasingly awarded on a competitive bidding, or price, basis, at least for those types of transactions involving what are deemed to be commodity-like loans, securities, or other financial instruments.

The restructuring of companies and portfolios has been a natural outcome of the increased attention to financial performance. To attract investors (in order to raise their share prices) companies have undertaken mergers and acquisitions, dispositions of ill-fitting businesses, and a more adventurous use of financial leverage to increase returns on investment. Money managers, under increased performance pressure themselves, have undertaken increased trading in their portfolios, looking to equal or beat the indexes.

Globalization of financial markets has occurred through the linking of major market centers in the United States, Europe, and Japan. It is increasingly difficult for major banks to continue to service their traditional clients without being able to offer access to global markets and services.

Securitization, the process of converting an illiquid asset into a liquid, tradeable one, has accompanied these other events. Partly in response to the need to provide new investment vehicles to a rapidly expanding world liquidity pool, and partly as competition to banks, insurance companies, and savings institutions, the securities markets have developed ways to convert short-term commercial loans, mortgages, customer receivables, and other assets into marketable securities. This evolution, among other effects, has added to the substantial blurring of distinctions between traditional banking and securities institutions.

The growth in the asset base and the capital requirements of financial service firms attempting to compete in the new, more performance-oriented market environment has been considerable. Firms have had to expand greatly the number of market-making activities in which they were engaged and the number of market locations in which they operated. One result of these developments has been to increase substantially the amount of capital that all firms need to maintain in order to participate actively in all major markets.

Table 22-2. Principle Effects of the Developments

- Great liquidity created in the markets
- Enormous growth in the volume of transactions
- Difficult competition
- Emphasis on innovation and specialization
- Internationalization of the business
- Difficult risk exposures
- Rapid growth in the size of firms
- Management complexities

All of these developments forced the firms into dependency on their telecommunications and data processing systems, not just for communicating market information and orders around the world, but also for settlement procedures and for the analytic capability that had to accompany new product development. Those firms that emerged from the period with superior systems capabilities found themselves in possession of a valuable competitive weapon.

Finally, as a growing share of the basic business of banks and securities firms fell into the tough trench warfare of financial commodities, many found relief in moving into merchant banking, in which much greater returns could be earned by exposing the firm to greater credit and market risks, which it was hoped could be skillfully and profitably managed. Many firms were attracted to make bridge loans for highly leveraged acquisitions and to take stakes themselves in these transactions.

STRATEGIC IMPLICATIONS OF THESE DEVELOPMENTS

These various developments resulted in a number of changed competitive conditions to which financial service firms had to adapt in order to protect their existing market positions. Some of the more important of these changed conditions are listed in Table 22–2.

These changed conditions carry with them a number of strategic implications for financial services firms. Foremost among these is the change in the basic economics of the banking and securities businesses. These changes (1) threaten the continuing profitability of firms, (2) have resulted in the development of certain competitive rigidities, and (3) have shifted financial power from banks to securities firms (see Table 22–3).

Table 22–3.   Changing Economics

Profitability Threatened

- Spreads decline as volume increases, especially for traded products
- Innovative products enjoy high spreads, but these are quickly copied and discounted
- Many investment banking products are becoming commodities
- Services to clients require positioning and/or research coverage
- Large profit opportunities are available from trading, but risks are high and competition increases them
- Personnel cost continues as the greatest expense of the business, but systems costs are catching up quickly
- International expansion costs several times more than domestic expansion, and revenues are slower to develop

Developing Competitive Rigidities

- Investment banking business is becoming increasingly concentrated in a small number of firms
- High-margin advisory businesses are hard to break into
- Increasingly complex risk management capability requires high level of market expertise as well as computer and mathematical capacity

Financial Power Is Shifting from Banks to Securities Firms

- Securitization has transferred substantial assets from banks and insurance companies to the market
- Many U.S. banks have experienced loan losses, capital problems, and regulatory constraints that have adversely affected their competitiveness and growth potential relative to securities firms and foreign banks
- Many U.S. and other securities firms enjoy lower costs of capital than banks
- Top U.S. securities firms will control more financial assets by 1992 than top banks (See Figure 22-1)
- U.S. and Japanese securities firms are still afforded substantial protection from Glass-Steagall Act and Art. 65

Pressures on Profitability

Because recent years have been mainly characterized by expanding, bull markets (until October 19, 1987) with the parallel development of financial and trading capacity in the markets, it became common to see lending spreads and brokerage commissions lowered, as new competitors sought to establish themselves in the market. To make money, it was thought, firms had to innovate, that is, be the first to introduce a successful new product or financing idea. As a result, many innovative financings occurred. These, however, were quickly copied by others, after which the innovators could no longer command premium commissions, leading the market on to the next product. Some firms preferred to compete by offering more aggressive market-making services instead, but soon, as competition increased, the risks began to outweigh the rewards in this area also. During 1982–1986 especially, many firms inserted themselves into the newly globalized markets and invested heavily in increased financial capacity (i.e., the capital and the staff to conduct substantial activities in the markets). When the volume and activity in the markets began to recede below the capacity that had been created, conditions became very competitive. Facing such conditions, many firms chose to withdraw from some or all of the more dangerous international trading markets. Dropouts from the post–Big Bang markets in the United Kingdom in gilt-edged securities and equities became numerous. Likewise, many firms elected to withdraw capacity from the U.S. government securities and the Eurobond markets when the trading conditions began to harden in early 1987. However, most firms have elected to take a wait-and-see approach, neither withdrawing nor advancing much until the next turn in the market can be foreseen. Under these conditions, firms will not rush headlong into underpriced transactions, but they will pop in from the sidelines from time to time, whenever a trade can be made at a small profit. The result, as of the end of 1989, is that the markets continue to possess excess capacity for the level of business being done.

Competitive Rigidities

One reason for competitive inertia is that serious players are reluctant to withdraw from the field if in doing so they would leave it to be dominated by a small coterie of large-firm competitors who, in surviving current conditions, may be very difficult to displace later on, once the market recovers. Moreover, many firms believe that by losing visibility in the markets, they might also lose the capability to land high value-added advisory business, or become rusty in key skill areas that are linked to their ability to perform in the markets. Some firms simply believe that more favorable conditions will return soon, so that a comparatively short wait can be justified.

Shifting Power

Finally, a shift of financial power from banks to securities firms has occurred as a result of securitization activities, the deterioration of the creditworthiness of many banks, which has increased their cost of funding, and a substantially more rapid growth in securities market activity than in traditional banking activity until late 1987.

U.S. banks in particular have had to endure disadvantageous regulatory conditions, extensive foreign competition in their home markets and in Euromarket loans, and Third World debt and other problems in their loan portfolios, while U.S. securities firms enjoyed a prolonged bull market; the introduction of CMOs, junk bonds, and other profitable new instruments; and the largest merger and acquisition and corporate restructuring activity ever. New opportunities were promised as a result of the reorganization of the London and other stock exchanges, but these opportunities were mainly to be in the area of securities market transactions. Although many U.S. and other commercial banks were permitted increased opportunity to participate in securities markets in the United States, Europe, and Japan (and in Canada and Australia) the principal beneficiaries of these reforms were thought to be the American investment banks and a few others who were in a position to best capitalize on the new opportunities.

Securities firms, too, were attracting and retaining substantial amounts of capital from earnings, new issues, joint ventures, and other means, and the capital was being employed as a base for expanding the total amount of assets carried on their books as inventories of securities traded, customer receivables, and other investments. Although stock exchanges maintain minimum capital requirements for member firms, these were not restrictive; indeed, many large securities firms principally (because they could offer high-grade collateral on loans) were able to borrow 30 or more times their capital, while most regulated banking institutions (except in Japan) were for the most part unable to borrow much more than about 20 times their capital.

As a result of these factors, the total amount of assets carried by U.S. securities firms (a proxy for the financial potency of any financial institution) increased rapidly relative to the rate at which the total assets of the leading banks were increasing. At the rate of overtaking prevailing during 1988, it could be expected that within a few years the total assets of the 10 largest U.S. securities firms would exceed the total assets of the 10 largest U.S. banks (see Figure 22–1).

Such a condition would have been considered inconceivable 10 years before and is probably inconceivable today in the United Kingdom or in Japan. The remainder of Europe and most other countries permit universal banking, so the matter of shifting influence does not arise in these countries except to the important extent that the increasing activity of securities markets at the expense of banking activity has created changes in the way universal banks conduct their business.

Because of especially competitive conditions in the securities markets since 1987, some commercial banks have backed away from securities activities, and some securities firms have backed away from

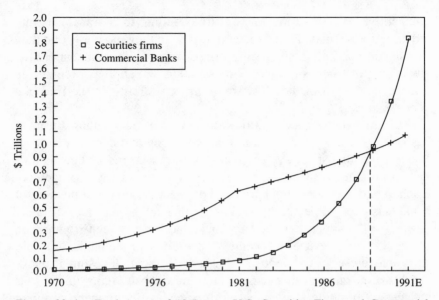

Figure 22–1. Total Assets of 10 Largest U.S. Securities Firms and Commercial Banks.

efforts to become large, global financial institutions in their own right. Increasing convergence of banking and securities businesses, especially among the larger firms, poses special problems for financial strategists. The convergence is likely to both increase and hasten if, as anticipated, U.S. and Japanese banks are provided relief from the constraints of the Glass-Steagall provisions of the 1933 Banking Act and the Japanese equivalent of the Act, Article 65 of the Securities and Exchange Act.

Unprecedented Competition

The principal effect of the many changes in the financial services businesses that have occurred over the past several years has been the extraordinary increase in competition. Those firms from relatively free-market areas such as the United States and the United Kingdom have felt the change in competitive pressure the most. But as international linkages increase, even firms in protected areas are able to feel the difference.

Many firms anticipate that they will have to compete vigorously in the future just to maintain the business they already possess. As their historical franchises come under attack, they will have to fight hard just to stay even. Other firms, perhaps more confident of their competitive abilities, look forward to extending their franchises into territories previously denied to them, although they too know that they will have to defend their existing market base while at the same time advancing into those of others. This situation will apply particularly in Europe as a result of the 1992 single-market reforms in the financial services area.

Such an extensive competitive upheaval in the banking business has been virtually unknown throughout its long and complex history. Banks have almost always been subject to some kind of licensing or regulation that restricted their activities and limited their competitive reach to national or regional arenas. For years the financial position of banks has been protected by regulation of lending and deposit rates. "Excessive" competition between banks has always been frowned on by regulators for fear of weakening the abilities of the banks to safely carry and preserve the deposits entrusted to them. Investment banks and brokers, on the other hand, not being deposit-taking institutions and generally being too small to offer much of a competitive threat to other institutions, were left substantially unregulated.

Characteristics of Individual Firms

Today's competitive upheaval forces banks of all types to reconsider the basic business strategy of their firms. In doing so, each bank must reevaluate various individual attributes of the firm, including (1) its comparative advantages (or disadvantages), (2) its managerial capacity, (3) its tolerance for risk, (4) its tactical situation relative to its principal competitors, and (5) the time-frame over which the competitive results are to be achieved, before fitting all of these factors together with the goals and objectives of the firm.

Having considered these factors, firms arrive (perhaps without realizing it at first) at the most important of their strategic decisions, one that becomes very difficult to reverse after it has been made— the choice of whether the firm is to aim at becoming a "world-class player," a "major national leaguer," or a "niche player" (see Chapter 20). Should none of these shoes fit, or the principals in the firm be unable to select one, then the firm's destiny may instead be to be sold, broken up, or liquidated.

Firm-specific Attributes and Comparative Advantages

Strong firm-specific attributes constitute potential competitive "weapons" to be used in the struggles ahead. Singly and in combination,

---

Table 22–4. Review of Strategic Comparative Advantages or "Competitive Weapons"

Fixed Resources

1. Branch and affiliate network
2. Computer hardware
3. Telecommunications hardware

Intangible Resources

1. Business franchise
2. Knowledge (see Chapter 19)
   a. Client specific
   b. Arena specific
   c. Product specific
3. Systems and procedures
4. Placing power

Human Resources

1. Professional
2. Nonprofessional

Financial Resources

1. Capital base
2. Deposit or funding base

---

these weapons constitute the "arsenal" that each competitor brings to the battle. No two competitors are alike in the content and quality of their arsenals, though each can be assumed to emphasize those weapons that provide the greatest comparative advantage.

The arsenals, however, comprise only weapons—the weapons themselves being only instruments of strategy, not the reason for the strategy. In time, one's opponents can remake their own arsenals, upgrading them or adding new weapons that one's own arsenal lacks. Strategies between competitors differ in being different routes to the same destination (i.e., financial leadership and world-class standing), and the choice of routes may (and should) be influenced by the competitors' comparative advantages at the time. Some of the proximate competitive weapons in global competition are discussed in the previous chapter and summarized in Table 22–4.

In assessing the strength of a firm's specific competitive attributes, it is essential that management undertake every effort to obtain an objective result. This may mean opening some doors to criticism by internal management or by outside observers, either of which can disturb internal harmony among management and staff. Nevertheless, honest answers are necessary to such simple questions as "How do we measure up relative to our immediate competitors?"; "What are we better at than everyone else?"; and "Where are our vital weaknesses?"

Important Intangibles

Unmentioned per se, but nonetheless to be included in the various categories of intangible resources listed, are a variety of special characteristics that individual banking institutions may or may not possess and that can have major significance in their choice of strategy. Among these would be special cultural or language requirements that may have to be handled, such as the need for continental European banks to adapt to a much more transactional (as opposed to relationship) nature of business in the future, or the need on the part of Japanese banks to bridge both language and cultural aspects of business when operating abroad. Unique parental relationships that may affect business acquisition or other franchise characteristics also apply here, such as the tripartite association of American Express, Shearson Lehman Hutton, and Nippon Life, which may alter greatly the resultant global strategy of these firms.

Other intangible differences among banks include the quality of management systems in place at all levels necessary for competitive excellence. Normally, this would be a question only of whether the bank had sufficient good managers to undertake the strategic challenge ahead. However, in view of the massive changes in the global banking environment—the need to operate in markets, environments, and cultures substantially different from those in which a firm has operated in the past—the issue of management adequacy often turns on whether the firm has educated and trained the talent necessary to manage the institution in the future.

Highly structured organizations, like certain European and Japanese banks, will have to adapt to a looser, more flexible, and decentralized style of management to succeed in the capital markets parts of their businesses. Investment and merchant banks, on the other hand, will have to adapt to tighter central controls as vital risk management and other organizational requirements increasingly apply across entire firms. In some respects, such managerial adaptations cannot be accomplished without a great deal of internal turmoil and displacement. For many institutions, the sooner they pass through this difficult period of adaptation the sooner they will be able to address

The important strategic issues ahead of them; without such changes, they may not be able to do so.

Extensive managements shifts take time to accomplish, and they must be accompanied by appropriate institutional changes (such as in performance evaluation, promotion, and compensation schemes) that support the systemic changes that have been made and emphasize the necessary development of teamwork and a firmwide awareness of competitive issues. Bankers Trust, for example, has effected a substantial change in its business strategy over the past decade and has received much favorable comment for its attention to the necessary parallel changes that had to be made in its managerial system in order for the new strategy to be implemented.

Tolerance for Risk

In addition to these intangibles, most firms must adapt their tolerance for risk to those risks that will be appropriate for their future competitive efforts. The risks involved in today's global banking strategies are numerous. They include position risks from trading activities all over the world and credit risk associated with expanding product lines, client exposures, and penetration into new arenas. Systems risks of various types accompany these. Often, commercial bankers have difficulty adapting to a trader's mentality, while traders are either bored or intimidated by the vast control infrastructure necessary to keep on top of credit risks, systems risks, and regulatory compliance and quality control in general.

Starting Position

In addition to the firm-specific issue noted here, assessment must be made of the tactical position from which the institution's new strategy will evolve and the urgency with which it must be implemented. The starting tactical position might be centered on defending a superior position in at least one of the markets in which the bank is competing. The Deutsche Bank, BNP, Citibank, and Nomura Securities, for example, each enjoy a superior market position in their home countries and in certain other market sectors, such as parts of the Eurobond or the Euro-CD market. These firms attract business because of their high franchise value, are able to attract and retain considerable resources, and are free to exploit these advantages in challenging the market share of other banks for clients, arenas, or products.

Other banks, however, such as Dresdner Bank, Morgan Stanley, or Nikko Securities may have nearly (but not quite) achieved a superior position in their preferred and most important home market, in which case they may expend a disproportionate amount of their own resources, for example, on achieving leadership in this "case" market rather than on attacking competitors in other markets. Morgan Stanley, as an illustration, did not join the gilt-edged securities business in London after Big Bang, presumably to conserve resources and to concentrate its focus on the international markets for equity securities. Nikko Securities undertook an all-out effort in the 1980s to catch up with or displace Nomura's leadership position in domestic Japanese securities markets, one result of which was that it underemphasized its Euromarket activities, allowing Daiwa Securities to pull ahead.

The great majority of banks and investment firms, however, are not leaders in any substantial market or market segment, and thus fall into neither category mentioned above. Such firms must be classified as struggling in the middle of the market with many other similarly positioned firms. Such firms as Kidder Peabody, Dean Witter, Westdeutsche Landesbank, Credit Commercial de France, and Standard Charter are among those that might be placed in such a category, despite being fully capable of retaining substantial prestige and recognition within their home countries. Finally, there remain those banks that are just starting to supplement their usually narrowly focused business with an international capability of some sort. Such banks as Wasserstein Perrella (New York), Charterhouse (London), or the Bank of Yokohama might fall into this category.

It is possible, indeed normal, for banks to belong to several different strategic categories at the same time—different ones for different C-A-P cells and clusters in terms of Figure 20–1. Deutsche Bank, for example, would be considered as being in a superior market position insofar as global merger and acquisition activities of German companies are concerned, but in a just-getting-started position for non-German transactions in Europe and the United States. Nonetheless, in aggregate, banks must have an overall competitive position that provides a basis of strength and resources, that tends to infuse their overall attitudes and self-confidence, and that, in the end, shapes the kind of global strategies they adopt. As in all else regarding strategy, cold-blooded objectivity is essential. Not only must the bank have a clear idea of where it is headed over the coming years, it must also have a realistic understanding of where it is coming from. The route to the destination varies depending on the point of departure.

Strategic Urgency

The route may also vary according to the speed at which the journey is planned, that is, on the urgency given to the implementation of the strategy by the bank's directors. Some bank boards feel that immediate results are necessary in order to gain the high ground in competitive markets before everyone else gets there, or to be able to take advantage of sudden openings in the markets or special opportunities created by regulatory or other considerations.

In 1986, the Tokyo Stock Exchange announced that it would select a limited number of foreign securities firms for membership, which resulted in many firms from the United States, Europe, and Asia dropping what they were doing to make their case for acceptance. Six ultimately were chosen in the initial round, and these firms then were given about six months to commence trading on the Exchange or risk losing their memberships. First there had been a panic to respond to the process of selection, then another panic to hire and train the people necessary to protect the memberships that had been won.

Urgency is not always desirable, of course, but sometimes it is unavoidable. Those firms that have adapted to a fast-moving, opportunistic pace, one in which urgency is the norm, may have certain advantages over their slower moving competitors. But not always. The hare is sometimes the first one to fall into the trap, or become disoriented, leaving opportunities for the tortoise.

Some firms are surely more adapted to, and happy with, a pace of gradual progress. Some are not in a hurry at all, not being concerned with market shares, and thus move at an even slower but surer speed. J.P. Morgan was the last of the major U.S. commercial banks to enter the Eurobond business, and by most accounts is regarded as the most successful. Some of Morgan's competitors had moved quickly to set up investment banking operations alongside their syndicated loan business and never were able to separate the two, which tended to result in the bond side of the business being run by commercial bankers who were not all that competitive. Other banks rushed into Eurobond activities, took substantial positions, lost money, frightened top management, and were forced to retrench. Morgan learned from the errors of the others. Some banks inevitably confuse movement with progress but rarely find that a quick start results in the strong and profitable market position they fully expected to enjoy five years later. Others seem always to be late and underpowered, struggling to wrest a meager market share from those other firms that compete in the middle of the pack.

Effective Implementation

If a bank is to favor a rapid pace of strategic development, it needs to plan accordingly and equip itself with the human, financial, and management resources necessary to accomplish the task. Those firms, for example, that have prided themselves on running on a limited, lean overhead (without "excess" management talent) are not going to be capable of simultaneously implementing aggressive expansion strategies in Europe, Japan, Australia, and Canada, except on an inefficient and expensive basis that will have to be reworked later.

It should be clear, therefore, that for all of the parts of the strategic plan to be in place, the institution undertaking the plan has to think through not only where the strategy is to take it and from where, but also how quickly and by whom. The pace of implementation has to fit the people who are going to implement the strategy. A group of 60-year-old former regional bank managers from Leeds, or Phoenix, or Sapporo, or Rotterdam, or Dusseldorf will not necessarily be the best people to put together global futures and options trading in six overseas locations or to manage mergers and acquisitions in the United States or equity warrant financings for Japanese corporations.

THE STRATEGY FORMULATION PROCESS

All of the factors that shape strategies must ultimately be tied together, as illustrated in Figure 22–2. Doing this is the job of top management. Others can advise and help in analyzing the options, but only top management can decide whether (and why) a firm should commit substantial capital and other resources to expanding its operations into new areas or cut back on such activities to conserve its strength in domestic markets.

Top management must also assess whether the firm has enough of the requirements for success in pursuit of its strategy to make a go of it, or whether it should delay things until such time as it does. Often, aggressive and ambitious executives responsible for functional or geographic areas of business will feel an urgency to move ahead before the firm is ready to do so. Equally, domestic executives are often reluctant to see resources diverted to lower yielding international activities, while profitable business is abundant at home. Whereas most senior executives are fully aware of what it takes to succeed in connection with a major league national strategy or a niche strategy, the full requirements to become a world-class player are not always as well understood.

Figure 22–2. Strategy Formulation Process.

Table 22–5 enumerates some of these requirements for success, which boil down to plenty of capital, plenty of talent (much of it foreign), and plenty of time. As activities become more extensive and widespread and institutions are required to adapt more often to fast-changing market environments, greater emphasis on management and control systems become essential. But these cannot cost more than the business is capable of supporting. And, finally, there is never a satisfactory substitute for leadership—in this case, of the global enterprise—both in the overseas locations and in the head office.

After management has thought these matters through carefully and fought over and argued them vigorously for a good while, a consensus can emerge as to the right strategy for the institution. Even so, the

---

Table 22–5. Succeeding as a World-Class Player

- At least $1 billion of capital
- Comparative advantages that can be developed and sustained
- Large number of trained and talented personnel, especially leaders
- Acculturation and role models
- Ability to manage a large, complex organization without suppressing the talent
- Ability to manage large risk exposures without flinching
- Ability to manage technology successfully
- Ability to maintain cost discipline and controls
- Realistic time frame
- Ability to react quickly to changing developments

strategy needs to be monitored to reflect changing conditions (including changes in the goals and objectives of the institution) and management's progress in implementation. Numerous midjourney course changes can be anticipated. Indeed, the environment in which global banking is conducted changes so rapidly and extensively that plans have to be revised frequently. The basic strategy must therefore be flexible and capable of substantial alteration on short notice to take advantage of developments as they arise in the markets—and to allow for correction of inevitable, earlier mistakes and misjudgments.

SUMMARY

Whereas different firms may have similar goals and objectives, few will have similar strategies for achieving them. Each firm brings a different set of individual strengths and weaknesses to the task, a different set of management and financial capacities, and different tolerances for risk that affect the ultimate choice of strategy. Financial services constitute at best an overpopulated industry, with great ease of entry and constantly changing conditions that favor innovation and entrepreneurial efforts. So strategies tend to wrap around the personalities and the resources available for the campaign. They are also affected, however, by the firm's competitive or market leadership position at the beginning of the period at which a new strategy is to be implemented. Urgency is also a factor, as is the need to constantly monitor how the strategy is working out and whether the strategy is still appropriate. Top management is the key player in strategy-setting exercises. It is often the only group in the firm with the overall visibility and the authority to make the tough decisions that always come up.

Strategies in the context of global financial service operations are as necessary as a chart in long-distance navigation. When one is sailing within sight of land (one's own land in particular) charts may be nonessential, but not when venturing into far away and unfamiliar seas.

SELECTED REFERENCES

Walter, Ingo. *Global Competition in Financial Services*. New York: Ballinger Publishing Co., 1988.

Walter, Ingo, and Roy C. Smith. *Investment Banking in Europe*. Oxford: Basil Blackwell, Ltd., 1990.

Robert G. Eccles and Dwight B. Crane. *Doing Deals*. Cambridge, MA: Harvard Business School Press, 1988.

23

Organization and Management

All international financial services organizations have had to adjust to the major developments in financial markets that have so dramatically affected their businesses and their working environments. Globalization of markets, deregulation, a continuing stream of innovation and transactional opportunities, and the constant threat of competitive encroachment, among other developments, have profoundly and irreversibly changed the nature and functions of international banking.

Banks have been pushed into market-driven transactions as never before, involving counterparties from various parts of the world and requiring transactions made under highly competitive conditions in volatile markets. These transactions and the origination and market-making functions that the organization must have in order to make them often result in large securities inventories or lending positions being carried with commensurate risk. The banking business (in whatever form) has changed a great deal over the years, and organization and management systems and procedures have had to be changed to fit the times. These changes, however, have not been easy, especially considering the conditions prevailing in the financial environments in which they had to be made.

Because of volatile and competitive markets, businesses that used to be safely conducted from a few, well-controlled branch offices abroad today require greater autonomy in the field. Yet the scope of globalized financial markets and the extensive participation in them by the major players have become such that head offices, concerned about the risks and costs of burgeoning international activities, have become more directly engaged in varying overseas activities. How to organize and manage international financial organizations, always a difficult issue, has risen to the top of the list of key issues that must be resolved in order for firms to be able to compete effectively.

The pace of change and the requirements imposed on financial service firms to keep up with this pace have resulted in many managerial shortcuts. Many "temporary" arrangements have been made, only to be changed repeatedly as the firms have searched for the optimal balance between control and competitiveness, between profit and market-share improvement. So far, very few (if any) organizations have perfected an organizational and management system that even they themselves believe works very well in the increasingly complex international environment.

This is perhaps especially true for investment banks, which tend to believe that the only way to change "things" is to change key people. This approach differs from that of commercial banks, which are known for changing reporting arrangements (and sometimes changing people) through periodic reorganizations. In the past few years there has been a steady change of people and of organizations by all types of banking institutions from all sorts of countries. The right organizational balance, alas, is difficult to establish and soon changes once it is.

Among recent changes and developments in international finance that organizational shifts have had to accommodate has been the build-up of great liquidity in the markets, which has led to an enormous growth in the volume of transactions—all of which had to be processed and accounted for in back offices. Competition has become intense even for business with one's own clients, requiring more attention to marketing, innovation, and client service. As markets have become globalized, individual banks and securities firms have had to internationalize their own businesses by providing global capital market coverage and execution and by responding to new opportunities created by deregulation around the world. With all this, new and difficult exposures to risk have had to be assumed and dealt with. The task of managing firms under these conditions has become a formidable one indeed.

MANAGEMENT COMPLEXITIES IN COMMERCIAL BANKS

International business is a relatively new enterprise for most U.S., Japanese, and European commercial banks. Only a relative small number have been active overseas for more than about 25 years. As the Eurodollar market grew after the early 1960s, more became involved. Branches were set up in London and other European cities. Gradually, these spread to all of the OECD countries. Meanwhile, of course, overseas branches in Latin America and Asia were expanding as banks followed their clients into these markets as well.

In the 1970s, many international banks, large as well as regional, entered into Euromarket lending consortiums to share the risks and the loan-generating capabilities of the participants. After a few years, virtually all of these consortium banks were disbanded—there were too many management problems, too little central direction, and too many occasions when a consortium bank found itself competing directly against one or more of its shareholders.

Next came a wave of "merchant banking" subsidiaries of major U.S., European, and Japanese commercial banks. For the most part, these subsidiaries were formed to avoid regulatory restrictions—as in the case of German banks setting up Luxembourg subsidiaries and Japanese banks setting up London and Hong Kong subsidiaries—or to broaden the scope of their international syndicated lending while avoiding intrabank turf and authority questions. Although the purpose of the merchant banks was to incorporate Euromarket investment banking activities, the main reason that many U.S. banks entered merchant banking was to create a portfolio of loans that were more entrepreneurial and imaginative than those normally offered by the parent. During the late 1970s and early 1980s, many of these loans went into default or were unprofitable after including overhead charges. Subsequently, most of these banks took steps to take these troublesome loans under the more stringent control of parent officials or sell them off. Few had found their merchant banks to be top competitors of investment banks in the securities field. A number of U.S. banks disbanded or sold their merchant banking affiliates. Others retooled them.

In the early 1980s several German, Swiss, and French banks had set up powerful London-based subsidiaries to participate in the Eurobond markets, and Japanese commercial banks had been seeking ways to increase their influence in this market by leading the underwritings of those limited transactions that the Ministry of Finance permitted. Most U.S. banks were looking to swaps, revolving underwriting facilities, and various special types of lending to earn their keep, although a few—for example, J. P. Morgan, Citicorp, and Chase Manhattan— were succeeding in various types of Euromarket transactions.

Still, by the mid 1980s the American and some European and Japanese banks were begining to look at the Euromarket as a tough place to make money. Lending spreads had narrowed to the lowest level in years. There were better lending opportunities in the United States. Some continued to participate actively in the underwriting and trading of Eurobonds, especially in floating rate notes, but on the whole this market turned difficult as well, especially with the declining dollar. Merchant banking subsidiaries experienced trading losses. Many were reined in or sold.

With the coming of Big Bang in October 1986, many commercial banks found themselves committed in various ways to the London securities markets. Some had bought London brokers, others had decided to develop their own capabilities required for membership on the Stock Exchange. These developments, however, occurred at the time when U.S. and British (and certain other) banks were increasing their loan loss reserves and were under considerable pressure to increase capital and earnings. Several banks, including Continental Illinois, Bank of America, Standard Chartered Bank, and Midland Bank, have been required to dispose of important overseas assets and businesses in order to meet capital requirements. In 1988 the Bank for International Settlements announced the report of its Basel Committee on bank capital adequacy (see Chapter 25), the result of which will require many banks in many countries to strengthen their capital bases further. This action came at an inconvenient time for many banks with important aspirations to establish themselves in the international securities markets in London and Tokyo prior to repeal of the Glass-Steagall Act in the United States, which many believed was likely to occur in the near future.

Meanwhile, the scrambling international activities of banks has resulted in a wide spectrum of international cross-holdings of bank shares (see Chapter 3). Japanese banks have acquired many smaller banks on the West Coast of the United States and elsewhere, and some British banks (Lloyds, Standard Chartered and Midland Bankers) have sold holdings and branches in the United States while others (National Westminster) have been active acquirers. Bank of America sold its large Italian subsidiary to Deutsche Bank, which has also acquired other holdings in Europe; Irving Trust, before being taken over by Bank of New York, sold its interest in Banca Svizerra Italiana and ended up inviting Banca Commerciale Italiana to acquire 51 percent of its shares. On the whole, acquisition of controlling interests or stakes in banks by banks from other countries was an area of great activity during the 1980s.

For many commercial banks conducting extensive foreign operations certain organizational and management problems became generic. Foreign branches began to profilerate, credit approval processes were cumbersome, and a large number of expatriates began to accumulate on payrolls. These expatriates were expensive, required frequent reassignments, and were often hard to reintegrate into the head office when their traveling days were done. A kind of cumbersome bank "foreign service" grew up. Overseas living arrangements for branch managers and other senior personnel became excessive. Large, elegant housing and chauffeured cars were resented by head office staff, not only for the expense, but also for the colonial airs that seemed to be part of the package.

Senior head office personnel were not always happy with the risk exposures that their foreign resident personnel had created. After the unwinding of the early consortium banks many bank loans of inferior quality were discovered. Merchant banking and securities activities sometimes produced further loans of questionable quality or trading exposures or losses that provided unpleasant surprises to the head office. On several occasions in the late 1970s and 1980s senior representatives of (mainly) American banks abroad were replaced by executives more in tune with head office thinking. Merchant banking affiliates, although attempting to be active in the Eurosecurities markets, were usually headed by a reliable commercial banker whom the head office could trust to look after the sometimes shaky loan portfolio in the merchant bank and not to do anything too rash in the risky securities markets. After a time, the attitude would change—a quest for greater market share in the syndicated loan, Eurobond, or other securities markets would become official, and someone with suitable experience would be invited to take charge of the merchant banking affiliate. Then, the inevitable trading losses would be experienced and the system would refocus on commercial banking skills.

Commercial banks also had to contend with much higher compensation being paid to Euromarket personnel by investment banks and certain of the continental banks. The Euromarket attracted those who were transaction oriented, risk-taking individuals. Commercial banking had for the most part attracted a more conservative, risk-averse variety of employee.

Despite the fact that there were very few regulatory restrictions inhibiting the participation of U.S. and most other commercial banks in all types of international financial markets, commercial banks did not make much of an impact on the Eurosecurities markets. In the end, banks that were large, permanent institutions reacted slowly to the many changes affecting their environment. When they did react, it was often (for most commercial banks) not in such a way as to rank them among the most competitive providers of securities services. This, of course, was not the case for the Swiss and German universal banks, which had been very active in securities markets for years.

Indeed, it can be argued that the comparatively poor showing in the Eurobond and Euroequity markets on the part of U.S. and U.K. commercial banks, despite their relatively free access to the market for more than 20 years, is chiefly the result of the inability of these banks to manage the organizational changes that were necessary to accommodate a major new nonbanking business.

It is now clear, however, that commercial banks are trying harder to master these management issues. The need to be able to offer similar securities market services in their home countries is a pressing incentive to learn. Some have made remarkable progress in a relatively short time, by reorganizing their banks into a small number of large divisions that handle bankwide activity in distinctly different functional areas, for example, lending, trading, money management and fiduciary activities, advisory activities, etc. They have also learned that a bright, young banker in whom the rest of the bank has confidence can successfully be put in charge of a securities business. He or she will have to hire experienced traders, get engrossed in the business, and be willing to start small, but it can be done. Of course, it is equally important that top management develop a tolerance for the trading and other risks associated with the securities business, so that the new venture can participate in the markets on a basis that is fully competitive with other major players.

MANAGEMENT COMPLEXITIES
FOR INVESTMENT BANKS

While the commercial banks have been adapting to a slowing growth in their traditional lending businesses and a need to reorient their activities into fee-generating and trading activities, the investment banks have been experiencing at the same time both major structural changes in their business and explosive growth in it. Between them, these two factors have greatly complicated the management tasks of investment banks.

The principal complication comes from the rapid increase in the size of firms. Services now embrace government finance, real estate, mortgage finance, leveraged buyouts and bridge financing, junk bonds, and foreign exchange, in addition to the traditional business of underwriting corporate stocks and bonds. To this must be added the increase in the scope of the firms' activities caused by globalized markets and the growth of international activities. Such growth has been accompanied by greater requirements for capital, trained personnel, good leadership, and more operating space and support systems.

In addition, the shift toward transactional preeminince has created a greater need for block trading and positioning capacity, and the ability to finance large amounts of securities inventories both in home markets and abroad.

Risk exposures of investment banks are much more complex than they were a few years ago. Market-making risks must be managed for an expanding variety of instruments, some of which may be little understood or nearly illiquid. Credit risk exposure is much greater than before, as are risks of systems failures and the malfeasance of employees, as a number of firms have learned to their dismay.

The pace of change in the investment banking business, of innovation and obsolescence, and the need for rapid communications are all additional burdens that firms that a few years earlier were small and entreprenurial organizations have had to learn to live with and manage effectively.

In a strictly international context, however, investment banks face a number of special problems that complicate management's task. During the 1960s and 1970s, U.S. investment banks, U.K. merchant banks, and European universal banks were the principal market leaders in Euromarket transactions. Cross-border mergers, private placements, and other advisory transactions also sometimes occurred, and these firms would normally handle them. The volume of such transactions was small by contemporary standards but the fees, commissions, and underwriting profits were relatively stable.

After 1980, however, the markets became at once more volatile, more active, and more competitive. The increased volatility of interest rates and exchange rates contributed greatly to the increased volume of new issues and of secondary market trading. More competitors were attracted to the markets, including second-tier U.S. investment and commercial banks, and especially Japanese securities firms and merchant banks owned by commercial banks. The market rediscovered the floating-rate note, which was usually purchased by banks, and volume of activity in this instrument soared. New securities, new underwriting methods, and new trading ideas proliferated, putting greater emphasis on competitive transactional capability (speed, aggressiveness, and risk-taking capacity) as well as on innovation.

Spreads and profits came under pressure. New entrants, hoping to build up their market share by using their New York marketing and trading skills only lost more money. Trading positions had expanded enormously; firms tried to perfect the art (often elusive) of hedging Euromarket inventories, but they were not always successful. Losses, the rapid pace of expansion, fear of losing control, and finally, a sharp reduction in market volume caused by the collapse of the dollar in 1987 led the head offices of many firms to take control of the London (and Tokyo) "madness" and restrain it.

Once one firm was seen to be reining in its international activities, many others copied it. This led to sharp and substantial reductions in personnel throughout the industry too and greater efforts to control costs. Firms settled in to a less aggressive posture for some businesses while exiting others. Conventional wisdom now concluded one could not do everything and should not try to.

As a result of all this, investment and merchant banks' organizational structures (and senior international managers) changed, and senior head office personnel asserted greater control over international operations, regardless of how poorly they themselves were informed about unique characteristics of international business or the territories, clients, and the personalities involved. Competitive personalities of individuals added to the tendency of some to blame others for past difficulties or to protest that lack of support in difficult times was the source of the trouble. In any event, the axes fell, as they always do, with an undisputed finality.

Different Organizational Approaches

Organizing international operations so they can be managed effectively has always been a difficult task. It is not a static matter that, once organized, can be left in place indefinitely. The organizational structure changes constantly, irrespective of whether such changes are desired by the firms' top management. Many things cause the organization to change: the relative importance of the international activity of the firm to its overall business; how dynamic and competitive the international business environment is at any particular time; and, perhaps most important, the personalities of the international managers of the firm and how these individuals are able to interact with the rest of the firm. Good organizational design will take all of these factors into account and will provide for flexible adjustments from time to time to accommodate new situations.

Any international organization has to balance both the *geographic* and the *functional* aspects of the firm's business. Geographic considerations apply to those factors that are unique to the international environment. These embrace culture, language, and other indigenous factors, but also knowledge of the persona and the practices of local markets and the particular relationships that exist between the firm and its clients in the area. These elements are not only oriented to the marketing of the firm's products, but pertain also to local transaction execution, trading and support activities of the firm, at least insofar as these are carried out in the geographic area and not in firm's head office. Geographic factors vary considerably between, say, the United States, Europe, Japan, and the Middle East. They all vary much more from domestic business (and from each other) than the same sort of factors vary between New York and Chicago, for example, or between London and Edinburgh. Within the organization a number of people, including one or more senior people, can usually be found with responsibility for maintaining and enhancing the geographical aspects of the firm's business.

Functional aspects pertain to a particular line of business or products, regardless of where they are transacted. A bond issue has certain quality control and risk features that have to be managed regardless of whether it is launched in New York, London, Paris, Tokyo, or Sydney. Functional aspects come in bundles—bond new issues have to be supported by distribution, trading, and perhaps research if the new issue activity is to be successful. Bond people know about these things, whether they are stationed in New York, London, or Tokyo. If the volume of bond new issues business is small or not important, then the geographic team can manage the bond business on a part-time basis with its own people or perhaps with newly hired geographic/bond specialists. As the business grows, however, the people in charge of the bond business at the firm's head office may be asked to take over supervision of the growing bond business in the distant geographic area, so that it can be managed more competitively and with less risk exposure.

At various times, some aspects of a firm's international business will be in a geographic mode (i.e., where the product is principally controlled by the geographic side) while others may have passed into functional hands. Not all products and services will be at the same stage of development or require the same level of attention. However, the more products there are and the more unfamiliar the geography is to functional operatives (and vice versa) the more difficult will be the management function. Many who have experienced this type of international matrix organizational structure have come to believe that, like democracy as described by Winston Churchill, it is the worst and most inefficient form of government, except for all the others.

Most financial services organizations own 100 percent of their overseas operations and thus can manage them as they wish. Usually the foreign operation occupies one of a series of ever-changing points on the spectrum between geographic and functional control of particular products and services and, in the aggregate, of the overall international operations of the firm. As in most things involving a balance of power between two poles, if the international operations are dominated by either extreme, great organizational difficulties can ensue.

Excessive Functional Control

In the early days of the Eurobond market, from 1965 to 1972, two U.S. commercial banks attempted to carve out for themselves a preeminence in the market that equalled (or perhaps exceeded) their standing in the commercial banking field. The banks appointed as head of their respective London-based "merchant banks" individuals who had been employeed there for many years and who were regarded as solid. Before long, these bankers became caught up in Euromarket activities, initiated a number of innovative deals including some of the first floating-rate Eurobond issues, and in general became visible personalities on the small but disproportionately visible Euromarket stage.

The businesses of their banks were expanding and they added staff. However, they also added problems—their colleagues and superiors in New York wanted to know about positioning and secondary market risks and wanted to approve credit extensions before they were granted by the London merchant bankers. When trading losses occurred, as was inevitable, detailed explanations were required. Ultimately, the functional side won, and the aggressive heads of their London merchant banks were discharged and their staffs drifted off. They were replaced by more conventional, less controversial people. These banks have never regained the market leadership position that they enjoyed at the time.

There are many cases in which the head office, coming alive after a long period of comparative disinterest, exerts its authority over branch operations overseas but in doing so kills the special thrust that in part resulted in the conditions that caused the intervention in the first place. Sometimes this occurs because of serious problems in the branch, sometimes because changes within the geographic region have been so pronounced that the head office fears losing control, and at other times it occurs because of a change in management (and therefore in the personalities involved) at one end or the other. Whatever the reason, once the head office takes over, its influence can be heavy-handed and destructive of important geographic components needed for ultimate success.

Excessive Geographic Control

The problem of course, can be on the other end as well. The geographic unit may become remote and isolated from the parent. There have been a number of cases of U. S. investment banking firms setting up international subsidiaries in Europe with a sufficient degree of autonomy so as to appear to be separate, self contained businesses linked to the parent only by a telephone line. Perhaps the classic example of such an occurrence was the experience of White, Weld & Co., a New York investment bank (since merged into Merrill Lynch) that had a Swiss subsidiary, Cie Financiere White Weld, which in turn owned a London merchant bank, White Weld Ltd. The European end of the firm comprised a number of long-standing White Weld managers, many of whom were European.

They got off to a very fast start when the Eurobond market became active with issues for U.S. companies, and they secured a large share of the market. They were dealing with first-class "names," for which first-class receptions were granted by investors. In time, the business of White Weld Ltd. expanded, and its employees were able to negotiate with White, Weld & Co. a substantial degree of independence from the parent and a separate compensation system. Ultimately they were allowed an ownership interest in the European subsidiary.

White, Weld & Co. was not a first-rank competitor in the investment banking field in New York, and gradually its ability to contribute business to the subsidiary declined. The firm began to specialize in smaller company investment banking business, while White Weld Ltd. continued to attract top people and to expand into the growing areas of international finance. Eventually White Weld Ltd. forced its parent to take in Credit Suisse as a partner, and the firm became Credit Suisse White Weld. Finally, White, Weld & Co., after a series of losses and setbacks in the United States, merged with with Merrill Lynch, and Credit Suisse White Weld became Credit Suisse First Boston.

More recent examples of problems arising from too much geographical autonomy involve those firms that have allowed the European branch or subsidiary to build up their own "duplicate" staff of salespeople, traders, back office personnel, and bankers, all of whom report only to the geographic chief. Although such a system can indeed work well, it usually involves extensive commitment to overhead in the subsidiary (which in an international context can be more expensive than domestic overhead because of the high number of professional employees needed to handle a comparatively small volume of business). This also often creates disinterest in and a lack a cooperation between the firm's U.S. and European businesses. Such attitudinal differences can create serious difficulties in effecting coordination and assistance between markets.

For example, suppose a major U.S. client wants to issue bonds. It will need the firm's recommendation as to whether it should issue in Europe or in the United States, a situation that can create conflict between competing units. Or suppose an important client of the firm wants to sell an operating division and may need to know which European companies should be considered as possible buyers and how each would finance the transaction. The domestic investment bankers handling the transaction will probably not know the answer to these questions but will want to provide them anyway in order to preserve the business relationship with the client. The European subsidiary may feel that the probability of a European company buying the division is so low as to be a waste of time. If the subsidiary is too autonomous and too self-sufficient, it may be very difficult to control situations where coordination and assistance is mandatory.

The approach most often used to provide incentives for cooperation is fee-sharing, but it should be clear that in cases such as that mentioned above, the U.S. bankers are not going to be eager to share part of a large domestic merger fee with their European colleagues only for supplying some necessary but not crucial information. If they are forced to share fees when they do not think they should, they will find other ways to get the information they need, including setting up their own groups that duplicate some of the client coverage or research functions of the European unit. Once fee-sharing is introduced as an incentive to cooperation, every incidence of cooperation becomes a negotiation subject to economic considerations.

Joint Ventures

Notwithstanding the earlier experience of consortium banks, some institutions have been able to make jointly-owned international finance companies work successfully. The best known of these is the CS First Boston venture that is 44.5% owned by Credit Suisse. As indicated above, Credit Suisse First Boston came into being when White Weld was merged into Merrill Lynch. Credit Suisse did not want Merrill Lynch to succeed to White Weld's interest in Credit Suisse White Weld, so it arranged for First Boston to acquire Merrill's interest. At the same time, the new enterprise, Credit Suisse First Boston, would acquire a 39 percent interest in First Boston itself, which was then experiencing serious financial difficulties.

As part of the arrangement, First Boston and Credit Suisse First Boston divided up the world. First Boston was not to operate in Europe; Credit Suisse First Boston was not to operate in the United States. If a European client of Credit Suisse or Credit Suisse First Boston wanted to sell securities in the United States, then First Boston would handle the issue. If a U.S. client of First Boston wanted to issue Eurobonds, then CSFB would take care of it. In either case, the referring party would be credited with part of the fee by the executing party. The issue of market primacy in time became clouded by other factors, including the complexities associated with sharing merger and other advisory fees fairly and the complications arising out of business done in Japan, where First Boston had historical strength, and in Europe, where Credit Suisse First Boston and First Boston vie for stock brokerage and related commissions associated with foreign investors' purchases of U.S. securities and the reverse.

The relationship between Credit Suisse First Boston and its parents was a stormy one. All of the main parties are aggressive, strong-willed individuals who represent their particular interests well. Credit Suisse First Boston was headed by a former vice chairman of First Boston. His deputy was an executive director of Credit Suisse. The chief executives of both Credit Suisse and First Boston were deeply and continually involved in the relationship. It was time-consuming, at times abrasive, and frequently frustrating to all concerned. However, Credit Suisse First Boston long remained the most successful participant in the Euromarket, and First Boston one of the premier houses in New York, and they each contributed substantially to the other's profits. The arrangement was an economic success but strenuous to maintain. It became highly questionable whether First Boston would enter into such a dramatic arrangement again, one requiring it to give up its European business, unless, as before, the firm were in such a weakened position financially as to have little choice. In October 1988, after long negotiation, First Boston and Credit Suisse First Boston agreed to merge into a new holding company—CS First Boston.

There have been other efforts to put together jointly owned international operations. In the late 1970s the French bank Paribas and the British merchant bank S.G. Warburg combined forces, among other things to acquire a controlling interest in the U.S. investment bank A. G. Becker & Co., which, like First Boston at the time of its arrangement with Credit Suisse, was experiencing financial and other difficulties. Unlike First Boston, however, Becker was a second-tier firm, known mainly for its commercial paper business and its Chicago origins. The surviving entity was called Warburg-Paribas-Becker. Its franchise was to be the United States, but the threesome was expected to cooperate everywhere.

This venture was not a success. Warburg and Paribas invested substantial sums in the firm and spent endless hours trying to figure out an appropriate Anglo-French-American management style and control system, but without success. Finally Warburg sold out to Paribas, and Paribas in turn, after a further unrewarding effort, sold the firm to Merrill Lynch.

There were several problems with the venture from the start. First, Becker was a weak (not just a weakened) player with a limited range of business to bring to the party. Second, Warburg and Paribas, although cooperating in Europe under the terms of a complex and difficult entente, did not have any particular European execution capability to contribute, such as the Credit Suisse White Weld Eurobond business that was in place at the time of the First Boston transaction. Both firms had much to offer in their respective national markets, but their broad international businesses were not strong. Finally, a three-way management consortium of a company, with serious financial problems to begin with, can only be regarded as adding serious further complications to the task at hand.

These two ventures notwithstanding, most international financial joint ventures have been confined to minority investments (sometimes without voting rights) of one financial firm in another. These investments almost always result in a satisfactory financial return to the investor, but very little if any participation in the transactional flow or in reciprocal referrals of business. An exception might be the tripartite investment arrangement among the New York, Paris, and London operations of Lazard Freres, which differs from other examples in that the firms come from a common heritage, are relatively small in size and lines of business, and each strongly influenced by a very small number of powerful individuals who personally own shares in each of the firms.

Isolation and Impotence

Some firms set up or maintain small branches or subsidiaries abroad to look after their interests in the particular country, but without the mandate to compete aggressively to achieve a prominent market share. Many merchant banking affiliates of U.S. and Japanese banks located in Europe fall into this category, along with a large number of European firms with modest operations in the United States. Such operations, by being so limited, are unable to compete in their host market and thus are doomed to isolation and impotence.

Some firms that have inherited such affiliates have closed them or attempted to upgrade them. To succeed, they need to assemble at least four ingredients: (1) They must (obviously) be licensed to compete in the appropriate business—most commercial banks have not been permitted to conduct certain investment banking businesses in the United States but 15 such banks (non-U.S. banks that were grandfathered under the International Banking Act of 1978) are free to compete; (2) They must have a particular product or service that is marketable in the local environment they are trying to penetrate—for example, many European firms want to sell Eurobonds, European mergers, or investment management services in the United States; (3) They must have a competitive spirit that is backed by the head office; and (4) They must have an organizational structure that lets a new business grow in the shadows of older and more established businesses.

As an example of the last ingredient, some European commercial banks that were grandfathered to conduct a securities business in the United States have tried to develop this business but have encountered organizational problems in doing so. These involve conflicts between the struggling investment bank and the more established, more profitable commercial banking business. The conflict arises, for example, when new and often outside leadership is implanted at the investment bank. An invigorated approach follows in which the investment bank draws up a strategic plan. This plans involves the gathering under the investment bank's roof all advisory fee-related and complex "financial engineering" products. In today's context these are defined to include leveraged buyouts, bridge financing, real estate finance, asset-backed securities, etc. In addition to any securities that result from these categories of products, related bank credit facilities are also to be bundled in.

In the eyes of the investment bank, products requiring special knowledge and market making capabilities should be properly grouped for marketing to clients, execution, and credit extension. Revenues from these transactions will accrue or be transferred to the investment bank, where they will be combined with brokerage and underwriting commissions as they would be in any U.S. domestic investment bank. The commercial bankers may regard some of this as excessive encroachment into their territories and revenues. First, they might argue, nothing should be marketed to any of the bank's existing clients or prospects without going through the relationship officers first, otherwise client confusion and loss of control of the relationship might result. Second, they may express concern that skills they have already developed in connection with extending credit facilities for sophisticated transactions will be set aside and the work done to successfully launch the bank into these lending areas will be wasted if these businesses are "given" to the investment bankers. Lastly, there may be a resentment on the part of the commercial bankers that the investment bankers act in a superior way and seem to be looking down at them. When these problems surface, as inevitably they will when something as significant as a new corporate emphasis on investment banking is undertaken, it is important that the wishes of the top management of the bank is clearly known and expressed and that senior geographic and functional managers be charged with implementing, preferably jointly, a workable solution.

Buying the Talent

It is sometimes necessary to go outside a bank's own organization to recruit specialists. This occurs every time a firm decides to strenghten its capabilities in a nontraditional line of business. This is very normal and only creates special problems when too great a reliance on hired experts occurs. Hired-in talent can be very beneficial—the people involved can help to train others, bring contacts and a network through which business can be done, and may be able to contribute immediately to the profits of the firm.

However, unless the bank can make a convincing case that it is offering fast-track career opportunities to those who join, and shows some regard for the individuals' concerns about long-term job security and benefits, the talent thus secured will have been attracted only for the money and may be attracted away again by someone else for more. Employers of such people need to decide what sort of opportunities, benefits, and upward mobility they wish to offer to locally recruited personnel and stick to it. The basic rule may be that old-time commercial bankers assigned to a tour of duty as head of an investment banking affiliate will probably not get the bank or anyone else in trouble, but he or she is unlikely to accomplish much of any value, either. Conversely, a much bigger risk is taken to support a Young Turk hired from another firm, but this may be the only way to achieve the objective of significant participation in a new market.

Keys to Success

The management and organization of multiline international banking businesses are difficult to get right. And when one does, it doesn't last long. What worked well under one set of circumstances and personalities may not work at all under a different set. Partly, the task is difficult because the environment and the competition change continuously. Partly, it is difficult because the people change, both those on the line and those in the head office to whom they report. And it is especially difficult when a commercial banking and an investment banking business are operating under the same roof, and the pressure for each to succeed is great.

The principal key to success in managing such organizations is recognition of the need for flexibility. All sorts of changes, compromises, and accommodations should be considered acceptable if they work. If an existing structure doesn't work, it should be discarded in favor of one that might. Some organizations, typically large commercial banking organizations that have not experienced the need for major organizational change in many years, may find the result of this flexibility chaotic and disorderly. If so, they will benefit by learning to live with a tolerable amount of chaos. They will certainly hobble their own organization more by insisting on principles and rigidities that no longer represent virtues in the business than they will by letting things get stirred up a bit.

Some other keys for success may include the following:

1. *People management is vital.* In a highly competitive market in which international financial services are sold, the most important roles are played by the individuals assigned to the intersection of geographic and functional roles in the firms. The ability to attract the best people, motivate them, train them to accept greater responsibilities, and develop them into leaders of the firm is critical to the firm's success. Unless this part of the machine is functioning properly, little else will happen right. Unless the right people are tapped to be leaders—of product or service units or of client rela-

tionship teams—the firm's productivity will suffer. To develop the best individuals and get them into the right jobs, it may be necessary to bend the organization to fit the particular people involved. Investment banks have been doing this successfully for years, commercial banks less so.

2. *Getting comfortable with the risk.*   The new and larger exposures to risk that international financial services entail is something to which senior management must become accustomed. Although there are various types of risks involved, most will be unfamiliar to executives who have risen in their firms within one line of business. Investment bankers are reasonably comfortable with market risks, but they are less familiar with credit risks. Commercial bankers may be the reverse. There are system risks, personnel risks, and risks to the firm's reputation that both types of bankers may be untrained to deal with. Unless top-management understands and can be made comfortable with the kinds of risks that top-ranking players must accept every day, it is unlikely that its firm will ever rank among the top players.

3. *Make the operations consistent with the strategy.*   Naturally, it is essential that a sound and workable competitive strategy be devised and implemented. Less obvious, however, is the need to support the strategy operationally. A sufficient number of revenue producers and their supporting personnel must be provided, along with telecommunications equipment, and the necessary amount of capital must be allocated. Equally important, however, accounting and control systems, risk monitoring and performance evaluation systems, and adequate back office and financing facilities to make the operation capable of functioning effectively. Without these often overlooked systems and operational capabilities, it will be difficult if not impossible to know whether the operation is achieving its objectives.

4. *Have realistic expectations.*   The most effective operation needs time to establish itself, even if it is not having to do so by wresting market share away from competitors. Most new undertakings require years to become effective. Expectations of instant results are not realistic. Equally, operations that are excused from high expectations are also unrealistic. The best programs involve a combination of measuring annual progress against management-by-objectives standards, with continuous analysis of how one is doing against the competition. Severe standards for market penetration and excellence can still be maintained and may be more likely to

be achieved if expectations are realistic and made known with a judicious degree of patience.

SUMMARY

There are many different types of organizations, involving different nationalities and cultures, all striving to participate in the same global Financial services businesses. Many different approaches to organization and management issues will be tried. There probably is no right or wrong way, though either can apply to a particular situation at a particular time. Many experiments will be made. Firms will emulate others and be emulated. Through this multinational migration across the newest financial frontiers of all sorts of competitors, however, we can expect to observe convergence. The competitive process, gradually, is making the competitors more alike.

24

Megabanks in the Year 2000?

A popular parlor game among financial people in the mid 1980s was making lists of the top 10 global banks at the end of the century. The presumption, widely accepted, was that globalization of financial markets would draw to the center a handful of banks or financial services firms that would be so much stronger and so much more globally integrated than the others that they would constitute a new financial "oligopoly."

Everyone who was a major player in his home market and who aspired to global prominence in the future had his eye on making the all-world team in the year 2000. The effort to do so would have to be great, and sustained, but the result would be worth it—a market position that could last for generations. With nearly 15 years to go, there was still ample time to catch up or to consolidate one's position among the world's leading fully internationalized financial institutions of the next century.

Many banks and investment banks thought like this in 1987: At least a dozen from the United States, a dozen from Japan, ten or so among the continental giants, five or six from the United Kingdom, perhaps one or two from Hong Kong and Singapore. In addition, there were half a dozen insurance companies from the United States, Europe and Asia that also had their eyes on becoming world-class players in a wide range of financial services.

There were others, too, who appeared interested in securing places for themselves at the top. Industrial corporations with substantial financial activities were looking at the same markets as the banks. Companies such as Ford, General Electric, Volvo, American Express, Sears Roebuck, and BAT Industries already controlled substantial financial assets, provided an extensive array of services, and were looking to expand them further.

Altogether, 60 or 70 serious, apparently qualified candidates for the millennium's financial Olympic games could be identified. Of these, perhaps only 10 or 15 would make it into the oligopoly. The object of the parlor game was to see whom informed observers would tap for the top spots. There was reasonable agreement as to which institutions would be included among the top 20. After that, narrowing down to the top 10 was a matter of individual taste.

In one such survey in 1987, two firms were mentioned for the top ten more often than others—Citicorp and Nomura Securities. In the next tier, those most often named included Deutsche Bank, Salomon Brothers, and Morgan Guaranty. Then came Credit Suisse/CS First Boston and a collection of U.S. investment banks and the other Swiss banks. These were followed by British and continental banks and more Japanese. Out of this crowd, most people thought, would come the megabanks of the twenty-first century.

The players, however, were for the most part predicting the future based on what they knew about the present. The ones picked are basically the global finance oligopoly of today, the market leaders in banking from around the world.

Perhaps there is one thing we can be sure of regarding today's consensus oligopoly for the year 2000—it will be wrong. Fifteen years is a very long time in finance. Over such a long period many unexpected but dramatic things occur that change the ranking of prominent firms.

Two 15-year periods before, in 1957, there was no thought of globalization. The top 10 list would have been the list of the largest banks in the world, which was dominated at the time by American banks and did not have any Japanese on it at all. The most prominent American banks then included Bank of America, Continental Illinois, and Mellon Bank. Securities firms and merchant banks were too insignificant in size to be on the same list with the large commercial banks. If there had been a listing of top securities firms from around the world, which were then not considered significant enough to rank, it would have included only a few U.S. and British houses. The U.S. firms would prove to be an impermanent lot; of the top seventeen investment banks in the United States at the time of the ruling by Judge Harold Medina dismissing the government's antitrust suit against the industry in 1954, only five were still in business under the same name 30 years later.

If the survey had been made 15 years later, in 1972, the American banks would still have been prominent, and the Japanese would still have been absent, but perhaps Merrill Lynch, Morgan Stanley, Warburg, Deutsche Bank, UBS, and Paribas would have been talked about. If the list had been made just a few years later, it might also have included one or more of the London based consortium banks, such as Orion Bank, that had sprung into being for a short time as the best answer to the internationalization of banking. Orion was formed in 1970 by six prominent banks from different countries. It succeeded for a while, but coordination among shareholders became difficult, and in time the individual shareholders became competitors of the consortium. Orion was unwound in 1981 when it was purchased by one of its shareholders, Royal Bank of Canada.

The list in 1989 shows not only the displacement of American banks by European and Japanese banks, it also underscores the rapid rise through the ranks of Nomura Securities, Salomon Brothers, CS First Boston, Goldman Sachs (with or without Sumitomo), and American Express–Shearson Lehman Hutton.

The list of the top 10 or 20 global bankers, in other words, is quite volatile. Perhaps only four or five of the original twenty would have remained on the list throughout the full 30-year period—banks such as Citicorp, Deutsche Bank, Morgan Guaranty, and one or more of the larger Swiss banks.

The list of top bankers in the year 2000 is bound to be as different from the list of 1985 as it and its predecessors were from those taken 15 years before. Already in the few years since 1985, important changes are being registered in the top 10. Since 1985 there were two years of bull markets followed by a sickening crash of the stock markets in 1987 and a volatile recovery thereafter. The dollar sank so low as to render the Euromarket ineffective until its recovery. The United Kingdom had both Big Bang and the crash within a year. The commercial banks made large additions to LDC loan loss reserves only to encounter the Basel Committee's new rules on capital adequacy (see Chapter 26). Some firms, like Nomura, Warburg, and Goldman Sachs have grown bigger and stronger, while others like Salomon Brothers, Merrill Lynch, CS First Boston, and Shearson Lehman Hutton have felt profit pressures or the hot breath of a predator. Ahead lay 1992 in Europe, probable repeal of the U.S. Glass-Steagall Act (and possibly its Japanese cousin, Article 65), further deregulation of markets and commissions in Japan, much more restructuring within the financial services industry, and, no doubt, a further calamity or two somewhere in the global financial marketplace.

The principal requirements for membership in the global top tier, many thought, would be a strong base of profits and capital, a permissive regulatory environment, and the ability to participate in a major capacity in each of the world's capital market centers: New

York, London, and Tokyo. These qualities are unevenly distributed among the world's leading financial service institutions.

U.S. Commercial Banks

The principal U.S. commercial banks understand the globalization trends that are affecting their business quite well. These banks have been operating large units abroad for the past 20 or 30 years. They have networks of branches, contacts with clients, internationally acclimated personnel, and good entrenched positions in the key markets. What they lack so far are the skills of the securities markets into which so much of their clients' business is being driven and the legal authority to participate in the securities business in two of the world's three key arenas.

At home, however, U.S. commercial banks have been taking a pounding. Deregulation has allowed money market funds, savings institutions, credit card companies, and stock brokers to compete with banks for retail business. Their domestic lending business has also been under attack from foreign banks in the United States and from the securities markets.

Securitization became an important factor in the financial services industry during the 1980s. Ever since commercial paper developed into the principal source of short-term unsecured credit for large corporations, the threat to banks of having their corporate lending business displaced by the securities markets has been a serious one. Commercial paper outstandings in the United States grew to exceed $500 billion at the end of 1989; whereas major money center banks made only about $320 billion of commercial loans that same year. At the same time, banks were also losing business to the capital market as high-yield bonds issued by corporations with below investment-grade bond ratings—"junk bonds"—had developed into a $200 billion market. Securities backed by home mortgages and other assets also grew into a very large business in the United States. Securitization was eroding deeply into the mainstream corporate lending business of U.S. banks.

While others were allowed to enter their businesses, the banks were still restricted from expanding across state lines or from entering different financial and nonfinancial service areas by a web of entangling legislation, Federal Reserve regulations, and Comptroller of the Currency and Federal Deposit Insurance Corporation requirements. The domestic banking regulatory base in the United States is confused, changeable, inconsistent and generally hard on the banks. Nor does there appear to be much hope that the mess that represents American banking regulation will be simplified and improved in the near future.

The banks, however, have for years been free to compete in virtually any business outside the United States. Banks have had unrestricted access to the Eurobond business since the beginning. One or two have made names for themselves in this market, but for the most part U.S. commercial banks have been unimpressive in the free-wheeling world of Eurobonds. Banks have suffered from the fact that Eurobonds have been a sideshow business compared to their main lending operations. Their top people in Europe are bankers, not traders. Their operations, the personnel they recruit, their compensation structures, their control systems, everything about their business has reflected its leadership by commercial bankers, with no training in or stomach for aggressive trading practices, position risks or hedging techniques.

Also, by not being able to participate fully in the U.S. capital markets—which after 1984 provided for instant market access through the SEC's Rule 415—the commercial banks were not able to offer the full range of global alternatives to their clients and therefore were distinctly uncompetitive with investment banks for the capital market business of U.S. corporations. Not being able to service the principal companies from their home countries, where their market position and influence with clients was at its highest, was a serious disadvantage.

Unless the banks can escape the chains of Glass-Steagall and orient themselves properly to the capital markets environment that is sure to dominate corporate and governmental financing until the next century, their prospects for being included among the few perched on the financial Mount Olympus of the twenty-first century seem dim. Knowing this, the banks have made a mighty push to encourage Congress to repeal Glass-Steagall in 1988.

It almost succeeded. The banks argued that the law blocked their necessary strategic development. They also argued that respected academic studies had shown the entrance of banks into the securities markets would increase competition, lower fees, and provide better services for issuers, "with small and medium sized companies being the prime beneficiaries of the heightened competition."[1]

It seemed a clear case for repeal: The Treasury was for it. The Federal Reserve was also and became more vocal on the subject after Alan Greenspan replaced Paul Volcker as chairman. And the banks had good academic and free-market arguments supporting their case.

Some observers, however, noted that the banks were much weaker institutions than they had been a few years before. Most of the money-center banks had seen their bond ratings reduced to the extent that in 1989 not one major U.S. bank holding company retains a triple-A Moody's rating, while as recently as 1980, nine had had them. In early 1988, Standard and Poor's downgraded Chase Manhattan's senior debt to A from AA−, Manufacturers Hanover Trust went to BBB from A−, and the Bank of America to BBB− from BBB. These new ratings certainly brought into question the traditional reputation of bankers as being pillars of financial stability and probity. A BBB− rating is only one notch above a junk bond.

Domestic lending difficulties over the past several years had reduced a number of large and important American banks to even humbler circumstances. Banks such as Continental Illinois, Interfirst Republic, and the once proud Mellon Bank, among others, had to be rescued or substantially restructured by the FDIC. If this weren't enough, Third World loans became a more serious problem. Citicorp's May 1987 addition of $3 billion to its loan loss reserves and J. P. Morgan's $2 billion reserve in 1989 forced most other banks with substantial exposures in Latin America to make similar charges. The capital positions of the banks did not look very strong to many in Congress, who at the time were busy working out the rescue of the savings and loan industry in the United States, which some expected would cost the taxpayer upwards of $50 billion.

U.S. banks were probably the hardest hit among all international banks by the BIS' new capital adequacy standards. Though the amounts to be raised are modest in most cases, the profitability of the banks has not been high enough in recent years for retained earnings to fully cover future capital requirements. Meanwhile, market conditions in the United States continue to be unfavorable for the sale of new equity securities by the banks. The BIS capital requirements could become especially burdensome for some U.S. banks, however, if further large charges to loan loss reserves are made for Latin American loans or if a bank wants to invest in new areas, such as the securities industry, where such investments would be subtracted from the bank's core capital.

Some in Congress felt that the banks already had too much on their plates in 1988 to be able to compete in the tough business of investment banking, which, if anything, was yet another capital-intensive business. However much the banks may wish to be free-market operators, they remain regulated financial institutions with the

U.S. Government standing behind their deposits. If things should go wrong, the stability of the U.S. banking system as well as taxpayers' dollars are at stake.

Compromises were offered to keep the focus on getting rid of Glass-Steagall. "Firewalls" were proposed to keep the securities business of the banks and its noninsured financing separate from the banking business. Restrictions were suggested that would prevent banks with insufficient capital from participating in the securities business, and disallow mergers between the largest banks and securities firms. The Senate passed a bill 94–2 in the spring of 1988 that substantially did away with Glass-Steagall. The House Banking Committee passed a bill through committee during the summer of 1988 that gave the banks securities powers, but with many more restrictions than were in the Senate bill. This version was quite disappointing to many commercial bankers. In September, the House Energy and Commerce Committee, whose Telecommunications and Finance Subcommittee was also given a say in the matter, proposed amendments to the Banking Committee's bill that tightened the restrictions further and confused the issue as to which committee in the House had jurisdiction over the legislation.

However, it was very late in the congressional calendar of an election year. Congress recessed in early October, 1988 without passing the repeal of Glass-Steagall. Still, it had been close. The 55-year-old legislation had only barely survived the most effective of many assaults. Surely, however, the matter will be addressed by the next Congress where, among other new arguments, emphasis will be placed on the need to provide reciprocal banking and investment banking privileges to banks operating in the United States in order for U.S. banks to be granted access to the large and important post-1992 European banking market.

In the meantime, banks rely upon the Federal Reserve as their source for further liberalization of the rules restricting banks in the securities area. Chase Manhattan Bank announced that, absent repeal of Glass-Steagall, it would file for permission from the Fed to increase its investment banking activities to 10 percent or more of the business of its securities affiliate and to be permitted to underwrite corporate debt and equity securities.

By the end of 1989, U.S. banks had fallen well behind the leading banks of other countries in terms of the value of their assets. Their domestic losses, their capital constraints and slower growth, and the weakness of the dollar drove even the best of the American banks well down the list in 1989. Citibank fell to eighth place in the assets league table, Chase Manhattan to thirty-third, J. P. Morgan to fifty-fourth, and Bankers Trust to seventy-sixth in the world standings, in which 9 of the top 15 banks were Japanese.

Ranked by an even more demanding standard, the market value of the bank's stockholder's equity at December 1988, the results were somewhat worse. Only five U.S. firms were among the top 100.

The U.S. banks have fallen into a bind. Pressured on one side by increasing competition for their traditional business and on the other by an unsatisfactory regulatory environment, the banks have lost profitability and the ability to raise additional equity capital. Many banks have been forced into mergers; others have mapped out strategies for restructuring their businesses through combinations with banks in other regions or with other banks similar to themselves that would permit greater profitability through economies of scale. As regulatory relief is granted, albeit piecemeal as has been the practice in the United States, further combinations, perhaps even with investment banks, will no doubt be considered. Without restructuring, however, most of today's major U.S. banks will not be in strong enough positions in the future to capture any of the medals.

Japanese Commercial Banking

Japanese banks, by contrast, appeared to be the ascending stars of the global scene, certainly at least in the rankings. These banks, however, suffer from problems similar to those of the U.S. banks.

On the whole, Japanese banks are undercapitalized, but they are not capital constrained; they are much more limited by regulatory factors than by anything else. The Japanese Ministry of Finance exercises exceptionally close control over the banks, with respect both to their permitted activities and new domestic business opportunities in Japan and to all of their activities abroad. They are further constrained by Article 65, which prevents them from competing in Japan with securities firms. The authorities, however, under the constant threat of being denied reciprocal banking privileges abroad, have allowed foreign banks to find back-door entrances to the securities businesses in Japan. Vickers da Costa, a U.K. brokerage firm specializing in Japanese securities that had been acquired by Citicorp, was allowed to continue doing business in Japan after the acquisition and subsequently became a member of the Tokyo Stock Exchange. Several Hong Kong companies that are joint ventures between banks and nonbanking companies have been granted securities licenses in Japan, and some of these, including six European universal banks, have joined the exchange. Japanese banks have still not been allowed such opportunities.

Japanese banks have been prevented by the Ministry of Finance from keeping pace in the securities field abroad. They have been allowed small European merchant banking affiliates but not the freedom to manage underwritings without restriction. With little else to do, the affiliates became big players in the ill-fated floating-rate note and preferred stock market that seized up during 1986 at considerable cost to their parents. The banks barely keep these affiliates afloat now with small participations in Euromarket offerings of Japanese companies.

Though a few Japanese banks in the United States invested in government securities dealers, most stuck to traditional commercial banking in their overseas activities. Here they have been able to acquire significant shares of U.S. and other lending markets because of aggressive pricing practices.

Japanese banks, consequently, own a large quantity of Latin American loans. Although they have not been hobbled by them so far, most of these loans have not been very fully reserved against. The new BIS standards will require most major Japanese banks to seek additional capital. This will not be difficult for them, however, because of their ability to raise large amounts of new equity through the sale of shares in the high-priced Japanese market, and because of the banks' considerable holdings of appreciated real estate and equity securities in other Japanese companies.

Like the U.S. banks, the Japanese seek regulatory relief in order to enhance their ability to compete in the coming world. Financial regulation in Japan, however, is an intricate, interwoven construction that is not easily changed in substantial ways without a consensus among the principal affected parties that can take years to develop. For the time being, though the Japanese banks have access to more funds than they can use in lending and great incentives to enter the globalized securities markets, they are not permitted to do so. They are all dressed up with nowhere to go. Hence investments such as Sumitomo Bank's in Goldman Sachs appear to make sense.

European Banks

European banks approach the year 2000 with a number of strengths and weaknesses in common, plus, of course, the varying individual characteristics of their national backgrounds. Among their common strengths are their secure capital bases, profitable businesses at home that underwrite their continuing stability, and, for many, a long history of international activity and substantial experience in the securities business.

Very few of the major European banks will require additional capital to meet the new BIS standards. Most continental banks have written off most of their Third World exposures, and many have raised additional capital in the markets in the past few years.

Banks in Europe, like those in Japan, have been the subject of regulatory protection through preclusion of competition from sources outside the domestic banking system. Retail money market funds, as they are known in the United States, do not exist widely in Europe. In many European countries, regulators are not unwilling to see large spreads between deposit and lending rates, knowing that the differentials are used to provide profits and strength to the banking system. They know, however, that in the tradeoff they have given up some of the competition, efficiency, innovation and invigoration that might otherwise have entered the banking industry.

Many major European banks, especially British, French, and Dutch banks, have been active abroad since colonial days, and many have extensive overseas branch networks. Continental banks, operating throughout their history as universal banks, have accumulated substantial experience in underwriting and brokerage activities and investment management. In their home countries these banks exert considerable power and influence in corporate boardrooms, in the legislature, and in the markets.

However, after years of being large, powerful, and profitable, many of these banks have grown inefficient, overly centralized, and conservative. Swiss banks, for example, make most of their interest income from lightly competitive domestic lending businesses and most of their fee income from safekeeping and managing investments for foreigners. Many find the risk exposures and the comparatively poor profitability of business abroad to be discouraging. Yet they persevere, knowing that they have to develop their international business, but they are reluctant to delegate all of the authority that their colleagues outside Switzerland may need to be fully competitive. The same is true for many other European commercial banks.

For the same reason, many European banks have been somewhat timid in expanding into areas permitted to them, such as the post–Big Bang market in the U.K. and the U.S. securities markets, where about 15 European banks are grandfathered to conduct both banking and securities activities. Those banks with the right to conduct universal banking in the United States have not extensively exploited the opportunity, although one bank, Credit Suisse, controls a 44.5 percent ownership of CS First Boston, into which First Boston Corporation was merged in December 1988. The pace of change in world financial markets has been much greater so far than the pace at which European banks have reacted to it. Perhaps their unconscious strategy is to play the tortoise in the race with the hare.

The problem for the European banks is the 1992 liberalization. This will have major implications for the larger banks. They will have to both advance into other countries and defend their profitable domestic business from new competition. If domestic banking is truly deregulated in Europe, the ensured domestic preeminence of the large banks may come into question. The banks will have to change, which may be an invigorating, positive experience that enhances competitiveness (and the desire of the banks to become more aggressive globally) or it may not be.

No doubt most European banks will give first priority to getting their 1992-related position straight and worry later about their competitive postures in the United States and Japan. As the steady process of globalization of markets continues, however, banks may find their strong relationships with their clients weakening. Clients all over the world, influenced by the ways of the modern chief financial officer, are already accustomed to look daily for the best deal. Unless the large European banks develop their linkages with financial markets in the United States and Japan while they are reorganizing their businesses in Europe, they may find themselves less competitive than they need to be to satisfy their traditional clients' emerging global requirements long before the year 2000 arrives.

European Merchant Banks

The other type of bank in Europe, the merchant bank, or banque d'affaires, will be affected quite differently by the proposed 1992 reforms. These banks are oriented to the securities businesses—underwriting, brokerage and trading, and merger and other financial advisory services—that are likely to grow with further deregulation and integration within Europe. The problem for them is developing the size and capital base to perform as a global player in the face of tough competition, dangerous markets, and generally low profitability from their basic businesses.

Such a prospect has discouraged many a merchant bank in the United Kingdom from seeking to become a global investment bank. Such firms are scrambling instead to find niches in which they can hope to protect a reputation for excellence that comes from specialization. Others recognize that merchant banks must become U.S.-style integrated investment banks capable of handling all types of market transactions if they are to win the big prizes.

Of all the merchant banks, only a few have attempted to position themselves as U.S.-style integrated firms operating internationally from the outset. Three of these are part of large commercial banks. Two others, Warburg and Kleinwort Benson, have a long history of prominence in investment banking in the United Kingdom. They are both seeking to expand their activities further in Europe, in the United States and in Japan. None of the leading merchant banks has yet developed a heavyweight capability in the United States, nor of course, in Japan. They hope to survive on an international scale as they always have, by living by their wits.

U.S. Investment Banks

U.S. investment banks were among the first to discover and exploit the effects of globalization on the markets. Unlike most U.K. merchant banks and European universal banks, the U.S. firms were in Europe to be salespeople. They had no "captive" accounts in Europe, no in-house placing power. They did not manage major amounts of money in Europe until the early 1980s, when Morgan Stanley was given several billion dollars of Kuwaiti funds to manage.

Their original aim was to help U.S. corporations raise money through the issuance of Eurobonds. They were also active in selling U.S. stocks to clients in Europe. For both purposes they needed sales forces that were aggressive, capable, supported by research and trading capabilities, and which covered every appropriate nook and cranny in Europe, Asia, and the Middle East.

The sales forces gave the firms the contact with the market they needed to be able to come up with the best ideas, the best timing, and the courage to "buy" deals from their clients. The investment banks also were the first to integrate Euromarket and other information into their overall global trading and underwriting activities.

In the late seventies, Saudi Arabia was a major influence on the markets. A high proportion of the Saudi reserves were being invested in U.S. treasuries. Being part of the group of brokers that were servicing the Saudis at the time was an attractive source of trading profits, but more important, being in close contact with the Saudis meant that one knew enough about what they were doing in the markets to position one's trading book accordingly. This meant that a firm trading U.S. government securities in New York would be at a significant disadvantage, relative to its competitors, if it did not know what the Saudis were doing at the time.

Soon after the period of exceptional Saudi activity passed, it became obvious that foreign influences affecting the U.S. government markets would continue to be considerable. After the Saudis, the central banks of various countries became substantial open-market buyers and sellers of treasuries and other securities. Then, of course, came the Japanese era, by which time it was totally clear to everyone that the globalization of securities markets was here to stay.

Indeed, it became clear before long that globalization had affected almost all of the other businesses of U.S. investment banks. They could not represent a company that was for sale without providing the seller a list of possible foreign buyers that should be shown the offering papers. They couldn't advise a buyer as to the price he should offer for a company without knowing who the potential competitors would be in the transaction, including the likely foreign buyers. The same was increasingly becoming true in the real estate field, where Japanese investors in particular had been extremely active.

Institutional investors, especially the pension funds, had by the mid-1980s become convinced of the wisdom of acquiring foreign equities for their portfolios. They were in fact selling U.S. stocks and buying foreign ones. Staying with one's clients when they moved from one market to another had always been a fundamental business practice of most brokerage firms. Now the firms would have to become competent suppliers of international securities as well as of domestic ones.

By moving quickly—something investment banks are traditionally good at doing—the U.S. firms were able to occupy some of the high ground in the early days of globalized securities markets. But this progress was probably achieved at much greater cost than any of the firms expected at the time.

Their expansion was explosive, occurring simultaneously in London, Frankfurt, Zurich, Toronto, and Tokyo. Overheads went virtually out of control. All of the firms had hired large numbers of new employees at the same time, competing with each other in the employment market and running compensation to unprecedented levels. Many of these new people would take several years to become productive members of the teams they had joined. Others never would, either because there was no system for properly training new people, or because they would leave to join a competitor before they had contributed very much to the business. Offices were filling with expatriates, especially experienced hands from New York, who were far more expensive to maintain abroad than locals. Also, the back offices had to expand radically; new and larger computer systems, more operations personnel, and more space in budget-busting London and Tokyo were needed. And after 1985, the collapse of the dollar added considerable foreign exchange cost to all the rest.

Early in 1987 it became evident that the firms could not continue to expand at the same pace of the past few years. Slowed expansion, and indeed some retraction, was necessary. Repairs necessitated by the rapid advance would have to be made, or the firms would lose too much money. Layoffs began, efficiencies were pursued. Cost control finally had its turn.

The experience, however, made several things clear. The blind rush into new territories had made much less net progress than had been thought at the time. A more gradual, tortoiselike approach might have been a better alternative. Management competence and control are vital in securities operations, mainly in setting priorities and directing traffic. There are many international temptations that look good to the newly arrived New Yorker, but that, he later learns, should have been avoided.

Most U.S. firms, however, have not backed away from their commitment to globalizing their businesses at all. The speed of advance has been slowed across the board by tough competitive and cost conditions, but it will surely resume. The investment banks, though gradually becoming larger, more bureaucratic institutions, still manage their businesses on a much more immediate, ad hoc basis than do more traditional banking institutions. This makes the investment banks much more opportunistic and responsive to changing market and competitive conditions than others. However, they may still be too transaction driven and chaotic to install the cost management systems that they must have if they are to rise to become part of a future oligopoly. Short of that important requirement, however, they perhaps have a head start over the other types of banks in assimilating global financial conditions and performing effectively in markets outside of their home country.

Investment banks also have become quite large on an absolute basis and now appear to possess the scale needed to be major players on a global basis. As of the end of 1989, four of the ten largest U.S. investment banks had total assets in excess of $40 billion, and one, Shearson Lehman Hutton, had total assets in excess of $70 billion. At the rate at which investment banks have been increasing their capital and their leverage—and therefore their total assets—it is likely that within a few years the top 10 U.S. investment banks will show more assets on their balance sheets than will the top 10 commercial banks. The same would also be true for assets managed by the firms. Shearson Lehman alone manages more than $100 billion of assets for others.

Japanese Securities Firms

Japanese securities firms are different from all others. They are enormously profitable: Each of the "big four" firms earned more than $1.8 billion before tax in 1989. The most profitable U.S. firm earned less than half that amount. The firms are well capitalized: The smallest of the four had capital in excess of $5 billion at the end of 1989, more than all but two U.S. firms. They are also well valued by the market: Nomura's market capitalization alone exceeded $50 billion at year end 1988, more than the market value of all the major U.S. securities firms put together.

Such financial power makes these Japanese firms intimidating, but they really have not used much of it so far. Though there are some government regulations in place that might restrict their freedom of action, so far the securities firms have not acquired other international firms or (with a few exceptions) top professionals from such other firms. They have bought a few deals as lead manager from non-Japanese companies in Europe and in the United States, but almost all of their market power comes from handling Japanese transactions.

Their great size and profitability comes from their domestic business. The Japanese stock exchanges still maintain fixed commission rates. Profitable retail transactions are the major part of Japanese stock market activity, which now exceeds the trading volume of the New York Stock Exchange. The big four firms dominate the primary and secondary markets and cannot fail to earn prodigious profits.

Overseas, the Japanese firms are leading the league tables in the Eurobond market because of the large volume of Japanese debt and equity issues and because of the low volume in the non-Japanese dollar sector of the market. The Japanese firms have developed other capabilities in the Euromarkets and they are by no means limited to just Japanese business. However, the new issue business that they do now puts them at the top of the market share tables. Without it their rankings would be much less impressive.

While selling Japanese shares to foreigners, the firms also developed the capability to underwrite and distribute new issues of Japanese securities internationally. During the last 10 years more issues of securities have been made by Japanese companies in the Euromarket than by companies from any other country, by a large margin. Most of these issues were brought to Europe to avoid stringent new-issue queuing and pricing regulations in the domestic Japanese market. Currently, with large financial surpluses, Japanese investors have been the principal purchasers of Japanese Euroissues. These issues are basically domestic capital market issues that detour through Europe to avoid the technicalities of issuing at home.

Handling all of these new issues, which Japanese securities firms invariably do, has been both profitable and educational for the Japanese houses. This has prepared them to underwrite and distribute non-Japanese securities. Much, but not all, of such distributions are to investors in Japan that, like the Saudis of a decade earlier, all major issuers want to be able to reach. With investors and issuers from Japan both exceptionally active, the securities firms have become extremely visible.

The Japanese firms, however, suffer from some of the difficulties of the European banks: With profits so easy to make and the Japanese-related business so abundant, why do anything else? The firms are not risk takers, except in isolated cases, nor do they have to be. They are not especially creative—most of the innovations and new securities in the Eurobond market are introduced by non-Japanese firms. Nor are they especially efficient. It is generally understood that most Japanese securities firms' overseas operations lose money and always have, despite their continuous flow of profitable business. The offices are usually overstaffed and spend large amounts on entertaining a continuous flow of Japanese visitors.

In the last few years these firms have begun to hire senior personnel from among experienced financial people in the countries in which they have operations. These people, however, are never made part of the top management of the firms' Japanese parents, nor do they visit Japan often or impart their advice to colleagues in Tokyo with much effect. The firms remain totally Japanese in their global outlook. Very few decisions are made at the local level; everything has to be passed back to Tokyo where decisions are finally taken, according to Japanese consensual practice.

In the long run, Japanese securities firms face dangers from deregulation of their domestic business, especially the end of fixed commission rates, from the exclusion of banks from the securities business, and from more competitive and efficient capital markets in Japan that will preclude the need for Euromarket round-tripping by issuers of securities.

Perhaps they will also face the more distant dangers of being required to provide the same level of performance-enhancing services for their clients that U.S. and some European bankers do. Such services as block trading, off-the-shelf underwriting and providing first-rate research and support activities will someday be demanded by Japanese corporate and investor clients. Japanese firms do not provide such services today. Their emphasis is on service and loyalty to clients, not on price and objectivity. They are used to having their clients do as they say. The swing from relationship banking to transactional relationships could be very traumatic for some of the Japanese securities firms.

Of course these firms are quick learners and by nature extremely competitive. They are likely to adjust as the times change and to use their formidable wealth to good effect by acquiring major firms in other countries and hiring teams of people to make them run well. For the moment, however, this is not the Japanese way and therefore it won't happen.

Requirements for Success

To succeed in the coming environment of the twenty-first century, global banking firms will have to be competitive, above all. The freshest ideas, the best rates, and the quickest executions will be what matters most to the clients, who are themselves under increasing pressure to demonstrate that they are performing their jobs well in comparison to their competitors.

To be competitive, firms will have to be prepared to find the best ideas from all over the world and to be willing to risk their own capital as part of the process of serving the client. The business will be risky, and some firms will fail or be displaced in the ranks of the leaders by others. There will be a premium value placed on firms that are large and strong enough to recover from losses or mistakes and on firms that have grown wiser from their international experiences. There will also be a premium, as there usually is, on good management, solid business judgment, and sensible strategic thinking.

No one can be all things to all clients. None of the potential leaders of the year 2000 is yet so global in scope and competence that it could hope to provide all services equally well. The mighty Europeans are still ill-equipped to handle competitive capital market services in the United States and Japan. The long-dominant American banks have been battle-weakened by poor quality loans, domestic regulation, and competition from the securities markets. The Japanese banks are still tied too closely to the home market and too tied up by regulation to have become effective in any business but lending. U.S. investment banks are just beginning to learn what it takes to compete on a world scale, but may lack management ability and staying power when times are tough. Japanese securities firms are still too heavily dependent on Japanese business to compete on equal grounds in Europe and America. The nonbanking financial institutions are maneuvering, but haven't yet committed themselves to the battle.

SUMMARY

The odds are that there will not be a global financial services oligopoly in the year 2000, at least not any more so than there is one now. The parlor game played 10 years hence will no doubt result—as does the same game played today—in a selection of the leading banks and securities firms from each of the major regions. These institutions will still derive the bulk of their business, their profits, and their claims to fame from their domestic prominence. They will not likely be the same ones on today's list, however. The increasingly cruel and unforgiving requirement to perform competitively will drop some well-known names into the great realm of mediocrity. Others— aggressive, determined, and probably lucky—will find their way into the top ranks.

It is ever thus in free markets. It appears that one legacy of the turbulent 1980s will be freer markets in the twenty-first century; we can expect exciting times and bountiful opportunities but also many slippery and hazardous roads ahead.

NOTES

1. Pugel and White, p. 130

SELECTED REFERENCES

Carson-Parker, John. "Tomorrow's Superbanks." *Global Finance*, November 1987.

Lascelles, David. "Specialize if you are not a Global Player." *Financial Times,* Sept. 26, 1988.

Pugel, Thomas A., and Lawrence J. White. "An Analysis of the Competitive Effects of Allowing Commercial Bank Affiliates to Underwrite Corporate Securities." In *Deregulating Wall Street,* edited by Ingo Walter. New York: John Wiley and Son, 1985.

V

Public Policy Issues

25

Financial Deregulation and Reregulation

The principal aim of this book has been to convey an impression of the workings of the international financial services industry—its structure, conduct, and performance as they affect strategies and tactics of suppliers and users of investment banking and commercial banking products. There is, of course, an important regulatory dimension as well. This is not an industry where *laissez faire* is the order of the day. The industry has important characteristics of a public utility: It can create significant social benefits and social evils over and above those accruing to those directly involved—namely shareholders, creditors, employees, managers, and customers. The fact that what happens in banking and finance usually has much broader economic and social implications ensures that society, through governmental structures, will take a keen interest in its workings, sometimes for good and sometimes for ill. It is also clear that there are important regulatory distinctions between domestic and offshore financial activities, if only for the fact that a government's regulatory reach usually stops at its borders.

This chapter considers the broad issues of regulation and public policy toward the financial services industry, while Chapter 26 focuses specifically on the critical issue of capital adequacy as a determinant of financial stability in this industry.

The first issue involves onshore, or domestic, markets for financial services that are fully subject to domestic supervisory, regulatory, and monetary policy controls. Whether and how foreign-based financial institutions may compete in onshore markets is strictly a matter for national political decisions. When domestic institutions are systematically protected from outside competition, they are frequently highly profitable. But they can also use that "artificial" profitability to cross-subsidize the penetration of other markets for financial services. These may also be relatively uncompetitive and inefficient by international standards.

The second issue involves offshore markets for financial services that are substantially beyond the reach of national authorities. They include Eurocurrency and Eurobond markets, along with the peripheral financial services that complete the Eurocredit business. These are largely untaxed, unregulated, and highly efficient markets—in both static and dynamic terms—in which any number can play. While it seems fair to say that such characteristics have exposed the international economic and financial system to certain risks from time to time (some of them serious), offshore markets nevertheless set standards of performance in financial efficiency against which all other financial markets must be measured.

It is important to recall that the Eurobond market and more recently the Euroequity market are the outcomes of confused and often muddled behavior on the part of national regulators since the 1960s. Authorities in EC member nations were unable to agree, for example, on the establishment of an integrated European capital market in fulfillment of their obligations under the Treaty of Rome until 1990. Individual national authorities permitted increasing freedom of capital movement, yet excluded foreign borrowers and issuers from their national capital markets and drove them offshore. As capital markets moved offshore in the 1960s and 1970s, there were successively fewer reasons for returning to the various national markets as regulations were liberalized.

These same considerations ought to apply to the broader context as well. The highly developed state of the Euromarkets and the deregulated state of most of the major onshore markets (Japan, the United States, and the United Kingdom) have threatened to turn some of the banking centers of other countries in Europe, Asia, and Latin America into financial backwaters. Unless they too deregulate and permit world-class players to operate in their markets, value added in the process of capital allocation will move abroad—particularly as it affects the prime names among borrowers and issuers. Equally, they must afford their own financial institutions adequate opportunity to compete in international markets that are appropriate to their specific clients and product strengths.

The global environment for the provision of financial services has been and continues to be complex—and, in recent years, subject to rapid change. Shifts in the pattern and volume of international trade, protectionist trends, regional economic integration, changing exchange-rate regimes, and balance-of-payments measures, as well as general monetary and fiscal policies, have telling effects on the industry both in the short term and over longer periods of time. Perhaps more than most others, firms dealing in financial services need to react quickly and decisively to perceived threats and opportunities. Competitive success or failure hinges to an extraordinary degree on the value of information and on being able to move faster and more accurately than the competition.

MEASURES OF MONETARY CONTROL

Firms in the business of financial services are to a significant extent constrained in terms of competitive behavior within the context of onshore financial systems. Certain common patterns are apparent in the way these systems have evolved. The most obvious is the integration of banks and other firms providing financial services into the formation and execution of national monetary and fiscal policies, as well as balance-of-payments policies. The tools of monetary control range from "sledge-hammer" techniques such as changes in reserve requirements and mandatory asset ratios, open-market purchases and sales of securities by the central bank or monetary authority, and moral suasion, to rather selective credit controls such as margin requirements on borrowings against securities purchases, limits on loans to certain sectors, ceilings on deposit and lending rates, and "corset" restrictions limiting the expansion of loans. Within an overall policy, financial institutions also carry a fiduciary responsibility: They hold assets in trust, as it were, for depositors and investors.

Profitability in the financial services industry depends on astute management of assets and liabilities that often entail very high leverage ratios; the acceptance of carefully controlled interest-rate, exchange-rate, and liquidity risks; imaginative design and marketing of fee-earning services; and the resolution of agency problems in carrying out satisfactorily the wishes of the ultimate holders of the assets with which they are dealing.

All of these characteristics have combined to make financial services at the national level a "sensitive" industry, both as a central vehicle for the implementation of economic policy and as an industry subject to collective crises and failures by individual firms. The history of the United States, for example, records well over 15,000 bank failures—5,000 during the Great Depression of the 1930s alone and an average of well over 100 during the 1980s.

Mismanagement or outright fraud have left prominent names like Banco Ambrosiano, Bank Bumiputra, Credit Suisse, Franklin National, Herstatt, Schroder Munchmeyer Hengst, Seafirst, and Continental Illinois among the failed or seriously damaged in recent years. Others, such as BankAmerica, have seen their competitive standing seriously impaired, at least for a while. The $150 billion taxpayer bailout of the U.S. thrift industry in 1988–89 was nothing short of a national scandal, although its political fallout fell far short of what would have happened in the face of a comparable scandal in other areas of public life. And with close interinstitution financial links, a crisis for one player can quickly become a crisis for many, producing negative externalities that subsequently result in damage to depositors, commerce and industry, and to the economy at large.

PRUDENTIAL CONTROL

Governments are well aware of the inherent risks and potential conflicts involved in national and international banking, securities underwriting, and trading and dealing in financial instruments, foreign exchange, precious metals, and the like. Most notably in banking, these risks focus on the solvency of borrowers and the liquidity of institutions that are highly geared. Banking crises always carry with them negative externalities: damage imposed on individuals and institutions outside the firms directly involved and, in some cases, outside the industry itself. It is conventional wisdom that major banking crises can lead to severe damage to employment, income, economic growth, and related goals of society.

In order to protect themselves against such adverse external consequences, therefore, countries have built elaborate "safety net" systems that are designed to provide liquidity to institutions in trouble, insure depositors, and sometimes bail out borrowers to help the bank maintain solvency. The operation of domestic financial safety nets invariably creates problems of efficiency and fairness; for example, how to distinguish between institutions that are TBTF (too big to fail) and those TSTS (too small to save) and how to neutralize competitive distortions that may result from people's expectations about the operation of the safety net. Even more important, the existence of a safety net creates potential "moral hazard" problems where managers of financial institutions, knowing that they are likely to be bailed out, will behave in a less risk-averse manner and thus impose substantial contingent liabilities on those who hold up the safety net—the taxpayers and the general public.

To cope with this problem, and to ensure the safety and stability of national financial systems, governments apply various techniques of financial surveillance and control, ranging from careful bank examination procedures, reserve requirements, mandatory asset ratios, and maximum lending limits to risk-related deposit insurance premiums, disclosure provision, securities laws, and moral suasion. Countries deal with this problem in different ways. Some simply nationalize all or major parts of the domestic financial services industry. Regulation and control usually damage the efficiency of the domestic financial system, but this loss in efficiency can be considered as something of an "insurance premium" and is usually considered to be more than offset by the resulting gain in the safety and stability of the system. Figure 25–1 summarizes the financial safety net that, in one form or another, typically provides stability to national financial systems.

Problems arise, however, when national financial institutions take some of their activities offshore into the Euromarkets and foreign markets. Though home countries are supposed to regulate offshore branches and host countries are supposed to regulate subsidiaries and other affiliates, the effectiveness of government regulation and control with regard to these activities remains the subject of intense debate. The oil shocks of 1973 and 1979, dramatic changes in the monetary policies of the United States and rising real rates of interest beginning in 1979, the severe recession of the early 1980s, and economic mismanagement on the part of borrowers along with intense competitive pressures in offshore lending and gaps in risk/return assessments of financial institutions all combined to produce the international banking crisis that began in 1982. The stability of the international financial system as a whole was called into question, while holders of assets began a mass "flight to quality."

As central banks and other government authorities sought to stabilize the system through direct, bilateral financial infusions to countries in trouble, short-term lending by the Bank for International Settlements (BIS), and increases in the lending resources of the International Monetary Fund (IMF), the inevitable question of regulation and control of offshore financial activities arose. Legislation, such as the United States International Lending Supervision Act of 1983, has been enacted, and tighter cooperation among national regulatory authorities has been sought.

While the precise design of an *international* financial safety net that goes beyond the moral obligation of governments to extend their support to offshore problems of domestic financial institutions remains in doubt, any such arrangement will certainly entail greater regulation and control on the part of national authorities and, thus, an erosion of efficiency in the delivery of offshore financial services. Spreads

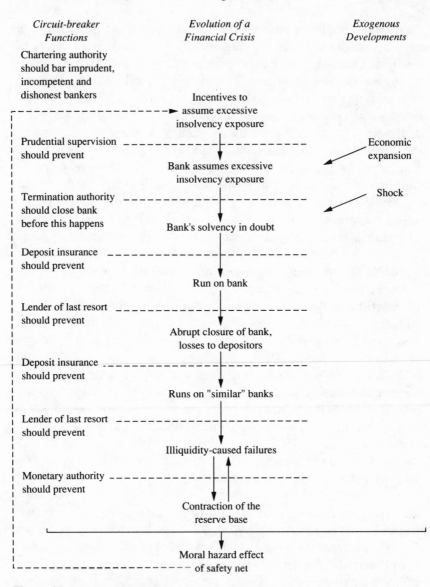

Circuit-breaker Functions	Evolution of a Financial Crisis	Exogenous Developments

Chartering authority should bar imprudent, incompetent and dishonest bankers

Incentives to assume excessive insolvency exposure

Prudential supervision should prevent

Bank assumes excessive insolvency exposure

Economic expansion

Termination authority should close bank before this happens

Bank's solvency in doubt

Shock

Deposit insurance should prevent

Run on bank

Lender of last resort should prevent

Abrupt closure of bank, losses to depositors

Deposit insurance should prevent

Runs on "similar" banks

Lender of last resort should prevent

Illiquidity-caused failures

Monetary authority should prevent

Contraction of the reserve base

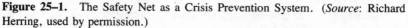

Moral hazard effect of safety net

Figure 25–1.   The Safety Net as a Crisis Prevention System.   (*Source*: Richard Herring, used by permission.)

between what borrowers pay and what savers receive will tend to widen, and financial innovation will be impaired. Whether another major oil shock in the 1990s and the accompanying need for financial recycling can again be absorbed by the offshore activities of financial institutions can only be conjectured. Such adverse implications have to be regarded as a price to be paid for greater financial stability.

Whether financial regulation is in some sense optimal and the cost of regulation therefore minimized is arguable. Characteristics of financial efficiency in the larger, unregulated offshore markets can often yield useful insights into the nature and magnitude of these losses in efficiency in individual domestic regulatory arrangements, and periodic offshore crises can indicate the nature and magnitude of some of the benefits of a more controlled domestic financial environment.

Regulation of Country Exposure and Portfolio Allocation

A good example of regulatory response in international banking involved cross-border credit exposures—a central issue distinguishing international from domestic banking, as discussed in Chapter 19. With the rapid growth in international banks' country exposures during the 1970s came increasing concern on the part of the regulatory and supervisory authorities that sound banking practice be maintained, including adequate information on exposure to country risk, its assessment, and its implications for portfolio diversification and loan pricing. This general concern was amplified by the size of bank lending to particular non-oil-producing developing countries. Figure 25–2 indicates the exposure of a number of international banks in several of these countries, in total and as a percent of bank capital.

In terms of the discussion in Chapter 15 the regulatory function on the part of supervisory authorities in this case focuses exclusively on the expected value of interest and principal recovery and its variance—usually with reference to potential impairment of bank capital—without regard to the other types of returns that are relevant to bank portfolio decisions. One might therefore envision a scenario whereby influence of regulators on bank lending decisions could well move them *away from* efficient international loan portfolios, particularly given that different banks have different sets of returns, access to information, perceptions of risk, and risk preferences. In the process, certain borrowers could be closed out of international credit markets who would otherwise have continued access. U.S. bank regulators have moved toward a uniform system of segregating country risks from other lending risks and dealing with them separately in their bank examination reports. The emphasis has been on diversification of country exposure within a bank's international loan portfolio based on capital ratios and on an assessment of the bank's own country analysis and monitoring capabilities. This supervisory aspect necessitated

Figure 25-2. Developing Country Loan Exposure of Major International Banks, 31 December 1988

	Gross Exposure	Pct. of Equity	Reserve Coverage	Net Exposure	Pct. of Equity	U.S. $ Exposure (in Millions)
Australia (Australian dollars in millions) [a]						
Westpac	A$ 275	5%	41%	A$161	3%	US$ 220
National Australia	–	0	–	–	0	0
ANZ Banking Group	1,331	36	41	786	21	1,065
Total	A$1,606	12%	41%	A$947	7%	US$1,285
Canada (Canadian dollars in millions) [b]						
Bank of Montreal	C$ 4,733	119%	42%	C$2,755	69%	US$ 3,944
Canadian Imperial	1,614	32	52	770	15	1,345
National Bank	1,305	75	40	783	45	1,088
Royal Bank	4,551	81	50	2,278	40	3,793
Scotiabank	4,013	116	45	2,257	64	3,419
Toronto-Dominion	370	9	45	204	5	308
Total	C$16,676	69%	46%	C$9,047	38%	US$13,897
France (French francs in millions)						
Banque Indosuez	Ffr 7,000	73%	40%	Ffr 4,179	44%	US$ 1,156
Bq. Nat. de Paris	43,000	156	52	20,640	75	7,102
Groupe Paribas	14,000	39	47	7,420	21	2,312
Banque Paribas	11,640	109	47	6,170	58	1,922
Credit Agricole	3,200	13	61	1,250	5	528

706

Cr. Ind. et Comm.	3,700	37	47	1,976	20	611
Cr. Comm. de France	5,186	89	47	2,749	47	856
Credit Lyonnais	37,000	168	51	18,270	83	6,111
Societe Generale	31,910	136	53	15,011	64	5,270
Total	Ffr144,996	91%	51%	Ffr71,495	45%	US$23,946
Italy (Lire in billions)						
Bca. Comm. Italiana	Lit 630	14%	50%	Lit 315	7%	US$ 488
Bca. Naz. del Lavoro	1,414	37	37	889	23	1,096
Ist. Ban. San Paolo	196	4	53	92	2	152
Credito Italiano	432	13	30	302	9	335
Total	Lit2,672	17%	40%	Lit1,598	10%	US$2,071
Japan (Yen in billions)[a]						
Bank of Tokyo	¥ 664	98%	15%	¥ 564	84%	US$ 5,008
Dai-Ichi Kangyo	339	26	15	288	22	2,557
Fuji Bank	329	24	15	280	20	2,485
Ind. Bk. of Japan	262	23	15	223	19	1,977
Mitsubishi Bank	339	26	15	288	22	2,558
Mitsui Bank	131	18	15	111	15	988
Sanwa Bank	300	26	15	255	22	2,264
Sumitomo Bank	380	30	15	323	25	2,868
Total	¥2,743	31%	15%	¥2,332	26%	US$20,705
Spain (Pesetas in billions)						
Banco Popular	P1	1%	84%	P0	0%	US$10
Banco Santander	–	0	–	–	0	0
Total	P1	1%	84%	P0	0%	US$10

(continued)

Figure 25-2. (cont.)

	Gross Exposure	Pct. of Equity	Reserve Coverage	Net Exposure	Pct. of Equity	U.S. $ Exposure (in Millions)
Switzerland (Swiss francs in millions)						
Credit Suisse	Sfr3,000	42%	35%[d]	Sfr1,950	27%	US$1,995
Swiss Bank Corp.	2,400	26	50[d]	1,200	13	1,596
Union Bank of Switz.	4,040	40	75	1,010	10	2,686
Total	Sfr9,440	36%	56%	Sfr4,160	16%	US$6,277
United Kingdom (Pounds in millions)[c]						
Barclays	£ 1,988	30%	48%	£1,028	16%	US$ 3,081
Lloyds Bank	4,185	130	44	2,359	73	6,487
Midland Bank	4,785	172	50	2,371	85	7,417
National Westminster	2,800	46	48	1,454	24	4,340
Total	£13,758	74%	48%	£7,212	39%	US$21,325
United States ($ in millions)[c]						
Bank of New York	US$ 2,225	73%	US$ 540	US$ 1,686	55%	US$ 2,225
Bankers Trust NY	3,900	151	995	2,905	81	3,900
Chase Manhattan	7,300	142	1,900	5,400	105	7,300
Chemical Banking	5,732	141	1,246	4,486	110	5,732

Citicorp	11,600	111	2,600	9,000	86	11,600
Manufacturers Hanover	8,000	232	1,480	6,520	189	8,000
J. P. Morgan & Co.	4,500	75	1,020	3,480	57	4,500
Republic NY Corp.	388	27	130	258	18	388
Bank of Boston Corp.	800	36	263	537	24	800
First Chicago	1,866	72	784	1,082	42	1,866
Money Center Composite	US$46,311	139%	US$10,957	US$35,353	84%	US$46,311
West Germany (Deutschemarks in millions)						
Commerzbank	DM 6,300	119%	37%	DM3,938	34%	US$ 3,552
Deutsche Bank	5,200	40	77	1,196	9	2,932
Dresdner Bank	7,634	99	50	3,817	49	4,304
Total	DM19,134	73%	53%	DM8,951	34%	US$10,789

a. As of March 31, 1989.

b. As of July 31, 1989.

c. As of June 30, 1989.

d. Minimum standard that the bank has confirmed that it exceeds; actual coverage is probably higher.

SOURCE: Various.

agreement by the U.S. regulatory authorities in November 1978 on a uniform country risk screening procedure for use by bank examiners. The agreement took the form of a joint effort by the Federal Reserve System, the Comptroller of the Currency, and the Federal Deposit Insurance Corporation.

The regulatory approach uses a nine-member committee of international bank examiners of the three supervisory authorities meeting several times each year to reach a consensus on the riskiness of exposure in selected countries based on a set of "briefing notes" generated by Federal Reserve economists in New York and Atlanta. These notes are prepared in a three-stage process: (1) There is an initial "screening" of some 80 countries on the basis of a limited number of reasonably current and readily available quantitative measures, such as the debt-service ratio, and an identification of countries falling above and below the sample median. (2) A "priority list" is drawn up of countries regularly showing up at or above the sample median, plus individual countries suggested by the international examiners' committee or through special situations identified by the Federal Reserve economists themselves. (3) A detailed country analysis is developed for the "priority" countries, which focuses on prospective debt-service capabilities and the various sources of internal and external strengths and weaknesses, political factors, competence of economic management, and adaptability to changing economic circumstances. The quality of these assessments is probably no better or worse than those of the major money-center banks, and the lack of continuous Federal Reserve "presence" in the individual target countries or day-to-day contact may be in part offset by superior information about them from official sources. The detailed country studies are distilled into a uniform briefing format jointly developed with the examiners, which stresses the perceived risks of reschedulings or other debt-service problems *relative to the other countries in the sample*. The emphasis on relative assessment of risks appears to be based on countries' anticipated access to financial markets if and when extensive refinancing of external debt is required.

The written briefings and oral supplements form the basis of "comments" in bank examination reports and, perhaps more important, of the examiners' discussions with senior bank management. Although the purpose of the exercise is explicitly *not* to preclude certain countries from additional U.S. bank lending or to suggest "superior" international loan portfolios, the inherent "second-guessing" function of the examination process may well affect bank exposure decisions and the allocation of international credit. There is the undeniable advantage of forcing the less well managed banks to conduct independent country monitoring in order to justify individual exposures and to pay careful attention to risks and returns in prudent international lending. But beyond this, aversion of banks to having particular country exposures subject to "listing" or "comment" in examination reports may well drive them away from desired loan portfolios that still meet acceptable standards of risk from a public-policy point of view. This may involve implicit imposition of the supervisory authorities' own views of appropriate risk and diversification patterns on banks' management of international loan portfolios.

The United States has played a leading role in making country assessment an integral part of the bank examination process. Regulators in other nations today likewise make distinctions among international lending risks pertaining to different countries, although in the past they relied almost entirely on uniform capital-asset ratios. Supervisory pressure on banks to develop defensible, independent country assessment and monitoring systems has likewise become in evidence outside the United States, and there is often a good deal of moral suasion present in the informal discussions between banks and their supervisory authorities, an important part of the regulatory process in a number of countries. Clearly, international differences in the supervisory function, as it embodies elements of country risk, potentially influence both the flow of international credit and competitive relationships in international banking.

An interesting example occurred as early as October 1979, when the Japanese Ministry of Finance clamped an embargo on further overseas foreign currency lending by Japanese banks, exempting only export credits and loans for energy imports. The authorities apparently feared the vulnerability of the banks, 80 percent funded in the interbank market, to a repetition of the 1974 Euromarket credit squeeze. A return of the Japanese banks to the market in June of 1980 was accompanied by ceilings on Euroloans, American-type lending limits, and far sharper surveillance—to the point, apparently, of imposing Ministry of Finance judgments on loan size and borrower qualifications.

There has been some movement toward achieving a degree of international regulatory uniformity with respect to country exposure. The supervisory authorities in the United States have pushed hard to expand and refine data on cross-border exposure of American banks, and to some extent this has been paralleled by similar improvements elsewhere, including international efforts to compile and publish the relevant data. For instance, the Bank for International Settlements (BIS) has assembled a great deal of information on country debt and provides guidance for national supervisory authorities on how to interpret it. The consensus seems to be that authorities should apply bank supervision on a consolidated balance sheet basis, as is done in the United States. Generally, the view took hold that, even though foreign subsidiaries are legally independent entities, in case of debt-service problems the liabilities would nevertheless fall due to the parent bank. Both Switzerland and the United Kingdom moved in this direction, for example. There is, however, no consensus on formal, systematic guidelines for diversification of loan portfolios exposed to country risk.

Besides the supervisory role at the national level, there is the possibility that country risk evaluations on the part of international organizations may influence the management of loan portfolios by international banks. Among the international institutions concerned with this issue are the Bank for International Settlement; the Institute for International Finance (a private organization set up after the onset of the debt crisis by the banks themselves); the Berne Union, which focuses on government export credit guarantees; and the so-called Paris Club, which is involved in rescheduling official debt of countries in trouble. All are concerned one way or another with assessment of country risk. While no direct links yet exist, attitudes emerging in such forums have the potential of influencing bank regulators at the national level and, through them, bank exposure management decisions.

Of possibly greater importance are the International Monetary Fund and, to a lesser extent, the World Bank, which maintain detailed country evaluations used in their respective decisions on balance of payments and project financing. While these assessments are nominally confidential, important elements are available to member governments, and there is the possibility that IMF opinion will gradually add a certain degree of uniformity to bank-lending decisions via the IMF's links to national regulators as well as its "stamp of approval" on country plans. A strong argument can be made for the widest possible dissemination of data collected and analyzed by international institutions. But this hardly justifies, on either technical competence or portfolio grounds, undue influence of IMF staff assessments of country risk on the private banks' international lending decisions.

At the same time, in actual or potential problem situations there is great value in coordinated lending by the IMF and the banks, assuming reasonably thoughtful application of IMF conditionality. If the problems are serious enough, the banks are naturally more than anxious to have a country approach the IMF and often await the outcome of such negotiations before committing themselves to further financing. Indeed, additional bank loans may depend on successful discussions with the IMF, and drawdowns of such facilities may be tied to the borrower's observance of conditions attached to parallel drawings on its IMF standby facility. In this way, added weight can be given to the IMF's influence in pressing for effective adjustment and economic discipline in deficit countries, while the implicit value of the bank's exposed assets is supported. Such parallelism, however,

Table 25–1. Inspection of Foreign Establishments' Returns

Country	Methods Used for Verification of Domestic Banks' Establishments Abroad [a]	Country's Attitude toward Direct Inspection by Parent Authorities [a]
Australia	na	na
Austria	A	na
Belgium	A + H	Allowed (R)
Canada	H A	na
Denmark	H	Allowed (R)
Finland	H	Forbidden
France	H	Forbidden by law (1980)
West Germany	A	Allowed (R)
Greece	na	na
Iceland	na	na
Ireland	I	Allowed (R)
Italy	H	Allowed (R)
Japan	na	na
Luxembourg	H + A	Forbidden
Netherlands	H (R)	Allowed
New Zealand	na	na
Norway	na	na
Portugal	I	Allowed
Spain	H + A	Allowed (R)
Sweden	na	na
Switzerland	A	Forbidden by law
Turkey	na	na
United Kingdom	A	Allowed
United States	I	Allowed

a. The following codes are used in this table: na = not available; I = on-site inspection; H = head-office inspection; A = external auditors; and R = based on reciprocity.

SOURCE: R. M. Pecchioli, "The International of Banking" (Paris: OECD Secretariat, 1983).

has so far appeared only in serious problem situations. Its extension to ordinary country lending situations could superimpose IMF country assessments on the private banks, distorting loan portfolios by influencing risk perceptions and affecting the direction and volume of international bank lending.

Table 25–2. Inspection of Foreign Establishments' Returns

Country	Solvency	Liquidity	Risk Concentration	Currency Exposure
Australia	na	na	na	na
Austria	yes	—	—	—
Belgium	yes	*b*	yes	*b*
Canada	yes	yes	yes	yes
Denmark	yes	yes *a*	yes	yes *a*
Finland	yes	yes	—	—
France	yes	—	yes	—
West Germany *c*	*a*	—	*a*	*b*
Greece	na	na	na	na
Iceland	na	na	na	na
Ireland	yes	yes	—	—
Italy	*b*	—	—	—
Japan	yes	yes	yes	—
Luxembourg *d*	yes	yes	yes	yes
Netherlands	yes	—	yes	yes
New Zealand	na	na	na	na
Norway	na	na	na	na
Portugal	—	—	—	—
Spain	*b*	*b*	*b*	*b*
Sweden	yes *a*	—	—	—
Switzerland	yes	—	—	—
Turkey	na	na	na	na
United Kingdom	yes	—	yes	*e*
United States	yes	yes	yes	yes

Notes: In the table na = not available and − = not applicable

a. Legal proposal.

b. Under consideration.

c. In West Germany, foreign branches of West German banks are supervised on a fully consolidated basis. With regard to foreign subsidiaries, supervision based on consolidated returns applies to a limited extent (solvency and risk concentration on the basis of a gentleman's agreement).

d. Branches only.

e. Partial consolidation as supervision of currency exposure extends to foreign branches of banks registered in the United Kingdom, but not to subsidiaries.

SOURCE: R. M. Pecchioli, "The International of Banking" Paris: OECD Secretariat, 1983.

The regulatory aspects of the country exposure problem illustrate both the issue of formulating regulatory structures that contain the problem without major distortions in market-driven financial flows, and the problem of reaching international consensus on regulatory approaches in an environment where the regulatory function is essentially national but the business itself is international.

While alignment in a number of regulatory and supervisory areas has been impressive, major differences remain. This is illustrated in Table 25–1 with respect to inspection of the accounts of foreign-based banks in various countries and in Table 25–2 with respect to various regulatory criteria on a global consolidated basis in the early 1980s. Gaps in the regulatory net maintain opportunities for "regulatory arbitrage" and hence for potential stability problems in the future.

FINANCIAL DEREGULATION

Deregulation in financial services has become a fact of life in the United States and in various other countries such as Japan and the EC under the 1992 initiatives. Information and transactions costs are falling. New competitors are entering the financial services field, while others seek exit or combine with viable players as elegantly as possible. New financial products come on-stream almost daily, their number and variety limited only by the human imagination. Artificial barriers to competition, some of which have been in place for decades, are being subjected to steady erosion. Competitors bid actively for human as well as financial resources, even as product, process, applications, management, and marketing technologies evolve faster than ever before. In short, the environment is one of vigorous competition, based at its core on concepts like institutional competitive advantage, specialization, and economies of scale and scope.

What are often archaic systems of financial institutions rapidly become streamlined under deregulation, as major wholesale and retail financial institutions spread geographically and across products while regional as well as local institutions plot defensive and collaborative strategies. Disintermediated financial flows link ultimate savers and ultimate investors, large and small, directly via the capital markets, even as financial intermediaries scramble to enhance value added in order to retain in some form their traditional role. Commercial banks become active in the government bond markets, in private placements, in financial advisory work, in arranging standby facilities, in selling loan participations, and in various other dimensions of investment banking. Investment banks, brokerage firms, insurance companies, retailers, and even manufacturing firms are developing lines of financial services where each thinks there is a profitable market niche. Banks, meanwhile, press on the real estate business, insurance, and even direct involvement in commercial transactions. Traditional "industry" lines become blurred, even though financial "activity" lines remain as sharp as ever.

If the process is permitted to work itself out, a far stronger and more efficient national financial system will eventually evolve, where excess profits ultimately disappear, transactions costs are driven to a bare minimum, information becomes much more readily available, the basis for rational decision making improves, and only the fittest competitors are able to prosper for very long. The process of financial allocation in the national economy will improve materially, and the gap between what the ultimate saver receives and what the ultimate investor has to pay for funds will be narrowed to the finest possible margin. Perhaps even more important, deregulated financial systems will improve availability of resources to new and emerging industries, strip away resources from declining and uncompetitive sectors and firms sooner, quite possibly enhance the underlying incentives to save and to invest, accelerate technological change, bolster the ability to lay off risk and perhaps swallow economic and financial shocks with less social damage, and generally support the process of sustainable economic growth.

If deregulation is to be justified in economic terms, that justification must come in large part through substantive change in competitive performance in the provision of corporate financial services. For example, the Glass-Steagall provisions of the Banking Act of 1933 in the United States (or Article 65 in Japan) notwithstanding, the 1980s saw substantial competition between securities firms and commercial banks for a wide variety of financial services, especially in the international capital market. In areas where there has been an absence of artificial barriers to competition, the efficiency and innovativeness that characterize the various competing financial services firms have been very high indeed, with commensurate benefits accruing directly to the users of the services and more broadly to the economic and financial system as a whole.

Economists generally work under the assumption that any limitation of competitive opportunity favors those who benefit from protection but also reduces the efficiency with which financial and human resources are allocated—the so-called *static* deadweight losses associated with protected markets. There are also adverse *dynamic* consequences (such as reduced financial innovation) that make themselves felt over a period of time and that ultimately are likely to be substantially more important. Evidence on the size and stability of underwriting fees, artificially wide banking spreads, the quality of services provided to small issuers, and the underpricing of new issues in protected markets usually follow the pattern one would expect to see in such situations.

The conclusion that more competition is better than less comes as no great surprise either from the standpoint of efficiency or fairness and seems well justified in terms of the inferential evidence presented on concentration and competitive structure. The evidence does suggest that statutory competition barriers generate costs and that deregulation generates material benefits to the users of financial services and to the economy at large.

POTENTIAL COSTS OF FINANCIAL DEREGULATION

If there are potential benefits associated with the deregulation of financial services, there are also potential costs with respect to both economic efficiency and equity dimensions. Potential costs include lessened stability of the financial system and the exploitation of conflicts of interest on the part of financial institutions engaged in both commercial and investment banking activities.

The magnitude of the first of these potential costs depends, in part, on the riskiness of various transactions that might be undertaken by financial institutions. That many financial activities involve risks is clear; if there were no risks, they would produce few gains, either to the direct participants or to society at large. However, risk can be managed through astute evaluation, diversification, and exposure limits, as well as through a growing array of hedging vehicles. In the securities business, for example, the major risks involved concern the potential losses associated with securities underwriting and dealing, their bearing on the safety and soundness of individual financial institutions and the system as a whole, and the nature of the risk/return tradeoffs in the market for corporate securities. However, by adding a new range of financial services activities whose returns are not perfectly correlated with those of traditional banking activities, the ability of commercial banks to engage in corporate securities business may well enhance the earnings stability of the institutions as a whole. It suggests that safety and stability of financial environment depend fundamentally on careful balance and breadth of scope of activities, more so than on traditional notions of narrowly defined activity limitations and controls.

In recent years various events have rocked the U.S. financial markets, ranging from the failure of Winters Government Securities in 1977, Drysdale Government Securities and Lombard-Wall Inc. in 1982, Lion Capital Group in 1984, and E.S.M. Government Securities in 1985, to 79 commercial bank failures in 1984 (including Continental Illinois) and the closure of 71 Ohio thrift institutions in 1985. Shaky foreign loans, agricultural and real estate credits, and the energy bust, alongside imprudent and sometimes sloppy or even fraudulent management practices, have all raised questions about the financial system's safety and stability. And there was the thrift debacle of 1988–89. Each crisis has brought with it a tightening of supervision and control under existing statutes, but no major moves toward reregulation. In this way, even major shocks have been absorbed relatively smoothly without incurring losses in the system's core efficiency and dynamism. Indeed, the case for continued deregulation has in some ways been strengthened to the extent that it fosters greater activity diversification and earnings stability on the part of the most viable, best-managed players in banking as well as securities markets.

In addition to questions relating to the potential impact of market interpenetration between financial institutions on financial stability, there is also the nagging issue of potential conflicts of interest when various types of activity are housed in the same institution, for example, investment banking, commercial banking, and trust banking. Various institutional and legal safeguards exist to limit conflict exploitation, and these safeguards can be made adequate to cope with significant deregulation of activity limits.

A careful examination of the structure of incentives and disincentives that underlies the exploitation of conflicts of interest usually shows that such exploitation is fundamentally inimical to the economic interest of the firm and its shareholders—the value of the enterprise as a going concern. Insulation of commercial banking units from securities affiliates of universal banks, for example, as well as the competitive nature of the markets for financial services and the ready availability of performance information, provides sanctions against deviations from this standard that are both timely and painful. Moreover, institutional factors that influence the behavior of managers, such as the structure of bonus schemes, the use of profit centers, and the market for corporate control, tend to ensure that behavior at variance with basic corporate and client interests is not tolerated for long.

BALANCING THE BENEFITS AND COSTS

If the evidence on the characteristics of a particular type of financial service is that the risks are both limited and manageable, if activity diversification enhances the earnings stability of financial institutions, and if economic incentives and legal constraints provide effective insulation and safeguards against conflicts of interest, then the case for permitting financial institutions to engage in a broad range of activities in order to maximize economies of scale and scope would appear to be very strong indeed. Enhanced static and dynamic benefits from more competitive financial institutions and markets would be the result.

The available evidence suggests that efforts to foster financial safety and soundness through activity separation, as Glass-Steagall in the United States and Article 65 in Japan have attempted to do, sacrifice the diversification (and hence stability) gains from interpenetration of commercial and investment banking activities. Any stability benefits attributable to activity separation are thus partially or wholly offset by stability losses due to reduced diversification of earnings streams.

The evidence also suggests that financial regulation generates efficiency losses. At the level of the firm, regulation prevents management from optimally deploying the institution's capital and human resources, designing optimal financial and organizational structures, and developing optimal business strategies. At the level of society, regulation fosters misallocation of resources, stifles innovation and international competitiveness, and constrains the contribution of the financial system to economic growth. The objective is to capture for society the efficiency gains from greater competition and market interpenetration between commercial and investment banking *without* at the same time compromising the safety and stability of the nation's financial system.

SUMMARY

Banking and finance constitute a highly sensitive sector. Fractional reserve banking embodies an inherent element of liquidity risk, as do maturity mismatching in asset and liability management, trading, and merchant banking activities. Despite careful diversification in asset deployment, exposures incurred in lending activities always involve solvency risk. The very role of financial intermediation entails the assumption of risks. Moreover, fraud, misrepresentation, financial collapse, predatory behavior, self-dealing, bubbles, busts, and shocks have afflicted financial systems over the centuries in the United States, Europe, and elsewhere in the world. Problems that afflict an individual institution may spill over to damage the entire fabric of the national financial and economic system. To cope with this problem, countries have tried to establish safeguards that are robust enough to contain external damage triggered by crises in the financial sector, yet that do not at the same time materially impair financial efficiency or the creative forces of private enterprise. Deposit insurance limits erosion of confidence by banking customers. The central bank as official lender of last resort exists to inject liquidity to individual institutions in trouble (e.g., via its discount facilities) and to the financial system as a whole (via open market operations and changes in reserve requirements).

Along with institutional safeguards comes regulation to further support the safety and soundness of the financial system. The apparatus is familiar: Reserve requirements, bank examination and supervision, maximum lending limits, securities regulation, activity limitations on commercial and investment banks, mutual savings banks and savings and loan institutions, and interest rate ceilings have been among the traditional techniques. Countries use different kinds of safeguard structures, but the need for them is universally recognized. Indeed, some use bank nationalization to "socialize" both the risks and the returns and not coincidentally to achieve a direct government role in credit allocation.

The problem with financial regulation is that it invariably erodes the *efficiency* of the system. All regulatory and supervisory measures have the potential of displacing financial resource allocation from that which is most efficiently driven by the free interplay of market force. This is as true of reserve requirements as it is of interest rate ceilings on deposits. Further costs are associated with eroded innovativeness and competitive vitality of the industry. So the combination of financial safeguards and regulation results in a lessening of financial efficiency and dynamism. Greater security is never free—there is always a price to be paid. Here we are buying increased safety with respect to the national financial system and paying for it in the form of reduced financial market efficiency. This is a logical tradeoff, yet there is always the question of whether we are paying too high a price for the increased financial stability we are purchasing through regulation and control. Many countries would surely regard bank nationalization as an extortionate price to pay for any prospective increase in financial safety that it would create.

These issues become especially difficult in the international environment, although much progress has been made to create a more coherent regulatory apparatus and at the same time a more level playing field. This has focused on more careful assignment of regulatory responsibility to branches and affiliates, coordination of national prudential policies, and perhaps most importantly, alignment of capital adequacy standards. This is discussed in the following chapter.

SELECTED REFERENCES

Bank for International Settlements. *Recent Innovations in International Banking*. Basel, Switzerland: BIS, 1986.

Cooper, Kerry, and Fraser, Donald R. *Bank Deregulation and the New Competition in Financial Services*. Cambridge, MA: Ballinger, 1986.

Goldberg, Ellen S., et al. *Off-Balance-Sheet Activities of Banks: Managing the Risk-Reward Tradeoffs*. Philadelphia: Robert Morris Associates, 1983.

Guttentag, Jack, and Herring, Richard. "Provisioning, Charge-Offs and the Willingness to Lend." The Wharton School, University of Pennsylvania, Philadelphia, PA, 1986. Mimeographed.

Guttentag, Jack, and Herring, Richard. "Funding Risk." The Wharton School, University of Pennsylvania, Philadelphia, PA, 1986. Mimeographed.

Guttentag, Jack, and Herring, Richard. "The Lender-of-Last-Resort Function." The Wharton School, University of Pennsylvania, Philadelphia, PA, 1986. Mimeographed.

Heimann, John. "The Problem of Confidence in Domestic and International Banking Systems." *Journal of Banking and Finance*, September 1982.

Pecchioli, R. M. *Internationalization of Banking*. Paris: OECD, 1983.

Walter, Ingo, ed. *Deregulating Wall Street*. New York: John Wiley & Sons, 1985.

Wellons, Philip A. *Passing the Buck: Banks, Government and Third World Debt*. Cambridge, MA: Harvard Business School Press, 1987.

26

Bank Capital Adequacy Controls

Banks are regulated institutions in all countries. Most governments either guarantee deposits to some extent or stand ready to offer assurances of solvency to depositors and customers who need to feel certain that their banks are safe. Without such assurances a banking system becomes volatile and unstable. Governments unavoidably have had the job of backing up the banks, at least since the collapses of the 1930s—"banks," of course, being those institutions that accept deposits of funds owned by the general public and make commercial and individual loans. To the extent that governments are involved in backing up or insuring banks' depositors against losses they are appropriately entitled to regulate the terms under which the banks take financial risks, including the business activities and capital structure of banks. The extent to which such regulation exists has varied considerably among countries.

As global banking activities have expanded, new financial products have proliferated (with many of these being tradeable in the market) and as competition between banks from different countries has grown, the difficulties in maintaining uniform standards for bank safety as well as "level" competitive conditions between banks from different countries became a serious problem. Regulatory differences, particularly those pertaining to capital adequacy, encouraged banks subject to less restrictive conditions to compete aggressively against other banks, which in turn pushed the more thoroughly regulated institutions to increase other forms of exposures as a way of keeping up.

ACHIEVING A "LEVEL PLAYING FIELD"

It should be obvious that the implementation of a truly level playing field in the financial services sector depends both on there being similar sets of restraints on the various different types of lending that banks perform and on common definitions as to what is and is not bank "capital." The task is complicated by the structure of regulatory and prudential constraints already in place and accepted in all of the countries involved. These differ with respect to both lending practices and capitalization. For example, there is a wide array of rules as to bank reserves—some countries permit "hidden" reserves against loan losses (in the form of deliberately undervalued assets)—and in the regulation of domestic deposit rates, deposit insurance, and domestic competition policies and a variety of other rules that can affect an institution's competitive positioning internationally. While these differences are comparable in nature to the competitive effects of subsidies and governmental participation in other industries, the differences are perhaps more serious in the banking sector. Moreover, in no other industry have uniform global standards been attempted.

Bank regulators have discussed the issue of standardization for years, confronting time and again the fact of national sovereignty in banking supervision and monetary control and the entrenched interests of banks themselves. At a meeting in Amsterdam in October 1986, however, banking supervisors resolved to work toward the same minimum capital standards for all banks that do business across national borders, as a matter of both competitive fairness and prudential soundness. Such a minimum would most probably also represent the maximum capital standards that countries will impose if their banks are not to suffer in international competition. Supervisors also agreed to work toward a uniform definition of capital, which in many cases included not only equity but also various forms of long-term debt, as well as greater commonality in loan loss provisioning. Although the new standards, discussed below, have accomplished these tasks, it is nonetheless clear that the job is not finished. Regulatory coordination cannot stop at this point, but must also go on to involve agreement on sanctions (including exclusion from specific businesses and markets) for institutions that violate or circumvent the rules and in due course address the problems of one set of standards applied to the bank sector and another, looser set of rules for the nonbanking financial services sector.

THE BASEL COMMITTEE GUIDELINES

In January 1987, following three months of discussion, the Bank of England and the U.S. federal banking regulatory authorities (the Federal Reserve, the FDIC, and the Comptroller of the Currency) announced that they had reached agreement on proposals for a common measure of capital adequacy. The proposals were for a risk-related approach similar in many respects to that already in use in the U. K. and to that proposed in papers published by the U.S. regulatory authorities in January 1986. The proposals also drew on work produced over the previous two years by the Banking Regulations and Supervisory Practices committee of the Bank for International Settlements (BIS) in Basle. This committee was called the "Basel Committee" or the "Cooke Committee" (in honor of its chairman, Peter Cooke of the Bank of England).

The Basel Committee's approach was to seek a convergence of the various regulatory methods to form a package that could be used by banking regulators from all of the Group of Ten (industrialized) countries plus Switzerland and Luxembourg.[1] The issues involved were controversial, and the goal of the Committee was thought to be ambitious. The 1987 U.S.-U.K. proposals were circulated for comment, then adopted by the Basle Committee as a whole in July 1988, and subsequently ratified by each country. The Federal Reserve announced its final version of the guidelines in January 1989.[2] In its announcement of the new guidelines, the Fed noted that they had been designed to achieve certain important goals:

1. Establishment of a uniform capital framework applicable to all federally supervised banking organizations
2. Encouragement of international banking organizations to strengthen their capital positions
3. Reduction of a source of competitive inequality arising from differences in supervisory requirements among nations

The guidelines establish a systematic analytical framework that makes regulatory capital requirements more sensitive to differences in risk profiles among banking organizations, takes "off–balance sheet" exposures into explicit account in assessing capital adequacy, and minimizes disincentives to holding liquid, low-risk assets.

Off–balance sheet items represent contingent assets (or liabilities) that the accounting profession does not require to be entered on the face of a bank's financial statements because of the uncertain nature of the contingencies that determine whether these items become due and payable (i.e., move onto the balance sheet). Most accountants do require that, as contingent items, they be disclosed in footnotes to the financial statements, but they escape being included in regulatory ratios. Some typical off-balance sheet transactions are listed in Figure 26–1.

Because many new financial products such as note issuance facili-

Contingent Claims	Financial Services
Loan Commitments	*Loan-related services*
Overdraft facilities	Loan origination
Credit lines	Loan Servicing
Backup lined for commercial paper	Loan pass-throughs
Standby lines of credit	Asset sales without recourse
Revolving lines of credit	Sales of loan participations
Reciprocal deposit agreements	Agent for syndicated loans
Repurchase agreements	
Note issuance facilities	*Trust and advisory services*
	Portfolio management
Guarantees	Investment advisory services
Acceptances	Arranging mergersw and acquisitions
Asset sales without recourse	Tax and financial planning
Standby letters of credit	Trust and estate management
Documentary of commercial letters of credit	Management of pension plans
Warranties and indemnities	Trusteeships for unit trust, pension
Endorsements	plans, and debentures
Financial support to affiliates or subsidiaries	Safekeeping of securities
	Offshore financial services
Swap and hedging transactions	
Forward foreign exchange contracts	*Brokerage/agency services*
Currency swaps	Share and bond brokerage
Currency futures	Mutual fund (unit trust) brokerage
Currency options	General insurance brokering
Cross-currency swaps	Life insurance brokering
Interest rate swaps	Real estate agency
Cross-currency interest rate swaps	Travel agency
Interest rate options	
Interest rate caps, floors, and collars	*Payment services*
	Data processing
Investment banking activities	Network arrangements
Securities underwriting	Clearing house services
Securities dealership/distribution	Credit/debit cards
Gold and commodities trading	Point of sale systems
Market-making in securities	Home banking
	Cash management systems
Export/import services	
	Correspondent banking services
	Trade advice
	Export insurance services
	Countertrade exchanges

Figure 26–1. Summary of Off-Balance Sheet Activities.

Table 26–1.   Selected Off–Balance Sheet Activities of U.S. Banks, 1980–1987^a

Year	Capital	Loan Commit- ments	Standby Letters of Credit	Commercial Letters of Credit	Foreign Exchange Commitments Outstanding	Interest Rate Swaps Out- standing
1980	108	na	47	20	177	na
1981	118	na	72	20	189	na
1982	129	na	100	17	215	na
1983	141	432	120	30	464	na
1984	154	496	146	30	584	na
1985	170	531	175	29	735	186
1986	183	572	170	28	893	367
1987	187	574	167	31	1241	451

a. In billions of dollars; through the first quarter of 1987.

SOURCE: Federal Deposit Insurance Corporation.

ties, swaps, and financial futures transactions involve contingent obligations, they are not included on balance sheets. The rapid growth in off–balance sheet items, however, has been a cause of concern to regulators.

Table 26–1 shows the growth of off–balance sheet items recorded by U. S. money-center banks since 1980. The concern led to an effort to "capitalize" off–balance sheet items so as to include them in the overall grasp of bank supervisory regulations.

Risk Categories

In principle the new system is a simple one, although by the time all of the modifications adopted were taken into account the implemented structure was fairly complex. However, the basic idea was to assign each asset owned by a bank (or accounted for on an off–balance sheet basis) to one of four "risk categories." Each risk category is assigned a "risk weight," which is used to multiply the amounts in each risk category to determine the amount of capital required by the bank. Table 26–2 shows risk categories and risk weightings and examples of the types of assets in each category.

Capital Tiers

Capital is divided into "Tier 1," or "core" capital (consisting of retained earnings, common stock, and qualifying perpetual preferred stock and minority interests in equity accounts of consolidated subsidiaries, minus "goodwill") and "Tier 2" capital (various forms of

Table 26–2. Summary of Risk Weights and Risk Categories for State Member Banks

Category 1: Zero percent

1. Cash (domestic and foreign) held in the bank or in transit.
2. Balances due from Federal Reserve Banks (including Federal Reserve Bank stock) and central banks in other OECD countries.
3. Direct claims on, and the portions of claims that are unconditionally guaranteed by, the U.S. Treasury and U.S. government agencies [a] and the central governments of other OECD countries, and local currency claims on, and the portions of local currency claims that are unconditionally guaranteed by, the central governments of non-OECD countries (including the central banks of non-OECD countries), to the extent that the bank has liabilities booked in that currency.
4. Gold bullion held in the bank's vaults or in another's vaults on an allocated basis, to the extent offset by gold bullion liabilities.

Category 2: 20 percent

1. Cash items in the process of collection.
2. All claims (long- or short-term) on, and the portions of claims (long- or short-term) that are guaranteed by, U.S. depository institutions and OECD banks.
3. Short-term claims (remaining maturity of one year or less) on, and the portions of short-term claims that are guaranteed by, non-OECD banks.
4. The portions of claims that are conditionally guaranteed by the central government of OECD countries and U.S. government agencies, and the portions of local currency claims that are conditionally guaranteed by the central governments of non-OECD countries, to the extent that the bank has liabilities booked in that currency.
5. Claims on, and the portions of claims that are guaranteed by, U.S. government-sponsored agencies. [b]
6. General obligations claims on, and the portions of claims that are guaranteed by the full faith and credit of, local governments and political subdivisions of the U.S. and other OECD local governments.
7. Claims on, and the portions of claims that are guaranteed by, official multilateral lending institutions or regional development banks.

---

a. For the purposes of calculating the risk-based capital ratio, a U.S. government agency is defined as an instrumentality of the U.S. government whose obligations are fully and explicitly guaranteed as to the timely payment of principal and interest by the full faith and credit of the U.S. government.

b. For the purposes of calculating the risk-based capital ratio, a U.S. government-sponsored agency is defined as an agency originally established or chartered to serve public purposes specified by the U.S. Congress but whose obligations are not *explicitly* guaranteed by the full faith and credit of the U.S. government.

(continued)

Table 26–2. (cont.)

8. The portions of claims that are collateralized ^{c} by securities issued or guaranteed by the U.S. Treasury, the central governments of other OECD countries, U.S. government agencies, U.S. government-sponsored agencies, or by cash on deposit in the bank.

9. The portions of claims that are collateralized ^{c} by securities issued by official multilateral lending institutions or regional development banks.

10. Certain privately issued securities representing indirect ownership of mortgage-backed U.S. government agency or U.S. government-sponsored agency securities.

11. Investments in shares of a fund whose portfolio is permitted to hold only securities that would qualify for the zero or 20 percent risk categories.

Category 3: 50 percent

1. Loans fully secured by first liens on 1–4 family residential properties that have been made in accordance with prudent underwriting standards, that are performing in accordance with their original terms, and that are not past due or in nonaccrual status, and certain privately issued mortgage-backed securities representing indirect ownership of such loans. (Loans made for speculative purposes are excluded.)

2. Revenue bonds or similar claims that are obligations of U.S. state or local governments, or other OECD local governments, but for which the government entity is committed to repay the debt only out of revenues from the facilities financed.

3. Credit equivalent amounts of interest rate and foreign exchange rate related contracts, except for those assigned to a lower risk category.

Category 4: 100 percent

1. All other claims on private obligators.

2. Claims on, or guaranteed by, non-OECD foreign banks with a remaining maturity exceeding one year.

3. Claims on, or guaranteed by, non-OECD central governments that are not included in item 3 of Category 1 or item 4 of Category 2; all claims on non-OECD state or local governments.

4. Obligations issued by U.S. state or local governments, or other OECD local governments (including industrial development authorities and similar entities), repayable soleley by a private party or enterprise.

5. Premises, plant, and equipment; other fixed assets; and other real estate owned.

6. Investments in any unconsolidated subsidiaries, joint ventures, or associated companies—if not deducted from capital.

7. Instruments issued by other banking organizations that qualify as capital—if not deducted from capital.

8. Claims on commercial firms owned by a governmant.

9. All other assets, including any intangible assets that are not deducted from capital.

c. The extent of collateralization is determined by current market value.

SOURCE: Federal Reserve Board.

"supplementary" capital). Table 26–3 presents a summary of definitions of qualifying capital for Federal Reserve supervised banks.

Before these proposals were adopted, the principal means of assessing capital adequacy for banks in the United States had been to divide "total capital" (which included retained earnings, common and preferred stock, and certain forms of subordinated debt) by "total assets." The Federal Reserve and other banking supervisory bodies set different ratio requirements for different types of banks. At the beginning of 1989, when the final guidelines were announced, U.S. money-center banks were required to maintain a 6 percent capital-to-total-assets ratio, although many banks were not in compliance.

Off–Balance Sheet Items

The face amount of an off–balance sheet item (such as a letter of credit, a swap, or a foreign exchange obligation) is taken into the risk-based capital ratio by multiplying it by a "credit conversion factor." The resultant "credit equivalent amount" is assigned to the appropriate risk category (according to the identity of the obligor or guarantor). Among those items converting to credit risks at 100 percent of face value are all direct credit substitutes, risk participations in bankers acceptances or direct credit substitutes (such as letters of credit), sale and repurchase agreements, and certain forward agreements.

Those items entitled to 50 percent conversion factors include transaction related contingencies, revolving credit agreements, and note issuance facilities and similar arrangements. Items converted at 20 percent include short-term self-liquidating trade-related contingencies. Items converted at zero percent include unused portions of commitments that either have an original maturity of one year or less or that are unconditionally cancellable at any time.

Interest Rate and Foreign Currency Contracts

The guidelines include among off–balance sheet items all interest rate and foreign exchange contracts of the following types:

Interest Rate Contracts	Foreign Exchange Contracts
Single currency swaps	Cross-currency swaps
Basis swaps	Forward contracts
Forward rate agreements	Currency options purchased
Options purchased (including caps, collars, and floors)	Any other instrument giving rise to like credit risks

Table 26–3. Summary Definition of Qualifying Capital for State Member Banks [a] **Using the Year-end 1992 Standards**

Components	Minimum Requirements After Transition Period
Core Capital (Tier 1)	Must equal or exceed 4% of weighted risk assets[c]
Common stockholders' equity	No limit
Qualifying noncumulative perpetual preferred stock	No limit; banks should avoid undue reliance on preferred stock in Tier 1
Minority interest in equity accounts of consolidated subsidiaries	Banks should avoid using minority interests to introduce elements not otherwise qualifying for Tier 1 capital
Less: Goodwill[b]	
Supplementary Capital (Tier 2)	Total of Tier 2 is limited to 100% of Tier 1[c]
Allowance for loan and lease losses	Limited to 1.25% of weighted risk assets[c]
Perpetual preferred stock	No limit within Tier 2
Hybrid capital instruments and equity contract notes	No limit within Tier 2
Subordinated debt and intermediate-term preferred stock (original weighted average maturity of 5 years or more)	Subordinated debt and intermediate-term preferred stock are limited to 50% of Tier 1;[d] amortized for capital purposes as they approach maturity
Revaluation reserves (equity and buildings)	Not included; banks encouraged to disclose; may be evaluated on a case-by-case basis for international comparisons; and taken into account in making an overall assessment of capital.

(continued)

Table 26–3. (cont.)

Deductions (from sum of Tier 1 and Tier 2)	Minimum Requirements After Transition Period
Investments in unconsolidated subsidiaries	
Reciprocal holdings of banking organizations' capital securities	
Other deductions (such as other subsidiaries or joint ventures) as determined by supervisory authority	On a case-by-case basis or as a matter of policy after formal rulemaking
Total Capital (Tier 1 + Tier 2 – Deductions)	Must equal or exceed 8% of weighted risk assets

a. See discussion in Section II of the Guidelines for a complete description of the requirements for, and the limitations on, the components of qualifying capital.

b. All goodwill, except previously grandfathered goodwill approved in supervisory mergers, is deducted immediately.

c. Amounts in excess of limitations are permitted but do not qualify as capital.

d. Amounts in excess of limitations are permitted but do not qualify as capital.

SOURCE: Federal Reserve board.

Credit equivalent amounts are calculated for each individual contract of the types listed above. Table 26–4 shows credit conversion factors for various types of off–balance sheet items. To calculate the credit equivalent amount of its off–balance sheet interest rate and exchange rate instruments, a bank sums the following amounts:

1. The marked to market value (positive values only) of each contract (that is, the current exposure)
2. An estimate of the potential future credit exposure over the remaining life of each contract

The potential future credit exposure on a contract, including contracts with negative mark-to-market values, is estimated by multiplying the notional principal amount by one of the following credit conversion factors, as appropriate (see Chapter 15):

Remaining Maturity	Interest Rate Contracts	Exchange Rate Contracts
One year or less	0.0%	1.0%
Over one year	0.5%	5.0%

Table 26-4. Credit Conversion Factors for Off-Balance Sheet Items for State Member Banks

100 Percent Conversion Factor

1. Direct credit substitutes. (These include general guarantees of indebtednss and all guarantee-type instruments, including standby letters of credit backing the financial obligations of other parties.)

2. Risk participations in bankers' acceptances and direct credit substitutes, such as standby letters of credit.

3. Sale and repurchase agreements and assets sold with recourse that are not included on the balance sheet.

4. Forward agreements to purchase assets, including financing facilities, on which drawdown is *certain*.

5. Securities lent for which the bank is at risk.

50 Percent Conversion Factor

1. Transaction-related contingencies. (These include bid bonds, performance bonds, warranties, and standby letters of credit backing the nonfinancial performance of other parties.)

2. Unused portions of commitments with an original maturity[a] exceeding one year, including underwriting commitments and commercial credit lines.

3. Revolving underwriting facilities (RUFs), note issuance facilities (NIFs), and similar arrangements.

20 Percent Conversion Factor

1. Short-term, self-liquidating trade-related contingencies, including commercial letters of credit.

Zero Percent Conversion Factor

1. Unused portions of commitments with an original maturity[a] of one year or less, or are unconditionally cancelable at any time, provided that a separate credit decision is made before each drawing.

a. Remaining maturity may be used until year-end 1992.
SOURCE: Federal Reserve Board.

The guidelines note that no potential exposure is calculated for single-currency interest rate swaps in which payments are based on two floating-rate indexes—that is, so-called floating/floating or basis swaps. The credit exposure of this type of contract is taken strictly on the basis of their mark-to-market value. The only form of "netting" (or offsetting one position against another) is netting by "novation," in which all obligations of one party to another party are automatically amalgamated with all other obligations for the same currency and value date. Table 26-5 shows sample calculations of credit equivalent amounts for interest rate and currency swaps.

**Table 26–5. Calculation of Credit Equivalent Amounts
Interest Rate and Foreign Exchange Rate Related Transactions for State Member Banks**

Type of Contract (remaining maturity)	Potential Exposure				Current Exposure		Credit Equivalent Amount (dollars)
	Notional Principal (dollars)	× Potential Exposure Conversion Factor	= Exposure (dollars)	+	Replacement Cost [a]	= Current Exposure (dollars) [b]	=
120-day forward foreign exchange	5,000,000	.01	50,000		100,000	100,000	150,000
120-day forward foreign exchange	6,000,000	.01	60,000		–120,000	–0–	60,000
3-year single-currency fixed/ floating interest rate swap	10,000,000	.005	50,000		200,000	200,000	250,000
3-year single-currency fixed/ floating interest rate swap	10,000,000	.005	50,000		–250,000	–0–	50,000
7-year cross-currency floating/ floating interest rate swap	20,000,000	.05	1,000,000		–1,300,000	–0–	1,000,000
TOTAL	$51,000,000						$1,510,000

a. These numbers are purely for illustration.
b. The larger of zero or a positive mark-to-market value.
SOURCE: Federal Reserve Board.

Implementation

The guidelines include a schedule for implementing the new system. No later than the end of 1990, total capital to risk-weighted assets must be not less than 7.25 percent (of which at least 3.25 percent must be in the form of Tier 1 capital). By the end of 1992, a ratio of 8 percent (of which at least 4 percent must be in the form of Tier 1 capital) must be in effect. The guidelines note that during the transitional period through the end of 1992 banking supervisors may allow some forms of supplementary capital to be included in the Tier 1 category on a temporary basis.

Appendix A to this chapter shows sample calculations of capital to total assets ratios and the new risk-based capital ratios. Table 26–6 shows the year-end 1990 and the final, year-end 1992 standards that the guidelines specify.

THE EFFECTS OF THE GUIDELINES ON BANKS

In general, several effects desired by the regulators are likely to occur as a result of the imposition of the BIS guidelines. One intent, for example, was to make riskier instruments become more costly to hold, lessening the chances of excessive exposure and the prospect that regulators will have to step in to provide support in a crisis. Another was to limit underpricing of off–balance sheet commitments.

It is likely that the BIS guidelines, now accepted by all of the OECD countries as providing a common standard for safe and prudent banking capitalization, will lead to further deregulation and unwinding of protectionism in domestic banking in many European countries (see Chapter 27). Once all agree on the same minimum base, there is no advantage for institutions to be undercapitalized or for countries to unduly subsidize banking institutions, for example, by setting interest rate controls to allow banks to accumulate excess profits as a cushion against future losses at the expense of economic growth and efficiency. In the post-1992 European marketplace, when member countries of the EC hope to enjoy their much-heralded single internal market, freed-up banking regulations will be a necessary accompaniment.

Given the rate of financial innovation over the past decade and the deluge of new instruments, both marketable and non-marketable, that resulted, it was necessary that the guidelines provide regulators with a coherent framework into which to slot new types of exposures as they evolve, instead of lagging events by as much as several years, as was often the case. Each new type of instrument will be assigned to the highest risk category until such time as the regulators rule otherwise. In the past, the more frequent occurrence was for new types of instruments not to be assigned to any category whatsoever.

The guidelines are intended to force most banks to increase their capital reserves. Regulators, concerned by the large increases in underperforming and nonperforming loans that many banks have experienced as a result of domestic industrial and real estate problems and extensive exposures to Latin America and Eastern Europe, intended that substantial amounts of new capital would be raised for the global banking system, especially by American and Japanese banks, both of which tended to score poorly on the basis of the new risk-related capital calculations. Capital, however, would be more stringently defined than before and divided into core and supplementary categories that further tightened the standard. Banks, on the other hand, had several ways to acquire more capital—and several years to do so—including (1) shifting assets, for example from the 100 percent to lesser weighted (i.e, more creditworthy) categories; (2) raising more capital from the sale of equity securities or other assets in which unrealized gains existed; (3) increasing earnings by investing in high-yield assets whose risks could be hedged through syndication and/or diversification; and (4) increasing earnings by recapitalizing the bank, usually by merging or combining with another bank in one of many possible ways.

Appendix B to this chapter is a reproduction from the 1987 financial statements of J. P. Morgan Inc. (the banking holding company for Morgan Guaranty Trust Co.) showing in detail how the various categories of assets and capital are determined and how the new guidelines affected them.

Some Difficulties Imposed by the Guidelines

The risk-based capital approach was expected to put greater pressure on banks to charge higher spreads or fees for financial transactions in which they participate, in order to recover the incremental cost of the additional capital needed to support specific loans and advances or simply to recover the higher overall cost of capital that the bank would now incur. This condition was seen by many banks to place them at a substantial disadvantage relative to securities firms, with whom they are increasingly in direct competition. Securities firms, not being regulated by authorities that must look after the deposits they are guaranteeing, are not subject to the new rules or to any similar constraints.

Table 26-6. Comparison of Standards Specified by the Basel Committee: Initial, 1990, and 1992

	Transitional Arrangements for State Member Banks		Final Arrangements
	Initial	Year-end 1990	Year-end 1992
1. Minimum standard of total capital to weighted risk assets	None	7.25%	8.0%
2. Definition of Tier 1 capital	Common equity qualifying noncumulative perpetual preferred stock, minority interests *plus* supplementary elements *a less* goodwill	Common equity qualifying noncumulative perpetual preferred stock, minority interests *plus* supplementary elements *b less* goodwill	Common equity qualifying noncumulative perpetual preferred stock, and minority interests *less* goodwill
3. Minimum standard of Tier 1 capital to weighted risk assets	None	3.625%	4.0%
4. Minimum standard of stockholders' equity to weighted risk assets	None	3.25%	4.0%
5. Limitations on supplementary capital elements			

a. Allowance for loan and lease losses	No limit within Tier 2	1.5% of weighted risk assets	1.25% of weighted risk assets
b. Qualifying perpetual preferred stock	No limit within Tier 2	No limit within Tier 2	No limit within Tier 2
c. Hybrid capital instruments and equity contract notes	No limit within Tier 2	No limit within Tier 2	No limit within Tier 2
d. Subordinated debt and intermediate team preferred stock	Combined maximum of 50% of Tier 1	Combined maximum of 50% of Tier 1	Combined maximum of 50% of Tier 1
c. Total qualifying Tier 2 capital	May not exceed Tier 1 capital	May not exceed Tier 1 capital	May not exceed Tier 1 capital
6. Definition of total capital	Tier 1 *plus* Tier 2 *less:* reciprocal holdings of banking organizations' capital instruments investments in unconsolidated subsidiaries	Tier 1 *plus* Tier 2 *less:* reciprocal holdings of banking organizations' capital instruments investments in unconsolidated subsidiaries	Tier 1 *plus* Tier 2 *less:* reciprocal holdings of banking organizations' capital instruments investments in unconsolidated subsidiaries

a. Supplementary elements may be included in Tier 1 up to 25% of the sum of Tier 1 plus goodwill.

b. Supplementary elements may be included in Tier 1 up to 10% of the sum of Tier 1 plus goodwill.

SOURCE: Federal Reserve Board.

Nor are the provisions of the accord uniform between banks of different countries. For example, it continues to permit British banks to count "silent" reserves (which do not exist in the United States) as part of capital under the presumption that such reserves, along with other peculiarities of individual EC countries, will be phased out over time as part of the harmonization of EC banking regulations. Wide international differences also exist in the availability of information on bank performance, which may influence their relative competitive positioning and certainly affects the ability to determine whether the international competitive playing field is in fact relatively level.

Transparency in U.S. accounting for banks is ensured by the regulatory structure, and any disclosure problems are relatively quickly remedied, including cross-border exposures and off–balance sheet exposures in such transactions as swaps. In other countries, disclosure is far less extensive and in some cases relatively meaningless. Disclosure of off–balance sheet exposures in many cases is absent altogether, and many home countries of multinational banks fail to disclose their worldwide operations on a consolidated basis at all.

The question also remains open whether other banks may emerge among the nonparticipating countries (or located outside them in tax havens) to challenge banks from the participating countries for business. Such banks, which could be from Austria, Lichtenstein, or Kuwait, would possess a competitive edge over the participating banks through less rigorous regulatory standards. Conceivably, banks could migrate to unregulated areas for the purpose of competing with the banks from the major countries. However, since only a small percentage of the world's international banking assets are booked outside the participating countries, the impact of such a migration would not appear to be large.

It is also clear that coordination with authorities regulating the securities industry is essential if competitive rules under which firms in the two sectors (banking and securities) of the industry operate are not to serve as further distortions to competitive conditions in the case of financial services that are performed by both banks and nonbanks.

As part of its mandate to regulate British wholesale markets under the Financial Services Act, the Bank of England in July 1987 issued a "grey paper" outlining a regulatory framework for gold bullion and large sterling and foreign currency deposits, spot and forward foreign exchange commercial transactions, and various other wholesale instruments, as well as a code of conduct for market participants. Institutions covered by the rules must be "fit and proper" according to the criteria laid down by the Bank of England, specifically with regard to capitalization, management and operational capability, and standards of business conduct. The intent of the risk-based capital requirements for nonbanks was to have them as closely aligned as possible to those agreed to under the emerging Basel accord, in order to avoid competitive distortions between banks and nonbanks active in the same financial markets. The so-called London Code of Conduct is designed to cover a specific set of financial instruments that would adhere to the Code wherever they are traded, thus representing a uniform level of quality. These include swaps, sterling and foreign exchange deposits, gold and silver bullion, options, and futures. The Code also governs relationships among market participants and between them and their customers. As efforts continue by the EC to formulate more exact rules and standards under which securities firms must operate in Europe, it is equally likely that these efforts will encounter the London Code of Conduct, and it is likely that something along those lines will eventually be applied across Europe.[3]

Finally, it has also been argued that coordinated risk-based capital requirements can actually be counterproductive, since assets categorized in the same risk class may have vastly different risk profiles. Moreover, since different assets and off–balance sheet exposures require different levels of capital, the result may well be distortions in banking decisions—for example, loading up on highly interest-sensitive U.S. government securities that require less capital backing than perhaps less volatile asset deployments that require more capital—decisions that ultimately may lead to increased, rather than decreased, vulnerability of individual institutions. It could also reduce financial innovation and, as noted, place banks at a competitive disadvantage against nonfinancial institutions operating in the securities markets that are not subject to similar requirements.

U.S. banks were probably hit hardest by the Basle standards. Major money-center banks appeared to be substantially undercapitalized in 1987 after most had made large additions to their loan loss reserves for Third World debt. Table 26–7 shows that the 10 largest U. S. banks had an average capital to total assets ratio of about 3 percent in 1987. By contrast, the 10 largest U.S. regional banks had an average ratio about twice that of the money center banks. In 1987, about 30 percent of the top 50 U.S. banks were estimated to need additional core

Table 26–7.   Capital to Assets Ratios for 10 Money-Center Banks and 10 Regional Banks

Money-Center Banks

Bank Holding Company	Total Assets in billions [a]	Net Tangible Common Equity
Citicorp	$194.4	2.16%
Chase Manhattan	98.9	2.54
BankAmerica	96.9	2.10
Chemical New York	78.4	2.17
J. P. Morgan	74.7	5.95
Manufacturers Hanover	73.8	1.56
Security Pacific	64.7	3.15
Bankers Trust	54.7	4.12
First Interstate	51.8	3.93
Wells Fargo	44.7	2.53

Regional Banks

Bank Holding Company	Total Assets in billions [a]	Net Tangible Common Equity
Bank of Boston	$30.5	4.65%
PNC	28.3	6.13
Bank of New England	27.1	4.46
Suntrust	25.6	5.66
NCNB	24.5	4.86
First Union	24.5	6.40
NBD	22.6	5.04
Barnett Banks	20.4	4.37
First Wachovia	18.8	6.43
Banc One	17.7	6.92

a. As of June 30, 1987.

SOURCE: Keefe, Bruyette & Woods.

capital by 1992, and almost all would need additional supplementary capital.[5]

The problems experienced by most money center banks in 1987–1989 were reflected in historically low stock prices, thus making it extremely expensive for most of the banks that needed additional capital to raise it by issuing new shares of common stock. Instead, they were required to utilize the other methods for boosting capital noted earlier. Most of the major money center banks were required to sell assets to realize capital gains or to reduce the size of the asset base being supported by their capital. Some, such as Manufacturers Hanover Trust Company and Bank of America, were required to sell off substantial parts of their nonbanking businesses in order to "shrink down" to a level that was supportable by their diminished capital base. Thus, in order to comply with the new regulations, many banks were forced to accept low-growth strategies, the disposition of strategically important activities, and to sharply reduce costs and services. The net result was a drop in the competitive power of U.S. banks relative to non-U.S. banks, especially in the commercial lending market, and relative to securities firms that grew rapidly in size and competitiveness during the 1980s.

Indeed, U.S. banks faced such severe problems during most of the 1980s that their cost of funds had increased substantially relative to the cost at which their customers and competitors could secure funds. This disequilibrium was forcing money-center banks out of the lending business and into higher spread business, for example with middle market or lower quality companies. Figure 26–2 shows the deteriorating spreads over U. S. Treasury securities at which bank financing was available during 1987.

At the same time bank stock prices were trading at very low multiples, on a historical basis, of their earnings. In part, this was

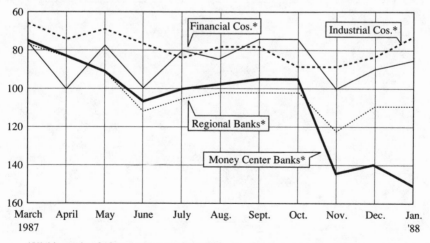

*Yield margin of 10-year notes rated single-A over Treasury notes due in 10 yrs.

Figure 26–2. Deteriorating View of Major U.S. Banks. Yields Margin over Benchmark Treasury Securities. Margins Are Measured in Basis Points. A Basis Point Is 1/100th of a Percentage Point. (*Source:* CS First Boston, Inc.)

because the market did not believe the earnings figures it saw—more "surprises" were expected in the future, and real balance sheet strength was emerging as a primary factor in setting bank stock prices.

When first announced in early 1988, the new guidelines caused the stock market to tighten further around those banks with high risk-based capital ratios (see Figure 26–3). In some ways this was a great irony. Banks had been selling themselves to investors as growth companies, capable of dynamic and aggressive activity in the United States and of unrestricted activity abroad. For years they had been striving to escape the image of regulated public utilities that they had after the Banking Act of 1933 had been enacted. During the high point of the stock market's appreciation of the future potential of modern, technically sound money center banks, price/earning ratios reached nearly 20 times current earnings. After the problems of domestic loan writeoffs and large exposures to Latin American credits, money center bank p/e ratios declined to around 5 times earnings, and the market placed highest values on those money-center banks that had the soundest balance sheets, not the greatest growth prospects.

Japanese banks awoke to find themselves far behind even the 1990 Basel capital standard: The average capital ratio of Japanese banks in

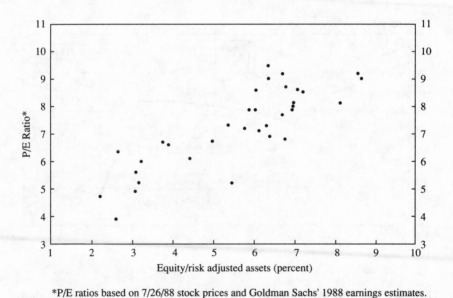

*P/E ratios based on 7/26/88 stock prices and Goldman Sachs' 1988 earnings estimates.

Figure 26–3. Relationship between Capital Adequacy and Stock Valuation. (*Source:* Goldman, Sachs and Co.).

1986 was less than half this level, or about 2.7 percent. The Japanese banks argued that because of differences in the way they operate, as well as interbank support and protection from the Bank of Japan, they did not require the same level of capitalization as European or American banks in order to ensure stability—in effect acknowledging the existence of a *de facto* public subsidy. The Ministry of Finance, however, stuck to the Basel accord and, although numerous "concessions" were made to Japanese banks during the transition period, they are to comply with the standards on schedule.

The Japanese banks have been aided in this undertaking by their relatively conservative asset holdings (approximately 80%of all assets are estimated to survive as "risk-adjusted assets") and by their ability to dispose of marketable common stocks held in client companies and other investments, such as land and buildings, at very substantial capital gains.

Accordingly, Japanese banks have been allowed to apply an "adjustment factor" of 45 percent to unrealized gains in their securities portfolios in calculating "supplementary capital." Alternatively, of course, they could sell the portfolio and apply the proceeds to core capital. The banks, however, have a long tradition of holding shares in client companies and are reluctant to sell these shares. In addition, as the Japanese stock market rose substantially after the announcement of the guidelines, the value taken into supplementary capital by the banks has risen accordingly.

Japanese banks also have been able to sell shares of their own common stock, or securities convertible into common stock, at the exceptionally high prices that were typical of the Japanese stock market. These sales were in very large amounts—often in several hundred million dollar offerings—in Japan itself and in the Eurobond and Euroequity markets. It was quite likely that the capital shortfall of Japanese banks would disappear entirely if nonbanking assets were marked to market values and a comparatively modest amount of new shares were sold. An example of this is shown in Figure 26–4, which demonstrates how Mitsubishi Bank calculated its compliance with the guidelines in September 1988.

European banks met the new situation quite differently. Each country had substantially dissimilar banking equity to asset ratios. In 1985 the ratio was 4.0 in Belgium, 4.8 in France, 1.8 in Germany, 8.8 in Italy, 1.7 in the Netherlands, 8.1 in Spain, 5.6 in Sweden, 3.2 in Switzerland, and 5.7 in the United Kingdom. Some of these ratios

	Tier 1	Tier 2
	Core capital	Supplementary capital
	Yen 1,176 billion	Yen 1,918 billion
	($9 billion)	($15 billion)
	Risk adjusted assets	Risk adjusted assets
	Yen 36,467 billion	Yen 36,467 billion
	($280 billion)	($280 billion)
	3.22%	5.26%
Benchmark:	4.00%	4.00%
Shortfall:	.78%	0.00%
	Yen 283 billion	
	($2.2 billion)	

Total assets	X 80%	Risk adjusted assets
Yen 45,584 billion		Yen 36,467 billion
($350 billion)		($280 billion)

Unrealized gains	X 45%	Supplementary capital
Yen 4,263 billion		Yen 1,918 billion
($33 billion)		($15 billion)

Figure 26–4. Basel Committee Guidelines Compliance Calculations, Mitsubishi Bank (Sept. 1988).

would be improved if hidden reserves, acceptable in some countries such as Germany and Switzerland, were included.[6] Most of the European banking authorities have allowed substantial write-downs of Third World debt, as a result of which the German and Swiss banks, in particular, appeared well reserved.

European banks likewise have been seen working on their capital positions and 1988 estimates, as Figure 26–5 indicates, reflected good progress. However, they not only adjusted their capital positions but also their entire business strategies as a result of the coming need to adapt to changed business and banking conditions in Europe attributable to the EC 1992 initiatives. Consequently, many bank mergers and acquisitions, joint ventures, and stakeholdings occurred, which in most cases strengthened capital positions.

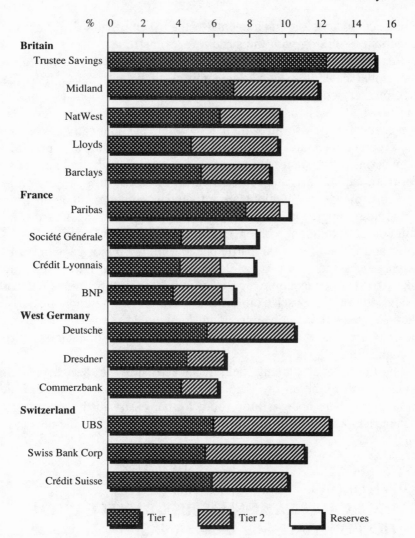

Figure 26–5. Raising the Standard: Capital Adequacy Ratios, 1988 Estimates (capital expressed as percentage of assets). (*Source:* Merrill Lynch Capital Markets Inc.)

SUMMARY

The risk-based bank capital adequacy system is a major achievement for several reasons. First, it appears that it will work; that is, it will incorporate in its framework all on–and off–balance sheet assets at suitable risk weightings. It will not damage innovation, nor will it remain inflexible. Periodically the ghosts of the Basel Committee will announce accords on amendments to the system that will reflect the benefits of working with the system for some time.

Second, it will result in the addition of substantial new capital to the global banking system. How this is to be raised is left to the free-market actions of individual banks, whose freedom to conduct their own business as they see fit is comparatively unrestricted by the regulations. Also, it will sort through the innovative types of bank capital invented by bankers mainly as loopholes to previous regulations rather than because of intrinsic merit and eliminate those forms of capital that cannot be relied on to do the job.

Third, the new regulations are influential, coming as they do from an ad hoc group of banking supervisors who worked together to find solutions to common problems. The effectiveness of their deliberations and the ability of the participants to bridge major gaps in banking practices and regulatory philosophy is impressive. The results are likely to stand as examples for other regulatory deliberations and for extensions of the Basel Committee's work to nonparticipating jurisdictions, both those concerned with banking in other countries and those concerned with the regulation of nonbanking financial service organizations.

Fourth, a level playing field has been more or less achieved. Competitive conditions will be almost entirely equal by 1992, and in any case there appears little room for banks to substitute competition in risk-bearing for competition in interest rates under the new system.

APPENDIX A
SAMPLE CALCULATION OF RISK-BASED CAPITAL RATIO FOR STATE MEMBER BANKS

Example of a bank with $6,000 in total capital and the following assets and off–balance sheet items:

Balance Sheet Assets

Cash	$ 5,000
U.S. Treasuries	20,000
Balances at domestic banks	5,000
Loans secured by first liens on 1–4 family residential properties	5,000
Loans to private corporations	65,000
Total Balance Sheet Assets	$100,000

Off–Balance Sheet Items

Standby letters of credit (SLCs) backing general obligation debt issues of U.S. municipalities (GOs)	$10,000
Long-term legally binding commitments to private corporations	20,000
Total Off–Balance Sheet Items	$30,000

This bank's total capital to *total* assets (leverage) ratio would be:

$$\frac{\$6,000}{\$100,000} = 6.00\%.$$

To compute the bank's weighted risk assets:

1. Compute the credit equivalent amount of each off–balance sheet (OBS) item.

OBS Item	Face Value		Conversion Factor		Credit Equivalent Amount
SLCs backing municipal GOs	$10,000	×	1.00	=	$10,000
Long-term commitments to private corporations	$20,000	×	0.50	=	$10,000

2. Multiply each balance sheet asset and the credit equivalent amount of each OBS item by the appropriate risk weight.

0% Category

Cash	$ 5,000
U.S. Treasuries	20,000
	$25,000 × 0 = 0

20% Category

Balances at domestic banks	$ 5,000
Credit equivalent amounts of SLCs backing GOs of U.S. municipalities	10,000
	$15,000 × 0.20 = $3,000

50% Category

Loans secured by first liens on 1–4 family residential properties	$5,000 × 0.50 = $2,500

100% Category

Loans to private corporations	$65,000
Credit equivalent amounts of long-term commitments to private corporations	10,000
	$75,000 × 1.00 = $75,000
Total Risk-Weighted Assets	$80,500

This bank's ratio of total capital to weighted risk assets (risk-based capital ratio) would be:

$$\frac{\$6,000}{\$80,500} = 7.45\%$$

APPENDIX B
BASEL COMMITTEE GUIDELINES CALCULATIONS OF RISK-ADJUSTED ASSETS: J. P. MORGAN INC., 1987

In accordance with the proposed guidelines, J. P. Morgan's risk-adjusted assets would be approximately $46.5 billion at December 31, 1987, as follows:

Risk asset grouping	Balance	Risk weight	Risk adjusted balance
Cash claims on U.S. government (less than 90 days) and other zero-weight assets	$ 1,192 [a]	0%	—
Claims on U.S. government (over 90 days) and other claims collateralized by U.S. government securities	3,482	10%	$ 348
Claims on domestic banks and short-term claims on foreign banks	19,052	20%	3,810
Claims on U.S. government-sponsored agencies and local currency claims on foreign governments	5,673	20%	1,135
General obligations of state and local government units	4,466	20%	893
Public purpose revenue bonds	141	50%	71
All other assets [b]	40,195	100%	40,195
Total assets [c]	74,201		46,452

a. Dollars in millions.

b. At December 31, 1987, total assets were below the 1987 average balances. Accordingly, the amounts presented above have been adjusted to more closely reflect 1987 average balances by adding approximately $3.8 billion to "All other assets." If calculated based on actual period-end balances at December 31, 1987, the risk-adjusted capital ratio would be higher.

c. In accordance with the proposed guidelines, the assets, off–balance sheet exposures, and equity of certain consolidated subsidiaries which are subject to capital requirements of other U.S. regulators have been deducted for the purpose of calculating J.P. Morgan's risk-adjusted capital ratio. If such assets, off–balance sheet exposures, and equity were included, the risk-adjusted capital ratio would be higher.

J. P. Morgan's total combined risk-adjusted assets and off–balance sheet exposures at December 31, 1988, excluding the assets and off–balance sheet exposures of J. P. Morgan Securities Inc., were approximately $61.9 billion as follows:

	Contract amount[a]	Credit conversion factor	Credit-equivalent amount	Risk weight	Risk-adjusted balance
A. Total risk-adjusted assets, per previous table					$38,760
B. Commitments and contingencies:					
Financial guarantees and standby letters of credit	$ 3,793	100%	$ 3,793	20–100%	2,417
Nonfinancial guarantees	4,827	50%	2,414	100%	2,414
Other letters of credit	135	20%	27	20–100%	17
Commitments to purchase securities, assets sold with recourse, and securities lending indemnifications	5,571	50–100%	5,296	0–100%	1,832
Commitments to extend credit:					
One year or less	1,424	0%	—	0%	—
Over one year	26,385	50%	13,193	20–100%	12,546

	Contract or notional amount	Current exposure	Potential exposure		
C. Foreign currency contracts: (*including currency swaps*)	$156,642	$7,142	$3,230	10,372 0–50%	3,273
D. Interest rate contracts: (*including interest rate swaps*)	109,936	1,578	319	1,897 0–50%	601
Total risk-adjusted assets and off–balance sheet exposures					61,860

a. Dollars in millions.

	Capital	Risk-adjusted capital ratio [b]
Tier I	$6,027 [a]	8.55%
Tier II	2,513	3.57%
Total	8,493	12.05%

a. Dollars in millions.

b. See notes to the risk-adjusted asset.

Tier I:		
Common stockholders' equity [b]	$4,520 [a]	
Tier II capital includable as Tier I	1,507	
Total adjusted Tier I capital		$6,027
Tier II:		
Preferred stock	250	
Subordinated notes due 1994 to 1997	683	
Other qualifying term debt	1,379	
Allowance for credit losses [c]	1,708	
Tier II capital includable as Tier I	(1,507)	
Total adjusted Tier II capital		2,513
Investments in unconsolidated banking and finance subsidiaries		(47)
Total qualifying capital		8,493

a. Dollars in millions

b. In accordance with the proposed guidelines, the equity in certain consolidated subsidiaries which are subject to capital requirements of other U.S. regulators has been deducted from common stockholders' equity at December 31, 1987.

c. J. P. Morgan believes that its entire allowance for credit losses should qualify for inclusion as Tier II capital during the initial phase of the transition period.

SOURCE: J. P. Morgan Inc.

NOTES

1. Belgium, Canada, France, Germany, Italy, Japan, Netherlands, Sweden, the United Kingdom, and the United States.
2. The remainder of this section draws heavily, and sometimes literally, on the final text of the guidelines released by the Federal Reserve Board on January 19, 1989, entitled "Federal Reserve System, 12 CFR Part 208, Appendix A and 12 CFR Part 225, Appendix A [Regulation H, Regulation Y; Docket No. R-0628], 'Risk-Based Capital Guidelines'."
3. *The Economist*, March 19, 1987.
4. Goldman Sachs Research Group, February, 1988.
5. *The Economist*, op. cit.

27

Problems of Access to International Markets

Controls over the operations of foreign firms in financial services affect either their entry into the national market or their freedom of operation.[1] There are basically two types of barriers to market penetration in the financial services sector: entry barriers and operating barriers. Both limit access to all or some segments of the market, although some act to make market access more costly than it would otherwise be. Here we shall briefly describe the impact of the two types of barriers to international trade in financial services.

INTERNATIONAL DISTORTIONS AND COMPETITIVE PERFORMANCE

Returning to the basic C-A-P model introduced in Figure 20–1, we can ask how competitive distortions affect the individual cells in the matrix, the ability of financial institutions to serve various markets globally and, therefore, the formulation and execution of strategies. These questions can be discussed in terms of entry barriers, of operating restrictions that affect access to client groups (Type A), and of operating restrictions that affect the ability to supply the market with specific products (Type B)(see Figure 27–1).

First, and most obvious, entry barriers restrict the movement of financial services firms in the lateral arena dimension of the matrix. A firm that is excluded from a particular national market faces a restricted lateral opportunity set that excludes the relevant tranche of client and product cells. To the extent that it is the outcome of protectionist political activity, the entry barrier itself will create supernormal returns in some or all of the cells in the tranche. It may, of course, have this effect even if there is no protectionist intent. Foreign-based institutions already in the market will, as noted earlier, tend to have a vested interest in keeping others out. Opportunities created by coun-

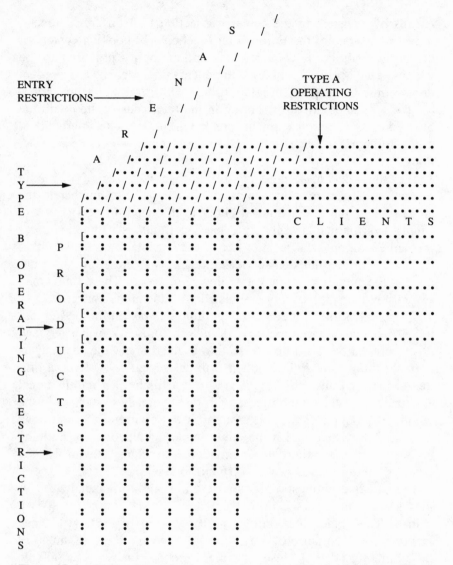

Figure 27–1. Market Access Barriers in the International Financial Services Activity Matrix.

tries relaxing entry barriers will be seized by institutions envisioning potential supernormal returns in some of the previously inaccessible cells.

Second, firms that are allowed into a particular market only through travel or representative offices may nevertheless be able to access particular client/product cells in that tranche, securing business and returns by transferring the actual transaction to a different arena—for example, one of the Euromarket functional or booking centers or the institution's home country. This option applies primarily to the wholesale and private banking components of the client and product dimensions. Correspondent relationships with local banks are probably the only alternative for sharing in the returns associated with the blocked cells in product dimensions having to do with international trade, foreign exchange, syndications, and other wholesale transactions.

The story becomes more complicated in the case of operating restrictions. The firm now has access in one form or another to the arena tranche but is constrained either in the depth of service it can supply to a particular cell (e.g., lending limits, staffing limits, or restrictions on physical location) or in the feasible set of cells within the tranche (e.g., limits on services foreign banks are allowed to supply and the client groups they are allowed to serve). These limits may severely reduce profitability associated with the arena concerned.

To the extent that horizontal integration is important in the international financial services industry, despite the presence of barriers and other competitive distortions affecting a given arena tranche, supernormal returns may still be obtained in unaffected cells. Even a limited scope for transactions with the local affiliate of a multinational enterprise may generate business with that company elsewhere in the world, for example. The value of a physical presence of any sort in an otherwise restricted market may thus support competitive positioning elsewhere in the institution's international structure. Obviously, the value of these linkages is very difficult to assess.

The strategic implications of barriers to trade in financial services thus seem clear. They reduce the feasibility set within the C-A-P matrix. They place a premium on windows of opportunity. They increase the importance of horizontal linkages and the assessment of their value. And they raise the importance of lobbying activity to open up markets where cells having potentially supernormal returns are blocked or restricted, and to keep them restricted when barriers to competition are the source of such excess returns.

BARRIERS TO ENTRY

Entry barriers act to inhibit foreign-based firms in the financial services industry from servicing the needs of domestic clients. As discussed below, they range from complete embargoes (including visa denial to foreign bankers) and limiting foreign presence to allowing representative offices only (with no banking powers), to restrictions on the forms a foreign presence can take and limits on foreign equity positions in local financial institutions.

Global versus Selective Entry Barriers

As with other quantitative restrictions of international trade, entry barriers can be either *global* or *selective*. Global measures apply equally to all foreign-based institutions, while selective measures apply differently depending on the specific foreign institution involved or its home country. Global entry barriers may prohibit a foreign presence entirely (embargo) or limit foreign presence to certain forms of involvement in the domestic financial system *ab initio*.

Selective measures may permit differential entry for institutions from different home countries, based on considerations of banking reciprocity or general reciprocity in bilateral trade relations. They may also allow entry by institutions singled out on the basis of "desirability" criteria such as past or potential future contributions to the development of the national financial system.

It is sometimes difficult to determine whether the administration of entry barriers is indeed global or selective. A case in point is Australia's decision in 1985 to permit for the first time foreign bank entry. A total of 16 banks were selected from an extensive list of applicants, based on composite criteria combining reciprocity considerations and assessed potential contributions on the part of individual applicants. While nominally discriminatory, the selection process appears to have been carried out in a substantially open manner, giving it some of the characteristics of a global quota.

As things developed, however, the Australian market at least initially did not quite live up to the hopes of the foreign bankers. First, the Australian economy and its currency went into a serious decline, limiting profitable banking opportunities. Second, the competition from the Australian banks was considerably more vigorous than expected, narrowing margins and market opportunities. Third, the number of foreign banks admitted was much larger than many of the 16 successful applicants had expected, further increasing competitive pressure. Fourth, deregulation stiffened competition for corporate clients from the 150-odd merchant banks operating in Australia, about 60 of which had entered the business since deregulation. The result was wholesale scaling down of growth objectives and retargeting of business strategies under tight cost controls, although few showed any inclination to disengage. At the end of 1986, foreign banks had captured about 10 percent of the total assets of the Australian banking system.

Selectivity in entry into domestic financial services markets is heavily based on reciprocity considerations. Domestic financial institutions, in developed as well as developing countries, usually find it necessary or desirable to establish a presence abroad. This may involve foreign countries with intensive trade, investment or migration links, locations of major significance for foreign-currency funding requirements, or a necessary presence in the important financial centers of the world. Domestic institutions thus face an inherent conflict between their interest in accessing foreign markets for financial services and their desire to keep foreign-based players out of domestic markets. This assessment and the domestic lobbying activity that results obviously depend on the stakes involved in each case, as well as the probability that the foreign government will demand reciprocity (and that its own institutions will lobby for it).

Some cases in point are the the more or less explicit linkage of foreign banking entry into Brazil with the interests of Brazilian institutions in expanding abroad and the highly selective linkages between the opening of various parts of Japan's financial system to outside competitors and the growing activities of Japanese financial institutions in Europe and the United States.

Japan has been perhaps the most attractive among the various banking arenas from the perspective of foreign-based players. Driven by an extraordinarily high savings rate, Japanese investments in foreign securities rose from $4.1 billion in 1966 to $145.7 billion at the end of 1986 (in addition to $435 billion in foreign real estate and direct investments), and projections were that they could reach $1 trillion by 1995.

As of early 1987 there were 79 foreign banks and 36 investment firms established in Tokyo, with 6 foreign firms admitted to the Tokyo Stock Exchange at the end of 1985. Goldman Sachs, Jardine Fleming, Merrill Lynch, Morgan Stanley, S.G. Warburg, and Vickers da Costa (a British subsidiary of Citicorp) were the foreign-based players among the 93 Tokyo Exchange members in 1987.

In 1987 some 36 foreign-based firms had been licensed as securities dealers. In March 1987 the Ministry of Finance announced its decision to permit U.S. commercial banks to operate securities affiliates in

Japan—powers not allowed these same banks at home under the Glass-Steagall Act or their Japanese commercial bank competitors under Article 65. The U.S. banks would be permitted to trade in all kinds of securities, with no limits on allowable business volume. This gives major U.S. players such as Bankers Trust, Morgan Guaranty, Chemical Bank, and Manufacturers Hanover powers in Japan that have been accorded their European universal bank competitors since 1985. In 1987 there were 11 banks based in Germany, Switzerland, France, Great Britain, and the Netherlands with securities licenses in Japan. The securities affiliate must be a branch of an offshore subsidiary that is 50 percent owned by the parent bank, with the other half owned by a "friendly" corporate partner. Expectations were that around 50 foreign-based firms would have securities licenses in Japan by 1988.

Foreign players are permitted to trade in some kinds of securities but are limited to dealing with the 120 largest Japanese financial institutions and prohibited from securities dealing with corporate or retail clients, as well as being restricted to a minuscule share of government bond underwriting. They also must execute stock trades through members of the Tokyo stock exchange, which were subject to a 27 percent fixed commission and limited price competition.

Controls on deposit interest rates, fixed commissions on stock transactions, the absence of stock index futures and commercial paper markets, and separation of commercial and investment banking impeded full integration of Tokyo into the global financial markets for a number of years. In April 1987 the Japanese Ministry of Finance announced that financial institutions based in Japan could henceforth use foreign futures and options markets to hedge their investment portfolios. This represented a major step in further integrating Japan into the international financial market and increasing the scope for Japanese financial houses to develop further their global market presence. Given the assets of Japanese trust banks, investment trusts, and insurance companies, as well as securities firms and other financial houses, the impact promised to be very significant indeed.

Gradual deregulation in Japan thus has proceeded in each of the salient regulatory dimensions, but always with an eye to maintaining the preeminence of Japanese players in the home market. Besides the slow pace of market liberalization, foreign firms faced the "buy Japan" mentality so familiar in the industrial sector on the part of Japanese consumers, corporations, and investors.

It should be emphasized once again in this context that foreign-based institutions that are already in a particular market, either because they were grandfathered at the time entry barriers were imposed or because they have achieved entry in some other manner, will have an unambiguous incentive to resist further opening of the market to foreign players. They have no reciprocity incentive with respect to their home country or third countries, and unless they perceive significant external benefits from additional entrants they have every reason to resist additional, potentially powerful competition.

Of 141 countries surveyed by the U.S. Department of the Treasury in 1984 (including 24 former colonies of European powers) 13 had no explicit entry restrictions to foreign banks and 3 others prohibited only the acquisition of a majority interest in an existing indigenous bank. Eighteen others prohibited additional foreign presence, or allowed none at all, and 23 limited foreign banks to representative offices — the most passive form of foreign banking presence.[2] Representative offices may not hold deposits or make loans and are useful mainly for developing new business contacts, conveying local market information to head office, maintaining a relay service with correspondents, and providing a visible presence of the parent bank to clients.

From such surveys, it is quite clear that barriers to the entry of foreign financial institutions vary greatly among countries. At one extreme is exclusion: the complete prohibition of all foreign presence, extending even to representative offices. Frequently such an embargo coincides with the existence of a nationalized domestic banking industry in which all private banking (domestic or foreign) is prohibited. More common is some form of conditional restriction on the entry of foreign banks, which usually relates to the type of presence that is permissible and to the nature of the associated banking powers. Even conditional restrictions are not entirely unambiguous. Within a set of domestic regulations and laws there often exists a substantial element of discretion. In the same vein, policies may mean different things in different situations and precedent is certainly not an infallible guide to future policy responses.

In general, entry restrictions can be described as essentially "quota-like." They specify whether a foreign financial institution may operate in the domestic market and, if so, how. The form of participation specified may be a representative office; a separately capitalized and locally incorporated subsidiary; a nonbank, such as a finance company that cannot take deposits but can make certain types of loans; a minority foreign equity participation; mandatory partnership with the government; and the like. Occasionally, new foreign financial institutions are limited to certain home countries, based on past colonial relationships or existing regional economic arrangements such as the European Community. Most-favored-nation treatment is certainly not characteristic of the rules imposed by countries on entry of foreign financial institutions. Often a complete moratorium is placed on new entrants because "there are already enough banks," or because of the "frailness of the domestic banking structure," an infant industry argument. And red tape in processing new applications is a perennial problem.

Sometimes an explicit price may be exacted for entry, for example, a U.S. $10 million foreign currency deposit with the country's central bank for each branch to be established, with the same deposit also forming the basis for the legal lending limit in local currency. Exceedingly high capital requirements for new subsidiaries may be used as an entry barrier as well, as may a mandatory volume of foreign currency loans to the government or to specified domestic institutions, a commitment to set up a national branch network or to rescue failing local institutions, or a commitment to enter or render certain types of financial services that are not yet domestically well developed.

Bargaining leverage may extract certain benefits perceived to be of value by the host government, benefits that might not materialize as quickly under open market access. But once safely in, foreign financial institutions can exact a heavy price in terms of high profits from the continued monopolistic climate of the domestic financial industry. Indeed, these same institutions are sometimes in the forefront of the ranks lobbying for continued policies of exclusion once their own entry has been achieved. Restrictive entry policies, selectively applied, may thus provide leverage to help a country achieve certain developmental goals, but at a substantial potential cost in adverse shifts in its effective terms of trade.

DISTORTIONS OF OPERATING CONDITIONS

Similar to entry restrictions, operating controls can seriously influence competition in domestic banking and financial markets, so that even if liberal entry is possible it is by no means certain that foreign competitors will be permitted to meet rival firms on equal terms.

Incidence of Domestic Regulation

Once having gained entry to a particular market, foreign-based financial institutions generally become fully subject to domestic monetary policy, supervisory, and regulatory controls (see Chapter 25). At this point there are three possibilities: (1) domestic controls, in law or in administrative practice, fall less seriously on foreign players than on their domestic competitors; (2) the nominal incidence of regulation is identical for both; or (3) foreign players are subjected to more restrictive regulation than their local competitors.

The first option seems to be a relatively rare occurrence. Probably the most important case in point involved foreign banks in the United States prior to the passage of the International Banking Act of 1978 (IBA). Foreign-based institutions were exempt from membership in the Federal Reserve System, from the Bank Holding Company Act and the McFadden Act restrictions on branching across state lines, and from the Glass-Steagall prohibitions against an institution's involvement in both commercial and investment banking. The IBA eliminated this discrimination in favor of foreign players, except that institutions already involved in both commercial and investment banking — and those already having branches in multiple states — were grandfathered. This created a degree of tension that has become more important with the continued securitization of financial flows in the United States.

Given the continued restrictive effect of Glass-Steagall in the U.S. domestic market on their American competitors, the 15 foreign banks that were grandfathered under the International Banking Act of 1978 (and could thus maintain both a commercial and investment banking presence in the American market), as well as foreign-based securities houses that are principal competitors to U.S. commercial and investment banks, intentionally generally tread softly in exercising their full potential power in the U.S. capital market. In 1986, however, some began to flex their muscles. Nomura Securities and Daiwa Securities led significant issues in the U.S. market for prime names. Sumitomo Bank and Trust Company purchased a 12.5 percent share in Goldman Sachs, in the face of Article 65, Japan's version of Glass-Steagall, albeit under tight restrictions on the part of the Federal Reserve. Securities affiliates of Swiss Bank Corporation, Union Bank of Switzerland, and Deutsche Bank led 15 debt issues amounting to over $2.5 billion during 1986. American commercial banks that were attempting to become major players in global finance saw some of their principal rivals do deals in their own market that were prohibited to them—a rare case of foreign firms being treated significantly more favorably than domestic firms and being able to exploit that treatment to good effect in developing their worldwide competitive positioning.

In a similar vein, we have already noted that foreign-based commercial banks in Japan were allowed to enter the domestic securities business despite Article 65 barriers that continued to restrict local banks in this critical area. And certain developing countries, such as India, have required that local banks become actively involved in providing financial services to clients in rural agriculture, a requirement that does not bear on foreign-based institutions. But except for a few such anomalies, usually based on historical reciprocity considerations, preferential treatment is not likely to be encountered.

The second case applies in many developed countries and a number of developing countries as well. Foreign institutions here are subject to precisely the same nominal operating constraints as are domestic institutions. This applies to reserve requirements, asset ratios, lending limits, exposure constraints, capital adequacy, banking powers, access to funding sources and central bank lending, etc. Despite nondiscrimination *de jure*, the incidence of such measures may in fact fall more heavily on newcomers or on foreign players that are forced to enter the market through affiliates rather than branches, therefore being relatively poorly capitalized. These may in some cases be unintentional operating barriers and can either directly limit market access or raise the cost of doing business.

The third case involves the explicit use of operating barriers to restrict the competitive positioning of foreign-based institutions after they have achieved access. The measures range from restrictions on expatriate employment, number and location of offices, client groups that may be served, types of business that may be handled (including trust business, lead management in securities underwriting, and retail deposit-taking), mandatory linkage of allowable business to international transactions, and the like. Most are paraquantitative restrictions in that they place positive limits on the nature and scope of activities. Some, however, may be paratariffs, as in the case of funding restrictions that raise the cost of funds in the local market relative to domestic competitors.

Four basic types of operating restrictions can be identified: (1) market delineation acts to restrict market access directly by identifying groups of clients that may or may not be served (or that must be served) and how they are to be served; (2) growth limits set maximums on the size of a foreign financial institution's presence in the local market, either in absolute terms or by market share; (3) funding limits increase the cost of debt and equity capital (including bank deposits) taken up in the local financial markets, either to restrict market share or to adversely affect profitability; and (4) nuisance measures may raise the cost of doing business in the local market or compromise the quality of products.[3]

Market Delineation

Some operating restrictions are quota-like in that they limit the markets that foreign-based financial institutions are allowed to serve. A "permitting" procedure, for example, may subject all loans beyond a certain size to the scrutiny of the central bank. The institution's presence may be limited to a few cities (usually the capital and major ports), to a single city, or even to a single office. Additional offices may be permitted only after five to ten years of satisfactory operations.

In 1983, for example, the Brazilian authorities told foreign banks that they could open two offices in provincial cities for each one they closed in Rio de Janeiro and Sao Paulo, an opportunity promptly grasped by some in anticipation of a resumption of Brazil's resource-based economic growth later in the 1980s.

Various types of profitable business may be reserved for state-owned banks, and foreign banks may be prevented from letter of credit business involving the government. Foreign institutions may be prohibited from taking liens on real property (effectively banning asset-based financing), or they may be prevented from entering the trust and investment management field or from holding the proceeds of equity sales. They may also be forced to divest themselves of finance companies or other nonbank affiliates in order to prevent their use as banking outlets.

The host government may direct domestic public and private enterprises not to do business with foreign institutions or to limit any such business to areas not adequately served by local institutions. Foreign banks may be excluded from participation in the government's export credit guarantee program and subsidized export financing may have to be done only through domestic banks. Foreign institutions may be restricted to export/import financing, foreign exchange, and foreign currency lending only. A certain proportion of total assets may have to be placed in government bonds. Some types of large financings may have to be lead managed by local banks, disallowing foreigners lucrative income from fees. Advertising may be limited in various ways and mandatory financing of certain economic sectors or nationalized enterprises may be imposed. And the list goes on.

Under a rule promulgated in 1984, for example, advertising for new deposits in the United Kingdom for banks based outside the European Community was restricted by requiring a warning about the absence of deposit insurance, possible transfer risks and exchange risks, and detailed information on their financial condition. While this action was clearly a matter of prudential control, the discriminatory competitive side effects represented a potential threat.

As noted earlier, foreign banks in Japan have long felt systematically discriminated against in an opaque structure of financial control that delivered much the same sort of protection that has traditionally shielded favored manufacturing and agricultural interests. The foreign banks, for example, have been discouraged from taking aggressive leadership roles in yen-denominated syndicated loans for foreign borrowers. Although foreign banks had been present in Japan for over three decades, they still accounted for only 3 percent of total lending and 2 percent of total deposits in 1982. Whereas the foreign banks were long protected through a monopoly on so-called impact loans aimed at financing Japan's foreign trade, removal of this protection in 1981 was not matched by liberalization in other areas, particularly funding.

Nevertheless, various foreign banks entered into the trust banking business in Japan through joint ventures with local security houses, but these were rendered far less attractive when in late 1984, under strong pressure from the Reagan administration, the government decided to permit five American and three European (British, German, and French) banks to enter the trust business in Japan directly. Swiss banks apparently were initially excluded because of secrecy laws that were said to prevent the Japanese authorities from adequately judging bank performance. Japanese trust banks professed to be "shocked" at the prospects of increased competition and American negotiators thought they had an agreement to open the Japanese market to all qualified institutions. Nevertheless, the highly controlled market opening suggested continued protectionism. Japanese pension funds amounted to about $60 billion in 1984 and are expected to grow rapidly to at least $260 billion within a decade.

How difficult it is to separate discrimination against foreign financial institutions from the legitimate exercise of national economic and financial policy prerogatives came to light in Korea during 1986. The 47 foreign banks operating in the country had survived in large part on swap facilities made available to them by the central bank, which encouraged foreign currency lending to the country, as well as government guarantees covering lending to the major Korean industrial groups. Concern over the size of the country's foreign debt led the Ministry of Finance in 1986 to freeze dollar loans by all banks operating in the country, to seriously discourage local currency financing of business by issuing Bank of Korea "monetary stabilization bonds" at extremely attractive interest rates, and to curtail swap facilities. Also included was a requirement that 35 percent of all new lending go to small and medium-sized local businesses, an increase from a previous requirement of 25 percent.

On the funding side, foreign banks in 1986 obtained the right to sell certificates of deposit, but they could sell only up to 7 percent of their capital and were required to give up an equal amount of swap facilities. Meanwhile, the interest rate they could pay on local currency deposits was linked to a range set by a cartel of domestic banks. They were also required to give up swap facilities in the amount of one-half of any discount-window borrowings. The authorities indicated that these were simply steps on the way to phasing out swap facilities entirely.

All of this was taken by the foreign banks as partial revocation of a 1984 agreement, reached with considerable U.S. trade pressure, to (1) reduce barriers to competition, particularly in local currency lending, (2) provide partial access to discount-window facilities, and (3) partially lift legal lending limits. A variety of other government interferences in the operation of foreign banks, however, were not in fact liberalized by Korea as agreed or were made ineffective by other discriminatory rules and regulations. Korean officials, on the other hand, viewed the measures simply as elimination of "special privileges" that had afforded unusually favorable treatment of foreign banks during a time when Korea was in serious need of foreign currency financing for its industrialization—a need that had come to an end.

Asset Growth and Size Limits

Besides telling foreign-based financial institutions where they may not (or must) do business, governments have shown great ingenuity in limiting the share of the overall market that foreign competitors may obtain. Leverage (gearing) ratios, reserve requirements, and capitalization limits may be set at different levels for foreign and for domestic institutions, all in order to constrain their overall market share. Foreign currencies may have to be placed with the central bank in some proportion to the volume of domestic lending, or explicit quotas may actually be placed individually or collectively on foreign institutions to limit their share of the overall market. Such limits may be either static or dynamic, thereby permitting a gradual and controlled expansion of growth in their share of the market and in their portfolio loans. Restrictions on growth have both quota-like and tariff-like effects, depending on whether they physically limit the overall value of business or raise its cost. In some cases, they increase costs progressively as the volume of business grows and thus they are somewhat akin to tariff quotas in commercial policy.

The Canadian Banking Act of 1980 limited all foreign banks to an 8 percent share of total domestic Canadian assets, about C$11 billion in 1981. At the same time, several dozen additional foreign banks applied for charters as full branches, further dividing the asset ceiling imposed on them. In effect, the ceiling excludes foreign banks from funding a major part of Canadian financing needs, particularly in resource-based industries, at the very time Canadian banks were moving aggressively to expand their market share in the United States and other countries. This obvious lack of reciprocity generated a great deal of criticism at the time.

Funding Limits

Besides restricting overall growth and the markets to be served, which generally affects the asset side of the balance sheet, there may also be restrictions placed on the liability side. In addition to capital-related restrictions, foreign financial institutions may be prevented from accepting only deposits altogether, certain types of deposits (for example, time, savings, or demand deposits), or deposits from certain types of customers (for example, individuals in the retail banking market). They may be denied access to deposits from the government, which may direct its own business (and that of firms over which it has some influence) to domestic banks or only to those banks in which it has an equity interest.

All such restrictions force foreign institutions to fund themselves in the local interbank market, certainly resulting in higher costs and, given the limited depth and breadth of that market, in the periodically restricted availability of funds as well. If the interbank market is dominated by a few large and powerful domestic institutions, those domestic institutions can easily have the foreigners over the proverbial barrel if they become nettlesome. Indeed, a few governments actually *require* foreign-based financial institutions to borrow significantly from domestic banks.

Additionally, foreign-based financial institutions may be denied eligiblity for interest subsidies made available by the government, thus effectively narrowing loan spreads, and foreign institutions' bankers' acceptances arising from trade financing may not be acceptable for discount in the domestic money market. Foreign banks may be prevented from having access to the discount services of the local central bank, thereby forcing suboptimal asset and liability management. All such measures increase the difficulty in arranging local sources and uses of funds in such a way as to erode the profitability of foreign-based institutions.

An example of discriminatory capital requirements applied to foreign banks occurred in Portugal in 1986. In order to protect overstaffed and inefficient but heavily capitalized domestic institutions, the government increased capital requirements by 64 percent for "new banking institutions," mainly foreign, which had been operating profitably. Maximum leverage for foreign banks was set to five times capital, and 44 to 60 times capital for the nationalized Portuguese banks. Combined with other regulatory measures favoring indigenous banks and severe branching restrictions applied through refusal to act on applications, Portuguese policy was seen as a clear protectionist thrust, in conflict with a 1984 law that was basically aimed at nondiscrimination, as well as with Portugal's obligations as a new member of the EEC with respect to the right of establishment.

Nuisance Measures

Besides acting on the core element in the business of financial services (the size and shape of the balance sheet), governments have found other ways to restrain foreign competition. Access to telecommunications facilities, to electric power, to transportation, to postal services, and to building permits may be restricted. Transborder data flows, which are the competitive lifeblood of multinational financial networks, may be impeded or taxed. Foreign financial institutions may be saddled with discriminatory rates of profit tax, stamp duties, or transfer fees, or they may be forced to do all their foreign exchange business through local banks, sometimes at government-prescribed rates.

Not least important, there are frequent staffing and managerial restrictions. Job quotas for local people may be imposed either in the aggregate or by the level of employment. All managers and/or directors may have to be local residents or nationals and senior expatriate personnel may have to be vetted on an individual basis by the authorities. Sometimes work and residence permits are employed in this connection and even the issue of visas may be used to restrict visits of home office or third country personnel. If, indeed, banking and financial services is a "people business," as suggested, then such measures can have extraordinarily harmful effects by raising costs, reducing the quality of products, and constraining the ability to expand. Throughout, red tape plays a major role, both in raising transactions costs and in elevating the level of uncertainty surrounding the business.

There is in various countries an impressive range of operating restrictions on banking and the provision by foreign-based institutions of other financial services. It should be noted, however, that not all the restrictions are intended solely to discriminate against them. Nevertheless, even under such circumstances, a handicap may still exist.

An unintentional differential impact can occur because of specific variations that may exist between the character of domestic and foreign operations. Some countries, for example, set maximum permissible limits on the size of bank loans to individual borrowers. These limits are usually specified in terms of the size of the bank's capital. If a bank's local office is treated as a separately capitalized entity instead of on a consolidated basis with its parent, its ability to extend loans to large corporate borrowers can be severely constrained, although direct loans from the parent may be a way of circumventing this problem. Moreover, if local requirements include minimum capital asset ratios, treatment of foreign banks as separate entities may deprive them of a significant advantage, if not impose a severe handicap.

General constraints on bank growth and on certain types of lending, as well as limits on the profitability of banks, may constitute *de facto* discrimination against foreign banks because (1) they tend to be among the later market entrants, except perhaps in excolonies, (2) they tend to have a heavier concentration of their business in the wholesale end of the market, and (3) they often have the potential to attain a faster rate of growth than indigenous banks. Unintended discrimination also exists when limits are placed for balance-of-payments reasons on the repatriation of bank profits.

A good example of such a problem arose in Argentina during 1986. The country had over 200 banks with over 5,000 branches and 150,000 employees at the end of 1985, and its financial industry was generally regarded as free-wheeling, bloated, and poorly supervised. The system's fragility was demonstrated after revelations of bank fraud, unsound banking practices, and negligence caused a number of private institutions to fail and resulted in a rush to deposit in state banks. Their share of deposits rose from 38 percent to 60 percent in 1986, while their share of banking assets rose from 34 percent to 66 percent. To cope with the problem the authorities significantly increased reserve requirements, thereby causing an increase in lending rates and stimulating the rapid growth of a parallel market of intercompany and other loans totally outside the banking system, which in turn threatened a loss of government control of the domestic credit system.

In response, the authorities encouraged 23 mergers between weaker and stronger banks. They also sharply cut reserve requirements and proposed a law that would increase the central bank's supervisory authority and effectiveness, restrict banks to activities specified in the law and spell out which institutions are in fact banks, and define banking as a "public service." Foreign-based banks in Argentina, which had largely stayed clear of the problems, vigorously objected to some of the proposed restrictions as well as to the public-service definition of banking. In particular, they objected to the imposition of capital requirements double those applied to local banks, and to a provision tying their deposit-taking ability to their volume of international trade credits.

An example of how the existence of a direct presence in a foreign market opens up the possibility of external political pressure on operations exerted by the local government occurred in the Philippines in early 1987. During the renegotiations of the Philippine debt, Citibank took a relatively hard line and refused to go along with other banks in accepting a relatively low interest margin on the $8.6 billion of restructured debt. This prompted the local authorities to discuss what actions could be taken against Citibank's Philippine business, including closing offices and limiting the permissible range of business. Brazil had previously closed Mellon Bank's representative office in Rio de Janeiro for its refusal to renew about $150 million in trade credits to that country. Citibank had a presence in the Philippines for 85 years and operated three bank branches; a subsidiary, CityTrust, was one of the major Philippine banks. However, most observers viewed this threat as posturing by the government during tense negotiations in which the role of Citibank was considered critical.

On the other hand, "foreignness" can be beneficial if liabilities denominated in other currencies are excluded from the base used to compute required reserves. Similarly, exclusion of foreign financial institutions from the requirement to make (possibly unprofitable) priority sector loans or to support government debt issues may have a favorable effect on their position in the market.

Besides operating barriers affecting conventional banking services, impediments may also hinder foreign-based firms offering such financial services as charge cards. One type of operating barrier facing foreign-based credit, debit, and T&E card issuers (see Chapter 11) is lack of access to the domestic bank clearing system. In order for their cards to be usable in automatic teller machines, charge card issuers usually must have access to that system. In some countries where payments clearing is controlled by the government or by a cartel of local banks, access to the system may be denied to foreign-based issuers. Canada and Malaysia have been cited by American Express Company as examples of two countries imposing operating restrictions of this type.

In addition, foreign-based firms may be prohibited entirely from offering charge cards. In Taiwan, for example, only debit cards are allowed (whereby charges are debited from the cardholder's bank account), thus limiting issuance of charge cards to a cartel of local banks, most of which are controlled by the Taiwanese government. Without access to domestic bank accounts foreign-based firms cannot therefore issue debit cards and are therefore excluded from the charge card business in Taiwan.

Another impediment, seen, for example, in Norway and Denmark, concerns controls on the pricing of charge card services, which involves fees paid by merchants and other clients accepting the card for charge purchases. Such fees may be prohibited entirely, and any fees may be imposed solely on the card user. This can put the issuers of charge cards at a severe disadvantage against the issuers of credit cards, where returns are largely derived from interest charges on purchases. If the latter are predominantly issued by local banks, such policies may constitute discrimination against foreign-based suppliers of charge card services.

Occasionally the government or government-owned entities may supply financial services in competition with the private sector and hence foreign-based card issuers. Air Canada, for example, issues a charge card that is given preference in bidding for the government's card and related travel services contracts.

On balance, then, foreign-based financial institutions can probably expect to operate at a disadvantage with respect to indigenous competitors in most countries because of intentional or accidental discrimination against them. Sometimes these disadvantages will wane with time. As noted earlier, such organizations generally seek entry into national markets at the wholesale end of the business and will pursue activities that have some trace of internationality, such as foreign currency loans, trade financing, or loans to multinational enterprises. Local retail and middle-market business will tend to become more important only after the enterprise has been more or less fully integrated into the national financial environment. This may give pioneer international financial institutions a competitive edge over new entrants into the international banking arena and over new banking competitors in general. Yet, even when foreign banks have been long established as retail competitors, local banks often resist innovations involving new technologies or ones that promise to alter banking practices radically, such as automated teller machines and credit cards. Table 27-1 presents a compilation, as of 1990, of the principal aspects of the legal setting in which banks operate in various countries.

THE ISSUE OF RECIPROCITY

The Oxford English Dictionary defines reciprocity as "mutual or correspondent concession of advantages or privileges, as forming the basis for the commercial relations between countries." The principle of reciprocity as it is conventionally applied to trade in financial services implies that a country discriminates in its treatment of foreign firms by affording each of them exactly the same treatment the country's own firms receive at home. Reciprocity is therefore analogous to retaliation in international trade policy. By treating foreign-based firms the same as the foreign government treats home country firms there a country may hope to improve the mutual investment climate. One of the arguments in favor of reciprocity in the provision of financial services is that it will maintain overall barriers at a lower level than passive acceptance of unilaterally imposed impediments to open competition.

Reciprocity is certainly easier to define in the case of trade in goods than trade in services. Swaps of tariff concessions on particular volumes of trade have formed the basis for reciprocity in past trade negotiations. But there is no comparable standard for measuring reciprocity in financial services. Access to a particular market for a particular set of firms may carry entirely different significance from access to another market for another set of players. Understanding reciprocity in this context clearly requires an intimate knowledge of markets, products, and competitors.

Nor is it always clear that reciprocity is in the interest of firms seeking access to foreign markets, in whose interests it is ostensibly being applied. Strict reciprocity, for example, would require foreign countries to apply geographic branching limitations and Glass-Steagall–type restrictions to U. S. financial institutions doing business there, which even Japan does not do.

On the other hand, reciprocity is often espoused as the most equitable standard for a foreign presence in the domestic provision of financial services. In practice, however, full reciprocity encounters a number of pitfalls that make it virtually impossible to administer in its narrowest form, and very few countries appear to adhere strictly to such a policy, although many include reciprocity in their consideration of other factors related to the entry of foreign banks.

In drafting the International Banking Act of 1978, for example, the United States Congress in effect rejected reciprocity in favor of "national treatment," putting foreign-based financial institutions on the same competitive footing as domestic institutions. To apply the concept of reciprocity in its strictest sense would conceivably have required 33 different policies covering foreign banks from the 33 different countries represented in the United States at the time. Such a policy would necessarily have been largely reactive in nature and would have resulted in an incoherent amalgam of petty regulations entirely inconsistent with the objectives of equity and efficiency of the American financial system.

While reciprocity may be impractical as a policy for large and internationally oriented financial systems, it is nevertheless frequently used as a justification for various national policy actions concerning the entry of foreign banks. Brazil, for instance, applies the concept to United States banks on a one-to-one basis, permitting an American bank in Brazil for every Brazilian bank in the United States. And, if existing American or British banks in France or Mexico were nationalized, it would be very surprising if their governments failed to retaliate against French or Mexican banks in their own countries.

Reciprocity has perhaps been most widely used in recent years with respect to Japan, perhaps in part a reaction to the perceived lack of Japanese reciprocity over the years with respect to trade in industrial

Table 27–1. Summary of Laws Affecting Domestic Activities of Commercial Banks in Major Industrialized Countries

	Japan	European Community (EC)	West Germany	United Kingdom
Principal Regulators of Commercial Banks	Ministry of Finance (MOF); Bank of Japan.		Federal Banking Supervisory Office (FBSO); Deutsche Bundesbank.	Bank of England.
Branching Restrictions				
Geographic	None.	None for EC-based banks, which can branch Community-wide effective no later than January 1, 1993. Banks not based in the EC may branch only as permitted by each country's supervisory authorities.	None.	None.
Regulatory	Prior authorization by MOF required. Number of new branches limited by MOF.	EC-based banks must notify their home state's supervisory authorities.	Notification to the FBSO and the Bundesbank required.	Prior notice to the Bank of England required.
Scope of Permissible Activities				
Securities	Japanese banks are limited to (1) purchasing and selling securities for customer accounts or for the investment purposes of the bank; (2) underwriting and dealing in commercial paper and government, government-guaranteed, and municipal securities; (3) dealing on behalf of institutional clients. Non-Japanese banks may conduct securities activities through 50%-owned affiliates.	The Second Banking Directive (SBD) permits an EC-based bank to engage in securities activities anywhere in the EC to the extent permitted by the bank's home state supervisor. An Investment Services Directive has been proposed.	Unrestricted.	Unrestricted powers. Activities usually conducted through subsidiaries of parent banks Firms carrying on securities activities are regulated by the Securities and Investments Board (SIB) and by self-regulatory organizations (SRO's).
Insurance	Not permitted.	Permitted only if permitted by the bank's home state supervisor and by the country where the bank proposes to engage in the activity.	Unrestricted powers. Activities generally conducted through subsidiaries of parent banks.	Unlimited powers. Activities usually conducted through subsidiaries of parent banks.

France	Italy	Canada	United States
Banking Commission; Committee on Bank Regulation; Committee on Credit Institutions.	Ministry of Treasury; Interministerial Committee for Credit and Savings (CICR); Bank of Italy.	Office of the Superintendent of Financial Institutions (OSFI).	Federal Reserve Board (bank holding companies; state member banks, consumer protection regulation), Comptroller of the Currency (national banks), FDIC (insured banks), State banking regulators (state-chartered banks).
None.	None.	None.	Intrastate branching allowed only to the extent permitted by State law (McFadden Act). Interstate branching by national banks is generally not permitted. However, bank holding companies may own bank subsidiaries in more than one state if expressly permitted by state law (Douglas Amendment).
Notification to the Banking Commission required.	Authorization by Bank of Italy required.	None for widely-held Canadian banks and for U.S. owned Canadian bank subsidiaries. Prior authorization required for other banks.	Authorization by federal or state agencies required.
Unrestricted powers.	Unrestricted powers, except that banks are not permitted to execute transactions on exchanges.	Unrestricted powers when conducted through subsidiaries of parent banks.	May underwrite & deal in government securities. May underwrite and deal in other debt & equity securities provided that (1) the activities are conducted in a bank holding company subsidiary; (2) the revenues of such activities do not exceed 10 percent of the total revenues of the subsidiary and (3) bank affiliates are insulated by appropriate firewalls.
Unlimited powers. Activities usually conducted through subsidiaries or affiliates.	Not currently permitted.	Not permitted. The government has proposed unlimited activities through subsidiaries of parent banks.	Restricted powers for national banks. Powers for state banks vary according to state law. Bank holding companies generally limited to credit-related insurance activities.

Table 27-1. Summary of Laws Affecting Domestic Activities of Commercial Banks in Major Industrialized Countries (cont.)

	Japan	European Community (EC)	West Germany	United Kingdom
Industrial Investments	Limited to holding 5% interests.	SBD forbids a bank from investing more than 15% of its own funds in a non-financial company; such investments are limited, in the aggregate, to 60% of the bank's capital.	Unrestricted powers. Activities generally conducted through subsidiaries of parent banks.	Permitted subject to consultations with Bank of England.
Restrictions on the Structure of Banking Operations	Japanese banks must be corporations; foreign banks are exempted. Bank holding companies are prohibited.	None. However, in countries where access to organized securities markets is restricted to non-banks, banks can obtain access through wholly-owned financial services subsidiaries.	Banks may not be organized as sole proprietorships.	Banks may not be organized as sole proprietorships.
Capital Requirements	Statutory minimum of 1 billion yen for city banks, regional banks, trust banks, and branches of foreign banks and 10 million yen for long-term credit banks and the specialized foreign-exchange bank.*	Proposed directive provides uniform risk weights for EC banks, with one exception: West German and Danish banks may weight commercial loans secured by real estate at 50% instead of 100% until January 1, 1996.*	Banking Act requires "adequate" capital as determined by Principles issued by the FBSO, in agreement with the Bundesbank. Initial capital of at least DM 10 million is expected. New guidelines in accordance with the Basle Agreement will be issued in the second half of 1990.	Banks incorporated in the U.K. must have a minimum capital of £1 million. There is no minimum capital requirement for branches of foreign banks. The Bank of England establishes minimum capital for each bank to reflect its own circumstances.*
Deposit Protection Scheme	Deposit Insurance Corporation.	Recommended to be in place in all Member states by 1990.	Deposit Protection Fund.	Deposit Protection Fund.
Administration and Membership	Mixed public-private control; mandatory.		Private; voluntary. Most banks are members.	Mixed public-private; mandatory.
Maximum Protection Per Depositor	10 million yen (US $69,000).		30% of bank's capital and disclosed reserves.	75% of £20,000 (75% of US $34,000).
Annual Cost/Premiums	0.012% of deposits (1989).		0.03% of deposits (1988).	Depends on payments made by Fund in prior year.
Special Features	Unlike most schemes, includes coverage for deposits of foreign branches of domestic banks. Excludes deposits of Japanese branches of foreign banks.		Unlike most schemes, includes coverage for deposits in foreign branches of domestic banks.	
Reserve Requirements	Yes; interest-free.		Yes; interest-free. 4.15% to 12.1% as of February 1, 1987.	Yes, for banks with more than £10 million in sterling liabilities (excluding interbank deposits) maturing in less than two years. (0.45% of eligible liabilities as of Sept. 1988.)

* Regulators from 17 countries (including all those listed in the table) agreed in 1988 ("Basle Agreement") to implement a minimum capital requirement of 8% of risk-weighted assets by January 1, 1993. Different countries may use different risk-weighting schemes, however.

France	Italy	Canada	United States
Require prior authorization by the Banking Commission.	Require prior approval of Bank of Italy.	Require approval of Minister of Finance.	Require prior approval of appropriate federal agency (Bank Merger Act). May be challenged by the Department of Justice. State banks may also need state approval.
Crossing the 5% threshold requires prior notification to the Committee on Credit Institutions. Crossing the 10, 20, and 33 1/3 percent thresholds, or obtaining a "controlling interest" requires the prior approval of the Committee.	Acquisition of more than 2% of the voting stock of a bank, as well as subsequent increases or decreases in excess of 1%, must be disclosed to the Bank of Italy.	Domestic banks must be widely held. There is 10% ceiling on group and individual ownership, except on newly incorporated banks. Total holdings by nonresidents (other than U.S. residents) may not exceed 25%, with no individual owning more than 10%.	Crossing 10% or 25% threshold generally requires prior notification. Any company acquiring 25% or some lesser amount that constitutes control requires prior approval. Bank holding companies are required to obtain prior approval to acquire 5% or more of a bank's shares.
Yes.	None as of 1980.	Yes.	Yes.
Yes.	Yes.	Yes.	Yes.
	Banks are prohibited from seeking new customers by "undignified" methods, such as distributing advertising circulars and making house-to-house visits. Banks are required to show the amount of their paid-in capital and reserves on all letters, publications, and advertisements.	Banks may not charge for cashing government checks.	Community Reinvestment Act requires supervisory agencies to assess banks' records of meeting the credit needs of the bank's entire community, including low- and moderate-income neighborhoods. Among other laws (the Federal Reserve Board administers more than a dozen) are the Equal Credit Opportunity Act and the Home Mortgage Disclosure Act.
Non-EC banks whose home countries do not have treaties of establishment with France may be required to obtain a commercial card for their non-EC officers which authorizes the banking subsidiary to employ foreign nationals. In addition, non-EC banks may be denied access if the bank's home country does not grant French banks reciprocal access.	Entry is through the establishment of branches or subsidiaries. The minimum capital for a new foreign branch is 25 million lira. Foreign banks' home countries must offer Italian banks access to the home countries' markets in order to do business in Italy. (Reciprocal national treatment.) As of December 15, 1989, new banks will be authorized provided they meet minimum capital, management, and operations requirements.	Entry is through Canadian bank subsidiary, not a branch. "Similar competitive opportunity" reciprocity requirement. Non-U.S. foreign banks may not hold more than 12% of all domestic bank assets. Beyond the first office, non-U.S. foreign bank subsidiaries may not open additional branches without the prior permission of the Minister of Finance.	None. National treatment standard, except in obtaining primary dealer status, which requires reciprocal national treatment.

NOTE: Although the information contained in this table is based on sources believed to be reliable, the preparers disclaim any expertise as to the banking laws and regulations of foreign countries or international organizations. Because banking laws and regulations are constantly changing, not all information may be current. In addition, presentation of this material in this format substantially oversimplifies the topics addressed.

Source: Federal Reserve Board, February 21, 1990.

goods and in part a response to the attractiveness of the Japanese capital market as the second-largest in the world. It is doubtful that 36 foreign firms would have obtained securities licenses or that the Tokyo Stock Exchange would have accepted 6 foreign members in December 1985 without threats of retaliation from the United States, the United Kingdom, and Switzerland. Foreign players have used this opening to good advantage. Salomon Brothers, for example, had become one of the top-tier securities traders in Tokyo by 1986. At the same time, foreign banks have been permitted to enter the trust business, bond futures trading, and bankers' acceptance business in Japan, while the authorities have eased debt-to-equity limits.

In December 1986 the Federal Reserve Bank of New York awarded licenses as primary securities dealers to only two Japanese securities houses, Nomura and Daiwa, (instead of all four that applied) and made it clear that even these licenses could be revoked in the absence of significant further progress in opening Japan's securities industry to U.S. firms. A third Japanese firm, the Industrial Bank of Japan, had already gained access to this market by acquiring a U.S. dealer, Aubrey Lanston & Co., through its subsidiary, J. Henry Schroder Corp.

In response, change was sought—for example, in the prevailing system of government bond allotments to an underwriting syndicate of 775 firms (including 42 foreigners). Even as outsiders, Japanese securities firms purchased at least half of all U.S. government securities, while American firms' allotments in Tokyo amounted to only 0.07 percent. Complete liberalization of membership in the Tokyo Stock Exchange was also sought, as was liberalization of commercial banking—in 1986 a total of 76 foreign banks held only 5 percent of Japanese banking assets.

The issue of reciprocity came up once again in the context of Japanese direct participation in Wall Street financial houses during 1987, when Nippon Life Insurance bought a 13 percent share of Shearson Lehman Hutton from the American Express Company for $538 million, following the 1986 acquisition of shares in Goldman Sachs by Sumitomo Bank. Together with other foreign participations and joint ventures such as Credit Suisse First Boston, the Japanese purchase of Aubrey Lanston & Co. (a primary government bond dealer), European holdings in Drexel Burnham Lambert, South African holdings in Salomon Brothers, and Arab investments in Smith Barney, the political profile of a strong foreign presence in the U. S. securities industry has grown significantly. The specter was raised of a repeat in the financial services industry of the foreign "domination" of the American markets for steel, garments, consumer electronics, and automobiles as foreign (especially Japanese) players developed a strong foothold in U.S. capital markets and acquired world-class training and financial technologies.

This became a fertile ground for raising the issue of reciprocity, and an amendment to a House international trade bill would require strict reciprocity in the financial services sector. The focus appeared to be on specific lines of activity. For example, while all of the Big Four Japanese securities houses had primary dealer status for government bonds in the United States, no U.S. firms had comparable status in Japan in 1988. The number of seats on the Tokyo Stock Exchange held directly or indirectly by U.S. firms was another matter of contention, challenges being made to the Japanese assertion that physical space and efforts to computerize the trading floor precluded increasing the number from the existing six firms in the near term.

Despite some Japanese liberalization moves, including permission for foreign banks to establish 50 percent owned securities firms in the face of prohibitions against local banks to do likewise, allegations of market distortions persist. This includes the allocation system for government bonds that relegates foreign players to a minor role in primary markets and the massive role played by the postal savings system in the allocation of individual savings in Japan.

The fact that only the Japanese securities houses had relatively free access to each of the three major world financial centers—London, New York, and Tokyo—was viewed as an unacceptable state of affairs in an increasingly globalized financial market.

The reciprocity issue also arose during a dispute between the United Kingdom and Japan in March–April 1987, extending the concept beyond the financial services sector itself. Like the United States, Britain had long pressed Japan for increased access for U.K. securities firms to its capital markets, in view of the virtually unrestricted access of Japanese banks and securities houses to London markets. At the end of 1986, 29 Japanese banks, 9 insurance companies, and 58 securities firms operated in the United Kingdom. All four of the largest securities firms were members of the London Stock Exchange. At the same time, 5 British banks and 14 securities firms (including some taken over by foreign interests as part of London's Big Bang) were operating in Japan. Of the six foreign members of the Tokyo Stock Exchange in 1986, one (S. G. Warburg) was British and another (Vickers da Costa) was a wholly owned British subsidiary of Citicorp.

In addition, British authorities were upset about the apparent exclusion of Cable and Wireless PLC, a telecommunications company, from significant access to the Japanese market for long-distance communications. The Japanese government proposed merging two rival consortia into a single new international telecommunications carrier, limiting the 13 interested foreign companies (most of them not international carriers) to a 20 percent stake and denying Cable and Wireless "meaningful" participation. This stance was justified by the Ministry for Post and Telecommunication as a matter of national security, but appeared clearly aimed at limiting competition from C&W's strong global network.

Hampered by EC membership in retaliating in the telecommunications sector—for example, by reducing the 28 percent share of Japan in the U.K. market for imported equipment—and by the limited role of Japanese firms in British telecommunications services, the Department of Trade and Industry, backed by the Treasury and many MPs, sought a broader retaliatory approach that focused on the powerful position being established by Japanese banks and securities firms in London. The U.K. authorities threatened to revoke the licenses of some of the 58 Japanese firms in London and proceeded to secure the necessary punitive powers under the U.K. Financial Services Act to do so. The government also made it clear that Japanese applications for new bank licenses would be refused, a move evidently intended to pressure Yamaichi and Nikko Securities, whose main competitors, Nomura and Daiwa, already had banking licenses in the United Kingdom. Under the Act, the retaliation could be triggered only by restricted access to the Japanese market for financial services, so that the C&W case was only a proximate trigger for the British threats.

Concern about the use of retaliation in financial services came mainly from the Bank of England, given the possible erosion of London as a world financial center at a time of growing importance of Japanese players. The prospects of Japanese firms moving to Frankfurt, Amsterdam, or Paris were raised, given the fact that, unlike Tokyo and New York, London is the only global financial center not founded on a massive base of domestic capital. The debate proved to be lively, with popular sentiment appearing to be lined up against the central bank's cautious view and the bankers lined up behind it in a "forest of pinstripes" accused of ignoring the fact that financial services should properly be viewed as part of the broader system of international trade.

In some countries, the principle of reciprocity is applied at the sub-national level as well, as is true in several American states. A number of them restrict the entry or operations of foreign banks, sometimes citing considerations of reciprocity as their motive, despite the consistent approach oriented toward national treatment at the federal level. Japan, for example, denied Texas-based banks permission to establish branches in Tokyo because Texas did not allow foreign bank branches, although there were a number of Japanese representative offices there.

But many developed and some developing countries seem to favor some form of national treatment of foreign financial institutions after they have overcome whatever entry barriers exist. Thus, the principles of reciprocity and national treatment in fact coexist and are often complementary. As noted earlier, the former is sometimes negative and often punitive, while the latter is generally positive and constructive.

The Reciprocity Issue and the EC Single Financial Market

Perhaps the most important case of reciprocity came up in connection with the 1992 initiatives in the European Community (EC), under which a single market is to be created for substantially all goods and services, including commercial and investment banking. In commercial banking, the EC's Second Banking Directive gives the EC Commission the power to bar entry or restrict the operation of banks from countries that discriminate against banks that are home based in the EC or that do not accord them national treatment. Virtually identical wording was included in the Directive covering securities and investment firms.

The reciprocity provisions sparked controversy especially by the United Kingdom and Luxembourg, where they were viewed as essentially protectionist in character and potentially damaging to the two country's roles as open and fully competitive financial centers—with some even arguing that more liberal establishment rules should apply to London and Luxembourg than in the rest of the EC. France, on the other hand, took a hard line on the reciprocity issue, possibly in the hope that it could improve the competitive position of Paris against London. In some ways the issue reflected weak liberal home country establishment regulation versus tough host country rules governing the creation of a viable commercial presence.

Under full implementation of reciprocity, banks and securities firms from a given country would be excluded from the entire EC if the home country of the applicant were found to discriminate in any respect against financial institutions firms from *any* EC member country. The home country so concerned could then retaliate and presumably exclude from its markets firms from *all* EC members, and in both the banking and securities directives the Commission specifies conditions under which foreign banks and securities firms are permitted to operate on a level playing field with their EC competitors under a single banking license. Under the reciprocity provisions, non-EC institutions' home countries would likewise be required to offer EC institutions reciprocal or "nondiscriminatory" access to their own market. By attaching reciprocity conditions, the EC Commission thus fell short of *de jure* "national treatment" in both the banking and securities industries (whereby foreign and domestic firms are treated identically, and hence the general equivalent of liberal trade in regulated industries) as the operating standard for financial services under the 1992 initiative.[4]

EC member governments were urged by the Commission to apply reciprocity tests immediately, both to facilitate later implementation of reciprocity at the EC level and to preclude an end run around reciprocity via grandfathering, a suggestion evidently aimed at Japan. Despite the tough language, reciprocity is likely to be implemented with considerable discretion on the part of the Commission. Rather than insisting on full reciprocity, the Commission is likely to pressure third countries for treatment of EC players on a par with indigenous firms and therefore effectively apply a national treatment standard to a significant extent. Under the directives, the EC will have to enter negotiations with offending countries and, barring a successful conclusion, could restrict market access on the part of institutions from those countries—albeit not retroactively.

The dangers of reciprocity were nevertheless readily apparent, although they were somewhat ameliorated by grandfathering provisions for any firm established in the EC by the end of 1992. Nevertheless, reciprocity remained an important feature of the EC unified financial services market, and is likely to be raised when new authorizations are requested after 1992, as well as when established non-EC firms ask to conduct new kinds of activities.

Universal banking practices in the EC versus the separation of commercial banking from investment banking in the United States and Japan, for example, gave rise to a potentially major reciprocity issue. If reciprocity is either waived or grandfathered by the EC, it could result in exceptional pressure on the U.S. Congress to formally repeal the Glass-Steagall provisions of the Banking Act of 1933 or become a matter of serious dispute between the EC and its U.S. and Japanese trading partners. According to one observer, reciprocity is "a missile aimed at Tokyo which will land in New York and explode on Capitol Hill."[5]

Realistically, American financial institutions, some of which have been established in Europe longer than many European institutions, probably had little to fear from the reciprocity issue. Informed Europeans recognized the contributions these American firms have made to the evolution of the financial system, the importance of the United States to their own financial institutions, and the potential costs of delinking Europe's financial system from markets that have become truly global in nature. Japanese had greater cause for concern, given the perceived lack of reciprocity shown European institutions in their attempts to establish a viable presence in Japanese financial markets. Consequently, Japanese firms rapidly increased their presence in the EC, broadening their networks especially in the United Kingdom and Germany in the expectation that grandfathering would prove to be an important safeguard for them. In late 1988, 18 leading international bankers, mainly American and Japanese, issued an appeal for open access to European financial markets in the 1992 context.[6]

A hint of things to come appeared in mid-1989, when a trade group, the European Banking Federation, identified 26 countries that imposed restrictions against foreign banks. The list included Japan, the United States, Canada, Australia, Norway, Sweden, China, Singapore, Thailand, Taiwan, South Korea, India, Indonesia, Malaysia, Pakistan, Argentina, Brazil, and Mexico.

In part, the final story on reciprocity will depend on the outcome of the ongoing Uruguay round of trade negotiations under the auspices of the GATT. For the first time, multilateral trade negotiations include financial services, with national treatment representing the financial services industry's equivalent of the GATT most-favored-nation principle. This standard implies equality of opportunity in market access, including the right to establish a viable commercial presence no less favorable than that accorded to local firms, as opposed to treatment no less favorable than foreign firms receive in the applicant's home country.[7] If national treatment is accepted in any future GATT agreement, the reciprocity issue for EC investment banking should effectively drop away for all countries that become signatories.

THE EUROMARKET BENCHMARK

The existence of a substantially free offshore market—at least in the wholesale commercial and investment banking segments of the industry—provides policy makers with a better tool with which to assess the implications of domestic distortions in the financial services industry than is, perhaps, available in any other sector of the international economy.

To a significant extent, the Eurobond and Eurocurrency markets remain subject to limited taxation, regulation, and control, with protection essentially unknown and keen competition being continuously waged among countries that have decided to establish Eurofacilities in the form of offshore banking centers.

The Euromarkets are basically efficient, in both a static and dynamic sense, and exist as useful benchmarks for comparing the losses in efficiency associated with protection, as well as general prudential and regulatory controls that exist in domestic financial systems. They also serve in part to limit the damage that protection imposes on international financial institutions, since it is often possible to transfer transactions for clients out of the national environment and into the Euromarkets. Indeed, this option and the fear of competitive erosion of national financial centers have triggered a spate of deregulation in many countries.

Market Access Liberalization in Financial Services

Given the structure and motivations underlying distortions of competitive conditions in the financial services industry, national treatment would seem to be the substantive equivalent of liberal international trade in this sector. This means that foreign-based players are subject to precisely the same regulatory and prudential controls as domestic players. Yet even this standard can produce differential effects on domestic and foreign-based institutions because of different starting positions and operating characteristics. Further unintended distortions can arise because of stringent home country capital requirements for institutions doing business in international and foreign markets, where they may compete with players based in other countries who may be treated much more leniently.

What is really required is "equality of competitive opportunity," in the sense of a level playing field—an extraordinarily difficult concept to define, much less to deliver, in the case of an industry as complex as financial services. This can be viewed as comprising the following components:

1. Freedom to establish branches, agencies, subsidiaries, representative offices, or other affiliates within a national market on a basis identical to that applying to locally owned financial institutions. In terms of Figure 27–1, freedom of establishment is critical to competitive equality in serving the C- and A-cells within a country and maximizing the positive linkage effects to cells in the rest of the global matrix. National antitrust and other policies relating to establishment would bear identically on foreign players and domestic players.
2. Regulatory symmetry, insofar as possible, with respect to domestic and foreign competitors. This includes the incidence of prudential controls such as capital requirements, asset ratios, lending limits, and reserve requirements. It also involves equality of access to the domestic securities markets, including lead managing local currency issues in the local and offshore markets, as well as equal access to the national payments clearing system, money markets and central bank discount facilities, and trust and investment businesses.
3. Freedom to import critical resources. This includes travel and resettlement of professional staff, subscriptions of capital in the case of certain nonbranch affiliates, and access to data processing and telecommunications equipment on the same basis as local firms. Also included is equality of access to transborder communication and data transmission.
4. Symmetry with respect to the application of exchange controls, if any, as between foreign and local players. This bears on capital outflows such as foreign borrowing in the local markets and local investments abroad, as well as remittances of earnings.
5. Equality of access to domestic client groups, financial institutions, and product markets. This entails branching privileges equal to those of local firms and the right to purchase shares in local financial institutions consistent with domestic laws regarding competition.

Together, these elements would provide a consistent set of benchmarks for equality of competitive opportunity that, as noted, is the equivalent of liberal trade in the financial services sector. This does not mean that foreign-based financial institutions should be able to avoid the effects of national tax, prudential, and monetary control policies, and it is clear that the implementation of a truly level playing field is made vastly more complicated because of these considerations.

SUMMARY

Foreign-based financial institutions of necessity operate in one of the more highly regulated environments in international trade. Restrictions are often justified by the need for effective domestic prudential or monetary control. They can also reflect strong protectionist pressure emanating from indigenous financial institutions and political pressure relating to national control of the "commanding heights" of the economy. When the financial systems of countries are opened to foreign involvement, it is sometimes only for a brief period in order to accept new entrants and these windows of opportunity can lead to a mad scramble among international financial institutions to establish themselves before the windows are closed again. Once in, operating restrictions can also severely limit the activities of foreign-based financial institutions.

Entry as well as operating barriers, whether imposed for reasons of financial control or protection, may constrain financial efficiency and the prospects of economic growth for the host country. Yet the restricted competition itself can be highly profitable to those foreigners who have managed to find a niche in the market. This helps explain the ambivalence that even the most international of financial institutions have exhibited toward the prospects of aggressive liberalization of international trade in banking and other financial services.

Unlike international trade in goods, trade in services generally, and financial services in particular, tends to be directed toward taking the product directly to the customer and this usually requires a supplier's presence in the host country. Because the rules of the game for foreign direct investment are ill-defined and not covered by internationally accepted principles of conduct, GATT-type rules of nondiscrimination do not apply.

Given the structure of entry barriers and distortions of operating conditions, it would appear that national treatment is the substantive equivalent of free trade in a highly regulated industry such as financial services, an industry whose sensitivity to systemic problems will ensure that it will continue to be subject to regulatory controls. This is not necessarily the case, however. As we have noted, even nominal national treatment can have differential effects on domestic and foreign-based institutions because of their different starting positions and operating characteristics. What is really required is "equality of competitive opportunity" in the sense of a level playing field. This is an extraordinarily difficult concept to define, much less to deliver, in the case of an industry as complex as financial services. But as a goal, it is this sector's equivalent of free international trade.

Discriminatory barriers imposed on foreign competitors in national financial markets are analogous to protection in merchandise trade and, as we have seen, include tariff-like and quota-like distortions. Finally, reciprocity in rules governing financial services is similar to that found in conventional merchandise trade, except that the principle tends to be far more narrowly defined at the subsector and even the individual enterprise level.

NOTES

1. Ingo Walter, *Global Competition in Financial Services* (Cambridge, MA: Ballinger–Harper & Row, 1988).
2. U.S. Department of the Treasury, *Report to the Congress on Foreign Government Treatment of U.S. Banking Organizations* (Washington, DC: Department of the Treasury, 1979). Updated in 1984.
3. Ingo Walter, *Barriers to Trade in Banking and Financial Services* (London: Trade Policy Research Centre, 1985).
4. Ingo Walter, *Global Competition in Financial Services* (Cambridge, MA: Ballinger–Harper & Row, 1988).
5. John Heimann, Quoted in John Plender, "Towards a Bigger Bang," *Financial Times*, October 28,1988. For a full discussion, see Ingo Walter and Roy C. Smith, *Investment Banking in Europe: Restructuring for the 1990s* (Oxford: Basil Blackwell, 1989).
6. Stefan Wagstyl, "Japanese Decide to Hedge Bets," *Financial Times*, December 19, 1988.
7. "The City Leads, But Brussels Conducts." *The Economist*, November 19, 1988.

SELECTED REFERENCES

American Bankers Association. *The Future Development of US Banking Organizations Abroad*. Washington, DC: American Bankers Association, 1981.

Cohen, Michael, and Morante, Thomas. "Elimination of Nontariff Barriers to Trade in Services: Recommendations for Future Negotiations." *International Law Journal*, 1981.

Cooper, Kerry, and Fraser, Donald R. *Bank Deregulation and the New Competition in Financial Services.* Cambridge, MA: Ballinger, 1986.

Corbet, Hugh. "Prospect of Negotiations on Barriers to International Trade in Services." *Pacific Community*, April 1977.

Diebold, William, and Stalson, Helena. "Negotiating Issues in International Service Transactions." In *Trade Policy in the 1980s* edited by William R. Cline. Washington, DC: Institute for International Economics, 1983.

Leutwiler, Fritz, et al. *Trade Policies for a Better Future.* Geneva: General Agreement on Tariffs and Trade, 1985.

Morgan Guaranty Trust Company. "America's Banking Market Goes International." *Morgan Economic Quarterly*, June 1986.

Neu, C. R. "International Trade in Banking Services." Paper presented at a NBER/CEPS Conference on European - U.S. Trade Relations, Brussels, June 1986. Mimeographed.

Office of Technology Assessment, U.S. Congress. *International Competition in Banking and Financial Services.* OTA, Washington, DC: July 1986. Mimeographed.

Organization for Economic Cooperation and Development. *Trade in Services in Banking.* Paris: OECD, 1983.

Pecchioli, R. M. *Internationalization of Banking.* Paris: OECD, 1983.

Sagari, Sylvia B. *"The Financial Services Industry: An International Perspective."* Dissertation Graduate School of Business Administration, New York University, 1986.

Saunders, Anthony, and Walter, Ingo. "International Trade in Financial Services: Are Bank Services Special?" Paper presented at the Symposium on New Institutional Arrangements for the World Economy. University of Konstanz, 1987. Mimeographed.

Tschoegl, Adrian E. *The Regulation of Foreign Banks: Policy Formation Outside the United States.* New York: Salomon Brothers Center for the Study of Financial Institutions, New York University, 1981.

Tschoegl, Adrian E. "Foreign Bank Entry into Japan and California." In *New Theories of the Multinational Enterprise,* edited by Allen M. Rugman. London: Croom Helm, 1982.

Tugendhat, Christopher. "Opening-up Europe's Financial Sector." *The Banker*, January 1985.

U.S. Comptroller of the Currency. *A Critical Evaluation of Reciprocity in Foreign Bank Acquisition.* Washington, DC: U.S. Government Printing Office, 1984.

U.S. Comptroller of the Currency. *US Banks' Loss of Global Standing.* Washington, DC: U.S. Government Printing Office, 1984.

U.S. Department of the Treasury. *Report to the Congress on Foreign Government Treatment of U.S. Banking Organizations.* Washington, DC: Department of the Treasury, 1979. Updated in 1984.

Walter, Ingo. *Barriers to Trade in Banking and Financial Services*. London: Trade Policy Research Centre, 1985.

Walter, Ingo, and Gray, H. Peter. "Protectionism in International Banking." *Journal of Banking and Finance*, December 1983.

Walter, Ingo. *Global Competition in Financial Services*. Cambridge, MA: Ballinger–Harper & Row, 1988.

Walter, Ingo, and Smith, Roy C. *Investment Banking in Europe: Restructuring for the 1990s*. Oxford: Basil Blackwell, 1989.

Index

The Institutional Investor Series in Finance

The Institutional Investor Series in Finance has been developed specifically to bring you—the finance professional—the latest thinking and developments in investments and corporate finance. As new challenges arise in this fast-paced arena, you can count on this series to provide you with the information you need to gain the competitive edge.

Institutional Investor is the leading communications company serving the global financial community and publisher of the magazine of the same name. Institutional Investor has won 36 major awards for distinguished financial journalism—including the prestigious National Magazine Award for the best reporting of any magazine in the United States. More than 560,000 financial executives in 170 countries read Institutional Investor publications each month. Thousands more attend Institutional Investor's worldwide conferences and seminars each year.